California's topography is characterized by great variety. Its coastline varies from the low, sandy beaches of Southern California to the rocky headlands of Cape Mendocino and other northward protrusions. The Coast Ranges, one of the state's two great mountain systems, runs generally parallel to the coast.

Within the spurs of the Coast Ranges lie many of the state's most fertile and agricultural valleys. Eastward is the Central Valley, California's richest agricultural region, which has a width of up to fifty miles. The Central Valley is walled in to the east by the Sierra Nevada rampart, which at Mount Whitney, the highest mountain in the continental United States outside Alaska, reaches an altitude of 14,496 feet.

From the summit of Mount Whitney one can see the weird sink known as Death Valley, 282 feet below sea level, the lowest spot in the United States. Stretching southward are the nation's two largest deserts, the Mojave and the Colorado. By contrast, the topography of northern California contains such large bodies of water as Lake Tahoe and Clear Lake.

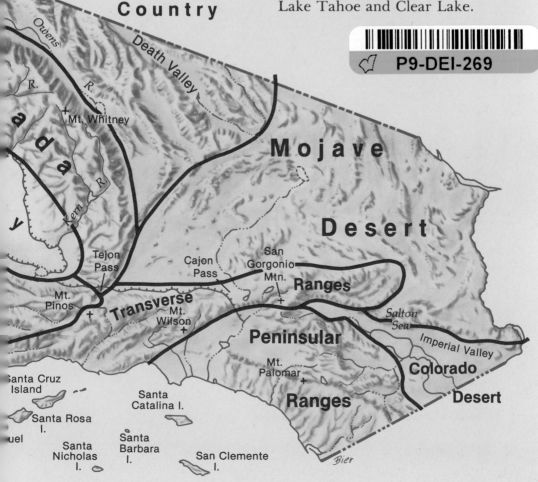

Range

Country

Owens

R.

R.

Death Valley

Mt. Whitney

ada

Kern

R.

y

Mojave

Desert

Tejon Pass

Cajon Pass

San Gorgonio Mtn.

Ranges

Mt. Pinos

Transverse

Mt. Wilson

Peninsular

Salton Sea

Imperial Valley

Mt. Palomar

Colorado

Santa Cruz Island

Santa Catalina I.

Ranges

Desert

Santa Rosa I.

uel

Santa Nicholas I.

Santa Barbara I.

San Clemente I.

Bier

California

California

A HISTORY

FOURTH EDITION

Andrew Rolle
CLELAND PROFESSOR OF HISTORY
OCCIDENTAL COLLEGE

HARLAN DAVIDSON, INC.
ARLINGTON HEIGHTS, ILLINOIS 60004

Library of Congress Cataloging-in-Publication Data
Rolle, Andrew
California: a history.

Includes bibliographies and indexes.
1. California—History.   I. Title.
F861.R78   1987   979.4   86–4790
ISBN 0–88295–839–9

Contents

Maps, Tables, and Photographs

Maps and Tables

Photographs

Preface

A HISTORY OF CALIFORNIA must first do justice to its Indian beginnings and then to the long years of Spanish colonialism and the Mexican era, which contributed so much to the shaping of past and present. It must consider enrichment by later immigrants, too—the Chinese, French, Germans, Italians, and Japanese. It must describe and analyze the many dramatic changes brought by California's American era, especially in the twentieth century. Such a book must also give special attention to minority unrest and the population explosion, as well as to industrial and cultural expansion.

The aim of this book is to recount the state's history from its origins to the present. It seeks to interpret every phase of the story, for both students and general readers, without recourse to burdensome detail.

Since its publication in 1963, and new editions in 1969 and 1978, this volume has enjoyed many individual printings. The complex changes that recently have swept over California have made a fourth major revision absolutely necessary.

The selected bibliographies of periodical and book references which follow each chapter have been brought up to date. An "Index of Authors Cited" recapitulates these bibliographies. New maps and illustrations are also provided.

Among the specialists who aided the improvement of this work are the following colleagues: the late Professors Alfred L. Kroeber, Robert Glass Cleland, Ray A. Billington, Oscar O. Winther, Allan Nevins, and John A. Hawgood. Three previous editions benefited from the suggestions of Professors Doyce B. Nunis, Jr., John H. Kemble, Abraham P. Nasatir, Joseph A. McGowan, James Jensen, Ward M. McAfee, Richard D. Batman, Iris Engstrand, Roger Daniels, Clement Meighan, John B. McGloin, John E. Baur, Theodore Grivas, D. E. Livingston-Little, and W. H. Hutchinson. Frances and Alec Rolle, Albert Shumate, Fred B. Rogers and Governor Edmund G. Brown, Sr. were also more than helpful. More recently others who aided my progress include Professors Robert F. Heizer, John Gaines, David Leary, Richard Orsi, Otto von Sadovsky, and Myra Moss. I am grateful as well to Rosalind Isuji, Roy Hayes, Sydney Allen, and Katherine Kratz.

Modern scholarship has better illuminated the role of women and minority groups in shaping the state's history. I received valuable aid from Professor Gloria Lothrop and Heather Draughon Green in preparing material on women in California. I have also expanded the sections on the environment, and about blacks, Chicanos, and Asians.

This fourth line-by-line revision is more thoroughgoing than previous ones. The chapters covering modern California have been completely changed. The elimination of extraneous details has produced a more direct narrative, one better suited to today's generation of students.

A. R.

CHAPTER 1

The Distinctiveness of California

THERE IS A LARGENESS about California that transcends its open style of life, unpredictability, and expansive tone. First, the name brings to mind extremes and paradoxes in both geography and climate. California's mountains are the highest in the continental United States outside Alaska, its rains, floods, and fires often the most catastrophic, its droughts among the driest, its fogs the densest, its earthquakes the most damaging; its redwoods are the oldest and tallest, and its deserts among the most naked and forbidding in the western hemisphere.

Just as California's geography is grand and diverse, so is its history. The record of man in California offers the historian a dimension and significance equal to that of a sovereign nation. The nineteenth-century English observer James Bryce once wrote of California that no other American state would, if isolated, be so truly a nation in itself. A 1906 article in *Munsey's Magazine* put it this way: "It will never be easy for an Easterner to believe that this one state is larger than the six kingdoms of Belgium, Holland, Greece, Denmark, Portugal, and Rumania; that it is as long as from New York to Indianapolis." California's development, furthermore, has been influenced by all manner of people—explorers, Indians, *padres*, trappers, traders, whalers, miners, cattlemen, and farmers of every nationality.

Among the regions of America, California contributes great richness to our national life. It stands in contrast to the crisp quietness of New England, the leisurely courtesy associated with the Old South, the agrarian sobriety of the Middle West; California connotes that scenic grandeur and sense of newness of the Far West. California literature expresses a distinctive regionality which underlies the "local color" of Bret Harte, the wit of Mark Twain's tales, the humor and tragedy of John Steinbeck, as well as the celebration of nature

1

in the poetry of Robinson Jeffers. In architecture, the fusion of the New England and Spanish heritages has produced the Monterey-style house, with its balconies, adobe walls, and white woodwork. Like the southwestern states of New Mexico and Arizona, California represents a mingling of a Spanish colonial influence with the mainstream of an increasingly mechanized way of life.

Land, People, Geographical Diversity

Land and population are at the heart of California's history. Among the states, California is third in size (153,693 square miles). Only Alaska and Texas have a larger landmass. The ten counties that make up southern California are nearly as large as all six New England states combined, and larger than Illinois, Iowa, or Alabama. If southern California alone were a separate nation, it would rank tenth in the world in gross national product, ahead of Brazil, India, and Mexico.

Even by American standards, California's recorded history is relatively brief. Not until 1769 was the first Spanish mission in California founded—150 years after the Pilgrims landed at Plymouth, 250 years after Hernando Cortés invaded Mexico. Population growth has been phenomenal. When admitted to statehood in 1850, California had only 92,597 residents. But for more than a century the state doubled its residents about every twenty years. By 1986 California's population numbered over 25 million, and the state was growing by 250,000 persons each year. As California's frontier rurality moved toward an industrial and urban culture, the missions and the ranchos of the Spanish period made way for such expressions of modernity as Hollywood, oil derricks, aircraft factories, steel mills, residential subdivisions, and television studios. The grape vineyards and orange groves of the early twentieth century have surrendered space to tourist attractions, housing projects, and jet-propulsion laboratories. Crowded highways, the noxious fumes of smog, and serious state and municipal problems have damaged the charm California once held for health seekers, tourists, and lovers of the out-of-doors.

Yet the allure of California remains. It has drawn to it the nation's richest citizens, who wintered at Santa Barbara or Pasadena, especially before World War II, and some of its poorest, including Middle Western "Dust Bowl" refugees of the 1930s, disparagingly called "Okies" and "Arkies." California's present population represents the culmination of an intense westward migration, rapid acculturation, high social mobility, and frenzied material growth. California's contrasts in climate, in topography, in flora and fauna, all contribute to the state's appeal. It offers virtually every physical, climatic, geologic,

Desert flora. (From the author's collection.)

and vegetational combination: the wettest weather and the driest; poor sandy soil in the southeastern desert regions and rich loam in the Central Valley; some of the hottest recorded temperatures on earth and also the coldest; the highest mountain in the United States outside Alaska (Mount Whitney, 14,496 feet) and the lowest point in the country, only sixty miles distant in the grim wastes of Death Valley (at Bad Water, 282 feet below sea level); scrub brush in southern California and the world's largest trees in the rugged High Sierra. In the summertime it is actually possible to leave a temperature of well over a hundred degrees in the Central Valley and in half an hour travel by car to San Francisco Bay, fogbound at less than fifty degrees. Similarly, the orange groves of Southern California are in the wintertime seen against a backdrop of snowy peaks in the distance. One can travel from snow- and ice-clogged Idyllwild, a resort atop the San Jacinto mountains, to the burning sands of Palm Springs in less than an hour. (In fact, a direct funicular line connects these spots.)

Three-fourths of the surface of the state consists of hills and mountains; the remaining fourth of fertile valleys and deserts. California has more diversity of natural resources than many foreign nations. As a result, although more than half the people and industry are in southern California, much of the raw materials and 90 percent of the water are located in northern California. Each section, thus, is highly dependent upon the other.

Industrial areas—north and south—occupy only a small percentage of the state's surface. California is a major producer of the nation's lumber. It is also the top agricultural state in the nation. For decades it has ranked first in the production of lemons, apricots, avocados, figs, grapes, olives, peaches, pears, plums, and many other fruits. Because it is possible to raise crops during three growing seasons— instead of the usual one—agriculture continues to flourish. Yet today only 5 percent of California's people live on farms. Many orange groves, once the major producers of citrus fruit in the United States, have toppled before the axes of subdividers; nevertheless, more oranges are grown in California today than ever before. Moving out of zones of high population density, growers have opened up agricultural areas in the San Joaquin and Imperial valleys and on the western slopes of the Sierra foothills. The same decentralization has occurred with other crops, including grapes. Despite urban encroachment upon vineyards, California produces most of the nation's wine. Los Angeles ranks sixth among the counties of the United States in total income from farm products but is number one in dairy production. Similarly, the El Monte, Petaluma, and San Fernando regions continue to be important in the production of poultry and eggs. Sebastopol remains a major apple-growing center. But the Santa Clara Valley, although still a region full of apricot and prune orchards, is now surrounded by the computer firms of Silicon Valley. The Sierra foothills are renowned not only because of earlier gold-mining activities, but also because of the peach and pear trees their slopes sustain. In California's river-delta zone, rice, asparagus, and sugar beets grow in profusion. And the Salinas area is the nation's major producer of lettuce.

California's natural resources were virtually unexploited by either the Indians or the Spaniards. Magnificent timber stands remained untouched. The melting snows of the Sierra ran wasted in rivers rushing to the sea; the power of California's waterfalls was unharnessed. Subterranean reservoirs of petroleum were untapped. Gold remained locked in the Sierra awaiting the picks and shovels of miners. The Spaniards, who lived off flocks and herds, were—almost unknowingly—the wardens of California's wealth. Under the Americans, after the gold rush of 1848–1849, mining techniques were developed in California that were used throughout the world. American mining law, too, was largely evolved in California. Early in the twentieth century oil and gas displaced gold as a cornerstone of the state's mineral wealth. California has, however, depleted much of its oil resources and ranks behind Alaska, Texas, and Louisiana in its production. Once California produced about a million barrels of petroleum daily, some 6 percent of the world's annual crude oil production. For a long time after 1900, the state was second among the states in total mineral output. California still leads the nation in the production of chromite, diatomite, quicksilver, metals of the platinum group, sand and gravel, sodium carbonate and sodium sulphate, as well as tungsten, mercury, iodine, and borate minerals.

Topography and Climate

California spans the Pacific seaboard for 1,200 miles, counting coastal indentations, between the thirty-second and forty-second parallels. The maximum length of the state is 824 miles; the maximum width 252 miles. The chief surface features, apart from its coastline, are the two mountain chains that traverse almost the entire length of the state, and the great Central Valley lying between them. The mountains of the Coast Range are generally below 4,000 feet in height, but a few peaks—San Antonio, San Bernardino, San Gorgonio, and San Jacinto—range from 10,000 to 11,600 feet. Inland, more than forty peaks of the Sierra Nevada mountain chain rise to 10,000 feet in height; a dozen peaks exceed 14,000 feet. The western slope of the High Sierra is seamed by watercourses, turbulent in their youth, calm and serene in maturity. The Sacramento and San Joaquin, however, are the state's only navigable rivers.

Like the people who inhabit it, California is a restless, ever-changing land which has both grown and shrunk over millions of years. Its coastal ranges are in their geological infancy, and their formation presents us with a gigantic jigsaw puzzle. Millions of years ago the Pacific coastline extended from southwest Idaho through Nevada down to southeastern California. Although some rocks found in the San Gabriel and San Bernardino Mountains and Mojave Desert have been dated back 1.8 billion years, most of present-day California is less than 200 million years old.

Six million years ago, Baja California was part of the Mexican mainland. There was no Gulf of California, and what we now call Los Angeles lay 400 miles south of its present location. If today's earth motions continue for 10 million years, Santa Barbara, Los Angeles, and the Baja Peninsula will be moving slowly past San Francisco, and in about 30 million years they will be jammed up against Alaska.

Except for its dividing plain, California is mostly mountainous. Numerous mountain passes, including the Tehachapi, the Cajon, and the San Marcos, as well as long, narrow valleys, nestle between the summits of the Coast Range. Much of the agricultural wealth of California lies in such valleys as the Napa, Salinas, and Santa Inez, as well as in the Los Angeles Basin. Easily the most important of California's agricultural areas is its San Joaquin-Sacramento Valley. In 1843, when John Charles Frémont first saw this valley, it was a natural bed of wild flowers four hundred miles long and fifty miles wide where herds of antelope grazed. The valley is today one of the best granaries of the world, as well as an area of increasing industrialization.

It is more accurate to speak of California's "climates" than to refer to one single climate. Scores of microclimates give California more little climates per mile and more miles of specialized climate than perhaps any other equal area. No traveler in the Sierra in midwinter would find the arid or almost subtropical climate that tourist advertisements ascribe to California. What is usually thought of as "California climate" prevails south of San Francisco to the Mexican border, and between the coastal mountains and the Pacific Ocean. In this region the seasons drift mildly from one to another, almost unperceived. Frost is not heavy enough to stop winter greening of the hills. Light breezes and cooling fogs generally keep the temperature at a comfortable level. The heat of the day is fanned by prevailing westerly winds. In summer, near the coast, climatic equability is also maintained by low clouds, known as *veloes*.

California's coastline is cooled by a meteorological process called "upwelling." Warm winds blow inward from a northwesterly direction, bringing colder ocean waters to the surface. When the warm air contacts the cold waters, condensation forms fog and low clouds. These are usually confined to within a few thousand feet above the ground. The fog sits over the ocean, creeping inland at night and retreating seaward by day. The heat of the landmass helps to dissipate this fog. California's climate is rarely humid or soporific. Less than 1 percent of the earth's surface enjoys such ideal weather.

Rain varies markedly. Annual rainfall in the northwest corner of the state, above Eureka, reaches 110 inches, making the area a virtual rain forest. Precipitation in the central valley is heavier at Sacramento and Stockton than at other cities farther south, including Fresno and Bakersfield. At San Francisco, the average annual rainfall is nearly

23 inches; at San Luis Obispo it falls to 19 inches, and then to less than 15 inches at Los Angeles. At San Diego, near the Mexican border, rainfall generally amounts to only 10 inches per year. Seasonal precipitation averages only 6 inches at Bakersfield and as little as 1 or 2 inches in desert areas. Drought conditions sometimes exist from Monterey southward to San Diego. Practically all of California's precipitation—both rain and snow—falls between November and April. Water must be stored carefully and transported over long distances for the steady distribution not provided by nature.

The coastal mountain ranges partly control California's weather. In winter, North Pacific storms, moving counterclockwise, sometimes cyclonic in their fury, crash down on the Coast Range. The rain clouds, carried by heavy winds, push through the canyon gaps in these mountains into the central valley. Because eastward-moving storms are broken up on the Sierra's crest, there is less rain east of the Sierra; on their western slopes dams impound water for urban use. Below the eastern Sierran cordillera the temperature rises as high as 134 degrees, and so little water falls upon areas like Death Valley that there exists hardly any substantial vegetation. Along the volcanic plain in northeastern California, agriculture and animal grazing are also limited by climate and a rocky topography.

The uneven distribution of water has given rise to the tongue-in-cheek observation that California's unusually "high fogs" sometimes cause drowning among the unwary. In the north the danger of floods is no joking matter. Since Gold Rush days the communities of Sacramento, Stockton, Oroville, and Marysville have been plagued by winter inundations which burst through artificial dikes raised along the sides of the American, Sacramento, and San Joaquin rivers. Paradoxically, one of the most serious flood threats also exists in semiarid southern California. There, although the rainfall is the lightest in the state, the scarce, burned-out chaparral provided poor cover for the watershed. Inexperienced people build their homes on low flats, alluvial fans, or in canyon mouths, making themselves vulnerable to disasters.

The key word to describe California's climate—as well as most of its other natural characteristics—is variety, indeed grandiose variety. Newcomers sometimes express disappointment over California's prolonged spells of dryness, heat, and, quite rarely, cold. Some critics even persuade themselves that the one normal characteristic of California's weather pattern is summed up in the word "unusual."

Flora and Fauna

The wide range of climate in California makes possible a corresponding variety in vegetable and floral products. Almost every plant, tree, or shrub that grows in temperate zones, and many indigenous to the tropics, can be grown somewhere in California. The state also is known for unique forms of vegetation, especially for its giant sequoias, which have their roots deep in the past. Along with the ancient bristle cone pines of the White Mountains, these lords of the forest are probably the oldest living things on earth. Some sequoias now standing were in their prime at the time of Christ. In fact, their age may be 5,000 or more years. Most "big trees" that have perished have been the victims of human ravages, or of fire, lightning, or fierce storms. Sequoias are virtually immune to diseases that afflict other trees, and their tannic bark is resistant to fire.

The gnarled Monterey cypress, a picturesque denizen of the seacoast, likewise commands attention. It is found only along a rugged section of the Monterey shoreline. These trees, clinging precariously to promontories like Cypress Point, are totally exposed to the Pacific storms. Heavy winds have twisted them into fantastic forms, and yet they survive. Similar in tenacity are the Torrey pines of the coastline above San Diego.

California's skies were once darkened by flocks of geese, ducks, and other migrating birds who wintered there. The wildlife has been greatly depleted by the ravages of man. Nevertheless, 400 species of mammals and 600 varieties of birds make the state their home. From the horned toad and desert tortoise to the bobcat, weasel, and black-tailed deer, California's fauna is as diversified as its other features. In the wilderness, coyotes, mountain lions, wolverines, and cougars still roam. Big-horn mountain sheep and wapiti, or elk, once common, are now rare, and the California grizzly bear is virtually extinct. The condor and sea otter have barely escaped extinction. Perched on the brink of extinction, the condor—largest land bird in North America—reminds us of the way in which California is both old and new.

Geology and Scenic Grandeur

Geologically, California is young. The 400 mile-long Sierran scarp, caused by uplifting and faulting, and the volcanic Cascades and the nonvolcanic Klamaths in the north are in youthful stages of development. The California coastline, pushed up out of the Pacific's depths at Points Pinos and Lobos, as well as at Cape Mendocino, is a rocky one, with headlands jutting out to sea. California's coastline, unlike our eastern shore, is one of emergence, rather than submergence; in fact, the entire Pacific shoreline, down to Cape Horn in South America, is sharply uplifted. This geologic pattern has produced few navigable rivers or estuaries and harbors comparable to Boston, New York, Philadelphia, or Baltimore. With the exception of San Diego in the south, San Francisco in the middle, and Humboldt Bay in the northern corner of the state, natural harbors are virtually nonexistent in California. Los Angeles is not a natural harbor.

Stupendous changes, frequently abrupt, sometimes gradual, have shaped the face of California in past geologic ages. The two principal mountain chains, the Sierra Nevada and the Coast Range, were titanic upheavals from beneath the earth's crust. The fiery origin of the Cascade mountains to the northeast is revealed by their lava formations and extinct cinder cones. One supposedly dead volcano, Lassen Peak, came alive in 1914 and spouted out a holocaust of hot mud and ash which devastated everything in its path. At intervals, Lassen floats a pennant of smoke from its summit to warn hikers that its inner fires still smolder. Indian traditions still exist of former eruptions in California's northern mountains. John Muir once wrote of these, "They tell of a fearful time of darkness, when the sky was black with ashes and smoke that threatened every living thing with death, and that when at length the sun appeared once more it was red like blood." Seething geysers and hot sulphur springs—safety-valves of subterranean heat and pressure—testify that underlying fires are far from extinguished at Geyserville.

Physical forces have combined to change the configuration of California's mountain chains. The movements of glaciers, changes of weather and temperature, volcanic and chemical action, eroding running water, successive earthquakes—all have had a part in sculpturing the mountains of California. The Yosemite chasm, in particular, is noted for its domes, peaks, and glacier-formed perpendicular walls nearly a mile high, with their waterfalls—all within a radius of half a dozen miles. The Yosemite Valley was not officially seen by white men until 1851, a year after California became a state. For decades the remote interior remained a frontier. The scarred Sierra, created by avalanche, earthquake, rasping glaciers, gale-force winds, rain, and frost, stands aloof with ice and snow on its peaks.

Serious earth tremors, as in 1812, 1870, 1906, 1933, 1952, 1957, and 1971, indicate that these forces are still strong, and that shocks may be expected to occur again. The sheer precipice that forms the eastern walls of the Sierra, facing Owens Valley and Nevada, drops 10,000 feet in the Mount Whitney region. This area provides a striking example of vertical faults caused by earthquake shocks.

Although the California coastline is in an emergent stage, its geologic story has been one of repeated rising and sinking. Seashells, whale bones, and beach boulders are to be found on mountain tops far above the present level of the sea. Ages ago ocean waves washed the base of the Sierra Nevada, but as geological forces heaved up the floor of the Central Valley, ocean waters were forced to recede. The most recent phase of the geologic development of the coastline

Floor of Yosemite Valley before silting of Mirror Lake occurred. (From the author's collection.)

was the flooding of the mouths of streams that helped form San Francisco and San Diego bays.

Prehistoric California went through numerous transitions of climate, including both arctic cold and tropic heat. A few small glaciers still exist in the Sierra, as mementos of the ice age. The tropical past is locked into the asphalt beds at Rancho La Brea, now a municipal park in Los Angeles. During the tertiary age, the quaking, sticky surface of this prehistoric swamp became a death trap for animals and birds long since extinct. The blackened skeletons of creatures caught in the mire of these tar pits furnish evidence of the tropic life that once existed. Museum dioramas can only partly portray the mammoths, camels, horses, saber-toothed tigers, and ground sloths that once roamed through California's primeval forests of vines and palmetto fronds. Carbon-dating techniques have established the age of animal and mineral objects taken from La Brea as more than 28,000 years.

Isolation

California's discovery came late in history. Its remoteness from civilizations both East and West, as well as the tremendous physical difficulties of approaching the area, kept it isolated. To the east was a vast, unexplored continent with rugged, often snow-covered mountain ranges, almost unfordable rivers, and waterless deserts. Added to these obstacles were widely dispersed, fierce Indian tribes. Even after the eastern half of North America had been settled, travelers faced numerous barriers in attempting to cross the great western stretches of country. When Frémont entered California early in 1844, he and his troop of men narrowly escaped death from exposure and starvation amid the snows of the Sierra. The tragic story of the Donner Party, lost and starving in these mountains two years later, is even better known. Death Valley acquired its lugubrious name from parties of travelers whose horses and cattle perished in its arid wastes. California did not invite exploration or settlement.

The seemingly endless waste of water to the west kept sailors away from its shores. When Ferdinand Magellan sailed out of the Atlantic through the straits that bear his name and came upon an unknown ocean, he called it the "Peaceful Sea" (Pacific). Later navigators who experienced its frequent tempests thought it should have been called the "Restless Ocean." As European mariners crawled along the Pacific coastline from the south, head winds drove their ships hundreds of miles off course, sometimes far out to sea. Only by the patient tacking of sails and beating to windward, at times for weeks at a stretch, could tiny vessels make a northing. In 1539, Francisco de Ulloa, the first white man to round the point of Lower California, complained bitterly of the northwest wind, which so hindered him from making progress that he angrily called it the "king of all that coast." Added to the wind and weather was scurvy. On the earliest Spanish expeditions so many sailors were incapacitated from this disease that not enough were left to man the vessels, which were obliged to drift at the mercy of wind and wave.

Though Spain's mariners died by the hundreds, and ship after ship sank, nothing could halt the spirit of its navigators. League by league, each expedition reaching a slightly higher latitude, these men made their way up the coast, from the early sixteenth century onward. In time they won the distinctive and still unexplored "terrestrial paradise at the left hand of the Indies" named California.

Selected Readings

For descriptions of the geologic and natural wonders of California see: John Muir, *The Mountains of California* (New York, 1894); Mary Austin, *The Land of Little Rain* (Boston, 1903), and, with Sutton Palmer, her *California: The Land of the Sun* (New York, 1914); Roderick Peattie, ed., *The Pacific Coast Ranges* (New York, 1946), and his *The Sierra Nevada* (New York, 1947).

David Hornbeck and Phillip Kane, *California Patterns: A Geographical and Historical Atlas* (Palo Alto, 1983), is the most modern geography of California. See also Warren A. Beck and Ynez D. Haase, *Historical Atlas of California* (Norman, Okla., 1973). Consult also David W. Lantis, Rodney Steiner, and Arthur E. Karinen, *California: Land of Contrast* (Belmont, Calif., 1963).

Discussion of California's earth tremors is in Robert Tacopi, *Earthquake Country* (Menlo Park, Calif., 1964). A classic guidebook was produced by the Federal Writers Project of the WPA as *California: A Guide to the Golden State* (New York, 1939, revised, 1954).

Early multi-volume histories of the state include Hubert Howe Bancroft, *History of California* (7 vols., San Francisco, 1884–90); Theodore H. Hittell, *History of California* (4 vols., San Francisco, 1885–97); and Zoeth S. Eldredge, ed., *History of California* (5 vols., New York, 1915). These were followed by Charles E. Chapman, *A History of California: The Spanish Period* (New York, 1921), and its companion volume, Robert G. Cleland, *A History of California: The American Period* (New York, 1922). Rockwell D. Hunt and Nellie Van de Grift Sanchez, *A Short History of California* (New York, 1929), for its time a distinct contribution, preceded Cleland's later books, *From Wilderness to Empire* (New York, 1944), and *California in Our Time* (New York, 1947).

Still later, after John Caughey (1940), came a variety of new state histories by Andrew Rolle (1963), Walton Bean (1968), as well as Warren Beck and David Williams (1972). James D. Hart, *A Companion to California* (New York, 1978) is encyclopedic. Also consult two brochures by Andrew Rolle, *California, A Students' Guide to Localized History* (New York, 1965) and *Los Angeles, A Students' Guide to Localized History* (New York, 1965).

Valuable as bibliography is Robert E. Cowan's *A Bibliography of the History of California and the Pacific West, 1510–1906* (San Francisco, 1914, 1933).

CHAPTER 2

The Indian

THE CALIFORNIA INDIANS have been portrayed in an unfortunate manner. It was once believed that they could not be compared favorably with other tribal groups in North America. But they should not be measured only against Caucasian standards. From ancient times, these Indians arrived at a more than harmonious adjustment to their environment.

Though their culture was simple, the California Indians acknowledged no peers in certain specialized activities. Among these were complex cult religions, intricate basket designs, acorn-leaching operations, and their skill in flint chipping. Dependence upon acorns as a basic food discouraged organized agriculture. Similarly, their serviceable basketry work may have accounted for the neglect of pottery, an art form brought to a high state of achievement by tribes living to the south and east. Like other North American Indians, these first Californians did not understand the principle of the wheel, had no real system of writing, and led a Stone Age existence. But material achievements form only part of their story.

Living close to the soil, the natives achieved stability. Peaceful in outlook, they possessed an uncomplicated yet successful culture, in tune with their environment. A few tribes, among them the Hupa and Yurok, showed some highly developed culture traits. These Indians preferred their basic way of life to systematic agriculture or handicrafts. It is difficult to generalize about so many different tribal groupings, but the basic fact about the California Indians is that, isolated from other North American Indian cultures by mountain barriers and deserts, they developed a society well suited to their geographic needs. Theirs was a style of living built around food gathering and fishing, rather than sowing, planting, or harvesting. Instead of describing that way of life in terms of a culture lag, it is more

13

accurate and contemporary to speak of the California Indians' culture as effective in providing them with a livelihood. Their social system remained intact for thousands of years.

As to the origins of California's Indians, the bones of "Laguna Man" are thought to be 17,000 years old. Flint chips from another site near Calico were dated by the anthropologist L. S. B. Leakey at 20,000 to 100,000 years old.

In recent years Professor Otto von Sadovsky has established evidence of a link between California's Indians and certain Asian tribes. He asserts that up to 80 percent of the languages used by two tribes in northwest Siberia and nineteen California tribes are related. This link involves more than 10,000 different words and forms of grammar. The invaders probably traveled toward the Bering Straits by water at a time when the climate was warmer than today. They may have also used a then-existent land bridge. Although the earliest origins of America's Indians have been traced back for thousands of years, the Penutians (or Costanoans) who lived from Monterey northward appear to have arrived only 3,000 years ago. They may have pushed tribes already there into the mountains south and north of their new culture area. In addition to linguistic similarities with the Siberians, their mothering, marriage, religion, and magical beliefs echoed those imported to California.

Physical and Ethnic Characteristics

Short, and with small skulls, most California Indians did not possess the copper complexion, aquiline features, or proud bearing associated with the American Indian. Instead, according to anthropologist Alfred Louis Kroeber, they "were flat-nosed and broad-faced, with an apathetic carriage." Yet they were sturdy and long-lived, and there were handsome individuals among them. Chief Solano of the Suisunes, for whom Solano County is named, was six feet, seven inches in height and broad in proportion. Such a chieftain would have done honor to any tribal society. The Colorado River tribes were among the tallest groups of California.

That these Indians were not dull-witted is shown by the facility with which they acquired use of the Spanish language, which they soon learned to speak correctly. The Spaniards also taught them to read music and to sing church chorales, and they learned to intone Latin with astonishing accuracy.

Because California's aborigines were without education in any modern sense, such accomplishments as they acquired in a few years of mission instruction seem remarkable. Their ability to learn mechanical arts finds a silent but impressive witness in the remains of

Indian Population Table[1]

Pre-1542	300,000[2]
1769–1822	100,000
1870	30,000
1880	16,277
1890	16,624
1900	15,377
1910	16,371
1920	17,360
1930	19,212
1940	18,675
1950	19,947
1960	39,014
1970	91,018
1980	198,275[3]

[1] Population census statistics are muddled by changing criteria. Indians were not included in census data before 1890. Early data are approximate. Later figures include in-migration from other areas.
[2] Only 133,000 to 150,000 according to A. L. Kroeber. The larger figure is based upon Sherburne F. Cook's estimate of 310,000.
[3] Includes some Yumas, who also live in Arizona. The figure is also confused by Chicanos being numbered as Indians.

California's missions, erected almost entirely by Indian workmen under the direction of friars. In the mission schools, Indians became carpenters, weavers, and farmers. There were no better cattle herders, although the Indians had never seen domesticated animals, including horses, before the coming of the Spaniards. There is reason to feel amazement at their capacity, rather than shock at their lack of it.

Native Arts and Dwellings

Native Indian crafts or arts were few in California. Basket making was largely in the hands of the women, who were also expert in dressing skins and in making rush mats for beds. California's coastal Indians built dugout canoes with no better tools than wedges of elk horn and adzes with mussel-shell blades. Household utensils included basket pots into which hot stones were dropped, stone mortars and pestles for grinding seeds and acorns, horn and shell knives, and flat spoons or paddles for stirring acorn gruel. The Indians also used looped sticks for cooking with red-hot stones, nets of vegetable fiber for fishing and carrying small objects, and wooden trays and bowls.

Indian dwellings were of the simplest construction, varying in accordance with the climate. In northwest and central California, they were sometimes partly excavated, with sides and roof of heavy wood slabs split or hewn from trees; center posts held up the roofs of larger structures. These "houses," half above and half below ground, kept the Indians warm in cold weather, but the damp, fetid atmosphere of their interiors would have been unendurable to modern whites. The dwellings of the Klamath River tribes were built above the surface; they were rectangular, with walls and roof constructed of redwood planks. The Yurok and Hupa built frame houses. Mountain Indians preferred bark or wood-slab buildings. Among the Chumash, along the Santa Barbara coast, houses of "half-orange" shape were built of poles drawn together and tied at the top. Thatched grass, foliage, or wet earth covered these dwellings, whose light construction was suited to the mild climate of the area. Cave habitation was also practiced by various Sierran Indians, but in the warmest parts of California the natives were satisfied with a thatch or brush shelter, piled up heavily on its windy side.

As a result of these latter habitations, the Indians' interest in housing has been described as deficient—a basically incorrect indictment in view of the different dwellings they constructed. When the collection of bones and other refuse strewn on the floor became too offensive, and the fleas and vermin too numerous, an Indian family sometimes set fire to their "house" and built a new one elsewhere.

Food and Clothing

The food of the primitive Californians was more often vegetable than animal, but roots formed only a part of it. Thus these Indians do not deserve to be called by the epithet "diggers"—a term first applied to them, in contempt, by Americans.

The first sound to be heard on approaching an Indian village was the pounding of pestles in mortars. The major food staple of the Indians, corresponding to the maize consumed elsewhere, was the acorn. Carefully gathered in season and stored in raised cylindrical cribs, acorns constituted, with dried salmon and nuts, the basic provisions stored by natives for winter. Before acorns could be eaten they had to be hulled, parched, and pulverized, and the tannic acid leached out. This last operation was done in a basket, or in a sand basin. Next, the Indians boiled the sweetened ground acorn meal. The Shastas roasted moistened meal, while the Pomo and other groups mixed red earth with their meal and baked it; the resultant mixture was eaten or stored. The Indians also ate, after boiling, the green leaves of plants. Roots, otherwise poisonous, were made fit for food by long roasting underground. The natives possessed no intoxicating drinks, but a mild form of inebriation was produced by prolonged smoking of wild tobacco and jimson weed.

California's Indians ate the flesh of animals whenever they could obtain it. Weapons were few in number and relatively poor in quality—usually small bows and arrows, and flint-tipped lances. When hunting large game, the Indians made up for lack of weapons by strategy. Wonderfully deft and skilled in stalking game, they contrived disguises with the head and upper part of the skins of animals. They also set out decoys to attract birds within arrowshot. Game drives were organized, with the animals directed past hidden hunters. Less common was the technique of running down a deer by human relays, until it fell from exhaustion. Pits and traps were used to catch larger game, except the grizzly bear. The Indians held this animal in such fear that they let it alone, believing it possessed of a demon. Wood rats, squirrels, coyotes, crows, rabbits, lizards, field mice, and snakes were all, however, fair game. Cactus apples and berries were a special treat. The Indians were not fastidious in their tastes, and did not disdain to eat snails, caterpillars, minnows, crickets, grubs found in decayed trees, slugs, fly larvae gathered from the tops of bushes in swamps (these had a texture rather like tapioca pudding), horned toads, earthworms (used in soup), grasshoppers (roasted and powdered), and skunks (killed and dressed with due caution). Fish, especially salmon and shellfish, formed an important part of the diet of coastal Indians, often excellent fishermen who guarded their "salmon waters," as the northern rivers where these fish spawned were called. Incursions upon salmon fishing areas by intruders caused bloody conflicts.

Food, whether animal or vegetable, was provided almost wholly by nature. Although the Colorado River Indians were settled agricultural tribes, most of the other natives of California followed no form of agriculture, except scattering seeds of wild tobacco. Indeed, after the coming of the padres, male Indians frequently opposed such radical notions as organized crop cultivation, involving backbreaking labor in the fields.

Nature, in addition to furnishing the Indians with food, gave them the ingredients for their clothing. Originally most of the men went naked, wearing not even a breechclout, although rude moccasins, sandals, and (in the north) snowshoes were worn. The Indians' complexions were dried and cracked by exposure to wind, sun, and water. Only in the coldest weather did they utilize rabbit or deerskin cloaks and skin blankets. Some natives were known to roll in the mud and to wash off the surface of their bodies when the sun came out. Women wore a pretense of a skirt made of tule grass from the waist to the knees, or narrow skin aprons, front and back. In cold weather they wore a cape of deerskin or rabbit fur and sometimes covered their breasts with furs, including those of the otter and wildcat. They were fond of ornamentation, and painted faces and bodies in patterns.

They decorated their hair with small shells, bones, and even stones. For ceremonial occasions they used elaborate headdresses of feathers and beads. Some Indians wore basketry hats, while those of the central region bound their heads with hairnets.

Social Customs

The women and children did much of the drudgery among the California Indians, while the men, when not engaged in hunting and fishing, sometimes roamed from house to house and from village to village. The women hunted small animals, gathered acorns, caught fish, scraped animal skins, fashioned robes, hauled water and firewood, wove baskets, barbecued meat, and constructed some dwellings. Creation of a male paradise on earth seems almost to have been the Indians' objective. Yet it is incorrect to label the males as lazy. They specialized in certain occupations. Among the Hupa Indians, for example, these included making bows, arrows, nets, and pipes, dressing hides, and preparing ceremonial fire-sticks from cottonwood roots.

California's natives were different in behavior from the taciturn Eastern Indians of James Fenimore Cooper's Leather-stocking tradition. They impressed visitors as a joyous race, among the happiest and most gregarious of all American aborigines. Far from resenting the coming of most white men, they gave them a friendly welcome. Indeed, the Spaniards complained that the singing and dancing was so continuous, day and night, that they had little opportunity for sleep. The Indians, of course, were not always joy-ridden or garrulous. A day might pass in some villages with nothing more than a few grunts exchanged.

The Indians were fond of dancing, in which they engaged not only for amusement, but also in connection with ceremonials. The northwest Indians had the salmon dance; special dances for the newborn child, the black bear, the new clover, the white deer, and the elk; the dance of welcome to visiting Indians; the dance of peace; and of course war dances, for which the braves were painted and dressed in finery of plumes and beads. Dancing also took place at the separate puberty rites for boys and for girls. The Yurok held a first-salmon dance at the mouth of the Klamath River. The Hupa, in addition to a first-eel ceremony, also held an autumnal first-acorn feast. Some of these first-fruit ceremonies bore a resemblance to the Thanksgiving feast of the Puritans of New England.

Dancing, singing, and chanting formed a significant part of the lives of the Indians, who possessed a greater power of tonal imagery and lyric sense than is credited to them. Musical activities became spirited whenever the Indians indulged in the chewing or smoking of jimson weed, whose narcotic effect is similar to that of mescaline or marijuana. Some religious rituals, such as those of the Toloache cult, made use of music as an adjunct to narcotics. Accompanied by the hum of bull roarers (a slat of wood swung at the end of a thong), chanting and singing would go on late into the night.

Among other types of celebrations were those at which the Indians boasted about the huts they had built, the victories they had won; defeats were duly glossed over. All achievements were recounted by wizened elders in long orations, to which people listened in solemn silence. Afterwards they did not gorge themselves with a great feast, in our fashion, but often ate abstemiously. The California Indians had good reason to be proud of their achievements. A source of pride was watercraft, which they handled with dexterity and skill. One of the most common types was the tule balsa, a sort of raft made out of river rushes; this craft, used for fishing, was usually poled or paddled on inland waters. The Indians also made use of plank canoes, which were burned or chopped out of large trees.

A special ceremony took place each summer when the southern California and Sierra Nevada tribes held a memorial dance for the dead in the village cemetery. There they built a large fire into which clothing, baskets, and other possessions were thrown as offerings to the departed. Indian braves then danced in a circle around the fire, accompanied by the rattle of the mourning chant.

Organized mourning for the dead by close relatives was practiced by nearly all tribes. This took the form of smearing the face with a wet paste mixed from the ashes of the deceased. The Indians kept this facial covering on until it wore off, for as long as a year. A few tribes buried their dead; others practiced cremation.

Many customs might seem strange to us. In northwestern California a wife could be purchased for strings of shell money or deerskins. A man was disgraced if he secured his wife for nothing. Polygamy was practiced by some who could afford the price of more than one wife, and rich men sometimes had many wives. Some Indians were inveterate gamblers, who would risk their last possession, even their wives, in games of chance. A "strip poker" guessing game was popular, as were other gambling games involving the use of stone pebbles under sea shells. The Indians were also fond of athletics. In various ball games, and in leaping, jumping, and similar contests, they accepted defeat with the same sportsmanship as they did victory; but there was familial and local pride in achievement.

Each family was a law unto itself, and there was no fully systematic punishment for crime. Yet atonement for injury was not unknown. Sometimes serious offenses could be excused for "money." A murderer could even buy himself off by paying the family of the deceased in skins or shells, after which friendship might be restored between him and the aggrieved.

In these days of super-nationalism we best understand social organization as practiced by the nation-state. In Indian California, where approximately 135 different dialects were spoken, a strict political or tribal system cannot easily be discerned. Kroeber cautions that it is wise to avoid the term "tribe." Except for a minority of well-defined tribes or tribelets, including the Yumas and some of the Indians of California's northwest coast, the basic political unit was the village community settlement. The Spanish called these village units *rancherías*. They were loosely knit groupings of several hundred aborigines; within each there were clans, identified by individual totems. A *ranchería* had a patrilinear leader, who was paid ceremonial deference, but whose authority was limited to giving advice. One can apply the term "chief" to him only with qualification. Sons of clan chieftains inherited the father's power only if they were potentially of similar capacity.

California's Indians were not generally nomadic. Boundaries were defined, and to pass beyond a local boundary sometimes meant death to the trespasser. This led mothers to teach children the landmarks of their own family or tribal limits. These lessons were imparted in a singsong enumeration of the stones, boulders, mountains, high trees, and other objects on the landscape beyond which it was dangerous to wander. Women and children, of course, depended upon husbands and fathers for protection against enemies. Controversies between families sometimes led to "wars," at times over the abduction of women or quarrels about food sources. Rock and arrow fights took place around acorn groves or salmon streams. The name of one of California's northern counties, Calaveras ("skulls"), was given to one of its streams by the Spanish Lieutenant, Gabriel Moraga, who found skulls scattered along its banks.

Because the California Indians seemed less warlike than Eastern tribes, their comparative mildness of character led early writers to speak of them as cowardly. Actually the Spaniards had sharp encounters with them before they were finally subjugated. Moraga led forty-six campaigns against them. Americans, later finding them already subdued by the Spaniards, failed to realize how much "frontier work" had been accomplished before their arrival. On those occasions when the Indians fought systematically, they never tortured prisoners of war, though some of them took the scalps of dead opponents.

An institution that the Californians had in common with other Indians was the sorcerer, or "medicine man," and they had profound faith in his ability to cure illness. His shamanistic treatment consisted mainly of reciting incantations, after which he placed one end of a hollow tube, a basic tool of the trade, against the body of the patient. He then pretended to suck out the cause of the disease, which might be a sliver of bone, a sharp-edged flint flake, or a dead lizard or other small animal, which he had previously secreted in his mouth. His success, in fact, depended partly upon his ability to fabricate incredible stories. Notwithstanding the pretenses of these practitioners, they had knowledge of the medicinal properties of herbs, roots, and other natural remedies, and used it to benefit their patients. Even the Spanish consulted medicine men when other means failed to cure them of afflictions such as dysentery. Until the coming of the Spaniards the Indian seems not to have suffered from such white man's diseases as smallpox, influenza, and measles. Tuberculosis was unknown to them, the common cold was rare, and venereal disease did not exist. Constant scratching from lice and fleas, however, bloodied their bodies, and they were kept awake nights by the vermin from the filthy animal skins they used as bedclothes.

Though not universally used, one of the favorite treatments of Indian illnesses was the *temescal,* or sweathouse; this was a mound-like structure, usually made of timbers hermetically covered with earth, with only one small opening. A large fire was built inside the sweathouse, the patient entered, the door was closed, and there, among steaming hot stones, a sick Indian remained until dripping with perspiration. Then he rushed out and leaped into the nearest lake or stream, sometimes into ice-cold water. This was a sort of "kill or cure" remedy. The Spaniards attributed to its use large numbers of deaths among the Indians from smallpox and similar diseases. The cold-water plunge was, however, effective in eliminating vermin. Personal odors also were thereby diminished. Because the *temescal* was restricted to men, one chronicler wrote that the women smelled like long-dead fish. (Among some tribes, however, both sexes were accustomed to take a daily plunge in the nearest stream.) Some men preferred to sleep at the *temescal* baths rather than at home.

Religion

Indian religion, as moderns prefer to understand it, was primitive. Yet tribal groups had a well-defined system of shamanism, designed not only to cure disease, but also to serve a religious purpose. There were cults based on distinct ideas about the creation of the world and about the primeval flood. Each family unit believed that the creation took place at a spot within their local territory. A tradition held that at a remote time in the past a billowing sea rolled up onto the plains to fill the valleys until it covered the mountains. Nearly all living beings were destroyed in this deluge, except a few who had gone to the high peaks. There was some notion of a supreme being, known by various names among different groups. They also held to a concept of immortality: in eternity good Indians would go to a happy land beyond the water, where food would be plentiful and there would be nothing to do but eat, sleep, and dance. When the coming of the new moon was celebrated, an old man would dance in a circle, saying, "As the moon dieth and cometh to life again, so we also, having to die, will live again."

California Indian mythology was extensive and complex. About it Kroeber wrote: "Their legends evince a higher power of primitive speculation than might be anticipated in view of their being largely animal tales, with [a] coyote as the chief figure." The most unusual of Indian folktales and village traditions were preserved and passed on, garbled at times, to invading whites.

In the practice of religion, the Indians sometimes conversed with a supernatural being while in a trance. Dreams too were a source of communion with heavenly deities, as in a vision. Individuals sought to cure themselves of disease, actual and imagined, by rituals involving singing, dancing, and smoking. A guardian spirit oversaw one's quest for freedom from pain, aided, of course, by medicine men, who engaged in a "doctors' dance"; there were rain, rattlesnake, and bear doctors, possessing clairvoyant and curative powers.

The Toloache and Kuksu cults were among those that figured significantly in the religious life of California's Indians. The Toloache ritual featured smoking jimson weed, an ancient rite that induced supernatural visions, even hallucinations. The Kuksu cult was originally a male secret society with an esoteric set of initiation rites. So complex were these that young boys were schooled in the use of masks, disguises, and ritualistic dancing. Ritualistic chambers, usually earth-roofed, were designed for use by the Kuksu faithful. Other esoteric "closed cults" also existed in California, the most prominent of which was the "World Renewal" religious system of northwest California.

The Indian Languages

The Indians possessed a veritable babel of languages. No less than twenty-two linguistic families are identifiable. All but one of these (Yukian) extended beyond the borders of California. Within its present boundaries there were, as already noted, 135 regional dialects. This confusion of tongues was one of the principal difficulties with which the missionaries had to contend. Because it was laborious to learn so many dialects, native interpreters were not easily found. Many Indian groups could not understand one another's speech, though separated sometimes by only the width of a stream. It is a feat of memory merely to list the dozens of different groups in California. Among the better known linguistic classifications are the Hupa or Hoopa, Pomo, Modoc, Maidu, Mono, Yurok, and Yuma (see map on the following page). Many smaller groups have become extinct.

The Indians of California have left behind little of greater permanence than the place names taken from their dialects. The meaning and origin of most of these place names remains cloaked in mystery; linguistic scholarly investigation was not instituted until most of the aborigines were dead. Those who remain had forgotten almost everything connected with their tribal past. Thus an "unanalyzed residuum of meaningless names," to quote Kroeber, was lost forever. Not until the Indians had almost vanished did the white man realize the loss.

Considering the disregard in which the Indian was held by whites, it is remarkable that the names of nine California counties—Colusa, Modoc, Mono, Napa, Shasta, Tehama, Tuolumne, Yolo, and Yuba— have been taken from the language of the Indian. Two more county names—Inyo and Siskiyou—are of possible native origin. In general, the significance of the native names borne by towns, rivers, mountains, and counties has been hopelessly lost. Modern man must be content with the historic interest that the sound of these names gives to California. They remain the only enduring monument to the first lords of its soil.

Indian Population

As compared with most regions of North America, California had a dense native population, doubtless as a result of the mild climate and abundant food supply. An early estimate placed the number of Indians when California was discovered at from 100,000 to 150,000,* or one-eighth the entire Indian population in the area now covered by the United States, although the territory these Indians occupied was only one-twentieth of that total land area. After disastrous diseases were introduced among the Indians by the Spaniards, their numbers were drastically reduced. Despite a reputation for cruelty given the Spanish by their enemies (the "Black Legend," or *leyenda negra*), they were not generally hard taskmasters. When the Indians

---

*Professors Alfred L. Kroeber, C. Hart Merriam, and S. F. Cook have all given different figures concerning the California Indian population prior to the arrival of the first Spaniards. In a letter of January 22, 1960, to the author, Kroeber stated: "The population has been estimated, after detailed analysis, at around 133,000, and again at about a quarter of a million."

Major Indian Linguistic Groups in California

Adapted from A. L. Kroeber, *Handbook of the Indians of California* (Bureau of American Ethnology Bulletin 78, Washington, 1925), Plate I.

entered the confinement of the missions, however, they gave up the habit of burning down their "houses" occasionally, as well as their use of the sweathouse. The abandonment of these practices removed the only methods of sanitation the Indians had known, and increased the incidence of disease.

The record of Indian decimation is examined in a later chapter. Anthropologists have come to reject the romantic notion of the missions as proper Indian homes, regarding those establishments as slave-labor camps. Some suggest that if a native returned to his tribe—and sin—soldiers were sent to shoot him while he was still in a state of grace. Following secularization of the missions in California's Mex-

Members of the Diegueño tribe, Mesa Grande, 1906. (Museum of the American Indian.)

ican period (1834), the condition of the Indians deteriorated further.

The natives' numbers diminished severely after the discovery of gold in the American period, which brought more disease, as well as mining operations that destroyed food sources. Northern salmon no longer swam up California's streams to spawn. Miners cut down acorn groves for firewood. The whites also seized valuable Indian campsites. The Indians, alas, developed a vulnerable culture. When slaves are property, they are usually taken care of as valuable assets. In the American period, Indians were considered to be not quite persons; hence they were sacrificed and their death toll grew heavy. Induced to sign treaties they did not understand, the natives were moved off fertile lands into rocky deserts. Starvation and malnutrition brought down their numbers to a remnant estimated at only 16,000 by the year 1900.

Selected Readings

Basic to an understanding of the California aborigines are Stephen Powers, *Tribes of California* (Washington, D.C., 1877); Alfred L. Kroeber, *Handbook of the Indians of California* (Bureau of American Ethnology, Bulletin 78, Washington, D.C., 1925); and Frederick W. Hodge, *Handbook of the American Indians North of Mexico* (2 vols., Washington, D.C., 1907–10; repr. New York, 1959). Kroeber published numerous monographs in the University of California's *Publications in Archaeology and Ethnology*. Especially useful is his "California Culture Provinces," in volume 17 of this series (Berkeley, 1920). One of Kroeber's last efforts, written with S. A. Barrett, is entitled *Fishing Among the Indians of Northwestern California* (Berkeley, 1960). Most useful also is *Aboriginal California: Three Studies in Culture History* (Berkeley, 1963), the combined work of A. L. Kroeber, James T. Davis, Robert F. Heizer, and Albert B. Elsasser. Consult Sherburne F. Cook, *The Conflict Between the California Indian and White Civilization* (Berkeley, 1943), and his *The Population of the California Indians, 1769–1970* (Berkeley, 1976), as well as C. Hart Merriam, *Studies of California Indians* (Berkeley, 1955). These studies attempt to gauge the effects of white contact upon the Indians, as do C. Alan Hutchinson, "The Mexican Government and the Mission Indians of Upper California, 1821–1835," *The Americas* 21 (April 1965), 335–62, and Daniel Garr, "Planning, Politics, and Plunder: The Missions and Indian Pueblos of Hispanic California," *Southern California Quarterly* 54 (Winter 1972), 291–312.

Consult also Fray Gerónimo Boscana's "Chinigchinich" in the appendix to the first edition of Alfred Robinson's *Life in California* (New York, 1846) and Helen Hunt Jackson, *Ramona* (Boston, 1844). There is a reprint of her 1887 volume, *A Century of Dishonor*, edited by Andrew Rolle (New York, 1965). See also, in Zoeth Skinner Eldredge, ed., *A History of California* (5 vols., New York, 1915), 5, the essay, "Types of Indian Culture in California"; and Robert F. Heizer, "The California Indians, Archaeology, Varieties of Culture, Arts of Life," California Historical Society *Quarterly* 41 (March 1962), 1–28, and Heizer's *Languages, Territories and Names of California Indian Tribes* (Berkeley, 1966).

More specialized interpretations are Nils Christian Nelson, *Shellmounds of the San Francisco Bay Region* (Berkeley, 1909); Galen Clark, *Indians of the Yosemite Valley and Vicinity* (Yosemite, 1904); and R. F. Heizer and M. A. Whipple, *The California Indians: A Source Book* (Berkeley, 1951). See also R. F. Heizer and J. E. Mills, *The Four Ages of Tsurai* (Berkeley, 1952), as well as C. D. Forde, *Ethnography of the Yuma Indians* (University of California *Publications in Archaeology and*

Ethnology 31, Berkeley, 1928), and, in the same series (volume 1), P. E. Goddard, *Life and Culture of the Hupa* (Berkeley, 1903).

Religious values are discussed in James R. Moriarty, "A Reconstruction of the Development of Primitive Religion in California," *Southern California Quarterly* 52 (December 1970), 313–34. A discussion of the Indian's traditional stories of the creation of the world, vision of man, fire, sun, thunder, and meaning of life appears in Edward W. Gifford and Gwendoline H. Block, *California Indian Nights Entertainment* (Glendale, 1959). In a more literary vein is Theodora Kroeber's *The Inland Whale* (Bloomington, 1959), and her exciting *Ishi in Two Worlds: A Biography of the Last Wild Indian in North America* (Berkeley, 1961). See also Edith B. Webb, *Indian Life at the Old Missions* (Los Angeles, 1952).

The origin of Indian and other place names can be determined from Erwin G. Gudde, *California Place Names* (Berkeley, 1960); Phil Townsend Hanna, *The Dictionary of California Land Names* (Los Angeles, 1951); Nellie Van de Grift Sanchez, *Spanish and Indian Place Names of California* (San Francisco, 1914); and A. L. Kroeber, *California Place Names of Indian Origin* (Berkeley, 1916).

Recent scholarship on Indians includes: George H. Phillips, *The Enduring Struggle: Indians in California History* (San Francisco, 1981), a handy abbreviated account, and James J. Rawls, *Indians of California: Their Changing Image* (Norman, Okla., 1984). Robert F. Heizer, *California Indians* (Washington, D.C., 1978) is the most important work published since Kroeber's *Handbook of the Indians of California* more than half a century ago. Finally, an overview of forgotten sites throughout California is provided by Joseph and Kerry Chartkoff, *The Archeology of California* (Stanford, 1984).

CHAPTER 3

Discovery

CALIFORNIA'S NAME was derived from a sixteenth-century Spanish book, *Las Sergas de Esplandían (The Exploits of Esplandían)*, written by García Ordóñez de Montalvo. This volume was one of those impossible romances of chivalry, similar to King Arthur and his Round Table, which grew out of the Crusades of the eleventh century. Although these romances had Christian knights for their heroes, they also featured Amazons, giants, griffins, and other mysterious creatures living on land, sea, and even in the air. During the sixteenth century a semipagan literary craze ran to such extremes in Spain that there was talk of prohibiting fiction that featured the supernatural. Had the Spanish Crown banished the chivalric romances entirely, California might not today be called by its present name. Such literature finally received its death blow from the ridicule heaped upon it by Cervantes in his *Don Quixote*.

Las Sergas de Esplandían centers around Esplandían, a perfect knight, the son of Amadís of Gaul, bound to vows of courage and chastity, and sworn to follow in his father's footsteps as *conquistador* of all his enemies. In this second-rate novel the word *California* appears as the name of a wonderful island of tall, bronze-colored Amazons, ruled by a pagan queen, Calafía, who goes to the assistance of the pagan forces besieging the city of Constantinople. The fact that these women repelled all male suitors excited the Spanish imagination.

Las Sergas de Esplandían was at its height of popularity when Hernando Cortés was carrying on his explorations; he and his men were familiar with it. The fact that he asked for the prohibition of such romances of chivalry in the American colonies indicates that the craze affected the discipline of his soldiers. Following the conquest of Mexico in 1519–1521, Cortés wrote to the Spanish King about a rumored "island of Amazons or women only, abounding in pearls and gold,

28

lying ten days' journey from Colima." The Spaniards then still believed the peninsula of Lower California to be an island.

Most historians give credit for the first use of the name California
to the explorer Francisco de Bolaños, who in 1541 explored the coast
above the tip of Lower California. But in the mid-1530s, the mariners
of Cortés had already landed in Lower California. Whoever first
named the province, there is no reason to doubt that California was
so called not in mockery, but in anticipation of finding pearls, gold,
and other riches mentioned in Montalvo's romance about the mythical island of Queen Calafía.

California and the Orient

There might have been Oriental contact with California well before
1542, when the first Spanish navigator, Juan Rodriguez Cabrillo,
arrived. Sailing junks crossing the northern Pacific could utilize the
Japanese current to drive them as much as 100 miles per day. The
longest distance between the Commander and Aleutian Islands is
about 150 miles. Sinologists have long believed that early Asian mariners traveled to a mysterious land known as Fusang, possibly the
Pacific Coast of North America.

In 1972 a thirty-five kilogram doughnut-shaped stone, which appears to be of Chinese origin, turned up off Point Conception. In
ancient times such stones were used to clear seaweed from anchor
chains. Other artifacts found over the years include an early Chinese
bronze fan and ancient Chinese coins. Glass Japanese globes, used
to hold up fishing nets, continue to wash ashore in California. Mayan
and Incan rope bridges in Peru resembled those constructed of similar fibers in Asia. There was also a similarity between the Aztec
priesthood and the monastic societies of the East; and certain Indian
hieroglyphics were like those employed in China. From the third to
the fifteenth centuries A.D. the Chinese improved their skills in navigation and cartography, becoming adventuresome sailors in both
the Indian and Pacific Oceans. From the tenth century onward they
possessed a crude magnetic compass.

Chinese legendry records that in the fifth century A.D., Hwui Shan
and some Buddhist monks discovered a far-off land they called Fusang. As late as 1697, Francesco Giovanni Gemelli-Careri, an Italian
who traveled in a Manila galleon along the California coastline, believed that North America "bordered upon Great Tartary," in the
Far East. Today—in an age when the Kensington Stone, the Cardiff
Giant, and Piltdown Man have been exposed as hoaxes—modern historians are highly skeptical. Once such flights into a fantasy past as
the "discovery" of California by the Chinese were given greater cre-

dence. Despite the Vikings, the first *effective* discovery of America was made in 1492 by Columbus; so can it be said that California was first *effectively* found by the Spaniards fifty years after that date, within Spain's New World colonial system. Meanwhile, the Western Hemisphere blocked the path of Columbus and seemed to him a vast land-obstacle, rather than a stupendous find.

A Northern Passage to the Orient

Columbus's original purpose of finding a route to the Orient was not abandoned. In 1513 another explorer, Vasco Nuñez de Balboa, sighted "the great mayne sea heretofore unknowen" lying west of the new continent. His discovery gave rise to an active search for a way from the Atlantic around the continent to the Pacific. In 1520 the difficult passage of Ferdinand Magellan around the South American continent and into the Pacific through the strait that now bears his name made it clear that this entrance was too stormy for the small European ships of that period. This encouraged a search for still other routes, north and south. As eagerly as Ponce de León looked for the fountain of youth in Florida, his countrymen sought the mythical passageway to the Orient, the "Strait of Anián" (or "Northwest Passage," as it was called by other explorers).

Rich cities and other marvels were rumored to lie on the banks of the great northern strait that led to Cathay. Other legends spurred the Spaniards onward, similar to those that had goaded them to make explorations farther south—including dramatic tales of the Seven Cities of Cibola, the Kingdom of La Gran Quivira, and even the gold hoard called El Dorado. During the 1520s and 1530s highly colored reports led the Spaniards into a futile search for a group of wealthy interior villages of the Zuñi Indians, said to be called the Seven Cities. As for La Gran Quivira, it was rumored to be a place where even common kitchen utensils were made of gold. The story of El Dorado (the Gilded Man) was based on the reputed existence of an Indian chief in the mountains of Bogotá, today located in Colombia, whose body was painted with gold dust every morning and washed off again in the evening, and whose followers allegedly threw objects made of gold into a nearby lake (Lake Guatavita); this fable too had its counterpart in a North American setting. More important than these mythical tales was Spain's realization that some enemy nation, particularly England or Russia, might find the Strait of Anián before they did and that such a power might fortify it.

The Pacific Explorations of Cortés

Once Cortés completed his conquest of Mexico (1519–1521), he turned toward the newly discovered western sea. He had been commissioned by the king of Spain, Charles V, to search for the legendary Strait of Anián, and it seemed that the best plan was to launch exploratory voyages from the western coast of Mexico. He proposed to equip a fleet at his own expense with which to subdue the Moluccas and Spice Islands, hoping also to find the isle of the Amazon Queen. Cortés, in his orders to one of his lieutenants, wrote that on the coast near Colima "there is one province which is inhabited by women without any men; and it is said of them that they produce their progeny in the same manner as is related in the ancient histories of the Amazons." His men never reached Upper California during a series of discouraging expeditions from 1527 to 1539.

For the Philippine trade, Cortés did establish a ship-building station at Zacátula, on the western shore of Mexico. There he sent carpenters and shipwrights to build stout vessels. The construction of these primitive ships was a remarkable feat. All their ironwork and rigging had to be laboriously brought from the Atlantic port of Vera Cruz on the backs of Indians and animals.

In 1532, Cortés sent out two ships into the Pacific. This expedition ended in mutiny and its commander was never heard of again. The mutineers landed in the Bay of La Paz above the southern tip of the gulf shore of the peninsula, at a place inhabited by savage Indians. When the Spaniards, twenty-one in number, went ashore to get water they were attacked, and all were killed but two sailors who had been left on the ship. The survivors brought back rumors of pearl beds off the Lower California cape, which stimulated later exploration.

After this third expedition, Cortés determined to send no more captains into the Pacific, but to go himself. On the third of May, 1535, he entered the Lower California bay where the massacre had occurred and took formal possession in the name of the king of Spain, calling the place Santa Cruz. At this time, however, Cortés found himself surrounded by political enemies both in America and in Spain. To a degree his New World successes had aroused jealousy, and he was harassed by the intrigues of opponents. Frustrated and discouraged by constant opposition, and desiring to rejoin his wife and children in Spain, he decided to return there. He had not, however, abandoned hopes of mighty treasures, and in 1539 he ordered Francisco de Ulloa to make a further voyage to the north.

Ulloa's little fleet consisted of three small vessels. According to the quaint contemporary English translation of the expedition's diarist: "We imbarked ourselves in the haven of Acapulco on the eighth of July in the yeere of our Lord 1539, calling upon Almighty God to

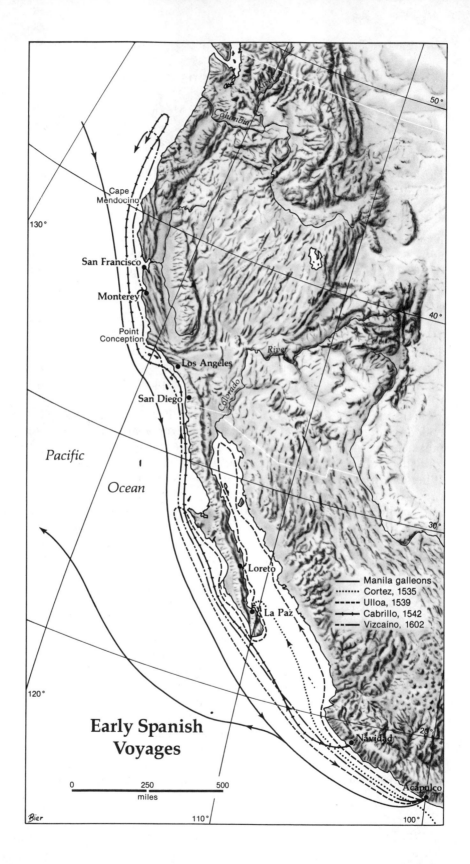

50°

Columbia

Snake

130°

Cape
Mendocino

San Francisco

Monterey

Point
Conception

Los Angeles

San Diego

River

Colorado

Pacific

Ocean

40°

30°

Loreto

La Paz

Manila galleons
Cortez, 1535
Ulloa, 1539
Cabrillo, 1542
Vizcaíno, 1602

120°

**Early Spanish
Voyages**

20°

Navidad

0   250   500
miles

Acapulco

Bier   110°   100°

guide us with his holy hand into such places where he might be served and his holy faith advanced." Ulloa's men turned their prows towards the Sea of Cortés, or Vermillion Sea, as the Gulf of California was then called. Following the mainland shore, Ulloa made his way to the head of the gulf, expecting to find a passage around the "island" to the open sea. After vain efforts to find this passage, he returned southward, carefully hugging the eastern shore of the peninsula.

The failure to find the passage at the head of the gulf weighed heavily upon the minds of the voyagers. The expedition's diary reads: "Whereat we were sorry, because we were always in good hope to find some outlet in some place of that land, and that we had committed a great error in not searching out the secret whether that were a strait or a river which we had left behind us unsearched at the bottom of this great sea or gulf." The "strait or river" mentioned was the Colorado River, into which the gulf then ebbed and flowed.

Ulloa's men, in their attempt to round the point of the peninsula, met a violent tempest that forced them to navigate on the open sea. For eight days they beat up and down the coast, praying for a wind that would take them forward. Finally they reached the point of Lower California and turned northward. On January 5 Ulloa's men came in sight of Cedros Island, so called because of the tall cedars on its summit. Here they landed and took possession in spite of Indians who attacked with sticks and stones. The Spaniards stayed at Cedros only a short time. Battling opposing winds, they sent back the largest ship to its home port. Ulloa continued in a smaller vessel. At 30 degrees north latitude he was compelled by northern winds and lack of provisions to turn about, missing by a narrow margin the chance to be the first white man to see Upper California. The geographical error representing California as an island appeared on maps as late as 1784.

Cabrillo's Discovery of Alta California

When Cortés departed from Mexico, he left behind his bitterest personal enemy, Viceroy Antonio de Mendoza. In charge of future explorations, Mendoza, who had been sent to apply restraints on him, eradicated the memory of Cortés's exploits. The viceroy eagerly launched his own search for the Strait of Anián. Mendoza also sponsored new quests for the "Seven Cities" reported by Fray Marcos de Niza, a priest who in 1539 had penetrated northward on foot to the land of the Pueblo Indians, and whose reports had been wildly exaggerated in passing from mouth to mouth.

Numerous sea and land explorations or the early 1540s represented a continuation of Cortés's search for treasure. Expeditions in and around Lower California, however, extended but slightly Spain's knowledge of northern waters. And they hardly led to the discovery of new riches. Similarly, the military expedition of 1540, led by Francisco Vázquez de Coronado into today's Kansas, failed to find riches.

Viceroy Mendoza, in yet a further attempt to discover the Strait of Anián and the treasures to which it might lead, decided to send another exploratory party north by sea. This one would proceed with orders to explore the coast beyond the latitude reached by Ulloa. A leader was found in Juan Rodríguez Cabrillo, described as a "navigator of great courage and honor and a thorough seaman." Little is known of the actual discoverer of California, except that he was Portuguese by birth and had participated in the expedition in which Cortés conquered Mexico. It was common practice for Spain to employ seamen from other countries; Columbus, a Genoese, had navigated under the protection of the king and queen of Spain.

The two small vessels to which Cabrillo entrusted the lives of his men along an unknown coast were poorly built and badly outfitted. Their anchors and ironwork had, like those of the ships built by Cortés, been carried across Mexico to the Pacific. They were manned by conscripts and were sparsely provisioned; the crews were subject to that deadly peril of the sea, scurvy. Weather was another constricting navigational factor. Today's satellite photographs, taken from a height of several hundred miles, suggest how coastal fog banks kept tiny vessels at sea, far away from the coastline.

The usual prayers having been offered to Almighty God for the success of the voyage, Cabrillo's sails were unfurled and the start made at midday on June 27, 1542, from the port of Navidad, on the western coast of New Spain. Seven and one-half months were spent in this voyage, during which the Pacific Coast, as far as 41 degrees and 30 minutes north latitude, was explored. It was folly to start the expedition so late in the season. Cabrillo's two ships, repeatedly beaten back by the northwest wind, at other times becalmed, rocked idly on the waves for days, unable to make a northing. Their captain, the documents say, paced the deck, peering anxiously into the mists ahead. He did not realize that he was about to make a great discovery and to lay down his life in doing so. The adventurers were on the threshold of an important event.

On Thursday, September 28, 1542, after three months at sea, Cabrillo's two ships entered a "very good closed port," the future harbor of San Diego. Their entrance into this bay formally marked the discovery of California—or Alta (Upper) California, as it was called in distinction to the peninsula of Baja (Lower) California.

When Cabrillo's party landed, all the natives fled but three, from whom the Spaniards learned that people like themselves, bearded and wearing clothing, had apparently been seen toward the interior.

The Indians made gestures to show how the white men threw their lances, and by galloping along the ground showed that the strangers had been on horseback. They also indicated that the white men had killed some natives. Writers have speculated that stories about the Ulloa expedition several years before, or perhaps even the Coronado land expedition of 1540, may have reached these Indians.

Cabrillo gave them gifts of beads and other trifles, to win their confidence. At Santa Catalina Island the Spanish visitors encountered other astonished but passive natives. Along the shoreline opposite Santa Monica, Cabrillo noted an indentation on the mainland that he called "the Bay of Smokes": even in those days before smog, Indian campfires covered the bay near today's Los Angeles with spirals of smoke. Cabrillo's party found the Santa Barbara Channel above Ventura teeming with a dense Indian population, whose seaworthy boats presented a marked contrast to the primitive rafts the Spaniards had seen on the Lower California coast.

Upon rounding Point Conception, above today's Santa Barbara, a heavy northwest wind forced them out to sea, and they came in sight of the islands now known as San Miguel and Santa Rosa. Seeking refuge from the wind, they ran into a snug port on San Miguel Island, known later as Cuyler's Harbor. They took possession of this port, calling it La Isla de la Posesión, and the harbor became a sailors' refuge during many a storm. This island too was populated by Indians, who traded beads manufactured from fish bones with natives on the mainland. In their long hair were intertwined cords into which were thrust daggers of flint, bone, and wood. They wore no clothing, and painted their faces in squares, like a checkerboard. Cabrillo spent a week on this island, in the course of which he suffered a fall, breaking his arm near the shoulder.

Despite this painful accident, and the severe storms, the commander gave orders to continue the search for the Strait of Anián. Next the Spaniards beat their way to a cape, near Fort Ross, having skirted Monterey Bay and the Golden Gate without seeing them. They then drifted south again, and on November 16 discovered what is now Drake's Bay thirty-eight years before Drake landed there. But, because of heavy seas, they dared not land. After two days they set sail once more, again missing the Golden Gate, and ran southward. Also unable to make a landing on the rocky coast north of Point Conception, Cabrillo's crew were relieved to reenter the snug harbor at San Miguel Island. Continuing high winds over the next two months compelled them to winter on the islands of the Santa Barbara Channel, chiefly at San Miguel.

Here the expedition sustained a grave misfortune. On January 3, 1543, its commander died, probably as a result of his earlier fall and the exposure he suffered during the hard northern voyage. After his men laid Cabrillo to rest they renamed the island La Isla de Juan Rodríguez. Drifting sand and cliffs which have since fallen into the sea obliterated his last resting place; not even the name of the island has been retained to commemorate his achievement. That Cabrillo was beloved of his men is implicit in a statement found in the expedition's records: "They returned to Navidad sorrowful for having lost their commander."

As he lay dying, Cabrillo had charged his men to resume their quest and to explore the coast as far northward as possible. His pilot, Bartolomé Ferrer (or Ferrelo), took command and the expedition set sail again. Scudding northward before a storm, Ferrer reached the northern limit of his voyage, possibly at the Rogue River in Oregon, but at least as far north as the Eel River of California. At this point the crews, crazed from scurvy, forced Ferrer to turn back. He returned to the harbor of Navidad in New Spain on April 14, 1543.

The first voyage to Alta California had failed to find the Strait of Anián, or the gold sought by Mendoza. Cabrillo had seen no cities with gold and silver walls—indeed no advanced Indian civilization with treasure lying in its streets, no lands so rich as the Aztec and Inca empires. Yet the expedition had proved a magnificent success. Cabrillo had opened the sea route to a province now familiar to all the world.

Selected Readings

About the origin of the name California, see Herbert D. Austin, "New Light on the Name California," Historical Society of Southern California, *Publications 12* (Los Angeles, 1923); Ruth Putnam, *California, the Name* (Berkeley, 1917); Irving Berdine Richman, *California Under Spain and Mexico, 1535–1847* (Boston, 1911), pp. 362–66; and George Davidson, *The Origin and Meaning of the Name California* (San Francisco, 1910).

See also Donald C. Cutter, "Sources of the Name 'California,' " *Arizona and the West* 3 (Autumn 1961), 233–43.

Discussion of Oriental contact with California is in Charles E. Chapman, *A History of California* (New York, 1921), pp. 21–42; Edward Payson Vining, *An Inglorious Columbus; or Evidence that Hwui Shăn and a Party of Buddhist Monks from Afghanistan Discovered America in the Fifth Century A.D.* (New York, 1885); Naojiro Murakami, "Japan's Early Attempts to Establish Commercial Relations with Mexico," in *The Pacific Ocean and History* (New York, 1917), pp. 467–80; and Zelia Nuttall, "The Earliest Historical Relations Between Mexico and Japan," University of California *Publications in Archaeology and Ethnology*

4 (Berkeley, 1904), 1–47. On this theme see also Douglas S. Watson, "Did the Chinese Discover America?" *California Historical Society Quarterly* 14 (March 1935), 47–57, and Charles G. Leland, *Fusang, or the Discovery of America by Chinese Buddhist Priests in the Fifth Century* (London, 1875). Further conjecture is in C. W. Brooks, "Report of Japanese Vessels Wrecked in the North Pacific Ocean From the Earliest Records to the Present Time," *Proceedings, California Academy of Sciences* 6 (San Francisco, 1876), 50–66.

Basic works on the discovery and exploration of California are Francisco Preciado, *Diary of the Voyage of Ulloa to Baja California in 1539-1540,* in Hakluyt's *Principal Navigations* (Edinburgh, 1885–90), volume 3; Miguel Venegas, *Noticia de la California y de su conquista temporal y espiritual hasta el tiempo presente* (Madrid, 1757); Henry R. Wagner, *Spanish Voyages to the Northwest Coast of America in the Sixteenth Century* (San Francisco, 1929), as well as his *Juan Rodríguez Cabrillo, Discoverer of the Coast of California* (San Francisco, 1941) and *Cartography of the Northwest Coast of America to the Year 1800* (2 vols., Berkeley, 1937); Francisco López de Gómara, *Historia de la conquista de Mexico por Hernando Cortés* (Mexico, D.F., 1943); Robert R. Miller, "Cortés and the First Attempt to Colonize California," *California Historical Quarterly* 53 (Spring 1974), 5–16; Martín Fernández de Navarrete, *Colección de viajes; documentos inéditos* (Madrid, 1825–27); Juan Paez, *Relation of the Voyage of Juan Rodríguez Cabrillo,* translated and edited by Herbert E. Bolton in *Spanish Exploration in the Southwest* (New York, 1916); and Antonio Pigafetta, *The First Voyage Around the World 1519, '20, '21, '22* (London, 1874). Other useful references regarding exploration are: Maurice G. Holmes, *From New Spain by Sea to the Californias, 1519–1668* (Glendale, Calif., 1963); Jack D. Forbes, "Melchior Díaz and the Discovery of Alta California," *Pacific Historical Review* 27 (November 1958), 351–57; and two volumes of basic documents concerning such mariners as Pedro de Unamuno, Vizcaíno, and Cermenho, *California: Documentos para la Historia de la Demarción Comercial de California, 1583–1632,* ed. by W. Michael Mathes (Madrid, 1965). Examples of the most modern scholarship on discovery are Harry Kelsey, *Juan Rodríguez Cabrillo* (San Marino, Calif., 1985), and Kelsey's "Mapping the California Coast: The Voyages of Discovery, 1533–1543," *Arizona and the West* 26 (Winter, 1984), 307–26. See also R. V. Tooley, *California as an Island: A Geographical Misconception Illustrated by 100 Examples from 1625 to 1770* (London, 1964).

On the Spanish northward advance by land see Herbert E. Bolton, *The Spanish Borderlands* (New Haven, 1921), and Philip W. Powell, *Soldiers, Indians and Silver: The Northward Advance of New Spain, 1550–1600* (Berkeley, 1952). The flavor of the Spanish mining frontier comes to life in Bernard Moses, *Flush Times at Potosí* (Berkeley, 1910).

CHAPTER 4

Continued Exploration

SPAIN, constantly obliged to protect its North American provinces, including California, against the expansionism of other nations, continued exploration along the shores of the Pacific Ocean. After discovery of the Philippine Islands by Magellan in 1521, the lure of profits from trade with the East Indies produced a new movement of Spanish ships from ports on the western coast of the New World. Though the outbound voyage was relatively easy, the return from Asia was extremely difficult. Favorable winds blew the ships toward the Orient, but on the return trip the same gusty winds beat them back.

The Philippine Trade

In 1564 King Philip II ordered a Spanish fleet sent from New Spain to find a practicable return route from Asia to America. This task could be entrusted only to the most skilled navigator in New Spain, Andrés Urdaneta, who had taken holy orders. He consented to leave his cloister to serve the king, ostensibly as chaplain of the fleet, but in reality as chief cartographer and sailing master. On November 24, 1564, the expedition left the port of Acapulco. It reached the Philippines and succeeded in making its way back to Acapulco after a voyage of 129 days. After leaving the Philippines, the Spanish vessel took advantage of heavy westerly winds and ran before them to the North American coastline. Establishment of this route, with its first landfall on the coast of Upper California, at about the latitude of Cape Mendocino, was to speed the settlement of California.

Trading ships henceforth, for two and a half centuries, carried silver bullion from Acapulco to be exchanged for Oriental goods at

Manila, the collecting point for spices and silks from the Orient. Slow, lumbering galleons returning from the islands were also filled with riches of the Indies—precious stones, musk, aromatic resin, wax, amber, porcelain, metals, carved and inlaid chests, knickknacks of all kinds, and exotic birds that talked and played tricks. Bales and chests were piled so high in cabins, and on the decks up to the gunwales, that one traveler wrote: "We had hardly room to stand. Nobody could live under deck, it was so full of provisions and commodities. All men lay exposed to the sun and air."

The rarities brought to America found a ready sale among the Spaniards in Mexico and Peru who had enriched themselves from mining silver. Some Oriental luxuries were also reshipped to Spain by way of Mexico. The Philippine trade was originally a government enterprise, maintained at royal expense; in time however, it came under the control of private merchants. Even today the name "Manila galleon" conjures up thoughts of adventure by men who risked their lives on small and insecure craft. Eventually, the Spanish crown restricted this traffic, limiting it to one galleon a year—standard mercantile practice for Spain. The mother country did not welcome competition from its colonies. Finally, in 1815, after lending peripheral color to California's history for 250 years, the galleons ceased to sail altogether.

Although the outward trip from Acapulco required only two or three months of fair sailing, the return took from seven to nine miserable months. The food became rancid or filled with maggots, and the water supply failed altogether, compelling reliance upon rainwater, caught in sails, barrels, or any other handy receptacle. Scurvy then set in; as some galleons approached the coast of America, body after body was thrown into the sea. Crews were so decimated that by the time they sighted California there were often not enough able-bodied men left to go ashore for fresh water, or to raise an anchor if it were dropped—even though they were tantalized by the sight of the land. So the ships limped on, without stopping, with their battered, leaky hulls, spoiled provisions, putrid water, and sick and dying crews, until they reached Acapulco. The loss of each vessel cast a deep gloom over both Manila and Acapulco; nearly every citizen had a stake in its cargo, or relatives among its crew. Moreover, the failure of one of these ships to arrive caused a great scarcity of the exotic commodities to which the Spaniards had become accustomed.

After 1564, the government in Mexico grew troubled at the loss of so many men on the return voyage from the Orient, and the miserable condition in which they arrived at the home port. Sorely needed was a safe harbor on the coast of Upper California, and a way station where ships could stop for repairs, fresh food, and water.

The quest for such a port made the Manila galleon important in the subsequent settlement of California.

Drake and Cavendish

The need for wood, water, meat, and repairs was not the only reason for Spanish determination to seek a haven for the galleons on the coast of the Californias. The intrusion in those waters of the English privateers Drake and Cavendish rudely shocked the Spaniards. By the late sixteenth century, when the English achieved access into the "Spanish lake" known as the Pacific, news of Spain's rich galleons in the Pacific had spread around the world. English privateers, little more than licensed pirates, then began to brave passage through the Strait of Magellan in order to reach the western coast of the Americas. There they could lie in wait for galleons returning from Manila. Henceforth the Spanish ships were armed with small cannon, muskets, and catapults for hurling stones, ineffective though these weapons were against fast corsairs.

In 1577 the magnificent sea dog Francis Drake, bearing a secret commission from Queen Elizabeth to "annoy the King of Spain in his Indies," set sail from Plymouth in England on a voyage that would last several years. In his vessel, the *Golden Hind,* he made his way through the Magellan passage, and swooped down upon unsuspecting Spanish outposts on the Pacific like a hawk among barnyard fowl. Boldly attacking both coastal settlements and vessels, Drake captured ship after ship, sending them to run before the wind with all sails flying after taking off their treasure and crews. He stopped in the ports of Lima—in present-day Peru—and Guatulco—today in the Mexican province of Oaxaca—long enough to sack these towns before the terror-stricken populace of either could collect their wits sufficiently to make any defense. He was a courtly robber, and in his operations on the western coast of the New World never killed a man; instead, he treated his prisoners like honored guests, even giving them money and clothing after he set them free.

The *Golden Hind* was loaded almost to the sinking point with treasure—some say to the amount of 800,000 English pounds. In constant danger of capture, Drake finally set sail for England, by way of California and the northern Pacific. Fearing that Spanish ships would be lying in wait back at the Strait of Magellan, Drake sought a passage through the Arctic. According to some accounts, this was a major purpose of his voyage. Drake sailed north along a route that took him to the Upper California coast. On June 17, 1579, his lookout sighted a "convenient and fit harborough," at 38 degrees and 30 minutes latitude on the California shoreline. He entered this sandy

bay for the purpose of repairing his ship. Drake remained there until
July 23, during which time his men tipped the vessel onto her side,
caulked and careened her, and mended a bad leak. The exact location
of Drake's anchorage in California has long been a matter of controversy. Strong arguments have been advanced for the bight under
Point Reyes, today called Drake's Bay, a white-cliffed harbor then
held by the Miwok Indians. Some believe that Drake anchored at
Bodega Bay, a few miles farther north.

As to San Francisco's spacious bay, no evidence has been produced
that Drake or his men laid eyes upon it, even though his landing
parties went ashore north of the location of the present city. The
Englishmen probably did not anchor in a spot where shore parties
could see San Francisco Bay. Books and articles on the subject of
Drake's anchorage still debate its whereabouts. A basic contemporary
source (not listed in the bibliography of this chapter) is *The World
Encompassed by Sir Francis Drake* (London, 1628) written by persons
closely connected with that expedition.

Anthropologists generally conclude that Drake landed at Drake's
Bay. In 1775 the Spanish *San Carlos*, the first ship to enter San Francisco Bay, was seriously damaged by battering against rocks and tides,
a clear indication that Drake's earlier expedition entered a bay distinctly more sandy.

During his stay on the California coast, Drake established friendly
relations with the Indians, exchanged gifts with them, and went
through ceremonials that the English later chose to regard as acceptance by the natives of England's sovereignty. These symbolic acts
probably corresponded to the smoking of a "peace pipe." After com-
pleting repairs on their ship, Drake's party held religious services,
during which—the documents of the expedition solemnly assert—the
natives made loud responses, possibly incantations similar to those
of their own medicine men. Before he departed from California,
Drake claimed title to the country for his Queen by leaving behind

> a plate of brasse, fast nailed to a great and firm poste, whereon is en-
> graven her grace's name and the day and year of our arrivall there, and
> of the free giving up of the province and kingdome, both by the king
> and people, into her Majestie's hands; together with her highnesse pic-
> ture and armes in a piese of sixpence currant English monie shewing
> itself by a hole made of purpose through the plate; underneath was
> likewise engraven the name of our General.

In 1934 such a plate of brass was allegedly found near the Laguna
Ranch on Drake's Bay; after being thrown away it was supposedly
"rediscovered" in 1936 under circumstances that led skeptics to question its authenticity. For more than forty years, however, most historians considered this artifact genuine. Professor Herbert Bolton

of the University of California, Berkeley, fatuously pronounced it "one of the world's long lost historical treasures."

Only in 1977 did metallurgists reexamine the plate, pronouncing it a modern forgery. It contained too much zinc and too little copper or lead to be genuine sixteenth-century brass. A few historians, furthermore, had been suspicious about the quality of the lettering, believing that Drake's gunsmiths could have done a far more elegant job; the plate was obviously cut by modern machine tools. It now seems incredible that Professor Bolton could have become a victim of his own enthusiasm.

The first English chroniclers who described Drake's contacts with the California Indians also possessed a vivid imagination. Their accounts made a princely personage out of an Indian chieftain, who would actually have been attired poorly in rabbit skins; his rude basketwork hat was transformed into a royal crown, and every gesture into a courtly mannerism. The three main accounts of the Drake voyage were set down by writers who did not hesitate to embroider the original reports, so that their descriptions of California's geography and primitive people conformed to seventeenth-century European standards of etiquette. Drake's own full account was never printed; in all probability it was suppressed lest it cause England further complications with Spain.

Drake turned his back upon the shores of California, to which he gave the name "New Albion," and continued westward around the world via the Moluccas. The chief result of his stay in California was to hasten its occupation by the Spaniards. Drake did not add much to knowledge of the Pacific, for he used Spanish navigational charts taken from captured ships.

Controversy continues over where Drake actually landed. Some 600 bits of delicate Ming porcelain, discovered at former Miwok Indian sites, show no signs of having been tossed about in the surf. These have been pointed to as further proof of Drake's landing north of San Francisco Bay. Presumably these shards would have been part of the *Golden Hind*'s ship china, brought ashore by Drake's men. Real estate developers, antiquarians, and charlatans alike remain anxious to substantiate a variety of landing sites—including San Francisco Bay itself, usually for pecuniary gain.

The Voyages of Gali and Cermenho

In 1584 the viceregal government at Mexico City, aroused by the continued threat of foreign interlopers, ordered Francisco de Gali, the seasoned commander of the Manila galleon, to sail along the Upper California coast on his return from the Philippines. Gali was

to look for a new port in California waters that could offer temporary
protection for the galleons. On his return, Gali reported observing
a "very fair land, wholly without snow and with many rivers, bays,
and havens." His survey stimulated further explorations; among these,
perhaps the most significant occurred ten years later, when a Portuguese navigator, Sebastián Rodríguez Cermenho, explored and
marked out Gali's entire course, beginning where the galleon bound
from the Philippines reached the Channel Islands off the California
coast.

On July 5, 1595, Cermenho's ship, the *San Agustín*, sailed out of
Cavite in the Philippines, its decks crowded with boxes of merchandise, chicken coops, and barrels of ship's stores. On November 4 the
first North American landfall occurred a little north of Eureka. Cermenho entered the same bay in which Drake is supposed to have
anchored sixteen years before, went ashore with a party, and took
possession of the land and port in the name of the king of Spain.

At this shallow roadstead, Cermenho met with disaster. On November 30 the *San Agustín* was driven ashore by a squall and wrecked,
scattering the fine silks and porcelains in her cargo along the beach
for the Indians to pick up—as a chronicler says, "like pearls before
swine." Fortunately the crew had completed building a launch for
shore use. Into this craft they crowded themselves, seventy in all,
with such provisions of acorns as they could obtain from the Indians,
and proceeded to make their precarious way down the coast. The
meager accounts of this voyage in the launch *San Buenaventura* reveal
it to have been remarkable for endurance and courage. Cermenho,
notwithstanding uncomfortable conditions, continued to make careful observations. He noted the entrance to Monterey Bay, qualifying
as its real discoverer rather than the later explorer Vizcaíno, to whom
credit is usually given. On January 7, 1596, Cermenho's launch arrived at its home port of Navidad with the crew almost dead.

Cermenho was threatened with a lawsuit by the owners of the lost
cargo of the *San Agustín*. His effort, however, was not wasted; he not
only brought back a quite accurate description of the California coast,
but his disastrous voyage awakened the government to the folly of
trying to make such explorations with unwieldy galleons that risked
the loss of their precious cargoes. It became clear that future expeditions to California should make use of ships of light draught, to
facilitate shore observations. Such vessels would sail directly from
New Spain, loaded only with provisions. This plan was tried with
complete success seven years later when Viceroy Monterey sent out
another California expedition under Sebastián Vizcaíno, a Basque
merchant-navigator with experience on the galleon route and in
Lower California waters.

Vizcaíno at Monterey

Sailing under the protection of Our Lady of Carmel, Vizcaíno's "fleet" of three tiny vessels passed out of the harbor of Acapulco on May 5, 1602. The party proceeded up the coast, stopping at many of the points visited by Cabrillo and renaming them. To the Vizcaíno expedition we owe many familiar place names—San Diego, Santa Catalina Island, Santa Barbara, Point Conception, Monterey, and Carmel. At 36 degrees latitude Vizcaíno, on December 16, 1602, sailed into Monterey Bay. This became the principal event of Vizcaíno's voyage and he named the place after the viceroy who sponsored his expedition. Under an oak tree that stood so close to the shore that its branches were wet by the incoming tides, the explorers took part in a religious ceremony.

As Vizcaíno looked about him at the ring of hills, dark with the growth of pines covering them from base to summit, he became so enamored of the place that he wrote a fulsome description of it to the viceroy. His praise of a harbor defended from all winds was so misleading that the Spaniards who next saw Monterey, in 1769, failed to recognize it. Vizcaíno, continuing the voyage to the north, passed Cape Mendocino; then he decided, due to the miserable condition of his crews, to turn about for Acapulco.

On the way down the coast Vizcaíno's men were unable to land. The number of able-bodied men was so reduced that they dared not let go of their anchors lest they not be able to raise them again. Crew members died like flies from scurvy and starvation. Because of their sore mouths and loss of teeth, Vizcaíno's crew could not eat the coarse food they had on board. At Cedros Island most of them were able only to crawl ashore on their hands and knees; by a supreme effort, they managed to take on wood and water. Forty-five men, half the crew members, died on the voyage, which lasted eleven months. Yet they had made a detailed exploration as far north as Monterey. They had also reached and sketchily mapped the northern limit to about the latitude of Drake's Bay.

A lessening of Anglo-Spanish tensions occurred after Vizcaíno returned to New Spain from his California voyage. A new viceroy, the Marqués de Montesclaros, proved lukewarm toward colonizing California. In the years from 1602 to 1769 no ship is known to have entered California waters from the south, while the Manila galleons left few records of what they saw of the area, refusing to risk valuable cargoes by venturing too near Alta California's unfamiliar coastline. As a result, the miles slipped by, as these ships usually turned southward as soon as they sighted the floating seaweed that signaled the presence of rocky shoals. For more than a century and a half, there was little addition to the knowledge produced by Vizcaíno's voyage.

Selected Readings

A basic source on the Manila galleon trade is by Dr. Giovanni Francesco Gemelli Careri, an Italian passenger who published the gruesome details of his voyage in *Narrative of a Voyage on a Spanish Galleon from Manila to Acapulco in 1687–1688;* a translation is in *Churchill's Collection of Voyages and Travels* 4 (London, 1752). See also William L. Schurz, *The Manila Galleon* (New York, 1939).

Useful to an understanding of Drake are Henry R. Wagner, *Sir Francis Drake's Voyage Round the World: Its Aims and Achievements* (San Francisco, 1926); C. G. Fink and E. P. Polushkin, *Drake's Plate of Brass Authenticated. . ., California Historical Society, Publication No. 14 (San Francisco, 1937);* R. B. Haselden, *"Is the Drake Plate of Brass Genuine?" California Historical Society Quarterly* 16 (September 1937), 271–74; Robert F. Heizer, *Francis Drake and the California Indians* (Berkeley, 1947), and his *Elizabethan California* (Ramona, Calif., 1974). Wagner's *Drake on the Pacific Coast* (Los Angeles, 1970) puts forth the idea that Trinidad Bay was the landing site, while Heizer rules out that location entirely. Richard Hakluyt's *Principal Navigations . . .* (London, 1903–5) contains the three eyewitness narratives of Drake's voyage to California.

The Drake literature continues to expand. An entire issue of the *California Historical Quarterly* (volume 53, Fall 1974) was devoted to the Drake landing in California. A strong plea is Robert H. Power, "Drake's Landing in California: A Case for San Francisco Bay," *California Historical Quarterly* 52 (Summer 1973), 100–30. See also Frank M. Stanger and Alan K. Brown, *Who Discovered The Golden Gate?* (San Mateo, 1969). Earlier scholarship is Francis P. Farquhar and Walter A. Starr, "Drake in California: A Review of the Evidence and the Testimony of the Plate of Brass." This appears in volume 36 (March 1957), 21–34. Robert H. Power, "Portus Novæ Albionis Re-Discovered?" *Pacific Discovery* 7 (May–June 1954), 10–12, puts forth the view that Drake anchored in northern San Francisco Bay. Walter A. Starr, "Drake Landed in San Francisco Bay in 1579, the Testimony of the Plate of Brass," California Historical Society *Quarterly* 41 (September 1962), 1–29, reopens the controversy unconvincingly. The most well-reasoned summary article on Drake is Adolph S. Oko, "Francis Drake and Nova Albion," California Historical Society *Quarterly* 43 (June 1964), 135–58. Warren L. Hanna, *Lost Harbor: The Controversy Over Drake's California Anchorage* (Berkeley, 1979) is a balanced résumé. Two careful appraisals of material objects found in Marin County, where both Drake and Cermenho probably landed, are Edward Von der Porten, *Drake and Cermeno in California: Sixteenth Century Chinese Ceramics* (Point Reyes, Calif., 1973) and his *Porcelains and Terra Cottas of Drake's Bay* (Point Reyes, Calif., 1968). Most important is the Bancroft Library publication *The Plate of Brass Reexamined* (1977) and *Supplementary Report* (1979), both of which appear to confirm that the plate alleged to have been left by Drake is not authentic. See also N. B. Martin, "Portus Novus Albionis: Site of Drake's California Sojourn," *Pacific Historical Review* 48 (August 1979) 319–34 and two summary essays published as: *Early California: Perception and Reality* by Henry J. Bruman and Clement W. Meighan (Los Angeles, 1981).

On Cermenho see Sebastián Rodríguez Cermenho, *Diario* (1595), in manuscript form at the Bancroft Library, University of California, Berkeley. This and other documents at the Bancroft Library are transcripts from the Archivo General de Indias, Seville, Spain. Consult also Henry R. Wagner, "The Voyage to California of Sebastián Rodríguez Cermenho in 1595," California Historical Society *Quarterly* 3 (April 1924), 3–24. In the same journal Robert F. Heizer's "Archeological Evidence of Sebastián Rodríguez Cermenho's California Visit," 20 (December 1941), 315–28, offers a fascinating identification of artifacts, including Chinese pottery shards left after the wrecking of Cermenho's *San Agustín* at Drake's Bay. On Vizcaíno, see W. Michael Mathes, *Vizcaíno and Spanish Exploration in the Pacific Ocean, 1580–1630* (San Francisco, 1968).

A general, but imperfect, account of buccaneering in Pacific waters is Peter Gerhard, *Pirates on the West Coast of New Spain, 1575–1742* (Glendale, 1960). Michael E. Thurman, *The Naval Department of San Blas, New Spain's Bastion for Alta California and Nootka . . .* (Glendale, 1967), is a useful study of a key supply base.

CHAPTER 5

The First Colonizers of the Frontier

DURING THE PERIOD between the Vizcaíno expedition of 1602 and the permanent settlement of California in 1769, New Spain's northern border extended in a sort of arc, from a series of garrisons located along the Red River in present-day Louisiana to a remote chain of Jesuit missions spread throughout northern Mexico and Lower California. Along this colonial frontier were missions, mining camps, cattle ranches, and crude adobe *presidios*, or forts. Most of the colonization took place below the present border of California, but it laid the groundwork for later advances toward the north.

Three Jesuit clerics contributed to colonization of the approaches to California. Foremost of these was Eusebio Francesco Kino (sometimes spelled Chino or Chini), a native of Trento, Italy, who had been highly educated in German universities. As explorer, cartographer, and mission builder, Kino was responsible, in the years 1678–1712, for the founding of numerous missions on New Spain's northern frontiers. It was also Kino who, by his explorations and maps, proved in 1702 that California was not an island. Aiding Father Kino was another Italian Jesuit, the square-jawed, flinty Juan María de Salvatierra, who in 1697 founded the first of a chain of missions in Lower California. Salvatierra went on to become provincial of the entire Jesuit order in New Spain. The third major blackrobe was Father Juan de Ugarte, a cleric so strong that he could lift two men simultaneously and bump their heads together. Ugarte labored for years among the Indians. These priests, hardened by missionary work, gave a solid foundation to the frontier establishments from which later military and clerical officials would move toward Upper California. Kino's surveys had revealed much about Lower California, the tip of which had been occupied steadily since the first mission

was built. It would only be a matter of time before the coastline of
Upper California would be more fully explored and settled.

In spite of the success achieved by its colonizers, Spain was still
beset by fears of competition from other nations. At the end of the
Seven Years' War between France and England, in 1763, the British
took over most of North America from the French. As a result, Spain
came to share a common frontier with England in the Mississippi
Valley. Might this advance of the British encourage them to attempt
colonization further west, perhaps from ports in California? Or might
the Russians, probing across the northern Pacific in search of furs,
decide to enter California waters?

Gálvez and the Occupation of California

In 1765, Charles III, a vigorous Spanish monarch appointed José de
Gálvez *visitador-general,* or inspector general, of New Spain. Gálvez's
chief mission was to increase the royal revenues. As an enthusiastic
expansionist, he was also interested in fortifying New Spain's northern frontier. Gálvez sailed to Lower California on a personal inspection of the peninsula. During this tour he reorganized missions
and repaired the royal revenues. He also developed plans for a land
expedition to Upper California. While Gálvez was in Lower California in 1768, King Charles expelled the Jesuits from the Spanish colonies because of fear and distrust of their political power on the part
of various European monarchs.

They were replaced in Lower California by fourteen gray-robed
Franciscan friars under the fifty-five-year-old Junípero Serra, who
arrived at La Paz to continue the work begun earlier by Kino. As
mission builders and instructors of the Indians, these men would
serve a useful colonizing purpose for Gálvez, an ambitious leader
who became absorbed with plans to mount an assault upon Upper
California. The Russians provided him with his best excuse for this
projected expansion.

Russian encroachments from the north upon Spain's Pacific preserves—particularly the voyages to the American Northwest by Vitus
Bering and Alexei Chirikof in 1741, disturbed the Spanish lethargy
that had prevailed since Vizcaíno's trip to Monterey in 1602. As
Russian otter-hunting ships extended their cruises farther southward
each year, simultaneously the English became entrenched in the lower
Ohio Valley. Meanwhile, Dutch and English corsairs lurked off the
coast of Lower California. Gálvez, therefore, had to safeguard Spain's
future on its northern frontiers, and felt a pressing need to occupy
Upper California, thereby countering enemy powers.

So, Inspector General Gálvez planned a four-pronged expedition to occupy San Diego and Monterey. Two divisions were to go by sea and two by land; if one party should fail, another might succeed. The four groups would meet at San Diego and press onward to Monterey. Religious supervision of the expedition was entrusted to the Franciscan order, which had yielded control of Lower California to the Dominicans. This trust was joyfully accepted by the Franciscans; when these missionaries heard they were to turn over the peninsula to the Dominicans and move on to Upper California, they celebrated the news by ringing bells and holding a thanksgiving mass. Gálvez himself never saw Alta California, for he remained occupied with more important matters in Mexico City.

Serra and Portolá, Torchbearers

Gálvez took great care to select the right man to lead the Franciscans into the new land. His choice was Fray Junípero Serra. Selection of Gaspar de Portolá to head the military branch of the expedition was equally wise. Serra, idealist zealot, and Portolá, dutiful soldier, were to become the first colonizers of California. Serra, a native of the Mediterranean island of Majorca, had first come to America in 1749 to labor among the Indians of the New World. Before he was called to take up the presidency of the missions of both Californias, he served for nine years among the Pamé Indians in the Sierra Gorda mountains of Mexico.

In carrying out a plan for the occupation of California, Serra brushed aside obstacles that would have stopped lesser men. One of the worst of these was his own frail health, aggravated by a lame leg, from which he suffered nearly all his life. When he set out on the 1769 expedition to Upper California, he was so weak that two men lifted him into the saddle of his mule; but when his friend Fray Francisco Palóu, discouraged by the sight, bade him an eternal farewell, Serra gently rebuked him, and insisted that with the aid of God he would reach Upper California and there raise the cross.

Serra's military companion, Portolá, was from Catalonia and had served in European campaigns as a captain of dragoons. He was Lower California's first governor at the time of the expulsion of the Jesuits. On hearing of Gálvez's plan, he volunteered to lead the expedition to occupy the unknown north. In addition to occupying San Diego and Monterey, Portolá and Serra hoped to establish five missions. Church ornaments and sacred vessels did not constitute all of Serra's cargo, however; seeds, flowers and vegetables formed the basis of future mission gardens. The two land expeditions took 200 cattle from the northernmost mission of the peninsula. From these few animals were descended the herds that in time roamed the hills and valleys of Upper California—the chief source of wealth for several generations during its pastoral era. The peninsular missions were called upon to contribute all the horses, mules, dried meat, grain, cornmeal, and dry biscuits they could spare. Two small vessels, the packets *San Carlos* and *San Antonio* were made available for the two prongs of the sea expedition. On January 9, 1769, the *San Carlos* was ready to start at La Paz in Lower California. Added to her crew were twenty-five Catalan volunteers, a military party that could overcome any native resistance in landing. After a solemn mass and address by Gálvez, the little ship unfurled its sails, doubled the Lower California cape, and was off. Five weeks later after another exhortation from Gálvez and a last shout of *buen viaje* from those who remained ashore, the *San Antonio* also shook out her sails for San Diego, far to the north.

Meanwhile, preparations for the two land expeditions were under way in Lower California. By the latter part of March, Captain Fernando Rivera y Moncada, in command of the first division—his force strengthened by twenty-five leather-jacketed soldiers and forty-two Christian Indians—was ready to start from the northern frontier. This division was accompanied by Fray Juan Crespi, an associate of Serra. Crespi eventually accompanied Portolá all the way to San Francisco and left a journal of the entire march. On March 22, 1769, Rivera's small army, made up of veterans seasoned in frontier life, set off northward into the desert; it became the first overland party to reach California. The other land contingent, with Serra and Portolá, bronzed and bearded, riding at its head, set out for San Diego on May 15, 1769.

San Diego was, of course, also the objective of the two sea expeditions that had gone in advance. The *San Antonio*, which started a month later than the *San Carlos*, was the first to arrive, on April 11. When the *San Antonio* sailed into port, the Indians at first mistook it for a great whale. On April 29, to the joy of those on the *San Antonio*, the long-delayed sister ship sailed alongside and dropped anchor. The lengthy voyage—110 days—had caused such severe scurvy on the *San Carlos* that there were no men aboard able to lower a shore boat when it finally arrived.

Ashore, tents of sails sheltered the sick. Pedro Prat, who came on the *San Carlos* as surgeon, scoured the shore in search of green herbs with which to heal dysentery. Because of so many deaths, all thought of continuing the voyage to Monterey was temporarily abandoned. Each available man was occupied in caring for the sick. Those who died were buried at a point which has since borne the name *La Punta de los Muertos*, or Dead Men's Point.

A third ship, the *San José*, had also been dispatched by Galvéz but was lost at sea.

The Settlement of San Diego

On May 14, 1769, the gloom was lightened by the appearance of Captain Rivera, with his leather-jackets and native bearers from Lower California. To get a better water supply, Rivera moved the entire camp nearer the river, at the foot of today's Presidio Hill. He also built a handful of crude huts for the sick. At the end of June the camp was thrown into confusion by the sound of musket shots, announcing the approach of Portolá and Serra. Their party arrived in good condition. They had not left Lower California until a day after the arrival of the first land party at San Diego. More than a third of the 300 men who had set out for Upper California, by land and sea, had failed to survive the trip. Half of those still alive were physically incapacitated. The loss of so many men made a change in plans absolutely necessary. Leaving behind the friars with a guard of soldiers in care of the sick at San Diego, Portolá pressed on to Monterey with the main force.

Most of the men were seriously weakened by hunger, dysentery, and scurvy. But Portolá, a dedicated soldier, set to work at once to prepare for the advance to Monterey. Serra, equally determined, and remembering the thousands of natives living in heathenism, declared that if necessary he would remain in Upper California alone to carry on his labors among them. Portolá wrote a friend about his preparations for the journey to Monterey, "Leaving the sick under a hut of poles which I had erected, I gathered the small portion of food which had not been spoiled in the ships and went on by land with that small company of . . . skeletons, who had been spared by scurvy, hunger, and thirst.

After singing a final *Te Deum*, Portolá left San Diego on July 14, 1769. The sixty-four members of the expedition included family names later well-known in California's history—such as Ortega, Amador, Alvarado, Carrillo, Yorba, and Soberanes. These troops wore leather jackets of seven thicknesses of deerskin and carried bull-hide shields on their left arms. Lances and broadswords were among their weapons, as well as short muskets. Portolá's party made frequent stops to rest the men and animals. Their route may be traced by the place names left by this expedition—Santa Margarita, Santa Ana, Carpintería, Gaviota, Cañada de los Osos, Pajaro, and San Lorenzo.

Failure to Recognize Monterey

The Indians were friendly, and they furnished the party with food. Portolá pressed on until he reached the shallow Salinas River. He then marched along its banks to the sea, near Monterey Bay. There

he stood upon a hill and saw an open *ensenada,* or gulf. Although in
the latitude of Monterey, it did not fit the descriptions of Monterey
Bay given by Vizcaíno as "a fine harbor sheltered from all winds."
The bay of Monterey cannot be called a well-protected port. Mys-
tified, the little company gazed over the expanse of dark blue water
that lay before them. The sand of the long curving beach glistened
in the sun. But where was the grand landlocked harbor Vizcaíno had
described? Great swells from the ocean rolled in without obstruction,
and there was no safety from the wind except in the small hook of
the horseshoe where the town of Monterey now stands. The party
failed to recognize the bay of Monterey.

After holding mass at the mouth of the Salinas River, Portolá's
group concluded that their only hope of finding Monterey was by
continuing north. The party pushed on up the coast, with eleven of
the men now so ill that they had to be carried in litters swung between
mules. Near Soquel they had their first sight of the "big trees," which
Portolá named *palo colorado,* or redwood, because of the color of
their wood. At one stopping place they saw a giant tree of this species,
which they called *Palo Alto* (high tree), and the town located there
still bears that name.

Discovery of San Francisco Bay

Portolá's men passed northward over land never before trodden upon
except by Indians. Their path was hindered by *arroyos,* or gulches,
over which bridges had to be built to permit the animals to pass.
After exploring in the direction of Point Reyes, an advance party
excitedly reported to Portolá their discovery of a "great arm of the
sea, extending to the southeast farther than the eye could reach."
This, of course, was San Francisco Bay, whose magnificent panorama
the whole party viewed for the first time on November 2, 1769.
Astonished by the sight of so vast a body of water, the explorers
concluded that Monterey Bay must now be behind them; this was
yet another large estuary. For decades ships had passed by the opening of the bay of San Francisco. Yet it remained for a land expedition
to discover the greatest harbor on the Pacific Coast.

Around San Francisco Bay wild geese were so abundant and tame
that they could be knocked down with a stick. After a feast of mussels,
ducks, and geese, the group decided to return southward to Point
Pinos, taking nearly the same route by which they had come. When
Portolá and his men reached Carmel Bay, they set up a large cross
near the shore, with a letter buried at its base; if future ships should
come into the vicinity they would be informed that Portolá's expe-

dition had been there. His men then crossed Cypress Point, and near the bay which they still did not recognize as that of Monterey they erected another wooden cross. On its arms they carved these words: "The land expedition is returning to San Diego for lack of provisions, today, December 9, 1769."

Winter covered the Santa Lucia Mountains, which they had to cross. In their plight the party welcomed any sort of food. Portolá wrote: "We shut our eyes and fell to on a scaly mule (what misery) like hungry lions. We ate twelve in as many days, obtaining from them perforce all our sustenance, all our appetite, all our delectation." The party fortunately obtained fish from the Indians.

"Smelling frightfully of mule," they finally returned on January 23, 1770, to the makeshift wood and adobe walls of their San Diego palisade, not knowing whether any of the company they had left behind were still alive. Mercifully, when they fired their muskets as a salute, those who were still alive rushed out to exchange greetings.

The accomplishments of this expedition were significant. The first mission in Upper California had been founded on July 16, 1769, and named San Diego de Alcalá. A good part of the coast to the north had been explored. Back at San Diego, however, the Indians had lost their awe of white men and began to steal even the bed sheets from under the sick. Then a boy belonging to the garrison was killed and several men wounded by arrows. Death continued its ravages, and provisions grew alarmingly short. Earlier, Portolá had sent the *San Antonio* back to San Blas on the Mexican west coast for supplies. As it had not yet returned, on February 10, 1770, he ordered Captain Rivera and a small party of the strongest men back to Lower California to seek supplies. Portolá decided to return to the peninsula himself if no relief ship should arrive by March 20. Little could be obtained from the Indians, who lived off the countryside. As for hunting wild game, ammunition was scarce and had to be saved for defense against possible attack.

The whole camp waited tensely to see if new supplies would arrive by the appointed time. Each day the missionaries knelt in supplication for the coming of a supply ship and began a nine-day prayer, or novena, to San José, patron saint of the expedition. On the afternoon of the last day of grace, March 19, 1770, as twilight began to obscure the horizon, a loud cry of "The ship! The ship!" rang through the camp. For a moment a sail was dimly seen, then it disappeared. This supply vessel appears to have been ordered to Monterey. On reaching the Santa Barbara channel, where an anchor was lost, its captain stopped to take on water, and he learned from Indians that Portolá's land party had returned from the north. Four days after being sighted at San Diego, the ship reappeared and dropped anchor there.

Rediscovery of Monterey

With hunger and despair relieved by a feast, Portolá again started preparations for a new expedition to find Monterey. Sending the *San Antonio* ahead by sea, he led a land party over the same route as before and reached the spot where they had set up the second cross, near Monterey Bay, the previous winter. They found the cross still standing, but now surrounded with a circle of feathered arrows thrust in the ground, as well as some sticks on which were hung sardines. This they accepted as an offering of friendship on the part of local Indians.

This time Portolá recognized the bay of Monterey. He, Crespi, and Pedro Fages, as they walked along the beach, observed that its bay resembled a round lake. The *San Antonio* arrived a week later. On June 3, 1770, beneath the very oak tree under which the Vizcaíno expedition had held services in 1602, Father Serra conducted a solemn mass amid the ringing of bells and salvos of artillery. Here was founded the second mission in Upper California, dedicated to San Carlos Borroméo. For convenience in obtaining wood and water, the mission was later removed to the little bay of Carmel, about four miles from Monterey. From Carmel, which became Serra's headquarters, he wrote his friend Father Palóu, "If you will come I shall be content to live and die in this spot." A presidio was established overlooking Monterey Bay.

On July 9, 1770, Portolá turned his command over to Fages and sailed away on the *San Antonio;* California heard no more of him. In its history he must always be a prominent figure, as the first of its governors, leader of the first expedition over the thousand-mile trail from the peninsula, and discoverer of San Francisco Bay.

Selected Readings

The best portrayal of Kino is Herbert Eugene Bolton's *Rim of Christendom* (New York, 1936). Another biography is Rufus Kay Wyllys, *Pioneer Padre: The Life and Times of Eusebio Kino* (Dallas, 1935). See also Eugenia Ricci, *Il Padre Eusebio Chini, Esploratore Missionario della California e dell'Arizona* (Milan, 1930), and Kino's own *Favores Celestiales,* translated and edited by Bolton as *Kino's Historical Memoir of Pimeria Alta* (2 vols., Cleveland, 1919). See also Bolton's *The Padre on Horseback* (San Francisco, 1932), and Frank C. Lockwood, *With Padre Kino on the Trail* (Tucson, 1934). Kino's astronomical activities are discussed in Ellen Shaffer, "The Comet of 1680–1681," Historical Society of Southern California *Quarterly* 34 (March 1952), 57–70, and in Kino's own *Esposición astronomica de el cometa* (Mexico, D.F.,

1681). Finally, on Kino, consult Ernest J. Burrus, trans. and ed., *Kino Reports to Headquarters* (Rome, 1954). On Salvatierra see Miguel Venegas, *Juan María de Salvatierra,* translated and edited by Margaret Eyer Wilbur (Cleveland, 1929). For other early Jesuit activity in the Southwest, see J. J. Baegert, *Observations in Lower California,* translated and edited by M. M. Brandenburg and Carl L. Baumann (Berkeley, 1952); see also the following volumes by Peter M. Dunne: *Pioneer Black Robes on the West Coast* (Berkeley, 1940), *Pioneer Jesuits in Northern Mexico* (Berkeley, 1944), *Early Jesuit Missions of the Tarahumara* (Berkeley, 1948), and *Black Robes in Lower California* (Berkeley, 1952). See also Theodore E. Treutlein, ed., *Pfefferkorn's Description of Sonora* (Albuquerque, 1949).

On Gálvez see Herbert I. Priestley, *José de Gálvez, Visitador-General of New Spain* (Berkeley, 1916). See also the translation of Father Javier Clavigero's *Storia della California* (1789) in Sara E. Lake and A. A. Gray, *The History of Lower California* (Stanford, 1937).

Regarding the Russian threat to California see Frank A. Golder, *Russian Expansion on the Pacific, 1641–1858* (Cleveland, 1914), and the same author's *Bering's Voyages* (2 vols., New York, 1922–25). Good accounts of the first colonization of California are Charles E. Chapman, *The Founding of Spanish California* (New York, 1916), and Irving Berdine Richman, *California Under Spain and Mexico, 1535–1847* (Boston, 1911). See also Douglas S. Watson, *The Spanish Occupation of California* (San Francisco, 1934).

Missionary activity has been widely chronicled. The *diario* of Fray Francisco Palóu appears, in translation, in Herbert E. Bolton, ed., *Historical Memoirs of New California* (5 vols., Berkeley, 1926). Crespi's *diario* (or journal) is also in these volumes. The relationship of Governor Fages with the padres is treated in Herbert I. Priestley, ed., *A Historical, Political and Natural Description of California by Pedro Fages* (Berkeley, 1937). See also Donald Nuttall, "Pedro Fages and the Advance of the Northern Frontier of New Spain," Ph.D. dissertation, University of Southern California (1964). Lives of Serra include Abigail H. Fitch, *Junípero Serra* (Chicago, 1914), and *Junípero Serra: Pioneer Colonist of California* (New York, 1933) by Agnes Repplier. An adulatory treatment of Serra and his fellow Franciscans has been written by a member of the order, Father Zephyrin Engelhardt, *The Missions and Missionaries of California* (4 vols., San Francisco, 1908–15). See also Charles J. G. Piette, *Evocation de Junípero Serra, fondateur de la Californie* (Washington, D.C., 1946). The best work on Serra is Father Maynard J. Geiger's *The Life and Times of Fray Junípero Serra* (2 vols., Washington, D.C., 1959); the same author has translated and edited Palóu's *Life of Fray Junípero Serra* (Washington, D.C., 1955). See also Geiger's "Fray Junípero Serra: Organizer and Administrator of the Upper California Missions, 1769–1784," California Historical

Society *Quarterly* 42 (September 1963) 195–220, as well as Geiger's *Franciscan Missionaries in Hispanic California, 1769–1848: A Biographical Dictionary* (San Marino, Calif., 1969). Serra's successor has rated a biography, Francis Guest's *Fermin Francisco de Lasuén (1736–1803): A Biography* (Washington, D.C., 1973).

Regarding Portolá, see Robert Selden Rose, ed., *The Portolá Expedition of 1769–1770; Diary of Vicente Vila* (Berkeley, 1911); and the *diario* (1770) of Miguel Costansó in its English version, *The Spanish Occupation of California*, edited by Douglas S. Watson (San Francisco, 1934), as well as Costansó's *The Narrative of the Portolá Expedition of 1769–1770*, edited by Frederick J. Teggart (Berkeley, 1910). Also useful is Zoeth S. Eldredge, ed., *The March of Portolá and Discovery of the Bay of San Francisco, Log of the San Carlos, and Original Documents* (San Francisco, 1909). Also consult Theodore E. Treutlein, "The Portolá Expedition of 1769–1770," California Historical Society *Quarterly* 47 (December 1968), 291–313; Janet R. Fireman and Manuel P. Servín, "Miguel Costansó: California's Forgotten Founder," California Historical Society *Quarterly* 49 (March 1970), 3–19; and *The Costansó Narrative of the Portolá Expedition: First Chronicle of the Spanish Conquest of Alta California*, translation, introduction, and bibliography by Ray Brandes (Newhall, Calif., 1970).

Spanish techniques of claiming discoveries are discussed in three articles: Henry Raup Wagner, "Creation of Rights of Sovereignty Through Symbolic Acts," *Pacific Historical Review* 7 (December 1938), 297–326; Manuel P. Servín, "Symbolic Acts of Sovereignty in Spanish California," *Southern California Quarterly* 45 (June 1963), 109–21; and Servín's "The Instructions of Viceroy Bucareli to Ensign Juan Pérez," California Historical Society *Quarterly* 40 (September 1961), 243–46.

CHAPTER 6

Missions, Presidios, and Pueblos

AMONG THE THREE INSTITUTIONS used to colonize California—the mission, the presidio, and the pueblo—the mission must take first place. The other two served mainly to support and defend this primary establishment. Spain's ostensible purpose in the operation of its missions was the saving of the souls of aborigines, but actually it sought to win their allegiance. By 1776, the central role of the church was evident in the recommendations made by Father Serra to the governor of California. He suggested a survey for a new overland route from Sonora. Serra hoped for an increase in the population of California, expansion of its agricultural possibilities, and exploration along its northwest coast. Without these developments, California would not grow and prosper. The claims of Serra as "Founder of California" rest upon such secular contributions, as well as on his missionary labors.

Establishment of the Missions

California's missions were among the youngest of those scattered from Buenos Aires to Sonoma and from Tallahassee to San Diego. Though the mission system operated practically the same elsewhere in the Spanish empire, the circumstances of its founding in California were somewhat different. From the time of Kino, it was foolhardy for individual missionaries to face the dangers of the frontier alone. Those priests who went to Upper California were accompanied by guards, and supplied with provisions until the missions could gather Indian colonies around them and become self-supporting. Twenty-one missions were established in California, forming a chain from San Diego to Sonoma. They were separated by about a day's travel

*Mission San Luís Rey, from Robinson's "Life in California before the Conquest,"
1846.* (C. C. Pierce Collection; by courtesy of The Huntington Library, San
Marino, California.)

on horseback—some thirty miles apart. The King's Highway, or *El
Camino Real* of the tourist literature, was then scarcely more than a
dusty path, the only road from mission to mission and from presidio
to presidio. Serra founded nine missions. The succeeding nine were
established by Fray Fermín de Lasuén, a name as important in California's development as that of Serra.

Three requisites determined the choice of a mission site—arable
soil for crops, water supply, and a large local Indian population. By
the time the twenty-one missions were established, the friars had in
their possession much of the choicest land in the province, which led
to later resentment.

The first mission buildings were of rude thatch construction, huts
of sticks, plastered with mud or clay, and roofed with tule. Mission
chapels had only an altar and other crude wooden church furniture.
The permanent adobe-brick or cut-stone buildings, with which tourists are today familiar, still appear dignified. These missions were
slowly built with Indian labor after the era of the pioneer missionaries. Today's stone walls at Mission San Carlos Borroméo were never
seen by Father Serra, even though he died there.

Architecturally the missions are distinctive, differing in many par-
ticulars from those in other parts of America. The California padres,
in their isolation, evolved a plan of their own; the result was a combination of Moorish and Roman influences, with modifications appropriate to the environment. Isolation prevented the overdecora-

San Francisco Solano
de Sonoma (1823)

San Rafael Arcángel
(1817)

San Francisco
(1776)

San Francisco de Asís
(1776)

Santa Clara (1777)

San José de Guadalupe
(1797)

Branciforte (1797)

Santa Cruz (1791)

San Juan Bautista (1797)

San Carlos Borromeo
(Carmel) (1770)

Monterey

Nuestra Señora de
la Soledad (1791)

San Antonio de Padua
(1771)

San Miguel Arcángel
(1797)

North

San Luís Obispo
(1772)

La Purísima Concepción
(1787)

Santa Inés (1804)

Santa Barbara (1786)

Santa Barbara (1782)

San Buenaventura (1782)

San Fernando Rey de España
(1797)

Los Angeles (1781)

San Gabriel Arcángel
(1771)

The California Missions

with dates and order of founding

● Mission

⬡ Presidio

■ Mission pueblo and civic
municipality

0   50   100

miles

San Juan Capistrano
(1776)

San Luís Rey de
Francia (1798)

San Diego de Alcalá
(1769)

Bier

Colonnades in quadrangle, Mission San Juan Capistrano, founded 1776; photograph taken 1885. (C. C. Pierce Collection; by courtesy of The Huntington Library, San Marino, California.)

tion rampant on the Iberian peninsula, inherited by Spain from the Moors. "California mission architecture" is characterized by open courts, long colonnades, arches and corridors. The typical red-tiled roofs were one solution to bitter experiences with fire. Destruction of earlier buildings by earthquakes led to the use of thick walls reinforced with buttresses.

Governing the Natives

The missionaries instituted patriarchal government, assuming a paternal attitude toward the Indians and treating them as wards. There were usually two friars at an establishment, the elder of whom had charge of interior matters and religious instruction, while the younger attended to agricultural and outside work. Each mission administrator was subject to the authority of a father-president for all of California. He in turn bowed to the orders of the College of San Fernando, headquarters of the Franciscans in Mexico. Except in the punishment of capital crimes, the friars had full control of the destinies of their Indian charges, and these padres became virtual rulers of their mission domains. Floggings and other corporal punishments were occasionally administered to the Indians for various offenses. The missionaries defended their discipline on the ground that it was the only effective means of controlling the childlike natives.

Modern clerical scholars, among them Father Francis Guest, have offered alternative explanations to accusations of bestiality by the Franciscans toward California's aborigines. Flagellation, or use of rope *disciplina* whips and hairshirts, formed part of the routine clerical mortification of the flesh. Guest finds it understandable that they should inflict similar punishments upon their charges. As to charges of medical abuses by the missionary padres, he does not find them to have been callous and indifferent witnesses to the early death of many natives. Instead, he points to the primitive state of medicine in the eighteenth century, especially in a frontier environment. Although delinquent Indians were whipped, sometimes excessively, and some lost their lives due to poor sanitation, one needs to place punishment and high mortality rates at the missions within the context of eighteenth-century Spanish standards. Most historians have seen treatment of the Indians by the clergy or the military as victimization. Later, in the American period, misuse of them multiplied. The natives were perceived as primitives who were useful as cheap labor. Because they were docile and exploitable, farmers, ranchers, and miners could easily take over Indian lands. The natives, furthermore, had become obstacles to "white progress." Ultimately, they were expendable.

The missions were not devoted entirely to religious instruction. Each was also a sort of industrial school, in which natives learned the formal meaning of work and where they were taught trades. Native strength, harnessed with missionary inventive genius and mechanical skill, produced remarkable irrigation works. The Franciscans were the pioneers of California's water system.

The friars served as teachers, musicians, weavers, carpenters, masons, architects, and physicians of soul and body. Putting their own hands to the plow, they raised enough food for mission use, and occasionally a surplus of meal, wine, oil, hemp, hides, or tallow. This was shipped down the coast to New Spain; at Acapulco these products were exchanged for articles needed in Alta California—clothing, furniture, and tools. At mission farms and orchards the missionaries tried to adapt various crops to the climate and soil. Semitropical fruits, such as oranges, lemons, figs, dates, and olives, flourished in mission gardens, and their cultivation preceded the development of California horticulture. Even cotton was grown at some missions.

In Mexico City a strong new viceroy, Antonio María Bucareli, helped the struggling mission establishments greatly. Serra's reputation also stands high, but he had several remarkable companions, among them Francisco Palóu, founder of Mission San Francisco, and Lasuén. Palóu had been among the last of the Franciscans to turn over their Lower California missions to incoming members of the Dominican order, and in 1773 he joined Serra in Upper California. Palóu was not merely a missionary, but also author of the first book ever written in California, *Noticias de la Nueva California;* this and his *Vida de Junípero Serra,* are basic works about its early history. Lasuén, another cleric of talent and character, filled the post of president with distinction after Serra died.

At Serra's death, in 1784, he and his followers had been in California sixteen years. Their nine missions claimed a total of 5,800 converts. Flocks and herds ranged over thousands of acres, and Indians labored at spinning, weaving, carpentry, and masonry, besides raising crops for daily sustenance. The missionaries had also been associated with establishment of the first towns in California. These were of three types: the military, which grew up around such presidios as those of San Diego and Monterey; the civic, founded under secular, civilian auspices; and those that developed around the missions themselves—the "mission pueblos."

Presidios and Military Towns

California's presidios, or frontier fortresses, were built to protect missions from Indians and to guard Spanish claims to the area against foreign aggression. These presidios were located at strategic positions, generally at the entrances of the best ports. Small groups of houses, inhabited principally by settlers, traders, and the families of soldiers, grew up around the presidios, and such "military towns" developed into colonial centers. These presidial pueblos included San Diego, founded July 16, 1769; Monterey, June 3, 1770; San Francisco, September 17, 1776; and Santa Barbara, April 21, 1782. At first they were under military rule, but each acquired its own civil government. An early presidio consisted of a square enclosure, surrounded by a ditch and rampart of earth or brick, within which were located a small church, quarters for officers and soldiers, civilian houses, storehouses, workshops, wells, and cisterns. Outside were grouped a few dwellings, crops, and pasturage for horses and mules.

In addition to military pursuits, such as exploring, hunting, capturing runaway neophytes, and carrying the mails, the duties of the soldiers who manned the presidios included the erection of buildings, the care of herds and flocks, the cultivation of the soil. These occupations were not always to their liking, and they soon learned to employ Indians for many services. The neophytes received such pay as a string of beads, a dish of porridge, shoes, or a bit of cloth.

With a few bronze cannons mounted on ramparts, and often without powder to charge them, soldiers were equipped to resist attack only by still more poorly armed Indians. Not one of the presidios could have stood up against a well-equipped ship of war. Indeed, they were maintained more as a warning against possible enemies than with any expectation of making a fight. In time the cannon rusted and the presidios took on an air of dilapidation.

Even the officers lived under primitive conditions that awakened the pity of foreign visitors. Like exiles in a strange land, they waited for the day when they might return to more comfortable homes. The Englishman George Vancouver, visiting in 1792, described the house of the *comandante* at San Francisco as consisting of two rooms with earth floors, not boarded or even leveled; the windows had no glass, and furniture was almost completely lacking. Yet such was the warmth of hospitality of the officer's family that the visitor admitted he forgot their lowly surroundings.

Portolá's discovery of San Francisco Bay was to lead to the establishment of a military outpost on its peninsula largely through the efforts of Juan Bautista de Anza.

Anza was, like Portolá, a military man—one of the significant trail-breakers and tough Indian fighters of the West. He learned his vocation from his father and grandfather, also frontier captains. Anza had long planned to explore a route northwestward from Sonora to the ocean, believing that such a land passage would obviate the delay and perils of the sea voyage, on which California still relied for major contact with the outside world. Viceroy Bucareli, convinced of the importance of strengthening the California settlements, saw in Anza's proposal an opportunity not only to open a new land route, but also to send colonists under protection of a capable leader. Women settlers, provisions, and domestic animals were in particularly great demand in California. Bucareli therefore empowered Captain Anza to reconnoiter the proposed route. In January 1774, with the trails-priest Father Francisco Garcés as his guide, and a band of thirty-four men, Anza set out westward from Tubac in northern Mexico. Theirs was the first sizable crossing by white men into southern California from the Colorado basin through the San Jacinto Mountains. Another key to the success of this party was Garcés, a fearless missionary who three years before had penetrated into California beyond the junction of the Colorado and Gila rivers, to the walls of the southern Sierra. (Later this trail would be followed by some of the United States gold seekers of 1849.) On March 22, 1774, Anza's party reached Mission San Gabriel in California, where they were received with enthusiasm by the padres. Anza and his men then moved on to Monterey, returning later that year to the Sonora frontier. An overland route to California some 2,200 miles long had now been opened.

In 1775, preparations were made to send Anza with another party of colonists, recruited throughout Sinaloa and Sonora, and so impoverished that they had to be given clothing and pay in advance. On October 23 Anza left Tubac at the head of this second company, consisting of 240 men, women, and children. Their commander led them and a herd of 200 cattle beyond the Colorado River once more to Mission San Gabriel, and on to Monterey. A few colonists then accompanied him to the site of the future San Francisco. At the lagoon known as Dolores, Anza built brush huts and celebrated mass. He had made this second trip with the loss of only one life. Indeed, eight more persons had been added to his party by births along the way. Anza did not remain long at the Golden Gate, returning to frontier service in Sonora and Sinaloa.

On September 17, 1776, the presidio of San Francisco de Asís was formally dedicated, and on October 9 the mission was founded by Father Palóu, acting for Serra. Palóu helped build its first chapel, a wooden structure with a thatched roof. This building served the mission for eight years, until the present adobe structure was finished. Because it was located near Dolores Creek, it became known as Mission Dolores. The year this mission was established also saw the signing of the American Declaration of Independence.

Though a mission and presidio now existed at the future site of San Francisco, the community was not yet a real pueblo. In March 1775, the viceroy had also sent Captain Juan Manuel Ayala, in command of the vessel *San Carlos*, to explore further the vast bay which still had no name. No ship had yet passed through the Golden Gate, and Ayala feared danger along its narrow, rocky shoreline. At nightfall on August 5, 1775, the *San Carlos* moved into the entrance of the bay, cautiously dropping her lead line every few moments. The wind blew strongly, and threatened for a time to tear out a mast; but the little vessel moved on until it reached a point one league within the mouth, near North Beach. Then the wind suddenly died down. Ayala remained in San Francisco Bay a total of forty-four days. He named two of its islands—*Nuestra Señora de los Angeles* (Our Lady of the Angels) shortened later to Angel Island, and *Alcatraz*, or "Pelican," because of the large number of those birds flying over it.

Civil Pueblos

In addition to mission and presidial pueblos, there was a third category of early towns, those established under a definite civil government. The first of these were San José, founded in 1777; Los Angeles,

1781; and Branciforte (now extinct), 1797. The civil pueblos are considered the first real municipalities of California. They were established according to a plan by Governor Felipe de Neve in his code of laws, or *Reglamento*, issued in June 1779. Neve's regulations, derived from the Laws of the Indies, theoretically granted each pueblo four square leagues of land, laid out according to the topography of the country. First a plaza was marked out—a rectangular space in the center in inland towns; on the waterfront in the case of a town on a river or bay. Facing upon the plaza were the council house, church, storerooms, and the jail; the remaining frontage was occupied by houses. The life of the community revolved around these central squares; even bullfights took place in them.

Valuable inducements were offered settlers who would make their homes in these pueblos. Each was entitled to a house lot, stock and implements, an allowance in clothing and supplies amounting to $116.175 for each of the first two years and $60 for each of the next three, the use of government land as common pasture, and, finally, exemption from taxes for five years. The settler was required to sell surplus agricultural products to the presidios, and to hold himself, his horse, and musket in readiness for military service in any emergency. He was also required to build houses, dig irrigating ditches, cultivate the land, keep his implements in repair, and maintain a specified number of animals. Each pueblo was to construct dams, canals, roads and streets, church and other town buildings, and to help till the public lands. From the town's agricultural production municipal expenses were theoretically to be paid. These arrangements were provisional for the first five years, at the end of which settlers were to receive title to their lands. As a safeguard against carelessness, no one had the right to sell or mortgage his land.

Municipal officers—consisting of an *alcalde* (similar to a powerful mayor), or two *alcaldes* in the larger towns, and a board of councilmen (*ayuntamiento*)—were first appointed by the governor, but were afterwards elected by the people. The *alcalde* decided all cases of minor importance, punishable by fine or imprisonment, while other high crimes were brought before the governor at Monterey. His judicial decisions were final. Anyone could demand trial by "good men" (*hombres buenos*)—three or five jurors, as ordered by the magistrate. The powers of an *alcalde* were almost unlimited, and generally these officials were honest in the administration of justice. The *alcalde* was in effect the "little father" of a town, to whom all carried their troubles.

The *ayuntamiento* managed the public business not only of the town but also of a large contiguous territory. The Los Angeles *ayuntamiento* had jurisdiction over territory as large as that of Massachusetts. It was a dignified body whose members were attired in black. The *ayun-*

tamiento received petitions and complaints from dissatisfied citizens, ranchers as well as townsmen.

There was no pay attached to the office of *alcalde* or *regidor* (councilman). The honor of holding public office compensated the holders for their labors. As a badge of office the *alcaldes* carried a silver-headed cane. They and the *regidores* were entitled to public respect. Functioning within the *ayuntamiento*, they were the arbiters of town life, socially as well as governmentally. Later, under Mexican rule, *alcaldes* and *ayuntamientos* were suppressed, and justices of the peace exercised functions originally performed by *alcaldes*.

San José de Guadalupe (now San Jose), founded November 29, 1777, was California's first civic pueblo. It consisted of a few mud huts, erected on the banks of the Guadalupe River, occupied by soldiers and their families. Not until 1786 did the residents receive legal possession of their lands. Further south the second civic pueblo, Nuestra Señora la Reina de los Angeles de Porciúncula, abbreviated today to Los Angeles, was founded at sundown on September 4, 1781, by eleven couples and their twenty-two children—a total of forty-four *pobladores*, or settlers. Recruited at Álamos in Sonora by authorization of Governor de Neve, they settled in the new "pueblo of Our Lady, the Queen of the Angels." Nothing could be more humble than the beginnings of this city. Its first citizens were of Indian and African blood, with a moderate admixture of Spanish; it was difficult to induce colonials of standing to accept exile to such a distant wilderness as California. Yet, by 1784 this band of colonists had replaced their first rude huts with adobe houses and laid the foundations for a church and other public buildings. Two years afterwards, when land titles were finally issued them, each Angeleno affixed his cross to these documents (not one of Los Angeles's first citizens could write his name). Later the town assumed importance from its overland trade with New Mexico over what came to be known as "The Old Spanish Trail."

California's third civic community, Branciforte, named after a viceroy and designed for defense, was founded in 1797 near the present Santa Cruz. It was a failure and soon passed out of existence. The colonists who founded it were mostly convicts sent by officials in Mexico to serve out sentences of banishment in California.

Selected Readings

Basic to understanding the mission is Herbert E. Bolton, "The Mission as a Frontier Institution in the Spanish American Colonies," *American Historical Review* 23 (October 1917), 42–61. See also Frank Wilson Blackmar, *Spanish Institutions of the Southwest* (Baltimore, 1891).

Later works that treat the settlement of the California frontier include Theodore Maynard, *The Long Road of Father Serra* (New York, 1954), and Omer Englebert, *The Last of the Conquistadores: Junípero Serra, 1713–1784* (New York, 1956). One should consult *The Writings of Junípero Serra* (4 vols., Washington, D.C., 1954), edited by Antonine Tibesar, as well as Maynard Geiger's carefully edited translation of *Palóu's Life of Fray Junípero Serra* (Washington, D.C., 1955), and Francis J. Weber, "The Pious Fund of the Californias," *Hispanic American Historical Review* 43 (February 1963), 78–94. Additional data concerning the missions is in *The Letters of José Señan, O.F.M., Mission San Buenaventura*, translated by Paul D. Nathan and edited by Lesley Byrd Simpson (San Francisco, 1962). Francis J. Weber, "The California Missions and Their Visitors," *The Americas* 24 (April 1968), 319–36, lists foreigners who visited the missions.

The founding of Los Angeles is discussed by W. W. Robinson in *Ranchos Become Cities* (Pasadena, 1939), as well as in his *Panorama: A Picture History of Southern California* (Los Angeles, 1953). A less successful example of pueblo founding is studied in Florian Guest, "The Establishment of the Villa of Branciforte," California Historical Society *Quarterly* 41 (March 1962), 29–50. The most important official at the local level is portrayed in Theodore Grivas, "Alcalde Rule: The Nature of Local Government in Spanish and Mexican California," California Historical Society *Quarterly* 40 (March 1961), 11–32.

See also Francis Guest, "Municipal Government in Spanish California," California Historical Society *Quarterly* 46 (December 1967), 307–35, and Guest's "Cultural Perspective on California Mission Life," *Southern California Quarterly* 55 (Spring 1983), 1–65, which should be compared with Harry Kelsey, "European Impact on the California Indians," *The Americas* 61 (April 1985), 494–511. These sources concern governance by the padres of Indians. See also James Sandos, "Levantamiento: The 1824 Chumash Uprising Reconsidered," *Southern California Quarterly* 57 (Summer 1985), 109–33. The best account of founding Los Angeles is Edwin Beilharz, *Felipe de Neve, First Governor of California* (San Francisco, 1972).

On Anza see Herbert E. Bolton, ed., *Anza's California Expeditions* (5 vols, Berkeley, 1930). A diary of the last Anza expedition was by its chaplain, Fray Pedro Font, edited by Frederick J. Teggart as *The Anza Expedition of 1775–1776* (Berkeley, 1913). For the Yuma massacre consult Douglas D. Martin, *Yuma Crossing* (Albuquerque, 1954).

An updated survey of early California is John Schutz, *Spain's Colonial Outpost* (San Francisco, 1985).

CHAPTER 7

California and Its Spanish Governors

THE SPANISH GOVERNORS in California were men of intelligence and character who served their king faithfully. In 1770 Pedro Fages followed Portolá as military commander of Upper California. Fages, a sturdy officer, labored hard to put the new colony on its feet. He was also an Indian fighter of repute and an explorer who, in 1770 and 1772, led two expeditions to San Francisco Bay and made a thorough reconnaissance of its shores. Fages kept the California colony alive, during a period when supply ships were delayed, by providing bear meat from the Cañada de los Osos (Bear Canyon), near San Luís Obispo. His brusque manners and hot temper involved him in many disagreements with the missionaries and with his young wife, Doña Eulalia, all of which the padres recorded in entertaining detail in the mission archives. Petty wrangling occurred between the religious and the military, a result of trying frontier conditions and divided political authority. Friction between Fages and Serra became so acute that Serra asked for his removal. Fages's replacement as military *comandante* of Upper California was Captain Rivera y Moncada, leader of the first land party during the 1769 Portolá expedition.

The change turned out to be a mistake; Rivera was not only erratic in disposition, but also a procrastinator by nature. He even neglected to carry out specific orders of the viceroy, although in at least one case his obedience caused unfortunate results. In 1773 elaborate instructions were given him for the conduct of his office, including important regulations for the control of shipping. According to these, severe restrictions were to be imposed on the admittance of vessels into California ports, except those from San Blas and the Philippine Islands. This policy, which Rivera enforced, interfered with California's future trade with foreigners and aroused discontent among its inhabitants. In 1775 an uprising of the Indians at San Diego occurred; Fray Luís Jaime was killed in the fracas. Rivera, however, quelled the outbreak before it could spread and life resumed its peaceful tenor.

Under Rivera a royal decree reversed the dominance of Lower and Upper California. In 1777 this decree established the governor's residence at Monterey, sent Rivera to Loreto in Lower California to rule that peninsula as lieutenant governor, and brought in a new and vigorous governor for Upper California. This active, enterprising administrator, Felipe de Neve, may well have been the best of the Spanish governors. Like his predecessors, Neve was a soldier, but he had a statesman's mind. His fame is based chiefly upon the code of laws which he drew up for regulation of the civic and military affairs of California.

The Yuma Massacre

Connected with the founding of these pueblos, notably San José and Los Angeles, is one of the most tragic occurrences in the history of the American West. Rivera received orders in 1781 to conduct a party of settlers bound for the proposed pueblos from Sonora and Sinaloa. At the Colorado River, Rivera sent the colonists ahead, while he and his soldiers, accompanied by the trails-priest, Father Garcés, stopped at the river. On July 17, 1781, the Yuma Indians attacked two missions—Purísima Concepción and San Pedro y San Pablo—which had been established as way stations near the river crossing. All the friars at the mission, all the male settlers in the area, and all the men in Rivera's command, including himself and Father Garcés, were shot or clubbed to death by the Yumas while women and children were herded off into slavery. The Yumas saw the Spanish invaders as mortal enemies. Though they had been promised supplies and good treatment by Anza, when they saw the Spaniards marching through their cornfields and pumpkin patches, their resentment rose. As a result of the Yuma Massacre, neither pueblos nor missions were reestablished on the Colorado River; the route opened by Anza grew more dangerous than ever before. Governor Neve joined Fages in a campaign against the Yumas, which was a failure. The Indians, who took refuge in impenetrable country, remained unpunished and hostile.

Serra's Successors

During the second gubernatorial term of Fages, which began in 1782, California suffered a heavy loss in the death of Father Serra, on

August 28, 1784. Of the seventy-one years he had lived, thirty-four had been spent in missionary work. His immediate successor, Palóu, occupied the presidency of the missions for only a year, which he spent chiefly in the preparation of the two volumes already mentioned. He was succeeded by Lasuén, who labored for eighteen years thereafter to carry out Serra's plan for the extension of the California missions.

Governor Fages's second administration came to an end in 1790, when, worn out by anxieties connected with his office, and harrassed by the constant urgings of his wife to leave this rough frontier post, he offered his resignation. In 1794 after a succession of governors (named in the Appendix), a most able new California leader arrived. He was a Basque named Diego de Borica. One of the most progressive of the Spanish governors, Borica was also a good soldier and administrator. He was, in addition, agreeable, fond of jest, and so delighted with California that he never lost an opportunity to sing its praises. "To live long and without care come to Monterey," he wrote his friends. "That is the most peaceful and quiet country in the world; one lives better here than in the most cultured court of Europe."

Among Borica's first acts was to inaugurate a system of public education; but he received little encouragement from either the government or people. The governor was friendly to the friars, with whom, in spite of disagreements, he established a harmonious relationship. Borica authorized Father Lasuén to have the regions not served by the existing missions explored for new mission sites; and together they decided that five more establishments could be founded. Borica believed that conversion of all the Indians west of the Coast Range would make it possible to reduce the number of provincial guards. Hitherto the missions had been isolated units; Borica now proposed to link them into one chain, nearer together. Under supervision of Governor Borica and Father Lasuén, the new missions were established in a short time.

Lasuén placed great emphasis on instructing the neophytes in artisan trades, as well as in agriculture and stock raising. Carpenters, blacksmiths, and masons were sent from Mexico to the province at royal expense, and this new talent helped develop further the mission architecture and economic progress of California.

Borica induced the missionaries and inhabitants of the pueblos to experiment with planting hemp and flax, which later became moderately successful crops, and sheep-grazing.

The years 1797 to 1799, however, also were a time of anxiety over the increasing numbers of foreign ships arriving in California ports. Although their ostensible purpose was trading or exploration, the Spaniards considered the real motivation to be espionage. The appearance in particular of vessels sailing under the flag of the new

American Union, to take on wood and water, caused alarm among Spanish authorities, who knew how poor their defensive potential was. Attempts were made by Governor Borica to repair fortifications. He issued instructions to soldiers to resist attacks as long as possible; then they were to retreat toward the interior, driving livestock before them and taking all other supplies, so that these would not fall into the hands of the enemy. Borica erected shore batteries at San Diego and Yerba Buena, instituted irrigation works, guarded provincial revenues, and acted as censor of public morals. A steadfast friend of the Indians, he did what he could to see that they were not despoiled of their lands. He was a merciful magistrate who believed that no capital punishment should be inflicted upon them, even for murder; only imprisonment and labor were meted out as sentences for Indians. Borica also had a hand in the separation of Upper from Lower California: at his recommendation, a dividing line was fixed below San Diego, and this afterwards helped determine the boundary between the United States and Mexico. Lastly, along with his busy official life Borica found time for society, and his genial personality helped make his administration one of social distinction at Monterey.

Upon Borica's retirement in 1800, José Joaquín de Arrillaga served a second term as governor, one marked by continuing cordiality between the military and religious officials, but the Mexico City government had lost interest in the missions and was sending no money to support them. The presidios and civil establishments too were allowed to fall into deplorable state; buildings were half ruined by wind and rain; cannon rusted from exposure and disuse; already spiritless troops remained badly equipped, barely able to keep down miscreant Indians. California's soldiers were left without pay for years. These conditions are to be ascribed not to inefficiency on the part of any one Spanish governor, but to prolonged neglect by the central government.

As for the missions, their period of expansion came to an end with the death of Father Lasuén on June 26, 1803. The missions served the area from San Diego northward to San Francisco and between the Coast Range and the ocean. One could travel safely over a distance of 500 miles and enjoy the hospitality of the missions each night without having to carry along provisions. Horses were plentiful en route.

One of the principal worries of Governor Arrillaga's administration was the founding of a Russian settlement in California in 1812. The Russians had arrived in 1806 to examine trading opportunities. Now they established Fort Ross, north of Bodega Bay, as a post to supply their Alaskan settlements. The Russian threat to California had, at last, become real. Such cares as these lay heavily upon Arrillaga, who died on July 24, 1814.

Solá, Last of the Spanish Governors

California's next governor was Pablo Vincente Solá. His arrival at Monterey in 1815 was marked by days of feasting and dancing, exhibitions of expert horsemanship, gory bull and bear fights in the capital's muddy arena, and a grand finale in which Indians danced in their best feathers, beads, and war paint. The royalist governor considered this fiesta an expression of California's loyalty to Spain, when such allegiance was growing weaker. Furthermore, Solá, a haughty official, expected the homage he was tendered.

The new governor found a multitude of troubles in California. His popularity diminished after his condescending attitude became publicly known. He was proud of his Spanish birth and inclined to look with contempt upon colonials as incompetent whelps. He was also angered by the smuggling that had grown up between the inhabitants and foreigners. Yet, when he himself faced scarcities of clothing, furniture, tools and other necessities—as a result of the shortage of supply ships during the colonial rebellions against Spain—he grew more sympathetic to the plight of the Californians and began to wink at smuggling.

Solá's personal wishes would soon be immaterial. Spain's empire was about to crumble throughout Latin America and in California too during his governorship.

Selected Readings

The Spanish governors are the topic of Donald A. Nuttall, "The Gobernantes of Spanish Upper California," California Historical Society *Quarterly* 51 (Fall 1972), 253–80. Palóu's *Serra* and his *Noticias* are, of course, basic. The latter work has been translated into English by Herbert E. Bolton, as *Historical Memoirs of New California* (3 vols., Berkeley, 1926). See also Pedro Fages, *A Historical, Political and Natural Description of California*, translated by Herbert I. Priestly (Berkeley, 1937), and *Letters of Captain Don Pedro Fages and the Reverend President Fr. Junípero Serra at San Diego, California, in October, 1772*, translated by Henry R. Wagner (San Francisco, 1936). Another valuable compilation is the *Writings of Fermín Francisco de Lasuén*, translated and edited by Finbar Kenneally (2 vols. Washington, D.C., 1965).

After the 150th anniversary of Los Angeles, the Historical Society of Southern California *Annual Publications* 15 (1937) published articles concerning Governor Felipe de Neve, including Lindley Bynum's "Governor Don Felipe de Neve, a Chronological Note" and his "Four Reports by Neve, 1777–1779."

The Yuma Massacre is discussed in Douglas D. Martin, *Yuma Cross-*

ing (Albuquerque, 1954); and in Pedro Fages, *The Colorado River Campaign 1781–1782*, translated and edited by Herbert I. Priestly (Berkeley, 1913). Father Garcés has been treated biographically in Elliot Coues, *On the Trail of a Spanish Pioneer* (2 vols., New York, 1900). Consult also John Galvin, ed., *A Record of Travels in Arizona and California, 1775–1776 by Fr. Francisco Garcés* (San Francisco, 1965).

The founding of San Francisco is the subject of Herbert E. Bolton's *Outpost of Empire* (New York, 1931).

The architecture of the missions has been treated by Kurt Baer, *Architecture of the California Missions* (Berkeley, 1958), and in his *Paintings and Sculpture at Mission Santa Barbara* (Washington, D.C., 1955), as well as in Baer's "Spanish Colonial Art in the California Missions," *The Americas* 17 (July 1961), 33–54. Colored photos of Edwin Deakin's paintings are in *A Gallery of California Mission Paintings*, edited by Ruth Mahood (Los Angeles, 1966).

A glimpse of the mission system appears in Herbert I. Priestley, *Franciscan Explorations in California* (Glendale, 1946). See also Henry R. Wagner, "Early Franciscan Activity on the West Coast," Historical Society of Southern California *Quarterly* 23 (September 1941), 115–26. Useful also is John A. Berger, *The Franciscan Missions of California* (New York, 1948), and Maynard Geiger, *Mission Santa Barbara, 1782–1965* (Santa Barbara, 1965), as well as his "New Data on the Buildings of Mission San Francisco," California Historical Society *Quarterly* 46 (September 1967), 195–205. An appraisal of the "Spanish heritage" is attempted in Manuel P. Servín, "California's Hispanic Heritage: A View Into the Spanish Myth," *San Diego History* 19 (Winter 1973), 1–9.

CHAPTER 8

Exploration and Foreign Interference

SPANISH EXPLORERS along the California coast pursued their aims so energetically that much of its geography had been mapped before other Europeans made a significant appearance there. Charting of the northwest coast, opening of the interior valleys, and pacification of the natives were achieved during the Spanish occupation.

Exploring the Northwest Coast

After San Francisco Bay had been charted, Father Serra suggested to Viceroy Bucareli that other explorations be undertaken north of San Francisco. The viceroy had received reports from Madrid of Russian designs upon California. He appointed Captain Juan Pérez to investigate both Russian and English activity above California as well as to chart its northwest coastline. Pérez set out from San Blas on January 24, 1774. Above San Francisco his ship crept along a rocky, uncharted coastline but he succeeded in reaching Queen Charlotte Island. There Pérez was compelled, by the suffering of his men from scurvy and exposure, to turn about and head for home. Although the fog, rain, and headwinds made it impossible for his expedition to land, Pérez made many observations. Coastal Indians came out to his vessel in dugout canoes to barter dried fish, furs, carved wooden boxes, crude images, and hair mats for Spanish beads, iron, and sheets of thin copper. The Indians sang and scattered feathers on the water as a token of friendship. The ship was at one point encircled by as many as two hundred natives, whose concerted chanting and thumping of wooden drums stunned the whites.

When, late in August of 1774, Pérez's frigate dropped anchor in

Monterey Bay, he had surveyed part of the coastlines of British Columbia, Washington, and Oregon, in addition to that of northern California. Pérez was deprived of renown because of Spain's policy of keeping such voyages secret. Thus even the names that Pérez gave to points on the northwest coast were eventually discarded in favor of place names left by other navigators.

In March of 1775 two other explorers set out from San Blas. These were Captain Bruno de Heceta and Juan Francisco de la Bodega. At latitude 41 degrees their ships headed into a fine bay. Its shores, covered with wild roses, iris, manzanita, *yeraba buena* (literally "good grass"), and tall pines, were inviting, and the Spaniards landed and took possession in the name of the king. Since this event took place on the day of the Holy Trinity, they called the bay Trinidad, by which name it is still known. Friendly Indians wearing wreaths of flowers and feathers trooped to the beach and assisted the strangers in taking on wood and water.

Farther north, the Spaniards encountered less friendly natives. When a boatload of six Spaniards went ashore for water, they were set upon and cut to pieces before the eyes of their helpless companions on the ship, who had no other small boat in which to go to their aid. The natives next went out in canoes and surrounded the schooner; they had to be driven off with musket fire.

To Heceta belongs the discovery of the Columbia River, on July 27, 1775, although the achievement is sometimes ascribed to the United States sea captain Robert Gray in 1792. Three days after Heceta first sighted the Columbia, his two ships were separated in a driving rain and mist. They did not meet again until they returned to Monterey. Heceta eventually reached Nootka, on the west coast of Vancouver Island. Because of the miserable condition of his crew, Heceta decided to turn about; he remained in sight of land on the way down, exploring the coast as he went.

Bodega, though short of food and water, and with a crew also crippled by scurvy, ran far to the north. When the cold autumn rains set in, however, the men suffered so severely from insufficient clothing that Bodega was also compelled to return southward. The trip was a stormy one and great seas rolled over the ship, carrying away everything movable and filling the hold with water. On October 3, 1775, his vessel found itself in a bay about four leagues north of Point Reyes, on whose banks bear and deer could be seen feeding. The local Indians welcomed the wary Spaniards, who named the bay Bodega.

In the years 1774–1775, the northwest coast, as far as 57 degrees 58 minutes, had thus been explored and formally taken into Spanish possession by Pérez, Heceta, and Bodega.

The Nootka Sound Controversy

To defend its rights on a coast which it claimed up to 60 degrees latitude, Spain sent two more expeditions into the region in 1788–1789. Under the command of Estavan José Martínez, these parties had orders to establish a fort and mission on Nootka Sound as a symbol of Spanish sovereignty in the region. Ten years before, the English mariner Captain James Cook had first landed at Nootka.

At Nootka, Martínez found several English vessels already at anchor. He explained that Spain regarded the region as an extension of its California colony. Next Martínez seized the English vessels at Nootka and made prisoners of those on board. This act later nearly led to armed conflict between the two countries and created a diplomatic incident with repercussions in Europe. Martínez eventually released the English vessels, having meanwhile taken possession of the port. A Spanish post, maintained at Nootka for five more years, was provisioned by transport, as an extension of the California colony.

While Martínez was at Nootka in 1789, he encountered the American ships *Columbia* and *Lady Washington*. (The term *American* refers here and subsequently to the United States, not to the entire Western Hemisphere.) The captains of these ships, Robert Gray and John Kendrick, wisely did not involve themselves in the Nootka Sound controversy. Although relations between the Americans and Spaniards remained outwardly cordial, this appearance of the ships of the new republic caused uneasiness among the Spanish. America, an expanding new country in search of world markets, would one day base its territorial sovereignty in the Far West partly upon the voyages of Spanish navigators.

In 1795 both the Spanish and English posts at Nootka Sound were abandoned. This withdrawal was one of the most evident steps in the progressive decline of Spanish power and influence, especially along remote Pacific shores, including California.

La Pérouse and Malaspina

Geographic separation from Spain's other colonies, plus rigid mercantilist trade policy, forced Californians to lead calm, even dull, lives. They knew the name of their king and that of the pope but little more about events abroad. Only ships flying the flags of other nations could bring them sorely needed goods which the decrepit Spanish supply system failed to provide.

Foreign vessels began to appear in California waters as a result of the activities of a man who never set foot in that province—Captain

Cook. When he landed at Nootka to obtain furs for sale in China, his voyage attracted almost as much attention as his discovery of the Hawaiian Islands. A great fur trade on the northwest coast began to attract European and American ships to ports further south, in California.

In August 1785, the French scientist and navigator Jean François de Galaup de la Pérouse sailed from Brest, heading an expedition whose objects were geographic, scientific, and commercial. In addition to making a survey of the flora, fauna, native population, and geology of various Pacific regions, its commander was to inquire about the new North American fur trade. On September 15, 1786, La Pérouse's two vessels anchored in Monterey Bay among a school of whales spouting vile-smelling water. Since Spain and France were on cordial terms, California officials had received orders to accord the foreigners the same hospitable welcome as vessels of their own nation. During La Pérouse's ten-day stay his crew took on wood and water while geologists and botanists collected specimens and made drawings. The Californians supplied the visiting ships with cattle, vegetables, milk, poultry, and grain; for none of this would they accept even a *peseta*. The visitors reciprocated with cloth, blankets, beads, tools, and seed potatoes from Chile.

La Pérouse's report commended California's agricultural fertility and mild climate, which were compared to those of southern France. Although he testified to the high purpose of the missionaries, he thought they erred in attempting to enforce a disciplined life upon a people whose self-reliance suffered from the mission system.

The Frenchmen, having finished charting of the coast, prepared to resume their cruise to undiscovered parts of the Pacific. *Comandante* Fages filled the hen coops of the departing vessels from his own poultry yard, while the fathers at Carmel Mission supplied the La Pérouse expedition with vegetables and fruit. The expedition departed after a farewell that turned out to be final; except for a letter written by La Pérouse on February 8, 1788, at Botany Bay on the coast of Australia, giving the news of the murder of twelve of his men by natives of the Navigator Islands, nothing more was heard of the party until 1825, when the wreckage of two French ships was found on the reefs of Vanikoro, an island north of New Hebrides. Had it not been for the forethought of La Pérouse in forwarding installments of his journal to France, the records of his voyage would have been lost. This expedition is notable because it was the first official visit to Spanish California from the outside world, and it resulted in the first scientific description of the province.

A few years later, in September of 1791, California received a two-week visit from another scientific expedition, this one a Spanish project led by an Italian, Alejandro (Alessandro) Malaspina. He was on

a round-the-world mission with instructions to inspect the Pacific
Coast more thoroughly than any Spanish explorer had yet done, and
to find the long-sought Strait of Anián. Malaspina met Father Lasuén,
president of California's missions; the cartographic staff of the expedition made nautical observations, described the avifauna of the
region, and recorded the customs of the Indians and Spanish settlers.
Malaspina wrote an account of his visit which, while valuable, is not
as complete as that of La Pérouse or, later, of Vancouver. His voyage
is incidentally notable as having brought to California the first American to land on its shores. This was John Green, a sailor from Boston
who had shipped as a gunner's mate; he died while in California.

Vancouver's Voyage

English interest in California was high during the eighteenth century.
The poet John Dyer's book *The Fleece* (1757) forecast that there
would come a day "when, through new channels sailing, we shall
clothe the California coast, and all the realms that stretch from An-
ian's streights to proud Japan." George Vancouver had orders to
examine the extent of Spanish possessions, and to seize unclaimed
territory. He made his first landfall below Cape Mendocino, and
sailed northward from that point. On November 14, 1792 he entered
San Francisco Bay in the sloop-of-war *Discovery*. Despite strained relations between Spain and England, Vancouver was given a cordial
reception by the padres and military officials.

Vancouver's party visited Mission Santa Clara—the first foreigners
to penetrate so far into the interior—and were stuck by the physical
beauty of California's northern valleys. They returned to San Francisco, where they gave the Spaniards English culinary and table utensils, bar iron, and a few ornaments for the church. At Monterey
Vancouver was received as hospitably as he had been in San Francisco
Bay. At Carmel Mission, only a few leagues from Monterey, the fathers constructed a ceremonial bower of green branches and enter-
tained their foreign guests in the mission garden. This gesture was
returned by a dinner that Vancouver tendered aboard the *Discovery*;
next came a picnic in the garden of the Monterey presidio, and fire-
works furnished by the visitors.

Despite this cordiality, Vancouver was in Pacific waters to advance
British interests. Upon a return visit to California in 1793, he was
greatly offended not to receive the same welcome as on the year
before. Governor Arrillaga objected to allowing foreign officials to
penetrate into the interior. Vancouver remarked in his report on
this trip to California: "The only defenses against foreign attack are

a few poor cannon, inconveniently placed, at San Francisco, Monterey, and San Diego."

Sea Traders and Whalers

In 1796, the first United States vessel to anchor in a California port, the *Otter* of Boston, took on wood and water near Monterey. It secretly landed ten men and a woman on the Carmel beach at night, forcing them from a rowboat with a pistol. They were convicts from Botany Bay, an English penal colony in the South Pacific, who had used the *Otter* to escape. Governor Borica was offended at what he regarded as a dishonorable trick on the part of the Yankee captain. Finding it, nevertheless, necessary to provide for the newcomers, Borica put them to work as carpenters and blacksmiths at nineteen cents per day; the ex-prisoners turned out to be so industrious and well-behaved that he would have kept them in California had not royal orders obliged him to send them to Spain. In 1798, four sailors who had been left in Lower California by the American ship *Gallant* were also brought to San Diego and set to work while awaiting a vessel to take them to San Blas. In 1799, the *Eliza*, also an American ship, anchored at San Francisco and obtained supplies on the condition that it would not touch at any other port in the province. Although not really welcomed officially, American masters kept putting into California ports, where the natives were delighted to receive scarce supplies. A new world of contact with foreigners was coming alive for the Californians. During the years between 1808 and 1821, when Spain's colonies were in rebellion, Otto von Kotzebue, the Russian sailor-scientist, who made two visits to the coast during this period, described the people of California as almost without clothing and neglected by their mother country. Their plight afforded rare commercial opportunities for American traders, who grew steadily bolder. Furthermore, the Spaniards never became a commercial people. Their background was pastoral and agricultural. Despite regulations against contact between foreign vessels and the Californians, a contraband business sprang up.

Local officials were powerless to prevent trade with the "Boston ships"; their own wants were as dire as those of any other resident. In 1817, James Smith Wilcox, a Yankee trader, lean and lank, dressed in a beaver hat and swallow-tailed coat, excused his illegal smuggling operations on the ground that they "served to clothe the naked soldiers of the king of Spain, when for lack of raiment they could not attend mass, and when the most reverend fathers had neither vestments nor vessels fit for the church nor implements wherewith to till the soil." Other poachers and traders, especially Americans, came to feel equally self-righteous about the role they played in smuggling goods to California.

The arrival in California of increasing numbers of foreign ships occasionally roused the viceroy at Mexico City to issue stricter orders against trading with them. Since, however, he had no means of carrying out such *pronunciamientos*, Yankee poachers continued to operate—although at peril to themselves and their ships. On March 22, 1803, shots were exchanged between the American vessel *Lelia Byrd* and a shore battery at San Diego after part of its Yankee crew had been captured while trading ashore. Although several shots struck the sails, rigging, and hull of the American ship, no one was hurt. The Yankee captain, William Shaler, got his men safely away to the Hawaiian Islands and China. The next year the *Lelia Byrd* was back doing a flourishing fur business; but Captain Shaler and his leaky, worm-infested ship were careful this time to avoid the fortified ports of San Diego and Monterey.

The contraband "Boston ships" form a fascinating record of the invasion of a culture by another society. The American traders became important in breaking down the restrictions imposed by the Spanish Crown, and they sometimes suffered severe consequences when caught. In 1813, Captain George Washington Eayrs of the ship *Mercury* ran into a Spanish longboat in California waters. Unarmed, Eayrs and his men were captured and taken to Santa Barbara, where they were interned for two years. The captain wrote pleading letters from his squalid California prison, but he languished there at the pleasure of his captors.

Illegal coastal trafficking, by which New England wares or Chinese luxuries were exchanged for sea-otter furs, steer hides, tallow, and cow horns (to be made into buttons), continued to be dangerous. Yet the rewards were great. In the first few decades of the nineteenth century the price of prime otter pelts at Canton, China, was from $50 to $100. As many as 18,000 skins were delivered to the China market from California in a single season. This traffic became a significant branch of the great American China trade. Out of it grew also the fortunes of several prominent New England families.

One further economic link connected New England with California—Yankee whalers. These seamen stayed away from their home ports as long as four years. Battered and bruised by the gales of the North Pacific, they were grateful to find in California protected ports of call in which they could repair their ships and spirits. Fresh meat, fruit, grains and other provisions for the long homeward voyage around the Horn were readily obtained there. Richardson's Bay, near today's San Francisco, was an early rendezvous for whaling vessels, known by their fishy odors. These ships carried manufactured goods to exchange for coins or for local products. Out of their sea chests came needles, stockings, thread, bolts of cloth, and other comparatively luxurious commodities. Whalers undercut the prices of other traders and served as forerunners of the commerce that developed later during the hide- and tallow-trading era. At Monterey, these men of Nantucket and New Bedford left behind a permanent souvenir of their stay—a whalebone sidewalk—as a token of their appreciation for the shelter the town had afforded them. Whalers, furthermore, carried home glowing accounts of pastoral California, which helped popularize the province.

Arrival of the Russians

The Russians came into California, not with sword in hand, threatening violence, but, like their American competitors, as traders who gradually won tolerance if not an official welcome. Since the 1740s, when Vitus Bering had prepared the groundwork for the Russian-American Fur Company in Alaska, the Russians expanded their sphere of influence. They accumulated valuable caches of furs at their trading station in Sitka, but they were frequently on the verge of starvation in the midst of riches; the harsh climate and barrenness of the country made agriculture virtually impossible. Cold, forlorn, and eager to purchase supplies from Yankee sea captains, who also sought sea-otter and seal furs in the North Pacific, the Russians listened carefully to American reports about the abundance of wheat and other cereals in California.

In 1803, the Russians sent a company of natives of the Aleutian Islands to California to hunt otter. The Russians foresaw danger as a result of Spain's aversion to foreigners in California waters; but the abundance of otter to the south proved to be profitable enough for them to risk confrontation with the Spaniards. This marked the beginning of the contract system by which Russians and Americans hunted land and sea otter on the southern coasts for a decade or more. The furs were secured by Aleut hunters and partly by contraband trade with the Californians for goods. In 1805, Nikolai Petrovich Rezanov, chamberlain of the czar, was sent out to inspect the Russian colonies in the North Pacific. At Sitka he found the settlers reduced to eating crows and almost anything that could be swallowed; Russian supply ships had faltered in caring for the colony. Rezanov decided to go to California in search of supplies. His party was courteously received at San Francisco, but Governor Arrillaga feared that furnishing such foreigners with supplies would be considered an act of disloyalty by his government. He thus balked at doing so, just as he had disapproved of Vancouver's visit. A novel element was, however, injected into the negotiations between the Russians and the

Spaniards: the Russian envoy fell in love with the vivacious fifteen-year-old daughter of the *comandante* of the port. Rezanov's private correspondence with his government suggests that in wooing this girl, Concepción Argüello, diplomacy as well as romance entered into his behavior; but there is no reason to suspect that his affections were not also involved. The betrothal of the couple required permission of the girl's parents, Arrillaga, and the friars; all of them consented, and thus Rezanov was placed in a new position. As a future member of the *comandante's* family, he had no trouble persuading the governor to furnish supplies for the starving Russian colony at Sitka.

Rezanov's ship, the *Juno*, was laden with wheat, barley, peas, beans, tallow, and dried meat, and on May 8, 1806, Rezanov sailed away, while the Argüellos, including Concepción, waved farewell from the fort. The understanding when Rezanov left was that upon his return to St. Petersburg he would go to Madrid as an envoy from the Imperial Russian Court, in order to smooth over misunderstandings between the two powers in the Pacific. Then he would return, via New Spain, to San Francisco to claim his bride and settle those matters relative to the commerce Russia wished to promote. Rezanov never returned to California; after years of waiting for news of him, Señorita Argüello, who had in 1850 taken the vows of the Dominican order at Monterey, learned of Rezanov's death in Siberia while on his way home from California. This romance has been used as a literary theme by Bret Harte and other writers.

Fort Ross

Although the objective of Rezanov was to obtain supplies and relieve the Russian food scarcity at Sitka, he hoped also to extend Russian power southward. In 1809, an officer of the Russian-American Fur Company, Ivan Kuskov, was sent to California from Alaska to select a site for a southern outpost. He landed at Bodega Bay, a good harbor and fine building site, possessing tillable lands, a mild climate, and an abundance of fish and furbearing animals. In 1812 Kuskov returned, this time with equipment for a trading station and with Aleuts to fish for the community. Kuskov made no pretense of consulting Spanish officials, but simply chose a strategic shoreline site, eighteen miles north of Bodega. He built a rectangular fort, surrounded by a palisade with bastions at the corners pierced for cannon and mounted with ten pieces of artillery. Inside the stockade a wooden house of six or eight rooms, furnished with carpets and a piano and boasting glass windows, was for the officers. In one corner of the enclosure was a chapel, which had a round dome and a belfry with chimes. Granaries, workshops, and redwood huts for the Aleuts were outside the stockade, and on the beach the Russians erected a wharf, a tannery, and a bath house. Fort Ross was, surprisingly, painted blue. The Russians named this place "Ross," a derivation from the word "Russia"; because of its fortifications, it became generally known as Fort Ross. It lacked a good anchorage, and consequently Russian ships wintered and made repairs at Bodega. Attempts at raising vegetables at Fort Ross were only moderately successful, and the Russians were forced to rely upon the Californians for grain.

While Kuskov was building Fort Ross, the Spanish officer Gabriel Moraga was sent to investigate Russian activity north of San Francisco. The Russians allowed the emissary to inspect the fort, and, after pointing out their deficiencies in wheat, indicated that they would like to improve trade relations with their neighbors to the south. Moraga, on his return to San Francisco, reported that the Russians seriously needed food. In January 1813 he returned with three horses, twenty head of cattle, several *fanegas* (a Spanish unit of measure) of wheat, and permission from Governor Arrillaga to trade with Fort Ross. A mixture of compassion and fear had led the governor to aid the Russians. However, California's Spanish officials never gave formal permission to the Russians to settle in the country or to trade directly with the people of California. As soon as the viceroy at Mexico City received word of the Russians' arrival there, he indignantly notified Kuskov that his occupation of territory was in violation of a treaty between Russia and Spain. The viceroy requested Kuskov to remove his settlement. But the Russians knew that Governor Arrillaga's weak garrisons were in no position to enforce the viceroy's order.

Later, Governor Solá, who was less friendly to the Russians than his predecessor, Arrillaga, again sent notice to them at Fort Ross to leave the country. The Russians paid no attention. Their colony continued to trade with the Californians, furnishing them articles of iron, wood, and leather in return for agricultural supplies.

The Russians tanned hides, fired brick and tiles, constructed barrels and kegs, and made rope from home-grown hemp. They also made a start at shipbuilding by constructing four small vessels. The Russians even raised delicate plants in a glass hothouse, and the flowers they grew on their foggy peninsula gave the place a look of permanence.

Discipline at Ross was strict, and temptations few, but the Russian colonists preferred life there to the privations farther north. The population of the post was never large, ranging from about one hundred to four hundred persons, including Aleuts and their wives, with whom the Russians mixed socially. With the Aleuts as hunters, the Russians pursued the sea otters so assiduously that before long these animals were cleared out of the coast between Trinidad and

San Francisco bays. From 1812 to 1840 the Russians also maintained an establishment at the Farallones Islands to secure fur seals and to kill gulls (as many as 50,000 per year) and sea lions—as food for the Aleuts.

Moraga and the Opening of the Central Valley

The area of California occupied by the Spaniards was generally limited to the coastal region extending from San Francisco to San Diego. Soledad was the farthest inland settlement in the province, some thirty miles from the sea. The vast interior valley lying between the Coast Range and the Sierra Nevada, where herds of antelope grazed on wild oats, was termed *tierra incognita* (unknown land) in early documents. The southern part of the Central Valley was better known than the northern because of previous expeditions between the Colorado River and California. In 1774, Anza had crossed the desert diagonally from southeast to northwest, and the next year he had again traversed this region to bring the first colonists to California. Garcés had once gone across the mountains to Lake Tulare, exploring present-day Kern and San Bernardino counties.

By the beginning of the nineteenth century, a few of California's most exposed settlements were occasionally threatened by tribes bolder and more aggressive than the mission Indians. Gabriel Moraga, an organizer of military expeditions into the interior, took part in as many as forty-six campaigns against Indians. He penetrated into the Sierra Nevada during a number of these forays, which began in 1806. His *entradas* into the interior can be traced by the names bestowed upon rivers. The Kings River was explored and named by Moraga, as were the Merced River and Mariposa Creek. The Feather River was called *El Río de las Plumas* (the river of the feathers) in 1820 because of the feathers of wild fowl floating on its waters. The county through which it flows has retained the original Spanish form of its name, Plumas, while that of the river has been translated into the English word, Feather.

Moraga, as a result of his pioneering leadership, is entitled to the credit for the opening of California's Central Valley. He could be ruthless when occasion demanded and has been called the best soldier of his time. In 1811, he was made a lieutenant for gallantry in an Indian battle at the Carquinez Straits. During the Mexican period other parties went inland to recover stolen animals and to suppress Indian uprisings. Neither the Spanish nor the Mexican government, however, established towns or missions in the interior.

Selected Readings

A major source regarding the explorations treated in this chapter is Theodore Treutlein, *San Francisco Bay, Discovery and Colonization, 1769–1776* (San Francisco, 1968). Regarding Heceta, see Benito de la Sierra, "The Hezeta Expedition to the Northwest Coast in 1775," *California Historical Society Quarterly* 9 (September 1930), 201–42. See also Francisco Antonio Maurelle, *Journal of a Voyage in 1775, to Explore the Coast of America, Northward of California* (London, 1781). An account of another Spanish visitor to California is *Journal of José Longinos Martínez–Notes and Observations of the Naturalist of the Botanical Expedition in Old and New California and the South Coast, 1791–92*, translated and edited by Lesley Byrd Simpson (San Francisco, 1961).

Later expeditions are described in Henry R. Wagner, *The Last Spanish Exploration of the Northwest Coast and the Attempt to Colonize Bodega Bay* (San Francisco, 1931), and in Cecil Jane, ed., *A Spanish Voyage to Vancouver and the Northwest Coast of America* (London, 1930). Vancouver's voyage and other English explorations are treated in George Godwin, *Vancouver: A Life, 1757–1798* (London, 1930), and G. H. Anderson, *Vancouver and His Great Voyage* (London, 1923). See also V. L. Denton, *The Far West Coast* (Toronto, 1924).

A reprinting, in French, of the La Pérouse expedition's report of 1786 is Gilbert Cinard, ed., *Le Voyage de Lapérouse sur les Côtes de L'Alaska et de la Californie* (Baltimore, 1937). An older version in English is *A Voyage Round the World, in the Years 1785, 1786, and 1788 . . .* (3 vols., London, 1798).

George Vancouver's *A Voyage of Discovery to the North Pacific Ocean and Round the World* (3 vols., London, 1798) is the basic source on Vancouver. The California portions have been edited by Marguerite Eyer Wilbur as *Vancouver in California, 1792–1794* (Los Angeles, 1953).

An account of the Malaspina expedition (containing translations from *Viaje politico-cientifico Alrededor del Mundo por las corbetas Descubierta y Atrevida . . .*, published in Madrid in 1885) is in an article by Edith C. Galbraith, *California Historical Society Quarterly* 3 (October 1924), 215–37. See also E. Boni, *Malaspina* (Rome, 1935), and Donald C. Cutter, *Malaspina in California* (San Francisco, 1960).

The *Lelia Byrd* episode is described in Lindley Bynum, ed., *Journal of a Voyage Between China and the North-western coast of America made in 1804 by William Shaler* (Claremont, 1935). Shaler's career is also treated in Roy F. Nichols, *Advance Agents of American Destiny* (Philadelphia, 1956). See also Andrew Rolle, "The Eagle Is Seized," *Westways* 46 (December 1954), 16–17. The California sea-otter commerce is described in Adele Ogden, *The California See Otter Trade, 1784–1848* (Berkeley, 1941), and in the same author's "New England Traders in Spanish and Mexican California," *Greater America: Essays in Honor of Herbert Eugene Bolton* (Berkeley, 1945), pp. 395–415. Consult also William Henry Ellison, ed., *Life and Adventures of George Nidever* (Berkeley, 1937), and Magdalen Coughlin, "Boston Smugglers on the Coast (1797–1821): An Insight into the American Acquisition of California," California Historical Society *Quarterly* 46 (June 1967), 99–120.

Regarding Russian contact with California, see T. C. Russell, ed., *The Rezanov Voyage to Nueva California in 1806* (San Francisco, 1926), and the same editor's *Langsdorff's Narrative of the Rezanov Voyage to Nueva California in 1806* (San Francisco, 1927). See also the biography by Hector Chevigny, *Lost Empire: The Life and Adventures of Nicolai Petrovich Rezanov* (New York, 1937).

A Russian account is Otto von Kotzebue, *A Voyage of Discovery in the South Sea* . . . (3 vols., London, 1821). Another contemporary narrative is by Rezanov's associate, George Heinrich von Langsdorff, *Voyages and Travels in Various Parts of the World During the Years 1803, 1804, 1805, 1806, and 1807* (2 vols, London, 1813–14). Recent Russian scholarship appears in S. B. Okun, *The Russian-American Company* (Cambridge, 1951), which builds upon P. Tikhmenev, *Historical Survey of the Formation of the Russian-American Fur Company* . . . (2 vols., St. Petersburg, 1861–63).

Regarding Moraga, see *Diary of Ensign Gabriel Moraga's Expedition of Discovery in the Sacramento Valley, 1808*, edited by Donald C. Cutter (Los Angeles, 1957). On the same subject see S. F. Cook, *Colonial Expeditions to the Interior of California's Central Valley, 1800–1820* (Berkeley, 1960), and his later *Expedition to the Interior of California's Central Valley, 1820–1840* (Berkeley, 1962).

Concerning the color of Fort Ross see Doyce B. Nunis, ed., *The California Diary of Faxon Dean Atherton, 1836–1839* (San Francisco, 1964).

CHAPTER 9

Arcadia

SPAIN'S COLONISTS were sustained by a paternal government. The Crown tried, sometimes without success, to send supply ships periodically until the Californians could become self-supporting. But Spain's custodial attitude deprived its colonists of self-reliance. Once the Latin American independence movement broke out, the Californians were on their own, obliged to govern themselves for the first time. Economically, too, as well as politically, the Californians had to learn how to care for one another. First under Spanish and then under Mexican rule, California faced a future that in large measure was to be determined by a combination of its heritage and its isolation. A glance at its pastoral way of life may help clarify the events that preceded and accompanied the revolt from Spain.

Ranchos and Land Grants

The sparseness of the frontier population severely limited markets available for agricultural products and manufacturing. Ranching conditions, however, were almost perfect in California: abundant pastureland and water existed, in addition to a large supply of Indian labor. The climate was mild enough to permit animals to live throughout the year with little shelter, and there was no necessity to fence in stock. Ranching, moreover, popular in the Spanish homeland, suited the disposition of the Californians, who liked outdoor life on horseback. The small band of 200 cattle brought to California by the Portolá expedition, and the few that survived the overland trip with Anza's party, provided the stock from which most of the California herds developed. These herds yielded hides and tallow in abundance for export.

In order to raise cattle, settlers had to have land. No phase of California history has produced more far-reaching consequences than the disposition of the large private land grants during the Spanish and Mexican eras. (The latter is generally considered as beginning in 1821, when Mexico declared its independence.) California land titles today are grounded upon these original grants, which the Californians regarded as the very origin of their wealth. Many land grants are still known by their original names, including, for example, *El Toro* (the bull), *Los Laureles* (the laurels), and *La Sagrada Familia* (the Holy Family). Land was at first granted for pueblos, less than thirty grants being ceded to private persons during the Spanish period. The missionaries enjoyed only temporary rights to land. Due to the impossibility of protecting outlying and scattered ranches from unpredictable native attacks, settlers were to live "in the pueblos, and not dispersed." In time, however, the private rancho became a needed institution. In 1784 Governor Fages was empowered to make private grants, not to exceed three square leagues, each beyond the limits of the existing pueblos and not conflicting with missions or Indian villages. The grantee had to build a storehouse and stock his holdings with at least 2,000 head of cattle.

It was during the Mexico regime, however, that most of the "Spanish land grants" were made; after the establishment of the Mexican Republic, more liberal policies caused the number of land-grant applications to increase rapidly. A colonization law of 1824 promised security of both person and property to landholders, as well as freedom from taxes for five years. Any Mexican of good character, or any foreigner willing to become naturalized and to accept the Catholic faith, might petition for eleven square leagues of land. Mexicans were preferred to foreign settlers, who could not obtain grants within ten leagues of the seacoast.

In 1790 there were only nineteen private ranchos in California; by 1830 there were some fifty in existence. The square leagues by which grants were measured comprised a little more than 4,438 acres each. By modern standards this would constitute a large ranch. A rancho of four or five leagues was considered small; the smallest contained a square league; the largest included eleven square leagues or nearly 50,000 acres. These ranchos were unfenced grazing ranges, devoted chiefly to raising great herds of half-wild cattle which supplied almost the only source of livelihood the Californians enjoyed.

The blossoming of the rancho era occurred during a brief span of thirteen years between secularization of the California missions by the Mexican government in 1833 and occupation of the province by the Americans in 1846.

Rancho boundaries were loosely defined by landmarks, such as a chain of hills, a clump of cacti, or the center of a stream bed; the whitened skull of a steer might also mark the limits of a grant. Beginning at a point marked by a pile of stones, called a *mojonera*, a horseman measured the tract with a fifty-foot-long *reata* trailing behind him. The quantity of land was guessed at, and the phrase *poco mas ó menos* (a little more or less) was used to cover any deficiency or excess. This vagueness caused protracted litigation when ranchos fell into the hands of American occupants.

Some Californians came to own several ranchos, each with herds of cattle and horses. Many family fortunes were founded on the success of the ranchos, especially after the beginning of the traffic with English and American vessels in search of hides and tallow. William Heath Davis, Jr., a resident of California during its Mexican era, once compiled a list of its largest land and cattle owners. Francisco Pacheco owned the San Felipe, San Luís Gonzaga, and other ranchos, totaling 125,740 acres. The two ranchos alone contained 14,000 head of cattle, 500 horses, and 15,000 sheep. David Spence, who married into the Estrada family, counted 25,000 acres in the Buena Esperanza rancho, with 4,000 head of cattle. Henry Delano Fitch held the Rancho Sotoyome of eleven leagues with 14,000 cattle, 1,000 horses and mares, and 10,000 sheep. The Swiss Johann Augustus Sutter enjoyed a full eleven leagues of land, extending sixty miles in length. Abel Stearns, an American, was the owner of a number of ranchos near Los Angeles, comprising thousands of acres on which grazed 30,000 cattle, 2,000 horses and mules, and 10,000 sheep. Mariano Guadalupe Vallejo of Sonoma had practically unlimited land. The sites now occupied by Oakland, Alameda, and Berkeley form only a part of what was once the Rancho San Antonio, the property of Don Luís Peralta; his lands furnished pasture for 8,000 head of cattle and 2,000 horses. Up until about 1840, Davis counted 1,045 ranchos. About 800 of these were stocked with an average of 1,500 head. According to Davis, there were 1,220,000 cattle at the height of California's pastoral period.

Cattle and Horses

Each ranchero had three brands for his stock: the iron of *fierro* burned upon a steer's hip; the *señal*, a notch, slit, or hole cut in the ear; and the *venta*, or counterbrand, placed upon an animal when it was sold to another owner. Every ranchero was also required by law to hold a *rodéo*, or roundup, of his stock at least once a year.

Cattle were the mainstay of the economy. Beef was the principal item of food. Leather hides provided harnesses, saddles, soles for shoes, even door hinges; the long horns of cattle were used as added protection on top of adobe walls or fences in towns, as well as for shoe buttons. Tallow went into molding candles, in an age before kerosene lamps or electric lights. Hides and tallow also became the main items of exchange. Trading accounts were in *pesos* and *reales*, but little cash was exchanged. The Californians obtained wearing apparel and manufactured necessities by bartering hides with foreign vessels. The term "California bank note," a dried steer hide, had a value of approximately one dollar.

The word *rancho* was used primarily to indicate a farm devoted to stock raising, although sometimes crops were planted on ranchos. Some ranchos employed over a hundred Indian laborers, under a *mayordomo* who himself might be Indian. Without Indians the ranchos could hardly have carried on. Despite their previous lack of experience with stock animals, Indians seemed to take naturally to handling horses and cattle.

Also indispensable in herding cattle were the rancho's horses, usually mustangs. Some were descendants of Arabian animals brought to the Americas by *conquistadores*. A horse could be bought for three dollars—less than the cost of saddle and bridle. Capable of speed and endurance, the California horses and their riders acquired great skill in rounding up cattle.

Cowboys, or *vaqueros*, were required in large numbers because of the absence of fences in the territory over which cattle ranged. Free-running stock became so wild that it was unsafe to venture among herds on foot or unarmed; any rider might need to defend himself against savage bulls or against ferocious grizzlies, then encountered near the mountains.

Because even a bountiful California could not furnish enough pasture in years of drought, it became necessary for ranch hands to "cut out" and kill older animals. Horses too multiplied at such a rate that they ran wild, so that similar measures were necessary to control them; some met their death by being driven over precipices into the sea and into rivers to drown. The lack of fences also led to institution of the *rodéo* (roundup) to separate and brand stock. Every rancher had his own registered brand.

No one could adopt or change a brand without permission of the governor. The *rodéo* was conducted under a *juez de campo*, or field judge, who settled disputes over the ownership of animals. Rancheros also held bloody *matanzas*, or cattle slaughterings. Men rode at full speed through the herds and killed the animals with one cut of a knife directed at a vital part of the neck. Next, skinners stripped off the hides, and butchers cut the meat into strips for drying. The tallow was melted and poured into bags made of hides, to be delivered to trading ships by floating these bags out to the vessels. Most of the bloody carcasses, for which there was no market, were left on the field to be disposed of by the Indians and wild animals, or to rot.

The artist Titian Ramsay Peale, who traveled to California with the Charles Wilkes expedition in 1841, noted that the hills and valleys of the province were dotted with carcasses in various stages of decomposition. So many bleached and brittle bones lay underfoot that when Peale traveled at night, he was struck by the eerie crushing of bones under the hoofs of his horse.

Primitive Agriculture and Industry

California's agricultural progress continued to be carried on at the missions, on whose land oranges and grapevines were first planted successfully. It was from Mission San Gabriel that the wheat traded to the Russians came; and at Mission San José the padres planted a tract about a mile square in wheat. Their methods of sowing and reaping, however, were extremely primitive. Indian laborers scratched the ground with a rude wooden plow, fashioned from the cooked limb of a tree and shot with an iron point; they harrowed the soil by dragging branches along the surface as the padres scattered grain in the furrows. Grain was cut with hand sickles and bound in sheaves, the missionaries being careful that enough seed was left for the field to replant itself. For threshing, a flat, circular piece of ground was fenced in and its surface watered and pounded until, after drying, it became very hard. The wheat was then thrown into the enclosure and seventy-five or a hundred mares driven around and around until the grain was trampled out. Next came winnowing by tossing the wheat against the wind. At first grinding was by hand, with stone pestles and mortars. The padres later built water-driven grist mills.

The most common method of grinding was by the *arrastra*, two circular millstones placed on top of each other. The lower stone remained stationary, while the upper rotated when the cross beam attached to it was dragged in a circle by a mule. Thus the grain was crushed between the two stones, by a process used in Spain for centuries.

California's colonials never held sheep in the same esteem as they did cattle; nevertheless, each mission and most of the private ranchos raised small flocks for mutton and wool. The wool was coarse and wiry, but strong, and was woven by the Indians on looms into cloth called *serga*, as well as into blankets. As for pork, neither Spaniard nor Indian was fond of it. Hogs were raised mainly for their lard, used in soap making, one of the few early industries. The padres also raised flax and hemp for manufacturing rope.

It seems remarkable that two of California's natural sources of wealth were neglected by its earliest settlers—fur-bearing animals and gold. The sea otter and the seal swarmed in the coastal waters of

California, but the inhabitants allowed this harvest to be reaped by American and Russian hunters.

Pastoral Simplicity on the Ranchos

Life on the ranchos was carried on in accordance with a simple, patriarchal system. The rancho family was a self-sustained economic and social unit, comparatively isolated from the outside world. The ranchero, the family's contact with life beyond the rancho, was the unquestioned master of his estate. He was obeyed by both his family and Indian retainers. Yet he did not generally abuse his authority, for he was, ideally, a born gentleman—kindhearted and mild-tempered.

Probably no society ever existed in which a stronger bond linked parents and children. Families numbered from fifteen to twenty, or even more, to which were added in-laws and orphans. In spite of affectionate ties, the family observed strict discipline; fathers could administer corporal punishment to sons even sixty years of age, and no son dared smoke in his father's presence. Children even asked permission to sit down. Dances were begun by elders, while young people stood by and awaited their turn. Even where no family relationship existed, older persons could inflict punishment upon young people when they saw fit.

Rancho life was a blend of abundance and barrenness. Supplies of clothing, furniture, and other manufactured articles were always insufficient. The mildness of the climate, however, made scarcity easier to bear than would have been the case in colder lands. The ranchero and his family, too, inherited austerity from their Spanish ancestors; when they could not get shoes, shirts, black silk stockings, *rebozos*, or *mantillas*, they learned to do without or improvised substitutes. If anyone needed meat or corn, he was encouraged to ask a richer neighbor for it and it was freely given, often without mention of price.

The ranchero was usually a man of abstemious habits, arising long before dawn to partake of a slight breakfast of bread and chocolate, then to mount his horse and be off on the daily round of his lands. Evening saw the return of the master, who sometimes had not eaten during the day, and the gathering of this *patron's* large family around a well-laden table.

Food on the rancho was plain but nourishing and plentiful, beef forming the principal dish. Meat and drink, as well as grain, a little fruit, and certain of the more ordinary vegetables, were all produced by the rancho.

Housing and Clothing

The houses on the ranchos, as well as in the towns, were oblong structures of *adobe* (sun-dried brick), unadorned inside or outside. The fact that lumber was not used widely as a building material, in a country so rich in timber, is best explained by the absence of saw-mills and woodworking tools. Adobe, however, offered advantages in addition to its availability: dwellings made of it, with thick walls and spacious rooms, were warm in winter and cool in summer. At first, homes were built on high spots, bare of surrounding trees or bushes, for defense against attacks by Indians. As this fear receded, the rancheros planted gardens and fruit orchards around the rancho buildings. Those who could afford it bought mahogany furniture made in South America or the Philippines and brought by trading ships. Almost every house had its altar for worship and a picture or two of Virgin and Child on the wall. Even in the poorest homes, beds were covered with intricate lace spreads and pillow cases.

The well-to-do ranchero was sometimes quite a dandy. One of these, José Arnaz, described a fiesta outfit:

> Shoes of deerskin embroidered with gold or silver threads; breeches of cloth, velvet, or satin reaching to the knee, and open on both sides, bordered with gold braid and silver buttons; vest of velvet, silk, or cloth, and over it a jacket of blue, black, or green cloth embroidered in gold and silver thread. Add to this outfit a gay sash of red satin bound around the wearer's slender waist, and a wide sombrero with a cord of silver or gold encircling the crown, worn jauntily tipped on one side.

The horse ridden by a ranchero had also to be equipped with ornateness. Embroidered trappings might nearly cover the animal, with a bridle mounted in solid silver and long stirrups all but sweeping the ground.

In comparison to the dress of the men, that of the women was rather plain—although colorful. Alfred Robinson, a trader, describes the costume of middle-class females in 1829 as consisting of

> a chemise with short embroidered sleeves, richly trimmed with lace, a muslin petticoat flounced with scarlet and secured at the waist by a silk band of the same color, shoes of velvet or blue satin, a cotton *rebozo* or scarf, pearl necklace and earrings, with the hair falling in broad plaits down the back. Others of the higher class dress in English style, and instead of the *rebozo*, substitute a rich and costly shawl of silk or satin.

Such fancy attire was not often seen, and fashions varied but little in a culture where clothing remained scarce. It was literally true that a man might wear his grandfather's hat or coat.

Amusements

For entertainment, hunting grizzly bear, elk, and other game was popular. It sometimes took many bullets to kill a grizzly, but the bear was not always pursued with a gun. Some hunters met a grizzly on foot and in single combat, armed only with a long knife and an oxhide shield; as a rule, however, they had the assistance of their constant companions, the horses. The large California elk, extinct today, was also a dangerous animal.

There were entertainments of a milder sort, especially *meriendas*, or picnics, in which entire communities joined. Young people and men rode their best horses, while the older ladies and the children were satisfied to climb into creaking two-wheeled *carretas* to bounce along to some grassy picnic place behind the slow oxen, with much chatter and laughter. These *meriendas* featured *carne asada* (roast meat), succulently barbecued on spits over a bed of glistening coals. After roast chickens, turkeys, *enchiladas*, or *tamales*, the rest of the afternoon might be spent singing and dancing to the music of guitars. Every event, public or private, from the birth of a child to the arrival of a new governor, was celebrated with dancing. As many as fifty guests would be accommodated at one rancho for days. On such an occasion steers were killed, and Indian women pounded corn in *metates* (stone mortars) to make *tortillas* (flat, thin corn cakes). It was a rare evening when there were no guests to join the family, old and young, in dancing the *jarabe* or *fandango*.

Pueblo Life

Pueblo life, though more elaborate than on a remote rancho, consisted of the same generous hospitality. A host might carry attention to a guest so far as to leave coins in a dish on a table in the spare room in order to save the visitor the embarrassment of asking for money. If the recipient neglected to return such a loan, good hosts forgot about it. A traveler who arrived with an exhausted horse found a fresh one ready in the morning, saddled and bridled for his use.

The number of persons who lived in pueblos and on ranchos grew slowly. The entire white population of the province as late as 1848 was an estimated 14,000, divided nearly equally between Californians and foreigners. By "Californian" is meant a person of Spanish birth or background who settled in the province as a resident during either the Spanish or Mexican era. In addition, a small percentage of the Indians lived in or near pueblos. Although mere hamlets, Los Angeles and Monterey were the social centers of the province.

Yerba Buena, as San Francisco continued to be called during its early years, was even smaller. It had grown up spontaneously on a spot known as *El Parage de Yerba Buena* (the place of good grass), taking its name from a weed that grew locally in profusion. The importance of the pueblo, located about three miles from the presidio that defended the area, consisted in the anchorage for ships furnished by its little cove, an anchorage that later became the greatest harbor on the Pacific Coast.

Government of the California pueblos remained in the hands of *alcaldes*. There were laws against gambling, as well as regulations concerning the manufacture and sale of liquor and keeping of late hours. A private citizen had to obtain a license before he could give a dance in a town house. Bull-and-bear fights, a form of entertainment somewhat varied from that of old Spain, were also popular. These bloodcurdling events were conducted in the public plaza, in front of the local church. A trapped bear was tied by one foot to a bull, after which the two beasts fought it out until one or the other was killed. The people gambled on the outcome. Cockfighting and horse racing afforded the Californians other ways to wager.

Pueblo attire tended to be more fashionable than on the rancho. Don Tomás Yorba, a ranchero who spent much time in town, wore a black silk handkerchief on his head, the corners of which hung down behind his neck. He also sported fine felt hats and an embroidered shirt, a cravat of white jaconet (a thin cotton fabric), tastefully tied, a blue damask vest, short breeches of crimson velvet, and a bright green cloth jacket with silver buttons. His shoes were made of embroidered deerskin. With his sword hanging by his side, he was every inch the Spanish *caballero*.

Education, Health, and Public Morals

Despite the efforts of various governors to encourage education, provincial schools were limited. School was sometimes held in empty granaries or in barracks. Among the teachers were superannuated soldiers, whose only qualification was some knowledge of reading, writing, and "figuring." Their chief instructional assistant was the *disciplina*, a cat-'o-nine-tails, which was liberally applied to youngsters. Ambitious young men managed to acquire additional education from priests, military officers, and foreigners. In the Mexican period the best-known foreign teacher was William E. P. Hartnell, an English trader with a knowledge of half a dozen languages. He settled near Salinas and taught his own and his neighbors' children.

The California governors could provide no better facilities for public health than they could for education. Although California boasted few doctors, some people lived astoundingly long. At a time when medicine was still in a primitive state, California probably would not have benefited greatly from the arrival of more doctors. Its major health asset was a salubrious climate, combined with the moderate labor and open-air amusements in which most of the people participated.

Theft, murder, and other crimes were rare in provincial California. Foreign sea captains would sometimes sell goods to rancheros along the coast on credit and return months later to receive their pay in hides and tallow. Banditry, except by Indians, was reputedly unknown until after the beginning of American occupation. The bandit Joaquín Murieta was said to have ascribed his criminal career to brutal treatment by American miners.

The padres did much to stabilize provincial life. Baptisms, confirmations, marriages, and other vital ceremonies were, of course, performed at the missions. Even wedding dinners were held there. The missions also served as a hospice for wayfarers, who could count on a night's lodging. Mission accommodations were of the barest sort— usually consisting of a bed of rawhide, scratchy flaxen sheets, and meals that were simple in the extreme. The warmth of greeting, however, made up for discomforts, and on a stormy night, as the wind whipped across mission tile roofs, travelers were thankful for the fragrant pine logs burning in their fireplace grates.

The Heritage of Spain

Modern California still retains cultural reminders of its provincial, pastoral era. As in every part of the Western Hemisphere in which Spain planted its characteristic civilization, it left its imprint in institutions and language. Rivers, mountains, and towns often are known today by names that originated with the Spaniards; and a number of social, religious, economic, and architectural terms are of similar origin. Words growing out of the Spanish heritage include *adobe*, or sun-dried brick; *arroyo*, a creek or its dry bed; *cañada*, a deep valley; *cañón*, a narrow passage between high banks; *chaparral*, a thicket of brambly bushes; *corral*, an enclosure for livestock; *embarcadero*, a landing place; *fiesta*, a celebration; *placer*, where gold is found free in the loose earth; *plaza*, an open square in a town; *pueblo*, a chartered town; *rancho*, land used for pasturage; *rodéo*, a roundup of cattle for branding; *sierra*, literally a saw, but applied to a range of saw-tooth mountains; *tule*, water reed; *vaquero*, cowboy. Some of these terms have been anglicized: *cañón*, for example, takes the form *canyon*. Spanish place names are clustered in the narrow strip of land between the Coast Range and the sea. They thin out markedly to the east, indicating the limits of Spanish settlement. The frequent use of the prefixes *San* and *Santa* (Saint) indicates the religious character of the first occupation, though variety characterizes the names chosen by soldiers. Place names were first applied to the most striking·natural features—the rivers, creeks, bays, mountains, and capes.

One of the earliest place names bestowed by the Spaniards was that of the bay of Monterey, so called in honor of Viceroy Gaspar de Zúñiga y Acevedo, Count of Monterey in Mexico. The Merced River was first called *El Río de Nuestra Señora de la Merced* (the river of Our Lady of Mercy) by Moraga's exploring party of 1806, as an expression of gratitude at the sight of its waters after an exhausting march through dry country. The same expedition named Mariposa Creek after the butterflies found on its banks. Moraga also named the Sacramento River after the Holy Sacrament.

Among California's counties, Mendocino was named after Antonio de Mendoza, first viceroy of New Spain; the term was first applied to the cape, probably by the crews of ships coming from the Philippines. Several counties were given the names of missions—San Diego, San Luis Obispo, Santa Clara. Other counties, like Merced and Sacramento, took the names of their principal streams. Among these is also Kings County (from *El Río de los Santos Reyes*, or river of the Holy Kings). Fresno (ash) County was named after the abundance of those trees in the region, and Madera (timber) County after the forests that covered its valleys.

A few towns and cities bear the names of prominent early Californians. Martinez from the family of that name. Suñol was christened for the owner of one of the most beautiful valleys in the state. Vacaville commemorates the Vaca family. Alviso bears the name of one of the Anza colonists, and Benicia that of the wife of General Vallejo; the town of Vallejo honors the memory of Don Mariano himself. An Alvarado Street, named after a Mexican governor, can be found in both Monterey and Los Angeles. One of the main streets of the latter city, Figueroa, honors another governor, and dozens of Los Angeles street names commemorate the past—among them Pico, Los Angeles, San Pedro, Aliso, and Sepulveda. In San Francisco, there is a Junípero Serra Boulevard, as well as streets named Noriega, Pacheco, Ortega, Rivera, Taraval, Ulloa, Guerrero, Valencia, and Palou. Oakland has two main avenues with Spanish names—Alcatraz (pelican) and San Pablo (Saint Paul). Santa Barbara has restored its Spanish street names, which had fallen into disuse; no city of California, in fact, clings more strongly to its colonial past, including its many red-tiled and whitewashed buildings. Spanish place names and architecture, however, are only the most conspicuous reminders of the past. The California legal system retains Spanish provisions concerning mining, water rights, trespass regulations, tribunals of conciliation, and the property rights of women.

Pageants and plays commemorating the Spanish past include the Mission Play of San Gabriel, the Portolá Festival of San Francisco, and "De Anza days" celebration at Riverside, and a yearly "Spanish" fiesta at Santa Barbara. In these events colonial dress is worn by the participants, who are often descendants of Spanish-Californians. In cookery, too, Spanish colonial dishes, including *tamales, enchiladas, tacos,* and *tortillas,* are widely consumed.

California's Hispanic background was submerged by the Anglo-American invasion, yet one cannot deny the Hispanic heritage. In this age of the television western one should not forget that the cowboy inherited his know-how, horse, outfit (including *reata,* spurs, and chaps), lasso, and lingo largely from the Spanish. Lingering aspects of the Hispanic past are also found in the very faces of Californians of Spanish background, in their names, customs, and local ordinances. With the best of intentions there is considerable public genuflection to and exploitation of California's colonial history by sentimental antiquarians, genealogists, artists, architects, historical societies, and tourist promoters.

Selected Readings

Basic sources for the study of Spanish-Mexican society in California are William Heath Davis's book *Sixty Years in California* (San Francisco, 1889), and *Seventy-Five Years in California* (San Francisco, 1929). See also Andrew Rolle, *An American in California: The Biography of William Heath Davis, 1822–1909* (San Marino, Calif., 1956). Two Yankees who came to California wrote accounts of their stay: Richard Henry Dana, *Two Years Before the Mast* (New York, 1840), a minor American classic, and Richard J. Cleveland, *Narrative of Voyages and Commercial Enterprises* (2 vols., Cambridge, Mass. 1842). Perhaps the most perceptive analysis of Dana's *Two Years Before the Mast* is in D. H. Lawrence's *Studies in classic American Literature* (New York, 1923). There is a somewhat unsympathetic biography of Dana by Samuel Shapiro entitled *Richard Henry Dana Jr., 1815–1882* (East Lansing, Mich., 1961). One can also consult such romantic treatments as Nellie Van de Grift Sánchez, *Spanish Arcadia* (Los Angeles, 1929), Gertrude Atherton, *Before the Gringo Came* (New York, 1894), and the more popular revision of the latter, *The Splendid Idle Forties* (New York, 1902). See too Tirey L. Ford, *Dawn of the Dons* (San Francisco, 1926), as well as John Steven McGroarty's romanticized *California: Its History and Romance* (Los Angeles, 1911), Charles F. Lummis, *The Spanish Pioneers* (Chicago, 1893), and another of his hispanophile volumes, *Flowers of Our Lost Romance* (Boston, 1929).

Other appraisals include Hubert Howe Bancroft's *California Pas-*

toral (San Francisco, 1888), and Alberta J. Denis, *Spanish Alta California* (New York, 1927). Useful also are Susanna Bryant Dakin's *A Scotch Paisano: Hugo Reid's Life in California* (Berkeley, 1939) and *The Lives of William Hartness* (Stanford, 1949). Medicine is described in George D. Lyman, *The Scalpel Under Three Flags in California* (San Francisco, 1925). An excellent reminiscence is *The Blond Ranchero: Memories of Juan Francisco Dana*, as told to Rocky and Marie Harrington (Los Angeles, 1960). *Don Pio Pico's Historical Narrative*, translated and edited by Arthur P. Botello (Glendale, Calif.), offers a special view of the Mexican era. Also see Jeanne Van Nostrand, *Monterey, Adobe Capital of California, 1770–1847* (San Francisco, 1969).

Raymund F. Wood, "Anglo Influence on Spanish Place Names in California," *Southern California Quarterly* 58 (Winter, 1981), 392–413 describes the origins of both Spanish and English names on the landscape.

CHAPTER 10

Mexican California

AFTER THREE CENTURIES of dominance by the homeland, the Spanish colonies in the New World grew restive. Discontent kindled the flame of revolution, which spread from province to province between 1808 and the middle 1820s. Almost to the last, California remained loyal. This was partly because little news reached provincial California of revolutionary activities in Mexico and elsewhere in Latin America. Pablo Solá, last of California's Spanish governors, was an aristocrat who looked upon revolutionary activities farther south as the work of misguided fanatics. Although opposed to independence, Solá was interested in the welfare of California and skillful in managing its affairs.

The first significant manifestation of discontent in California occurred when, after 1808, ships from San Blas failed to arrive in sufficient number to supply the populace. Revolutionary attacks against Spanish ships aggravated the situation, so that fewer and fewer were able to visit the California ports. Along with the American trading ships that helped fill the gap, a number of privateers began to appear in the Pacific, some fitted out in the United States; these roamed the high seas, ravaging the ships and shoreline of Spain's colonies. News of the blockade of the South American Pacific colonial ports of Valparaíso, Callao, and Guayaquil by revolutionists and privateers so worried Solá that he ordered a stricter watch along the shore for suspicious vessels. Although Californians made complaints against the viceroy in Mexico City for his failure to send supplies to the settlers and back pay to their soldiers, they had no initial thought of resisting his authority or that of Governor Solá. They were more concerned with pirates.

Bouchard's Visit to California

In November 1818, two mysterious ships were sighted by a sentinel at Point Pinos, near Monterey. The larger of the two vessels, the *Argentina*, was commanded by a Frenchman, Hippolyte de Bouchard, who had served in the patriot navy of the new "Republic of Buenos Aires." He was a big and brutal captain of fiery temper, who exercised an iron rule over his men. The other vessel, smaller in size, was the *Santa Rosa*. It was under the command of an English soldier of fortune named Peter Corney, whom Bouchard had picked up in Hawaii while Bouchard was trading gold chalices and silver crucifixes looted from churches throughout Latin America. Bouchard's crews were a motley lot of some 350 cutthroats, thieves, and revolutionists; among them were Malays, Portuguese, Spaniards, Englishmen, and Australians—all aiming to profit from the upset condition of the Spanish empire.

When the smaller of Bouchard's privateers, the *Santa Rosa*, dropped anchor in front of the presidio of Monterey (with its eight dilapidated cannon), the "visitors" looked formidable. The *Santa Rosa* opened fire on the presidio. Corney and his crew, expecting little resistance, were surprised at the brisk return of cannon balls from the battery hastily established on the beach by the presidio's forty soldiers. Then Bouchard moved in with the *Argentina*, and sent ashore a flag of truce, along with a demand for the immediate surrender of Monterey.

Bouchard received a defiant reply from Governor Solá, although the Californians had little means of resisting. The pirate landed several hundred men and a number of field pieces near Point Pinos. Greatly outnumbered, Solá retreated, with a supply of munitions and the provincial archives, to the Rancho del Rey, near the present site of Salinas. At Monterey many townspeople fled. Some took refuge at Missions San Antonio and San Juan Bautista until conditions should permit their return to the capital. While the inhabitants were away, the invaders sacked and burned both the presidio and town of Monterey. Few buildings escaped. Even orchards and gardens were destroyed.

Concerning the conduct of his crew during this pillage, Peter Corney later wrote, "The Sandwich Islanders, who were quite naked when they landed, were soon dressed in the Spanish fashion; and all the sailors were employed in searching the houses for money and breaking and ruining everything." Something over a week was spent by the attackers in burying their dead, caring for their wounded, and repairing the *Santa Rosa*. They also made efforts to win over to their cause those of the inhabitants who had the courage to remain in the pueblo; but such propaganda, ostensibly promoting the cause of liberty, failed to impress a people whose homes had been despoiled.

After replenishing their larders, the *Argentina* and the *Santa Rosa* set sail and Governor Solá returned to Monterey. The privateers next moved down the coast, stopping at points on the way to burn and pillage. Rancho del Refugio was burned in revenge for the loss of three pirates, who were lassoed and ignominiously dragged off by a party of *vaqueros*. San Juan Capistrano was one of the places sacked and robbed of its store of wines and spirits, much of which immediately went down the throats of the pillagers. After taking two apparently willing Indian girls aboard to brighten their voyage, the pirates sailed south from that mission, and California was finally relieved of their presence.

This attack by Bouchard constitutes California's only contact with outside revolutionists during the wars of independence. Once Bouchard left the province, life in California resumed its calmness; not long afterwards, events of great importance to the New World occurred in Mexico. In February 1821, Agustín Iturbide, a colonel in the royal army in Mexico City, suddenly defected to the insurgent cause, raised a revolutionary flag, and made New Spain independent.

Beginning Mexican Control

When news reached California of the seizure of political control in Mexico, it was at first received with disbelief. In April 1822, however, Governor Solá convened a *junta*, or caucus, consisting of officers from the presidios and padres from the missions and swore allegiance to the new government. Former royal officials and some of the padres took an oath to Iturbide without hesitation, although the friars sensed that a nonroyal government in Mexico would lead to decline of the mission system. The Californians had to face the fact that a new government was in actual control at Mexico City.

The California *junta* chose Solá as its delegate to the new Mexican *Cortés*, or congress. Before the governor could even leave for Mexico City, however, an official arrived at Monterey from that capital to preside over the transfer of authority from Spain to Mexico. Aware of California's royalist sympathies, this agent of the new regime arrived in a ship that flew a green, white, and red flag from its masthead. The eagle in the flag's center, the symbol of Mexico, indicated to the Californians who lined the Monterey docks to receive him that Governor Solá's control over California had clearly ended.

Succeeding Solá was California's first popularly chosen governor, Luís Antonio Argüello, a native Californian serving as commander of the port of San Francisco. Argüello announced that the decrees of the Mexican government would be accepted and the title *nacional* would be substituted for *imperial* in all documents; public and private letters were thereafter to be signed with the words "God and Liberty," and the old title *Don* was to give way to *Ciudadano*, or citizen.

California, far from the vortex of the struggle, was lucky to have received independence from Spain without the fratricidal blood-letting that drenched Mexico's soil. Yet the province did not escape the personal rivalries that afflicted the other Spanish colonies following separation from the homeland. Scarcely a California governor during the Mexican period served his term unharassed by outbreaks against him. The distance and the difficulty of communication, feelings of resentment against Mexican power, and strong local pride all encouraged sectionalism, for the Californians still did not identify with faroff Mexico.

Argüello's Government

Argüello, who came from northern California, had been chosen governor over a prominent southerner, José de la Guerra. This circumstance began a rift between north and south, at first scarcely perceptible, which continued for decades. Argüello established a *diputación*, or legislative body, sometimes called a *junta*. This consisted of six representatives, one from each presidio and pueblo district. The new governor had to see to it that a *disputado* (deputy) was sent to Mexico City; he had to repair the roads, support schools, feed troops, and control the Indians. To help solve the money problem Argüello in January 1824 convened another assemblage at Monterey, composed of representatives of the military, civil, and clerical phases of California life. According to the provisions enacted by the body, local crops as well as all branded cattle were to be taxed as never before—at least officially, though these provisions were not always fully enforced.

One element remained lacking in the general approval of the new measures made necessary in California by a changed political situation. This was the cooperation of the missionaries. When the padres heard of plans to tax the missions, they protested that these establishments, founded to care for Indians, in fact belonged to the natives and were untaxable. Since the missions, however, held much of the best land in the province, to exempt them would have deprived the government of a major means of support. Whether they liked it or not, the padres were destined to put up with increased surveillance over their operations. But compliance with regulations of the government violated, according to the friars, obligations of fidelity to the king of Spain. They feared that the new Mexican Republic would become a duplicate of postrevolutionary France, which had expelled its clerics from public life.

Some members of the new California *diputación* believed that the attitude of the friars merited rebuke, even that the management of the missions should be taken from them. While no direct steps toward secularization occurred during Argüello's administration, there were straws in the strong winds that blew out of Mexico that suggested missionary rule might be nearing its end.

With or without the cooperation of the missionaries, Argüello's new government had a number of serious administrative problems to settle. The second *junta* that the governor convened also decided to maintain a military force of 290 men, as well as a militia of males between the ages of eighteen and fifty. *Alcaldes* were still to administer civil justice, with appeals to the governor being permitted. Criminal trials were to be by courts-martial, but sentences were to be executed as soon as pronounced—in order to avoid legal delays. The Mexican *Cortés*, inefficient and inexperienced, was preoccupied with matters much closer to itself.

Increasing Foreign Activity

During Argüello's governorship, there arrived in California foreigners—both traders and settlers, and a number of people who were both. Although the authorities of the province had inherited much of Spain's suspicion against strangers, the revolutionary atmosphere tended to bring about somewhat more liberal policies.

Argüello had been friendly with the Russians since the days when Rezanov had courted his beautiful daughter, Concepción; and the Russians had long desired to enter into a partnership for fur hunting and trading with the Californians. As governor, Argüello signed a contract with the Russians that furnished his government with Aleut hunters, who were in return to be fed and supplied by the Californians. The Aleuts hunted in small skin canoes called *bidarkas*. The product of their hunt was divided between the Russians and the Californians. This official hunting was done chiefly in San Francisco Bay, which swarmed with sea otter, but was also carried on as far south as San Pedro.

There was increasing acceptance, too, of English and American trading enterprises. California's padres now signed an agreement with the English partnership of McCulloch and Hartnell, a subsidiary of the firm of John Begg and Company, today purveyors of Scotch whiskey. Hugh McCulloch and William E. P. Hartnell came to California from Lima in 1822. They were allowed to bring one cargo a year to the province and take out all the hides the missions had to offer for $1.00 each, as well as suet, lard, tallow, wheat, wine, furs, and pickled beef. Known as "Macala y Arnel" to the Californians, the company had entered into an agreement that launched the prosperous hide and tallow traffic.

In the same year Henry Gyzelaar and William A. Gale, already acquainted with the coast as smugglers, arrived in the ship *Sachem* from Boston and initiated the American side of the new hide and tallow trade. Gale, like his companion, was a trading supercargo, or roving merchant, representing a Boston trading syndicate; following the eventual secularization of the missions, however, ambitious Yankee middlemen—including Nathan Spear, William Heath Davis, Jr., John R. Cooper, Alfred Robinson, and Abel Stearns—replaced such supercargoes. These new resident merchants distributed goods on land as well as from aboard ships. Rancheros were no longer dependent upon the uncertain arrival of government supply vessels. Ship captains could now load and unload their vessels at central collecting points, rather than at secret landfalls scattered up and down the coast.

One Boston firm, Bryant, Sturgis and Company, maintained a chain of ships plying the sea lanes between that harbor, California, Hawaii, and China. With Gale as its resident agent, this firm alone carried probably half a million hides from California to New England's shoe industry. Other sizable Boston firms included Marshall & Wildes and William Appleton & Company, both of which kept vessels on the coast. Stocked with hundreds of commodities, from silk stockings to tobacco, these were veritable floating commissaries. For trading with these vessels, rancheros brought great quantities of hides in a "green" state, or at best carelessly dried, from the interior. The smelly skins were soaked in sea water by hide "droghers," really working traders. Then the hides were stretched on the ground and pegged fast with wooden stakes. When they were dry the "droghers," local Indians, or Kanaka sailors from Hawaii, would sprinkle them with salt, scrape them, and fold them lengthwise with the hair out. Next the skins were packed into the holds of the Yankee ships offshore, some of which held as many as 30,000 hides. Floated out to the ships beyond the surf went also the large cowhide bags filled with melted tallow.

Heretofore most of the foreigners landing on the shores of California had been visitors. After a short period of trading, their vessels had usually raised anchor and sailed away. Now a different type of outsider began to arrive, as a result of the 1824 act passed by the Mexican Congress which promised security to foreigners settling in California and obeying its laws. Such traders took advantage of this virtual invitation to conduct business in California; many settled in the province, married daughters of the country, and founded families. One of these men was John R. Cooper, who arrived in California in 1823 as captain of the American ship *Rover* and settled at Monterey. With Cooper came Daniel Hill and Thomas Robbins of Massachusetts, who decided to make their homes at Santa Barbara. David Spence, an Englishman, came to California from Lima to superintend the packing of hides, beef, and tallow for Begg and Company; like Cooper, he settled at Monterey, where he married into a California family. His countryman was William A. Richardson, who arrived in Yerba Buena on the English whaler *Orion*. Richardson was later baptized in the Catholic Church, married the daughter of the *comandante* of the port, and became a key figure in the settlement of that pueblo.

Among these foreigners, the most prominent group was composed of the dozens of "warm-water Yankee" traders, as distinguished from the "cold-water Yankees" of the eastern seaboard. These traders reaped rich rewards from the marketing of their all-year stock of goods. Almost everyone, in fact, profited from their activities—except Mexican customs collectors, who the traders were expert at avoiding. Long before the Gold Rush a whole generation of pre-pioneer Americans in California acquired a thorough knowledge of the province, established the friendliest relations with its people, and made themselves indispensable in the exchange of the necessities and luxuries of life. These Yankees, who settled California long before the first overland parties crossed the plains, came to represent a blending of California's Spanish and Anglo-American cultures.

The Indian Revolt of 1824

Although there had been occasional uprisings in the past, the natives were so disunited that no general revolt had ever occurred. Association with white men, however, gradually taught the Indians to appreciate the value of union, as well as to use firearms. In February 1824, a revolt started simultaneously among the neophytes of Missions Purísima Concepción, Santa Inés, and Santa Barbara.

The cause is obscure, but it probably followed some outrage perpetrated upon the natives. Soldiers at Santa Inés, attacked by the Indians without warning, were surprised to find their assailants well armed. The Indians set fire to the mission buildings, partly destroying them; but when Sergeant Anastasio Carrillo arrived with reinforcements from Santa Barbara, the attackers yielded. At Purísima there was a more determined fight. After seven Indians and four whites had been killed, the mission guards were compelled to surrender. Later, following a parley, they were allowed to go to Santa Inés, but Indians kept possession of the mission for nearly a month. At Purísima the rebels erected palisade fortifications, cutting loopholes in the church walls and mounting two rusty cannon used during fiestas. But inexperience in handling both guns and powder quickly brought about their defeat when they were attacked by Lieutenant José Mariano Estrada and a force of 100 men. At Santa Barbara, Indians also entrenched themselves in the mission buildings, from which they fired guns and arrows. *Comandante* de la Guerra attacked them there, and after a fight of several hours the Indians fled to the hills, taking with them all the property they could carry. Succeeding expeditions were required to quell the revolt. In mid-1825, Governor Argüello reported to the Mexican government regarding the miserable state of the Indians, calling attention to the injustice of keeping them any longer in virtual slavery.

Under Argüello the change to Mexican rule had been quietly accepted by the Californians, and a beginning was made at representative government. California had exchanged the paternalistic, conservative regime of Spain for the unsettled sovereignty of Mexico. Governmental instability resulted in factional fights.

Echeandía's Turmoil

José María Echeandía, Argüello's successor, was a a "tall, thin, juiceless man, possessing but little enterprise or force of character, and much concerned about the effect of the California climate upon his not too robust health." At first Echeandía so feared the foggy weather at Monterey that he came no farther into California than San Diego. As commander of both Californias, Echeandía claimed that the southern town was more centrally located for transacting the business of the two provinces. Nothing in his instructions required this hypochondriac to live at Monterey, so he was acting within his rights in conducting California affairs from the city of his choice. Though no formal transfer of the capital was made, southerners were delighted by Echeandía's residence at San Diego. Jealousy between north and south gained momentum, and the new governor started out handicapped by unpopularity in northern California. A rivalry between Echeandía, who was a bachelor, and the young American sea captain Henry Delano Fitch for the hand of Señorita Josefa Carrillo of San Diego indicates that a romantic motive as well as reasons of health had something to do with Echeandía's stay there.

A more pressing question facing Echeandía was that of supplies for soldiers and their families, who had to be clothed and fed. The missions were the traditional source for these necessities, but the friars no longer gave willing support. The padres were growing uncomfortable as they became aware of increasing distrust of them and of other persons of Spanish birth in a revolutionary and secularist Mexico. Only with difficulty was Echeandía able to persuade the missionaries to furnish food and clothing. Some of the California soldiers had not been paid for years. Once they saw they were no better off than before Echeandía's arrival, they blamed him for their misery. In 1828 part of the garrison at Monterey revolted. These troops were, however, persuaded to return to their duties. The more hostile of the mission padres likewise stirred up sentiment against Governor Echeandía. Opposition to Echeandía was forcefully expressed by Joaquín Solís, a former convict, and José María Herrera, who had been sent to the province from Mexico as a governmental financial agent. Together they issued a *pronunciamiento* accusing California's governor of tyrannical behavior toward the populace. Solís and Herrera led a "revolution," which began at Monterey; this movement was hardly more than a strike by the soldiers for their pay, but it extended as far south as Santa Barbara. Solís and fellow conspirators were arrested and sent to San Blas. So ended the first of a series of minor uprisings against Mexican authority in the province, conflicts of *pronunciamientos* rather than of guns.

The Mexican government's practice of sending criminals to California also had much to do with the antagonistic feeling between Californians and Mexicans. About the time of the collapse of the Solís rebellion, eighty convicts arrived, and were put ashore at Santa Cruz Island and given a few cattle and some fish hooks with which to maintain life. After experiencing a devastating fire, the convicts built rafts and made their way back to Carpinteria, below Santa Barbara. In July 1830, a vessel arrived from Mexico with fifty more criminals. They were distributed throughout the territory under the surveillance of local authorities. Echeandía was blamed for their arrival, and California's *diputación* voted to request Mexico not to send any more such colonists. The practice of sending criminals by the shipload ceased, although many continued to enter the province as soldiers, an affront that outraged the Californians.

During Echeandía's administration another Indian outbreak bedeviled the unlucky governor. The leader of this revolt of 1829, Chief Estanislao, put up an even more vigorous fight than had the rebellious Solís. Estanislao had at one time been *alcalde* of San José. He ran away and joined a band of renegades in the San Joaquín Valley. They fortified themselves in a dense wood and sent out defiant challenges. That summer, forty of Echeandía's soldiers armed with muskets and a swivel gun, found the rebels. The Indians killed two of the soldiers and wounded eight others; the rest were forced to abandon the siege when their ammunition ran out and the heat became insufferable. Estanislao's Indians were elated by the victory, and held a celebration with feasting and dancing.

Because the uprising threatened to become widespread, Echeandía sent a force of 100 cavalry, infantry, and artillery, under Mariano

Guadalupe Vallejo, commander of the military forces of California. Vallejo's troops were met by a cloud of arrows. Since the woods in which the Indians hid were impenetrable, Vallejo set them on fire, forcing the Indians to the edge of the thicket. Vallejo's reconnoitering revealed a series of Indian pits and ditches protected by barricades of trees. Entrenched behind these fortifications were more Indians. The Californians brought up cannon, and the Indians were driven from the entrenchments. In the darkness of the following night many escaped, including Estanislao. He took refuge with Father Narciso Durán, president of the missions, who concealed the Indian chieftain until a pardon was obtained from the governor.

Beechey and Du Haut-Cilly

Not the least important of the events of Echeandía's time were the visits of some notable foreigners. On November 6, 1826, the British ship *Blossom* having completed a year's cruise in the North Pacific and Arctic oceans, sailed into San Francisco Bay under the command of Captain F. W. Beechey. A comparison of Beechey's description of the place with that of Vancouver shows that surprisingly few changes had occurred in the surroundings—and those in the direction of decay rather than improvement. Beechey commented, for example, on the ruinous condition of the fort on the bluff. Like others before him, he was struck with the contrast between the natural advantages of the country and the lack of enterprise of its residents. Beechey also observed discontent among all classes, and he predicted that the Mexicans could not hold the land. Many of the friars dreaded the worst, and would willingly have quit the country. "Some of them were ingenious and clever men," wrote Beechey, "but they had been so long excluded from the civilized world that their ideas and their politics, like the maps pinned against the wall, bore the date of 1772, as near as I could read for fly specks." Beechey's visit is important for the detailed description of the country and its inhabitants given in his narrative. Some remarkable watercolors of California were painted by artists in his crew.

In January 1827 another distinguished visitor arrived in California waters: Auguste Bernard du Haut-Chilly, commanding the French ship *Le Héros* on a trading voyage around the world. An educated, close observer and an entertaining writer, this Frenchman was accompanied by Dr. Paolo Emilio Botta, an Italian archaeologist and scientist. More of the California mission and presidial establishments were visited by this party than by any of the foreigners preceding them.

Secularization

In 1826, Echeandía formulated a plan for secularization of the missions. Mexico desired to place the missions under secular rule and to convert mission towns into civic pueblos, but this action had to be approached cautiously. The friars were the only ones who could keep the neophytes in subjection and induce them to work. If these priests should leave, California would be deprived of its major means of support and its people exposed to raids by hostile natives. The friars were in an anomalous position—unwanted, yet not permitted to leave. Some of them wished to depart, but most were old men, attached to their Indian wards.

On January 6, 1831, Governor Echeandía published a proclamation putting into effect secularization of the missions. The missions were to become pueblos, with each Indian family receiving an allotment of land and livestock, and with the friars remaining as curates. The effect of this partial secularization was to make the Indians unruly and restive. Some thereafter refused to work at all; others gambled away their property. Still others were compelled to beg or steal.

Fulfillment of Echeandía's secularization plan was temporarily prevented by a change in the political administration in Mexico and the appointment of a new governor for California, Manuel Victoria, "a friend of the padres and foe to secularization." Yet the forces working for secularization could not be stopped.

Selected Readings

Peter Corney wrote a firsthand account of the Bouchard raid, *Voyages in the Northern Pacific* (Honolulu, 1896). The era during which Bouchard's raid occurred is the subject of an unpublished doctoral dissertation by Frances Carey Jones, "California in the Spanish-American Wars of Independence: The Bouchard Invasion" (University of California). See also the article by Lewis W. Bealer, "Bouchard in the Islands of the Pacific," *Pacific Historical Review* 4 (August 1935), 328–42.

For the transition from Spanish to Mexican control, the richest sources are in the Bancroft Library, University of California, Berkeley. Some of this material has been printed in the series edited by George P. Hammond, *The Larkin Papers* (10 vols., Berkeley, 1951–66). Suggestive is George L. Harding's *Don Agustín V. Zamorano: Statesman, Soldier, Craftsman, and California's First Printer* (Los Angeles, 1934). Another biography that transmits the flavor of the Mexican period is Terry E. Stephenson's *Don Bernardo Yorba* (Los Angeles, 1941). Robert G. Cleland's *The Place Called Sespe* (Los Angeles, 1940,

1957) is a local history with larger implications. See also Myrtle M. McKittrick, *Vallejo: Son of California* (Portland, 1944).

Regarding early Americans in California during the Mexican period, see Reuben L. Underhill's biography of Thomas Oliver Larkin, *From Cowhides to Golden Fleece* (Stanford, 1939, 1946), and Robert J. Parker's "Chapters in the Early Life of Thomas Oliver Larkin," California Historical Society *Quarterly* 16 (March and June 1937), 3–39, 144–71. For the hide and tallow trade consult Adele Ogden, "Alfred Robinson, New England Merchant in Mexican California," California Historical Society *Quarterly* 23 (September 1944), 193–218, as well as her "Hides and Tallow: McCulloch, Hartnell and Company, 1822–1828," in the same periodical 6 (September 1927), 254–64, and "Boston Hide Droghers Along the California Shores" 8 (December 1929), 289–305. See also Rolle, *An American in California*, and Raymond A. Rydell, *Cape Horn to the Pacific* . . . (Berkeley, 1952).

Regarding Indian disturbances, see Marion L. Lathrop, "The Indian Campaigns of General M. G. Vallejo," Society of California Pioneers *Quarterly* 9 (September 1932), 161–205.

The visits of Beechey and Du Haut-Cilly produced literary by-products: Frederick W. Beechey, *Narrative of a Voyage to the Pacific and Beering's Strait* (2 vols., London, 1831), and Auguste Bernard du Haut-Cilly, *Voyage autour du Monde* . . . (2 vols., Paris, 1934). See the translation by Charles F. Carter, "Duhaut-Chilly's [sic] Account of California in the Years 1827–28," California Historical Society *Quarterly* 8 (June-September 1929), 131–66, 306–36. Edmond Le Netrel's *Voyage of the Héros Around the World with Duhaut-Cilly in the Years 1826, 1827, 1828, and 1829* has been translated by Blanche Collet Wagner (Los Angeles, 1951).

Family life in Mexican California is the subject of Gloria Miranda, "Hispano-Mexican Childrearing Practices in Pre-American Santa Barbara," *Southern California Quarterly* 65 (Winter 1983), 307–20.

CHAPTER 11

Infiltration
and Revolt

The unrest that had led to revolution in Spain's former colonies was in part due to discontent caused by contact with foreigners. In California such contact came first by sea but also eventually by way of the seemingly impenetrable wilderness of desert and mountains that, for all practical purposes, had once sealed the remote province off from the east. California might have remained dormant and tranquil behind this barrier for another generation had it not been for a hardy band of American fur trappers. Since the founding of Jamestown and Plymouth, Yankees had been moving west. Englishmen, Frenchmen, and Indians had given way to their march; forests, deserts, wild animals, rugged mountains, and swollen streams had failed to stop the tide. It was only a matter of time before Americans would establish overland contact with the settlements founded by Spain in the Southwest.

Jedediah Smith, First Overland American

During Echeandía's governorship Jedediah Strong Smith, a young trapper of New England parentage, became the pioneer who blazed a trail from the newly formed United States to southern California. Smith, at the head of a small group of fur traders, was in search of beaver and land-otter pelts. His southwestward trek, undertaken twenty-odd years after Lewis and Clark penetrated the American Northwest, has kindled the imagination of historians. Smith has become a legendary figure, a brave and adventurous "Knight in Buckskin." He earned this reputation through his courage and capacity for withstanding the perils of the wilderness. On one occasion a ferocious grizzly bear attacked him, taking his head between its jaws and leaving an ear and part of the scalp hanging from his bleeding skull. One of Smith's men stitched up the lacerated trapper with needle and thread and he was on his way again.

In the early 1820s Jed Smith found his first employment at St. Louis—then the center of the burgeoning fur trade—with General William Henry Ashley, the most successful fur-trading entrepreneur in the trans-Mississippi West. In late summer of 1823, Smith undertook the first of many trips west for Ashley; his route made him one of the earliest white men to cross the continental watershed via South Pass, along what later became the Oregon Trail. In 1826, after an apprenticeship of several years with Ashley's trapping brigades, Smith and two other trappers, David E. Jackson and William L. Sublette, formed a partnership and bought Ashley's interests. Their new enterprise took the three men far beyond the fringes of the Western frontier in search of pelts. On August 22, 1826, Smith led a trapping expedition of fifteen to twenty men and fifty horses out of Bear River Valley, in today's northern Utah. This departure signaled the beginning of an extensive penetration of the region between the Great Salt Lake and the Pacific shoreline, via the unexplored deserts of present-day Nevada and Arizona. Smith's party was composed of rough adventurers, capable of almost inconceivable endurance. His own tenacity, tempered with a sobriety unusual among "mountain men," had brought him the respect of these men. The party moved along the chalky banks of the Sevier River southwestward toward the Virgin River, continued to the Colorado, and then to the desolate Mohave villages. Venturing across sandy alkali wastes, over part of the route today traversed by transcontinental railroads, they headed in the direction of the California coast.

At the age of twenty-eight, Smith became the first white to reach California overland, undergoing Indian attack and severe shortages of food and water. Once he entered that remote area, Smith's adversaries were no longer the blistering white heat of the desert by day and the chilling winds that blew by night. With these he knew how to cope. Quite another matter was the inquisitive Mexican bureaucracy, polite but supremely suspicious.

Guided by two runaway Indians from San Gabriel Mission, Smith's party moved across the desert area between the Colorado River and the California pueblos. On November 27, 1826, he and his bedraggled men reached San Gabriel. The astonished priests at the mission received the uncouth-looking strangers warmly. In exchange for the food, wine, and lodging extended them, the trappers provided the friars with bear traps with which to catch Indians who poached oranges from mission groves.

While his men relaxed for almost two months in the company of the padres, Smith rode southward to see California's choleric gov-

ernor, Echeandía, about permission to trap in the province. After
several days he reached San Diego, only to have Echeandía demand
an explanation of Smith's illegal entry into California. When Smith
failed to convince the suspicious governor that—lost and hungry—
he had simply stumbled into the province, Echeandía seized his weapons and placed him under arrest. Smith protested that he was "no
Spy"; he produced a passport and a diary listing all fifty-seven members of his original party in order to prove that they were bona fide
trappers. These and other documents concerning Smith were confiscated and have been lost; probably they are still in some remote
Mexican archive.

The governor, unable to reach a decision about Smith, sent to
Mexico for instructions as to whether this Protestant alien should be
allowed to return overland to his own country. Languishing, meanwhile, in a dirty San Diego *calabozo*, or jail cell, Smith scrawled a
letter in brown ink to the American minister at Mexico City, Joel R.
Poinsett, complaining: "I am destitute of almost everything with the
exception of my Traps (guns which I can not now call mine), Ammunition, etc." There followed a strong appeal by visiting Boston
shipmasters, to Echeandía and to the American consul at Mazatlán.
These sea captains maintained that, lacking food and water, Smith's
party would have perished if he had not entered California. Smith
was finally freed from imprisonment and allowed to return to San
Gabriel; there he was to pick up his men, upon condition that he
leave California posthaste, never to return. Echeandía considered
Smith and his men interlopers, and anticipated that, if this intrusion
went unchecked, countless other trapping parties might inundate the
province that he was sworn, as governor, to defend.

Via the Cajón Pass, Smith recrossed the Sierra Madre range by
which he had come, then moved northward along the eastern foothills of those mountains into the San Joaquin Valley. In order to trap
along the Stanislaus and Kings rivers, as well as other streams, the
party established a camp in California's Central Valley. Early in the
spring of 1827, near Mission San José, he addressed a letter to Father
Narciso Durán, assuring the padre that he had made several efforts
to cross the mountains, "but the snows being so deep I could not
succeed in getting over."

On May 20, Smith left most of his men in camp and, accompanied
by two companions, set forth with seven horses and several mules to
trudge through the High Sierra toward the Great Basin of Utah.
These were the first white men ever to cross the dangerous Sierra.
Smith reached his destination beyond the Great Salt Lake after about
a month of travel. He and his one surviving companion were reduced,
in Smith's words, to only a "horse and one mule remaining, which
were so feeble and poor that they could scarce carry the little camp

equipage which I had along. The balance of my horses," Smith wrote,
"I was compelled to eat as they gave out." Smith was happy to arrive
at Bear Lake in time for an Independence Day celebration.

California, however, had not seen the last of Jedediah Smith. On
July 13, 1827, after spending only ten days at the redezvous with his
fellow trappers, he began the trek back to rejoin the men he had
left west of the Sierra. Disregarding the warnings of Governor
Echeandía, this time Smith headed a group of nineteen men. Near
the Mohave villages, as Smith approached the Colorado River, his
trail was blocked by Indians. Smith and his trappers rested for a few
days in the vicinity; then, as they attempted to cross the river, the
Mohaves attacked. The Indians killed ten of the Americans and
wounded another. Despite the loss of more than half his group, Smith
finally succeeded in reaching Mission San Gabriel, where he obtained
new horses. When he reached the encampment on the Stanislaus, he
found the first party of trappers "in a very unpleasant situation; their
supplies were almost exhausted and he without any to assist them."
During Smith's absence the Americans had again fallen under the
displeasure of the Mexican authorities. Father Durán had warned
the trappers to move on.

Now Smith, at Mission San José in search of supplies, was once
more seized, this time by Father Durán. After being placed in the
custody of Mexican officials at Monterey, Smith and his party were
thrown into jail. Durán accused the Americans of enticing Indian
neophytes to desert from the mission. Stripped of his guns and under
heavy guard, Smith again appeared before Governor Echeandía, who
was then in the north. After much argument Smith was released for
a second time. The fortunate presence at Monterey of the English
trader William E. P. Hartnell and of four masters of American vessels
made it possible for Smith to secure the supplies he needed. In December of 1827 he departed from California under a heavy bond
not to return.

Smith's route northward through today's Humboldt and Trinity
counties, and onward via Del Norte, proved rough and difficult. He
took more than six months to traverse northwestern California, par-
alleling the coastline toward what is now the Oregon border. At one
place it took many hours to get the horses of the party down a slope
fifty feet high, and one animal fell and broke its neck. Smith's men
continued trapping as they journeyed northward.

On July 5, 1828, while in the Umpqua River country of southern
Oregon, Smith's group suffered an Indian massacre from which only
their leader and two other men were lucky enough to escape. The
trio fled to the Hudson's Bay Company post at Fort Vancouver. Finally, after two years of separation, Smith found his way back to his
partners, Jackson and Sublette, on the Snake River. Before long, he

was off again, and on May 27, 1831, while marching across more of the burning stretches of the Southwest, met his death—probably at the hands of Comanche Indians while searching for a waterhole along the Santa Fe Trail to New Mexico.

Jedediah Smith's influence upon the early history of western America overshadows even his dramatic adventures. He was a pathfinder whose descriptions of the terrain he crossed constitute a unique contribution to the development of overland communications. The geographic barriers that once gave the Californians undisputed ownership of a choice land began to fall rapidly. Hunters, trappers, and traders crossed into the farthest West over at least half a dozen new trails.

Tension in California

Outbursts continued in California against Mexican authority. Resentment toward the central government was increasing, not only because of its indifference and neglect, but also because of its overbearing and mediocre governors. Californians felt contempt for these officials. They also yearned for freedom. Successive revolts following the Solís debacle were halfhearted, bloodless affairs; but they might have become precursors of a movement for independence had not California's dissatisfaction been interrupted by American conquest.

Political changes in Mexico were reflected in California. Echeandía was supplanted by Lieutenant Colonel Manuel Victoria, a militaristic conservative and an opponent of secularization. Echeandía had already issued his decree of secularization of January 6, 1831, with the purpose of rushing the measure into effect before turning over the government to his successor.

When Governor Victoria arrived in California, he found a particularly unfriendly reception awaiting him after he took steps to annul Echeandía's secularization order. Arbitrary by nature, and accustomed to the direct methods of the soldier, Victoria was described as a lean man of such dark complexion (he was half Indian) as to inspire the people to dub him "the black governor." Convinced that everybody opposed to him was in the wrong, Victoria made no attempt to conceal his contempt for the Californians.

During the rule of Echeandía, justice had been carelessly administered, and crime had sometimes gone unpunished. Victoria had stricter ideas of discipline. He boasted that he would make it safe for any man to leave his handkerchief or watch lying in the Monterey plaza. The governor, however, set out to reform abuses without preparing the public for his changes, and with little concern for the constitution. In his haste to take a shortcut to justice, he ordered the death penalty put into effect for minor offenses. Californians were shocked, and began to look upon their new governor as a bloodthirsty monster.

Victoria also rode roughshod over political opponents, provoking a revolt. Several citizens—including the American Abel Stearns, who had become a naturalized Mexican, as well as José Antonio Carrillo, and José María Padrés—were exiled to Mexico, without trial. In refusing to convoke California's *diputación*, and in trying a local *alcalde* in a court-martial, Victoria overreached his constitutional authority. He took the government of the province into his own hands, and engendered hatred among the Californians. A movement to drive Victoria from office rapidly gained ground. Victoria's punishment of Indian offenders was especially hard for the padres to endure, for they stood between their wards and civil injustice. One missionary threw himself at the feet of the governor to beg for the life of a young boy who had stolen a trivial sum. He was refused.

The foreign residents remained, for the most part, discreetly silent, although some of them were more favorable to the governor than they thought it advisable to admit. Increasing numbers of the foreigners were becoming naturalized citizens, but they were nevertheless primarily concerned with financial success rather than with politics. Revolution was destructive to their interests; they needed stable conditions that were favorable to business. Victoria won their confidence by his stand against "evil-doers" and his efforts to keep public order.

Nothing aroused the anger of the native Californians so much as Victoria's refusal to convoke the *diputación*. The governor was convinced that this body would interfere with his policies, and he ignored petition after petition. He framed a manifesto stating that he was personally convinced of the illegal election of a large number of the members of the *diputación* and that he was determined it should not meet again. On hearing this statement, the Californians sent complaints to Mexico, calling upon the government to protect the province against Victoria's arbitrary measures.

The Revolt against Victoria

Active opposition to the governor was mounting. After taking possession of the presidio and garrison at San Diego, a force of about fifty rebels marched to Los Angeles, seizing control of that pueblo. There they found prominent leaders in jail, by order of Victoria, and they prepared to fight the governor. Victoria set out southward from Monterey with a detachment of soldiers. A few miles from Los Angeles, near Cahuenga Pass, he was surprised to encounter some of his own forces, accompanied by 150 insurgent recruits from San Diego and Los Angeles. Victoria called upon these soldiers to come over to his side. They refused, and he then directed his men to fire a volley over the heads of the "enemy," to frighten rather than to harm them. The southerners replied with a few shots; then, their courage failing, they turned to run away, but Victoria was due for another surprise.

Among the Angeleños was a popular daredevil, José María Ávila, noted especially for his skillful horsemanship. Ávila suddenly rode out alone toward Victoria and his subaltern, Captain Romualdo Pacheco, and rushed at them with his lance leveled, as if in chivalric personal combat. Ávila drew an ancient pistol and shot Pacheco through the heart. In the ensuing battle Ávila was unhorsed and killed, some say by Victoria himself, who received a deep lance wound in the face.

The opposition to Victoria forced him to give up the governorship. Echeandía took over the reins of government until the *diputación* at Los Angeles could choose another temporary governor. However, after Pío Pico was announced as its choice, on January 10, 1832, Echeandía refused to relinquish his office. Echeandía wanted no native son that he did not trust to take over the governorship.

When Victoria had marched against the insurgents at Los Angeles, he left in command at Monterey his secretary, Captain Agustín Vicente Zamorano. Zamorano took no part in the rebellion of 1831, and made no effort to defend Victoria. After Victoria was driven out of the country, Zamorano realized that popular feeling in favor of Echeandía was lukewarm. He won over to his side most of the foreign residents, who disliked Echeandía and distrusted Pío Pico. Zamorano was wily enough to conclude a truce with Echeandía. The two agreed to divide California's military command between them: Echeandía's authority was to extend south of San Gabriel, while Zamorano was to rule north of San Fernando. This arrangement, however, came to an end with the arrival of a newly appointed governor.

Figueroa

The choice fell upon the mestizo José Figueroa, prominent in Mexican politics as *comandante-general* of Sonora and Sinaloa. During six years in that position, Figueroa had learned something of California's disturbed affairs. The new governor's talent for administration, his superior education, and his affable manners won for him personal popularity, and helped overcome, temporarily, the prejudice against imported Mexican governors. Figueroa was unostentatious and democratic, making it a point to treat the poorest Indian with as much

consideration as the highest official. His first act was to issue a proclamation granting amnesty to all who had taken part in the disturbances of 1831–1832. Both revolutionists and conservatives hastened
to offer their allegiance to Figueroa.

Another important act of Figueroa's administration was his move
to take firmer possession of the territory to the north. By a treaty
of 1819 the Oregon region had been ceded by the Spanish government to the United States, and the northern boundary of Spain's
holdings on the Pacific Coast was fixed at the forty-second parallel.
Mexico had inherited a claim to territory extending more than 4
degrees latitude north of San Francisco; but the only establishments
by which it held its claim to this northern area were the missions of
San Rafael and San Francisco de Solano (commonly called Sonoma).
Figueroa took steps to open this region by sending Mariano Guadalupe Vallejo, afterwards known as "Comandante of the Line of the
North," to look for a suitable site for a presidio. Two colonies of
settlers were established by Vallejo, one at Petaluma and the other
at Santa Rosa, while he built up a great private estate near Sonoma.

Further Secularization of the Missions

All other issues of the administration of Figueroa were overshadowed
by the question of secularization. Figueroa has been attacked by historians as the destroyer of the missions. Yet he acted as the agent of
his government, attempted to mitigate evils that he saw could not be
avoided, and urged that the loosening of mission control proceed
gradually. Figueroa faced the fact that, originally, under the regulations of Spain, the Indians were eventually supposed to leave the
missions and to be settled in pueblos. He feared, however, that un-
conditional release of the Indians might lead to their destruction.
Actually, depletion of the Indian population had marred life in the
mission establishments. Also, the missions, based on a paternal system, could no longer continue. Indian servitude was incompatible
with Mexico's avowed republican principles. Conversely, the missionaries' contention that their Indian wards still required control
could not be wholly denied.

Figueroa approached mission secularization with reluctance. He
made a tour of inspection of the missions, asking the padres for their
opinions about plans to secularize their establishments. Their protests convinced the governor that the missions were not yet ready
for secularization, and he warned the Mexican government that the
Indians could not yet be placed on their own.

Figueroa's warning, however, came too late. Sentiment in Mexico
for emancipation of the Indians culminated in a sweeping decree of

August 1833. The missions were immediately to become parish churches. An unfortunate loophole for corruption was left by the decree's omission of any plan for disposing of mission properties. Wide ranges of valuable land suddenly became available to the public, and some of the best soil in California haphazardly drifted under the control of private persons.

Governor Figueroa attempted to make the emancipation as smooth and gradual as possible. He allowed only a few missions at a time to be converted into parish churches. Half the land and livestock of these he ordered distributed among the Indian neophytes, while all remaining property was placed in the care of administrators. The income from the latter property was to be used for the administrators' salaries and for the expenses of schools and welfare requirements—especially those benefiting the Indians. To the surprise of Figueroa, the Indians did not accept their new freedom with joy. Instead, they hung about the missions, reluctant to leave the places that had been the only homes they had known, in some cases for as long as sixty years. As for the friars, they realized that their cause was lost. It was impossible to obtain other clergy to take their places. And because, without the influence of the padres, outbreaks among the Indians were feared, Californians were not all willing to let the missionaries go.

The Padrés–Hijar Colonization Venture

During the year 1834, in the midst of his difficulties over secularization, Governor Figueroa experienced further troubles as a result of the arrival of a party of colonists from Mexico. These settlers were under the leadership of José María Padrés, who had been banished from the territory by Victoria. Padrés, with money given him from the Pious Fund (a sum of money allocated earlier for missionary activity by the Mexican government), had paid the traveling expenses of more than two hundred persons desiring to settle in California. The government had no legal right to use missionary funds for this purpose. Nevertheless, with the prominent Mexican José María Hijar backing him, Padrés planned a new colony. The background of the settlers he had assembled was superior to that of any group yet sent to California. Among them were doctors, lawyers, teachers, goldsmiths, and artisans, but they were for the most part persons not fitted for the rigors of frontier life.

Padrés and Hijar did not meet a warm welcome in California. They had brought with them twenty-one Mexicans to serve as administrators of the missions, whereas native Californians had planned to fill these places. Preparations were made to establish these settlers on the northern frontier, as a bulwark against the Russians. The majority of the new colonists finally were sent to Mission San Francisco de Solano, from which most of them went into the Sonoma Valley. Failing to obtain employment, they spent a very uncomfortable winter, compelled to live upon the charity of Figueroa's government. Some made violent threats to the governor, which caused Figueroa to take action against the most restless ones, especially after the Mexican central government withdrew its support of this hapless colonizing project. On May 8, 1834, the governor arrested both Padrés and Hijar as undesirables and sent them packing out of the port of San Pedro for San Blas, Mexico. Other colonists were, however, allowed to remain behind, and the descendants of some of them bear such well-known California family names as Coronel, Ábrego, Noé, Serrano, Prudón, and Covarrubias.

Completion of Secularization

As the process of secularizing the missions continued, Governor Figueroa, harassed and worn out, died on September 29, 1835. He left behind a reputation as probably the best of California's Mexican governors. Had he lived, some of the purposes of secularization might have been accomplished. Figueroa is not to be blamed if few Indians got the land intended for them under the key secularization law of August 1833.

Now government administrators and their friends, some of them members of the "first families," were enriched from the spoils of the missions. The natives had little respect for these administrators. Frequent disturbances occurred, especially in the south, when Indians took mission property they had been given and bartered it for liquor, so that they were left with no worldly goods. They failed to cultivate the land, and it passed to others. Buildings decayed from neglect, and the herds of cattle were depleted as the animals were killed by the Indians for food or sold to foreign traders in exchange for gewgaws. For a brief period, from 1840 to 1845, secularization was virtually suspended, partly as a result of the pressure asserted by church authorities in both Mexico and California. On March 29, 1843, the proclerical Governor Micheltorena actually ordered restoration of the missions to the church fathers. But the impoverished Mexican government renewed the secularization process. Soon California's governors would rent and sell certain missions, also turning them into pueblos. Outright looting of mission properties went unchecked. Repeatedly, knaves stocked their ranchos with animals filched from mission herds. The mission Indians stood apathetically by deeply confused. The dreams of Junípero Serra faded, and California's missions began to crumble into dust.

Selected Readings

Regarding Jedediah Smith, consult Maurice S. Sullivan, *The Travels of Jedediah Smith* (Santa Ana, 1934), and the same author's *Jedediah Smith, Trader and Trail Breaker* (New York, 1936). A more recent biography is Dale L. Morgan, *Jedediah Smith and the Opening of the West* (New York, 1953). Robert Glass Cleland, whose *Pathfinders* (Los Angeles, 1929) represented some of the first scholarship on Smith, later included him in *This Reckless Breed of Men* (New York, 1950). Also basic to an understanding of Smith are Harrison C. Dale, *The Ashley-Smith Explorations and the Discovery of a Central Route to the Pacific, 1822–1829* (Glendale, 1918, 1941), and Donald McKay Frost, "Notes on General Ashley, the Overland Trail and South Pass," *Proceedings of the American Antiquarian Society* 54 (October 1944), 161–312.

Articles regarding Smith include A. M. Woodbury, "The Route of Jedediah S. Smith," *Utah Historical Quarterly* 4 (April 1931), 35–46. Two articles that concern Smith in southern California, both by Andrew Rolle, are "Jedediah Strong Smith: New Documentation," *Mississippi Valley Historical Review* 40 (September 1953), 305–8, and "The Riddle of Jedediah Smith's First Visit to California," Historical Society of Southern California *Quarterly* 36 (September 1954), 179–84. George R. Brooks, ed., *The Southwest Expedition of Jedediah S. Smith* (Glendale, 1977) includes the long-lost personal account of Smith's 1826–1827 journey to California.

Gerald J. Geary, *The Secularization of the California Missions* (Washington, D.C., 1934), is the only book-length study of that subject. See also John B. McGloin, "The California Catholic Church in Transition," California Historical Society *Quarterly* 42 (March 1963), 39–48, as well as his life of Archbishop Joseph Alemany, entitled *California's First Archbiship* (New York, 1966).

Regarding Hispanic influence in northern California, useful is H. F. Raup and William B. Pounds, Jr., "Northernmost Spanish Frontier in California," California Historical Society *Quarterly* 32 (March 1953), 43–48. Several articles by George Tays appeared in the *Quarterly* during 1937 (volume 16) under the title "Mariano Guadalupe Vallejo and Sonoma—A Biography and a History." See also Madie Brown Emparan, *The Vallejos of California* (San Francisco, 1968).

Colonization is the motif of C. Alan Hutchinson, *The Hijar-Padrés Colony and its Origins, 1769–1835* (New Haven, 1969).

CHAPTER 12

On the Eve
of American Rule

GOVERNOR FIGUEROA had managed to retain the allegiance of the people more by personal charm than by the authority of his office. After his death Californians grew restless again, and this tendency was aggravated, as usual, by constant changes of governmental policies in Mexico. Nicolás Gutiérrez, who succeeded Figueroa as governor *ad interim*, filled the office for four months until the next appointee arrived. This period was marked by only one significant governmental event—temporary recognition of Los Angeles as California's capital. As a result of the persistent pressure of such southerners as José Antonio Carrillo and Pío Pico, an abrupt decree of May 23, 1835, announced the moving of the capital southward. This news was jubilantly received by Angeleños, but did little to assuage north-south relations.

Chico and His Ouster

California's next regular governor, the Mexican-born Mariano Chico, was a political reactionary and unpopular with the majority of Californians. Public resentment rose to the boiling point, and Chico was expelled from California after only three months in office. The ouster was clandestinely accomplished, with the insurgent Californians managing to avoid open conflict with the national government. Chico threatened to return with troops to take vengeance, but it was an empty boast.

Mexican governors were no longer welcome in California; one after another found the place hostile. Indeed, most provincials no longer called themselves *Mexicanos*, but *Californios*.

Upon the expulsion of Chico the civil and military commands again fell to Gutiérrez. This time he experienced a stormier tenure. Though easygoing and inoffensive, he was a Spaniard by birth, and was regarded as a foreigner. A petty quarrel between him and Juan Bautista Alvarado provided an excuse for his overthrow. The Californians were determined to secure home rule for the territory. Why should a Vallejo, an Alvarado, a Carrillo, or any other California leader be in a position of inferiority to an outsider whom he considered his inferior? Contact with foreigners had emphasized the backwardness of Mexico and awakened local ambitions. The ease with which the Californians had expelled Victoria and Chico emboldened them to act independently. But they did not yet feel strong enough to walk alone. Hence their struggle was to secure autonomy in internal affairs.

Alvarado, Home Rule, and More Foreigners

A leader anxious to leap into the fray was at hand. By late 1836 the twenty-seven-year-old Juan Bautista Alvarado had by virtue of his talents, education, and powerful family ties made himself prominent as a local patriot. He was a member of the *diputación* and an *hijo del país*, or native son, endowed with magnetism and eloquence. Alvarado and José Castro assembled a force of seventy-five men, armed with antiquated muskets. At Monterey the revolutionists recruited Isaac Graham, an American fur trapper and hunter of unsavory repute. Graham ran a whiskey distillery on the Rancho Vergeles. A backwoodsman from Tennessee, he was reckless, with a following of similar character. Graham was induced to join the revolutionists by promises of land and other favors. Though momentarily grateful for the American's loyalty, Alvarado was to rue the day when he availed himself of his services.

A little "army," made up of Graham's band of about fifty riflemen—Indians, Americans, and renegade Mexicans—together with 100 Californians under José Castro, quietly appeared at Monterey on November 3. Without bloodshed they took possession of the fort. One cannon ball struck the house of the governor. This so terrified Gutiérrez that he surrendered immediately. Once again a governor appointed by the Mexican government was put aboard a homeward-bound ship, the third such official to be expelled from California.

Alvarado thereupon wrote his relative Vallejo: "It is wonderful, Uncle, with what order our expedition has been conducted. Everybody shouts *vivas*, for California is free." On November 7, 1836, California's *diputación* proclaimed it a "free and sovereign State"—at least until Mexico should restore the Federalist Constitution of 1824 as a conditional "Declaration of Independence." Alvarado was named governor by the *diputación;* Vallejo was designated military chief; and Monterey again became the capital. Despite the fact that Alvarado had led a successful revolt, he was still sufficiently fearful of Mexican authority to keep the Mexican banner floating in public places. When news of the uprising reached the central government, it issued a swarm of proclamations threatening punishment to the participants.

Local patriotism and independence again were overshadowed by internal quarrels and sectional jealousies. In the extreme south, San Diego had a special grievance. It had long wanted the provincial customhouse to be located within its municipal confines, but had been unable to wrest that distinction from Monterey. Such disagreements resulted in an armed encounter between Californians; this took place near San Buenaventura, with Castro at the head of the northerners and Carlos Carrillo in command of the southerners. Only one man was killed. After another skirmish at Las Flores, in which the two factions met in "a battle for the most part of tongue and pen," Alvarado was able to persuade Carrillo to disband his troops, ending opposition to the Monterey government.

Alvarado, in August 1838, was confirmed as governor by Mexico. Some expressed surprise that the central government should confer this honor upon a man lately in rebellion against it. The authorities probably cared little who was governor of California so long as he was loyal and did not ask for money or troops.

A few years of respite from internal dissension followed, permitting Governor Alvarado to devote attention to affairs that had been sadly neglected. The missions continued to deteriorate, in spite of his appointing the honest and hardworking William E. P. Hartnell as a government inspector. The ruinous state of the missions was not altogether due to previous dishonest administrators. The mission Indians had in many cases disposed of the little property that had been distributed to them. With encouragement from the former neophytes, the non-Christianized Indians of the interior were conducting raids on the exposed and disintegrating missions, running off horses and mules and killing unguarded cattle.

Another problem of the Alvarado administration was continuing sentiment for insurrection, especially in the south. Among the leaders of this movement was Pío Pico, who still sulked at the refusal of California's junta to keep the capital at Los Angeles. Also, California's permanent foreign residents had changed since the arrival of the earliest traders, merchants, and rancheros. Most of these were pioneers were respected; among them were such names as those of Hartnell, Cooper, Fitch, Spear, Davis, Spence, Stearns, and Robinson. In the 1830s, however, troublemakers had come into the province. Some of these refused to settle down. Among them Isaac Graham, in particular, was distrusted by Alvarado, who considered that ruffian foolhardy enough to attempt seizure of California, this time his administration. Graham made his Monterey cabin a center for rabble-rousing former fur trappers and sailors. Alvarado got wind of an alleged plot to overthrow him whose origin he traced to Graham. Texas had become independent in 1836 largely through the efforts of such ambitious Americans.

In April 1840, Alvarado began to round up suspect malcontents. Out of a total of 120 foreigners that he arrested, he sent Graham and forty-five of his "dangerous" associates, in irons, to San Blas. The governor was subsequently accused of trumping up a false charge of conspiracy against these foreigners, as a pretext to rid the province of them. Yet many "respectable" foreign residents approved of Alvarado's clamping down upon Graham and his followers. They believed these restless men to be a menace to the stability of California. Ultimately the British consul at Tepic, in Mexico, took up the exiled Graham's cause with the Mexican government; the old hunter was ordered released and even given free ship passage back to California. This was a rebuke to Governor Alvarado by higher authority. In July 1841 the citizens of Monterey were astounded to see Graham and two dozen of his ragged companions disembarking from a ship in that port, as insolent as ever.

Mention has been made of the visits of La Pérouse, Vancouver, Beechey, and Du Haut-Cilly; in the 1830s and 1840s increasing numbers of such travelers appeared in California ports. The French naval frigate *Venus,* under the command of Captain Abel du Petit-Thouars, in 1837 remained for a month at Monterey. The captain's report included descriptions of the Alvarado Revolution and of California's weak government. Another visitor, also on a trip of observation for the French government, arrived in California three years later; this was Eugène Duflot de Mofras. These trips were more than pleasure tours. Interest in California was mounting, and foreign governments were eager to obtain information about the province.

The United States, as concerned as any other outside power over the future status of California, sent its first naval expedition to the Pacific Coast in 1841. The leader of this enterprise, Commodore Charles Wilkes, though dour and pessimistic in his report, wrote about what he called the greatest natural harbor in the world, San Francisco.

The Return to Mexican Rule under Micheltorena

Only for short periods of time did California escape being a dumping ground for unemployed Mexican officials. The joint rule of Alvarado as civil governor and Vallejo as *comandante-general* ended late in 1842. In August of that year a newly appointed executive, Manuel Micheltorena, now a general of brigade, arrived suddenly at San Diego. In appearance he was attractive, with an erect, military bearing, and in manner gracious. But Micheltorena came handicapped by a company of three hundred tough *cholos*, or half-breed ex-convicts. In a state of destitution, these "troops" had been sent with Micheltorena by the Mexican government partly to restrict further entry of foreigners into California. As irregulars, they had not received pay in a long time, and could not resist the temptation to steal kettles, pots, chickens, jewelry, and even clothing. Their depredations included molesting local señoritas. At San Diego, where the governor was first welcomed to California, local residents soon became anxious to speed him and his *rateros*, or scamps, northward to the capital of Monterey.

Before his arrival at Monterey, Micheltorena was met by startling news. Hostilities between Mexico and the United States seemed on the verge of breaking out. Commodore Thomas Ap Catesby Jones, in command of the American Pacific squadron, was under the mistaken impression that war had already been declared and he had made a hurried run from Peruvian waters to raise the flag of the United States prematurely at Monterey. Convinced of his error within only a few hours, Jones restored the Mexican flag and the difficulty was composed, for the moment, in a friendly manner.

Governor Micheltorena encountered more serious troubles. The old quarrel between Monterey and Los Angeles about the location of the capital kept cropping up. Outbreaks of the Indians continued, too, to cause anxiety. As for foreigners, Micheltorena tried to secure their loyalty by granting tracts of land in the Sacramento Valley to a number of them. As a consequence he was popular with some foreigners; yet he feared them.

Micheltorena's Expulsion

Micheltorena made every effort to win the favor of all Californians. He made up out of his own pocket losses resulting from the thievery of his men. He pleased the friars by restoring properties to their care, even though this action came too late to save the moribund mission system. Micheltorena also established better schools in the province than had ever existed. But the Californians regarded his convict troops as a bitter insult, one of many heaped upon them by the Mexican government. Micheltorena too had to go. The only question was when.

In November 1844 another revolt broke out, again under the leadership of Alvarado and José Castro. Vallejo held aloof from the conflict, attempting to keep the peace by urging Micheltorena to send his soldiers home to Mexico. On November 22 the governor marched against the rebels. After an encounter near San José, in which argument took the place of fighting, a treaty was concluded. Micheltorena agreed to send his *cholos* (tough *hombres*) out of the country within three months, but the harassed governor had no authority from Mexico to carry out this promise. It soon became evident that he was using the time gained to win over local foreigners in order to resist further revolts. By now there was a determination to drive him out of the province, as with Governor Chico.

Foreign residents were aligned on both sides in the quarrel with Micheltorena, depending on their personal motives. Isaac Graham joined Micheltorena's forces to avenge himself upon Alvarado, whom he never forgave for his exile in 1840. Stearns took sides with the localists Alvarado and Castro to gratify his hatred of Mexico and the rancor he still nursed for his treatment by Governor Victoria. Sutter, a Swiss adventurer who had come to California in 1839 to build a fort at New Helvetia on the Sacramento River, contracted to aid Micheltorena in consideration for a large grant of land, in addition to that which already obtained from Alvarado. Graham and Sutter, however, were persuaded by fellow foreigners that they could best serve their own interests by joining Alvarado. Fifty foreigners enlisted against Micheltorena, whose forces, congregating near Los Angeles, included 100 Indians from the interior armed with guns, bows, and arrows.

On February 20, 1845, the opposing armies, each 400 strong, met at Cahuenga Pass and engaged in a two-day artillery duel, at such long range that there was little danger of anyone being hit. The foreign contingents on both sides then awakened to the folly of shooting at each other over a quarrel in which they had little to gain. At Los Angeles the foreigners held a conference and resolved to withdraw from the conflict. On February 22 Micheltorena, his foreign support vanished, agreed to be deported from California. He also consented to take his jailbird army with him. With his departure the province achieved, before the American conquest, what amounted to independence.

Following these events, Pío Pico attained recognition as civil governor by Alvarado and other native sons. José Castro, as powerful at Monterey as Pico was in Los Angeles, became military *comandante*. California was determined to govern itself, but almost immediately the old rivalry between north and south flared up. Pico used his position to remove the capital to Los Angeles again. Meanwhile, Castro and his northern cohorts latched onto the Monterey customhouse as a center of power. California was a house divided. The finances of the government became hopeless; there were disagreements about allocation of revenues; debts piled up; salaries were seldom paid. Pico was in a position to control legislation, but Castro had possession of the funds. This quarrel between *comandante* and governor, between north and south, between customhouse and local officials, dragged on fruitlessly during 1845–1846. There seems little doubt that factionalism, which constantly threatened to erupt into actual warfare, helped reconcile the Californians to United States rule. Vallejo and other native sons became convinced that Americanization would and should occur. True, many Californians later remembered with nostalgia the pastoral era, supplanted by a driving, pushy American period. But some actually looked forward to this change of rule as the best hope for California's future.

Russian Abandonment of California

The increase in the number of Americans coming into California was accompanied by a Russian exodus. American settlers had moved closer and closer to Fort Ross. The Russians had found their way largely blocked by Yankees; among these was John B. Cooper, who, by 1837, had taken possession of a rancho in the upper part of the Russian River Valley. Furthermore, the Russian establishment at Ross had become a financial burden. In its last four years of operation, the fort had lost 45,000 rubles for its owners. The Russians were discouraged also, as early as December 2, 1823, by American President James Monroe's historic message in which he stated that lands in the Western Hemisphere were "henceforth not to be considered as subjects for future colonization by any European powers." During 1842 the Russians withdrew from California.

Since they had gone through the form of buying the lands from the Indians (although the price paid was a bagatelle), the Russians claimed they should be reimbursed for the territory. The Californians believed that, in view of the long, and illegal, occupancy by the Russians, all buildings, lands, and other property should be turned over to the provincial government without charge. A Russian commissioner who came to California from Alaska to oversee the withdrawal, however, threatened to burn Ross rather than give it away. In the autumn of 1841 the Russians concluded a sale with Sutter that solved this problem. Although the Swiss was heavily in debt, he arranged to purchase all movable property at Fort Ross—including a glass hothouse, farming implements, a small vessel, a few cannon, some old French flintlock muskets, military supplies, and munitions—for $50,000.

So ended thirty years of Russian occupancy of their outpost in California. Today the only relics of their tenure are a few buildings and some archival records. In addition, there remain various place names—among them Fort Ross itself, the Russian River, and Mount St. Helena, named for the empress of Russia. The Russian withdrawal occurred on the eve of American rule as a new day was dawning for California.

Selected Readings

The last days of Mexican rule are portrayed in J. J. Hill, *History of Warner's Ranch and Its Environs* (Los Angeles, 1927), and George William and Helen Pruitt Beattie, *Heritage of the Valley: San Bernardino's First Century* (Pasadena, 1939). Other books that reflect the era are Stephenson's *Yorba*, William D. Phelps, *Fore and Aft, or Leaves from the Life of an Old Sailor* (Boston, 1871), and Henry A. Wise, *Los Gringos, or an Inside view of Mexico and California* (New York, 1849).

The report of the *Venus* is entitled *Voyage autour du monde sur le frégate Vénus pendant les années 1836–1839 . . . par Abel du Petit Thouars* (11 vols., Paris, 1840–55). A translation by Charles N. Rudkin, covering the California portion of the expedition, is *Voyage of the Venus: Sojourn in California* (Los Angeles, 1956). Eugène Duflot de Mofras's narrative, *Exploration du territoire de l'Orégon, des Californies et de la Mer Vermeille . . .* (Paris, 1844) has been translated, edited, and annotated by Marguerite Eyer Wilbur, as *Duflot de Mofras' Travels on the Pacific Coast . . .* (2 vols., Santa Ana, 1937). See also the descriptions by Charles Wilkes in his *Narrative of the United States Exploring Expedition during the years 1838, 1839, 1840, 1841, 1842* (5 vols., Philadelpia, 1844), as well as the popularized biography of Wilkes, *The Hidden Coasts*, by Daniel M. MacIntyre (New York, 1953) and David B. Tyler, *The Wilkes Expedition* (Philadelphia, 1968).

The emergence of the southern counties into an American pattern is the theme of Robert Glass Cleland's *The Cattle on a Thousand Hills: Southern California, 1850–1870* (San Marino, 1941, 1951). Supplemental is Thomas Jefferson Farnham, *Travels in the Californias, and Scenes in the Pacific Ocean* (New York, 1844). See also Myrtle M. McKittrick, *Vallejo: Son of California* (Portland, 1944); several biographical sketches in Rockwell D. Hunt, *California's Stately Hall of Fame* (Caldwell, Idaho, 1950); and Richman's *California Under Spain and Mexico*. Literary aspects of the shift from a Hispanic to an Anglo-Saxon orientation are in James D. Hart, *American Images of Spanish California* (Berkeley, 1960).

CHAPTER 13

Trappers, Traders, and Homeseekers

THE OVERLAND MOVEMENT to California pioneered by Jedediah Smith was soon joined by a number of other adventurous American trappers, among them James Ohio Pattie, Ewing Young, William Wolfskill, the Sublette brothers, Kit Carson, and George Nidever. Many of these, and dozens of less renowned traders and home-seekers—including the obstreperous Isaac Graham—were to help transform the province into an American outpost.

The Patties

Prominent among the "mountain men" was the Kentuckian James Ohio Pattie, who in 1824 set out with his father, Sylvester, a Missourian, on a trapping expedition southwestward from the Missouri River frontier. On June 20 the little party, consisting of five persons, crossed the Missouri sixty miles above St. Louis. There they joined a larger party. Not all of these persons accompanied Sylvester and James Ohio Pattie into the unexplored Southwest, however; some struck off in other directions. For several years the Patties trapped for beaver along muddy and unattractive streams which no white men had even seen before. They reached the Mohave villages on the Colorado by March 16, 1826, some six months before Jedediah Smith, becoming the first Americans to trap along the California and Arizona frontier. As they made their way through the uncharted Southwest they took many furs. Future prospects of the party seemed excellent until Indians stole their pack animals and compelled them to cache the unwieldy furs, most of which they never recovered. Still worse, another cache was confiscated by the Mexican governor at Santa Fe, who pocketed the proceeds himself, on the ground that the Americans had been trapping without a license. Thus began a series of hardships which, in the end, brought death to the elder Pattie and poverty to the younger man.

Late in September 1827, the Patties, with about thirty companions, continued westward from Santa Fe to trap along the Gila. By the first of December they reached the junction of that river with the Colorado. Repeated misunderstandings caused the party to divide, until the Pattie group numbered but eight persons. These wandered haphazardly through what is today southern Arizona. At one camp-site a band of Yuma Indians, under cover of a heavy storm and the blackness of night, stampeded their horses. This left the Patties no choice but to build canoes from nearby cottonwoods for transport down the Colorado. Floating down that river, they set traps all along the banks, and their store of beaver skins again increased daily.

As the Patties approached the Gulf of California, they abandoned their handmade canoes, due to the "tumultuous commotion of the water." Burying their stock of furs, they set out on a grueling journey farther westward across Lower California, in the hope of reaching some sort of Mexican settlement. The fierce sun and scorching sand, the almost total lack of moisture, and their own extreme fatigue brought a sense of desperation to the little company.

With the assistance of friendly Indian guides, they came finally to the Dominican mission of Santa Catalina; but instead of being accorded relief by its padres, they were thrown into the guardhouse. They were, after all, foreign interlopers. After a week of scanty fare, they were sent under guard to San Diego, then seat of the California governor's residence. Like Jedediah Smith, they were amazed at the harsh treatment accorded them by Echeandía and dismayed when he remanded them to separate prison cells. The governor was especially suspicious of the trappers as a result of Smith's recent expedition. The impaired health of Sylvester Pattie was not equal to the poor food and execrable physical treatment, and he was seized with an illness that proved fatal.

After the death of his father, the younger Pattie was given a chance to serve the governor. The governor needed an interpreter to translate English-language documents and to deal with foreign visitors. Also, Echeandía relaxed his extreme rigor when a smallpox epidemic began to rage in the upper part of the province and casualties multiplied alarmingly, especially after he learned that Pattie had brought along some scarce vaccine. The governor promised him a passport for a year if he would vaccinate the people on the coast, and agreed to compensate him for the service and to grant him his liberty. Pattie accepted these terms, and traveled up and down the coast for Echeandía, vaccinating some ten thousand Indians and other California residents. For his efforts he was dubbed by another trapper "sometime

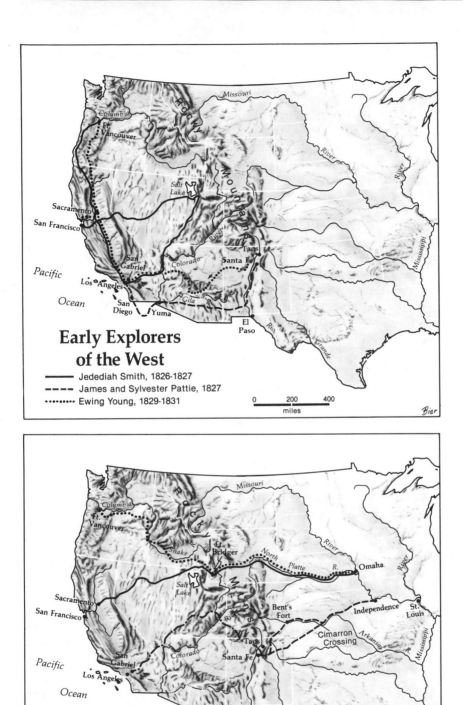

Early Explorers
of the West

—— Jedediah Smith, 1826-1827
---- James and Sylvester Pattie, 1827
········ Ewing Young, 1829-1831

0   200   400
miles

Bier

Missouri

Columbia
Ft. Vancouver

ROCKY Mountain

Salt Lake

Sacramento

San Francisco

Pacific

Ocean

San Gabriel

Los Angeles

San Diego

Yuma

Colorado

Taos
Santa Fe

Gila

El Paso

Rio Grande

River

Mississippi

Early Trails
of the West

---- Santa Fe Trail, 1821-
—·—·— Old Spanish (Wolfskill) Trail, 1829-
········ Oregon Trail, 1841-
—— Central Trail ('49'ers)

0   200   400
miles

Bier

Missouri

ROCKY

Columbia
Ft. Vancouver

Snake

Ft. Bridger

North Platte R.

River

Omaha

Salt Lake

Sacramento

San Francisco

Bent's Fort

Independence

St. Louis

Cimarron Crossing

Arkansas

Taos

Santa Fe

Pacific

San Gabriel

Los Angeles

Colorado

Ocean

Mississippi

surgeon extraordinary to his Excellency, the Governor of California."

Upon completion of his task, Pattie was thunderstruck when confronted with the demand that he become a Catholic before receiving
the favors promised him by the governor. He refused to change his
religion and left California early in 1830 by sea. Making his way
overland to Mexico City and then to Vera Cruz, he disappeared from
the pages of history. Pattie was significant because he not only pioneered the Gila River route to California, but also left for posterity
one of the most exciting records of Western adventure. His *Personal
Narrative*, first published in 1831, is a mine of unreliable but fascinating information.

Ewing Young

Among the fur traders of the Southwest, none was more active than
Ewing Young. For more than a decade he trapped along the streams
of the southern Rocky Mountains as well as the San Joaquin and the
Sacramento Rivers in California. Although he led an impressive number of trapping parties during this period, he remains one of the
least heralded of California's "mountain men." He learned his trade
early in life, trapping first mainly in the waters of the Pecos. In August
1829 he headed a party of twenty-nine men from Taos toward California; they went by way of the Zuñi villages and the Salt River,
traveling down the Gila and the Colorado.

Some of the men, among them Young's protégé Kit Carson, decided to cross the Mohave desert with Young to the settlements of
southern California. Following Jedediah Smith's trail, the party moved
through Cajon Pass and, early in 1830, reached San Gabriel Mission.
Hardy, and inured to physical danger, Young attained a reputation
as a trailblazer as a result of such treks.

In 1831 Young took thirty-six men to California along the old
Pattie route. Among them were Isaac Williams, Jonathan Trumbull
Warner, Isaac Sparks, and Kit Carson's brother, Moses. All would
leave their mark on California. On this expedition Young engaged
in otter and beaver trapping along the Kings River and stretches of
the San Joaquin. He then proceeded to the Sacramento and came
upon a Hudson's Bay Company brigade a few miles south of the
American River. American trapping competition with that English
company was already under way. Early in 1833, Young moved northwest, passing along the southern and western shores of Clear Lake
and reaching the coast about seventy-five miles north of Fort Ross.
He followed the seashore in search of beaver as far as the Umpqua
River in Oregon, before moving back southward down the Sacra-

mento Valley, entering the San Bernardino Valley in southern California during December of 1833. This itinerary may convey the wide scope of the travels, made under frightful conditions, of trappers and traders like Ewing Young.

Other Early Trappers

Part of the early fur trade in the Southwest was carried on clandestinely, since as a rule only Mexicans (including Californians) possessed licenses to trap legally. Milton Sublette was granted such a license, but only on condition that he teach "a certain proportion of Mexicans the art of trapping." Mexican Californians displayed little interest, however, in trapping, and by the 1830s hundreds of trappers from the United States were scattered all over the Southwest.

In 1824 William Wolfskill had joined Young and others to trap along the tributaries of the Colorado, collecting about $10,000 worth of furs. The legendary "Pegleg" Smith was a member of Young's party that trapped on the Gila in 1826. Another visitor to California at about this time was George C. Yount, a pioneer for whom the town of Yountville, in Napa County, was named. In 1829–1830, Christopher (Kit) Carson was, as already noted, a member of Young's expedition to California. Other fur men who became prominent in the future state included J. J. Warner, whose southern California ranch became a rendezvous for old-timers. Others were David E. Jackson, of Jackson Hole and Grand Teton fame, and Job F. Dye, who later wrote *Recollections of a Pioneer of California*. Thomas Fitzpatrick, known by his Indian name, "Broken Hand," was one of the most dependable of all the guides of his day. Joseph Reddeford Walker is remembered as the discoverer of Walker Pass, and Louis Robideaux, a trapper of French descent, as the man for whom Mount Robidoux in southern California is named. Other colorful figures among the fur men were "Uncle Billy" Waters, "Old Bill" Williams, Ceran St. Vrain, Isaac Slover, and Nathaniel Pryor. Each in his own way helped expand American influence in the Far West.

Sutter's New Helvetia

As California accommodated to foreign influence, a unique role was taken by Johann Augustus Sutter. Born in the Grand Duchy of Baden, Sutter left Switzerland for America in 1834 to escape a debtor's prison and an angry wife. After tarrying in Indiana and Missouri, and visiting parts of Mexico along the Santa Fe Trail—as well as Honolulu and the Russian colonies in Alaska—he arrived on the Pa-

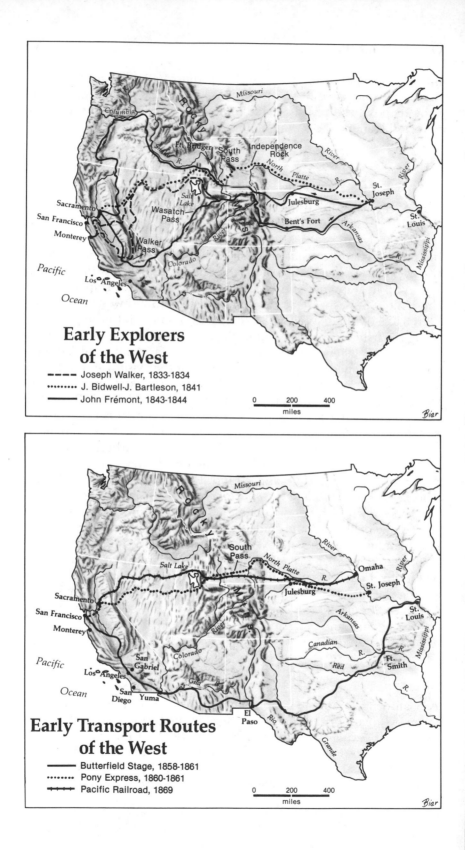

Early Explorers
of the West

- - - - Joseph Walker, 1833-1834
.... J. Bidwell-J. Bartleson, 1841
———— John Frémont, 1843-1844

0   200   400
miles

Bier

Early Transport Routes
of the West

———— Butterfield Stage, 1858-1861
.... Pony Express, 1860-1861
+++++ Pacific Railroad, 1869

0   200   400
miles

Bier

cific Coast. Called "a dreamer with a gifted tongue," Sutter achieved a distinctive place in California's history; he was shrewd and wily, as well as visionary.

Sutter brought with him to California Hawaiian, or Kanaka, laborers, hoping to build a self-sustaining colony and fort in the Sacramento Valley. In 1839 he obtained permission from Governor Alvarado to occupy a virtually unexplored 50,000-acre tract of land near the junction of the Sacramento and American Rivers, after convincing Alvarado that he could act as a semiofficial representative of the government in the interior. Impressed with the proposal, the governor also promised Sutter Mexican citizenship. The early American trader William Heath Davis, Jr., first guided Sutter's party to the site of the future city of Sacramento, where Sutter planned to build his fort. Sutter took two pieces of artillery with him into the wilderness. When, after eight days, the company reached their destination, they found seven or eight hundred Indians awaiting them. Sutter prepared his party to resist attack, but the Indians were more curious than hostile and numbers of them ventured out on the river to greet the foreigners in *tule balsas* (fibrous raft floats). Reassured, Davis and Sutter landed near today's Sacramento and pitched tents. When Davis took leave of the group the next morning, Sutter fired a salute in honor of this departing guide. Upon hearing the noise of the cannon, hundreds of Indians crowded into Sutter's encampment. Large numbers of deer, also startled at the sound, ran crazily out of the nearby woods; "the howls of wolves and coyotes filled the air, and immense flocks of water fowl flew wildly about over the camp."

In the midst of this wilderness, Sutter began construction in 1840 of an outpost. He had, it will be recalled, purchased from the Russians at Fort Ross the bulk of their equipment and supplies. Sutter now constituted himself as guardian of the Sacramento frontier, setting up an adobe wall eighteen feet high by three feet thick, enclosing a rectangular fortress. Sutter named his colony New Helvetia, in honor of his homeland.

Naturalized as a Mexican citizen, and clothed with authority to administer justice, Sutter took steps to repress Indian hostilities and to check illegal trapping and fishing. The new leader won the respect of the local Indians, whom he employed along with the Hawaiians he had brought with him. On his vaguely bounded grant of eleven square leagues, Sutter combined the occupations of trapper, trader, farmer, stock raiser, merchant, military ruler, and feudal magnate, even threatening on one occasion to raise the French flag and to march on the government garrison at Sonoma. At another time he broadly intimated that he would brook no interference with his plans by Mexican officials. When Sutter wrote to an acquaintance about California's officialdom, including its military commandant, he hinted

sarcastically that if "this Rascle of Castro" should undertake to interfere with his activities, "a very warm and hearty welcome is prepared for him." Sutter could not afford to be more explicit, lest his
message be captured. In a letter to Jacob P. Leese, an American
trader, the Swiss referred to the ten guns and two field pieces he
kept in readiness to protect his fortress; Sutter added significantly,
if not grammatically, "I have also about 50 faithful Indians which
shot their musquet very quick."

Sutter's friendliness for Americans coming into California over the
Sierra passes irritated California's Mexican leaders. In his *Autobiography* he wrote: "I gave passports to those entering the country, and
this they did not like. I was friendly with the emigrants, of whom
they were jealous. I encouraged immigration, while they discouraged
it. I sympathized with the Americans while they hated them." Within
a short time Sutter boasted a barony at New Helvetia of thousands
of sheep, cattle, horses, and hogs that roamed over his principality.
He also developed a profitable trade in beaver skins and other agricultural products and acted the role of lord of all he surveyed.

Because New Helvetia was located on the main line of overland
immigration, it was a rendezvous for newcomers winding down the
trails from the the Sierra Nevada. The name of Captain Sutter became commonplace to these immigrants, to whom it stood for generosity and goodness of heart. Later the gold discovery that enriched
others proved to be the undoing of Sutter. His laborers were lured
away from workaday operations by the higher wages associated with
gold. The validity of his land titles under American law was also
questioned as squatter riots occurred on his lands in the 1850s. Sutter
was reduced from affluence and power to bankruptcy.

Bidwell and the First Overland Migrants

Sutter was not the only foreigner to settle in the interior with Mexican permission. "Doctor" John Marsh, a young Harvard graduate,
had reached California in 1836 with a company of Santa Fe trappers,
and had settled on a rancho in northern California near the base of
Mount Diablo. The publication of some of Marsh's letters in Missouri
newspapers stimulated Midwestern interest in California. Then the
trapper Antoine Robideaux, upon his return from there in 1840,
started a campaign of publicity on behalf of the Pacific province,
arousing excitement in the little frontier town of Weston, Missouri.
The trapper claimed he had found "a perfect paradise, a perpetual
spring" out West.

One spirited pioneer, a twenty-year-old school teacher named John
Bidwell, had become imbued with the idea of seeing the great West

and California. He helped to ready a migration party, though he "had barely means to buy a wagon, a gun, and provisions." By May 1, 1841, Bidwell's company consisted of forty-seven emigrants, three trappers, a group of Catholic missionaries, their wagon freighters, a lone Methodist minister, and various adventurers. Fifteen women and children were in the party. Paul Geddes was elected its president, John Bartleson captain, and Bidwell secretary. Thomas Fitzpatrick ("Broken Hand"), who had trapped in the Rocky Mountains and was headed for that area again, was the only person familiar with the country to be traversed. The missionaries, headed by the later re-nowned Jesuit Peter De Smet, were making the westward journey in order to establish a mission among the Flathead Indians.

On May 19, 1841, the motley caravan, known as "the first emigrant train to California," started on its dusty way from Sapling Grove, Missouri. First came the missionaries, with four carts and one wagon. Next in line of march were eight wagons drawn by horses and mules. Then came the last unit, consisting of five wagons drawn by seventeen yoke of oxen. As clerk, Bidwell kept a journal, especially valuable for its account of daily life in a wagon train. He also recorded such less routine matters as the creation of "a new family" en route, an event that occurred on June 1, 1841, when one Isaac Kelsey married a Miss Williams. A week later Bidwell wrote that eight or ten buffalo were killed, their bones giving the camp the appearance of "one complete slaughter yard." On June 22, the party reached Fort Lar-amie, moving on to Independence Rock, near the Sweetwater River, within present-day Wyoming. The emigrants next crossed South Pass toward the Bear River Valley and on July 11 reached the turn-off point of the Oregon Trail near Soda Springs. There Father De Smet, the guide Fitzpatrick, and about half the party departed for Fort Hall, fifty miles to the north. The rest, thirty-two in number, pro-ceeded on toward California.

Staggering through the alkali flats near the Great Salt Lake, with constant mirages ahead, the travelers jettisoned their heaviest pos-sessions, including furniture, washpans, butter churns, baggage, and even wagons. By September 16, Bidwell wrote that "All hands were busy making pack-saddles and getting ready to pack." No one in the party had experience in packing animals; one can only imagine a caravan of loose packs, frightened horses, kicking mules, and bel-lowing oxen accompanied by their footsore owners. Inexperienced and trail-weary, the group wandered for days through the Humboldt Valley and Carson Sink, in today's western Nevada, most of their provisions gone. Then one night Bartleson, a blundering and selfish person, with eight of the other men took the best horses and aban-doned the party of which he was ostensibly leader. Several days later these nine deserters shamefacedly returned to camp near the Walker

River, having failed to find a better route toward the Sierra crest. By that time Bidwell had calmly taken command.

After slaughtering their remaining oxen, and jerking and drying the meat for the trip ahead, the group began the ascent of the High Sierra mountain mass. As they traveled through deep snows, they carefully kept together. Bidwell's diary reports, of the twenty-eighth of October: "We ate the last of our beef this evening and killed a mule to finish our supper. Distance six miles." Two days later, to their great relief, the travelers "beheld a wide valley," and on the last day of the month they killed two antelope and some wild fowl. They had come to the edge of the Sacramento–San Joaquin Valley, which they estimated incorrectly as some hundreds of miles wide. They reached Marsh's ranch on November 4, 1841, almost six months after setting out from Sapling Grove.

John Bidwell quickly found employment under Sutter at New Helvetia. The qualities that had made him a trustworthy leader on the overland trail brought him renown as a prince among California pioneers.

Other American Homeseekers of the 1840s

During the early 1840s, hundreds of Americans entered California by various overland routes; many of these came in small parties from Missouri and Arkansas, with Independence, Missouri, being the most usual gathering point for the caravans. One of these groups, which departed for California at about the same time as Bidwell's party, was "the Workman-Rowland Company." This group encountered comparatively little hardship, as a result of their decision to take the Santa Fe Trail rather than the lesser-known northern route. They also wisely drove along flocks of sheep for daily sustenance and were in good physical shape when they came through Cajón Pass in California and arrived at Mission San Gabriel—only a little after Bidwell reached Marsh's ranch. Promptly upon arrival, John Rowland sought out the local Mexican authorities, presented them with a list of the names of his party, and declared his intention of obeying all legal requirements for settlers. Notwithstanding a previous warning against emigration to California, these Americans were given a welcome by local residents. The ease with which some of them also received large grants of land encouraged others to immigrate.

Still another expedition across the mountains into California was that of the Chiles–Walker party in 1843. Led by the trapper Joseph Reddeford Walker and by Joseph B. Chiles, who had been with Bidwell's 1841 expedition, the main party came from Missouri by way of Fort Boise, and proceeded southwestward across the Sierra toward the Owens Valley. After encountering many obstacles, the company reached Walker River, Walker Lake, and then Owens Lake. At that point, because of the weakened condition of the animals, the travelers abandoned their wagons. About Christmas they reached the Salinas River, and continued on to the lower Santa Clara Valley. This party and such other pioneer groups as that of Lansford W. Hastings, which entered California from Oregon in 1843, scattered to different points as homeseekers after arrival.

In May of 1844, another party, the Stevens–Murphy group, left the Missouri River and proceeded to Fort Hall. About half of them decided to go to Oregon. The remainder—including about twenty women and children—headed toward California; they reached the Humboldt Sink about the first of November, to enter the High Sierra region. The first snow had made its appearance. Instead of pursuing the route along Walker River, they broke a new path into California. So great were the difficulties encountered, however, that three of the men were left at Donner Lake. Not until the middle of the following March did the last members reach the California rancho settlements.

During 1845, half a dozen more sizable groups traveled westward from the Missouri frontier. These companies included the Grigsby–Ide party, consisting of fifty men with their families, and the Hastings–Semple party, which reached Sutter's Fort on Christmas Day. In the latter group was Robert Semple, a six-and-a-half-foot Kentuckian who was to become editor of California's first English-language newspaper and president of its first constitutional convention.

By word of mouth, and through newspapers, magazines, and pamphlets, an uncoordinated publicity campaign developed, coaxing immigrants from all parts of the United States over the Western trails. Frequently small parties, meeting on the plains, joined forces to travel in long trains together for weeks on end. Early in 1846, Sutter, the master of New Helvetia, predicted the arrival of more than a thousand Americans that season.

It is impossible to trace the movements of the numerous parties of overland immigrants that year, or even to record all their leaders. Vivid portrayals of the experiences of these homeseekers are in such books as Edwin Bryant's *What I Saw in California* (1848) and Jessy Thornton's *Oregon and California . . .* (1849). During 1846 a number of Americans also reached California by water. Conspicuous among these was the party headed by the Mormon leader Samuel Brannan, who entered the Golden Gate with colonists on the last day of July. Part of the group had intended to go on to Salt Lake City, where Brigham Young planned to build a new Zion of Mormonism. During the voyage two children were born on board the *Brooklyn*, the ship which Brannan had chartered—one, a boy, named Atlantic; the other, a girl, christened Pacific.

Out of a total of 7,000 persons who migrated to the Pacific Coast during the years from 1843 to 1846, the number of immigrants who actually entered California probably did not exceed 1,500. The early settlers were generally more attracted by the Oregon territory.

Frémont

By 1842 the days of the mountain men had begun to wane. As independent trappers settled down to a life of trading, an era of exploration, shaped by government survey parties, began. In this new period the United States Army's Topographical Engineers played a large role. The year 1843–1844 saw the arrival in California of John C. Frémont, naturalist-explorer-scientist, on his second expedition to the Far West. Frémont's guide was Kit Carson. It was not the direct purpose of the Frémont expedition to induce homeseekers to emigrate toward the Pacific; nevertheless, Frémont produced a number of maps of the West that had precisely that effect. Furthermore, Frémont's father-in-law was the powerful Senator Thomas Hart Benton, an avowed expansionist who had backed his ambitious plans for exploration of the farthest West.

Frémont reached Fort Hall on September 19, 1843. From there his party proceeded by way of the Snake River to Fort Boise, down the Dalles, and via the Columbia to Fort Vancouver, where provisions for three months were laid in. Then Frémont returned to the Dalles. His intention was to explore Klamath Lake and to search for "a reported lake called Mary's, at some days' journey in the great basin; and thence still on southeast to the reputed Buenaventura River." Moving through northwestern Nevada, Frémont continued to the Truckee and Carson Rivers. He originally had no plans to cross the Sierra Nevada into California, but on reaching the mountains rashly decided to take his weary men over them. While ascending the eastern slope of the Sierra, on January 29, 1844, he found it necessary to discard a twelve-pound brass howitzer which his party, ostensibly a scientific venture, had lugged along.

After an icy crossing of the Sierra, Frémont's men reached Sutter's Fort, or New Helvetia, via Carson Pass, early in March. Frémont rested several weeks at New Helvetia, then moved southward along the San Joaquin Valley to the Kings River. He next crossed Tehachapi Pass toward the Great Salt Lake and returned to Saint Louis. The explorer's official report, thousands of copies of which were printed and eagerly read, brought Frémont new fame. Historians, however, continue to differ over whether he was truly "the West's greatest adventurer," "a man unafraid," the "pathmarker of the West"—as his biographers have called Frémont—or whether he was merely a follower of other men's trails under government auspices. Although his first entry into California was almost accidental, and scarcely a new venture, Frémont mapped, surveyed, and charted the trails of the trappers, publicizing their routes and attracting more overland travelers to the West. He also stirred up controversy over his third expedition, in 1845–1846, and came to embroil himself deeply in the American conquest of California, as we shall see.

The Donner Tragedy

In the spring of 1846 James F. Reed of Springfield, Illinois, with George and Jacob Donner, formed an emigrant party doomed to play a tragic role in the history of the American West. The struggles of this first overland train from Illinois were due in part to the in-eptness and lack of force of George Donner, who became nominal head of the group. Bad luck as well as bad judgment plagued the enterprise, although some of its participants displayed notable her-oism in the midst of disaster. Included in the party were well-to-do farmers and poor families, persons of learning and ignorant folk, descendants of colonial stock, as well as Irish and German emigrants. A disproportionate number of elderly people, women, and young-sters were among them, and the group was shy of able-bodied men.

The Donners prepared to join an Oregon caravan, proceed with it to Fort Hall, then branch into central California. The company's outfit included seed and implements for farming, and bolts of bright cotton cloth, handkerchiefs, flannels, beads, earrings, laces, and silks for trading with the Indians. The most important equipment con-sisted of large, strongly constructed wagons, whose curved frames were covered with tent cloth. The party also brought along livestock, as well as more than $10,000 in cash "stitched between the folds of a quilt for safe transportation."

The group was astir before dawn on April 15, and by noon the emigrants were well started on their trip. They reached the Missis-sippi within a few days; on May 11, in the best of spirits, they made camp at Independence. During early June all continued to go well. From a point near the junction of the North and South Platte, Mrs. George Donner wrote, "We are now four hundred and fifty miles from Independence. . . . I could never have believed we could have traveled so far with so little difficulty. The prairie between the Blue and the Platte rivers is beautiful beyond description." The travelers celebrated the Fourth of July in patriotic style, with songs, a reading of the Declaration of Independence, and an address by one of the

men in the party. Not the slightest hint of misfortune had yet occurred.

At Fort Bridger the leaders of the caravan decided to follow the
amateurish advice of Lansford W. Hastings's *an Emigrant's Guide to
Oregon and California* (1845), which decribed a new route to California, allegedly 200 miles shorter than by way of Fort Hall. This route,
"Hastings Cut-off" (which Hastings had never seen), terminated eight
miles west of today's Elko, Nevada. It ran south of the Great Salt
Lake via Fort Bridger and joined the California Trail on the Humboldt River. The illusory cutoff turned out to be a nightmare for the
Donner party.

On July 20, the Donners broke camp and plunged into an unknown
wilderness. Along an almost impassable route, they fought their way
through the Wasatch Mountains. At times the party was compelled
to use ten yoke of oxen to draw a single wagon up the sides of a
steep gulch. The emigrants were a month—instead of a week, as they
had planned—in reaching the shores of the Great Salt Lake. The loss
of time proved costly. West of Salt Lake it became apparent that the
supplies would give out before the group could reach California. Two
members of the party, Charles Stanton and William McCutcheon,
volunteered to proceed on horseback to procure food from Sutter's
Fort. Because of lack of water the party left thirty-six head of cattle
on the desert. A mirage, revealing the waters of a lake, turned disappointment into anguish. Return to Fort Bridger was impossible;
there was no alternative but to continue onward.

The tension increased when John Snyder inadvertently struck the
wife of James F. Reed with a bull whip. Reed, enraged, stabbed
Snyder to death; he then used the boards from his wagon to make
a coffin for the dead man. The Donner party passed a severe judgment on the murderer, who cried out that he had acted in self-
defense. There on the remote desert floor of Western America, miles
from the nearest habitation, Reed's companions forced him to leave
the train. With his gun and a few provisions he set out alone for
California. Each day thereafter Reed's wife and children looked for
traces of him along the way—the feathers of a bird killed, or an
occasional note pinned onto a bush. They wondered whether he
might be scalped by Indians, or whether he would ever make it alone
to some frontier outpost. The Donner party had banished one of its
most needed members.

In the Sierra Nevadas winter was coming on fast. Instead of pressing forward, the party tarried four days for a badly needed rest.
Truckee Meadows, near the present city of Reno, Nevada, was covered with grasses and clover of good quality. It was difficult to leave
such security behind and proceed toward the unknown. On October
19, Stanton returned from Sutter's Fort with two Indian guides,

seven mules, and limited amounts of beef and flour. He had left his sick companion, McCutcheon, behind with Captain Sutter. Three days later the Donners crossed the winding Truckee River "for the forty-ninth and last time in eighty miles." The party moved northward through barely passable canyons. Clouds high on the mountain crest gave a clear indication of approaching winter, and there was a nip in the air. As they moved into higher elevations their wagons could not be dragged through the early snows that fell in the Sierra that year. One wagon broke its axle and tipped over onto little Eliza Donner, three years old, and Georgia, age four; the children were almost crushed by the avalanche of household goods that fell upon them. There was further delay as the party repacked provisions onto cumbersome oxen.

A stormy winter descended upon upper Alder Creek almost a month early. One part of their train bogged down in the snow near today's Donner Lake. Another small remnant holed up under brush and canvas sheets about six miles away. There they waited four months until early spring, sheltered only by snow-covered pines on one of the Sierra's windiest passes. The snow that winter reached a depth of twenty-two feet. Scattered into small clusters, the Donners made repeated efforts to get out of the mountains. They improvised snowshoes from oxbows and strips of rawhide. In mid-December 1846, a party known as "The Fifteen" left the rest behind. After weeks of severe suffering, dazed and stumbling about in the snow, seven survivors emerged via Emigrant Gap.

On the nineteenth of February, 1847, those left behind on the Sierra crest were startled by shouts. The strongest of them, climbing to the top of a huge snow bank, witnessed the "most welcome sight of their lives"—a reconnaissance party of seven men, reprovisioned by Sutter, composed of formerly snowed-in survivors. Each bore a pack. Even Reed, banished earlier, arrived with a second relief group to save some of the very men who had cast him out. He was overjoyed to find his wife and four children still alive. Suddenly a third contingent appeared. By then George Donner was too weak and sick to travel. His wife refused to leave her husband, allowing her little daughters to be taken from her to safety. When the fourth and last relief party arrived in the spring they found that Mrs. Donner too had died. Only forty-five of the seventy-nine persons in the original Donner party survived.

No one knows the full extent of the harrowing experiences endured during their battle against freezing and starvation. Writers sympathetic to the Donner party later denied allegations of cannibalism, but apparently almost all of the marooned pioneers who survived ate the flesh of dead trailmates. An American naval officer in

California at the time, Henry Augustus Wise, described cannibalism among the Donners almost too graphically:

> . . . . The survivors were found rolling in filth, parents eating their own offspring . . . exchanging limbs and meat—little children tearing and devouring the hearts of the dead, and a general apathy and mania pervaded all alike. . . . One Dutchman actually ate a full-grown body in 36 hours; another boiled and devoured a girl nine years old in a single night. The women held onto life with greater tenacity than the men— in fact the first intelligence was . . . by two girls. One of them feasted on her good papa, but on making soup of her lover's head, she confessed to some inward qualms. . . . A young Spaniard, Baptiste . . . told me that he ate Jake Donner and the baby: 'eat baby raw, stewed some of Jake and roasted his head, not good meat, taste like sheep with rot; but, sir, very hungry, eat anything.' These were his very words.

A mixture of individualism, religious conviction, and incurable nationalism led such pioneers to believe it was their "manifest destiny" to build a new world beyond the mountains in California. "Here was a country," wrote Walter Colton in 1846, "where furlongs stretch into leagues." If only all this land could soon become a part of the United States! As tension between their country and Mexico mounted, American settlers naturally harbored such thoughts. The rate of American migration to California in the 1840s seemed almost to forecast its future control by *Yanquis*.

"Doctor" Marsh's estimate of California's population for 1845 included 7,000 persons of Spanish blood and 10,000 domesticated Indians. In addition, Marsh calculated that foreigners in the province numbered 700 Americans; 100 English, Scotch, and Irish; and another 100 Germans, French, and Italians. The American group far outnumbered all others combined.

Selected Readings

Regarding the overland fur trade see Hiram Martin Chittenden, *The History of the American Fur Trade of the Far West* (3 vols., New York, 1902), Paul C. Phillips, *The Fur Trade* (2 vols., Norman, Okla., 1961), and Robert Glass Cleland, *This Reckless Breed of Men* (New York, 1950). References concerning individual trappers include Joseph J. Hill, "Ewing Young in the Fur Trade of the American Southwest," *Oregon Historical Quarterly* 24 (March 1923), 1–35; T. D. Bonner, *Life and Adventures of James P. Beckwourth* (New York, 1856); Charles L. Camp, ed., *James Clyman: American Frontiersman* (San Francisco, 1928); William Henry Ellison, ed., *The Life and Adventures of George Nidever* (Berkeley, 1937); Alpheus H. Favour, *Old Bill Williams, Mountain Man*

(Chapel Hill, 1936); and *The Personal Narrative of James Ohio Pattie of Kentucky,* edited by Timothy Flint (Cincinnati, 1831). Richard Batman's *American Ecclesiastes: The Stories of James Pattie* (New York, 1985) unravels conflicting tales spun by Pattie and Timothy Flint. Stanton A. Coblentz, *The Swallowing Wilderness* (New York, 1961), a biography of Pattie, regrettably, has no index, bibliography, or scholarly apparatus. See also Clifton B. Kroeber, ed., "The Route of James Ohio Pattie on the Colorado in 1826: A Reappraisal by A. L. Kroeber," *Arizona and The West* 6 (Summer 1964), 119–36, and Rosemary K. Valle's "James Ohio Pattie and the Alta California Measles Epidemic," *California Historical Quarterly* 52 (Spring 1973), 28–36.

Iris Wilson, *William Wolfskill, 1798–1866: Frontier Trapper to California Ranchero* (Glendale, 1965) tells how one mountain man refound himself in a new setting. Others are examined in LeRoy Hafen, ed., *The Mountain Men and the Fur Trade of the Far West* (6 vols., Glendale, 1965–68). W. J. Ghent has written a life of Thomas Fitzpatrick entitled *Broken Hand* (New York, 1931). Doyce B. Nunis has dealt with Andrew Sublette in *Andrew Sublette: Rocky Mountain Prince, 1813–1835* (Los Angeles, 1960).

Other volumes on the fur trade are Bernard De Voto, *Across the Wide Missouri* (Cambridge, Mass. 1947), and Lewis H. Garrard, *Wah-to-Yah and the Taos Trail* (Cincinnati, 1850). George F. Ruxton, *Life in the Far West* (New York, 1859), is a novel that reproduces aspects of the fur trade. For an account of the Hudson's Bay Company in California see Alice Bay Maloney, *Fur Brigade to the Bonaventura* (San Francisco, 1945), and her earlier article, "Peter Skene Ogden's Trapping Expedition to the Gulf of California, 1829–30," California Historical Society *Quarterly* 19 (December 1940), 308–16. More on the Hudson's Bay Company in California is in Dorothy Blakey Smith, ed., *James Douglas in California, 1841* (Vancouver, 1965). A personal view of the fur trade, touching also upon California, is in Sir George Simpson, *Narrative of a Journey Round the World, During the Years 1841 and 1842* (2 vols., London, 1849). A. C. Laut, *The Story of the Trapper* (New York, 1902), is informative.

Sutter's autobiography, in German, is entitled *Neu-Helvetien: Lebenserinnerungen des Generals Johann Augustus Sutter* (Frauenfeld, Switzerland, 1944). Consult also Erwin G. Gudde, *Sutter's Own Story* (New York, 1936). Secondary accounts are James Peter Zollinger, *Sutter: The Man and His Empire* (New York, 1939); the less valuable work by Julian Dana, *Sutter of California* (New York, 1938); and Marguerite Eyer Wilbur, *John Sutter: Rascal and Adventurer* (New York, 1949). See also John A. Hawgood, "John Augustus Sutter: A Reappraisal," *Arizona and the West* 4 (Winter 1962), 345–56.

A biography of Bidwell has been written by Rockwell D. Hunt under the title *John Bidwell: Prince of California Pioneers* (Caldwell,

Idaho, 1942). Bidwell's own *Echoes of the Past,* edited by Milo M. Quaife (Chicago, 1928), and reprinted as *In California Before the Gold Rush* (Los Angeles, 1948), also gives one a picture of the first overland emigrant party to California, as do Edwin Bryant, *What I Saw in California* (New York, 1848), and J. A. Thornton, *Oregon and California in 1848* (2 vols., New York, 1849). An account of an overland expedition of 1843 is Overton Johnson and William H. Winter, *Route Across the Rocky Mountains* (Princeton, N.J., 1932). Marsh's role in receiving these overland parties is discussed in the biography by George D. Lyman, *Dr. John Marsh, Pioneer* (New York, 1930).

Thomas F. Andrews, "The Controversial Hastings Overland Guide: A Reassessment," *Pacific Historical Review* 37 (February 1968), 21–34, restores to that source some of the influence denied it by later historians.

A mine of information about the Donner tragedy, including diaries and correspondence of survivors (among them Patrick Breen and James F. Reed), is in Dale Morgan, ed., *Overland in 1846; Diaries and Letters of the California-Oregon Trail* (2 vols., Georgetown, Calif., 1963). See also C. F. McGlashan, *History of the Donner Party: A Tragedy of the Sierra* (Stanford, 1940, 1947); George R. Stewart, *Ordeal by Hunger: The Story of the Donner Party* (New York, 1936, 1960); and Walter M. Stookey, *Fatal Decision: The Tragic Story of the Donner Party* (Salt Lake City, 1950). A firsthand account is Eliza P. Donner Houghton's *The Expedition of the Donner Party* (Los Angeles, 1920). Virginia Murphy Reed, "Across the Plains in the Donner Party," *Century Magazine* 42 (May–October 1891), 409–26, is by the daughter of James F. Reed, who was banished from the party; she infers that virtually every family "was forced to eat human flesh to keep body and soul together." This confirms W. H. A. Wise, *Los Gringos, or an inside view of Mexico and California* (New York, 1849), 74–5. On the Donner route see David E. Miller, "The Donner Road through the Great Salt Lake Desert," *Pacific Historical Review* 27 (February 1958), 30–44, as well as George Keithley, *The Donner Party* (New York, 1972).

Overland trail maps with accompanying narrative are in J. Gregg Layne's *Western Wayfaring: Routes of Exploration and Trade in the American Southwest* (Los Angeles, 1954). Consult also George R. Stewart, *The California Trail* (New York, 1962).

CHAPTER 14

American Conquest

AMERICAN SENTIMENT for the acquisition of California had deep roots. As early as 1829 President Andrew Jackson had sent Anthony Butler as his envoy into Mexico to negotiate for the purchase of territory in the American Southwest. Butler's suggestion of a bribe that would lead to the acquisition of California, Texas, and New Mexico offended the Mexicans, and he returned home in disgrace. The idea of adding California to American territory, however, was never abandoned by Jackson, nor by his successors, Presidents Van Buren, Tyler, and Polk. The strategic location of San Francisco Bay alone, with its matchless harbor and rich surrounding country, greatly impressed all of these presidents.

Furthermore, the laxity of Mexican control over the province made it obvious that California might well fall into the hands of some outside power. The Russians had, of course, by 1842 withdrawn from their trading post in California, but other countries continued to take a keen interest in the future of the province. Even Prussia, as historians have recently discovered, had an acquisitive eye on California. French interest in the territory had been whetted by the voyages of La Pérouse and Eugene Deflot de Mofras. In 1841 Vallejo wrote Governor Alvarado, "There is little doubt that France is intriguing to become mistress of California." De Mofras, as a matter of fact, had expressed his explicit opinion that "a French protectorate offers to California the most satisfactory way of escape from the dangers that threaten its future." The account of his explorations made careful note of the number of Frenchmen residing at different points in the territory and emphasized the foreign character of Sutter's New Helvetia.

England's interest in California, as well as Texas and Oregon, was even stronger than France's. James Alexander Forbes, British consul

at Monterey, had sent strong suggestions to the British Foreign Office
that California be acquired by the Crown. Although an English invasion was never imminent, one can understand the anxiety of the
Californians. In 1846 they became apprehensive at the news that
Father Eugene McNamara, a Catholic priest, proposed to plant a
colony of one thousand Irish and English Catholic families in the San
Francisco Bay region. McNamara's purposes were stated to be those
of advancing the cause of Catholicism and of preventing usurpation
of California by the United States—"an irreligious and anti-Catholic
nation." Father McNamara never fulfilled his plan, and it has never
been explained how English imperial aspirations were supposed to
have been reconciled with these Irish Catholic ambitions.

Deepening United States Involvement

Two events that had occurred in California in 1839 and in 1840 were
significant in terms of the American position there—the founding of
Sutter's fort at New Helvetia, and the arrest of former trapper Isaac
Graham. Sutter's presence astride the overland trails became a definite threat to Mexico's authority in the interior. Graham's internment, along with that of his rough associates, preceded stationing of
United States naval forces in California waters. Under President Tyler a movement for purchase of the province became more definite.
A United States diplomat, Waddy Thompson, pointed out the advantages of possessing San Francisco Bay, calling it "capacious enough
to receive the navies of all the world." He contended, "It will be
worth a war of twenty years to prevent England from acquiring it."

In 1842 the Stars and Stripes had already momentarily supplanted
the Mexican eagle in California; Commodore Jones had, as previously
noted, raised the American flag over Monterey in the mistaken belief
that the United States was at war with Mexico. Although Secretary
of State Daniel Webster tendered the Mexican government a formal
apology, the embarrassing episode revealed that the United States
did not intend to be caught unprepared in any race between the
great powers to acquire California.

President James K. Polk was elected on a platform favoring annexation of Texas and settlement of the Oregon boundary with England. Implicit in the platform was strong interest in California. In
1845, when Polk came into office, foreign governments began to
understand that the United States was committed to an expansionist
policy; interference with American plans might cause war. At Monterey, Polk relied upon an alert consul, Thomas Oliver Larkin, to
send confidential reports about local conditions. The president wanted

Larkin to prepare the groundwork for peaceful American penetration.

Polk first hoped to attempt the purchase of California. If he should fail, there were three other possibilities: (1) a revolt instigated by leading Californians against Mexico, aided by American residents; (2) patient delay, while the province was occupied by more Americans; and (3) seizure in a war with Mexico. Polk's aggressive policy involved the appointment of John Slidell as his official representative in Mexico, partly to explore the possibility of purchasing or annexing Texas, California, and New Mexico. United States failure in negotiations for the Southwestern territories was due as much to disturbed internal Mexican political conditions as to Mexico's unwillingness to sell, although the Mexicans did regard the giving up these territories to Yankees as demeaning.

After the failure of the Slidell mission at the end of 1845, and American annexation of Texas that year, Mexican-American diplomatic negotiations deteriorated steadily. Mexico greatly resented this "seizure" of one of its provinces although, since 1836, the Texans had proclaimed themselves independent. On April 15, 1846, Mexican forces entered the disputed territory between the Nueces and the Rio Grande rivers. President Polk's administration now requested a declaration of war from Congress. This was forthcoming on May 12, 1846. When General Zachary Taylor crossed the Mexican border, the action inflamed the Southwest from Texas to California.

Frémont and Hawk's Peak

Frémont, aware that war with Mexico over territorial conflicts in the Southwest was possible, had left St. Louis in May 1845 with his third expedition. Its purpose, further exploration of the Great Basin and the Pacific Coast, was not likely to relieve the tension between the two countries. With a party of sixty-two soldiers, scouts, topographers, and six Delaware Indians, Frémont again crossed the Sierra to Sutter's Fort, reaching California on December 9, 1845. This time he traveled as far as Monterey, where he held a conference with Consul Larkin. José Castro, who commanded the garrison at the capital city, was suspicious of the motives that had brought Frémont there. Frémont explained that his expedition was scientific and peaceful, and that he had come to Monterey only to purchase needed supplies. Castro gave the expedition permission to winter in California, with the understanding that Frémont would keep his men away from the coastal settlements.

In early March 1846, Frémont demonstrated his flair for the dramatic. He withdrew toward a bluff named Gavilan, or Hawk's Peak, where he built a log fortification overlooking the Salinas Valley, only twenty-five miles from Monterey. Even after a warning from Castro, he raised the American flag, as if to defy expulsion from the province. At first Frémont ignored the possibility of trouble. Then a warning letter from Larkin, and the realization that Castro seemed to be preparing to dislodge him, persuaded Frémont to vacate Hawk's Peak "slowly and growlingly" and move his men northward toward the Oregon wilds. Frémont's rashness embarrassed Larkin and other American residents, who hoped for annexation of California by quiet, behind-the-scenes contacts. The feelings of California officials toward the United States, furthermore, were outraged by the incident at Hawk's Peak.

On his way north the young commander was overtaken by Lieutenant Archibald H. Gillespie, a United States Marine Corps officer who had crossed Mexico in disguise. He produced secret messages from officials in Washington, including Secretary of State James Buchanan, as well as from Frémont's wife, Jessie Benton, and her father, Thomas Hart Benton, the expansionist chairman of the United States Senate Committee on Territories. Verbal instructions from President Polk may well have been given Frémont as well. Historians will never be able to determine the precise orders Frémont was given.

Whatever the content of the communications he received, the effect of them was to turn him back southward toward California. Gillespie's dispatches probably warned that war with Mexico was inevitable and, in effect, directed Frémont to cooperate with land and naval forces of the United States. Concerning the messages from Benton, Frémont later wrote: "I was to *act*, discreetly but positively.

Frémont's decision to return to the Sacramento Valley transformed him from explorer into soldier. He has been strongly criticized for his conduct, and it is conceded he was wanting in tact. Yet the vague governmental instructions under which he was acting hardly specified what his relationship should be with the aggressive little group of Americans that had settled in California's Central Valley. As he approached the Marysville (now Sutter) Buttes, sixty miles north of Sutter's Fort, Americans flocked into his camp. All were disturbed and excited by rumors of approaching war between the United States and Mexico, but they were in the dark regarding United States intentions. They imagined that a band of Californians, intent upon expelling foreigners, planned to take over Sutter's Fort, their rallying point. For this reason they enthusiastically welcomed Frémont. The explorer, however, placed himself in an extremely delicate position. He had no instructions to support a revolt among American settlers in California. However, he did not want to see an incipient uprising dissolved, with Americans driven out of the province for lack of his support.

The Bear Flag Revolt

The fears of the disturbed settlers near Frémont's camp continued to mount. Even the conservative Consul Larkin wrote Secretary of State Buchanan that he refused to predict the course of events. Encouraged by Frémont, some of the Americans were spoiling for a fight. Sutter and Larkin were appalled by the conduct of these leatherjacketed frontier ruffians who saw themselves in the role of American patriots. Yet, neither Sutter nor Larkin would have accused them of lacking courage; instead, they considered them lacking in judgment.

Early in June 1846, the frontiersmen heard that a large *caballada*, or bank of horses, which José Castro had obtained from Vallejo, was being driven from Sonoma to the Santa Clara Valley by Mexican officials, via Sutter's Fort. The frontiersmen thought these horses were destined for use against the American settlers, as part of a movement for their expulsion. With the knowledge, if not the sanction, of Frémont, the ruffians intercepted the horses and took them to Frémont's camp. Sutter, anxious to avoid hostilities with the Californians, was disgusted by Frémont's support of these quarrelsome Americans in what appeared to be a warlike act.

A few days later, the Americans plotted the capture of General Vallejo's headquarters in northern California, at Sonoma. Vallejo was known to be a supporter of Americans in California. In fact, Consul Larkin had counted upon Vallejo's prestige with both the native population and settlers to help smooth the annexation of California to the United States. At dawn on June 14, the frontiersmen burst into Vallejo's home and routed the general from his bed. By their behavior, which included gulping down his brandy, they offended and confused his family and personal entourage. "To whom shall we surrender?" asked the general's wife, unable to comprehend the commotion. The Americans forced the humiliated Vallejo to sign vague articles of surrender and placed him and members of his entourage under arrest. They were taken to Sutter's Fort, much to the chagrin of the old Swiss.

As a result of his boldness at Sonoma, William B. Ide emerged as leader of the American revolt. His followers provided themselves a flag with which to dignify their movement. They would have liked to use the American Stars and Stripes, but Frémont would not authorize them to do so, however much he sympathized with them. Therefore, Ide and his men improvised a red and white banner on which a grizzly bear faced a red star. The grizzly was the strongest animal in California. The framers of this crude ensign wrote about it, "A bear stands his ground always, and as long as the stars shine we stand for the cause." On the day they captured Sonoma, the Bear Flaggers raised their standard over its plaza. They spoke of themselves thereafter as representatives of the "California Republic," and made Sonoma their base. On June 24 they engaged in a relatively bloodless skirmish with the Californians between the pueblos of San Rafael and Sonoma. The engagement received the name "Battle of Olompali" but it was unimportant, except in consolidating the position of the Bear Flaggers.

Ide's men desired to be known as other than a band of filibusters. He therefore issued a proclamation giving his "inviolable pledge" that all persons "not found under arms" should remain undisturbed. The extralegal situation of the Bear Flaggers had become daily more evident. This independent group had staged a revolt far more severe than the Graham Affair half a decade before. To what lengths this revolution might have gone will, however, never be known. The Bear Flag movement came to a sudden halt when the American flag was officially raised at Sonoma after the capture of Monterey on July 7, 1846, by the naval forces of Commodore John Drake Sloat. (Sloat had heard of the outbreak of war early in June while anchored at Mazatlán, on the west coast of Mexico, and had quietly slipped out of that harbor and proceeded to California.) When the American ensign replaced the short-lived Bear Flag, the "California Republic" was terminated. Late in July the American military command nullified the actions of the Bear Flaggers, and Vallejo and his fellow prisoners were ordered released.

Provincial pride and historical romanticism created the legend that the Bear Flag Revolt produced an independent California, which then became part of the United States. Actually, the Bear Flag uprising was of limited significance in the acquisition of California; its conquest would have occurred anyway.

Early Success

One American who played a significant part in the conquest of California was Consul Larkin. He had come to the province as early as 1832 and had developed a thriving trading business along the coast. Following his appointment as United States consul in 1843, Larkin had kept his government informed as to conditions in California, with which he became thoroughly familiar. Larkin's policy was always conciliatory but faithful to his country's interests. His consular dispatches constitute a rich source of information about a confusing period in California history.

Commodore Sloat, as commander of United States naval forces in Pacific waters, had been instructed to seize various California harbors in the event of war with Mexico. He had learned from Larkin of the

Hawk's Peak incident involving Frémont; believing hostilities to be imminent, he had, early in June 1846, ordered naval forces toward Monterey to establish American control there. He set out eventually with them, in the flagship *Savannah*. At Monterey, Sloat received official dispatches and held extended conferences with Consul Larkin. These concerned revolutionary sentiment in California, the capture of General Vallejo, the Bear Flag uprising, and the activities of Frémont. Since Sloat did not at once raise the American flag, he has been charged with indecision. However, he had no idea by what authority Frémont had been acting, nor had he been informed as to the import of the messages that Gillespie had brought that commander. Yet Sloat had knowledge of hostilities in Texas along the Nueces River, even though he had not been officially notified of any formal declaration of war by Washington.

At 10 A.M. on July 7, 1846, Sloat landed some 250 marines and seamen at Monterey under Captain William Mervine. They marched directly to the customhouse, where the commodore's proclamation was read, the United States flag raised and cheered, and a salute of twenty-one guns fired from each American vessel. A week later the flag of the United States was flying at Yerba Buena, at Sutter's Fort, at Bodega, and at Sonoma, headquarters of the Bear Flaggers. Sloat's landing came just in time to prevent that group from further military action, which might have proved disastrous.

On July 15, 1846, Commodore Robert F. Stockton arrived at Monterey on the *Congress*, to replace Sloat. The new commander's vigorous actions were in contrast with Sloat's moderation. Stockton issued a more belligerent proclamation than Sloat's. This one announced that Stockton planned to march "against these boasting and abusive chiefs" of the interior and southern districts. Stockton reorganized the forces of Frémont, which included some of the Bear Flaggers, on a wartime footing. Although himself a naval officer, Stockton promoted Brevet Captain Frémont to the rank of major. Frémont then enlisted volunteers from the American settlers into a unit called the California Battalion of Mounted Riflemen, and, acting under naval orders, joined Stockton in a spectacular initial capture of much of the province. "We simply marched all over California, from Sonoma to San Diego," wrote John Bidwell afterward, "and raised the American flag without protest. We tried to find an enemy, but could not." This success was possible because the Californians had no organized army worthy of the name; Castro's immediate forces numbered scarcely a hundred men, disaffected and almost without arms. But Castro threatened that if Americans marched on Los Angeles they would find their grave.

Reversal

On the afternoon of August 13, 1846, American naval forces entered
Los Angeles and raised their flag without opposition. Stockton had
concluded what may be called the first conquest of California. Gillespie, the courier who had met Frémont with messages from Washington, now a captain, was left in command of Los Angeles with a
garrison of but fifty men. In enforcing an unrealistic local curfew
imposed by Commodore Stockton, he displayed an attitude of intolerance toward the Angeleños. Tact and friendliness would have
been more powerful weapons. Resentment at Gillespie's threats of
punishment stirred up the natives. With the encouragement of firebrand leaders, they proceeded from irritation to insurrection. On
September 23, Gillespie's small garrison was surrounded on a hilltop
in the middle of Los Angeles by several hundred excited citizens
determined to hold onto southern California. Besieged and short of
water, Gillespie was in a perilous situation. Under cover of darkness
he sent a courier on the long journey northward for aid from Commodore Stockton. The daring ride of an American soldier, reputedly
Swedish-born, has become almost legendary. This Paul Revere of
California history covered the distance between Los Angeles and San
Francisco in four and a half days. The dispatch he carried was written
on cigarette papers and concealed in his long hair. He was pursued
for miles by California horsemen, but kept riding. Despite lack of
sleep and difficulty in securing fresh horses, he finally delivered Gillespie's message of distress to Commodore Stockton.

That commander immediately ordered aid to Gillespie, and Captain William Mervine set sail for southern California with 350 men.
On October 7, 1846, his vessel, the *Vandalia*, dropped anchor at San
Pedro, outside Los Angeles. He was almost too late. Captain Gillespie's hilltop position had become untenable. Gillespie virtually surrendered to the Californians but had been allowed to retreat with
his men to San Pedro and to depart by sea when they reached that
port. Gillespie, however, promptly set aside the hasty agreement with
the Californians when he saw the new American military forces.

There followed "The Battle of the Old Woman's Gun," on the
nearby Dominguez Rancho. In this conflict the Californians fought
under the command of José Antonio Carrillo. They were mounted
on horses and armed with sharp willow lances and smooth-bore car-
bines; their most damaging weapon, however, was a four-pound cannon. This antique firearm, which had been hidden by an old woman
during the first American assault on Los Angeles, was tied with leather
reatas, or thongs, to the tongue and wheels of a mud wagon. The
cannon was whipped up and down a hillock facing the Americans
with great effectiveness. The Americans were forced to retreat to

their ships, having suffered five killed and a number wounded. They buried their dead on a small island near San Pedro, thenceforth known as "Dead Man's Island."

Anti-American opposition spread, and for a time the territory from Santa Barbara to San Diego was again in the hands of the Californians. Frémont had landed at San Diego from the U.S.S. *Cyane*, raised the American flag, and taken possession of that pueblo; he had then returned to Monterey. Further resistance broke out in southern California, however, and Stockton proceeded south while Frémont was raising reinforcements in Monterey.

At San Diego, Stockton began planning an attack on the "horse-covered" hills toward the north. Suddenly an important message arrived which modified not only his plans but the entire course of events in California. This was a desperate dispatch from General Stephen Watts Kearny. The War Department had ordered Kearny to proceed overland with an "Army of the West" from Fort Leavenworth, Kansas. He was to seize Santa Fe in New Mexico, then to move toward California. On Kearny's march of more than 1,000 miles from Sante Fe, he was accompanied by 300 men of the First United States Dragoons. These troops were followed by another company of dragoons and 500 members of an enlisted Mormon Battalion.

En route, General Kearny met the celebrated scout Kit Carson. Carson had taken part in the first stage of the conquest of California and was taking dispatches from Stockton eastward to Washington. These optimistic messages informed President Polk that Stockton had extended American control over the whole of Mexican California. Carson, who had left before renewed fighting in southern California broke out, told Kearny that the American flag was flying from every important position in California, that the war had ended, and that Mexican control of that province was over. Kearny decided to send a large share of his force back to Santa Fe, while he continued on toward California with about 100 dragoons and two small howitzers. Because Carson was such an experienced guide, Kearny turned him around and took him west. The general sent Stockton's dispatches eastward with one of his own scouts, mountain man Thomas Fitzpatrick.

The Battle of San Pascual

On December 5, 1846, northeast of San Diego, General Kearny ran into an unexpected hornet's nest of opposition. More than 150 armed Californians, under Andrés Pico, were encamped at the Indian village of San Pascual (near present-day Escondido). Kearny rashly ordered an attack before dawn, in a cold rain. At first the Californians seemed

to retreat from the field. Suddenly, however, they wheeled about
and charged Kearny's scattered, water-soaked forces with muskets
and long, sharp willow lances. The Americans, their carbine ammunition wet, tried to beat off the onslaught by hand-to-hand combat, but they were at a disadvantage. Eighteen Americans lay dead
in the mud before Kearny could repel the attackers. Nineteen other
soldiers were wounded and one was missing. Most of the fatalities
resulted from lance thrusts rather than from gun wounds. The total
number of Americans who died was twenty-two. General Kearny
himself received two ugly lance wounds. The Californians suffered
only minor injuries.

Kearny composed a message to Stockton pleading for help; he
described how the battle had been fought against heavy odds, how
his cumbersome, tired, and bony mules were no match for the quick
California ponies, and how his short sabres offered no defense against
the long lances of his mounted opponents. He sent this dispatch to
San Diego by Kit Carson and Lieutenant Edward F. Beale, early on
the day following the battle. He then resumed his march toward San
Diego, hoping that Stockton's reinforcements would soon reach him.
Kearny's progress was slow and his position precarious. After he
made his next camp on a hill near the San Bernardo Rancho, he was
virtually surrounded by hostile forces. His powder was damp, and
supplies were dangerously low; the tired dragoons were forced to
subsist for four days on mule flesh and a scanty water supply. But
their spirits were heartened when almost 200 sailors and marines
arrived from San Diego in response to the appeal Kearny had sent
to Stockton.

The Reconquest of Los Angeles

Worn by privation and embarrassed by his near-defeat at San Pascual,
Kearny reported the incident to the War Department as a victory in
which he had fought off a superior enemy under great odds. The
general considered that it was his mission to establish the supremacy
of the United States over California, and he behaved accordingly
toward Stockton and other Americans already there. Actually, prior
to his arrival the "first conquest" had occurred under Stockton, as
commander in chief and acting governor. Kearny let it be known
that the army was taking over, but Stockton declined to relinquish
command. Nevertheless, the two combined their resources of 600
army dragoons, marines, and sailors, and left San Diego to attack
Los Angeles. Officially, during their march northward, Stockton bore
the title of commander in chief of the expedition, while Kearny was
commander of troops. Frémont, now a lieutenant colonel, was also

Los Angeles, 1857. From a contemporary print.

about to approach Los Angeles, from the north. He moved southward from Monterey with 400 men and entered the San Fernando Valley near Los Angeles on January 11, 1847.

In their march on Los Angeles from the south, Kearny and Stockton met no real opposition until they reached the banks of a muddy little stream, the San Gabriel. There they encamped on January 7. General José María Flores was hoping to surprise the Americans with a last-ditch cavalry stand along the north bank of the river. Kearny and Stockton, however, forded the stream in the form of a square, and this strategy enabled them to capture the opposite bank quickly from the skirmishers. Two days later, in the *Cañada de los Alisos*, near the Los Angeles stockyards, the forces under Kearny and Stockton fought the Battle of La Mesa. Of slight importance as a military contest, it did confirm the victory at the San Gabriel River and permit the reoccupation of Los Angeles. The Californians abandoned the field, scattering in different directions; this was the end of resistance to the invading Americans. On January 10, 1847, American troops entered the City of the Angels and marched to its plaza, where Gillespie hoisted the flag he had been compelled to haul down the previous September.

Conclusion of Hostilities

Frémont, tardily arriving on the scene from the north, received the surrender of the last armed forces in California. Andrés Pico may have feared that Kearny and Stockton would place him before a firing squad; he preferred to surrender to Frémont, and did so on January

13, 1847, in the outskirts of Los Angeles. His brother, Pío Pico, last Mexican governor of California, had already fled to Sonora. José María Flores, hot-spur leader of the government in its last days, had also escaped. Frémont now entered into a truce with Andrés Pico. Although, in effect, he was acting over the head of Kearny, a brevet brigadier, Frémont personally pardoned Pico and other local leaders; the peace treaty he concluded with them, known as the Cahuenga Capitulation, was in fact a generous document. Pico's preference for surrending to Frémont, rather than to Kearny or Stockton, embroiled these American commanders in a three-way fight. An unfortunate conflict in orders from both the Navy and War Departments led to a savage quarrel over which of California's conquerors was commander in chief of the thousand or more men assembled under them at Los Angeles. Stockton relinquished his post as governor of California in favor of Frémont and traveled to the East Coast, leaving Kearny and Frémont to fight it out over who was commander of California. Ultimately Kearny established his authority over Frémont, against whom he prepared court-martial charges.

Some lesser American commands reached California too late to participate in the actual conquest. The Mormon Battalion, under Lieutenant Colonel Philip St. George Cooke, had followed General Kearny westward, reaching San Diego only on January 29, 1847. This unit marched to Los Angeles to be honorably discharged, after building a fort, Fort Moore, on the hill where Gillespie had been besieged. On the sixth of March another unit, consisting of two hundred fifty members of Colonel Jonathan D. Stevenson's regiment of New York volunteers, arrived in San Francisco. Within a few months their discharge was completed and many of these men were absorbed into the California population.

The war between the United States and Mexico came to an end with the signing of the Treaty of Guadalupe Hidalgo on February 2, 1848. A new southwestern boundary now gave the United States all of Upper California as well as New Mexico and Texas. Residents had the option of becoming American citizens. The United States agreed to pay Mexico the sum of $15 million for the land it took, and it politely disregarded the fact that American forces had partly conquered Lower California.

Selected Readings

The first nonheroicized study of the background of Americanization was Robert G. Cleland, *The Early Sentiment for the Annexation of California . . .* (Austin, 1915). More recent appraisals are John A. Hawgood, "The Pattern of Yankee Infiltration in Mexican Alta Cal-

ifornia," *Pacific Historical Review* 27 (February 1958), 27–37, and, in
the same journal, Norman A. Graebner, "American Interest in Cal-
ifornia, 1845," 22 (February 1953), 13–27. The role of President
Polk in developing official interest in California is made clear in E.
I. McCormac, *James K. Polk: A Political Biography* (Berkeley, 1922).
Polk's personal diary has been edited by Allan Nevins as *Polk: The
Diary of a President* (New York, 1929). The last days of Mexican rule
are the subject of George Tays's article, "Pio Pico's Correspondence
with the Mexican Government, 1846–1848," California Historical
Society *Quarterly* 13 (March 1934), 99–149. A perceptive but dull
study is Frederick Merk's *Manifest Destiny and Mission in American
History* (New York, 1963).

British interest in California is discussed in two articles by Sheldon
G. Jackson: "Two Pro-British Plots in Alta California," *Southern California Quarterly* 55 (Summer 1973), 105–40, and "The British and
the California Dream," *Southern California Quarterly* 57 (Fall 1975),
251–70. Also see Ephraim D. Adams, "English Interest in California," *American Historical Review* 14 (July 1909), 744–63. Prussian interest is treated in John A. Hawgood's "A Projected Prussian Colonization of Upper California," *Southern California Quarterly* 48
(December 1966), 353–68. The controversial Jones is the subject of
George B. Brooke, "The Vest Pocket War of Commodore Jones,"
Pacific Historical Review 31 (August 1962), 217–33.

Frémont's activities in California have been much debated. A useful starting point is the collection of Frémont's own reports by Allan
Nevins, entitled *Narratives of Exploration and Adventure* (New York,
1956). Nevins has also contributed two standard Frémont biographies, the latest of which is *Frémont: Pathmarker of the West* (New York,
1939). An early biography is John Bigelow's *Frémont: Memoir of Life
and Public Services* (New York, 1856). Cardinal L. Goodwin's *John
Charles Frémont: An Exploration of His Career* (Stanford, 1930) is dated
and strongly anti-Frémont. The most recent biography of Frémont
is Ferol Egan's *Frémont, Explorer for a Restless Nation* (New York, 1975).
Also consult Richard R. Stenberg, "Polk and Frémont, 1845–1846,"
Pacific Historical Review 7 (September 1938), 211–27. Jessie Benton
Frémont's *Souvenirs of My Time* (Boston, 1887) and *Far West Sketches*
(Boston, 1890), are interesting but unreliable. She, like her husband,
in his "The Conquest of California," *Century Magazine* 41 (April 1890),
917–28, and *Memoirs of My Life* (New York, 1887), argues *ex post facto*,
justifying each detail of his conduct. Thomas Hart Benton, *Thirty
Years View* (2 vols., Boston, 1854–56), is by Frémont's noted father-
in-law. On the conquest of California is the account of the *Proceedings
of the Court Martial in the Trial of (J. C.) Frémont* (Washington, D.C.,
1848). A psychiatric profile is Andrew Rolle, "Exploring an Explorer:

Psychohistory and John Charles Frémont," *Pacific Historical Review* 51 (May, 1982), 135–63.

One of Frémont's enemies was the philosopher Josiah Royce, who offered a critique of California's materialistic Americanization in his *California: From the Conquest in 1846 to the Second Vigilance Committee* (Boston, 1886), reprinted with an introduction by Robert Glass Cleland (New York, 1948). Aspects of the Bear Flag revolt are in Fred B. Rogers, *Bear Flag Lieutenant: The Life Story of Henry L. Ford* (San Francisco, 1951), as well as in William B. Ide's first-person narrative, *Who Conquered California* (Claremont, 1880). There is available a reprinted version of Simeon Ide's rare *A Biographical Sketch of William B. Ide*, with an introduction by Benjamin F. Gilbert (Glorieta, N.M., 1967).

A contemporary account of the conquest is James Madison Cutts, *The Conquest of California and New Mexico . . .* (Philadelphia, 1847). Kearny's march west is discussed in William H. Emory's *Notes of a Military Reconnaissance . . .* (Washington, D. C., 1848). Another contemporary description is Joseph Warren Revere, *A Tour of Duty in California . . .* (New York, 1849). Various articles in the *Pacific Historical Review* have dealt with participants in the conquest: William H. Ellison, "San Juan to Cahuenga: The Experiences of Frémont's Battalion," *Pacific Historical Review* 27 (May 1958), 245–61, and George Tays, "Frémont Had No Secret Instructions," 9 (June 1940), 159–71. The war in Lower California is described in Peter Gerhard, "Baja California in the Mexican War, 1846–1848," *Pacific Historical Review* 14 (May 1945), 418–24. Consult also John A. Hawgood's critical treatment, "John C. Frémont and the Bear Flag Revolution," *University of Birmingham Historical Journal* 7 (1959), 80–100. On the Battle of San Pascual see Arthur Woodward's *Lances at San Pascual* (San Francisco, 1948); Philip St. George Cooke, *The Conquest of New Mexico and California* (New York, 1878); and Justin H. Smith's *The War with Mexico* (2 vols., New York, 1919). Useful also is Walter Colton, *Three Years in California* (New York, 1950), a personal narrative by the first United States *alcalde* at Monterey. A revisionist view of the Mexican War is Glenn W. Price's *Origins of the War with Mexico: The Polk–Stockton Intrigue* (Austin, 1967).

There is a biased life of Sloat by Edwin A. Sherman, *The Life of the Late Rear Admiral John Drake Sloat* (Oakland, 1902). See also *A Sketch of the Life of Com. Robert F. Stockton* by Samuel J. Bayard (New York, 1856). Consult Robert J. Parker, "Larkin, Anglo-American Businessman in Mexican California" in *Greater America* (Berkeley, 1945) and John A. Hawgood, ed., *First and Last Consul, Thomas Oliver Larkin . . . A Selection of Letters* (San Marino, 1962). Other books touching on the conquest are Fred B. Rogers, *Montgomery and the Portsmouth* (San Francisco, 1959); Werner H. Marti, *Messenger of Des-*

tiny: The California Adventures, 1846–1847, of Archibald H. Gillespie (San Francisco, 1960); and Dwight L. Clarke, *Stephen Watts Kearny, Soldier of the West* (Norman, Okla., 1961). A discussion of military regimes that followed the conquest is Theodore Grivas, *Military Governments in California* (Glendale, 1963). The latest survey of the conquest is Neal Harlow, *California Conquered: War and Peace in the Pacific, 1846–1850* (Berkeley, 1982).

The history of an unusual army unit is told in Donald C. Biggs, *Conquer and Colonize: Stevenson's Regiment and California* (San Rafael, 1977).

CHAPTER 15

Gold

JAMES WILSON MARSHALL'S DISCOVERY of gold on January 24, 1848, was one of those events that influenced United States history as well as California's. Marshall's discovery occurred at Coloma, located on the south fork of the American River. This was not the first discovery of California gold. Minor finds had been made long before 1848, principally by mission Indians who brought the metal to the padres; but the friars reputedly cautioned the natives not to divulge the location of the gold, lest the province be inundated by money-mad foreigners.

In southern California, on an uncertain date during the year 1842, a ranchero, Francisco López, stopped to rest in San Feliciano canyon, near today's Newhall. He used a sheaf knife to dig up a few wild onions. When he noticed some bright flakes and nuggets clinging to their roots, he excitedly uprooted more of the plants. Hearing of López' find, several hundred men went up the canyon to seek gold. On November 22, the American trader Abel Stearns "sent to Alfred Robinson, Esq., 20 oz. California weight of placer gold to be forwarded by him to the U.S. mint at Philadelphia for assay." Unfortunately the San Feliciano lode was shallow; it "played out" within a few months. At about the same time another American trader, William Heath Davis, saw bits of gold ore in the possession of the California padres. However, until the arrival of the Americans, the Californians lived free from the gold fever that had afflicted the Spanish conquerors of Mexico and Peru.

Marshall's Discovery

It was James Marshall's later discovery that focused the attention of the entire world on a new El Dorado. Equipped with a modest education, a flintlock rifle, and his father's trade as a coach and wagon builder, Marshall had come to California from his native New Jersey by emigrant train in 1844. First he had gone to work for Sutter. Buying land later on nearby Little Butte Creek, he built and repaired spinning wheels, plows, ox yokes, and carts. In 1846, after participating in a campaign against the Mokelumne Indians, he joined the Bear Flag group and then enlisted in Frémont's California Battalion, continuing in military service until after the American conquest. Marshall then returned to Sutter's Fort, "barefooted and in a very sorry plight," to find that nearly all his livestock had strayed from his ranch or had been stolen. Like many another California combatant, Marshall had received no compensation for his volunteer war services.

The community around Sutter's Fort was growing with the influx of immigrants, and the demand for lumber was increasing. Sutter therefore agreed to supply the necessary capital for a community sawmill, in return for one-fourth of its future production. He sent Marshall to search for timber and a suitable location for the mill. The site chosen was on the south fork of the American River, forty-five miles northeast of Sutter's Fort. Local Indians called the place Cullomah.

In January 1848, after the discovery of gold, Sutter was at first incredulous about the many flakes of ore in the tailrace of the mill. Then he tried to keep the find secret. The baron of the Sacramento began to undergo a whole series of misfortunes. His diary tells how in early March a party of Mormons working for him "left for washing and digging Gold and very soon all followed, and left me only sick and lame behind." He complains that many other workmen left his service, hurting his business operations. Even the Indians, wrote Sutter, were "impatient to run" to the gold streams, and he was compelled to leave a year's wheat crop ungathered in the fields around New Helvetia. Moreover, he had spent large sums on the Coloma sawmill and on a flour mill, and he could find no one to operate them.

Marshall and Sutter's secret had proved too great to keep. Not long after the discovery, Sam Brannan, now a prominent merchant at New Helvetia, galloped from Sutter's Fort to San Francisco with dust and nuggets from the gold fields. As he rode along its streets he shouted "Gold! Gold! Gold from the American River!" swinging his hat wildly with one hand and in the other waving a medicine bottle full of bright dust. Soon a stampede started as people, singly and in bands, deserted their homes for the icy streams of the Sierra in quest of riches.

Labor costs in towns near the coast rose rapidly. Almost all business, except the most urgent, stopped. Seamen deserted ships in San Francisco Bay, soldiers departed from barracks, and servants left their masters, forfeiting accumulated wages in a frenzy of excitement. Threats, punishment, and money were powerless to stem this human tide. Forgetting to collect debts or to pay their bills, gold seekers rode, walked, and hobbled on crutches toward the Sierra. Amidst the hysteria San Francisco's early newspaper, the *Californian*, suspended publication on May 29, 1848, announcing: "The majority of our subscribers and many of our advertisers have closed their doors and places of business and left town. . . . The whole country, from San Francisco to Los Angeles and from the seashore to the base of the Sierra Nevada, resounds with the sordid cry of 'gold! Gold!! GOLD!!!!' while the field is left half planted, the house half built, and everything neglected but the manufacture of shovels and pickaxes. . . ." Thomas Oliver Larkin bitterly lamented the depopulation of Monterey, where buildings fell into disrepair and stores closed down. He wrote of the local scarcity of supplies: "Every bowl, tray, and warming pan has gone to the mines. Everything in short that has a scoop in it and will hold sand and water." "The gold mines," wrote Walter Colton, "have upset all social and domestic arrangements in Monterey; the master has become his own servant, and the servant his own lord. The millionaire is obliged to groom his own horse, and roll his wheelbarrow."

Within a few months news of California gold had found its way to every part of the globe. Exaggeration of the riches was so prevalent that one writer remarked, "A grain of gold taken from the mine became a pennyweight at Panama, an ounce in New York and Boston, and a pound nugget at London."

By May 1848 gold had been found at distances of thirty miles surrounding Sutter's Mill. By the first of June, 2,000 men were already digging for gold, and in another month that number doubled. The gold hunters of 1848, however, constituted but the vanguard of a human avalanche soon to descend upon California.

After President Polk mentioned the discovery of gold in his presidential message of December 5, 1848, even wider publicity was given the event. At the beginning of 1849 there were, exclusive of Indians, only some 26,000 persons in California. Before midsummer the number had reached 50,000. By the end of the year it was probably 115,000 notwithstanding the official but inaccurate census report of 92,597 for the year 1850. Possibly four-fifths of the population were Americans and most were men. Approximately half of the adult population was engaged in some branch of mining. Among the 20,000 foreign immigrants were contingents from Mexico, Great Britain, Germany, France, and Spain; and lesser numbers from Chile, Peru, and the Hawaiian Islands. Few nationalities were unrepresented. The Chinese were among the most numerous of the foreigners; by 1852 more than 20,000 had come to California.

San Francisco became the most rapidly growing city in the world. From only 812 persons in March 1848, by 1850 it was a boom town of 25,000 people. Upstream, Sacramento's waterfront area, to the west of Sutter's Fort, also took on intense activity. The route to the inland mines, it became a rendevous for throngs of adventurers who headed for the diggings. The overwhelming majority of Americans who reached California during those hectic days selected one or another of three main routes—"around the Horn," "by way of the Isthmus," or "across the plains."

The Routes of the Gold Seekers

The route around Cape Horn required up to nine months of travel. Sailing vessels were of light tonnage, and not all of them were seaworthy. Passengers made the best of monotony and seasickness. They amused themselves with banjo, fiddle, and games aboard ship; at landfalls en route, Rio or Callao, there were bullfights, cockfights, donkey rides, and the *fandango* for their entertainment. On one ship, the *Rising Sun*, the Fourth of July was celebrated during the passage around Cape Horn by blowing bugles, playing martial music, a mass reading of the Declaration of Independence, speech making, and a dinner of roast goose, plum pudding, mince pie, figs, and nuts. The actual passage through or around Cape Horn was hazardous. It might take a vessel days to break through the choppy Strait of Magellan, which was enveloped by strong currents and dense fogs. Yet thousands made it to California via what became known as the "white-collar route," because lack of exercise softened up seasick passengers.

Americans by the thousands reached California via the Isthmus of Panama or Nicaragua. Travelers crossing the isthmus, long before construction of the Panama Canal, used a watertight bag to transport clothing, and many took along a carbine, camping equipment, and medicines. Under favorable conditions, the isthmus route was the quickest way to California. The voyage from New York to the Panama Coast was 2,500 miles and the trip across the Isthmus 60 more; from Panama to San Francisco it was 3,500 miles. But travel conditions were seldom favorable.

Fully as dangerous as shipboard epidemics was crossing the Isthmus of Panama. Malarial fever was prevalent; amid unsanitary conditions there were victims of cholera, dysentery, and yellow fever. The typical American gold seeker, ambitious and curious, was not, however, easily swayed from his purpose, and the stifling 60 miles he had to traverse was full of interest. Part of the journey was made by water, in long canoes poled and paddled by native boatmen. Then, the journey overland on muleback proceeded through a vast tangle of

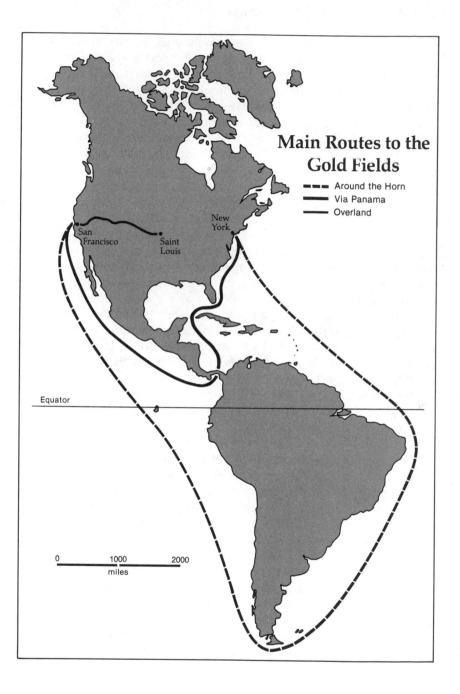

Main Routes to the Gold Fields

- - - Around the Horn
— Via Panama
— Overland

New York

San Francisco

Saint Louis

Equator

0   1000   2000
miles

luxurious greenness; one saw exotic varieties of birds among the coconut trees and tropical ferns, as well as forests of orange, crimson, and scarlet flowers. A rough overland ride on muleback finally brought the traveler to Panama. A shortage of coastal vessels, especially during the first half of 1849, sometimes stretched the traveler's stay into months, though later passenger service was better organized.

After Panama came the uncomfortable, hazardous journey to San Francisco Bay. Most ships had wretched accommodations and their food and water were vile. Pacific Mail Steamship Company ships powered by steam began gradually to supplement the sailing vessels, then to supersede them; but during the late 1840s most passenger service to California continued to be carried on in wooden sailing vessels, many of them old, worm-eaten, and leaky.

The covered wagon, or "prairie schooner," symbolized the vast population movement during the Gold Rush as much as does the clipper ship or steamer. Fortunately the principal routes across the Great Plains were marked out before the rush. Two of these were commonly followed by the "forty-niners." The favorite was a northern route leading directly west from St. Louis through South Pass in the Rocky Mountains. This was taken by 30,000 gold seekers in the year 1849 alone. A southern route proceeded first over the Santa Fe Trail, which ran from Westport (later called Kansas City), to Sante Fe; then it followed the Gila River to the Colorado, and finally crossed the desert into southern California. A party could trundle along some eighteen miles per day on this trail. Caravans averaged twenty-six wagons, each drawn by five yoke of oxen, or a span of ten mules.

With luck, the 2,000 miles to the gold fields over either of these routes could be covered in 100 days. Rivers had to be forded, food supplies conserved, the trains guarded against Indian attack. Not infrequently wagons had to be unloaded and reloaded several times in a single day while crossing rough terrain or streams. Many of the larger overland companies had to subdivide when more grass was required for the livestock than could be found in any one place.

Perhaps 10,000 persons chose yet another route, which began with a voyage of about eighteen days from New Orleans to Vera Cruz, Mexico. A horseback trip of 280 miles to Mexico City consumed another nine days; then one had to continue to Mazatlán, some 900 miles, or twenty days, of additional travel. The journey was concluded by a voyage to San Francisco taking thirty-five days. Total travel time from New York was frequently four months.

Death Valley in '49

Among the most tragic of all pioneer experiences were those encountered by overland gold hunters whose fate led them into Death

Valley. Comparatively few persons entered this "seventy-five mile strip of perdition," and those who did so usually went there unintentionally. Many of these unlucky travelers underwent sufferings similar to those of the Donner party. Death Valley, about one hundred and ten feet below sea level, stretches along California's southeastern Inyo County, east of the Sierra Nevada. Its atmosphere is almost without moisture. During many months of each year the heat is relentless. Constant hot winds blow across the sands, and the blinding glare of the sun parches the skin and induces a feverish, half-crazed state.

The story of one pioneer group will illustrate the horrors of America's most desolate valley. During the winter of 1848–1849, William Lewis Manly, a native of Vermont, accompanied a large and slow party westward over the California Trail. Innumerable delays during that season made it impossible for his party to reach the Sierra in time to avoid the fall snows. Manly and six companions were convinced that the Green River (a tributary of the Colorado) flowed westward, perhaps to the Pacific. At the Green they discovered a small ferry boat, possibly built by Mormon pioneers, and, after emptying some sand out of the boat, they attempted to navigate the treacherous stream. "We untied the ropes," wrote Manly, "gave the boat a push and commenced to move down the river with ease and comfort. . . ." Soon, however, the stream became a rapid, roaring torrent, dotted with dangerous rocks and shoals. The voyage down the Green came to a sudden halt when the clumsy boat jammed against a huge rock and was pinned so tight that it could not be budged.

Manly's little band was overjoyed to come upon another party near the Great Salt Lake. This group was headed by Asabel Bennett, an acquaintance of Manly's; they joined forces to plot a common strategy. Because it was late in the season, and they were aware of the plight of the Donner party in the winter snows of the Sierra Nevada, the Bennett–Manly group decided on a longer but supposedly safer route into southern California. From there they planned to move north to the California mines.

The party, however, became trapped in the endless wastes that led toward Death Valley. After wandering aimlessly in a sea of sand, they decided that, instead of trying to retrace their steps, they should travel toward the west. In the distance the party could see the Panamint Mountains, their summits white with snow, and these became a landmark for the travelers. Thirteen men, three women, and six children moved through the wastes of Death Valley, trying, again and again, to escape from Furnace Creek, their main camp. Canyons that led nowhere faced them at every turn. They were able to find a few brackish wells, but food supplies were running out. One after

Floor of Death Valley. (From the author's collection.)

another the oxen were killed for food. As the pioneers dipped into their last sacks of flour and meal, Manly confessed to a morbid despair. He thought he could escape by himself, but resolved that "all must be brought through or perish." Bennett proposed that Manly and John Rogers, the youngest and strongest men, go ahead on foot to seek help. The main party was to await their return from the California settlements with supplies.

Manly and Rogers struck out toward the Panamints across uncharted desert sands, then made their way over Walker Pass in the southern Sierra. After fourteen days they reached Mission San Fernando, where they obtained flour, beans, three horses, and a mule. Following a short rest, the two men started back toward Death Valley. Twenty-six days after having departed from their friends they finally found the camp once more, but came back to a dreadful sight. The survivors were huddled in the meager shade under their wagons, the covers of which they had taken off to make protecting tents for themselves and their animals. Weakness had so reduced the party that Manly and Rogers moved within 100 yards of the wagons without seeing a sign of life. A shot fired from Manly's rifle brought a man from under a wagon. "Then," Manly wrote in his narrative, "he threw up his arms high over his head and shouted—'The boys have come! The boys have come!' . . . Bennett and Arcane caught us in their arms and embraced us with all their strength, and Mrs. Bennett when she came, fell down on her knees and clung to me like a maniac, in the great emotion that came to her, and not a word was spoken." By their devotion and loyalty Manly and Rogers won the everlasting gratitude of their forlorn party.

About the first of February, 1850, the little band finally left Death Valley. They abandoned their wagons and all equipment that could be spared, and packed their meager belongings on the few remaining animals. The party crept along the eastern slopes of the Sierra, passed through Red Rock Canyon, crossed the Mojave River, and finally arrived at Rancho San Francisco over four months after leaving the Salt Lake trail. They had spent an entire year on their journey west, and they were still more than 500 miles from the mines. The story of the Bennett–Manly party, as told by William Lewis Manly in his *Death Valley in '49*, has become one of the classic accounts of Western history.

Life in the Diggings

The California placer camps hardly resembled the paradise envisioned by gold seekers as they made their way west. Mining was tiring work, accommodations were few, and conveniences practically nonexistent. Most "claims" lay along the banks of streams, where thousands of persons tried to strike "pay dirt." There was little subterranean work, or sinking of shafts, until later years, when the production of gold became heavily capitalized. "Dry diggings," found in flats and gullies where there was no water supply, were worked as eagerly as "wet diggings" along sand bars or stream beds. Lucky persons also struck it rich in "bench diggings," located on narrow tables along the hillsides, or in the innumerable "bars" (accumulations of sand and rock) opposite the bends of streams.

At first, miners had little experience or knowledge that would help them go about finding gold. They brought a variety of gadgets and equipment with them. Some prospectors achieved marvelous dexterity in simple "panning out" operations. Of all the instruments for washing gold ore, the pan was the simplest. It was made of tin or sheet iron, with a flat bottom about a foot in diameter and sides six inches high—rising at an angle of forty-five degrees. Other miners utilized the washing rocker, or "cradle." This machine extracted particles of gold from gravel by a washing operation. Gold-bearing sand dropped toward the bottom also of the "long tom" rocker, an elongated movable trough that supplemented gold pan or cradle. The "gold borer" was employed as one would use an auger or corkscrew, while the "waterwheel" had shaft, arms, and crossboards resembling the paddlewheels of a steamboat. The "boardsluice" was a long wooden trough, used where there was a plentiful supply of water. The larger these gravel-washing machines became, the more water was required for their operation. Sizable mining ventures involved extensive sluice and waterwheel systems, including "flumes," or open ditches constructed of boards, and later of iron pipe. Nearly all of the devices caused heavier gold sand to remain in the bottom of whatever vessel was being used. Lighter gravel was washed away by the action of the water. "Coyoting" was a form of mining in which each miner dug his own separate hole, a backbreaking task. It was a curious spectacle when red-shirted miners, diligently at work out of sight, suddenly reacted to an unusual noise—their heads popping out of the ground all over a hillside. But this was merely a variation, not the typical method of early California mining. The lonely prospector, equipped with gold pan, with canvas-covered supplies loaded haphazardly on the back of his surefooted mule, became the symbol of the Gold Rush.

California's principal gold quartz belt, known as the Mother Lode, ran northwest and southeast, between Mariposa and Amador, for seventy miles. The lode was characterized by its length, thickness, uniformity, and proximity to companion veins. This extensive ore-bearing region was divided into the Northern and the Southern Mines, with the watershed separating the Cosumnes and Mokelumne rivers. The many camps above the Mokelumne belonged to the Northern Mines; this region included the American River, with its forks, the Cosumnes, the Bear, the Yuba, and the Feather rivers, and smaller streams. Sacramento was the chief depot for provisions. The Southern Mines, whose headquarters was Stockton, included camps lying below the north fork of the Mokelumne, the principal rivers being the Calaveras, the Stanislaus, the Tuolumne, the Merced, and the mountainous portion of the San Joaquin, with its tributaries.

A number of picturesque place names came to be applied to the towns that mushroomed in the mining regions. These included Git-up-and-Git, Lazy Man's Canyon, Wildcat Bar, Skunk Gulch, Gospel Swamp, Whisky Bar, Shinbone Peak, Humpback Slide, Bogus Thunder, Hell's Delight, Poker Flat, Ground Hog Glory, Delirium Tremens, Murderers Bar, Hangtown (later Placerville), and Agua Fria ("cold water"). Placerville was first named Hangtown because of a hanging there in 1849 by lynch law; it has had the distinction of longevity, when as a rule mining towns appeared and disappeared astonishingly fast.

The first claimant of a piece of property was conceded to have the best right to it. Claim jumping has been exaggerated, as has the lawlessness of life in the diggings. Most people who went into the Mother Lode were law-abiding and eager to establish some system of order. While they awaited the arrival of a regular legal system, the miners enforced "district rules" which they themselves drew up. Criminal offenses argued before local courts meted out such penalties as ear cropping, whipping, and even branding and hanging. This system of extralegal justice obviously involved abuses. Almost certainly it did help to discourage crime, however. The regulations that each mining area made and enforced served, in fact, as a practical alternative to anarchy.

Despite the rowdy environment, fellowship and hospitality were found in the tents and dugouts of the miners. On Sunday, observed by most gold seekers as a day of rest, the men did their week's washing, baking, or mending, and, remembering wives and children back home, wrote letters. Sunday afternoons and evenings were enlivened by horse racing, yarn swapping, or gambling. A few miners had the hardihood to abstain from drowning their troubles in drink. Prostitutes were in great demand in the predominantly male society.

The bleak days the miners spent out of doors grubbing for wealth made them especially appreciative of traveling performers, among them Lotta Crabtree, Edwin Booth, and the flaming international celebrity Lola Montez. A more frequent means of entertainment for the lonesome men was singing in groups from a booklet entitled *Put's California Songster*. The lyrics of mining-camp songs were usually set to such well-known airs as "Pop Goes the Weasel," or "Ben Bolt." No song quite equaled "The California Emigrant" in popularity. The chorus of one version, set to the tune of "Oh! Susannah!" was especially popular:

> Oh! California!
> That's the land for me,

"Sundry Amusements in the Mines," 1848–1849. Contemporary print. (By courtesy of The Huntington Library, San Marino, California.)

> I'm going to Sacramento,
> With my washbowl on my knee!

A somewhat naughtier air, sung to the tune of "New York Gals," was entitled "Hangtown Gals":

> Hangtown gals are plump and rosy,
> Hair in ringlets mighty cosy;
> Painted cheeks and gassy bonnets;
> Touch them and they'll sting like hornets.
>
> CHORUS
> Hangtown gals are lovely creatures,
> Think they'll marry Mormon preachers;
> Heads thrown back to show their features—
> Ha, ha, ha! Hangtown gals.
> They're dreadful shy of forty-niners,
> Turn their noses up at miners;
> Shocked to hear them say "gol durn it!"
> Try to blush, but cannot come it.
>
> CHORUS
> Hangtown gals are lovely creatures, &c.

The Women Pioneers

Pioneer women were only occasionally acclaimed, as in the words from the song "Sweet Betsy From Pike":

> They swam the wide rivers and crossed the tall peaks,
> And camped on the prairie for weeks upon weeks.
> Starvation and cholera and hard work and slaughter,
> They reached California, spite of hell and high water.

Sarah Royce was one of these pioneer women, the mother of the Harvard philosopher Josiah Royce. They all faced a hard and scarcely rewarding life. Mary Bennett Ritter, one of California's first physicians, recalled that during the harvesting and haying seasons "there were from ten to forty men to be cooked for, beside the general housework, the washing and ironing, the churning, bread making and sewing for four children—plus making my father's shirts and underwear." She and her mother heated the water for Saturday night baths and made their own soap and dipping candles. All these workaday chores gave rise to yet another song:

> There's too much of worriment that goes in a bonnet.
> There's too much of ironing that goes in a shirt.
> There's nothing that pays for the time you waste on it.

Mary Jane Megquier, reputedly the first American woman to come to California (1849) via Panama, wrote a series of letters (later published as *Apron Full of Gold*) that give us a view of the difficulties encountered en route from there:

> Our party thought it best to have the natives cook their supper, it was rich to see us eating soup with our fingers, as knives, forks, spoons, tables, chairs are among the things unknown. They have no floors, the pigs, dogs, cats, ducks, hens are all around your feet ready to catch the smallest crumb that may chance to fall. As I was the *only* lady in the party, they gave me a chance in their hut but a white lady was such a rare sight they were coming in to see me until we found we could get no sleep, we got up and spent the remainder of the night in open air.

A woman's view of the gold rush did not feature the roseate sense of gain that male business types usually espoused. We have the reminiscences of Sarah Haight who, seeing the damage wrought by mining, wrote in her diary: "How unsightly it makes the country appear. How few flowers and how little vegetation there is where there is gold. . . . How often its blighting effects are on the human heart."

Boom or Bust

The majority of gold seekers averaged earnings of $100 per month—
a small return considering the conditions of extreme hardship and
the cost of living in the mining towns. There were, of course, those
who struck it rich. One man scooped up two and a half pounds of
gold in fifteen minutes, gold sold for $16 per ounce. But many miners
quickly used up their savings.

Prices for both luxuries and essentials were fantastic, especially in
an age when money in the Eastern United States had five times today's purchasing power. Copies of Eastern newspapers were grabbed
up at $1 apiece. A loaf of bread, which cost 4 or 5 cents on the
Atlantic seaboard, sold for 50 or 75 cents at San Francisco. Kentucky
bourbon whiskey leaped to $30 a quart; apples sold for $1 to $5
apiece, eggs for $50 a dozen (one boiled egg in a restaurant cost as
much as $5), and coffee for $5 a pound. Sacramento merchants sold
butcher knives for $30 each, blankets for $40, boots for $100 a pair,
and tacks to nail flapping canvas tents for as much as $192 a pound.
Medicine cost $10 a pill, or $1 a drop, and hotel accommodations
$1,000 per month.

Heaps of gold dust, kept in doeskin bags, piled up in San Francisco
stores. The traveling Eastern journalist Bayard Taylor complained:
"You enter a shop to buy something; the owner eyes you with perfect
indifference, waiting for you to state your want; if you object to the
price, you are at liberty to leave, for you need not expect to get it
cheaper; he evidently cares little whether you buy it or not." Another
observer described the merchant firm of Mellus & Howard as "so
surrounded with piles of gold dust" and as receiving "such enormous
rents from their landed property, it is said 400 to $500,000 per
annum, that they consider 10 to 12 thousand dollars for discharging
a ship a mere flea bite." Persons who lost both their grubstakes and
their courage quickly returned eastward whence they had come. The
most strong-willed and fortunate miners persevered.

After much of the loose ore had been panned out of California's
stream beds in the late 1840s, gold became more and more difficult
to isolate. No longer could penniless miners hope to wrest fortunes
from California's rocks and cliffs with primitive tools and by the sweat
of their brow alone. The technological changes in mining were to
affect both prices and wages. By the 1850s these changes required
heavy capital outlays from mining operators for new equipment. In
employing the technique of hydraulicking, which became common,
miners used canvas hoses and nozzles to wash down the sides of
canyons into troughs, whose riffles caught free-floating gold particles.
At Murderer's Bar and elsewhere whole rivers were diverted so that
their beds could be worked. Intricate paddlewheels operated bucket

Broadside advertisement of the Mormon Island Emporium, in the California mines, 1848–1849. Such stores also served as mail, express, and banking centers. (By courtesy of The Huntington Library, San Marino, California.)

pumps that drained the diggings. Hundreds of miles of canals and flumes carried water through sheet-iron pipes moving large deposits of ore to devices that could extract the gold. Stamp mills were also constructed, huge affairs weighing as much as 800 pounds each that clattered away as they reduced tons of rock to powder ore. The first stamp mills were made of vertical logs shod with iron, but these unimposing structures housed expensive imported machinery. The days of pick, shovel, pan, and burro were over.

Along with numerous technological changes there occurred a decline in gold productivity. By 1854 the "easy pickings" of placer mining had disappeared. Only much later, in 1880, after other placers developed in the Trinity–Klamath area of northwestern California, did gold production again soar. But it was mining companies, rather than individual miners, that raised the necessary capital for tunneling and timbering through bedrock, in the case of quartz mining, and for heavy machinery and hoses in hydraulic operations.

Once the gold bonanza drew to a close, prices declined rapidly. Traveling theater troupes that had been able to charge as much as $55 for stall seats now played to almost empty houses. Merchants found it difficult to sell the expensive "Long Nine" Havana cigars that had once commanded high prices. Shopkeepers threw sacks of spoiled flour into the streets of Sacramento and San Francisco to help fill muddy holes; unsalable cast-iron cookstoves were dismantled and used as sidewalks. No longer did a man need to send his laundry as far as Hawaii, and even China, to be washed. Discouraged miners, returning empty-handed from the diggings, left ghost towns behind them as they flocked back into the cities, anxious to find any sort of work. Others moved into the countryside. Some wisely bought farm lands after the rush and lived to amass fortunes they had not found in the placers.

Selected Readings

Rodman W. Paul's *California Gold* (Cambridge, Mass., 1947) explains the techniques of mining, and John W. Caughey, *Gold Is the Cornerstone* (Berkeley, 1948) is a general analysis. The discovery is treated in Erwin G. Gudde, *Bigler's Chronicle of the West: The Conquest of California, Discovery of Gold, and Mormon Settlement As Reflected in William Henry Bigler's Diaries* (Berkeley, 1962). One of many contemporary accounts by a California gold seeker is Alonzo Delano's *Life on the Plains and Among the Diggings* (Auburn, N.Y., 1854). Another volume that discusses conditions along the trails is the narrative by William Lewis Manly, *Death Valley in '49* (San Jose, 1894; New York, 1924). See also Manly's *The Jay Hawker's Oath and Other Sketches*, edited by

Arthur Woodward (Los Angeles, 1949). An appraisal of the make-shift governmental arrangement adopted in the diggings is Charles H. Shinn, *Mining Camps: A Study of American Frontier Government* (New York, 1885). Authentic descriptions of life in the mines appear in Baynard Taylor, *Eldorado, or Adventures in the Path of Empire* (2 vols., New York, 1850; repr. 1949).

Valeska Bari has edited contemporary accounts in *The Course of Empire* (New York, 1931), and Walker D. Wyman has compiled letters from the diggings in his *California Emigrant Letters* (New York, 1952). Under the pseudonym "Dame Shirley," Louise Amelia Knapp Smith Clappe wrote *The Shirley Letters from the California Mines* (see the edition with introduction and notes by Carl I. Wheat; New York, 1949). Other firsthand accounts include E. Gould Buffum, *Six Months in the Gold Mines* (Philadelphia, 1850); Carolyn H. Ross, *The Log of a Forty Niner* (Boston, 1923); James H. Carson, *Early Recollections of the Mines* (Stockton, 1852); and Franklin A. Buck, *Yankee Trader in the Gold Rush* (Boston, 1930). A descriptive volume is Thomas Jefferson Farnham, *Life, Adventures and Travels to California* (New York, 1849).

Other diaries include David M. Potter, ed., *Trail to California: The Overland Journal of Vincent Geiger and Wakeman Bryarly* (New Haven, 1945), and the illustrated *Gold Rush: The Journals, Drawings, and Other Papers of J. Goldsborough Bruff* (2 vols., New York, 1944), edited by Georgia W. Read and Ruth Gaines. The passage around South America is described in Rydell's *Cape Horn Route*, while that via Panama is discussed in John H. Kemble, *The Panama Route, 1828–1869* (Berkeley, 1943). Consult also Oscar Lewis, *Sea Routes to the Gold Fields* (New York, 1949) and Robert Samuel Fletcher, *From Cleveland by Ship to California* (Durham, N.C., 1959). Other accounts include Owen C. Coy, *The Great Trek* (Los Angeles, 1931), as well as Irene D. Paden, *In the Wake of the Prairie Schooner* (New York, 1943). See also Ralph P. Bieber, *Southern Trails to California in 1848* (Glendale, 1937). Popularizations include a book of pictures by Joseph Henry Jackson, *Gold Rush Album* (New York, 1949), and his *Anybody's Gold* (New York, 1941). Carl I. Wheat, *Books of the California Gold Rush* (San Francisco, 1949), discusses books relating to the Gold Rush.

Two articles that feature the gold rush as more than a California phenomenon are Ralph J. Roske, "The World Impact of the California Gold Rush, 1849–1857," *Arizona and the West* 5 (Autumn 1963), 187–232, and Ralph P. Bieber, "California Gold Mania," *Mississippi Valley Historical Review* 35 (June 1948), 3–28. See also Charles Bateson, *Gold Fleet to California: Forty-Niners from Australia and New Zealand* (East Lansing, Mich., 1964), an account of the rush from the Antipodes from 1849 to 1850, and F. P. Wierzbicki, *California . . . A Guide to the Gold Region* (San Francisco, 1933). A description of medical practices during the rush is George W. Groh, *Gold Fever* (New York,

1966). Appraisals of the discovery are Rodmann W. Paul, *The California Gold Discovery: Sources, Documents, Accounts, and Memoirs...* (Georgetown, Calif., 1966), and James S. Holliday, *The World Rushed In* (New York, 1982). Ralph Mann, *After the Gold Rush: Society in Grass Valley and Nevada City* (Stanford, 1982) is a comparative study of two important mining towns. Richard C. Wood and Leonard Covello, *Mother Lode Memories* (Fresno, 1979) is a pictorial depiction of such settlements.

Elza I. Edwards, *The Valley Whose Name is Death* (Pasadena, 1940) describes the perils of Death Valley.

CHAPTER 16

Approaches to Statehood

DURING THE MEXICAN WAR, California was treated as conquered territory, subject to military rule. Under international law, it retained its civil municipal institutions, while the conqueror issued temporary laws and regulations.

The *alcalde*, a remnant of Mexican bureaucracy, remained the major judicial officer of California at this period. His traditional functions were maintained, but his authority became variable. Walter Colton, an American who became *alcalde* of Monterey, referred to his position as embracing the manifold responsibilities of "guardian of the public peace." Nearly all California *alcaldes* were in time succeeded by Americans, who superimposed upon the Mexican institution the common law they had brought west with them. That law, then, began gradually to supplant the procedures of the past, providing, with the sanction of the military governor, such legal safeguards as trial by jury.

Military Government

In 1847, American rule over California was confused by the controversy between Commodore Stockton and General Kearny over their relative authority. Stockton regarded himself as possessing precedence; and, when Kearny stoutly asserted his own authority, Stockton refused to recognize it completely. As the controversy deepened, Kearny awaited instructions from Washington that were to place him in full charge. Meanwhile Stockton continued to be recognized as military commander and territorial governor until, following the Cahuenga Capitulations, he resigned in favor of Frémont, whom he commissioned as governor. Frémont acted as governor for some fifty days, during which Kearny continued to assert his claims.

Meanwhile instructions from Washington had reached Kearny directing that, as the senior officer of the land forces, he should be governor of California. Then there followed the Frémont–Kearny controversy, the upshot of which was the court-martial of Frémont, his conviction, and resignation. Although Frémont was found guilty of disobedience, conduct prejudicial to military discipline, and even mutiny, President Polk approved only part of the verdict, and he allowed Frémont to resign from the army.

American residents now complained about Mexican law, which continued to be enforced without benefit of courts. Frequent murmurings were heard over infringements upon the right of self-government. Kearny was succeeded as governor by Colonel Richard B. Mason. Mason recognized the popular discontent over government, but was obliged to rule under military restrictions. Nevertheless, a few days before he received news of a peace treaty with Mexico, he prepared for a new code of laws for California. This code unfortunately was not immediately issued, and, as American immigration into California increased, discontent among the settlers grew. The Treaty of Guadalupe Hidalgo, ratified May 20, 1848, concluded the Mexican War and resulted in the cession of California to the United States. Mason hoped that Congress would soon confer upon Californians their constitutional rights as United States citizens. Unfortunately the political machinery for a civil territorial government was slow to be authorized.

Californians grew in the conviction that some kind of self-government should be initiated with the least possible delay. Mass meetings at San Jose and elsewhere adopted by acclamation resolutions that a convention be held to nominate a candidate for governor. A public meeting at San Francisco, on February 12, 1849, even established temporary municipal government for that city. When General Persifor F. Smith superseded Mason as commander of the Army Division of the Pacific, he followed the example of his predecessors from Sloat onward. The military commanders sent to the region had been instructed to accommodate civilian desires, and had allowed wide local autonomy. Smith did not directly interfere with civilian gatherings. By this time Californians were living politically in almost as much a civilian environment as a military one.

General Bennett Riley, California's next military governor, was a mature, amicable leader, who knew both how to obey orders and how to deal with an upset population. Riley issued a proclamation that called for the selection of delegates to a general convention. Held at Monterey beginning on September 1, 1849, this would form a state constitution and plan a territorial government.

General Riley, however, had difficulty putting up with the San Francisco "Legislative Assembly," a fifteen-member body that refused to recognize civil power as residing in a military governor, and championed a temporary civilian government for that city. It also interfered with California's inadequate judiciary system and deposed a corrupt *alcalde*, creating and filling other offices as well. The assembly recommended that a general convention be held at San Jose on the third Monday in August to form a state constitution, for subsequent submission to popular vote. Finally Riley issued a proclamation denouncing the "men styling themselves the 'legislative assembly of the district of San Francisco.' "

Senator Thomas Hart Benton, still smarting from the court-martial of his son-in-law, Frémont, championed the rights of California's United States citizens. He and other senators claimed that the moment the Treaty of Guadalupe Hidalgo went into force, the United States Constitution extended over California. Congress, in failing to provide a territorial government, had encouraged the people to legislate for themselves. Early in 1849, President Taylor had sent a congressional leader, Thomas Butler King, to California as his personal agent. King was to acquire the fullest possible information regarding California's desire for statehood. He was also to encourage sentiment for the territory's admission into the Union. California was more than ready for statehood. King stayed on, becoming in 1851 collector of the port of San Francisco and later a senatorial candidate.

Californians kept clamoring for a constitutional convention. Fortunately for the peaceful settlement of differences, the troublesome San Francisco Assembly recommended that such a convention meet in September of 1849.

The Constitutional Convention of 1849

The constitutional convention at Monterey could be said to have opened even before its first session convened, so great was the enthusiasm of California residents for their political future. This made itself widely felt during the period when delegates were being elected, a process completed without accusations of regional or partisan advantage. The convention met on September 3, 1849, on the upper story of Colton Hall, a long, newly constructed white building overlooking the town of Monterey and the Pacific Ocean. Forty-eight earnest delegates, the majority of American birth, were sworn in as members of the convention. While none of the delegates were nationally known, they proved to be competent and devoted. The document they wrote was not the sudden creation of untutored gold hunters. It was the work of men deeply interested in the future of California.

Native Californians, earlier American settlers, and forty-niners reflected such divergent backgrounds that it seemed almost impossible to bring them to agreement. The task, however, fell to young and flexible men. The average age of the delegates was thirty-six; the oldest, José Antonio Carrillo, was fifty-three. There were few libraries to which they could refer for precedent; probably not more than fifty volumes of law and history were to be found in the locality of Monterey. These, however, included copies of some state constitutions.

The native Californians, who numbered seven out of the forty-eight delegates, were shown special courtesies, at least superficially. General Vallejo, dignified and popular, was acquainted with American institutions and laws; Vallejo was to render valuable services as a member of the first California senate. His personal fortunes suffered severely under American rule, with the loss of practically unlimited lands on which he employed hundreds of Indian laborers. Another native delegate to the convention, Pablo de la Guerra of Santa Barbara, had much in common with Vallejo: he too was tolerant and well educated, had been a prisoner of American troops during the conquest, and subsequently became a state senator. Even better known was Carrillo, a Castilian of strong character and intelligence. Antonio M. Pico, Jacinto Rodríguez, Manuel Dominguez, and J. M. Covarrubias were other native convention members. Sutter by now was regarded almost as an American. The most influential delegate was William M. Gwin, a Southern professional politician of wide experience. He had openly come to California for political reasons and soon sought election to the United States Senate. His ability in debate, added to his powers of leadership, marked him as the ablest politician of the group. Another political talent was Captain Henry W. Halleck, Riley's secretary of state. Thomas O. Larkin, "first and last American consul to California," also lent authority to the deliberations, as did men who had served in the San Francisco Legislative Assembly.

Debates of the Convention

Should the convention proceed at once to form a state constitution, or should it be content to establish a territorial government? A few native Californians, and conservative settlers from the South, opposed state organization. By an overwhelming majority the convention, however, voted to proceed with forming a state constitution.

This decision gave California the distinction of seeking admission into the Union without being an American territory.

The Committee on the Constitution reported a Declaration of Rights consisting of sixteen sections. A delegate moved to insert an additional section: "Neither slavery nor involuntary servitude, unless for the punishment of crimes, shall ever be tolerated in this State." This vital proposal was unanimously adopted. Because the miners did not want slaves working beside them, public sentiment was in favor of a free state; but the unanimous vote was rather surprising, since fifteen delegates had emigrated from Southern slave states. California, entering the Union as the sixteenth free state, was to destroy forever the equilibrium between North and South. The convention's vote, however, did not put an end to the slavery question. There was lively discussion about possible prohibition of the entrance of free Negroes into the future state. Slaveholders, it was urged, might bring their slaves to California and free them in great numbers. In such a case the Negroes would be likely to seek service in the mines, and thus compete with white labor to the detriment of the latter. These arguments, however, did not prevail. California became a completely free state.

Fiscal and monetary matters also occupied much of the delegates' attention. The convention voiced opposition to banks, based chiefly on suspicion of outside interference in California affairs. Providing a system of taxation was difficult because the large landholders of southern California objected to a land tax, which they feared would fall heavily upon them while a shifting population farther north and in the mines would enjoy the full benefits of a government they did little to support. Another issue attracting widespread interest was that of separate property rights for married women; this provision, finally adopted, was one of the first such guarantees embodied in the constitution of any state. Liberal arrangements were made for public education, and the income from certain state lands was set apart for establishment of a state university.

By far the most animated debate of the convention concerned California's boundary. When California was ceded to the United States by Mexico, its territory had not been strictly defined. The 42nd parallel of latitude, however, was conceded to form a boundary on the north, the Pacific Ocean on the west, and the treaty line between Upper and Lower California on the south. The point in dispute was the eastern border, which perhaps embraced the great desert east of the Sierra Nevada, and even the basin inhabited by the Mormons. In the opinion of the Committee on the Boundary, Mexican California, estimated at nearly 450,000 square miles, was too vast for one state. It recommended as the eastern boundary the 116th parallel. This would have placed the boundary at the eastern border of today's state of Nevada. The convention president, Robert Semple, argued that it was "not desirable that the State of California should extend her territory further east than the Sierra Nevada," a real natural boundary. A larger territory would prove unwieldy. Southerners felt that Congress, already reflecting sectional discord, would never permit one state to settle by itself the question of slavery in so large a territory. The convention, therefore, agreed upon a line of demarcation east of the Sierra crest, along the desert floor. Presumably this decision to restrict the size of California would make its new constitution more acceptable to the United States Congress, soon to debate California's prospective statehood.

The desire to secure California's immediate admission into the Union prompted the delegates to bring their deliberations to an end. As they affixed their signatures to the constitution, a salute of thirty-one guns was fired at the Monterey presidio just over the hill from Colton Hall, in honor of the states then in the Union (though California itself, the thirty-first, had not officially achieved that distinction). After the cannonade ended, the crowd assembled outside Colton Hall cheered, and men tossed their hats in the air as California's newly adopted Great Seal was displayed publicly for the first time.

This seal bears thirty-one stars, representing the states. Minerva, sprung from the brow of Jupiter, is the foreground figure, symbolic of California's admission to the Union without passing through territorial probation. A grizzly bear crouches at her feet; a miner, with rocker and bowl, illustrates "the golden wealth of the Sacramento"; and beyond the river, whose shipping typifies commercial greatness, rise the Sierra Nevada Mountains. At the top of the seal is the legend "EUREKA," the state motto.

A New Government and Statehood

California's constitution of 1849 endured for thirty years as the fundamental law of a growing state. Nevertheless, more was required to begin a new civilian government in California than the writing of a constitution. Copies of it were sent by messenger to virtually every town, camp, and ranch in California. After it was ratified by a vote of California's white males, Peter H. Burnett was elected governor, and San Jose was selected as temporary capital. General Riley gracefully resigned his powers as governor. California was in almost every respect a state, even though not yet admitted to the Union.

The legislature named two senators to be sent to Washington. One of these was Frémont, who had returned to California after his court-martial in order to supervise gold-mining operations on his tract of land at Mariposa. The other was Gwin. In March the two men laid copies of the new state constitution before Congress and requested admission of California into the Union.

Southern members of congress were, however, agitated at the prospect of admitting a free state occupying so vast a portion of the recent Mexican cession. Admission was rendered more complicated by California's involvement in the North–South struggle. Finally, after weeks of deadlock, a compromise "Omnibus Bill" assuaged the feelings of the South by allowing the future territories of New Mexico and Utah to decide for themselves their slave or free status. California was to be admitted as a free state. When news of California's admission reached San Francisco on October 18, all business was suspended, and the people poured into Portsmouth Square to hear local orators boast that California was a full-fledged member of the Union.

Locating the Capital

Several cities vied for the privilege of being selected as California's state capital. In addition to the claims of Monterey and San Francisco, support arose for San Luis Obispo, Benicia, Stockton, and Santa Barbara. San Jose was eliminated as a possibility because the legislators were not satisfied with the accommodations there; they were familiar with the town as the site of the first session of the legislature, dubbed after a trivial but highly publicized incident the "Legislature of a Thousand Drinks." A proposal by General Vallejo to lay out a new city between San Francisco and Sacramento along the Carquinez Straits received northern support, and in June 1851, Governor John McDougal actually moved the government archives from San Jose to this bleak site named Vallejo.

The state government was soon moved again to still another site. In February 1853, a resolution adopted by the legislature established Benicia as the capital. That town, which offered the dubious advantages of a two-story brick building in the middle of some river mud flats, was hardly more suitable than San Jose or Vallejo.

Meanwhile, Sacramento made such a strong bid for the capital that the legislature convened there in 1854. It had become one of the most populous cities in the state, and local pride ran high. A noisy procession marched through the principal streets, addresses of welcome were delivered, and Sacramento proved itself such a congenial place that it became firmly established as California's seat of government.

Selected Readings

The Frémont–Kearny–Stockton controversy over the governorship is portrayed in *Proceedings of the Court Martial in the Trial of (J. C.) Frémont* (Washington, D.C., 1848; republished Urbana, Ill.,1973).

Basic to understanding California's statehood are William H. Ellison, *A Self-Governing Dominion: California, 1849–1860* (Berkeley, 1950), and Cardinal L. Goodwin, *The Establishment of State Government in California, 1846–1850* (New York, 1914). Joseph Ellison's *California and the Nation, 1850–1869* (Berkeley, 1927) tells the story of the state's early relations with the country as a whole.

Events at the constitutional convention are related in J. Ross Browne, *Report of the Debates in the Convention of California on the Formation of the State Constitution* (Washington, D.C., 1850). Later treatments include Rockwell D. Hunt's *The Genesis of California's First Constitution* (Baltimore, 1895). Other accounts of these early years include Samuel H. Willey, *The Transition Period of California* (San Francisco, 1901), James A. B. Sherer, *Thirty-first Star* (New York, 1942), and articles by Joseph and William H. Ellison as well as by Bayrd Still, Earl Pomeroy, Grace E. Tower, and Hallie M. McPherson in the files of the *Pacific Historical Review*, the California Historical Society *Quarterly*, and the Historical Society of Southern California *Quarterly*.

The *Journals* of California's assembly and senate for 1850 are useful, as is the state constitution; a modern printing with an introduction by Robert G. Cleland is *Constitution of the State of California* (San Marino, 1949).

Notable also are Governor Peter H. Burnett's *Recollections and Opinions of an Old Pioneer* (New York, 1880), and William Day Simonds, *Starr King in California* (San Francisco, 1917).

CHAPTER 17

Social Ferment

CALIFORNIA SOCIETY REMAINED in turmoil after the gold rush in an unsettled culture without the foundations needed to give it stability. Discordant, brawling, and lawless elements had entered the new state and were bound to alter its future. The sheer numbers of California's new immigrants created a formidable problem of assimilation. By 1850, only about 8 percent of the white populace of over 100,000 were native Californians. Nearly one-fourth of these had come from foreign countries; the rest came from throughout the United States. Blacks numbered fewer than 1,000 persons. Thousands of uncounted Indians, confused and bewildered by the American conquest, were everywhere to be seen. Among the whites, men predominated over women at a ratio of twelve to one, few of the women and many of the men being unmarried. With so divergent a population, California faced grave social unrest.

Vigilantism and Its Roots

Although, in the absence of order, each man substituted his own notions of justice, "Respectable citizens" called for greater public morality; they were especially concerned with stamping out corruption at San Francisco, the state's first real city. But Californians did not always rid themselves gracefully of their social nuisances. In an atmosphere of legal amateurism, vigilantes devised callous legal remedies. The failure of duly constituted authorities to prosecute criminal offenders led to vindictive punishment of such persons at the hands of vigilantes.

Nevertheless, it would be inaccurate to speak of the activities of the vigilance committees as synonymous with mobocracy or lynch law. The vigilantes arose because the signing of the new constitution—and even the achievement of statehood—did not solve the problem of crime in California. Most vigilance committees considered themselves to be "popular tribunals" constituted as "the champions of justice and of right." A mob, in contrast, is a rabble animated by a common passion. The vigilantes did not usually operate where there was effective prosecution of the law.

After the discovery of gold, the influx into San Francisco included hundreds of young social parasites and criminals who paralyzed the weak municipal organization of San Francisco. In 1849 a band calling themselves the "Hounds," or "Regulators," terrorized the city with repeated acts of violence. These young men had been roaming San Francisco's streets as though they owned them. A similar group of hoodlums had their headquarters in Sydney Town, a notorious section of the city. Known as the "Sydney Ducks," this band was composed of former members of Great Britain's prison colony in Australia, newly arrived in California. Honest residents noted their troublesome activities by saying: "The Sydney Ducks are cackling."

Meanwhile, antiforeign sentiment flourished in California's new cities. This nativism, a form of racial hatred, became entwined with the sordid activities of San Francisco's gangs. On Sunday, July 15, 1849, a rowdy crowd of Regulators held a "patriotic" parade. After touring various saloons, where they demanded liquor and smashed windows, they began to assault Chilean families in tents on the city's sand dunes. They beat, kicked, and fired upon these foreigners, several of whom were seriously wounded. As news of these outrages spread, excitement in the town rose to a high pitch. Sam Brannan and other indignant city elders and property owners arrested and prepared to try the offenders. A citizens' court banished the Regulators from San Francisco. A delirium of criminality was to plague the city for several years. Murderers and thieves again went unpunished, and the city government showed no signs of acting against vice and corruption.

Vigilance Activity in the Early 1850s

Suddenly the civic conscience shook off its lethargy. In 1851, after a prominent merchant was assaulted and his safe burglarized, "The Committee of Vigilance of San Francisco" organized itself, with 200 members pledged "to watch, pursue, and bring to justice the outlaws infesting the city, through the regularly constituted courts, if possible, through more summary course, if necessary." The members determined that "no thief, burglar, incendiary, or assassin, shall escape punishment, either by the quibbles of the law, the insecurity of prisons, the carelessness or corruption of the police, or a laxity of those who pretend to administer justice." At the head of the committee to purge the city of vice was William T. Coleman, a successful young merchant and later one of the nabobs of San Francisco society.

Scarcely had the organization been formed when the city's fire bell brought the members to its headquarters, the Monumental Fire Engine House. John Jenkins, a former convict from Sydney, Australia, had burglarized a shipping office on Commercial Street, boldly carrying off its strongbox. Jenkins made the mistake of defying anyone to stop him. When several vigilantes sought to do so, he threw the strongbox into San Francisco Bay in an act of further contempt. When he was apprehended, the vigilance committee brought Jenkins to their headquarters, where the merchant Sam Brannan acted as his judge. Within a few hours, almost at the stroke of midnight, Jenkins was pronounced guilty. In the early morning hours the condemned man was taken to Portsmouth Square; a scaffold was hastily erected, a noose draped round his neck, and he was hanged. Although a coroner's jury charged Brannan and the other vigilantes with a rather hasty, indeed harsh, execution, San Francisco's "best citizens" approved the sentence heartily. The work of the vigilance committee continued until both the audacity and the power of the Sydney Ducks, and other criminal elements, were forever broken.

On the morning of July 11, 1851, the bell on the firehouse summoned the vigilance committee to consider a case involving another Sydney Duck, "English Jim" Stuart, a confessed criminal. Earlier, through mistaken identity, the committee had been about to execute an innocent man; but they discovered their mistake and found Stuart guilty instead. Stuart was led to the Market Street Wharf, where he was hanged aboard the deck of a ship anchored nearby. Two other men, Samuel Whittaker and Robert McKenzie, were soon afterward brought to trial for various crimes. Although they confessed and were condemned by the vigilantes to die, these prisoners were suddenly seized by the legally appointed sheriff and placed in jail. On Sunday afternoon, August 24, they were reabducted by a party of vigilantes, who took the men to their headquarters. The bell that summoned committee members soon sounded its death knell. Six thousand men witnessed in silence the execution of Whittaker and McKenzie.

The record of sentences imposed by the vigilance committee of 1851 is as follows, in addition to the four hangings: whipped, one man; deported, fourteen; ordered to leave the state, one; handed over to the "authorities," fifteen; discharged, forty-one. The final entry in the secretary's book is dated June 30, 1852. Even then the association was not formally dissolved, its members standing ready to resume their activities.

Apologists for "do-it-yourself justice" cite the remoteness or corruption of the police and courts. They continue to applaud the vigilantes. A reexamination of the record reveals that the distinction between vigilance activity and lynching was often lost sight of and that grave abuses were committed. Walter Van Tilburg Clark's *The Ox Bow Incident* splits sharply with the tradition that once glorified vigilantism.

During the early 1850s vigilante activities in the interior mining camps took on spectacular forms. The pages of the *Alta California*, the state's most important newspaper of the period, record many instances of the arbitrary administration of justice.

Whenever a mob got out of hand, foreigners were likely to bear the brunt of its fury, as in the lynching of Juanita, an "evil" Mexican woman. On the evening of July 4, 1851, at Downieville, a town on the north fork of the Yuba River, a group of American Independence Day celebrants smashed in the door of her shack. In the ensuing turmoil, Juanita knifed one of them. A vigilante jury speedily sentenced her to be hanged, although several of the miners who composed the jury were repelled by the idea of dealing so harshly with a woman. Juanita was "strung up" from a wooden bridge that spanned the Yuba.

Much of the persecution of foreigners, however, had an economic motivation. Immigrant miners, among them Chileans, Frenchmen, and Hawaiian Kanakas, were frequently chased out of select diggings. Yet these foreigners were too valuable a source of cheap labor to exclude permanently from the employment market. After 1850 Mexican labor could be obtained in the mines for as little as $1 per day. Thus, when restrictions, legal or extralegal, got so severe as to drive foreigners permanently out of California, some employers bridled. Groups of them sought to protect foreign laborers against mobs of jealous competitors and to repeal the legislature's "foreign miners' tax" of 1850. When this oppressive tax failed to produce more than $30,000 in its first year of operation (instead of a predicted $2,400,000), pressure for its repeal began to make sense.

In the early 1850s foreigners were not the only target of amateur law enforcers and guardians of middle-class respectability, who also turned their wrath upon suspected prostitutes, thieves, or drifters. At Sacramento 215 citizens formed themselves into a committee in order to police the city more efficiently. At Marysville, after seventeen murders had occurred within a week, another vigilance committee took "prompt steps in the premises." Because robberies were a particularly "frequent and alarming occurrence" around Mokelumne Hill, a scapegoat was executed in the presence of nearly one thousand witnesses. Presumption of guilt, in general equivalent to conviction, resulted in execution, ear cropping, or whipping.

The execution of Casey and Cora, 1856. Contemporary print. (H. G. Hills Collection; by courtesy of The Bancroft Library, University of California, Berkeley.)

San Francisco's Second Vigilance Committee

Only five years after San Franciscans dissolved their first vigilante brigades, another committee of vigilance came into being. This was the most reputable and orderly of all such groups. As the vision of the hangman's noose faded from memory, criminal activity again increased. About 1,000 unpunished homicides occurred in San Francisco from 1849 to 1856. In this period also, through the stuffing of ballot boxes and the use of "shoulder strikers," or city toughs, at polling places, corrupt officials became entrenched in municipal posts.

In this atmosphere the murder of James King of William, gadfly editor of the *Daily Evening Bulletin*, brought the city's corruption and lawlessness to still another climax. King had not hesitated to attack prominent personalities, including James P. Casey, a local politician and an unsavory business opportunist. King bluntly stated that his newspaper "would make certain parties writhe under the agony" of his exposures. Casey marched into the *Bulletin's* editorial room to demand an apology for accusations against him that had appeared in the paper. When ordered out of the building, Casey vowed he would kill the editor. King scoffed at this threat in his columns of May 14, 1856.

That evening, about five o'clock, Casey approached the newspaperman on the street, drew a revolver, aimed it, and pulled the trigger. King fell to the ground, mortally wounded. Shortly thereafter Casey was locked up in the city jail. Three days later several thousand vigilantes, enraged over this latest in a succession of homicides, seized

Casey and another accused murderer, Charles Cora, from the city jail and sentenced them to death before a tribunal. As King's funeral cortege moved through the city streets, the vigilantes executed Casey and Cora.

Within a fortnight almost 10,000 men had joined the vigilantes, with veterans of the 1851 group among the first to enroll. Each member, after taking a solemn oath, was known only by his assigned number. This San Francisco Vigilance Committee of 1856 again chose William T. Coleman as its head. After the election of officers, Coleman appointed a vigilante chief of police and twenty-five policemen to supplement local law-enforcement officers. Motivating the 1856 committee was its constitution, which described the association as existing "for maintenance of peace and good order of society." Coleman organized the membership into groups of 100 men each, with ten companies to a regiment. A letter from the vigilantes served notice upon San Francisco's Sheriff and his deputies that they would be held accountable for the custody of accused prisoners.

Mass meetings at Sacramento, Stockton, and San Francisco gave the vigilantes momentum, but there was also opposition to the movement. A Law and Order Party objected to the activities of the San Francisco committee on the ground that there was no real need of organized vigilance. State Supreme Court Justice David S. Terry lent his support to this countermovement of the Law and Order faction. Unfortunately for Terry and his cause, he became involved in a knifing fracas with one of the vigilantes, and was indicted by the vigilance committee. The judge's behavior ironically helped to discredit his argument that constituted law and order could cope with crime and public violence. Fortunately the man he had stabbed did not die, and after almost a month of embarrassing hearings Terry was acquitted. Few other officials opposed the vigilance committee of 1856.

Meanwhile, Governor John Neely Johnson, an antiforeign Know-Nothing Party leader, had taken cognizance of municipal crime in California, but he was inconsistent in combating it. Finally, on June 2, Governor Johnson asked William Tecumseh Sherman, commander of the second division of the California militia, to aid him in the enforcement of state law. By this time, however, the San Francisco vigilance committee was able to call upon 6,000 armed partisans and had firmly fortified its headquarters building, known as Fort Gunnybags.

Sherman, convinced of the military force and popularity of the committee's activities, did little to stem its power. Protected by bags of sand piled ten feet high and six feet thick, the committee stationed volunteer guards at key points. A great alarm bell was suspended on the roof, where cannon were also placed.

In its executive chamber, a spacious room in which were hung the flags of different nations, the vigilance committee continued to conduct its trials. Although the executive committee had a "black list," no action was taken except on the concurrence of at least two-thirds of all vigilantes present. The first deportations occurred on June 5, when three men were sent to Hawaii and three others to Panama. Persons so banished were warned not to return to California on penalty of death. Some undesirable characters preferred to depart rather than to risk rigorous penalties. With law and order restored, the committee voluntarily dissolved itself on August 18, 1856, ending three months of virtual control over the city.

Filibustering

Both vigilante activities and filibustering were typical of mid-nineteenth-century life on an unpoliced frontier. The term "filibuster," today applied to prolonged speech making in order to delay legislative procedures, had a more brutal connotation in that era. Filibusters went abroad to "free" unprotected territory from foreign control. The residents of such areas considered invading filibusters land thieves if nothing else. When successful, the filibuster might be acclaimed a hero at home; when he failed he was branded an outlaw.

Filibustering was a phenomenon of a restless, youthful America, convinced of its Manifest Destiny to expand toward the country's "natural frontiers." This expansionist enthusiasm had not abated with the acquisition of Texas and California. Rootless adventurers, anxious for new experiences, continued to be attracted to pursuits that would extend American rule over still more territory. During the 1850s it was as unpopular for a Westerner to be opposed to filibustering as it was for a Southerner to be against slavery. The two were not unrelated. Southerners among the filibusters were attracted to projects for spreading slavery farther south. Apologists for filibustering professed admiration for the courage of adventurers willing to shoulder rifles in foreign fields, seeing them as patriotic soldiers of fortune in an expanding America.

Unsettled conditions in California in the 1850s stimulated filibustering; disillusioned gold seekers looked covetously beyond American territory for adventure. However, the filibustering expeditions that originated from California after its admission to statehood were uniformly unsuccessful. The first one, in 1851 under the leadership of Alexander Bell, foolishly planned to reinstate a deposed president of Ecuador; before Bell reached Quito, rival factions in that country had composed their differences and united to rid Ecuador of Americans. Bell retreated to Panama, where his party was stranded; the expedition proved a fiasco. That same year Sam Brannan, an apostate from Mormonism, led a party of adventurers to Hawaii aboard the vessel *Game Cock*. In his attempt to capture those islands, Brannan was lucky to escape incensed Hawaiian pikemen, who threatened to run their spears through him. Joseph C. Morehead's plan to take the spiny peninsula of Lower California, also in 1851, proved equally futile. After most of Morehead's men deserted, he was fortunate to avoid Mexican imprisonment.

French Expeditions from California

Not only Americans were stirred by the possibility of filibustering. California's sizable foreign population included other footloose elements as well, among them Frenchmen who had taken leave of their native country as a result of the revolutionary movements of 1848. These failed aristocrats craved a life of adventurous treasure seeking and were especially interested in plans to colonize Mexico. Three such persons have left their mark upon the history of both California and northern Mexico: the Marquis Charles de Pindray, Lepine de Sigondis, and Count Gaston de Raousset-Boulbon.

De Pindray was a nobleman skilled in handling weapons. In 1851 he accepted an offer from the Mexican government to raise volunteers to protect the Sonoran mines against Apache Indians. This recruiting he did in California, where restless adventurers were in great supply. His men (all French immigrants) were to receive lands which Mexico hoped would serve as a buffer colony facing the United States. On the day after Christmas that year, de Pindray landed on the Mexican west coast at Guaymas with a force of 140. Their reception was at first enthusiastic. His band proceeded inland to Arispe; then he and his men began an arduous march toward the gold mines of the interior. Dissension developed, complicated by ill feeling between de Pindray's forces and the Mexicans through whose territory they passed. Suddenly de Pindray was mysteriously shot through the head. He may have been murdered by Indians, or by one of his men. The survivors of his party straggled back to the coast, where they made a hasty departure from the country.

The expedition of Lepine de Sigondis, another Frenchman, resembled that of de Pindray. Both men were promised land and met political conditions in the Mexican northwest that proved their undoing. De Sigondis, enlisting some sixty men, indeed was fortunate to escape death. Future filibusters from California would not always be so lucky.

The most renowned of all its French filibusters was Count de Raousset-Boulbon, nicknamed "Little Wolf." He was characterized by marked versatility, abounding energy, and great personal courage. Well educated and not entirely without idealism, he was at the same time prodigal and self-indulgent. He came to California in 1850 to seek his fortune, but met with only slender success in numerous jobs. Then, with an eye on the rich mines of Sonora, he turned to the promotion of a colonization enterprise with Patrice Dillon, French consul at San Francisco. Dillon, himself a filibuster at heart, became enthusiastic over the prospect of forming a buffer colony in northern Mexico to checkmate further advance of the United States. In 1852, after de Raousset-Boulbon obtained concessions in the area, underwritten by an anonymous banking house, both the French minister in Mexico and the governor of Sonora became financially interested in the filibuster's operations.

Raousset-Boulbon sailed for Guaymas on the Mexican west coast with 260 men on May 19, 1852. He received a warm welcome at that Mexican coastal town, but this was followed by a month's irksome delay due to political roadblocks. The count ignored warnings that he must placate rival Mexican political factions. Also, he refused to proceed to the interior by a circuitous route to avoid local Indian and Mexican opposition to him. When he received orders from one Mexican faction to report in person at Arispe, more than a hundred miles away from the seacoast, the Frenchman haughtily sent two underlings instead. These men returned with terms under which the party was warned to operate while in Mexico; but Raousset-Boulbon rejected the demands, making his company an armed enemy of local Mexican officialdom. There followed a period in which he was accused of organizing a rebellion in Mexico. He had indiscreetly offered to "liberate" northwestern Mexico and was actually able to capture Hermosillo. The count soon realized his hopelessly isolated position in a foreign land, and, after seventeen of his men were killed and twenty-three wounded, he retreated toward Guaymas on the seacoast and then to San Francisco.

During the next few years the count was in and out of Mexico, seeking land grants upon which to settle French, German, and Irish adherents. On the eve of a second expedition, however, his hopes were dashed by a report that President Antonio Santa Anna had sold part of Sonora to the United States. The rumor had a firm basis in the negotiations then being conducted between Mexico and the United States over a strip of land on the south side of the Mexican boundary. This territory, extending from the Gulf of Mexico to the Rio Grande, was the Gadsden Purchase; it became a part of the United States in 1854.

That same year Raousset-Boulbon led another expedition into Mexico. This time, when the Frenchman reached Guaymas with 500 men, he met unified resistance instead of the partial welcomes of the past. After part of his force had been killed, he was compelled to surrender. Tried on a charge of conspiracy, he was executed on August 12, 1854. At his own request the indomitable count faced a firing squad unblindfolded. His men were allowed to escape.

"The Gray-Eyed Man of Destiny"

A rival of Raousset-Boulbon and the best known of all California filibusters—indeed, one of the most melodramatic figures in United States history—was William Walker. A restless native of Tennessee, Walker completed medical studies at the University of Pennsylvania, then spent a year visiting various European cities. He did not find the practice of medicine to his liking, and, after further wandering, arrived at San Francisco in June 1850. Following a short venture into journalism there, during which a caustic pen sent him to jail, he entered into law practice at Marysville.

Accounts of French colonization in Mexico fired Walker with a passion that led him to be called "the gray-eyed man of destiny" and "the archfilibuster of California." In 1854, just as Walker was forming his own expedition, misfortune struck Raousset-Boulbon's last filibustering attempt. Both men competed for the limited funds available for such risky ventures. Walker's ambition was to bring about the independence of Sonora and Lower California for annexation to his own country, thus affording a new arena for the extension of slavery. He possessed an unquestioning belief in his own destiny. Yet his personal physique was far from impressive. A slight, red-haired, gray-eyed man, freckle-faced and slow of speech, below medium height, and weighing scarcely more than 100 pounds, Walker opened a recruiting office in San Francisco. There hundreds bought land certificates from him to be redeemed in Sonoran lands.

Walker, eluding United States government officials who did not want him to sail, left the Golden Gate with forty-eight followers and landed at La Paz, where he was reinforced by two hundred Mexicans. He then proclaimed the independent "Republic of Lower California." This short-lived "government" he quickly abolished, however, to launch the "Republic of Sonora," consisting of Lower California and Sonora, with himself as president. Reports of his activities brought him immense popularity in California. While Walker campaigned in Mexico the flag of the new republic waved over his San Francisco enlistment office and his bonds found a ready market there.

But soon there were reverses for Walker. Native Mexicans began to resent these California foraging expeditions; also some of his men deserted. Walker's harsh punishment of deserters added to his unpopularity. His force was reduced to thirty-five by the time they reached the Colorado River. This remnant finally reached the United States boundary near Tijuana in May 1854, and surrendered to American authorities. Tried at San Francisco on a charge of violating United States neutrality laws, Walker was acquitted and resumed the practice of law, though not for long.

Walker's next objective was Central America—Nicaragua in particular. One of the revolutionary factions in that country conceived the idea that, with Walker's aid, success would be certain. On May 3, 1855, he set sail for Nicaragua with sixty enlisted men. After landing, he declared himself to be the president of Nicaragua. Although he gained temporary power by this bold act, Walker overreached himself when he proclaimed a reversal of Nicaraguan antislavery laws that had been in existence for a generation. A series of revolts followed, and Walker surrendered in May 1857. Walker fled back to the United States, where he undertook other expeditions, despite his arrest on several occasions for violating American neutrality laws. His last enterprise involved a landing in Honduras, undertaken in hopes of returning to Nicaragua. Walker was shot as a foreign interloper in 1860.

The End of Filibustering

One of the last California filibusters was Henry A. Crabb, who had been a schoolmate of Walker's in Tennessee. A resident of Stockton after 1849, Crabb, like Walker, was intrigued by the possibility of spreading slavery abroad. In 1855 he enlisted swashbucklers and adventurers for his own expedition to Nicaragua; the exploit soured and he returned, a year later, to enter California politics. Following his marriage into a prominent Sonoran family, Crabb, in 1857, organized the Arizona and Gadsden Colonization Company with the purpose of taking over part of the Mexican state of Sonora. "General" Crabb outfitted his expedition in Los Angeles and El Monte, and proceeded overland past Yuma, and on to Sonora. Ambushed, Crabb surrendered. The Mexicans brutally executed him and his men, tacking their heads onto poles that faced northward. This was a warning that Mexico wanted no further filibustering expeditions. Invaded countries saw filibusters as marauders who personified economic rape and the destruction of property. These adventurers were also victims of poor planning and bad leadership. During negotiations that led to the Gadsden Treaty, they proved to be an embarrassment to United States negotiators. By then filibustering had become an outmoded stepchild of Manifest Destiny.

Selected Readings

A starting point for the study of California's vigilante activities is Hubert Howe Bancroft, *Popular Tribunals* (2 vols., San Francisco, 1887). An account of the 1851 vigilance movement, edited by Mary Floyd Williams, is entitled *History of the San Francisco Committee of Vigilance of 1851* (Berkeley, 1921); she also edited the *Papers of the San Francisco Committee of Vigilance of 1851* (Berkeley, 1919). Consult also Shinn's *Mining Camps*. William T. Coleman wrote the story of the Vigilance Committee of 1856 in an article entitled "San Francisco Vigilance Committees" in *Century Magazine* 43 (November 1891), 133–50. James A. B. Scherer's biography of Coleman, *The Lion of the Vigilantes: William T. Coleman and the Life of Old San Francisco* (Indianapolis, 1939), includes commentary on Coleman. A popular work is Stanton A. Coblentz, *Villains and Vigilantes: Story of James King of William and Pioneer Justice in California* (New York, 1936). See also George R. Stewart, *Committee of Vigilance: Revolution in San Francisco . . .* (Boston, 1964), and Robert Senkewicz, *Vigilantes in Gold Rush San Francisco* (Stanford, 1985).

Sherman's troubles with the vigilantes were reported in his letters in *Century* 43 (December 1891), 296–309, entitled "Sherman and the San Francisco Vigilantes." There is a quasi-history of the 1856 movement, *San Francisco Vigilance Committee of '56* (San Francisco, 1883), written by one of its members and edited by Frank M. Smith. Another treatment is James O'Meara's *The Vigilance Committee of 1856* (San Francisco, 1887). Government reports are in *Senate Executive Documents*, 34th Congress, 1st and 2nd sessions, volume 15 (Washington, D.C., 1857) and 3rd session, volume 7 (Washington, D.C., 1857). Also consult Alan Valentine, *Vigilante Justice* (New York, 1956).

Condemnations of vigilantism appear in Walter Van Tilburg Clark, *The Ox Bow Incident* (New York, 1942), in Ellison's *A Self-Governing Dominion*, and in John W. Caughey, *Their Majesties the Mob* (Chicago, 1960). Leonard Pitt, "The Beginnings of Nativism in California," *Pacific Historical Review* 30 (February 1961), 23–38, discusses the breakdown of law and order in the California mines.

Writers have treated filibustering as both a national and local phenomenon. Among older works are James Jeffrey Roche, *By-Ways of War: The Story of the Filibusters* (Boston, 1901), and *The Story of the Filibusters* (London, 1891) by the same author; W. V. Wells, *Walker's Expedition to Nicaragua* (New York, 1856); and Walker's own *The War in Nicaragua* (Mobile, 1860). Also useful for a study of Walker's career is William O. Scroggs, *Filibusters and Financiers* (New York, 1916). Laurence Greene, *The Filibuster* (New York, 1937), is a biography of Walker.

The best work on de Raousset-Boulbon and the French expeditions from California is Rufus K. Wyllys, *The French in Sonora, 1850–1854* (Berkeley, 1932). See also Wyllys' articles in the *Pacific Historical Review:* "The Republic of Lower California, 1853–1854," 2 (June 1933), 194–214; "Henry A. Crabb—A Tragedy of the Sonora Frontier," 9 (June 1940), 183–94; "An Expansionist in Baja California, 1855," 1 (December 1932), 477–82; and Diana Lindsay, "Henry A. Crabb, Filibuster, and the San Diego Herald," *San Diego History* 19 (Winter 1973), 34–42.

The Brannan expedition to Hawaii is treated in Andrew Rolle, "California Filibustering and the Hawaiian Kingdom," *Pacific Historical Review* 19 (August 1950), 251–63; some last manifestations of filibustering are described in Rolle's "Futile Filibustering in Baja California, 1888–1890," *Pacific Historical Review* 20 (May 1951), 159–66.

CHAPTER 18

A New Culture at the Golden Gate

SAN FRANCISCO—historically and culturally—deserves to be called California's first city. After the gold rush the old Spanish hamlet of Yerba Buena grew out of its sand hills, its flapping canvas tents, lean-tos, and rickety frame shacks to become a city. In the twenty years between 1850 and 1870, San Francisco also exchanged its cultural primitiveness for a cosmopolitan diversity of tastes and ideas. Recording this transformation of a trading post into a confident metropolis was the German traveler Friedrich Gerstäcker, who returned to a new gaslit San Francisco after only a year's absence in the mines, "I really did not know where I was, did not recognize a single street, and was perfectly at a loss to think of such an entire change. Where I had left a crowded mass of low wooden huts and tents, I found a city in a great part built of brick, houses, pretty stores."

By the time the "splendid idle forties" were past, San Francisco's harbor had become a forest of masts. In 1851 a visitor counted 600 ships there. Sailors, traders, and miners had displaced rancheros in the city's life, and "flush times" had come to the village by the Golden Gate. The weight of gold nuggets helped push open doors once closed to all but a few Yanquis by California's native society. Thousands of invading foreigners ushered out the Mexican past.

The Aftermath of the Gold Rush

Although the citizens of San Francisco voted themselves a charter in 1850, some American pioneers spoke of staying in California for only five years and therefore showed little interest in investing in durable housing. During the decade following the gold rush, a spirit of chance pervaded the city. Yet pressing civic problems demanded

North Beach, San Francisco, ca. 1860. (H. G. Hills Collection; by courtesy of The Bancroft Library, University of California, Berkeley.)

action. The fire hazard grew because of the large number of flimsy wooden structures that had been constructed instead of adobe dwellings. Housing became even more of a problem as the need for it increased drastically during the early 1850s. In 1850 more than 36,000 immigrants arrived in San Francisco by sea alone—representatives of every race, creed, and culture. Among them were spendthrifts, future soldiers of fortune like William Walker, bankers, bandits, and gamblers. "The very air," journalist Bayard Taylor wrote, "is pregnant with the magnetism of bold, spirited, unwearied action."

San Francisco's interconnected settlements made the administration of law and order difficult. A sheltered enclave called "Happy Valley" still contained about a thousand makeshift tents during the winter of 1850. "Pleasant Valley" opened onto a vast beachfront from the middle of town. "Sydney Town," around the base of Telegraph Hill, became a hangout of convicts and "ticket of leave" men, castaways from Australia. This district had been a particular target of the committee of vigilance in its drive against crime. There were other outlying settlements, "Little Chile," "Spring Valley," and "St. Ann Valley," in which criminal activity could easily be hidden. All of these eventually merged into the larger municipal unit of San Francisco.

Meanwhile San Francisco underwent a prolonged baptism by fire.

Six conflagrations swept over the city in a period of eighteen months. The first took place in December 1849, when a million dollars' worth of canvas structures and the merchandise stored in them were consumed. A second great fire occurred in May of 1850. After an interval of scarcely a month came a third fire. Further erection of inflammable tents and cloth structures was prohibited. But lumber, extensively used in local building, proved scarcely less combustible. Most damaging of all was the disaster of May 4, 1851, which destroyed a large part of the town. San Francisco would eventually rebuild itself in brick and stone, but until it did the city was subjected seasonally to full-scale fires.

The air of uncertainty after the gold rush was reflected in the San Francisco commercial market, where prices dropped sharply. Pickled beef and pork went from $60 to $10 per barrel; wheat flour decreased from $800 to $20 per barrel. Merchants could only guess what to expect in supply and demand. At least one storekeeper used surplus merchandise for filling ruts along the city's streets. Others dumped spoiled flour and unsalable cast-iron stoves into mud holes. Imports piled up at the wharfs and few items remained difficult to obtain.

The gold rush boom had coaxed bankers, and traders, as well as merchants into speculations that were to prove their undoing. The goal of most newcomers was to build themselves granite and marble mansions on Nob Hill. Unfortunately the unprecedented production of gold, which exceeded half a billion dollars from 1849 to 1855, had confused the economic fabric of California's largest city. A downward swing of the financial pendulum and the declining yield of gold from the placers decreased the influx of population, causing a reversal in property values. Housing sites that had cost $15 before the rush reached $8,000 during its height, only to plummet to less than $100 later.

Among the more profitable enterprises of the time, though it too had its risks, was the operation of saloons and gambling establishments. Gerstäcker described the *Cafés Chantants*, kept by Frenchmen, as "common drinking rooms," in the back part of which there was often a stage and a piano. Their function, he reported, was to encourage "loud laughter, riotous conversation," and to distract patrons from workaday responsibilities. Gambling also took place there, as well as in the bona fide gambling houses. Among the latter, Denison's Exchange, the Parker House, the St. Charles, and the Bella Union featured games of chance. Some gambling parlors were decorated with plush furniture, chandeliers, and mirrors; the El Dorado, with its eight gaming tables, velvet-upholstered chairs, and spacious bar, attracted perhaps the greatest crowds. Upstairs in these establishments there were prostitution cribs. In the plushier spots customers were expected to keep their derringers out of sight, unless attacked. Nowhere in the world were there so many billiard tables in proportion to the population. A few of the wealthiest citizens got their start as faro dealers or card men.

Another popular pursuit, in San Francisco as in the rest of the American West, was the practice of dueling. Only after years of public criticism were these avenging "affairs of honor" abolished. San Francisco was predominantly a city of young men, far away from home and removed from family restraints. Gambling, dueling, theatrical performances, and other forms of ostentatious living, had more appeal than churchgoing. For some, gambling became a mania. This, however, was not the whole story. In 1849 the Reverend Albert Williams organized the First Presbyterian Church of San Francisco. Mission Dolores served as a place of worship for Catholics of the town until 1849, when their first city church, named for St. Francis, was organized.

Cultural Growth

Regardless of unsteady economic and social conditions, San Francisco was concerned with culture. From the beginning, education was one of its major interests. In 1849 John C. Pelton arrived from Boston to open a municipal school on Portsmouth Square, based upon New England traditions of instruction; and in 1851 the city added a superintendent of schools and regular board of education. In addition, San Francisco early became known for its museums and libraries. By 1853 the first Academy of Science in the West was begun there. Later, this cultural impetus was supported by the mining fortunes of Nevada's Comstock Lode and by the riches of California's railroad kings.

California's first English-language newspaper, the *Californian*, had appeared at Monterey on August 15, 1846. Actually, this four-page weekly was only half in the English language, the other side being printed in Spanish. Because of the scarcity of paper, it had to be printed on any stock available, even on wrapping and tissue paper. In May 1847 the *Californian* moved to the future San Francisco. Only a few months after this paper appeared, Sam Brannan founded the *California Star*. The gold rush stopped publication of these pioneer journals, but in 1849 the two papers merged as the weekly *Alta California*, which became a daily the next year.

Mid-century California, with San Francisco as its cultural center, nourished travel accounts and books of reminiscence and recollection written by pioneers who had come to California by sea. Richard Henry Dana's *Two Years Before the Mast* (1840) was one of the first books to introduce the pastoral California of hide and tallow days to a wide reading public. Dana's views on California, however, reflect a New Englander's bias against a Hispanic society. A less well-known pioneer sea chronicle by a Yankee maritime trader was Richard J. Cleveland's *A Narrative of Voyages and Commercial Enterprises* (1842). Cleveland, a native of Salem, Massachusetts, admired the physical beauty of California but, like Dana, was not impressed by its early government and society. Both books represent gringo views of hidalgo culture. Another early work was Alfred Robinson's *Life in California* (1846). Robinson, long a resident of the Mexican province, wrote from the viewpoint of one who wished to refute the inaccuracies of the ordinary traveler.

Accounts that treat the period following the hide and tallow trading era include Edwin Bryant's *What I Saw in California* (1848), Bayard Taylor's *El Dorado* (1849), and Walter Colton's *Three Years in California* (1850). Joseph Warren Revere's *A Tour of Duty in California* (1849) is a description by a lieutenant in the United States Navy of both Lower and Upper California, including the "gold region," ports, and "Indian areas." Colton, in a later book, *Deck and Port* (1850), further describes Americanization.

Lonely Americans clamored for every sort of literary fare, from travel descriptions to pseudophilosophical gleanings. Most early writing appeared in local journals spawned in San Francisco. The *Golden Era*, founded in 1852, was California's first weekly of any literary pretension. It was followed by the *Pioneer* (1854), *Hutchings' California Magazine* (1856), and the *Hesperian* (1858). Such magazines, though unsophisticated, enjoyed a successful, if brief, career. The *Golden Era*, longest-lived of the early journals, continued to be published until 1893.

The real distinction among the journals, however, belongs to the *Overland Monthly*, a little brown-covered magazine with a grizzly bear on its masthead. The *Overland*, which began publication in July 1868 and continued intermittently until 1883, compared favorably with some of the best Eastern literary journals. Bret Harte was its editor. He had come to California in 1854 as a typesetter on the *Golden Era*; after he left that job, he wrote for the *Californian*. During his editorship of the *Overland* he achieved national status as a writer of short stories. As editor, he encouraged other authors to write for the *Overland* and gained Eastern audiences for them too. Harte had first attracted attention in the *Golden Era* by the publication of "*M'liss*," and went on, in 1868, to write "The Luck of Roaring Camp." This was followed by other local-color stories in the *Overland*, including "Plain Language from Truthful James." "The Outcasts of Poker Flat," published in that journal in January 1869, reaffirmed and strengthened the reputation created by his earlier stories, leading him to wider audiences. Harte created a stereotype of the Western miner as a bearded, red-shirted rowdy. In romanticizing this symbolic figure, he did for the miner what Owen Wister later did for the cowboy. Mark Twain's descriptions of miners and mining camps in his *Roughing It* are more realistic than Harte's, but Twain's *Roughing It* is not to be taken seriously. Although modern readers find Harte's work sentimental, mannered, and forced, he imparts the flavor of California's mining camps, cow towns, and interior.

A crude literature of burlesque was then fashionable. One of the exponents of this jokester style was an army officer stationed in California, Lieutenant George Horatio Derby, known under two pen names, "The Veritable Squibob," and "John Phoenix." In 1856 he wrote a salty book, *Phoenixiana*, which became immensely popular. Readers roared at such Derby remarks as "Absinthe makes the heart grow fonder," and "They came to cough and remain to spray"; the latter was adopted as an advertisement by a San Francisco druggist. Derby lampooned men and institutions with his coarse humor.

This tendency also characterized the writing of another forty-niner, Alonzo ("Old Block") Delano, a favorite of miners. Delano's *Pen Knife Sketches* (1853), his *Life on the Plains and Among the Diggings* (1854), and his melodramatic play, *A Live Woman in the Mines* (1857), were widely read. Educated and uneducated alike reveled in the literary horseplay brought into lonely and obscure camps. "Old Block" was also the proud possessor and exploiter of what was considered California's largest nose, widely known throughout the West. Rooted in his own experiences, his exaggerations and rustic humor were particularly attractive to contemporaries. Delano's books became best-sellers. Other gold rush favorites included John R. Ridge, a writer of half-Cherokee extraction who used the sobriquet "Yellow Bird"; Prentice Mulford, who took the name "Dogberry" as his pseudonym, and who became a spiritualistic hermit; and William H. Rhodes, who wrote under the name "Caxton."

Local colorists and frontier satirists remained popular in the period that followed the scramble for gold. Among them were J. Ross Browne, Rollin Daggett, and Dan de Quille. They were not great writers, yet they mirrored the unformed, innocent, and excitable society in which they lived. They boasted about the achievements of a proud generation, and wrote high-flown, facetious exaggerations. Their writings help the historian to understand an environment in which restless readers were emerging from primitive mining camps. This Southwestern group of writers used dialect, nostalgia, audacity, and extravagance to entertain their readers.

Mark Twain

A then-obscure writer was to become a literary immortal. This was Samuel Langhorne Clemens, or Mark Twain. He wrote with crafts-

manship and humor. Twain had come west with his brother following
a brief and irritating period of military service with a Confederate
Missouri home guard unit during the first months of the Civil War.
(Years before, Twain had been a river pilot.) Twain went into mining
in Nevada, and when bad weather kept him from work in the diggings, he amused himself by writing burlesque and caricature sketches.
These he signed "Josh" and sent to the *Territorial Enterprise*, the main
newspaper of Virginia City; this town was located in what is now
Nevada, but then was dominated by California culture. In 1862 he
walked 130 miles from a lonely mining site to Virginia City to take
a job on the *Enterprise* for $25 per week. Two years later Twain left
Virginia City and drifted into California, where he became a reporter
for the San Francisco *Morning Call*.

At San Francisco he met stimulating fellow writers, among them
Prentice Mulford, Bret Harte, Charles Warren Stoddard, and Joaquin Miller. Together they contributed pieces to the *Golden Era*,
which Twain once called "the best weekly literary paper in the United
States—and I suppose I ought to know." Twain, always an individual
among individuals, got into trouble with the San Francisco police
because of letters he sent his old paper, the *Enterprise*. In these he
assailed the corruption of San Francisco's police force, naming names.
Because of reaction to these charges, Twain decided to get away until
the feeling against him blew over. At a cabin retreat near Angel's
Camp in the Tuolumne uplands Twain lived a hermit's existence.
He read, wrote, and mined for gold, returning each night to sleep
in his slab-sided cabin. In the barroom of a dingy hotel at nearby
Angel's, Twain heard one Ben Coon—a former Illinois riverboat
pilot—tell a sprightly story about a rigged frog-derby. Although already printed in different versions in the California press, it was new
to Twain. He stayed on at Angel's that winter, and, on a plain table
in front of his rough stone fireplace, he wrote the first version of
"The Celebrated Jumping Frog of Calaveras County," adding a be-
guiling twist to the ending. This work was done at the request of the
humorist Artemus Ward, who wished to include the piece in a collection of tales to be published in New York. Without Twain's permission, the piece got submitted to an Eastern journal, the *New York
Saturday Press*. It made Twain famous almost overnight. In May 1867
it was published again, as the title story in Twain's first book, *The
Jumping Frog of Calaveras County and Other Sketches*.

During the long winter at Angel's Camp, Twain developed his art
of storytelling. He set himself the goal of writing incredible tales in
the same manner as he told them to lonesome miners. Returning to
San Francisco, he wrote a few more sketches for local journals, but
the publicity he achieved from the story of the jumping frog launched
him on a greatly expanded career. In 1866, at the age of thirty, he
sailed for the Sandwich Islands as a correspondent of the Sacramento

Union. Upon his return, Twain gave a series of comical lectures on Hawaii in California and Nevada. These started him on his way as a public speaker. Then he headed east.

Twain had made his mark in California and the West. His book *Roughing It* grew out of his experiences in the Nevada mines. He assembled his reports from abroad to the San Francisco *Alta California*, Sacramento *Union*, and New York *Tribune* in book form as *The Innocents Abroad* (1869). These writings helped him gain the international stature he came to enjoy. His satirical examination of society's shortcomings was at the heart of his success. Out west, where conditions were crude, was where he developed his famous narrative style.

Early Artists

San Francisco nourished, in addition to its prolific writers, a notable artistic colony. Among the foreign-born craftsmen associated with the area was the German etcher and printmaker Edward Vischer. Vischer traveled throughout California making sketches of the missions, which, after the gold rush, had been reduced to a state of "noble ruin." Another significant artist was the Scottish painter William Keith, sent west by the publishing house of Harper and Brothers in 1858 to execute engravings of the missions. The bear symbol on the masthead of the *Overland Monthly* is said to have been the work of Keith, who was a friend of Bret Harte. In 1866 Keith also painted an Overland Stage Coach poster which became known all over the nation. His water colors of the Yosemite, as well as his depicting of the California landscape, made him one of the most appreciated artists in the West, and the most renowned of California's landscape painters. Regrettably, most of Keith's best canvases were lost in the San Francisco fire of 1906.

Wealthy patrons also were attracted to the paintings of Charles Christian Nahl. Nahl, a German, had come to California in 1848. Taken with the grandeur of its scenery, he soon was producing a series of light-hearted sketches for San Francisco publishers. These sketches were printed on lithographed stationery used by miners who wrote home from the gold fields. They were also reproduced as etchings in books. Nahl's oils became popular on Nob Hill; his commissioned canvases were executed in a markedly romantic style.

John W. Audubon, youngest son of the noted naturalist, met with considerably less luck. He toured the California diggings after the gold rush making hundreds of realistic pencil and watercolor sketches of what he saw. Audubon decided to ship these paintings and sketches to the East Coast. Because they were too bulky to go overland, he

Residences of Mrs. Mark Hopkins and Governor Stanford, San Francisco. (H. G. Hills Collection; by courtesy of The Bancroft Library, University of California, Berkeley.)

Colton and Crocker mansions, San Francisco. (H. G. Hills Collection; by courtesy of The Bancroft Library, University of California, Berkeley.)

entrusted them to a friend traveling eastward in 1857 on the ship *Central America*. Audubon's friend and the bulk of his work went down with the ship.

Albert Bierstadt, like Vischer and Nahl a German artist, first came to San Francisco in 1858; he had traveled by way of the Rockies with a government exploring expedition. Bierstadt's canvases, in particular his exquisite paintings of animals in the mountains, plains, and forests of North America, grew very popular. His chief interest, like that of his contemporaries, lay in idealizing natural wonders: Yosemite Falls, the giant sequoias of the Sierra, and California's coastline. Later in life Bierstadt continued work in his New York studio near Irvington-on-Hudson. Some of his best oils, like those of Keith, were destroyed in the fire of 1906.

At San Francisco the tastes of its affluent citizens were reflected in the art they subsidized. Contemporary descriptions of the city of the "golden fifties and champagne sixties" stress its opulence as revealed in architecture and allied arts. There was uniformity in the buildings constructed by the rich during that period. The same Italian artists who painted the interiors of Mark Hopkins's baroque castle on Nob Hill also decorated theaters, hotels, saloons, and brothels along the city's Barbary Coast. Gilt-edged Victorian residences like that of Charles Crocker, with its ornate carvings, bell towers, and verandas, overlooked hilly lawns sprinkled with cast-iron animals. Popular legend has it that in the vicinity of the Hopkins mansion there were so many brass fences that one man was kept busy polishing them. The Flood mansion, across the street from Hopkins's, had such a fence as a memento of the days when its owner, James C. Flood, was a barkeep who prided himself on his brass bar rail.

The Theater

A prominent part of San Francisco's cultural scene was its Jenny Lind Theater, a favorite haunt of fans who flocked there to see the notorious Lola Montez. Lola, whose name was linked with many lovers, including King Ludwig of Bavaria, had been treated as a strumpet in the large cities of the Eastern United States. At San Francisco, however, her reception was ecstatic, even as compared with that accorded the great Shakespearean troopers Junius Brutus Booth and his son Edwin. Lola capitalized on the title given her by Ludwig— Countess of Landsfeld. But it was her beautiful figure, flashing eyes, and raven-black hair that captivated audiences. Her "Tarantula Dance," in which she shivered and trembled, was a lure for the crowds that assembled to see her. In 1853 she married Patrick Hull, an editor of the San Francisco *Whig*. At the primitive mining camp of Grass

Valley her husband, with whom she had quarreled violently, suddenly died. Lola agreed to resume performing, at $100 per admission. Even at this rate, she never lacked for customers. Brandishing a whip on stage, Lola defied and wooed the miners into a frenzy. After reputedly selling her jewels for $20,000 to the madam of a fashionable brothel, she left California behind for new conquests in Australia.

Lola Montez, however, was only one of the performers warmly received by early San Francisco audiences. In the two decades from 1850 to 1870 there was a great deal of interest in classical drama, and the Booths, among other actors, enjoyed tremendous popularity. Despite the crudity of the environment in which *A Midsummer Night's Dream* or *Romeo and Juliet* might be staged, audiences took these performances seriously, hurling both praise and maledictions at actors on stage. The number of performances staged and cast at San Francisco was staggering. Some 1,100 dramatic pieces were produced there from 1850 to 1859.

Whether a performer was in a melodrama or danced in an extravaganza, the star system emerged at an early date. A yearning for identification with individual performers characterized San Francisco's audiences. Players were amazed when gold nuggets and diamond brooches were thrown onto the stage by frontiersmen who had struck it rich. One of the artists on whom attention was showered was the flaming redhead Adah Menken. Clad in flesh-colored tights, she was probably the first woman to play the title role in *Mazeppa*, based on a romantic poem by Lord Byron. During 1863, at the Tivoli Theater, the shapely Miss Menken showed such consummate talent that the St. Francis Hook and Ladder Company made her a member of its fire-fighting brigade. This actress was wooed by international figures, including Alexandre Dumas and his son, as well as Dante Gabriel Rossetti. In later years Miss Menken was to be followed in popularity by Lillian Russell and Sarah Bernhardt.

Writers, artists, and actors all found San Francisco congenial. Its bohemian quarter stretched from North Beach across Telegraph Hill. Following the primitiveness of the gold rush years, a cosmopolitan culture flourished there.

Selected Readings

Among contemporary narratives of early San Francisco are Bayard Taylor, *Eldorado, or Adventures in the Path of Empire* (New York, 1850; repr. 1949), and Friedrich Gerstäcker, *Narrative of a Journey . . .* (New York, 1853), as well as T. A. Barry and B. A. Patten, *Men and Memories of San Francisco* (San Francisco, 1873). Useful for descriptive sketches of a later period is Robert E. Cowan, *Forgotten Characters of Old San*

Francisco (Los Angeles, 1938). For a visual impression see John H. Kemble, ed., *San Francisco Bay* (Cambridge, Md., 1957). Julia Altrocchi, *The Spectacular San Franciscans* (New York, 1949) and William M. Camp, *San Francisco, Port of Gold* (New York, 1947) also set the scene. In this same vein is Samuel Dickson, *San Francisco Is Your Home* (Stanford, 1947). Useful are Julian Dana, *The Man Who Built San Francisco* (New York, 1936); George D. Lyman, *Ralston's Ring* (New York, 1937); Amelia R. Neville, *Fantastic City* (Boston, 1932); and Miriam Allen de Ford, *They Were San Franciscans* (Caldwell, Idaho, 1941). See also Robert W. Lotchin, *San Francisco, 1846–1856: From Hamlet to City* (New York, 1974); Felix Riesenberg, *Golden Gate* (New York, 1940), and Charles Caldwell Dobie, *San Francisco, A Pageant* (New York, 1943). Educational advance is discussed in William G. Cain, *John Swett: The Biography of an Educational Pioneer* (Santa Ana, 1933) and in John C. Pelton, *Origin of the Free Public Schools of San Francisco . . .* (San Francisco, 1865).

For early journalism and literature see Franklin Walker, *San Francisco's Literary Frontier* (New York, 1939). The theater is treated in G. R. MacMinn, *The Theater of the Golden Era* (Caldwell, Idaho, 1941). Biographies include Bernard de Voto, *Mark Twain's America* (Boston, 1932); Justin Kaplan, *Mr. Clemens and Mark Twain* (New York, 1966); Ivan Benson, *Mark Twain's Western Years* (Stanford, 1938); and Edgar M. Branch, *The Literary Apprenticeship of Mark Twain* (Urbana, Ill., 1950). Regarding Harte, the best general book is George R. Stewart's *Bret Harte: Argonaut and Exile* (Boston, 1931). Stewart has also written about George Derby in *John Phoenix, Esq.: The Veritable Squibob* (New York, 1937). On Browne, see David Goodman, *A Western Panorama, 1849–1875: The Travels, Writings and Influence of J. Ross Browne* (Glendale, 1966). Francis P. Weisenburger has written a biography of Rollin Daggett, *Idol of the West* (Syracuse, 1965). Also see *The Western Gate: A San Francisco Reader*, edited by Joseph Henry Jackson (New York, 1952). A more specific piece of quanto-history is Peter Decker, *Fortunes and Failures: White Collar Mobility in Nineteenth Century San Francisco* (Cambridge, Mass., 1978).

Accounts of artists attracted to California are harder to come by. One of the few biographies is Eugen Neuhaus, *William Keith: The Man and the Artist* (Berkeley, 1938). Another biography, copiously illustrated, is Brother Cornelius's *Keith, Old Master of California* (New York, 1942). Helpful sketches of John W. Audubon, Albert Bierstadt, William Keith, Charles C. Nahl, and Victor Prevost are in *California Centennials Exhibition of Art* (Los Angeles, 1949). See also *The Drawings of John Woodhouse Audubon*, intro. and notes by Carl S. Dentzel (San Francisco, 1957).

CHAPTER 19

Post–Gold Rush Commerce and Industry

AFTER THE GOLD RUSH, California's commercial growth was sometimes erratic. Eventually a more settled, balanced pattern began to emerge. As the hide and tallow traffic, the overland fur trade, and sea-otter hunting receded into history, Californians turned toward more permanent means of livelihood.

One of the declining occupations was gold mining; the most precious deposits of ore were quickly exhausted. Individual miners moving from one rich lode to another gave way to organized mining companies, which could provide the machinery required to engage in deepshaft quartz operations. The percentage of the population engaged in mining continued to decrease. According to the 1850 census reports, 50 percent of California's working population was engaged in gold mining. Of these, many were employed in large-scale operations, either in quartz and stamp mills or in smelters and foundries. Some miners turned from gold to silver mining. A few entered professions that depended upon the mining industry—law, engineering, and banking. Former red-shirted miners also settled down to running hardware stores, livery stables, and saloons. Henceforth labor would become more skilled in the refining of raw materials and in the production of mineral and agricultural products. Greater numbers of people also began to earn their living by retailing, warehousing, and processing goods. To the occupations represented by the rancher and the miner were added such new trades as those of the gunsmith, tanner, collier, butcher, and baker.

Whaling and Fishing

By mid-century, Yankee sea captains had extended whaling operations beyond the waters of Alaska as far south as Peru. In 1855 alone 500 whaling vessels visited the Pacific Coast. Seventeen Portuguese firms at Monterey alone obtained 24,000 barrels of whale oil in a three-year period, the average yield from one gray whale being 20 barrels. The industry's center was still the Atlantic Ocean, but in the quarter-century after 1850 it shifted to the Pacific, where San Francisco became its principal base. By 1881, the California whaling fleet had dwindled to only forty vessels, though it lingered on into the twentieth century. (The vessel *Wanderer*, at the time she was lost on the rocks of Buzzard's Bay, August 26, 1924, was the last active American whaling bark to operate under sail.)

As new markets reflected the growth of population out West, the Pacific whaling industry was supplemented by commercial fishing. In 1855 at least three firms were already engaged in smoking and salting salmon in Sacramento. By 1880, some 850 boats caught 12,000 tons of salmon annually. Canned salmon production on the Pacific Coast amounted to $5 million per year. Monterey emerged as a terminus for the anchovy and sardine fleets, while San Pedro became a tuna-packing center. Other southern ports, too, were well known for their tuna catches, while the state's central ones handled sole, sand dabs, and other smaller fish. After the 1880s California fishermen made large catches of mackerel, skipjack, albacore, rockfish, and barracuda in order to meet increasing demands for fish. Shellfishing for clams, crabs, and abalone also grew into a significant industry.

Continued Mining: The Comstock Lode

From 1851 to 1855 the United States produced 45 percent of the world's gold, and most of this came from California, despite the great decline that followed its gold rush. Through the 1860s mining still employed as many persons as were engaged in any other single occupation in California. Even in the 1870s, with an annual production usually in excess of $15 million, California still surpassed other Western states in mining activity. As pan and cradle gave way to quartz-crushing and ore-pounding machinery, the chemist became a partner of the miner. The pulverizing of quartz, treated with mercury or quicksilver to form an amalgam, was a big technical advance in mining procedures.

The new technological developments in mining were accompanied by the discovery of rich silver deposits beyond the eastern boundary of California, in the Washoe region. Without California capital the

Placer miner on the Colorado River, ca. 1890. (C. C. Pierce Collection; by courtesy of The Huntington Library, San Marino, California.)

Comstock Lode would never have been developed. As early as 1853 hard-rock prospectors had poked about the brush-strewn slopes of Mount Davidson, east of the Sierra. They had dug up a bluish-tinged ore which interfered with washing operations, and which they cast aside as "that blasted blue stuff." In 1859 an assayer found that this "waste" was rich sulfide containing almost $4,800 per ton in silver as well as $1,600 per ton in gold.

Virtually overnight 10,000 persons moved eastward on hastily constructed wagon roads that wound precipitously down the Nevada side of the Sierra. Freighting into the Washoe mines became a big business and toll roads grew to be as valuable as mining claims. Until rail facilities could be built, supplies had to be hauled by mule and ox teams to Virginia City, center of the boom. That community quickly transformed itself from a tent mining camp into a proud town of frame and brick buildings.

For more than fifteen years the area around today's Carson City, Reno, and Virginia City was gripped by speculation. By the 1860s thirty mills were in operation, and as many companies floated mining stock on national security markets. William C. Ralston and his Bank of California invested heavily in the Comstock, transporting thousands of feet of timber as well as machinery and other equipment over the Sierra to shore up friable earth along tunnels that led to veins of silver fifty feet or more in width. Utilizing a German method of mine timbering, known as Philip Deidesheimer's cribbing technique, the San Francisco financiers who made up "Ralston's ring" turned the Comstock into a honeycomb of conduits and shafts. The Comstock swallowed up eighty million feet of lumber a year, aside from thousands of cords of wood to fuel its mills. Peak annual requirements reached the equivalent of 1,200 miles of 12 × 12 timber. The lode was justifiably called the tomb of the nearby eastern Sierra forests.

The Comstock was an interconnected series of volcanic and metallic fissures—a jumbled mass of veins that provided mystery for hard-rock miners lowered into its damp, hot tunnels. It took fourteen years to strip bare the richest ore pocket, known as the "Big Bonanza." In 1873 a mill owner and future San Francisco mayor, Adolph Sutro, began to build a tunnel into the heart of the Comstock's ore bodies. This impressive engineering feat provided the hot sumps below the ground with ventilation, better access, and vital drainage facilities. The tunnel also connected the network of existing "squirrel holes," as J. Ross Browne called the Comstock diggings. Completion of Sutro's tunnel in 1878 came many years too late, however, to reap for its stockholders the benefits promised by its builder.

A number of Western millionaires got their start in the Comstock. The combined efforts of George Hearst, E. J. ("Lucky") Baldwin, John W. Mackay, James Fair, James C. Flood, William S. O'Brien, John P. Jones, and Alvinza Hayward were needed to exploit the ganglia of ore bodies hidden beneath the surface. These men belonged to the same aggressive generation as the Vanderbilts, Carnegies, and Rockefellers. In an age of rugged individualism and laissez-faire economics, tough-minded tycoons created monopolistic economic empires, in the West as in the East. Half the mansions in San Francisco were constructed with Comstock silver and gold earnings.

By 1870, "The King of the Comstock," William Sharon—who controlled lumber and rail interests—had coaxed William C. Ralston into overcommitting himself in the "Washoe Madness." Ralston, Sharon, and Darius Mills by the mid-1860s had created the Union Mill and Mining Company, a syndicate that sank millions into a fight for control of the Comstock, in opposition to their archrivals, Flood, Mackay, and O'Brien. A national panic in 1873 resulted in slumps in both the production and the marketing of silver, signaling trouble for investors in the lode.

In California everyone from draymen to barkeeps had invested heavily in a mania of speculative irresponsibility. When Ralston's Bank of California failed, in 1875, the event set off a string of financial bankruptcies. For a time almost every bank in the state closed its doors, and serious unemployment added to the dark financial picture. Ralston himself (unlike some of his associates) was unable to save his own fortune. Distraught at the prospect of ruin, he met his death either by suicide or accident in the icy waters of San Francisco Bay.

The Comstock lode achieved its maximum output in 1877—almost $50 million—and afterwards slumped badly. By 1880 the Comstock had permanently failed. All things considered, it is possible that as much capital was put into developing the Comstock as was ever taken out in dividends or earnings.

Once the "blue stuff" of Six-Mile and Gold canyons gave out, and the Ophir and Crown Point mines closed down, speculators returned to San Francisco. They used their salvaged treasure to build a new city. Sutro became its mayor and bequeathed to it a noted library, still in existence. Mackay lent his energies and capital to an international cable and telegraphic system that bore his name. Flood and Fair had their family names perpetuated in San Francisco by other landmarks, including today's Fairmont Hotel.

Freight, Stage, and Mail Service

The Far West's two earliest mining rushes—to the California gold areas after 1848 and to the Comstock a few years later—accelerated progress in transportation. Staging and freighting were stimulated, even though good roads were not in existence. During the 1850s slow-moving mule and pack trains operated in California, gradually extending their services eastward and northward into the territories

Going into the Southern California mines by stagecoach, 1904. Diggings are in the canyon in the background. (C. C. Pierce Collection; by courtesy of The Huntington Library, San Marino, California.)

of Utah and Oregon. Freight outfits used three loaded wagons per unit, with a hitch of eight mules or oxen; one animal pulled about 1,000 pounds of weight. The grueling toughness of freighting produced a breed of "bull whackers" and "mule skinners" who, like the stagecoach drivers of the same era, were known for their colorful profanity.

The May 30, 1849, issue of the San Francisco *Alta California* announced the establishment of what was probably the first stage line in California, Maurison and Company's service from Stockton to the Stanislaus mines. In midsummer, 1849, James E. Birch established a stage line that operated from Sacramento to Coloma and to other mining centers. Miners paid Birch a stage fare each way of two ounces of gold, or $32. In 1850 John Whistman inaugurated service between San Jose and San Francisco, taking nine hours to make this forty-five mile run. His fare was also two ounces of gold. By the middle 1850s there were a dozen lines servicing mining centers. From 1854 onward the California Stage Company operated a profitable statewide integrated service. This firm grew out of a merger of five local lines, running stages over routes 1,500 miles long.

A monthly mail delivery had begun between Salt Lake City and Sacramento by 1851, utilizing mule-drawn relays over a 750-mile route. The Great Salt Lake Carrying Company hauled passengers from Sacramento to the Mormon settlements for $300 and freight for $250 per ton. In 1854, because the road across the Sierra was impassable during winter months, the route was changed, its terminus becoming San Diego, via the Mormon Trail.

Passengers on early stages were warned that the trip might be a bone-jarring experience. Routes were treacherous, crossing arid wastes and rapid streams. Crude ferries only gradually gave way to permanent bridges. Few stages traveled at night, for fear of both Indians and dangerous potholes. Drivers were well paid for their arduous work. It was no easy job to drive the large teams of mixed mustangs, hitched to heavily loaded stages, along the rough and stony roads and over the steep grades of the Sierra. Drivers were expected to keep on schedule and they had to know how to handle nervous teams of animals. A good driver communicated with his mules or horses through gentle movements of the reins. Among these "knights of the rein" were some famous drivers: Hank Monk, immortalized by Mark Twain, George Monroe, Baldy Hamilton, Buffalo Jim, Buck Jones, Curley Bill, "Old" Jim Haworth, "Uncle" Billy Mayhew, and "Charley" Parkhurst. Only after Parkhurst's death in 1879 was "he" found to be a woman named Charlotte. Tough as saddle leather and inured to the dust and heat of the trail, these "whips" raised stage driving to an art.

In 1851 there were few post offices in California. So poor was delivery service that for six weeks during the harsh winter of 1852–1853 Los Angeles received no regular mail. The employment of dependable drivers and establishment of new stage stations forced postal and parcel rates upward. Service remained so defective that a clamor went up in California during the 1850s and 1860s for improved schedules. As a result two Eastern staging firms, Adams and Company Express, and, beginning in 1852, Wells, Fargo and Company, absorbed much local mail service, including the shipment of gold. Both companies established branches in the mining camps and towns of the new state. With national connections by land and water, they were more dependable than the patchwork of local stage operations. In a five-year period Wells, Fargo transported $58 million worth of gold into San Francisco alone. In time both companies also took on banking functions.

Nevertheless, local lines continued to provide the bulk of passenger service, as well as to transport the mail. Gradually more stage stations

L. Lichtenberger's carriage factory, 147–149 Main Street, Los Angeles, 1883.
(C. C. Pierce Collection; by courtesy of The Huntington Library, San Marino,
California.)

were constructed, so that there was one every forty or fifty miles. At
these, drivers obtained fresh horses, enabling stages to run by day
and night, and passengers could rest briefly but primitively from their
journey. Although faster stages were shrinking travel time, they still
offered only a rugged alternative to walking. In fact, when a route
was hilly or muddy, passengers sometimes had to get out and push.
Travelers called Jared B. Crandall's Sierra stage firm "the line of
Foot and Walker." A week of travel through clouds of dust and in
the rain and snow upset many a passenger. In a few cases travelers
were driven insane; in others they stopped the stages to duel with
one another over some minor matter.

The best stage lines used Concord carriages, manufactured by Ab-
bott, Downing and Company in New Hampshire. The cabs of these
coaches rode on a leather cradle of "thorough braces" that cushioned
passengers against the buffetings of the road. Strongly constructed
of light New England ash and well-seasoned oak wood, and of iron
from Norway, the Concord coaches were sometimes ornately paneled
with clear poplar. One of these 2,500-pound carriages sold for as
much as $1,500, and required three spans of good horses, costing
up to $1,000 a span. Not until Phineas Banning began to manufacture

carriages at Wilmington in southern California were similar coaches built in the West. Banning began operation in 1867 of a stage connection between Los Angeles and Wilmington, which proved popular because of the quality of his coaches. Most stage lines adapted old mud wagons such as were to be seen on almost every ranch in California during the 1850s. These springless vehicles, fitted out to carry twelve passengers (as compared with fourteen to twenty-two in a Concord coach), were slow. Any driver who could cover sixty miles in six hours, handling six reins at one time, was a hero to youngsters along his route.

Stage lines, anticipating the coming of the railroads, eagerly sought federal subsidies. In 1857 a bill passed the United States Senate which authorized weekly mail service from Missouri River points to the Pacific Coast. The bill required "good four-horse coaches or spring wagons, suitable for the conveyance of passengers, as well as for the safety and security of the mails." The selection of a route through Texas, running in a semicircle from St. Louis to San Francisco, produced a storm of Northern criticism. Known as the Ox Bow Route, this had the advantage of being an "all-year route," whereas other trails westward were seasonal; but North–South tensions were strong.

Hard-driving John Butterfield, successful bidder for the franchise to carry the mails over the designated course, started his cross-country stages moving toward California in September 1858. Butterfield demonstrated that, by using relays of horses, his coaches could cover the 2,800 miles between Missouri and San Francisco in twenty-four days, eighteen hours, and twenty-six minutes. The schedule called for an average speed of five miles an hour, day and night, with fresh horses waiting at ten-mile intervals. The more than 1,000 men employed by Butterfield used two of the most famous vehicles of the mid-nineteenth century: Concord coaches and Troy carriages—or Celerity wagons. The passenger fare from St. Louis to San Francisco was $200. Overland travelers, however, were a secondary cargo in comparison to the mails; they had the option of either preparing meals en route themselves or purchasing inferior, and usually cold, food at stations. Passengers received scant attention at the hands of busy station men and preoccupied drivers.

As the Civil War approached, the Northern states became concerned with rerouting overland stages to California so that the Union could be sure of maintaining the mails. For strategic reasons this service was vital. Even before the outbreak of war, Butterfield, as operator of the route for the federal government, began to transfer equipment northward piece by piece. In 1861 the Butterfield Overland Mail's Southern course was abandoned in favor of a connection from St. Louis to California via Salt Lake City. Had not sectional tension kept the nation from settling upon a clear-cut railroad route, overland staging probably would have disappeared before the Civil War.

Ships of the Desert

A picturesque episode in the story of Southwestern transportation began in 1855 with a "Camel Corps," as recommended by Secretary of War Jefferson Davis. He believed that camels, which were successfully used in Africa and Asia, might also flourish in the "Great American Desert." The projected "lightning dromedary express" made its first trip westward to California from Arizona in fifteen days, with camels swimming the Colorado River on their way. On the eighth of January, 1858, the population of Los Angeles turned out to witness the appearance of this first camel caravan. The camels had come from Fort Defiance in Arizona and were on their way to Fort Tejon, where Lieutenant Edward F. Beale maintained headquarters. Beale supervised subsequent trips between that fort and Albuquerque, the camels being used principally to transport freight.

Because the camel experiment gave promise of success, the Army planned a regular caravan system. This project proved short-lived, partly because of Beale's recall eastward for Civil War duty. Also, the "ships of the desert" developed sore legs and feet from the Arizona and Nevada trails, which were covered with cacti, prickly pear, and sagebrush. Exasperated mule drivers, furthermore, wanted nothing to do with the smelly "humpbacked brutes." Two hard drivers, "Greek George" Caralambo, and an Arab, Haiji Ali ("Hi Jolly"), managed the stubborn camels. The project was abandoned in 1864 when the last of the animals was sold at San Francisco, after which they were used for pleasure riding and in circuses. There is a story that others were turned loose in the desert and that for years thereafter unbelieving travelers reported having seen their ghostly profiles in the shadowy night.

The Pony Express

Still another novel experiment in Western transportation was to be tried out. This was the use of fast relays of horses to carry mail more efficiently between distant points than was possible by stage service. The first "pony express," in 1858, delivered a message from President James Buchanan in Washington to Sacramento, California, in only seventeen days. The Pony Express proper, however, began operations in 1860 under the Central Overland California and Pike's Peak Express Company. This firm had been running a passenger and freighting business; a number of critics, angered by its failure to maintain schedules and equipment, had dubbed the COC & PPE the "Clean Outa Cash & Past Paying Expenses" line. The idea for a widespread mail operation originated with one of the line's officials, William Russell, who organized the subsidiary firm of Russell, Majors and Waddell to operate the new service. The Pony Express began to function on April 3, 1860, with the departure of a rider from St. Joseph, Missouri, for California. At the same time a packet of letters went eastward from San Francisco to Sacramento by riverboat, then forwarded by rail to Folsom, and next, by stage or pony via Placerville to Genoa (Mormon Station) in present-day Nevada where it began the long day-and-night journey to Missouri.

The westward route was, in general, the same as that taken by overland wagons. Both rider and horse went from the capital by steamboat down the Sacramento River and across the bay to San Francisco. The run of 1,966 miles was completed in nine days and twenty-three hours, less than half the time required by the best stages; these usually took twenty days to reach California from St. Joseph. The impressive record of Russell, Majors, and Waddell attracted national attention to their Pony Express.

The Pony Express comprised 80 riders, 190 stations, 400 station-men, and 400 fast horses. More than $700,000 was invested in the enterprise. Young, light riders were selected to deliver the mail, at salaries averaging from $100 to $200 a month. These boys were armed only with a six-shooter and a knife, and were required to take an oath against using profane language and intoxicating liquor. Each man rode about thirty miles, changing horses every ten miles, but "Buffalo Bill" (William F. Cody) is credited with a continuous ride of 384 miles. Jim Moore, another Pony Express employee, once rode 140 miles, and then, after a stopover of ten minutes, leaped again into the saddle, because of his partner's illness, for the return trip of 140 miles. Letters, transported in leather pouches, were written on the thinnest of paper; the rate of postage was at first $5 per half ounce, later reduced to $1.50 and finally to $1. Only one trip was completely missed and one mail lost, out of 650,000 miles ridden. Operating conditions were sometimes arduous. Riders found it necessary, during winter storms, to use pack animals along the Sierra trails.

The Pony Express, carrying its weekly mails without government subsidy, proved unprofitable despite its high postage rate. During its first eight months of service Californians sent east only 172 letters, and less than a dozen westward. Completion of a transcontinental telegraph line in 1861 ended the Pony Express. Though it had operated for only sixteen months, it had demonstrated the practicality of a central route, which would serve as a forerunner of the Central

Pacific Railroad. By 1862 Russell, Majors and Waddell, who had run the Pony Express as a sideline, were in such dire straits that they sold out their stage operation to a corporation headed by Ben Holladay.

Holladay, ruthless and tough, was a former mule skinner with financial interests in stagecoach, steamboat, and later, railroad transportation. He united various shaky remnants of the West's stage lines. By obtaining franchises, toll roads, and ferry rights, he briefly presided over the West's greatest transportation empire. Holladay, called the "King of Hurry," made staging a big business, dominating 3,300 miles of stage routes. He boasted during the Civil War that he operated overland stages to California at a loss, because of the personal request of President Lincoln. After 1862, he provided triweekly service at a cost of $225 per passenger over the 1,900 miles from Atchison, Kansas, to Placerville, California, a vital supply line. By 1865, through wartime inflation, the price of tickets had risen to $500. Anticipating a national railroad system, Holladay sold his staging operations to Wells, Fargo and Company, which gained control of other independent stage companies, including the old Butterfield Overland Mail Company.

Outlaws

Whether they worked for Ben Holladay or Wells, Fargo, Western riders and drivers ran the risk of road agents of all descriptions. The Wells, Fargo stages were robbed 313 times. Outlaws focused particularly upon the principal stage routes. They would appear suddenly at a coach door, masked and armed, quickly relieve passengers of their valuables and the stage of its strong box, then make off before the law arrived. Resistance meant instant shooting. Nor were the outlaws' activities restricted to harassment of the stages. The lone horseback traveler might fall prey to a skillfully thrown lariat.

Chief among the California banditti was Joaquín Murieta, the notorious brigand. Elusive and adroit, his name struck terror from one end of the state to the other. He has been called a cavalier as well as an outlaw, the superbandit of California's past. The Texas Ranger Harry S. Love, an experienced manhunter, was hired by the state legislature to track him down. Captain Love finally captured and killed a man supposed to be Murieta; the head of the victim was later exhibited in a jar of alcohol.

One of the highwaymen who infested the area around Los Angeles in the 1850s was Juan Flores, another expert with the pistol who was also "uncannily clever with the knife." But most feared of all in the southern part of the state was Tiburcio Vásquez, who was captured in 1874, after he had evaded the law for years. A sheriff's posse blasted him out of a hideout in the Cahuenga hills, and he surrendered after a volley of buckshot caught him in the left arm and leg as well as the side of his chest and head. To the jury that condemned him Vásquez testified that early in life "I got my mother's blessing and told her I was going out into the world to suffer and take my chances." When asked what he meant, he stated: "That I should live off the world and perhaps suffer at its hands." After twenty years of living off the world Vásquez was hanged until dead at San Jose.

In northern California Black Bart, a taciturn and gentlemanly road agent who wore a long linen duster and a flour sack over his head, achieved renown because of the invariability of four words he used upon stopping a stage: "Throw down the box!" In the eight years between 1875 and 1883 twenty-eight drivers threw down their express boxes for Black Bart. After nearly every robbery he left behind a taunting verse signed "Black Bart, the PO-8." To confuse his pursuers further, Bart's poetry was written in varying hands. One such poem, possibly apocryphal, was printed in a California mining paper:

> "So here I've stood while wind and rain
> Have set the trees a-sobbin'
> And risked my life for that damned stage
> That wasn't worth the robbin'."
> Black Bart, the PO-8

Bart inadvertently dropped a handkerchief at one robbery; its laundry mark led detectives to San Francisco, where he turned out to be a respected mining engineer named Charles E. Bolton. He was sent to San Quentin Penitentiary for five years, served his sentence, and then disappeared forever.

Many other stages were looted by bandits such as Dick Fellows, Tom Bell, and Rattlesnake Dick. As time passed, however, gold shipments became smaller and less frequent, and the incentive to pursue a life of crime diminished. The railroad made the stage less attractive and those coaches that continued to operate employed armed guards and detectives whose job it was to spot stage robbers.

The Telegraph, Banking, and Finance

In his book, A Tour of Duty, published in 1849, an early California visitor, Joseph W. Revere, predicted "the extension of the *Magnetic Telegraph*, with all convenient speed, from St. Louis to San Francisco."

Local telegraph service began with the completion in 1853 of a connection between the lighthouse at Point Lobos and San Francisco.

By 1860, Los Angeles was linked telegraphically with the Bay area. The next year the first telegraphic message arrived on the East Coast from California, addressed to President Lincoln.

Related to communications and staging was banking. Some frontier bankers began as saloon keepers, stage coach operators, or as businessmen with strong safes in the back of their stores. On their visits to town, miners who feared robbery, or the results of their own drunkenness, entrusted their hard-earned treasure to these crude repositories for safekeeping. In that day of the double-eagle twenty-dollar gold piece, and of two- and four-bit silver slugs, merchants charged 5 percent interest a month for storing money. As contrasted with modern banks, which profit by lending out the funds of depositors, early western banks considered keeping a miner's doeskin bag of nuggets or "poke" of dust a risky chore. Storage of another man's worldly goods might prove a touchy business should so much as a sneeze occur as precious gold dust was being handled.

The first banker at the mining camp of Mokelumne Hill was Gallant D. Dickinson; the vault of his "bank" was "an excavation a yard square" under his bed. He kept his gold in buckskin bags, with "a revolver of large caliber" nearby. Ore bags were tied with string, and "none was accepted unless labeled with the name of the owner." Dickinson offered his clients no guarantees against theft.

By storing money, lending it, transporting it, and manipulating both gold and other media of exchange, local hardware merchants and mill operators became flourishing banks. Yet only the large national express companies possessed the facilities for the safe transportation of money. Adams and Company and Wells, Fargo were joined in time by other firms that made the handling of money a major enterprise. By 1855, a financial panic was blamed on the haphazard business methods of these firms. The first of the banks to close its doors was Page, Bacon and Company, one of California's most prominent institutions. After depositors had begun their run on this bank, the panic snowballed. Most other San Francisco banks also had to cease operations when their gold resources were depleted by the demands of account holders for specie payment of their deposits. The Wells, Fargo interests weathered the storm, but among the banking houses that failed that year was Adams and Company. This firm had offices in almost every California commercial center. Since the company owed almost $2 million to depositors, charges of dishonesty were levied against Adams personnel by an irate public.

The banking panic of 1855 ushered in a decade of depression, during which Californians showed little faith in the stability of banks. In 1862 the legislature passed an act stipulating new conditions for the incorporation of savings and loan societies, and savings banks reorganized themselves under more responsible auspices in an age when a national bankrupt law did not exist. William C. Ralston's Bank of California was rechartered under a plan that guaranteed payment to depositors when, in 1875, Ralston and the bank suffered serious losses in the Comstock Lode.

By the 1860s, Los Angeles emerged as a new banking center, catering to the prosperous ranchers and farmers who populated the city's outlying districts. Prominent among the earliest banks there was Hellman, Temple and Company, formed in 1868. Isaias W. Hellman, a Los Angeles merchant, at first simply accepted for safekeeping the surplus funds of his customers. But a scuffle with a drunken Irishman convinced Hellman that he should keep more careful accounts in order to protect himself, and he was led into legitimate banking. Hellman's original firm was organized as the Farmers and Merchants Bank, later the Farmers and Merchants National Bank.

Early Manufacturing

Large-scale manufacturing in California appeared tardily on the scene. This fact can be partly explained by the unstable conditions of a new frontier and by its distance from large Eastern cities. Supplies too were often scarce. For the first few years following the American conquest, consumer needs continued to be met by imports. Then the market for manufactured goods became great enough to stimulate the development of industry. As early as 1849, the Union Iron Works of San Francisco was founded by James and Peter Donahue to meet local needs for wire, pipes, and machinery.

During the Civil War, the interruption of the flow of goods from Eastern states not only encouraged infant industries; it also converted San Francisco into an export center. Increasing numbers of ships entered the Golden Gate in ballast to load grain, flour, lumber, wool, mineral ores, quicksilver, and other products.

Even before the war, in 1860, California had 3,505 manufacturing establishments. Nearly 100 flour mills were then in operation, as were scores of lumber and textile mills, such foundries as the Risdon and Pacific Iron Works, the San Francisco chocolate factory of Domenico Ghirardelli, the sugar-beet refineries of the Oxnard Brothers and Claus Spreckels, cigar factories, tanneries, ship repair yards, gun powder works, and boot factories. That year San Jose, Stockton, Sacramento, Marysville, and Merced each possessed a woolen mill. Almost every town of similar size had a brewery or distillery and a metal or iron shop, and soon canneries would make their appearance. After the gold rush a flourishing wagon and carriage industry had begun with the early shops of John Studebaker at Placerville, and Phineas Banning at Wilmington. California needed blacksmiths, harness and saddle makers, wheelwrights, carpenters, and shoemakers. In short, the period after the 1850s saw a great advance in commercial development. Eastern capital was responsible for much expansion of productive capacity. The completion of a transcontinental railroad in 1869 also contributed, by making raw materials more accessible and by widening the export market. Manufacturing plants profited, too, from California's mild climate, which made year-round employment possible.

Selected Readings

California's economy after the gold rush is described in John S. Hittell's *The Resources of California* (San Francisco, 1863) and *Mining in the Pacific States of North America* (San Francisco, 1868), as well as in J. Ross Browne, *Resources of the Pacific Slope* (San Francisco, 1869).

The Comstock Lode is the subject of George D. Lyman: *The Saga of the Comstock* (New York, 1934) and *Ralston's Ring: California Plunders the Comstock Lode* (New York, 1937). The Washoe region is also discussed in G. B. Glasscock, *The Big Bonanza* (Indianapolis, 1931), and Lucius Beebe and Charles Clegg, *Legends of the Comstock Lode* (Oakland, 1950). Oscar Lewis, *The Silver Kings* (New York, 1947), tells what became of the Comstock fortunes. Julian Dana, *The Man Who Built San Francisco* (New York, 1936), is, in part, a biography of Ralston. Earlier accounts of the Comstock include Dan De Quille's *History of the Comstock Mines* (Virginia City, Nev., 1889) and Charles H. Shinn, *The Story of the Mine* (New York, 1896). The salting of mining claims with fake gems is described in Asbury Harpending, *The Great Diamond Hoax* (San Francisco, 1915). A fictionalized treatment of the Comstock is Mark Twain's *Roughing It* (Hartford, Conn., 1872). Also see Grant H. Smith, *The History of the Comstock Lode, 1850–1920* (Reno, 1943). A personal recollection is George L. Upshur, *As I Recall Them* (New York, 1936). See also Robert E. Stewart, Jr., and Mary Frances Stewart, *Adolph Sutro: A Biography* (Berkeley, 1962). Rodman W. Paul, *Mining Frontiers of the Far West* (New York, 1963) compares California and Nevada mining.

Books that depict freighting include Oscar O. Winther, *Express and Stagecoach Days in California* (Stanford, 1936), and Le Roy R. Hafen, *The Overland Mail, 1849–1869* (Cleveland, 1926). Frank A. Root and William Elsey Connelley, *The Overland Stage to California* (Topeka, 1901), is a standard treatment. Useful also is William Tallack, *The California Overland Express: The Longest Stage Ride in the World* (Los Angeles, 1935), a reminiscence, and William and George H. Banning, *Six Horses* (New York, 1930). See also Ernest A. Wiltsee, *The Pioneer*

Miner and Pack Mule Express (San Francisco, 1931), as well as Roscoe
P. and Margaret B. Conkling, *The Butterfield Overland Mail, 1857–
1869* (3 vols., Glendale, 1947). Walter B. Lang, ed., *The First Overland
Mail* (2 vols., East Aurora, N. Y., 1940–45), offers accounts of stage-
coach journeys over the Butterfield routes. See also M. H. B. Boggs,
My Playhouse Was a Concord Coach (Oakland, 1942), and Noel Loomis,
Wells Fargo (New York, 1969).

Regarding Holladay see Ellis Lucia, *The Saga of Ben Holladay: Giant
of the Old West* (New York, 1959), and J. V. Frederick, *Ben Holladay
the Stagecoach King* (Glendale, 1940). Also consult Edward Hunger-
ford, *Wells Fargo: Advancing the American Frontier* (New York, 1949).

The Pony Express is described in Glenn D. Bradley, *The Story of
the Pony Express* (Chicago, 1913). A popularized treatment is Samuel
H. Adams, *The Pony Express* (New York, 1950). See also William
Lightfoot Visscher, *A Thrilling and Truthful History of the Pony Express*
(Chicago, 1908). On the Pony Express and overland freighting see
Raymond W. Settle and Mary Lund Settle, *Empire on Wheels* (Stan-
ford, 1949), and their *Saddles and Spurs* (Harrisburg, Pa., 1955), and
War Drums and Wagon Wheels: The Story of Russell, Majors and Waddell
(Lincoln, Nebr., 1966). Consult also W. Turrentine Jackson, "A New
Look at Wells Fargo, Stagecoaches and the Pony Express," *California
Historical Society Quarterly* 45 (December 1966), 291–324. The camel
experiment is described by Lewis B. Lesley in *Uncle Sam's Camels*
(Cambridge, Mass., 1929) and by Harlan Fowler in *Camels to California*
(Palo Alto, 1950).

An imperfect biography is Maymie Krythe, *Port Admiral: Phineas
Banning* (San Francisco, 1957). Descriptions of travel are in William
H. Brewer, *Up and Down California in 1860–1864* (New Haven, 1930).
Government road-building activities are the subject of W. Turrentine
Jackson's *Wagon Roads West* (Berkeley, 1952). The telegraph is in
Robert L. Thompson, *Wiring a Continent* (Princeton, N. J., 1947).

Joseph Henry Jackson wrote two books about California outlaws:
Tintypes in Gold: Four Studies in Robbery (New York, 1939) and *Bad
Company* (New York, 1949). These can be supplemented by Ben C.
Truman's *Life, Adventures and Capture of Tiburcio Vásquez, the Great
California Bandit and Murderer* (Los Angeles, 1874). A popularized
biography of Murieta is Walter Noble Burns, *The Robin Hood of El
Dorado* (New York, 1932). Dane Coolidge, *Gringo Gold* (New York,
1939) is a novel about this bandit.

California's early banking history is in Ira B. Cross, *Financing an
Empire* (4 vols., Chicago, 1937). Consult also Robert G. Cleland and
Frank B. Putnam, *Isaias W. Hellman and the Farmers and Merchants
Bank* (San Marino, 1965); Robert G. Cleland and Osgood Hardy, *The*

March of Industry (Los Angeles, 1929). Harris Newmark's *Sixty Years in Southern California* (New York, 1916, 1930) tells the story of southern California's early development. So do J. A. Graves, *My Seventy Years in California, 1857–1927* (Los Angeles, 1929) and *California Memories* (Los Angeles, 1930).

CHAPTER 20

The Land Problem

FOR THE SPANIARDS, land was the basis for measuring wealth and status. Under the Spanish land system, newly discovered terrain belonged solely to the king, who did, however, authorize a few private grants to colonists, as trustees of the Crown. Later, the Mexican colonization law of 1824 (discussed in Chapter 9) increased the number of California land grants to more than 800. By the time of the American conquest, almost 14 million acres in all had been granted by Spanish and Mexican officials, with some of the grants overlapping each other. A few claims were gargantuan, up to 1,775,000 acres in size. The expense to grantees for handsome properties seldom exceeded twelve United States dollars.

The American Clamor for Land

Although the Treaty of Guadalupe Hidalgo, ending the Mexican War, guaranteed protection and security, dissatisfaction over the large land grants was expressed by settlers who had arrived recently, especially the Americans. Two different land traditions—the Spanish and the Anglo-American—were at loggerheads. For perhaps too long the rural Hispanic populace had clung to its silver-trimmed saddles and other symbols of the past. After 1850, old-time California residents, with herds of stunted cattle which had to be sold at a prohibitive price because of the high cost of raising them, faced imports of stronger Texas longhorns. Rancheros found themselves caught in a net of rising costs, falling income, and heightened competition as land-hungry American farmers streamed into this cattle frontier.

Ranchos located near a creek or on lake frontage were especially exposed to poachers. Overland cattle drovers stopped at such places to water their stock. American homesteaders who liked what they saw frequently became squatters, challenging the right of rancheros to hold large grants intact. Incoming Americans justified seizures of land by pointing out that, unlike other areas of the United States, California had made available to the public almost no arable free land. Squatters looked upon unoccupied lands as government property subject to occupation, claiming the produce of the land and even stray cattle. Other newcomers roamed about the country, living in wagons and using up water and grazing areas; these nomads picked up unbranded calves and other range animals.

In 1849 the secretary of the interior appointed William Carey Jones, like Frémont a son-in-law of Senator Benton, to investigate California's land grants. Jones, who like Frémont had bought former rancho lands, was not an unbiased source. He found the majority of the Mexican grants in conformity with the law; in short, the titles were "mostly perfect" and "equivalent to patents from our own government." A previous report on land titles, filed by Henry Wager Halleck, had reached a different conclusion. Halleck, an army captain, was serving as California's secretary of state under Richard B. Mason, military governor. His report, under army auspices, highlighted the doubtful validity of claims granted in the Mexican era. Halleck found unsurveyed tracts ill-defined as to origins and boundaries. In 1846, the last year of the Mexican era, eighty-seven grants had been made by Governor Pico, some to personal friends.

Viewed from the standpoint of the American pioneer, it was intolerable that "a few hundred despised Mexicans" should control vast tracts of the most desirable lands to the exclusion of American farmers. Squatters asked what right had the Vallejos, the Argüellos, or the Swiss Captain Sutter to regal estates of eleven or more leagues? Did not the land belong to "the hardy men who faced the dangers of desert and sierra" and brought American institutions to California?

The Federal Government and California Land

How much land might be opened up by the federal government: which parts of California would be declared public lands for sale? It took several decades to answer this question. Large tracts of federal land became available for sale after the Homestead Act of 1862 was passed by Congress. California itself became a gigantic land dealer. The state was granted 500,000 acres of land by the federal government for distribution, in addition to two sections in each township for school purposes. Individual purchasers were attracted by the low prices of these lands.

A congressional act of March 1851 ("to ascertain and settle the private land claims in the State of California") created a Land Commission to receive petitions from land claimants and to pass upon the validity of titles. Landholders failing to present claims within two years would forfeit rights to their lands, which would thenceforth be considered "a part of the public domain of the United States." This Land Act was mostly the handiwork of Senator Gwin, whose sympathies lay with American landseekers.

During reexamination of grant titles by the Land Commission, native landowners were subjected to unfair legal treatment. (The subject is discussed later in this chapter.) On the other hand, a few fraudulent claims were uncovered. One of the most astounding was that of José Y. Limantour, who, in 1853, asserted ownership of 600,000 acres, including islands and four square leagues within and adjoining San Francisco. A decade previous to this time he had given aid to Governor Micheltorena, who had, according to Limantour, signed his land-grant documents. Local residents, whom he suddenly asked to move off their lands or to pay him quitclaims, regarded Limantour's action as blackmail. When his claims were upheld by the federal Land Commission, alarm spread through San Francisco, especially since his claim included the lands on which the presidio, customhouse, mint, and other government property stood. Finally a federal district court adjudged Limantour's claims fraudulent. Arrested and awaiting trial for embezzlement, Limantour deposited a $30,000 bond. This he forfeited, fleeing the country for Mexico. The attorney-general of the United States pronounced his claims "the most stupendous fraud—the greatest in atrocity as well as in magnitude—ever perpetrated since the beginning of the world."

Continued Squatter Activity

American squatters were especially numerous around the bustling new city of Sacramento. When Sam Brannan and other businessmen tried to oust them, squatter leaders promptly responded that the land was public and that any settler would be protected by law. Nothing but superior force could dislodge the resolute squatters, who continued to seize vacant lots in the middle of the night, build weak "ribbon fences" around them, and erect flimsy shanties in the enclosures. Further conflict was inevitable. On August 14, 1850, forty armed squatters attempted to regain possession of a lot that one of their party had occupied, but from which he had been evicted. Sacramento's mayor, who asked the aid of all citizens in suppressing the riot, ordered the squatters to give up their arms and to disperse. They refused to oblige, and in the riot that followed the mayor was wounded. Martial law was then declared and an extraordinary police force of 500 men summoned for duty. In the hectic days that followed, Sacramento Sheriff Joseph McKinney was mortally wounded and several squatters killed. Not until two military companies arrived from San Francisco were the squatters removed and order restored. Squatting had also begun at an early date in San Francisco, and was not discontinued until land titles were settled by court decisions. Scarcely any part of the city was exempt from siezure by squatters. Victims of the San Francisco fire of 1851 even fenced in city lots while the ashes were hot, in order to prevent their property from being "jumped" by newcomers.

There were, in fact, "professional squatters" who hired themselves out to hold possession of coveted land. The usual equipment of such operators consisted of blankets to keep warm at night and firearms to fend off other poachers. This system was especially common in mining regions. A prospector could not leave his claim untended for so much as a week and expect to find it unoccupied on his return—especially if he had not set up on his property a written notice of ownership, with boundary stakes. "Claim jumping" sometimes occurred precisely because adequate notice of site ownership had not been made.

Not all squatters, however, were scoundrels. Many honestly believed that the grants on which they had settled were not actually the possession of others. Thus they took on in good faith the back-breaking job of land development. Accurate surveys of grants generally did not exist, and most original boundary marks had disappeared or become unrecognizable. The original title to Rancho San José read: "A large oak was taken as a boundary, in which was placed the head of a beef and some of the limbs chopped." Sometimes an owner's cattle brand was burned into a tree. Such marks were obliterated by nature. Further confusion arose because of duplications in the names and boundaries of grants. The *Californios* had built few fences and had almost never quarreled over boundaries.

As squatters increased in numbers, their votes were sought by politicians. In 1854, Governor John Bigler's annual message referred glowingly to "that enterprising and useful portion of our people"—the squatters. In 1856 a statute, entitled an "act for the protection of actual settlers and to quiet land titles in this state," passed by the legislature, provided that "all lands in the state were to be deemed and regarded as public until the legal title should be shown to have passed to private parties." In short, it was a piece of squatter legislation. This act was, however, pronounced unconstitutional by the state Supreme Court.

The 1851 Land Act

The Land Commission had opened its hearings in San Francisco on January 2, 1852; it adjourned on March 3, 1856. During that four-year period rancheros searched their homes for original grants from Mexican governors, ferreted maps out of the surveyor general's archives, called upon friends and relatives to testify to their long tenure on the land, and consulted lawyers—all to justify their titles. The burden of proof remained on them. They were at a disadvantage in other respects, too. None of the land commissioners spoke or read the Spanish language. Claimants in southern California were further handicapped by distance from the place of sessions. Rancheros mortgaged their lands at high interest rates to pay legal fees, made trips to appeal to Washington officials, and waited hopefully for confirmation of their titles.

Seemingly unending legal clashes provided much work for specialized law firms, among them Halleck, Peachy and Billings at San Francisco. These attorneys required large fees for unraveling landtitle snarls involving vaguely defined, poorly surveyed, or overlapping boundaries; still other properties posed complex tax-delinquency problems. Supposedly "final" decisions of the Land Commission were contested in both lower and upper courts, culminating in appeals to the United States Supreme Court. Legal delays ran into many years. Confirmation of the patent to the San José de Grácia de Simi Rancho, as an example, took fourteen years, or until 1865; and this was the first grant to be patented in what is now Ventura County after the Land Act of 1851 became operative. In another case a claimant had to wait thirty-five years before he could call his land his own. From 1865 to 1880, the owners of Rancho Palos Verdes underwent seventy-eight law suits, six partition suits, a dozen suits over the ejection of squatters, three condemnation proceedings, and other legal controversies outside the courts.

Litigation over pueblo land claims retarded municipal settlement of both San Francisco and Los Angeles. San Francisco answered several lengthy suits by claiming that, under Spanish legal tradition, it was, like every pueblo, entitled to four square leagues of land. The city received final title to its lands only after clearing up the Limantour claim. At Los Angeles, the city fathers voraciously staked out claims to four leagues square (considerably larger than four square leagues), but these claims were whittled down. In 1866, President Andrew Johnson finally confirmed that city's title to a tract of seventeen thousand acres.

Confusion over titles was compounded when squatter settlements were "platted" upon lands claimed by several owners. In several such cases squatters tore down fences, built makeshift shacks, and ripped out boundary and ownership markers. Knifings, shootings, and personal violence occurred whenever squatters were threatened with ejection from lands on which they had made improvements. When they received adverse court decisions, settlers organized themselves to influence the nomination of judges. Squatters, indeed, sought to form a new Settlers' Party.

Among those who championed the squatters were Governors J. Neely Johnson and John Bigler, as well as Senator Gwin, who had drafted the Land Act of 1851. On the other hand, Frémont, when a senator, lobbied for speedy confirmation of undecided land grants of a questionable nature, as did his brother-in-law William Carey Jones. Jones claimed one huge grant and Frémont another, the latter of which was confirmed by the Land Commission in 1855. This claim of Frémont's, in the Mariposa region, was so debatable that its confirmation raised some question as to the commission's fairness. Although the United States government acted in consonance with half a century of experience in land decisions handed down in frontier areas, some accommodation might have been expected of a supposedly superior system of law and order. Instead, the United States foisted rigid land-title examinations upon befuddled residents, who had only recently become citizens. Without knowledge of either American law or language, native Californians were understandably irritated. Congress, 3,000 miles away, and preoccupied with increasing tension between North and South, saw California as far out on the frontier, and considered Western problems only sporadically.

The fact that Congress could be pressured into rigorously sifting hundreds of land titles raised an unnecessary barrier between American claimants and the *Californios*. Threatened by violence over land seizure or cattle rustling, the rancheros, unused to moving about with revolvers strapped around their waists, generally yielded. An influx of frontier "bad men," enlisted by squatters, made rural areas dangerous. Though the *Californios* had recourse to the courts, the law was often interpreted by squatter judges and squatter juries and administered by squatter sheriffs. The power on the side of the squatters led to "squatter compromises" by which squatters could buy land that they already controlled with barbed wire and revolver. Though such sales altered the unity of a rancho, this was frequently the only way to accommodate self-invited squatters without actual violence.

The 1860s were difficult years on California's ranchos and farms. Land sales brought only temporary relief to the insolvent. In addition to a grasshopper invasion came floods, and then, in the middle of the decade, a period of bone-dry aridity. Five thousand head of cattle were marketed at Santa Barbara in these years for only 37 cents each. The annual income of land baron Abel Stearns fell to only $300. Desperate rancheros tried to raise vegetables, to sell out corrals of horses, to rent animals for plowing, to cut up cordwood for sale in nearby towns—anything to recoup losses. As if these disasters were not enough, a cattle disease, anthrax, grew so severe that Nevada stockmen would not purchase California hay during the 1861 Comstock mining bonanza.

The agricultural misfortunes of the 1860s were also due to the improvidence of some farmers; falling farm prices and mechanization were also responsible. New and oppressive property taxes also encouraged concentration of vast holdings in the hands of lawyers and bankers. Mobilizing their credit effectively, California's *nouveaux riches* formed tax-free, tight land monopolies from whose effects the state took decades to rid itself.

No genuine title to land could be established in some cases until after the 1870s. This situation led to the founding of flourishing state title-insurance businesses. Californians, however, weathered the many frustrations over land titles. And their descendants made real-estate development a major economic activity at the expense of California's rancho tradition.

Selected Readings

An introduction to the land problem is W. W. Robinson's *Land in California* (Berkeley, 1948), and his *Ranchos Become Cities* (Pasadena, 1939), a history of municipalities around Los Angeles. Also see Paul W. Gates, "Adjudication of Spanish-Mexican Land Claims in California," *Huntington Library Quarterly* 21 (May 1958), 213–36; Gates's "Pre-Henry George Land Warfare in California," California Historical Society *Quarterly* 46 (June 1967), 121–48; and his *California Ranchos and Farms, 1846–1862* (Madison, Wis., 1967); William W. Gwin, *Private Land Titles in the State of California: Speech in Reply to Mr. Benton* (Washington, D.C., 1851); and John Currey, *Treaty of Guadalupe Hidalgo and Private Land Claims . . .* (San Francisco, 1891). Indispensable is Ogden Hoffman, *Reports of Land Cases, Determined in the United States District Court for the Northern District of California* (San Francisco, 1862). Of similar importance is William Carey Jones, *Report on the Subject of Land Titles in California* (Washington, D.C., 1850). See also Henry W. Halleck, "Report on California Land Grants," in *California Message and Correspondence, 1850* (United States Congress, House Executive Document No. 17; Washington, D.C., 1850), and Royce's *California from the Conquest in 1846 to the Second Vigilance Committee in San Francisco: A Study of American Character* (New York, repr. 1948), 367–87.

More on land litigation is in Paul W. Gates, "The Fremont–Jones Scramble For California Land Claims," *Southern California Quarterly* 56 (Spring 1974), 13–44. See also Gates's "Carpetbaggers Join the Rush for California Land," *California Historical Quarterly* 56 (Summer 1977), 98–127, and *Letters of William Carey Jones in Review of Attorney*

General Black's Report to the President of the U.S. on the Subject of Land Titles in California (San Francisco, 1860). Central to this controversy is Henry George, *Our Land and Land Policy: National and State* (San Francisco, 1871).

A novel of conflict, reflective of land differences between the Hispanic heritage and the new American way, is Muriel Elwood, *Against the Tide* (New York, 1950). Similar in theme is William MacDonald, *California Caballero* (New York, 1936).

CHAPTER 21

California and the Union

CALIFORNIA WAS ONE of the few states that skipped the interim territorial stage of political organization. Its rapid growth was partly responsible for movement directly into statehood, and its population continued to increase at a prodigious rate—310 percent by the end of its first decade as a state. In 1860 California had a population of 380,000, of which residents born outside the state outnumbered the native-born by two to one.

With Zachary Taylor's election to the presidency in 1848 the Whig party took over many Eastern governmental positions, releasing a flood of unemployed Democrats. Among them was New York's Irish Tammany regular David C. Broderick, who sought to transfer that city's ward system to San Francisco. Other shrewd politicians, with years of political experience, helped tie the new state more closely to the Union, although full "economic statehood" was not achieved until the railroad linked California with the rest of the nation.

Another new leader was William M. Gwin of Tennessee, who became one of California's first two senators. Gwin and Broderick developed loyal followings. In an atmosphere of political simplicity such men attained power partly because of popular disinterest in state politics. In frontier areas settlers were absorbed in the process of daily life, mending leaks in their cabin roofs, lining wells with bricks, and fencing property boundaries.

The New State's Government

After California's constitution was ratified, the first legislature met at San Jose in December 1849, and Peter H. Burnett was sworn in as governor. He was a pioneer from Oregon, and, in politics, a Democrat. Burnett remained in office until January 1851, when succeeded by another Democrat, John McDougal. These early governors performed their duties for the most part ably but did not generally possess unusual capacity or color.

Among the earliest tasks to which California's early politicians turned their attention was the organization of new counties. The former military governor, General Bennett Riley, had divided the state into ten districts to be represented at the constitutional convention of 1849. These were subdivided by the first legislature into twenty-seven counties. By 1907 the number had grown to fifty-eight.

Equally important were the beginnings of party organization in California. The functioning of the Democratic party in the state dates from a meeting of its stalwarts at the temporary capital of San Jose during March 1851. Later that year a Democratic convention, meeting at Benicia, nominated a candidate for governor; this was John Bigler, who had worked at Sutter's Fort before the discovery of gold. Bigler's opponent, nominated by a Whig convention at San Francisco, was Pierson B. Reading, a former participant in the Bear Flag revolt who had worked his way up from the gold placers into political life. Bigler received the backing of his fellow Democrat, Senator Gwin, won the election, and was inaugurated governor January 8, 1852. The legislative practices of the time were venal. Corruption went unquestioned. For more than a decade there was but slight change in the relative strength of California's major parties, the state usually continuing Democratic.

In 1851 the legislature failed, after 142 ballots, to elect a successor to United States Senator Frémont, leaving Gwin for the better part of a year the only accredited representative at Washington. The proslavery Southern viewpoint that Gwin represented stood in contrast to California's "free state" admission into the Union back in 1850.

The Growing Democratic Split

Under Gwin's tutelage the next session of the state legislature was marked by persistent efforts to promote sentiment in favor of slavery. The passage both of a fugitive slave act and of discriminatory laws against blacks seem out of harmony with the antislavery record of California. Meanwhile, Broderick, a Democrat vigorously opposed to these pro-Southern measures, was stirring up statewide opposition to Gwin. The campaign of 1853–1854 brought a split in California's Democratic party, Broderick now entering into alliance with Governor Bigler and denouncing the "Southern democracy" of Gwin. It was a sordid campaign, resulting in the reelection of Bigler. He was also a political import, having been schooled in politics in Pennsylvania—where his brother became, like himself, a state governor. Perhaps the most salient feature of the intraparty controversy was Broderick's cutting rhetoric, especially evident at the Democratic state convention of July 1854, in Sacramento. There his faction faced Gwin's cohorts head-on. Delegates of both groups wore concealed pistols and bowie knives. When the factions could not settle their differences, two conventions emerged, each selecting its own candidates. By 1855 this rivalry between the two wings of California's Democratic party had almost wrecked it entirely; not until the threat posed by the new Know-Nothing party made cooperation necessary for survival did the two wings of the party extend token cooperation to one another.

In the middle 1850s the Know-Nothing sentiment against foreigners, manifested first in California's mining days, spread to almost every town and mining camp. The Know-Nothings concealed their tactics. This secrecy proved effective in keeping their principles veiled. The Know-Nothing motivation was anti-Catholic as well as nativist. When asked what they stood for, they stated that they "knew nothing." Operating behind the scenes, this little-understood party, which used secret handclasps, signals, passwords, and a ritual that emulated the Masons, pumped for Oriental exclusion and for delays in the naturalization of aliens. It was also Bible quoting and anti-liquor. The Know-Nothings persisted in power in California long after their strength dwindled nationally.

By 1856 the Know-Nothings caused California's Whig party virtually to disband. That year the state's tide of "Americanism," plus the promise to reform state government, swept a Know-Nothing, J. Neely Johnson, into the governor's mansion. But the real center of controversy during 1855–1856 was the contest for California's senatorial posts.

The Gwin–Broderick Rivalry

The political rivalry of Gwin and Broderick, both of whom had come West in 1849 full of ambition, has never been exceeded in intensity in California. Their differences on national issues and the clash of their personalities made cooperation by these two Democrats difficult. Gwin, standing more than six feet in height, was the picture of the dignified and courtly Southern gentleman. He was both a physician and a lawyer, as well as a politician. Dr. Gwin's followers in the Democratic party, who held strong proslavery views, were known as the Chivalry Wing, or "Chivs"; Gwin himself was called by his opponents the "arch-champion of the slave-holding interests in California." Broderick, a bold and bitter fighter, was schooled in the politics of Tammany Hall. A self-made man, he had worked in New York as a stonemason, a saloon keeper, and a volunteer fireman. At San Francisco he became a smelter of gold and silver, as well as a merchandiser of metals. Broderick was unequivocally opposed to slavery and its extension.

Broderick first made himself political master of San Francisco, then built up a powerful machine in the state, ruling political underlings by a combination of methods—some reprehensible. The Sacramento *Union*, which opposed Broderick, once called him a "Field Marshal" of politics. Broderick attempted to force the election of a successor to Gwin—a year before the normal date—and almost succeeded. Beaten back temporarily, he renewed the struggle for supremacy with Gwin. The Know-Nothings, calling themselves a "reform" group, sought to take advantage of the rift in the Democratic party created by the Gwin–Broderick fight. With a Know-Nothing elected governor in 1856, their goal was to persuade the legislature to name a Know-Nothing senator.

In the next few years the Broderick–Gwin feud dominated California politics. In March 1857 both Gwin and John B. Weller, who had succeeded Frémont as senator in 1851, would end their term of office. Both sought reelection.

The political situation at Sacramento was tense. After Broderick had captured the approval of the legislature for one of the senatorial seats, he held himself aloof from the deadlock over the other one. Then, after extorting from Gwin a promise that Broderick would have a virtual monopoly of the federal patronage, he grudgingly agreed to support his rival's reelection. Gwin was finally elected three days after Broderick, but only because the Irishman had given the signal. Broderick returned to San Francisco a conquering hero.

Gwin's "Chivs" were, however, vehement in their denunciation of Broderick. The old feud between the two men reopened. Politics in California descended to a new low, and the state Democratic party was split more widely than ever. Broderick ran into opposition from other quarters, too. President Buchanan disagreed with him politically, disliked him personally, and refused to honor Broderick's bargain with Gwin concerning patronage. Instead, the president showered his attentions on Gwin. On the floor of the Senate, Broderick was discredited by his own sharp tongue. He charged Gwin with graft and misappropriation of government money. Furthermore, Broderick was one of four senators on the national scene (including Stephen A. Douglas) who strongly opposed President Buchanan's pro-Southern views on the future territorial organization of Kansas. The national Democratic administration put strong pressure on the gritty Broderick to bring him to heel. Broderick found allied against him the president and a large segment of his party, which condemned him for repeated failure to cooperate with other Democrats. Despite support from Senator Douglas, and references to him as "the brave young senator," Broderick's star had set. He announced on July 25, 1859, "During the first session of the last Congress I attended all the caucuses of the Democratic party, until the door was shut in my face. . . ."

The Terry–Broderick Duel

In the summer of 1859 Judge David S. Terry, a close friend of Gwin and an unsuccessful candidate for renomination to the state Supreme Court, became incensed with Broderick and the "Douglas Democrats." Terry was irritated by Broderick's abuse of Gwin and by his unflattering public statements about Terry. These led to a demand for "satisfaction." Broderick at first declined the challenge to a duel. Terry thereupon resigned from the bench and demanded a retraction. When Broderick refused, a duel was almost inevitable in an age when "affairs of honor" were in vogue. On the morning of September 13 the principals met outside San Francisco, in the presence of seventy spectators. Broderick's pistol went off accidentally and the bullet struck the ground in front of him before he could take proper aim. Terry's shot lodged in his adversary's chest and Broderick fell to the ground. Three days later he died, at the age of forty. Now Broderick's faults were forgotten, and the duel in which he lost his life caused genuine remorse among those fellow Democrats who uncharitably had labeled him a "Black Republican." No longer could enemies within his own party stamp him as a collaborationist of President Lincoln. For at the national level, tension between North and South continued to create a seemingly unbridgeable chasm.

This bitter conflict temporarily wrecked the Democratic party in California. The California legislature of 1860 was the last ever dominated by the Chivalry wing of the Democrats. After the Terry–Broderick duel, Gwin's pro-Southern views became a political liability to the Democrats. In 1861 he was arrested as a disloyal person. In the last years of the Civil War both Gwin and Terry went into exile in Mexico.

Blacks and the Approach of the Civil War

In spite of the influence of the Southern Democrats, California's constitutional convention had determined that it was to be a free state. Relatively few slaves had been brought into California from the South. There were, however, blacks in the original pueblos and, later, a few black frontiersmen. Among the more prominent in California were Jacob Dodson, a volunteer with Frémont on his 1842 expedition, James P. Beckwourth, a scout and trapper who came west in 1844 and named Beckwourth Pass, and William A. Leidesdorff, vice consul to Mexico at Yerba Buena, who was of Danish-black parentage. During the Gold Rush Fritz Vosburg, Abraham Holland, Gabriel Simms, and other black miners operated the Sweet Vengeance mine profitably. Alvin Coffey used gold dust mined in the High Sierra to purchase freedom. Coffey had to pay $1,000 for his manumission and equal amounts to free members of his family. After accepting his money, Coffey's Missouri master took him back to St. Louis and sold him to a new owner. In 1854 Coffey, duped and reenslaved, returned to the California mines; after several more years of hard labor, he earned $7,000, with which he bought freedom for a second time. While California's 1849 constitution excluded chattel slavery, not until after the Civil War did federal courts guarantee those rights.

The census of 1850 lists about 1,000 black residents. By 1852 their number had grown to 2,200. Legally, none of these were slaves. The terms of California's admission to the Union prohibited slavery, long before Lincoln, in 1863, issued his Emancipation Proclamation. Yet California could not escape the side effects of slavery as a national institution. The California Fugitive Slave Act of 1851, passed at Gwin's behest, had provided that slaves brought in before the advent of statehood might be returned to slave states. This law was pronounced constitutional by the state Supreme Court. In numerous instances, however, slaves brought into California before its ban against slavery became effective were given freedom by masters who wished to remain in the state.

Darius Stokes, a black pastor who, by September 1856, had founded fourteen churches in California, claimed that the assessed valuation of property owned by the black population of San Francisco that year was $150,000. Three-quarters of a million dollars had been sent to the South by blacks to purchase freedom for members of their families. Stokes remarked that "men had paid as high as $2,000 each for their companions who were enslaved, to gain their freedom, and bring them to this State." Among them were mining engineer Moses Rodger and mine owners Gabriel Simms, Freeman Holland, and James Cousins. One black had purchased eight of his own children and had paid $9,000 for them, having earned the money by washing clothes. Another, Mifflin Wistar Gibbs, helped his people with money earned as a merchant. Mary Ellen Pleasant, known as "Mammy" Pleasant, in addition to running a house of prostitution, fought for civil rights. Recorded in her deeds were $30,000 she donated to buy rifles for the John Brown raid at Harpers Ferry, and for trips south to help blacks escape slavery.

In 1855 the "Convention of Colored Citizens of California" in San Francisco formulated plans for improving black status. This organization was responsible for repeal of restrictive laws. A militant newspaper owned and edited by blacks, *The Elevator*, which was published under the motto, "Equality before the Law," became the voice of the "Colored Convention's" executive committee.

A State Divided

As national disagreement between North and South grew, a majority of Californians remained loyal to the Union. An antislavery group within the state included Collis P. Huntington, Cornelius Cole, Mark Hopkins, Charles and Edwin B. Crocker, and Leland Stanford, while Southern sympathizers tried to kindle the fires of secession.

Among the Southern residents of California was Kentucky-born General Albert Sidney Johnston, Army commandant at the presidio of San Francisco. To him and other Southern officers the "coercion" of California into a state of war by the North was unconstitutional. General Johnston's loyalty came into question and he gave up his command to join the Confederate Army. Other Southern officers from California's Sixth Army Regiment followed him into the Confederacy.

There was other opposition to the Union in addition to the Southern one. Before Lincoln's inauguration there was talk of a "Pacific Republic" by Representative John C. Burch. This legislator urged Californians, in case of a fratricidal war, to "call upon the enlightened nations of the earth to acknowledge our independence, and to protect us. . . ." John B. Weller, who became governor in 1858, also advocated that California, instead of siding with North or South, should found on the shores of the Pacific "a mighty republic, which may in the end prove the greatest of all." In January 1861, a resident of Stockton hoisted a flag to represent the Pacific Republic. This touched off a general raising of the Stars and Stripes throughout the city. Union feeling remained strong. The dream of a Pacific Republic had finally died.

When hostilities began, California's legislature debated whether it would support President Lincoln. On May 17, 1861 the lawmakers resolved that "the people of California are devoted to the Constitution and the Union now in the hour of trial and peril." They allocated funds to train volunteers at Drum Barracks in San Pedro.

Nearby Los Angeles became a hotbed for secessionists, however. The Los Angeles *Star* was banned from the mails for its seditious editorials. The Bella Union Hotel on Main Street was out of bounds for Union troops because its bar was a gathering place for Southern sympathizers who toasted Robert E. Lee with their tumblers of bourbon and referred to Abraham Lincoln as "that baboon in the White House." The Los Angeles *News*, a pro-Union newspaper, editorialized: "Los Angeles County is disloyal, double-eyed in treason, and the inhabitants break out in broad grins upon hearing the news of a Confederate victory. . . ."

Secret supporters of the Confederacy included the Knights of the Golden Circle, Knights of the Columbian Star, and the Committee of Thirty. The members of these organizations avoided large meetings. Advocacy of secession sometimes also broke out in public speeches, in sermons and prayers from the pulpit, and at private celebrations of Confederate victories. During the war newspapers that went so far as to urge independence for California included the San Francisco *Herald*, Sacramento *Standard*, Alameda *Country Gazette*, Marysville *Gazette*, and Sonora *Democrat*. The Tulare *Post*, which changed its name to the Visalia *Equal Rights Expositor* printed such inflammatory editorials that the paper and its printing plant were destroyed by the state militia. Five "disloyal" papers were wrecked by mob violence.

To counteract secessionist sentiment the California legislature enacted emergency measures. A new law made it a misdemeanor "to display rebel flags or devices." Illegal behavior also came to include "adherence to the enemy" by "endorsing, defending, or cheering" the subversion of United States authority. State laws were enacted "to exclude traitors and alien enemies from the courts of justice in civil cases." Secessionist dissension at El Monte, Visalia, San Luis Obispo, Santa Barbara, San Bernardino, and Los Angeles was discouraged by federal troops.

Californians were spared actual warfare at home. Pro-Union demonstrations took place in all parts of the state, with resolutions of loyalty adopted at mass meetings in various towns and counties. San Francisco Home Guards promoted enlistments in the Union Army, kept an eye out for conspiracy, and worked vigorously for the election of a pro-Union war governor. Californians, having cast their vote for Lincoln in 1860, chose Leland Stanford as their wartime governor. Lincoln's popularity remained so great that in 1864 he would again receive the state's vote for the presidency.

California's gold provided indispensable financial strength for the Union cause. As a "hard-money" state it did not at first gracefully accept national laws making paper greenbacks legal tender. Californians, accustomed to gold and silver, did not trust greenbacks as a stable currency. California gold flowed into the federal treasury, bolstering the nation's economy during the stressful wartime period.

Leland Stanford, ca. 1875. (By courtesy of the Bancroft Library, University of California, Berkeley.)

The state also helped to supply the Union armies with wool, wheat, and other raw materials.

The war hastened California's integration into national life in other ways also. Passage of the Pacific Railroad Bill of 1862 by Congress was facilitated by the absence of Southern legislators who had blocked adoption of a Northern railroad route. During 1863, work on the Central Pacific Railroad began at Sacramento. Governor Stanford joined national party leaders in temporarily abandoning the name Republican; instead these sought the support of all citizens under a Union Party label. Anyone who deviated from such loyalty was apt to feel the whip of censure.

During the war years Californians were moved to new heights of sentiment for the Union cause by Thomas Starr King, a vigorous Unitarian preacher. As many as 40,000 persons came to hear him at mass meetings. Although King lived in California less than four years, he was an extraordinary figure in the history of the state. His reputation in Boston was so great that the First Unitarian Church in San Francisco had invited him to fill its vacant pastoral position. After his arrival in 1860, King became a major spokesman for the Union cause and raised funds for the Sanitary Commission, forerunner of the Red Cross. Over one-fourth of the money donated throughout the country came from California. King's eloquence was so great that his supporters said of him, "King saved California for the Union." He had also written books on the beauty of New England and was planning to do a similar work on the Sierra when he died of diphtheria in 1864 at the age of thirty-nine. In 1931, King was chosen, along with Father Junípero Serra, to represent California in Statuary Hall in the Capitol Building in Washington, D.C.

King was not alone in promoting the Union cause in California. An equally significant figure, Colonel Edward D. Baker, boldly affirmed that the state would be true to the Union, "to the last of blood and treasure." Baker and President Lincoln had been fellow lawyers in Illinois in the 1830s, and had represented the Springfield, Illinois district in Congress. Lincoln, in fact, had named his second son Edward Baker Lincoln out of respect for this good friend. Baker had joined forces with Cornelius Cole, editor of a newspaper in Sacramento, to publicize the Republican party; the two men had campaigned actively for Lincoln as president and for Stanford as governor. Baker rode in the president's carriage in Washington at the inauguration ceremony in 1861, introducing Lincoln on the occasion of his inaugural address. Later, as a Union colonel, Baker headed the California Battalion. He died in action at the Battle of Ball's Bluff.

Despite the enthusiasm of individual units, relatively few Californians saw active service. Conscription was never enforced. A total of about 15,000 men in California enlisted in the Union army. While most California volunteers spent the war years pacifying Indians in Arizona and New Mexico, a contingent did fight in the East. Massachusetts paid large bounties for volunteers out of a special fund earmarked for recruiting in California. A company, consisting mainly of native-born Californians, was organized at San Jose. They were equipped with lassoes, in the use of which they were expert. The "California Column," volunteers under the command of Colonel James H. Carleton, marched to Yuma, then into New Mexico, but too late to forestall a Confederate invasion there.

Another unit, the "California Hundred," sailed through the Golden Gate on December 11, 1862, leaving cheering crowds behind at dockside. Five weeks later, after a trip around Cape Horn, these troops reached Boston for service in the Union Army. Finally, during 1865 Californians rode with General Phil Sheridan in the defeat of Robert E. Lee's Army of Northern Virginia, and they were present for the surrender at Appomattox Court House.

The Postwar Political Scene

After the Civil War California governors and senators achieved national stature from the end of the war to the turn of the century. An exception was former Governor Stanford, who represented California in the Senate from 1885 to his death while in office in 1893. Railroad builder, politician, and philanthropist, Stanford had risen from humble origins to create one of the largest fortunes, political and economic, in the West. A legislator of similar stature, repeatedly reelected to the Senate, was George Hearst, father of the well-known publisher. Senator Hearst, too, died in office, in 1891. One other politician deserves mention, at least as a geriatric wonder. This was Senator Cornelius Cole—political fixture par excellence. Cole served in both houses of Congress. In his remarkable 102 years of life, from 1822 to 1924, he lived during the lifetime of every United States president from John Adams through John F. Kennedy, who had already been born when Cole died.

In the years before the turn of the century both parties remained conservative, and voters seemed satisfied to follow national trends rather than to create local ones. Except for the anti-Chinese issue, most public concerns were those of the nation as a whole. Among prevalent issues were the free-silver and other monetary controversies, a high tariff, distrust of labor agitators, and apathy toward reformers. Not until the era of the Progressives, spurred by the leadership of Theodore Roosevelt, would Californians be moved by reform.

Selected Readings

For politics in California see William H. Ellison, *A Self-Governing Dominion*. The Gwin–Broderick–Terry fracas is described in A. R. Buchanan, *David S. Terry of California: Dueling Judge* (San Marino, 1956), and A. E. Wagstaff, *Life of David S. Terry* . . . (San Francisco, 1911). See also David Williams, *David C. Broderick: A Political Portrait* (San Marino, 1969). Valuable are Winfield J. Davis, *History of Political Conventions in California, 1849–1892* (Sacramento, 1893); Jeremiah Lynch, *A Senator of the Fifties: David C. Broderick of California* (San Francisco, 1911); and James O'Meara, *Broderick and Gwin . . . A Brief History of Early Politics in California* . . . (San Francisco, 1881).

Articles that deal with California's political history of this period include William H. Ellison, ed., "Memoirs of Hon. William M. Gwin," *California Historical Society Quarterly* 19 (1940), 1–26, 157–84, 256–77, and 364–67; and Philip G. Auchampaugh, "James Buchanan and Some Far Western Leaders, 1860–1861," *Pacific Historical Review* 12

(June 1943), 169–80; Ellison has also written on "The Movement for State Division in California; 1849–1860," *Southwestern Historical Quarterly*, 17 (1914), 101–39. See, too, Walter R. Bacon, "Fifty Years of California Politics," Historical Society of Southern California *Annual and Pioneer Register* 5 (1900), 31–43, and Earl Pomeroy, "California, 1846–1860: Politics of a Representative Frontier State," California Historical Society *Quarterly* 32 (December 1953), 291–302.

The career of John McDougal, California's first American lieutenant governor and its second governor, is examined in H. Brett Melendy, "Who Was John McDougal? " *Pacific Historical Review* 29 (August 1960), 231–43. McDougal is sometimes confused with James A. McDougall, a later politician. See Russell Buchanan, "James A. McDougall, A Forgotten Senator," California Historical Society *Quarterly* 15 (September 1936) 204–5.

Civil War California is discussed in Percival J. Cooney, "Southern California in Civil War Days," Historical Society of Southern California *Annual* 13 (1924), 54–68, and, in the same series, Imogene Spaulding,"The Attitude of California to the Civil War," 12 (1912–13), 104–32; John J. Earle, "The Sentiment of the People of California with Respect to the Civil War," American Historical Association *Annual Report* 1 (Washington, D.C., 1907), 125–35; Horace Davis, "The Home Guard of 1861" in *The Pacific Ocean in History* (New York, 1917), pp. 363–72; and Helen B. Walter, "Confederates in Southern California," Historical Society of Southern California *Quarterly* 35 (March 1953), 41–55. A commemorative issue of the California Historical Society *Quarterly*, published in December 1961, contains Benjamin F. Gilbert, "California and the Civil War: A Bibliographical Essay"; see also Gilbert's "The Confederate Minority in California," California Historical Society *Quarterly* 40 (June 1941), 154–70. Unsophisticated accounts of the Western phases of the Civil War are Jay Monaghan, *Civil War on the Western Border* (Boston, 1955), and Oscar Lewis, *The War in the Far West, 1861–1865* (New York, 1961). See also Aurora Hunt, *The Army of the Pacific* (Glendale, 1951), as well as the same author's *Major General James Henry Carleton: Western Frontier Dragoon* (Glendale, 1958), which tells the story of the California Column. Consult also Gerald Stanley, "Civil War Politics in California," *Southern California Quarterly* 54 (Summer, 1982), 115–32, and Stanley's "Slavery and the Origins of the Republican Party in California," *Southern California Quarterly* 50 (Spring, 1978), 1–16; John W. Robinson, *Los Angeles in the Civil War* (Los Angeles, 1977); and Leo P. Kibby, "Some Aspects of California's Military Problems During the Civil War," *Civil War History* 5 (September 1959), 251–62. Relations with the federal government are in Milton H. Shutes, *Lincoln and California* (Stanford, 1943). See also Edward A. Dickson, "Lincoln and Baker: The Story of a Great Friendship," Historical

Society of Southern California *Quarterly* 34 (September 1952), 229–42; Shutes, "Colonel E. D. Baker," California Historical Society *Quarterly* 17 (December 1938), 303–24; and C. J. Stillé, *History of the United States Sanitary Commission* (Philadelphia, 1866).

Late-nineteenth-century politics emerges from Richard Frothingham, *A Tribute to Thomas Starr King* (Boston, 1865); E. R. Kennedy, *The Contest for California in 1861* (Boston, 1912); and George T. Clark, *Leland Stanford* (Palo Alto, 1931). Consult also such reminiscences as Cornelius Cole, *Memoirs* (New York, 1908), and Stephen J. Field, *Personal Reminiscences of Early Days in California* (San Francisco, 1880). See, too, Lauren E. Crane, ed., *Newton Booth of California* (New York, 1894). An account of Governor Frederick F. Low is Robert H. Becker, ed., *Some Reflections of an Early California Governor* . . . (Sacramento, 1959). Regarding King see also Ann Casey, "Thomas Starr King and the Secession Movement," Historical Society of Southern California *Quarterly* 43 (September 1961), 245–75, and Russell M. Posner, "Thomas Starr King and the Mercy Million," California Historical Society *Quarterly* 43 (December 1964), 291–307. An account of the activities of the American Party, which originated in California, is John Higham, "The American Party, 1886–1891," *Pacific Historical Review* 19 (February 1950), 37–46.

Regarding blacks in California, see the bibliography that follows Chapter 36 of this book as well as: Eugene H. Berwanger, *The Frontier Against Slavery* (Urbana, Ill., 1967). Consult also J. Max Bond, "The Negro in Los Angeles," a dissertation written in 1936 available in reprint (Berkeley, 1972); Delilah Beasley, *Negro Trail Blazers of California* (Los Angeles, 1919); and Rudolph M. Lapp, *Blacks in Gold Rush California* (New Haven, 1977). See also Sue Bailey Thurman, *Pioneers of Negro Origin in California* (San Francisco, 1952); Lionel U. Ridout, "The Church, the Chinese and the Negroes in California, 1849–1893," *Historical Magazine of the Protestant Episcopal Church* 28 (June 1959), 115–38; William E. Franklin, "The Archy Case," *Pacific Historical Review* 32 (May 1963), 137–54; Mifflin Wistar Gibbs, *Shadows and Light: An Autobiography* (Washington, D.C., 1902); and Clyde A. Duniway, "Slavery in California After 1848," *Annual Report*, American Historical Association (Washington, 1906).

A view of politics at the turn of the century and afterward is in Frank Hamilton Short, *Selected Papers* (San Francisco, 1923); George Lyttleton Upshur, *As I Recall Them: Memories of Crowded Years* (New York, 1936); Carl B. Swisher, *Stephen J. Field, Craftsman of the Law* (Chicago, 1930, 1969); R. Hal Williams, *The Democratic Party and California Politics, 1880–1896* (Stanford, 1973); Alexander Saxton, "San Francisco Labor and the Populist and Progressive Insurgencies," *Pacific Historical Review* 34 (November 1965), 421–38; Tom G. Hall, "California Populism at the Grassroots: The Case of Tulare

County, 1892," *Southern California Quarterly* 49 (June 1967), 193–204; and Eric Falk Petersen, "The End of an Era: California's Gubernatorial Election of 1894," *Pacific Historical Review* 38 (May 1969), 141–56.

Gerald D. Nash, *State Government and Economic Development: A History of Administrative Policies in California*, 1849–1933 (Berkeley, 1964) recounts how government agencies have stimulated economic activity.

CHAPTER 22

Ships and Rails

AFTER SETTLEMENT OF the Oregon boundary question in 1846 and the beginning of the California gold rush in 1848, thousands of persons sought cheap transportation to the American West. Travelers on the East Coast were told that, for $380, they could reach California in a matter of weeks via Panama. Rather than spend the longer time required to go around Cape Horn or to undertake the uncomfortable trip on the overland trails, thousands chose this Panamanian route. In 1849, ocean mail service began over the same route. From New York to the Isthmus of Panama, mail was carried aboard vessels of the government-subsidized United States Mail Steamship Company, and from Panama to San Francisco by the Pacific Mail Steamship Company. These firms, and the Aspinwall and Vanderbilt maritime interests, argued that ports like San Francisco could be made into unsurpassed gateways to the Orient.

During 1848 the Columbian government gave an American syndicate permission to build a trans-isthmian railroad. Construction was hazardous; workers, victimized by insects, were exposed to malaria and other diseases. Progress in cutting a roadbed through mangrove stumps and tangled vines proved incredibly slow. Near midnight on January 27, 1855, in a pouring rain, the last rail was laid. On the next day the first locomotive traveled from the Atlantic to the Pacific oceans.

More than 400,000 passengers and upwards of $750 million in precious metals were transported over the road during the thirteen years ending in December 1867. The bulk of this traffic was either headed for or returning from California. Upon the arrival of passenger steamships on the Atlantic coast of Panama, trains were dispatched in order to meet connecting steamships on the Pacific side.

The same was true for travelers and goods going in the opposite direction.

Completion of a more direct transcontinental line, however, eventually ended much of the need for this isthmian route to California. Smooth operation of the railroad was also impeded by sanitary and financial problems. Its American directors eventually sold their equipment to a French company that later began to build the precursor of the modern Panama Canal.

Inland Water Transportation

Pacific Mail Steamship Company operations extended also to inland transportation. Along the San Francisco waterfront, riverboat captains corralled many of the new arrivals, taking them up the inland streams to their ultimate destination. This service fanned out from the Golden Gate to interior ports, including Marysville, Sacramento, and Stockton. Utilizing a system of natural waterways, steamboat fleets and muddy scows alike ascended the San Joaquin, Sacramento, and the American rivers. At first haphazard, this traffic became systematized and better regulated. The owners of the best-known Sacramento steamboats, the *Senator, Cornelia,* and *New World,* found their vessels difficult to maintain due to shortages of parts. Because of the dangerous practice of racing, disastrous accidents occurred. Under high steam pressure, iron boilers exploded and decks buckled, strewing the bodies of passengers over the surface of the water. In 1854, a number of owners of steamers joined to form the California Steam Navigation Company. Until the railroads challenged its dominance, and hydraulic mining silted up its waterways, "California Steam" virtually controlled traffic in San Francisco Bay and along the inland rivers.

Some smaller competitors of the California Steam Navigation Company found it so powerful in prescribing freight and passenger rates that they actually welcomed the monopoly-breaking transcontinental railroad. In 1871, the company was, in fact, sold to railroad interests. Thus, eventually, Southern Pacific Railroad sternwheelers competed with the independents plying the inland waters.

Planning an Overland Railroad

By 1850 the expense of getting to California by sea averaged $400, and the trip sometimes took 120 days or longer. Overland stage service remained expensive, slow, and uncomfortable. Advocates of a transcontinental railroad pointed out that such a trip might be made by rail for as little as $150 and in only twenty days' time. Federal money would be needed in large quantities to complete so vast a project. Critics of the railroad maintained that the cost of construction would be prohibitive, with huge government land grants and loans required to compensate the builders, due to the financial risks involved.

Nevertheless the idea of a Pacific railroad gained acceptance in Washington. The deeply rutted and confusing trails to the West were clearly inadequate. For hauling mail, passengers, and freight more quickly, and for defense of the West Coast, a good rail route was seriously needed. There was no disagreement that such a route should traverse the shortest possible distance, because of the tremendous costs involved. Also, a decision was reached rather early that the terminus should be in California, rather than in Oregon. But the exact route westward was debated for years.

During the 1850s, debates in Congress over Western railroad legislation were interminable. Legislators had little experience with the colossal problems involved; congressmen mingled passion and interest with reason and judgment. Should construction and operation of the road be administered by the government outright? Or should the railroad be built and operated privately? How far should federal and state governments go toward financial encouragement and direct subsidies?

As early as 1852, a route that swung southward through Texas and then proceeded by way of the Gila Valley to Yuma and on to San Diego in California was advocated by Southern interests. This proposal, however, became only one of four that survived congressional debate. Finally, an appropriation was voted in 1853 to make surveys to determine the "most practicable and economical route." Various survey parties headed west for this purpose, but months ran into years, and by 1855 the goal seemed as distant as ever.

The railroad cause, however, did not lack spokesmen. The journalist Horace Greeley of the New York *Tribune*, who in 1859 made an overland trip to San Francisco, wielded an influential pen on behalf of a transcontinental railroad. In 1861 the outbreak of the Civil War had brought to an end all prospects of a Southern route. Military and political considerations now became paramount.

Organization of the Central Pacific

On June 28, 1861, three California merchants founded the Central Pacific Railroad Company at Sacramento: Leland Stanford acted as president, Collis P. Huntington as vice-president, and Mark Hopkins as treasurer. These three and Charles Crocker, who had joined them, came to be called the "Big Four." Originally, their enterprise relied less on their own efforts than on the determination of a young Connecticut-born civil engineer, Theodore D. Judah. Judah had laid out the rails of the Sacramento Valley Railroad to serve the mining regions along the slopes of the Sierra Nevada. Although that railway consisted of only twenty-three miles of track, it spurred Judah's ambition to promote a transcontinental system. By the late 1850s Judah was advancing some bold engineering concepts, which would make possible the construction of a railroad over the Sierra. He was often ridiculed in both Washington and California, some calling him "Crazy Judah," and others accusing him of promoting the operation purely for personal gain. Judah, however, had considerable construction experience, and this background gave his ideas persuasiveness. By personal lobbying in Washington, he was able to bring pressure to bear on Congress for passage of a railroad bill. Judah, because of the financial difficulties of his operations, had interested Stanford, Huntington, Hopkins, and Crocker in the railroad project. Judah's own line ran only from Sacramento to Folsom. He became chief engineer of the new Central Pacific Railway Company.

Congress on July 1, 1862, passed the Pacific Railroad Bill. In addition to the 400-foot right of way, a generous government land subsidy was given the railroad builders. Sections of this terrain stretched off in checkerboard fashion on either side of the track almost as far as the eye could see. In all, the railroad builders were entitled to 1,280,000 acres of public land for every hundred miles of track they laid plus $3 million in credit for each of two construction companies. Both the Central Pacific and Union Pacific companies were to construct at least twenty-five miles of road a year, and the thirty-year government bonds authorized for the railroad could not be redeemed for cash until forty miles of road had been constructed. Although the transcontinental railroad would be built by two separate corporations, Congress stipulated that the road should be operated "as one connected, continuous line." Actually the Central Pacific and Union Pacific companies remained separate entities.

Judah and his partners had also induced Congress to grant them a subsidy of $16,000 per mile for track laid across level land, $32,000 a mile in the foothills, and $48,000 per mile across mountain areas. Judah's partners devised a plan to collect twice the subsidy to which they were entitled. Their strategy was to convince Congress that the foothills of the Sierra Nevada began further west than was the case. This reasoning, written into the bill, "moved" the mountains to Arcade Creek so that they extended within only ten miles of Sacramento—near the center of the great valley of California.

Stanford was a thirty-six-year-old dealer in groceries and provisions when the partnership was formed; Judah was then thirty-five. Crocker, at the age of thirty-eight, was the owner of a dry-goods store; and Huntington, at thirty-nine, and Hopkins, at forty-seven, were partners in a hardware business. In a few years all except Judah were multimillionaires. Judah, the true originator of the enterprise, died prematurely in 1863. He was en route to seek Eastern capital with which to buy out his avaricious partners when he was stricken with a fatal attack of yellow fever.

The original intention of Judah's partners was to amass the lucrative federal subsidies by laying down the roadbed and track as quickly as possible. Crocker, who supplanted Judah as construction engineer, wanted to sell the company to others, who would operate the road. Crocker admitted in 1883, "We built that road for the profits we could make in building it, and when we got it done we didn't know what in the devil to do with it." Stanford stated, years later, that he and his colleagues would gladly have sold their railroad in 1869 for ten cents on the dollar. Judah fought some bitter battles against his partners' desire to substitute rapid contruction for sound engineering.

The provisions of the Pacific Railroad Act of 1862, generous as they were, were increased in 1864. In that year the Central Pacific, with backers of the Union Pacific, achieved passage of an amendatory act which doubled the land grants and increased financial inducements. The credit of both these companies was thereby greatly strengthened, enabling them to find a market for their mortgage bonds. The personal enrichment of the "Big Four" was made possible by the government's generosity. Yet some sort of subsidy was inevitable. The fact that enormous obstacles to construction of the railroad could be overcome only by vast sums of money, the pressure created by the war, and the inexperience of Congress in dealing with such a gigantic project—all explain why the legislation was so loosely written.

Construction of the Railroad

Building eastward from Sacramento, the Central Pacific had to ship machinery and supplies around Cape Horn, or via Panama, at great expense. Union Pacific crews, on the other hand, moving west from Omaha, were able to transport heavy supplies over track they had already laid. The Sierra Nevada presented a more formidable obstacle to the engineers of the Central Pacific than the Rocky Mountains were to offer the Union Pacific. The Sierra, however, did supply timber for ties, trestles, and the long snow sheds required in mid-

Chinese construction workers on the Central Pacific Railroad at "Cape Horn," a strategic point in the crossing of the Sierra crest. (From a contemporary print.)

winter—a resource lacking to the Union Pacific as it worked its way across the treeless Great Plains.

In order to cut a roadway through the rock walls of the Sierra, Central Pacific construction crews used picks, blasting powder, axes, and dumpcarts, in addition to thousands of laborers. Not only was mechanical equipment commonly employed today nonexistent, but little was known about the wilderness to be traversed. The Central Pacific relied on the labor of 15,000 Chinese, whom Crocker had imported.

Crews of these expendable "Celestials," a name taken from "the Celestial Empire" of China, tied by ropes around their middles, chipped at the sides of Sierra cliffs 7,000 feet high for wages of less than $2 per day. After they had chiseled out a footing along the steep canyon walls, other Chinese made use of this toehold in blasting out a roadway for the track. By September 1865, the Central Pacific extended fifty-six miles eastward from Sacramento into the Sierra Nevada. During the winter of 1865–1866 the only work possible was construction within tunnels. Crocker undertook to sledge three locomotives, forty railroad cars, and material for forty miles of track across almost thirty miles of winding, unfinished roadbed, blasted out previously, into the canyon of the Truckee River. There lighter snow made possible grading and track work on the eastern side of the Sierra. Despite irksome delays, due also to financial difficulties, the Central Pacific crossed the Sierra summit in December 1867, at an elevation of 7,047 feet; from there, the work of the crews was speeded by less rugged terrain.

The Union Pacific relied on Irish immigrants for its construction crews. There was a lively rivalry between the two companies, and it became especially intense when Crocker announced a schedule of a mile of track for every working day. His Chinese—known as "Crocker's Pets"—responded to every new demand made upon them. By June 1868 they had reached Reno, but it was not until early in 1869 that the most feverish construction occurred. On one day the Union Pacific's "Paddies" laid six miles of track; Crocker's Chinese countered with seven miles. The latter ultimately set a record with ten miles and fifty-six feet of track laid in under twelve hours. That day Crocker won a bet of $10,000 because of their labor.

The government subsidy was based upon mileage of track laid, and each railroad was eager to cover as much ground as possible. As the distance between rival construction crews lessened, their competition became ever more keen. For a time grading crews worked within a few hundred yards of each other along parallel lines, since they could not agree as to where the tracks should join. Early in 1869, railroad commissioners ruled that the two lines should meet at a place in northern Utah Territory called Promontory, 56 miles west of Ogden, 1,086 miles from Omaha, and 689 miles from Sacramento. There the gap was closed.

Driving the Golden Spike

It remained only to drive the last spike. On the tenth day of May, 1869, on desolate Promontory Point, the ceremony was performed, uniting Atlantic and Pacific with bands of steel. Two bonnet-stacked, wood-burning locomotives faced each other, on the new tracks, one headed east, the other west. Several hundred witnesses were present, including the Twenty-first Infantry Regiment, officials of both railroads, a photographer, and nearby settlers. Following the driving of Arizona's spike of gold, silver, and iron, and Nevada's spike of silver, California's laurel tie was put in place and its spike of gold produced. President Stanford of the Central Pacific and Vice-President Thomas C. Durant of the Union Pacific proceeded to drive this last spike while locomotive whistles screamed. Each blow of the silver sledge was announced via telegraph to Eastern cities, where the event was celebrated by the ringing of bells.

San Francisco gave itself up to three days of celebration. The telegraph announced: "The last rail is laid! The last spike is driven! The Pacific Railroad is completed!" At Sacramento the bells and whistles of thirty different locomotives joined in a chorus with the bells of the city's churches and fire houses. Bret Harte, envisioning a burgeoning trade with the Orient, wrote a poem to celebrate the driving of the last spike:

> What was it the Engines said,
> Pilots touching, head to head
> Facing on the single track,
> Half the world behind each back?
>
> You brag of the East. You do.
> Why I bring the East to you.
> All the Orient, all Cathay,
> Find thru me the shortest way;
> And the sun you follow here
> Rises in my hemisphere.
> Really—if one must be rude—
> Length, my friend, ain't longitude.

Now it took only seven days to travel the 3,167 miles, over separate railroad lines, from Sacramento to New York. The completion of the largest engineering job yet undertaken in North America was a decisive event. In 1869, 100 years after the settlement by the Portola–Serra expedition, California's frontier isolation had come to a close.

Development of the Southern Pacific

The builders of the Central Pacific had not intended to become the operators of it. But they later found their greatest fortunes in the hauling of freight and passengers. Not only did their Silver Palace Sleeping Cars carry thousands of excursionists and settlers West, but, also, long lines of boxcars transported shipments of wheat, gold, silver, lumber, and other commodities which brought the "Big Four" wealth undreamed of by Judah. In 1865, while still building the Central Pacific, they chartered the Southern Pacific Railroad Company, and, by acquiring smaller branch lines, constructing several others, and consolidating their enterprises, they created a railroad system covering hundreds of miles from San Francisco and Los Angeles to termini as far away as New Orleans and Portland. Its steamship connections would also link California with New York and Havana.

After completion of the Central Pacific, the "Big Four" extended their activities into San Francisco Bay, and then established north-south routes through California's Central Valley and along the coast from Oregon to southern California. The name under which the firm now operated was the Southern Pacific Railroad Company. The national panic of 1873 kept the company from building eastward outside the state. But in 1877 it reached out from Los Angeles to Yuma, via Colton and Indio. Instead of joining the Texas and Pacific Railroad at Yuma, as was once planned, the fiercely competitive Southern Pacific pushed on southeastward until it reached Tucson in 1880. It took advantage of the Texas and Pacific's construction and financial difficulties to lay its own track over some of the proposed route of the rival road. The first company to lay down its tracks gained the right of way. The Southern Pacific did carry out its agreement to join the Atchison, Topeka and Santa Fe Railroad; the lines were connected in New Mexico Territory in 1881, opening up a second transcontinental line. A third such route came into being when the Southern Pacific met the Texas and Pacific in Texas during 1882; another extension of the Southern Pacific's "Sunset Route" led from New Mexico eastward, and reached New Orleans in 1883.

Behind all this expansion was the rivalry between railroads for federal land. The Central and, later, Southern Pacific systems received over 11 million acres within California alone. The railroad also demanded county and city lands; the extent of a city's favors helped the "Big Four" decide what places they would service. Enticement of the railroad required money, with which a community would buy construction bonds. The Southern Pacific was accused of extorting funds from towns along railroad routes; the "Big Four" retorted that it needed this money for building bridges and overpasses, and for grading track beds. Without railroad connections to the outside world a community was "as good as dead." Among the interior towns that mushroomed because the railroad ran through them were Fresno, Merced, Tulare, Modesto, and Bakersfield. Some communities were bypassed and left to slumber. Los Angeles, today the largest city in California, almost met such a fate. However, in 1876, the city fathers allowed the Southern Pacific to acquire an existent twenty-two-mile line to Wilmington, and Los Angeles was permitted to join the railroad's network.

The Southern Pacific clung to its monopoly. Not until the 1880s was that hold challenged by the Atchison, Topeka and Santa Fe. Building westward, the Santa Fe reached El Paso in 1881, then crossed New Mexico and Arizona, sending its woodburning locomotives into Needles, where it bridged the Colorado River. Next the Santa Fe purchased and rented short lines, entering Los Angeles in 1887. A new track northward from Bakersfield to Stockton, called "The People's Road," was to compete with the Southern Pacific into San Francisco. The Santa Fe had built, bought, and negotiated its way into California, but construction costs, fierce competition with the Southern Pacific, and a depression in 1893 led to its bankruptcy and later reorganization. In California the Southern Pacific was to reign supreme for many years.

Selected Readings

The difficulties of traffic over the Isthmus of Panama are treated in F. N. Otis, *Illustrated History of the Panama Railroad* (New York, 1861). Inland water transportation is discussed in Jerry MacMullen's *Paddle-Wheel Days in California* (Stanford, 1944).

Basic to an understanding of railroad building are the *Pacific Railroads Reports* (13 vols., Washington, D.C., 1855). A one-volume condensation is George Leslie Albright, *Official Explorations for Pacific Railroads* (Berkeley, 1921). Among the earlier books on the railroad builders are Creed Haymond, *The Central Pacific Railroad Company: Its Relation to the Government* (Washington, 1888), a defense; Grenville M. Dodge, *How We Built the Union Pacific Railway* (Omaha, 1903); Lewis Henry Haney, *A Congressional History of Railroads in the United States* (2 vols., Madison, 1908–10); John Moody, *The Railroad Builders* (New Haven, 1921); and Robert E. Riegel, *The Story of the Western Railroads* (New York, 1926). A popularized account is Wesley S. Griswold, *A Work of Giants* (New York, 1962). More specific are Carl I. Wheat, "A Sketch of the Life of Theodore D. Judah," California Historical Society *Quarterly* 4 (September 1925), 219–71; John H. Kemble, "The Big Four at Sea: The History of the Occidental and Oriental Steamship Company," Huntington Library *Quarterly* 3 (April 1940), 330–58; and C. B. Glasscock, *Bandits and the Southern Pacific* (New York, 1929).

Other works include John D. Galloway, *The First Transcontinental Railroad* (New York, 1950); Stuart Daggett, *Chapters on the History of the Southern Pacific* (New York, 1922); and Oscar Lewis, *The Big Four* (New York, 1938), which is only partially satisfactory. An authorized history is Neill C. Wilson and Frank J. Taylor, *Southern Pacific: The Roaring Story of a Fighting Railroad* (New York, 1952). Glenn C. Quiett, *They Built the West: An Epic of Rails and Cities* (New York, 1934), and Gilbert H. Kneiss, *Bonanza Railroads* (Stanford, 1941), are informative. On the Santa Fe see: Glenn D. Bradley, *Story of the Santa Fe* (Boston, 1920); James Marshall, *Santa Fe: The Railroad That Built an*

Empire (New York, 1949); and L. L. Waters, *Steel Trails to Santa Fe* (Lawrence, 1950).

Business in the late nineteenth century is the subject of Mansel G. Blackford's *The Politics of Business in California, 1890–1920* (Cleveland, 1977).

CHAPTER 23

Agricultural and Urban Growth

THE ECONOMY OF MANY agricultural states depends heavily on some single crop, such as corn, cotton, dairy products, or beef. California, the nation's leader in agricultural output, produces more than two hundred farm commodities. The garden and field planting that went on at the missions was later complemented by cattle ranching, which became the most characteristic of California's agricultural activities. By the mid-nineteenth century, California's agricultural pattern had become genuinely diversified. Consumption within the state of beef, wheat, and, later, citrus and wine production, steadily increased. Forest reserves constituted yet another natural asset. California contained stands of Ponderosa pine, Douglas fir, spruce, redwood, and mesquite.

Cattle and Sheep Ranching

Before the close of the eighteenth century there were probably 100,000 head of cattle in California, and the number sharply increased during the gold rush boom. Ranching long remained California's main business. From 1849 onward large numbers of both cattle and sheep were driven overland from the Mississippi Valley, the New Mexico pueblos, and Salt Lake City. In 1849 the price of beef reached $500 per head at Sacramento; by 1851 cattle were still bringing from $50 to $150. These were flush years for California rancheros. By the early 1860s more than 3 million cattle roamed the hills and the valleys of California. By the 1850s several hundred thousand sheep also grazed on the state's ranges, and in the next decade the number of these animals rose to over a million.

When sheepmen erected sheds and fences, and their lambs over-

Vicente Lugo ranch house and some of its landlords and neighbors, 1892. (C. C. Pierce Collection; by courtesy of The Huntington Library, San Marino, California.)

cropped the ranges, trouble flared up between them and cattlemen. With ranges overstocked, cattlemen were in no mood to see the movement of their animals checked by barbed wire. In this conflict, which occasionally reached the stage of violence, sheepmen seldom emerged victorious. The cattlemen were more powerful and better organized. A few dry summers and severe winters drove small ranchers out, leaving behind the large cattle outfits, backed by Eastern, English, or Scottish, capital. Sheepmen often fell into the category of small operators, and suffered from the control of water by the large cattle baronies.

The pressure of the large cattle outfits made itself felt more strongly each year. Weakened by years of land-title litigation, the old rancheros had to cope with depressed agricultural prices. Oppressive state property taxes made it necessary for some to mortgage their lands, while high interest rates on farm mortgages drove them further to the wall. Feeling the hostility of squatters and the pinch of poverty, some sold out their lands, to become day laborers or to join the unemployed.

A devastating drought in 1863–1864 kept the skies cloudless for months on end. The dust on the ranges was so dense that it clogged the nostrils of dying cattle. The bleached skeletons of thousands of animals dotted the hillsides. Hundreds of thousands of cattle, starved for green grass and water, perished. Abel Stearns alone lost 30,000 head on his ranchos near Los Angeles. Sheep too died like flies. The price of land slumped, with southern California range lands selling for as little as ten cents per acre by the late 1860s.

In addition to the favorable price of Western land, crop failures and the harshness of life on the treeless prairies of Illinois and Iowa encouraged farmers to head for California. A piece of their popular balladry recorded the appeal it had for these Western migrants:

> Since times are so hard, I'll tell you, sweetheart,
> I've a mind to leave off my plow and my cart
> And away to California my journey I'll go
> For to better my fortune as other folks do.

California's cattle herds, roaming the ranges without proper care, had markedly deteriorated. As a result of inbreeding, they had become scrawny and bony. Their numbers had also been drastically reduced by the drought. Heavier, meatier strains began to be imported, new techniques of stock feeding and breeding were introduced, and fenced-in ranges became common. Powerful combinations of land barons took over choice pasture lands, which they forcibly guarded from encroachment. The cowhands of the Miller and Lux enterprises could boast that they rode over range—either owned or leased—stretching from Oregon to Mexico. At the Rancho Tejón in Kern County, Edward F. Beale ran cattle, after 1862, on 200,000 acres of land.

Improved methods of range management not only rescued the cattle industry but were also applied to sheepherding. California's flocks reached 7 million head by 1875. The breeding of stock with imported Merino strains produced a superior quality of wool. In the 1870s large profits from wool, which sold at twenty-five cents per pound, made it possible for sheep owners to hire Basque and Mexican sheepherders to tend their flocks while they lived more comfortably in town houses.

Dairying, Hogs, and Cereals

Little use had been made of either butter or milk during the Mexican period, the chief value of cattle being their hides and tallow. In a new era there developed a considerable production of dairy products. Toward the close of the century, existing dairies began to be supplanted by labor-saving devices. Some of the world's finest Holstein and Jersey herds were bred in California. Butter, milk, cream, cheese, and ice cream met increased demand. Stanislaus, San Joaquin, and Los Angeles counties were dairy zones of special importance. Dairies close to large centers of population, as at Norwalk, helped make Los Angeles County first in the nation in dairy production.

Part of the success of the dairy industry, as well as that of stock raising, depended upon the availability of feed for animals. A mechanical revolution in agriculture provided cast-iron and steel plows, mowers, reapers, and threshers; and horsepower was substituted for oxen to pull the new machinery. The introduction of commercial fertilizers also increased the productivity of farms. Philip D. Armour, head of the national meat-packing house that still bears his name, left the California agricultural scene because of inadequate feed stocks. Armour had raised hogs in the Mother Lode during the gold rush, but, finding that summer shortages of water limited his pasturage, had moved to the Middle West. In later years, however, the tremendous expansion of corn acreage in California resulted in a corresponding increase in the hog population.

Among the most important crops were grains, which could be grown without expensive irrigation equipment. Wheat and corn were in demand on international markets and had the advantage of being only partially dependent on local economic changes. California's climate and soil were splendidly suited to growing these and other grains in volume. Whereas the state had imported most of its grain during the gold rush, within a few years vast new ranches in California's Central Valley made it more than self-sufficient as a producer of oats, barley, and corn.

By the 1870s wheat had become an important export crop. The state produced an unusually hard, dry, white grain, popular with British millers. Much of the trade to Liverpool's Corn Exchange was controlled by Isaac Friedlander, California's "Grain King." Friedlander managed his own production, shipping terminals, and global marketing. With the aid of San Francisco financier William Ralston, Friedlander displayed genius in marshaling credit. Aboard sailing vessels he shipped durum wheat in burlap bags to Australia and China as well as to wheat-short Mediterranean countries. Italians milled California's wheat into pasta, while the French made it into their distinctive breads.

Annual wheat production grew to 40 million bushels in 1890; California ranked second by then among all states in wheat production. "Small-time farming," dependent upon weather, price fluctuations, and market saturation, had become excessively risky. Too many novices had turned to farming, and failure was inevitable for some—just as, earlier, inexperienced forty-niners had tried mining without success. Intensive capital was required for the purchase or rental of land and for the new farm machinery that had become necessary.

Harvesting in the San Fernando Valley, ca. 1900. (C. C. Pierce Collection; by courtesy of The Huntington Library, San Marino, California.)

In the 1870s and 1880s, fierce competition developed between large fruit, cattle, and wheat growers and small farmers. Large producers could make more favorable deals with middlemen and with railroad and steamship owners than could small growers. The big landowners were able to show much larger profits. They bought out farmers who could not meet the competition, and their operations came to resemble those of a corporation. Such agricultural combines turned to raising new crops, including rice, cotton, and hay.

Not all large landowners were monopolists, however. William S. Chapman, in the 1870s the largest landowner in California, actually encouraged the growth of small farms. Although there is evidence that he was a corrupter of land-office personnel in the Fresno area, Chapman sold part of his million acres to settlers for less than $2 per acre. He also introduced alfalfa as a "cover crop" in feeding cattle. By 1872, along with Friedlander, Charles Lux, and William C. Ralston, he was active in irrigation development in the lower San Joaquin Valley.

Cotton and Silk

Although experiments with the growing of cotton had been conducted since California's Spanish period, the crop did not attain commercial importance until much later. Attention to cotton cultivation increased during the Civil War, but in the early 1870s only about

2,000 acres were planted in cotton in all California. The yield varied from 250 to 500 pounds per acre. In the late 1870s a short-lived cotton "plantation" of about eighty acres existed within the Los Angeles city limits. But the production of this commodity was still quite limited. The raising of cotton depended upon favorable weather conditions, cheap irrigation, and finding markets. These conditions did not exist much before World War I. Not until the second decade of the twentieth century did cotton production boom in California. Then irrigation projects in the Imperial and southern San Joaquin valleys increased acreage suitable for the crop. Cotton was being grown on 138,000 acres in the Imperial Valley by 1918, and on 90,000 acres of the once-arid stretches of the San Joaquin by 1924. The quality of this cotton was superior even to some grown in the American South, and yield per acre was frequently higher. Eventually, relocation of automobile-tire factories close to sources of cotton supply boosted production (before the introduction of nylon, cotton was heavily used in tire manufacturing). As a result of these developments, California became a major cotton state.

No such success story can be told concerning silk raising in California. In 1854 a French immigrant botanist, Louis Prévost, introduced sericulture at San Jose. Several years later the experimental production of silk spread to southern California, and in 1862 the legislature offered a bounty for cocoons. Sericulture, however, never became more than a passing fad.

Development of the Citrus Industry

From the days when the padres first introduced fruit trees into mission gardens, horticulture expanded, albeit at a slower pace than raising cattle or the planting of wheat and cotton. Fruit growers, remote from large markets, found it impossible to ship perishable crops eastward until the development of the refrigerated railroad car. Then, however, some growers began to prosper spectacularly by raising and marketing one unique crop—citrus fruit.

California's citrus fruits include lemons, tangerines, and grapefruit. But the real symbol, and source of strength, of the citrus industry is the orange. In the mission period orange groves were small and undeveloped, producing pithy, thick-skinned, and sour fruit.

One of the earliest groves was planted at San Gabriel Mission in 1804. It consisted of six acres—about 400 trees—some of which were still bearing as late as 1885. About 1834, a Frenchman, Luís (or Louis) Vignes, transplanted thirty-five of these trees to his Aliso Street residence in Los Angeles, near the present Union Station. In 1841 another Angeleño, William Wolfskill, a former Kentucky trapper,

Orange groves in the 1920s. (From the author's collection.)

replanted a weed-wild two-acre orange grove and expanded his holdings to seventy acres. By 1872, there were 35,000 orange trees in Los Angeles county. Wolfskill's son sent the first trainload of oranges eastward to St. Louis in 1877, soon after the Southern Pacific Railroad made its services available to Los Angeles. The freight charges for the shipment were $500. The fruit arrived in good condition and Wolfskill sent other carloads to the East. His "export approach" to orange marketing, of course, depended heavily on the new rail facilities. The possibilities of advertising, which were just beginning to be realized, also proved a boon to orange growers. Wolfskill disposed of one crop for $23,000, which induced other growers to expand their acreages.

The most substantial experimentation in the cultivation of oranges occurred at Riverside. There, in 1870, Judge John Wesley North, who had served as President Lincoln's surveyor general and as a New York speculator, had been chased out of Tennessee by the Ku Klux Klan, bought 4,000 acres of barren land on credit. Some of this terrain was covered only by cacti, agave plants, and blooming yucca. In cooperation with the transcontinental railroads, which arranged special low fares, North was successful in bringing immigrants to California from Michigan and Iowa. These began, in the spring of 1871, to plant thousands of orange seedlings. Among the settlers in North's agricultural colony were an Eastern couple whose activities would drastically alter the infant orange industry.

To Luther Calvin Tibbets and his wife Eliza belong the credit for introducing, in 1873, the Washington Navel variety of oranges to California. This stock had been sent from Bahia, Brazil, to the United States Department of Agriculture in Washington, D.C.—hence its name. Under the care of Mrs. Tibbets, the tiny cuttings she and her husband had brought to California grew to maturity and produced a juicy, flavorful, seedless orange. The fruit attracted immediate attention at the first of a series of annual citrus fairs at Riverside. The two Tibbets trees became the parent stock for planting throughout the 1880s. California's climate and soil was especially suited to the Washington Navel, and growers won prizes for the quality of their fruit.

In the early days of the orange industry there was no crop-inspection or fruit-quarantine system. Destructive insects were introduced through nursery stock imported from various parts of the world. The cottony cushion scale came from Australia in 1868. In the next twenty years it spread throughout the orchards of southern California. So injurious was this pest that the orange industry was threatened with extinction. In 1888 the United States Department of Agriculture sent a special investigator to Australia to study the cottony cushion scale in its native land. The following year a small ladybird beetle (*Novius cardinalis*), which attacked the scale, was introduced into California. This Australian ladybug not only checked the spread of the scale, but almost eliminated the disease.

A second disease, black scale, also seriously damaged the citrus industry. In addition, sooty mold caused decay among individual trees. To fight the mold and black scale, growers had to wash tree trunks thoroughly. About 1901, they turned toward spraying orchards with distillate oil. This proved less effective, however, than fumigation, then considered the best protection against diseases affecting orange trees.

Another hazard to the orange industry was frost. In the winter months temperatures fall below freezing in California's groves. Protection against frost was found in the form of oil heaters burning cheap crude oil. Nearby city dwellers, however, whose house furnishings, draperies, and rugs were covered with soot from the oil burners, complained bitterly. Eventually, the orchards were protected against cold damage by wind machines, which keep air currents in motion to prevent frost.

The Success of Citriculture

To absorb increased production, new consumers had to be found outside California. As long as each grower marketed his own fruit, he remained easy prey to commission agents and speculators who secured rebates from railroad companies. The larger the grower's crop, the more indebted he became to middlemen and packers by the end of a growing season. After 1893 growers formed a cooperative marketing organization. Though not entirely satisfactory, this was a great improvement over old methods of marketing. It prepared the way for another organization, founded in 1895 as the Southern California Fruit Growers Exchange. In time the exchange was shipping eastward most of California's annual citrus crop. On March 27, 1905, an even more important cooperative was incorporated. This was the California Fruit Growers Exchange, which proceeded to make cooperative marketing general throughout the state, rather than only in southern California. Its trade name, "Sunkist," was used in the most vigorous advertising campaign the orange industry had yet attempted.

The California citrus industry, in fact, now set about to change the American breakfast diet. Specially decorated trains, which dispensed oranges at whistlestops in the Middle West, gaudy advertising billboards, free orange wrappers and spoons, and essay and poetry contests all helped carry the message of California's "golden fruit" eastward. As a result of this campaign a glass of orange juice, or sliced oranges or grapefruits, were widely adopted as substitutes for such starch and fat staples as buckwheat cakes, bacon, ham, porridge, and waffles. The orange became identified with California, as the slogan "Oranges for health; California for wealth" attested. The song "It's Always Orange Day in California," from Oliver Morosco's musical "Canary Cottage" (1914), runs:

> California, you were a Golden Country
>   Long before a man set foot on you.
> California, you had your Golden Poppies
>   .   When Cabrillo came in fifteen forty-two.
>
> California, you had your Golden Mountains
>   Back in eighteen forty-nine.
> And you've still a Golden plume,
>   For you wear a Golden bloom of oranges all the time.
>
> CHORUS
> It's always orange day in California,
>   Forget your winter snow,
>   Come out and see them grow
> The Golden sun is here to warm you
>   For every Golden fruit there's a Golden heart to boot
>
> Become a Booster—We'll make you used to the Golden climate.
> So hop a train, gol darn ya, and come out to California
>   On Golden orange day.
> It's always orange day in California.

California's chambers of commerce, the Los Angeles All-Year Club, and dozens of other booster organizations joined the advertising campaign begun by the citrus industry.

Success with the Valencia orange variety can be ascribed, in large part, to a Fullerton grower, C. C. Chapman. He found that his trees were such heavy bearers that they almost tore themselves to pieces by their production of fruit. Other growers who faced the same problem had disgustedly sunk much of their profits into propping up the overloaded limbs of their Valencia trees. Chapman worked out a system of pruning that checked rank growth and enabled his trees to carry a greater burden without damage to each tree.

Chapman was responsible for other innovations as well. It was the custom among growers to pay pickers and packers by the box. To forestall careless handling of his oranges, Chapman stationed himself among his men and began to pay crews by the day. He inaugurated fruit-inspection techniques that were a forerunner of the packing-house assembly line. Prevention of the bruising of fruit not only enriched Chapman; it also led to the discovery that blue mold could be controlled by wrapping oranges in paper.

Commercial introduction of the Eureka and Lisbon varieties of lemons rounded out the development of California citriculture. The Eureka lemon, native to Sicily and introduced into Los Angeles about 1870, is comparatively free from thorns, and has a tendency to early bearing and "setting" fruit on the tips of its branches throughout each year. The Lisbon lemon bears uniformly throughout the tree, and its heavy foliage protects the fruit from sunburn. Maturation of its largest crop in the winter also makes this tree attractive. Because of the superiority of these two species of lemons, and because of their climatic needs (warm days and cold nights), California has long produced almost 100 percent of the lemons grown in the United States.

Grapefruit production, however, experienced competition from Florida and Arizona. Unlike the lemon, the grapefruit tree requires a uniform night temperature; in the Texas and Mexican Gulf Coastal regions the climate approximates desired tropical conditions more closely than is the case in California.

California thus owes its success in citriculture to specialized growing and marketing methods, favorable climatic combinations, and to cooperative growers. Among those attracted were retired business professionals from the East and Middle West. Prominent people who had lost their health seemed especially attracted to the management of orange groves. For them a new life in California's sunshine and dry air often proved restorative and rewarding. Such folk brought needed capital to the state's agriculture. Many of these "retired" city dwellers, who built fine residences amid their orange groves, typified in their persons the slogan "Oranges for health; California for wealth."

Varied Crops in Varied Places

Within the spurs of the Coast Range and between the Sierra and the sea lie many of the most fertile valleys of California. Among these garden spots are the Napa, Livermore, Santa Clara–Santa Rosa, Salinas, San Luis, Santa Maria, Santa Inez, Santa Clara of the South, San Bernardino, and San Fernando valleys. In such fertile coastal areas some of California's most characteristic crops are grown. One of these is olives, whose cultivation dates from the Spanish period. By the end of the eighteenth century San Diego Mission alone had an olive grove of more than 500 trees. Olive oil, called *aceite de comer*, or edible oil, made La Mirada an olive center. At Sylmar, in the San Fernando Valley, a 2,000-acre grove was advertised as the largest in the world.

Like olives, walnuts were first cultivated in California by the Spanish padres. Rancheros were not ordinarily growers of tree crops. Vallejo's estate at Sonoma—"Lachryma Montis"—was an exception to the tree-barren ranchos elsewhere; and the Camulos Rancho near Ventura also grew fruits and vegetables before the American conquest. Following secularization of the missions, the groves of those establishments fell into disuse, and many trees died. Pruning, cultivation, and irrigation later restored a few mission trees, but it was basically a new fruit industry that emerged. In 1854 prunes were introduced into the Santa Clara Valley, which became the world's chief producer of Italian prunes. In 1867 at Santa Barbara the softshell walnut was planted commercially, and at Los Angeles, in 1873, William Wolfskill and Luís Vignes replanted the English walnut. This walnut, once called the Madeira nut, or Persian walnut, forms the basis of California's present crop, which accounts for almost 100 percent of the nation's walnuts. California also produces virtually all the almonds grown in the United States.

Enthusiasm over the size of the state's agricultural products led Californians into rapturous descriptions that seemed unbelievable to outsiders. In his book, *The Resources of California* (1863), John S. Hittell described potatoes that weighed four to seven pounds each, cabbages seven feet wide, and onions twenty-two inches in circumference. Hittell also claimed he saw a three-year-old red beet that weighed 118 pounds and was five feet long, in addition to a tomato twenty-six inches in circumference. Eastern readers were justifiably skeptical.

The pioneer botanist Luther Burbank, from 1875 until his death in 1926, carried on experiments with garden crops at Santa Rosa. Burbank's efforts, the details of which are recounted in his autobiography, *The Harvest of the Years* (1927), made possible increased production of tomatoes, lettuce, cauliflower, carrots, alfalfa, sugar beets, celery, and potatoes. Accompanying California's burgeoning agricultural productivity was the development of a canning industry; such trade names as Del Monte, Iris, and (in the case of sugar packaging) Spreckels became familiar in thousands of households. The growth of a hatchery industry at Petaluma and in the San Fernando Valley near Los Angeles also occurred.

"Vines in the Sun"

An important part of the agricultural history of California has been the development of its wine industry. A fortunate combination of climate and soil, particularly in northern California, gave viticulture a propitious start. Also, Europeans skilled in the care of vines arrived early in the region. Today, some 90 percent of the United States grape crop and most of the wine production comes from California.

In 1770, the year after the first Franciscans arrived in California, the missionaries set out a small patch of grape cuttings at San Diego. Vines of the European *vitis vinifera* stock were also planted at Missions San Gabriel, Santa Barbara, and San Luís Obispo, where they bore grapes for over a hundred years. The first vineyard planted at San Gabriel contained three thousand such vines. This stock, known as the *Vina Madre* (Mother Vine) or the "Mission variety," provided cuttings which became the basis of California's earliest vineyards.

In 1857 a group of Germans formed the Los Angeles Vineyard Society on lands they had bought about thirty miles southeast of Los Angeles, not far from the ocean. They gave their tract the name Anaheim, from its location in the Santa Ana Valley and the German word for home, *heim*. Around their property the Germans built a fence five and a half miles long, consisting of forty thousand willow poles, each eight feet long, of which six feet projected above the ground. They defended their fence by a ditch four feet deep, six feet wide at the top, sloping downward to a breadth of one foot at its bottom. The willow poles took root to form a living wall around the colony. Such "fortifications" were constructed mainly to keep out roving herds of cattle.

With water from the Santa Ana River, the Germans irrigated numerous twenty-acre vineyards. The colonists lived in a central plot. Among these settlers only one man originally understood the art of wine making, but they all went about the new work with patient industry. The year after the colony was begun, the Los Angeles *Star* (on April 18, 1858) printed the news that the colonists were planting more than 400,000 vines. Almost twenty years later, on December 11, 1877, the same paper announced one of the less desirable side effects, in the view of the California law, of all this planting: "Internal Revenue Collector Hall swooped down on an illicit distillery at Anaheim one day last week and captured the still and one thousand gallons of grape brandy spirits."

Also among the early wine makers was Agoston Haraszthy, a Hungarian of noble birth who is credited with the introduction, in 1851, of zinfandel grapes at his Buena Vista vineyard at Sonoma. Others included Etienne Thée and Charles Lefranc, two Frenchmen who were the founders of the Almadén Vineyards at Los Gatos. In 1858, Charles Krug, editor of the *Staats Zeitung*, first German newspaper on the Pacific Coast, bought land from Haraszthy and planted twenty acres of vines in the Sonoma Valley. Two years later he moved to the Napa Valley and founded the winery that still bears his name. Europeans who settled in California following the gold rush produced burgundies, clarets, sauternes, and champagnes in the state's northern valleys.

Large-scale production of wine, however, had to await the arrival of good vine cuttings from Europe. As early as the spring of 1862 the state legislature sent "Count" Haraszthy there to bring back 100,000 cuttings of 300 different varieties of select grapes. These he divided among the wine growers of the state. In spite of the impetus that such help gave the industry, the early wine producers encountered difficulties that resembled those of the orange growers. In the 1870s a dreaded enemy of the vine, the phylloxera, a soil-inhabiting aphid, practically wiped out California's struggling wine industry. Even more serious were the ravages in Europe of this plant disease. American root-stock rescued the European vineyards, whose decimation opened up a vast new market for California wineries.

No crop was better adapted than grapes to the climate of almost every California county. In the mid-1880s wine growing became quite fashionable, especially among the rich. Leland Stanford owned 3,060,000 vines near Mission San Jose. Senator James Graham Fair, a forty-niner and Comstock millionaire, built a winery near Petaluma. Senator George Hearst owned a vineyard in Sonoma County, and E. J. "Lucky" Baldwin grew grapes at Santa Anita in sandy and hot southern California.

By the 1880s no organization planted quite so many grapes as did the Italian-Swiss Agricultural Colony at Asti. It was founded principally by northern Italians from Genoa, Turin, and the Lombard vineyard towns, who had settled in the Napa and Sonoma Valleys. The workers of this semi-utopian colony were to receive free all the wine they could drink, in addition to a basic wage—an arrangement they chose in preference to receiving stock in the colony. After a few lean years this colony, like the German one at Anaheim, prospered. Its 1897 vintage was so large that there was insufficient cooperage in all California to hold the wine. A reservoir had to be chiseled out of solid rock, which became the largest wine tank in the world; when empty this vat could accommodate a dance floor for 200 persons.

As California wines began to win prizes for excellence, new wineries appeared, not only in the Sonoma Valley but at Napa, in the Livermore Valley, and in the San Joaquin–Sacramento Valley. At Cucamonga, in southern California, the Secondo Guasti family owned the largest (and probably the sandiest) vineyard in the world; they specialized in the production of such fortified dessert wines as ports, sherries, and muscatels. At Fresno, Modesto, Madera, and other interior towns, Italian and French immigrants established vineyards that were to increase further California's international reputation in wine production. The Inglenook Cellars at Rutherford, the Paul Masson winery at Saratoga, and the Beaulieu vineyards of Georges de Latour, also at Rutherford, became important after the turn of the century. A tradition for improved production and for wines of high quality grew out of patient techniques learned in Europe and transplanted to California. Although the Prohibition era of the 1920s temporarily put an end to wine making, the industry flourished again as soon as Prohibition was repealed. Two notable operations, those of Louis M. Martini and the Christian Brothers (the latter a religious order), began to produce creditable wines near St. Helena on a large scale during this period.

In the early years of the California industry the equipment needed to make wine consisted of tubs to receive the juice of the grapes, a small press, and half a dozen French "claret casks." Wine making takes place from about the middle of September to the first of October, according to the maturity of the grapes. Grapes must be picked only when fully ripe, and when there is no dampness on them. Upon their arrival at the press, all leaves and unripe or decayed fruit must be eliminated before crushing begins. Care must also be taken not to crush the seeds, which impart a bitter taste to the wine. If the wine is to be red, the pulp is left with its juice after the grapes are pressed. If the wine is to be white, the skins must immediately be separated from the juice. In either case, the juice flows into large casks where it is exposed to the air to hasten fermentation. Fermentation begins in three or four days; if the fermenting juice is not kept at 65° F. the wine either will be poor in quality or will spoil by souring. The liquid becomes "quiet" in a few days; then impurities are strained out, barrel bungholes are sealed, and the wine is left undisturbed for several months. In the next process, called "racking off," the wine is transferred into smaller oak casks for aging, which should improve it in mellowness. In the case of the best wines, aging, especially important for the red varieties, occurs in bottles rather than in barrels and casks.

A sizable part of the grapes grown in California are dried for sale as raisins. By 1941 California produced almost 75 percent of the raisins grown in the United States.

Reclamation and Irrigation

Extensive reclamation of swampy land and irrigation of dry terrain have opened up vast new areas for farming operations. All sorts of crops, from artichokes to watermelons, can now be grown in almost every one of California's fifty-eight counties. One of the first regions to undergo reclamation was the triangle of land formed by the Sacramento and San Joaquin rivers. This half million acres, consisting of a group of islands and swampy plains, had been transformed by the end of the nineteenth century. Individual farmers and the state built dykes, canals, conduits, and check dams to protect farms from floods. The delta has since become known for its output of deciduous fruits, rice, sugar beets, asparagus, spinach, celery, and other vegetables.

Irrigation is expensive and sometimes dangerous, but its importance in developing agriculture has been incalculable. The Imperial Valley is a notable example. Sometimes called the "American Nile" area, this valley is located in the dry and hot southeast part of the state. Much of the soil is sandy and alluvial. Up to 1891, the land under irrigation in the Imperial area was only 90,344 acres. This figure was more than doubled in ten years. George Chaffey, a Canadian who in the mid-1880s had built a self-sustaining irrigation colony at Ontario, near Los Angeles, planned this transformation of the Imperial Valley. By diverting the waters of the Colorado River, which ran unchecked into the Gulf of California, Chaffey made it possible for the Imperial Land Company to bring a large number of settlers into the valley by 1900. However, in 1905 a flood began that lasted almost two years, and created the Salton Sea. This torrent could not be stopped until the dangerous breach in the banks of the Colorado was sealed. The area was below sea level and the river threatened to inundate the valley. On February 10, 1907, with the help of Southern Pacific Railroad crews, rampaging flood waters were finally turned back after months of effort. Once the flood damage was repaired, the Imperial region grew into a model agricultural community. The novelist Harold Bell Wright's mediocre but popular novel, *The Winning of Barbara Worth*, made the valley nationally known.

By 1909 more than a thousand miles of canals had been constructed in the Imperial Valley. In 1913 this canal system covered more than half a million acres, extending below the border into Mexico. The operation was, for its time, the largest irrigation project in the United States. Barley, alfalfa, and other farm acreage rapidly expanded, and the valley became known as the "Winter Garden of the World." Imperial became equally famous for its cantaloupes and other melons.

Farther northward, east of Palm Springs, the Coachella Valley proved to be another marvel of productivity with the assistance of artificial irrigation. Crops in this valley have the advantage of early maturation. In the Coachella the harvest of table grapes, dates, melons, strawberries, and orchard fruits begins about May 25. Temperatures climb to above 110°, making the area notable as a producer of Red Emperor, Tokay, Ribier, and Thompson Seedless grapes.

Town Founding

As rancho holdings were broken up by controversies over legal titles, the lands fell into the hands of urban promoters, and the communities that sprang up on these sites took the names of the former ranchos. William Heath Davis converted part of Rancho San Leandro (acquired by marriage from the Estudillo family) into the central California community of San Leandro. He urged a neighboring native family, the Peraltas, to do likewise. Their claims, however, which covered part of the present sites of Berkeley, Oakland, and Alameda along San Francisco Bay, were disputed in the courts for years, and the Peraltas profited little from development of their terrain.

At first towns were little more than country crossroads, which became farm supply centers. In the 1850s, long before railroad connections with the outer world had been provided, Davis and other town founders strained their financial resources to the breaking point. They built houses, paved streets, constructed wharfs for visiting steamers, provided hotels for dusty overland travelers—in short, tried to transform a community of crumbling adobes into a city. At San Diego Davis, however, was doomed to failure. Later, in the 1860s, the real estate promoter Alonzo Erastus Horton constructed a "New San Diego," only to lose his fortune also. But some town developers succeeded from the start. Among these was Phineas Banning, founder of Wilmington. This community was on an estuary providing maritime access to the expanding pueblo of Los Angeles. Banning's Wilmington wharf and warehouses, built between 1851 and 1858, were sheltered by a rock jetty between Terminal and Dead Man's islands, near what was to become "New San Pedro." The harbor's channel was dug deep enough to float barges and steam tugs carrying freight and passengers from ocean vessels anchored offshore. During the Civil War the United States Army established Camp Drum and Drum Barracks near Banning's home at Wilmington. This government installation helped to assure the future of a new port for Los Angeles.

San Diego, ca. 1852. Possibly sketched by John Russell Bartlett. (Reproduced from his *Personal Narrative* . . . [1856].)

When incorporated as a city, San Buenaventura (abbreviated to Ventura) took its name from the nearby mission. Not far away was Oxnard, founded by the American Sugar Beet Company, begun by the Oxnard brothers.

Former ranchos became instant towns once the litigation over land titles was clarified in the late nineteenth century. Also in southern California, the city of Pasadena mushroomed out of Rancho San Pasqual, site of an Indian village. Throughout the 1850s Manuel Garfias, who held the grant to the rancho, had faced grave economic problems. Repeated borrowing, at ruinous rates of interest, forced Garfias to sacrifice the rancho property. In 1859 he sold San Pasqual for $1,800 to Benjamin D. Wilson, who had come to California with the Workman–Rowland party. Wilson interested a group of Indiana colonists who, by 1874, laid out a community complete with irrigation conduits leading into new orchards and grain fields. The settlers chose the name Pasadena from the Chippewa Indian language, a name touristically, and probably inaccurately, translated as "Crown of the Valley." In the twentieth century this town, once dotted with clumps of oak and fields of poppies, was to transform itself into a winter playground of millionaires, who would build mansions along its Orange Grove Avenue. Pasadena has profited handsomely from its almost prodigal land inheritance.

In the development of "rancho towns," it was the native Californians—the former owners of the land—who gained least, if at all. Various factors contributed to the rapid growth of such towns as Pasadena: the low cost of land, increasing population pressures caused by the railroads, and the energy of developers in establishing water facilities as well as transportation. These speculators turned an arid countryside into prosperous cities.

The Railroads and the Land Boom of the 1880s

The boom in California's urban growth, like that in agriculture, was closely connected with the railroads. The flood of population that descended on the state from 1870 to 1890, seeking to substitute sunshine for harsh winters, contributed to California's overall urbanization. It also helped determine where some of its future cities would be located. To southern California, in particular, there flocked unemployed cowboys and fruit pickers, farmers, engineers, health seekers, real estate promoters, and merchants.

On March 7, 1886 the Los Angeles *Times* reported that passenger fares, which had formerly been as high as $125 from the Middle West, were headed straight downward. Fares reached as low as $1 as 200,000 persons came to California in 1887 by railroad. Once the Atchison, Topeka, and Santa Fe reached Los Angeles that year, competition with the Southern Pacific remained brisk. Dozens of towns sprang up in Los Angeles County, and colleges, banks, and other institutions were also founded. Within less than two years 100 communities with 500,000 lots had been "platted" inside the county. Though lacking in coal and metals, and isolated on the far side of North America without a developed harbor, Los Angeles had embarked on a period of prodigious growth—the result of advertising and the lure of climate, as well as of railroad competition.

Promoters familiar with Italy exploited the similarities between California and ancient Tuscany or Campania. They pointed out resemblances along the Golden State's coastline, and tourists agreed that the terraced bluffs around Santa Barbara and Carmel were reminiscent of the Riviera's Santa Margherita and Rapallo. Blue skies, olive trees, and craggy cliffs took some back to the Bay of Naples. Even rainfall resembled Italy's, in that the least rain fell in the south. California's Hispanic past also contributed to the Mediterranean similarity. The resemblance became the subject of books, including Peter C. Remondino's health-stressing *Mediterranean Shores of America* (1892) and Charles Dudley Warner's *Our Italy* (1902). Grace Ellery Channing and Ernest Peixotto published articles entitled "What We Can Learn from Rome," in the magazine *Westways*, and "Italy's Message to Cal-

ifornia," in *Sunset*. Oscar Wilde referred to Los Angeles as "a sort
of Naples." The *Golden Era* of May 1888 reminded readers that San
Diego wanted to be called the "Naples of America." One county
emblazoned its 1905 *Sunset* magazine advertisement with the banner
heading: "The Italy of California, Glenn County." Both the San
Diego and Riverside chambers of commerce issued brochures that
advertised "their" Italy of America.

The comparison, which stressed the ancient and the romantic, carried over into the naming of new towns; California soon had its
Hesperia, Rialto, Tarragona, Terracina, and Verona. At one such
namesake, Venice, the real estate boom of the 1880s saw the building
of imitation lagoons and piazzas along an open beach. At Senator
James D. Phelan's Villa Montalvo, near Saratoga, Italian-inspired
rococo porticoes, cypress hedges, stone gryphons, and classical statues
sustained the mood. Similar in style was Henry E. Huntington's estate
at San Marino. Educational institutions, too, were affected by the
trend. The façade of Stanford University's chapel framed a mosaic
similar to that of the Rome church called St. Paul Outside the Walls.
The Occidental College campus was classical in its inspiration, while
a future UCLA was to use Romanesque construction. Later, also,
Scripps College bowed toward Italianate architectural design.

Selected Readings

Books that discuss agriculture as a factor in California's growth are
John S. Hittell, *The Resources of California* (San Francisco, 1863); Titus
F. Cronise, *The Natural Wealth of California* (San Francisco, 1868);
and J. Ross Browne, *Resources of the Pacific Slope* (San Francisco, 1869);
Edward J. Wickson's *The California Fruits and How to Grow Them* (San
Francisco, 1900) and his *Nurserymen and the Plant Industry* (Los Angeles, 1921) as well as Wickson's *Dairying in California* (Washington,
1896), and his *Rural California* (New York, 1923). Consult also the
agricultural chapters of Cleland and Hardy's *March of Industry*. A
symposium, edited by Claude B. Hutchison, is entitled *California Agriculture* (Berkeley, 1946). Persons interested in gardening should
consult Victoria Padilla, *Southern California Gardens* (Berkeley, 1961).

Featuring agriculture's interaction with the social milieu are: Richard Orsi, "*The Octopus* Reconsidered: The Southern Pacific and Agricultural Modernization in California, 1865–1915," *California Historical Quarterly* 54 (Fall 1975), 197–220; and Orsi's *A List of References
for the History of Agriculture in California* (Davis, 1974). On the founding of Riverside, see Merlin Stonehouse, *John Wesley North and the
Reform Frontier* (Minneapolis, 1965). The "orange culture" of California is described in Oscar Osburn Winther's "The Colonial System

of Southern California," *Agricultural History* 27 (July 1953), 94–103. The navel orange industry in California is the subject of Minnie Tibbets Mills, "Luther Calvin Tibbets, Founder of the Navel Orange Industry of California," *Historical Society of Southern California Quarterly* 25 (December 1943), 127–61. Regarding Burbank's agricultural experiments see Emma Burbank Beeson, *The Early Life and Letters of Luther Burbank* (San Francisco, 1927).

Regarding sheep, see Edward N. Wentworth, *America's Sheep Trails: History, Personalities* (Ames, Iowa, 1948); Earle Crow, *General Beale's Sheep Odyssey* . . . (Bakersfield, 1960), and L. T. Burcham, "The Advent of Sheep in California," *California Livestock News* 33 (May 1957), 13–15.

Useful for understanding the cattle industry are Edward F. Treadwell's biography of Henry Miller, *The Cattle King* (New York, 1931; repr. Boston, 1950). Also see L. T. Burcham, "Cattle and Range Forage in California: 1770–1880," *Agricultural History* 35 (July 1961), 140–49, and the same author's *California Range Land* (Sacramento, 1957). See also James M. Jensen, "Cattle Drives From the Ranchos to the Gold Fields of California," *Arizona and the West* 2 (Winter 1960), 341–52, as well as Dane Coolidge, *Old California Cowboys* (New York, 1939). Combining early agricultural land speculation with developments in ranching and farming is Gerald D. Nash, "Henry George Reexamined: William S. Chapman's Views on Land Speculation in Nineteenth Century California," *Agricultural History* 33 (July 1959), 133–37. Dennis Alward and Andrew Rolle's "The Surveyor General: Edward Fitzgerald Beale's Administration of California Lands," *Southern California Quarterly* 53 (June 1971), 113–22 also treats the disposition of land.

Early books about the wine industry include George Husmann, *The Cultivation of the Native Grape and Manufacture of American Wines* . . . (New York, 1866), and his *Grape Culture and Wine Making in California* (San Francisco, 1888). Another such work is Edna Eunice Wait, *Wines and Vines of California* (San Francisco, 1889). Early contemporary discussions include also Arpad Haraszthy, "Wine Making in California," *Overland Monthly* 7 (1871), 489–97, and, by the same author, *California Wines and Grapes* (San Francisco, 1883); a series of articles on the Haraszthy family of Paul Frederickson appears in *Wines and Vines* (July-October, 1947). Also see Joan Marie Donohoe, "Agostin Haraszthy: A Study in Creativity," *California Historical Society Quarterly* 47 (June 1969), 153–63.

On the Anaheim colony see Mildred Yorba MacArthur, *Anaheim: The Mother Colony* (Los Angeles, 1959), and Lucile E. Dickson, "The Founding and Early History of Anaheim, California," *Historical Society of Southern California Annual Publications* 11 (March 1919), 26–37. Consult also Iris Ann Wilson, "Early Southern California

Viniculture, 1830–1865," Historical Society of Southern California *Quarterly* 39 (September 1957), 242–50. Helpful on wine production is Vincent P. Carosso, *The California Wine Industry, 1830–1895* (Berkeley, 1951). Useful also is John Melville, *Guide to California Wines* (New York, 1955), as is M. F. K. Fisher, *The Story of Wines in California* (Berkeley, 1962).

Rodman W. Paul treats grain producing in "The Great California Grain War: The Granger Challenges the Wheat King," *Pacific Historical Review* 27 (November 1958), 331–49, and "The Wheat Trade Between California and the United Kingdom," *Mississippi Valley Historical Review* 45 (December 1958), 391–412. The struggle of farmers against hydraulic mining is the topic of Robert L. Kelley, *Gold vs. Grain: The Hydraulic Mining Controversy in California's Sacramento Valley* (Glendale, 1960). Irrigation is treated in Frederick D. Kershner, Jr., "George Chaffey and the Irrigation Frontier," *Agricultural History* 27 (October 1953), 115–22. See also J. A. Alexander, *The Life of George Chaffey: The Story of Irrigation Beginnings in California and Australia* (Melbourne, 1928). On growing silk see Nelson Klose, "California's Experimentation in Sericulture," *Pacific Historical Review* 30 (August 1961), 213–27.

The rural-to-urban transformation of California is explored by local histories. Some of the best are Gordon S. Eberly, *Arcadia: City of the Santa Anita* (Claremont, 1953); William Martin Camp, *San Francisco: Port of Gold* (Garden City, N.Y., 1947); Works Progress Administration, *Berkeley: The First Seventy-Five Years* (Berkeley, 1941); Chester G. Murphy, *The People of the Pueblo: or The Story of Sonoma* (Portland, 1937, 1948); Clara H. Hisken, *Tehama: Little City of the Big Trees* (New York, 1948); Hallock F. Raup, *San Bernardino, California: Settlement and Growth of a Pass-Site City* (Berkeley, 1940); Donald H. Pflueger, *Glendora—The Annals of a Southern California Community* (Claremont, 1951) and his *Covina: Sunflowers, Citrus, Subdivisions* (Claremont, 1964); Katherine M. Bell, *Swinging the Censer: Reminiscences of Old Santa Barbara* (Santa Barbara, 1931); and L. J. Rose, Jr., *L. J. Rose of Sunny Slope, 1827–1899* (San Marino, 1958). Regarding San Diego, there are six volumes by Richard F. Pourade: *The Explorers* (1960); *Time of the Bells* (1961); *The Silver Dons* (1963); *The Glory Years* (1964); *Gold in the Sun* (1965); and *The Rising Tide* (1967). Also see Andrew Rolle, *William Heath Davis and the Founding of American San Diego* (San Diego, 1953) and Max Miller, *Harbor of the Sun: The Story of the Port of San Diego* (New York, 1940). Regarding the capitol, see Joseph A. McGowan, *History of the Sacramento Valley* (3 vols., New York, 1961).

Histories of ranchos that became cities include Joseph J. Hill, *The History of Warner's Ranch and Its Environment* (Los Angeles, 1927); Robert G. Cleland, *The Irvine Ranch of Orange County, 1810–1950* (San

Marino, 1952); Ruth Waldo Newhall, *The Newhall Ranch: The Story of the Newhall Land and Farming Company* (San Marino, 1958); and W. W. Robinson, *Ranchos Become Cities* (Pasadena, 1939). Also see Hallock F. Raup, "Rancho Los Palos Verdes," Historical Society of Southern California *Quarterly* 19 (March 1937), 7–21, and Andrew Rolle, "Wagon Pass Rancho Withers Away: La Ballona, 1821–1952," in the same journal 34 (June 1952), 147–58. Consult also R. Louis Gentilcore, "Ontario, California and the Agricultural Boom of the 1880's," *Agricultural History* 34 (April 1960), 77–87, as well as Sheldon Jackson, *A British Ranchero in Old California: the Life and Times of Henry Dalton* (Glendale, 1977).

The basic work on the migration after 1887 is Glenn S. Dumke, *The Boom of the 'Eighties in Southern California* (San Marino, 1944). Development of a port before the "free harbor" fight is discussed in Richard W. Barsness, "Iron Horses and an Inner Harbor at San Pedro Bay, 1867–1890," *Pacific Historical Review* 34 (August 1965), 289–304. Although written by a non-professional, Joseph S. O'Flaherty, *An End and a Beginning: The South Coast and Los Angeles, 1850–1887* (Jericho, N.Y., 1972) is packed with information about the urbanization of Los Angeles. O'Flaherty's *Those Powerful Years* (Hicksville, N.Y., 1978) covers the period 1887–1917.

CHAPTER 24

Asian Discrimination

As WE HAVE SEEN, the railroad to the East was built largely with Chinese labor. California's growth was furthered, too, by Japanese farmers in the Central Valley, Italian and French wine growers in the north, as well as Swiss and German dairymen along the Coast Range. Such immigrants made California relatively receptive, especially in comparison with other Western states, to foreign ideas, food, styles of clothing, and patterns of life. Yet its history includes suspicion, harshness, and violence toward foreigners and minority groups. During the nineteenth century, Asians faced tough battles for acceptance. Their mistreatment is summed up in the phrase, "He doesn't have a Chinaman's chance."

Early Chinese Immigration

In 1847, the first small band of Chinese immigrants found their way into the state, attracted by stories of its great mineral wealth and of high wages paid in its mines and work camps. In 1870 there were 49,277 Chinese in California. California's first Chinese were treated with consideration. In 1850 they were invited to help celebrate the admission of the state to the Union. Governor McDougal once called the Chinese "one of the most worthy classes of our newly adopted citizens," and expressed a desire for further Asian immigration. This welcome was in part due to California's need for a dependable supply of common laborers. Asians showed themselves to be adaptable and faithful workers. In the mines, on ranches, in laundries and hotel kitchens, and in private homes, Chinese workers were content with meager wages.

The first serious dissatisfaction with the Chinese appeared in the

Chinese butcher shop in San Francisco, ca. 1890. (Wyland Stanley Collection, photography by I.W. Taber; by courtesy of The Bancroft Libaray, University of California, Berkeley.)

mines, where in spite of their small daily earnings, the Chinese through perseverance and frugality sometimes accumulated more gold than did whites. Californians in 1850 enacted the Foreign Miners' License Law, which imposed a monthly tax of $20 on immigrant miners. This measure had the effect of driving a horde of penniless foreigners away from the mines. The law was eventually repealed, and a milder tax substituted, to be followed in 1855 by a head tax of $50 to be paid by each foreigner upon entry in the state. As to the personal characteristics of "John Chinaman," as the individual Chinese came to be called, he was usually a patient, hard-working miner. He paid his bills promptly and was prudent enough to leave the richest mining claims to Americans. Nevertheless, when he got in the way of aggressive whites, he became the victim of accusations and violence. Some diggings were closed to Chinese and other foreigners.

"California for the Americans!" was a cry voiced in cities as well as in mining camps. Influenced by heightening public antipathy, Governor Bigler, who in 1852 succeeded McDougal, stigmatized the Chinese as scum "coolie" laborers. He called upon the legislature to prohibit contract immigration, becoming the first important official to display his anti-Chinese prejudice. When the financial panic of 1854 brought prices down with a crash, ruining business houses and causing unrest, feeling against the Chinese reached new heights. Miners by the thousands drifted back to San Francisco, only to find the labor market glutted. Large numbers of Chinese in "the City" were held responsible for its distressing unemployment. White workers complained that Orientals, by undercutting wages, deprived them of work—that they were, in fact, human leeches "sucking the very life-blood of this country." Governor Bigler, capitalizing on the prevailing public temper, rebuked the legislature in 1854 for its negligence in not voting for exclusion and deportation laws. Prejudice among whites extended even to little children, who were encouraged by their elders to practice public disrespect and insult against the Chinese. Mistreatment of the "pig-tail," or "almond-eyed Celestial," was of daily occurrence by the late 1850s. Sharply set apart by their physiognomy, dress, religion, mores, and exotic food habits (they ate bamboo shoots, salt ginger, dried duck liver, and seaweed), the Chinese were in no position to retaliate. The nadir of indignity was reached in San Francisco's notorious 1855 "Pig-Tail Ordinance." This regulation required Chinese men to cut off their queues one inch from the head. The Chinese fiercely protected the wearing of long hair, which contributed to the belief that they were unassimilable.

In spite of prejudice and persecution, from 1850 to 1900 a "Little China" was steadily growing on upper Sacramento Street and along Dupont Street. The mysteries of Chinatown held a great attraction for tourists. Smoke-filled gambling dens flourished, and back-room saloons, secret passages, deep basements, and hidden recesses teemed with hivelike activity, day and night. Opium smoking in filthy dens both fascinated and revolted Americans. The Chinese were also accused of importing prostitutes for the use of whites and of keeping these women in bondage.

When the Central Pacific railroad was being built, Mark Hopkins supervised the founding of the "Six Companies" to recruit, transport, and utilize Chinese labor on a large scale. This enterprise, operated by Hopkins's agents, was responsible for much of the immigration in the early 1860s—about 9,000 Chinese in all. Included among "Crocker's Pets," as these railroad workers were called, were undernourished, sometimes sickly, laborers bound to the "Six Companies" by contract. These came chiefly from southern China, where devastating poverty and ignorance existed. They were in no sense free laborers; rather, they were the tools of speculators who paid them a few pennies per hour. Shrewd brokers cooperated with railroad and steamship agents to exploit the Asians. Governor Stanford called the Chinese "peaceable, industrious and economical, apt to learn and quite as efficient as white laborers." Since their labors made a vast fortune for him, he would have been deficient in grace if he had said anything less.

Increased Anti-Chinese Sentiment

When the Chinese came into economic competition with laborers in various trades, resentment exploded into violence. In 1859 Governor Weller sent a company of state militia into Shasta County to put down riots by northern miners. By 1867 "anti-coolie clubs" had grown strong enough to dictate punishment for the misbehavior of Asians, and sheriffs, courts, and juries were generally passive in the face of such action. In December of 1867 Chinese were driven out of French Corral in Nevada County and their cabins destroyed. Out of a total of twenty-seven Caucasians arrested for this mob violence, one was tried and the rest set free. The guilty man was fined $100. On October 23, 1871, nearly a score of Chinese were massacred in a Los Angeles race riot, originating in a quarrel between two Chinese factions. This bloody episode was ignored by the law. Los Angeles earned a notoriety based on lawlessness both in its Chinatown and nearby "Nigger Alley."

The explanation of this hostility involved economic, social, and religious considerations. The press charged the Chinese with intolerable competition in mining, construction work, cigar making, and in the lesser trades. Moreover, critics accused them of draining substantial sums of money which was supposedly sent to China. The Chinese were the "yellow peril," living on inferior food in crowded, unsanitary dwellings, a threat to "Christian values and Republican government." They were said to be pagan, depraved, and vicious. It was believed they practiced a mysterious quasi-government among themselves that encouraged internecine wars. Their accusers found the Chinese lack of assimilation inexcusable. Although numerous Californians favored exclusion, a treaty negotiated in 1868 by Anson Burlingame eased the passage of Asians into the state and allowed the railroad kings to flood its labor market with more Chinese.

Agitation against the Chinese continued at both local and state levels. In 1871, Governor Newton Booth was elected to office on an anti-Chinese platform. Almost every time the state legislature convened, nativists proposed an "immigrant tax." There was strong feeling for repeal of the Burlingame Treaty, which had guaranteed free immigration. Such pressures were bound to affect legislation at the national level. In 1878 congress passed the "Fifteen Passenger Bill," restricting the immigration of Asians to fifteen passengers on any ship entering the United States. Although President Rutherford Hayes vetoed this legislation, an inflamed public in California pressed for a Chinese treaty with stronger exclusionist provisions. In 1882 the Democratic state convention passed a sweeping resolution against further Asian immigration. Both major parties were, in fact, anti-Chinese—on a national as well as a state level.

By the mid-1890s, the country was moving toward absolute exclusion. On April 30, 1902, despite stiff complaint from Chinese Minister Wu Ting Fang to Secretary of State John Hay, a new federal bill, "to prohibit . . . and to regulate the residence within the United States of persons of Chinese descent," was passed and approved by President Theodore Roosevelt.

California can take little pride in its history of exclusion. Its bigotry, race prejudice, and chauvinism were prime factors in national agitation against Asians. On the other hand, the United States, unlike leading European powers, refrained from carving up the Chinese Empire after the Boxer Uprising of 1900, and returned an indemnity fund levied against China so that it might be used to educate young Chinese in America. But such a tardy manifestation of good will could not immediately eradicate American guilt for the treatment of the Chinese.

California still has sizable Chinese colonies at San Francisco and Los Angeles. At the turn of the century, Fresno's Chinatown boasted 5,000 inhabitants and had its own Chinese opera house. Except for celebration of the Chinese New Year and the annual moon festival, Chinese activity in California's interior towns is not to be compared with that of earlier times. Yet, a former joss house in Weaverville functions not only as a state historical monument but also as a bona fide Taoist temple. Its altar, imported from China during the gold rush, is ancient. Chinese tongs, or welfare and fraternal organizations, continue strong, however, at Los Angeles and San Francisco. Chinese in these centers have remained a relatively homogeneous group, largely as a result of the success of their restaurants and shops, in artificially created "Chinatowns" rigged for tourists.

The Japanese Influx

Significant numbers of Japanese began to enter California in the late nineteenth century. Like the Chinese, they experienced reasonable treatment at first. Agitation against Asians had subsided during the Civil War. After the war, however, industrial discontent produced renewed hostility toward foreigners. "The front door has been off its hinges long enough," one California xenophobe of the 1870s declared. In this atmosphere, the Japanese posed a new cheap labor threat, and Californians once more applied the term "yellow peril" to them. In the 1880s another "American Party" was formed, in the tradition of the Know-Nothings, partly for the purpose of attacking Asians.

Not until 1891 did Japanese immigration into the United States for a single year exceed one thousand, but from that time on it increased markedly. Acquisition of Hawaii by the United States in 1898 was followed by a heavy two-year influx of Japanese and Chinese from these islands, and public opinion was aroused anew against all Orientals. Nevertheless, they still came. In 1900 alone, 12,626 Japanese entered the United States. By 1910 the number of Japanese had swelled to more than 40,000.

The first anti-Japanese exclusion meeting was held in May 1905 at San Francisco, resulting in the organization of an Asiatic Exclusion League. The next year the San Francisco Board of Education recommended establishment of special schools for Chinese and Japanese, separate from those for Caucasians. Before action on this proposal could be taken, the city experienced the great earthquake of 1906, which disrupted all civic activities except those devoted to recovery. When a "separate school order" was issued, requiring the transfer of a majority of San Francisco's ninety-three Japanese pupils to the existing Asian school, indignation was aroused in Japan, and diplomatic protests were promptly lodged with the American government. The Japanese objected as much to the inclusion of their children in a separate school with the Chinese as to any other discrimination. President Roosevelt insisted that the national government was a party to the controversy.

In accord with the president's view, the order of the San Francisco school board was rescinded. But, following a recommendation by a newly organized Japanese and Korean Exclusion League, the San Francisco school board passed a second resolution, on October 11, 1906, again announcing that Japanese children would be received only at an "Oriental" public school, along with the Chinese. This time the federal government's view was expressed by Secretary of State Elihu Root, who stated that the United States government "would not allow any treatment of the Japanese people other than that accorded the people of other nations." The attorney general of the United States brought legal action in California to enforce immigration agreements with Japan. However, since a legal decision (*Plessy* vs. *Ferguson*) had become the law of the land, the federal suit could affect only alien Japanese children, who had treaty rights, but not the native-born, who did not. Meanwhile the mayor of San Francisco and members of the school board journeyed to Washington to confer with President Roosevelt. The suits were dismissed, but only after the local board of education rescinded the objectionable order.

The arrival of Japanese laborers in large numbers, however, led to continued agitation against them. In 1908 demonstrations were such as to cause Ambassador Aoki to protest once more to the president, who telegraphed Governor James N. Gillett that restrictive measures then before the California legislature would strain relations with Japan at a time when the Roosevelt administration was already negotiating for the exclusion of labor immigrants. Accordingly, the bills were withdrawn.

By 1910 the Japanese population in California had reached more than 40,000. They were often ambitious and enterprising. Farmers among them worked impressively long hours, expecting the same of all the members of their families. The morale and drive of the Japanese, both as a nation and people, may have been due in part to pride over victory in the Russo-Japanese War of 1905. The press depicted the Japanese as efficient, shrewd, and conniving; they seemed to possess almost to excess the enterprise admired by Caucasian neighbors, with whom they had come into economic competition.

Obviously the major way to cut down further Japanese immigration was by diplomatic means. In order to avert an international crisis with Japan, Roosevelt called for further negotiations, which resulted in the well-known "Gentlemen's Agreement," part of the Root–Takahira accords, which became effective in 1908. Under these new provisions Japanese and Korean laborers who surreptitiously entered from Mexico, Canada, and Hawaii were excludable from the United States. Furthermore, the Japanese government agreed to restrict issuance of passports. California officials hoped this agreement would prevent the smuggling of Japanese into the United States. It did not. Immigrants subsequently entered the country illicitly in large numbers, especially from Mexico.

The institution of Japanese "picture bride" marriages further offended exclusionists. A Japanese laborer in America, unable to go home to be married, often made the acquaintance of his future wife through a go-between who arranged an exchange of photographs. The wedding ceremony was largely a matter of legal documents. This procedure allowed numerous potential immigrant mothers to be brought into the United States by an essentially evasive technique. In October 1919, the Japanese Association of America, aware of criticism, passed a resolution proposing abolition of such marriages. As of 1920, passports were no longer issued to "picture brides" by the Japanese government.

By 1913, anti-Japanese agitation led to proposal of a California alien land law known as the Webb Act. This bill sought to prevent aliens ineligible for citizenship from holding land. The measure seemed about to pass when a new president, Woodrow Wilson, dispatched Secretary of State Bryan to Sacramento to urge state legislators to draw up another bill. Intercession of the federal government resulted in removing some verbiage from the Webb Act, but its most drastic anti-Japanese clauses remained intact. Property acquired by such aliens would eventually be returned to the state, and agricultural lands could not be leased to them for periods to exceed three years.

The Japanese Problem after World War I

The Webb Act remained on the books, but there were ways in which the Japanese could evade its provisions. One of these was to gain control of land by registering it in the name of another landowner who was a citizen. By leasing and subleasing land, the Japanese came to control large truck-farm acreages. The more land the Japanese acquired, the more they were feared as an economic threat.

Laws resembling California's Webb Act were passed against Orientals in other Western states, but California's legislation was the harshest. After World War I, Secretary of State Robert Lansing wrote California legislators from the peace conference at Versailles that any further anti-Japanese legislation would seriously affect a settlement of peace terms. Again California was urged to moderate its attitude toward exclusion. But by 1920 the Japanese population in California had reached 72,000 because of loopholes in the "Gentlemen's Agreement" and the Webb Act. The legislature's Anti-Alien Initiative Measure of 1920 utterly prohibited the owning of land by Japanese or the leasing of farmland to them. Under its terms the Issei, or Japanese born in their native homeland, were forbidden even to hold an interest in any company owning real property.

Californians continued to fear the efficiency of the Japanese and the possibility that they might come to dominate the state's economic life. In 1917 Senator James D. Phelan charged that "because they work unremittingly—man, woman, and child, and participate in none of the activities of the community, they are capable of crowding out, and do crowd out the white population, until today the greatest production of potatoes, garden truck, beans and berries is controlled by them." Further resentment was caused because some Japanese refused to work for wages, preferring to bargain for a share of the crops. In this they differed from the Chinese laborers, as they did also in their quick adaptation to varied industries and in their land hunger. Nevertheless, the two groups together did much of California's farming. In some districts the Japanese and Chinese occupied up to 75 percent of irrigated areas.

After World War I, the Native Sons of the Golden West, the California State Grange, and other labor and patriotic organizations regarded the intermixture of Caucasians and Orientals as a grave danger. As thousands of young Japanese women began to come to the United States, California's exclusionists demanded a tighter federal immigration law. This led to provisions in the Immigration Act of 1924 which put an end to the "Gentlemen's Agreement." Henceforth scarcely any Asian alien ineligible for citizenship could be admitted into the country. The later deterioration of relations between Japan and the United States was in part caused by racist attitudes. In California the anti-Japanese agitation was to reach its most extensive proportions during World War II, when the rights of citizens of the United States of Japanese descent would be sorely tried.

Other Foreigners

Asians in California absorbed nativist antagonisms which might otherwise have been directed toward other immigrants. The French, Germans, Italians, and Irish encountered far fewer barriers to social acceptance and economic success. These foreigners cast off the traces of their immigrant origins more quickly in the West than in the large cities of the East. In rural environments especially, the folkways and customs of Basque sheepherders, Swiss dairymen, and Armenian fig growers merged with those of their neighbors. As immigrant languages fell into disuse, and connections with the "old country" became more remote, they put down California roots. As the population of cities grew, harvesters of prunes, tomatoes, cucumbers, grapes, and strawberries were needed in greater numbers. Europeans who came to California to pick crops frequently became owners of the very land they once were hired to work.

Other foreigners headed for the cities. The versatile Irishmen Denis Kearney and Frank B. Roney became labor organizers, and James McClatchy achieved prominence as a newspaper publisher. In the cities, the Italians and French were in the restaurant trades or, along with the Portuguese, in the fishing industry. Foreign-language newspapers enjoyed a wide circulation among the immigrants. While slanted toward issues and personalities of the nationality involved, this foreign press contributed to California's cosmopolitan flavor. By the 1870s the San Francisco Italians regularly published as many as five journals. At North Beach, in fact, the Italians formed the majority of the population after 1890. One Italian leader was Amadeo Pietro Giannini, founder of the modern Bank of America. In its earlier stage as the Bank of Italy, this organization contributed much to the rebuilding of the city after the fire of 1906 had destroyed banking and credit facilities. Another product of the Italian section was Angelo Rossi, a florist who became mayor of San Francisco.

The Irish and Germans seemed reluctant to give up native folkways. The Germans often pointedly sought to remain masters of their own fate; tradesmen, merchants, and farmers among them were admired for their thrift and industry. Among California's Germans were Adolph Sutro and Henry Teschemacher, both mayors of San Francisco. Theodore Cordua and Charles Weber became founders of Marysville and Stockton, just as the German-Swiss Sutter had, earlier, founded Sacramento. Heinrich Virmond was an outstanding merchant and trader. Claus Spreckels became the "sugar king" of California, and Edward Vischer and Charles Christian Nahl, artists.

Too much of California's immigrant past has been obliterated. Few issues of foreign newspapers published at San Francisco and Los Angeles have been preserved. Also, non-Asian foreigners frequently anglicized their names in an attempt to gain social acceptance. Many institutions and colonies founded by particular immigrant groups for their own protection rapidly disappeared. Little remains of the French utopian colony of Icaria Speranza, organized in 1881 near Cloverdale, or of the German colony at Anaheim. Above San Francisco, the Italian-Swiss colony at Asti exists only in a markedly different commercialized form. The Danes at Solvang, above Santa Barbara, have turned their community into a tourist center that imports most of the merchandise sold there. Yet the immigrant contribution lingers on, albeit diluted.

Selected Readings

Older works that deal with Chinese immigration include Mary R. Coolidge, *Chinese Immigration* (New York, 1909); G. F. Seward, *Chinese Immigration: Its Social and Economic Aspects* (New York, 1881); and William Speer, *China and California: Their Relations Past and Present* (San Francisco, 1853). A more recent appraisal is Elmer C. Sandmeyer, *The Anti-Chinese Movement in California* (Urbana, Ill., 1939). Consult also Gunther Barth, *Bitter Strength: A History of the Chinese in the United States 1850–1870* (Cambridge, Mass., 1964); Ping Chiu, *Chinese Labor in California, 1850–1880: An Economic Study* (Madison, Wis., 1963); Kwang Ching Liu, *Americans and Chinese* (Cambridge, Mass., 1963); and Thomas W. Chinn, ed., *A History of the Chinese in California: A Syllabus* (San Francisco, 1969). See also Luther W. Spoehr, "Sambo and the Heathen Chinese: California's Racial Stereotypes in the Late 1870's," *Pacific Historical Review* 42 (May 1973), 185–204.

For general understanding of California immigrants consult: Roger Daniels and Spencer Olin, eds., *Racism in California* (New York, 1972); Charles Wollenberg, "Race and Class in Rural California: The El Monte Berry Strike of 1933," *California Historical Quarterly* 51 (Summer 1971), 155–64; Commonwealth Club, *The Population of California* (San Francisco, 1946); and Doris M. Wright, "The Making of Cosmopolitan California—An Analysis of Immigration, 1848–1870," California Historical Society *Quarterly* 19 (December 1940), 323–43, and 20 (March 1941), 65–79.

The books of Carey McWilliams contain thought-provoking generalizations about foreigners. These include *California: The Great Exception* (New York, 1949); *Factories in the Field* (Boston, 1939); *Southern California Country* (New York, 1946); and *Prejudice: Japanese-Americans, Symbol of Racial Intolerance* (Boston, 1944).

Works concerning the Japanese include Yamato Ichihashi, *Japanese Immigration: Its Status in California* (San Francisco, 1915); T. Iyenaga and K. Sato, *Japan and the California Problem* (New York, 1921); K. K. Kawakami, *Japan in World Politics* (New York, 1917); H. A. Millis, *The Japanese Problem in the United States* (New York, 1915); and Sidney L. Gulick, *American Democracy and Asiatic Citizenship* (New York, 1918). About Asian exclusion see "California and the Oriental, Japanese and Hindus," *Report* of State Board of Control to Governor William D. Stephens (Sacramento, 1922). A helpful article is Thomas A. Bailey, "California, Japan, and the Alien Land Legislation of 1913," *Pacific Historical Review* 1 (March 1932), 36–59. Books that deal with later abuses against the Japanese include D. S. Thomas and R. S. Nishimoto, *The Spoilage* (Berkeley, 1946); D. S. Thomas, *The Salvage* (Berkeley, 1952); Jacobus ten Broek, Edward N. Barnhart, and Floyd W. Matson, *Prejudice, War, and the Constitution* (Berkeley, 1954); and Roger Daniels, *The Politics of Prejudice: The Anti-Japanese Movement in California and the Struggle for Japanese Exclusion* (Berkeley, 1962).

Regarding California's Italians, see Andrew Rolle, "Italy in California: A Mediterranean America," *Pacific Spectator* 9 (Autumn 1955), 408–19. See also Rolle's "Success in the Sun; the Italians in California," *Westerner's Brand Book* (Los Angeles, 1962), and his *The Immigrant Upraised: Italian Adventurers and Colonists in an Expanding America* (Norman, Okla., 1968), as well as Dino Cinel, *From Italy to San Francisco* (Stanford, 1982).

Erwin G. Gudde, *German Pioneers in Early California* (Hoboken, N.J., 1927), and Charles G. Loomis, *The German Theater in San Francisco, 1861–1864* (Berkeley, 1952) are among the few works on the Germans. On the French see Gilbert Chinard, ed. and trans., *When the French Came to California* (San Francisco, 1944), an English version of "Treny's" *La Californie Devoilée* (Paris, 1850), and Abraham P. Nasatir, *French Activities in California: An Archival Calendar Guide*

(Stanford, 1945). More chauvinistic than critical are three books on the Irish in California: Hugh Quigley, *The Irish Race in California and the Pacific Coast* (San Francisco, 1878); Thomas F. Prendergast, *Forgotten Pioneers: Irish Leaders in Early California* (San Francisco, 1942); and R. A. Burchell, *The San Francisco Irish, 1848–1880* (Berkeley, 1980).

Regarding California's Jews, see I. Harold Sharfman, *Nothing Left to Commemorate* (Glendale, 1969), as well as Robert Levinson, *The Jews in the California Gold Rush* (Los Angeles, 1978), and Max Vorspan and Lloyd P. Gartner, *History of the Jews of Los Angeles* (San Marino, 1970).

CHAPTER 25

Crushing the Indian

As HORDES OF SETTLERS Americanized California, assaults on the Indians by cattlemen, miners, merchants, and the military increased in number and gravity. Indian lands were overrun and tribal ways were challenged. Invading Caucasians, instead of accommodating to Indian prerogatives, demanded that the Indian change his way of life to suit them.

Friction between California's Indian groups prevented them from taking a united stand against whites, and they were able to launch only ineffective attacks. In contrast, Americans demanded protection and aid from their government. In the period after the Mexican War, the United States War Department ordered infantry and cavalry units to patrol pressure points and to deal sternly with Indian outbreaks. The result of white infiltration was decimation of the Indians; they had already suffered a decrease in numbers under Spain and Mexico, but their losses during the American era were appalling.

Starvation, disease, and liquor conspired with bullet and knife against the Indians. Pulmonary and venereal infections, smallpox, and other Caucasian imports wiped out even the marginal well-being that the Indians had enjoyed under Mexican rule. From 1849 to 1856 alone, California's Indian population was reduced to about 50,000.

Rarely had the Indian's land tenure been disturbed in pre-American times; the prevailing practice from the early Spanish period had offered legal protection against such action. But when the United States took over California from Mexico, aggressive Americans would not concede the Indians usufructuary rights to the lands they had formerly held. "Gringo" newcomers who had been shot at by warriors while crossing the Plains were scarcely in a conciliatory mood.

Driven from their homes and from the land of their fathers during

Mohave Indian family on the Colorado River, north of Needles. The unclothed man is the chief. (By courtesy of The Huntington Library, San Marino, California.)

the 1850s, Indians fled to inaccessible and desolate spots. Although most did not share the fierceness of the Plains Indians, some northern California Indians were resentful. Their resistance, resulting in attacks upon the property and livestock of settlers, was swiftly met with American armed might. An Indian might revenge any outrage suffered at the hands of Caucasians by killing the first white man he met thereafter. In turn, the Americans reacted with measures that included the wiping out of entire villages. In this pre-reservation era, Indians in the towns and cities fared perhaps worst of all. Their wages were miserable and the conditions under which they worked unspeakably bad. Even worse, however, were the disastrous effects of their gambling and addiction to "firewater."

Developing a Reservation Policy

After the gold rush, Indian raids on outlying ranches led to increased demands by harassed settlers that the natives be controlled. Beyond organizing posses to pursue marauders, some sort of countrywide reservation system seemed indicated. Travelers also demanded protection. As a result the federal government authorized treaties which specified that the Indians were to vacate their hunting grounds and live on reservations. In 1850 a United States Indian Commission, armed with an appropriation of $50,000, was to negotiate California's reservation system. Its members encountered numerous difficulties in persuading the Indians to move out of mountain homes onto the flat lands of the Central Valley. The Indians interfered with mining operations in the Sierra, but finally their hunger forced them to negotiate with the commissioners.

Eighteen treaties were concluded with the leaders of 139 native bands, representing practically the total Indian population of the state. The Indians agreed to recognize the sovereignty of the United States and to refrain from acts of retaliation. They accepted eighteen reservations, aggregating 7,500,000 acres, and promised at the same time to quitclaim and cede old land rights to the government. The commissioners, in turn, agreed to pay the Indians in agricultural implements and other goods, to retain the new reservations for the Indians' use in perpetuity, and to provide instructors and supervisors in farming, blacksmithing, and woodwork.

These California treaties were transmitted by President Millard Fillmore to the United States Senate. Fulfillment of the agreements was considered too costly; the commissioners had contracted claims of $716,394.79, at which most legislators balked. The Indians claimed they had promptly complied with the terms imposed, but the compensatory acreages promised them had, for the most part, not been forthcoming.

A few Indians had been herded into marginal strips of land after the federal government began to criss-cross their former preserves with roads. In a corrosive environment of shacks and shanties, they lived a life that was neither Indian nor white. "Never, in the poorest huts of the most poverty-stricken wilds of Italy, Bavaria, Norway, and New Mexico," protested Helen Hunt Jackson, had she seen anything "so loathsome as the kennels in which some of the San Diego Indians are living." It is a grievous truth that for years almost nothing was done to help these outcasts. In other words, only half a reservation system existed in California during the 1850s—and a mismanaged half, at that. Some writers have referred to this phase of the Indian story as one of virtual extermination.

Worsening Indian–White Relations

The management of California's Indian reservations, from their inception in 1853, is hardly a matter for pride. During the 1850s and 1860s, many of the Americans placed in charge of Indian affairs were clearly unfit for their posts, and in the case of some of them, personal venality accompanied inexperience. Too often, whenever a reservation contained valuable land, avaricious whites were permitted to swoop in and the Indians were driven onto rocky or sandy terrain. There they competed with squirrels for the acorns that fell from the oaks. Some Indians voluntarily left the reservations to become un-skilled laborers on ranches and farms, but they were often considered a shiftless and irresponsible element to be exploited by the whites. Early municipal ordinances encouraged a system of peonage under which a rancher, by paying the fine of an Indian arrested for drunk-enness, picked up a laborer who was required by law to work off the amount of his fine. Indians seldom understood the white man's reg-ulations under which they lived. Whenever land titles were trans-ferred, permission to remain on certain lands was often disregarded and the Indians were evicted.

The federal policy of dealing with the Indians was as unsuccessful in California as elsewhere—with one exception. In 1853 Edward Fitz-gerald Beale, the naval officer whose activities at the time of the conquest of California have already been mentioned, became the first superintendent of Indian affairs within the state. On a tract of 75,000 acres at Fort Tejón, in the Tehachapi Mountains, Beale began to convert a wild region into a model preserve for a remnant of Tejón and Castaic Indians. He believed that this small group could become self-sufficient and that such an experiment, if successful, might be influential throughout the West. Work at Tejón proceeded so well that Beale gave his Indian wards a voice in their affairs—almost un-heard-of in Indian relations. He met with selected chiefs to discuss such matters as the disposal of crop surpluses. Beale never hesitated to criticize whites, or to take disciplinary action against subordinates, when either treated the Indians unjustly. This policy resulted in com-plaints to Washington about his administration. After a change of Indian policy, charges of malfeasance forced him, in 1855, to relin-quish his superintendency. Fort Tejón was whittled down to 25,000 acres and its appropriation cut in half. Finally, in 1863, Tejón was abandoned.

California's other Indian preserves were soon reduced to marginal plots of unwanted land, where tribe after tribe deteriorated. The grubby reservations that continued to exist were utterly inadequate. Neither natives nor whites benefited from a system that settled the Indians in a cramped, stagnating environment. Such mismanagement of Indian affairs occurred partly because two agencies of the federal government, the War Department and the Department of the In-terior, quarreled over how to handle the Indian. "Pacification by feeding," or a closely regulated life on the reservation, was long the policy of the Interior Department. When, however, the Indian es-caped from inhospitable reservations, the War Department ordered the Army after him. The Army insisted that, unless it was given complete control of the Indian, it could not shoulder responsibility for the safety of whites.

It is remarkable that Indians displayed so little open hostility toward settlers. In the south there had been only one significant uprising, which took place near Warner's Ranch in 1851, under a subchief named Antonio Garrá. In the 1850s and 1860s skirmishing took place with some frequency in northern California, especially along the Humboldt, Eel, and Rogue rivers. For the most part, the whites (civilian and military) wanted to drive Indians into remote locales where they would be rendered harmless to white settlements. Another solution was to confine them to prescribed reservations. In one case, an expedition against retreating Indians led to a remarkable geographical discovery. Possibly the first whites to look upon the Yosemite Valley were members of Joseph Reddeford Walker's 1833 trapping expedition. But the effective discovery of the Yosemite was in 1851 by Major James D. Savage. That year Savage, volunteer leader of a group of whites known as the Mariposa Battalion, was deputized to pursue marauding Yosemite and Chowchilla Indians. Savage's posse chased about three hundred fifty Yosemites into their rugged Sierra hiding place, above the Merced River. Here the whites stumbled upon one of the world's most beautiful valleys. Soon thereafter Savage's men received the surrender of some of Chief Tenieya's warriors, but the Indians slipped away one night while their guard slept. This made necessary another stubborn military campaign. Only after Chief Tenieya's favorite son was killed did the old warrior himself finally surrender.

The Modoc War

The last and most dramatic of California's Indian conflicts was the Modoc War, the culmination of two decades of Modoc–white difficulties. The first bloodshed had occurred in 1852, when the Indians attacked an immigrant train en route to California, killing nearly half of this small party. Nearby miners demanded extermination of the natives who had participated. They formulated a plan for outwitting the Indians. Throwing the Modocs off guard by proposing a peaceful settlement of differences, the Americans retaliated against the offending Indians. The Modocs never forgot what they considered an infamous butchery, and for the next ten years hostilities continued intermittently.

In 1864 most of the Modoc tribe—seriously reduced in number— were persuaded by United States Indian agents to go to the Klamath Reservation in southern Oregon. But this northward migration caused the Modocs to trespass on the hunting lands of the Klamath Indians.

The Klamaths resented the presence of the Modocs and restricted their freedom of movement. Chief Kientepoos (Captain Jack) of the Modocs quickly led his people back southward to their ancestral preserves. Late in 1869, Alfred B. Meacham, superintendent of Indian affairs for Oregon, persuaded Captain Jack to return to the Klamath Reservation with two hundred Modocs. When, however, the Klamath Indians were as overbearing as before, the chief and his band returned again the following spring to their old camping grounds in northeastern California, along the Lost River in what is present-day Modoc County.

By coming back to California the Modocs defied United States authority, an act that invited military intervention. Disturbed settlers, in an atmosphere of confusion, spoke of organizing a force to protect themselves against the Modocs. By the winter of 1872 the Army moved in an observation force. On a November day in that year a Modoc girl named Wi-ne-ma caught sight of the military strength of the whites. Anxious to prevent bloodshed, she mounted a bay mare at Yreka and rode seventy-five miles to warn her people and to urge them not to resist. She thereby became a heroine of her tribe. An unfortunate clash, however, occurred when an Indian known as Scar-Faced Charley refused to give up his pistol to United States authorities. In the aftermath of this incident eleven settlers were killed by marauding Modoc bands, and the American cavalry closed in on the Indians. The Modocs, at the order of Captain Jack, retreated with their ponies and other property toward the lava beds to the southwest of Lake Rhett. There they sought the safety of caves guarded by jagged rocks and ledges. Though cut off from supplies, the Indians could subsist by eating field mice and bats found in the caves, and by drinking water from underground springs. Captain Jack announced that he would not molest settlers unless they entered his winter camp, claiming that it was the whites who were warlike. Nevertheless, the Army was determined to force the Modocs back onto the reservation. The cost of dislodging the small band of Indians, secure in their lava fortress and supplied with old muzzle-loading rifles and other antique arms, was to prove high.

On January 17, 1873, the army advanced on the Modocs, ordering volley after volley of cannon fired into the lava. This had little effect upon the Indians. Concealed behind rock breastworks, they returned fire against the charging Americans. The Army's losses compelled retreat. At this juncture the Quakers and other pacifist elements persuaded President Grant to create a peace commission. General E. R. S. Canby, commander of the Modoc operation, Superintendent Meacham, and two other commissioners made arrangements to meet Captain Jack.

With one thousand men surrounding the Modocs, General Canby

moved his camp to the edge of the lava beds and pitched a council tent between the opposing camps. However, at the Indian war council, Captain Jack was goaded by his tribesmen, despite his earnest protestations, into a treacherous promise. After the Modoc warriors had placed a squaw's hat upon Jack's head and taunted him as a coward and a fish-hearted woman, he had to prove his bravery. Although Wi-ne-ma made a plea to Meacham and Canby to remain in their own camp, a fatal peace conference was held on Good Friday, April 11, 1873. Both the Indian and the white emissaries had agreed to be unarmed, but not only did the Modocs bring along concealed pistols and knives, but several young warriors lay hidden in the nearby bushes, armed with rifles. After Captain Jack gave the signal for attack, he shot General Canby. Meacham was also stabbed and shot, though not fatally.

General Canby's troops determined to chastise the killer of their commander by pursuing Captain Jack through the lava beds. They, however, lost the greater part of a detachment of soldiers. Nevertheless, there could be but one end to the unequal struggle between the Modoc remnant and the Army. When Captain Jack's warriors finally could hold out no longer, a contingent surrendered and became government scouts. The other Modocs fought on until Captain Jack was captured. He and two of his accomplices were tried by court-martial and hanged at Fort Klamath. The Modoc War had cost the United States government half a million dollars, plus the lives of a general and about seventy-five men. All this might have been avoided if the Modocs had been allowed to remain occupants of a few remote lava beds and some marginal grazing land.

Befriending the Indian

The disappearance of the California Indians, especially in the latter half of the nineteenth century, is both tragic and pathetic. It seems incredible that between the beginning of the American period and the opening of the twentieth century their number declined from 100,000 to 15,500. In these few decades a proud people were utterly broken in health and morale.

After General Grant became president in 1869, he replaced all of California's Indian agents, and those in most Western states, with army officers. They found the condition of the former Mission Indians pitiable, scattered as they were over a wide region and living in small villages or rancherías. In 1870 four townships of land at Pala and San Pasqual were set aside for these Indians. Because of pressure from white citizens in San Diego County, these reservations were, however, abolished during the next year and army officers in the

Indian Service were replaced. Next, various churches were allotted Indian agencies to supervise, and the Mission Indians were assigned for a time to the Methodist denomination. The policy of appointing church agents, however, also gave way, as had the military super-intendencies, to appointees named by the commissioner of Indian affairs. As a result of pleas on behalf of the downtrodden natives, President Grant in 1875 established nine small reservations in San Diego County and later created additional reserves by executive order. These lands were, however, arid, brush-strewn, and unfertile.

Next, novelist Helen Hunt Jackson, an emotional champion of Indian rights, was appointed a commissioner to investigate Indian conditions. Her two influential books, *A Century of Dishonor* (1881) and *Ramona* (1884), focusing upon California, called attention to the mistreatment of the Indian. Other humanitarians then began, though tardily, to press for reform. Late in the nineteenth century Charles Fletcher Lummis, Southwestern author, editor, librarian, and an ac-quaintance of Theodore Roosevelt at Harvard, joined Jackson's cam-paign; he solicited funds with which the displaced Indians of the Warner's Ranch area in southern California were eventually settled on more fertile lands near Pala. In 1902 Congress appropriated $100,000 for the purchase of lands for the Warner's Ranch Indians and other homeless natives; part of this money could be spent to relocate them, or for subsistence and the purchase of agricultural implements, building materials, and farm animals. Hundreds of In-dians were resettled upon 3,438 acres of land at Pala. By 1903, the Indian Bureau set aside twenty-seven reservations for the Mission Indians, ranging in size from 280 to 38,600 acres, in addition to a reservation of 45,000 acres at Tule Lake.

Largely as the result of such reformers, the Dawes Act of 1887 had acknowledged federal responsibility for the care and sustenance of Indians. The legal fiction that the Indian population of the country was composed of separate nations, each with its own sovereignty, had long since ended. Under this congressional law, Indians were given many of the privileges of white citizens, including the right of each family head to own 160 acres of land. This land was, however, to be held in trust for twenty-five years, after which time the Indians were to receive ownership and full American citizenship.

Only a few reservations in California were, however, altered by the Dawes Act. The only significant reservation to be so affected was Fort Mohave, with some public domain allotments made also to the Washoe Indians. Otherwise, allotments, mostly of from five to ten acres, were made under separate acts passed from 1890 to 1910. Remaining nonallocated tracts were held in tribal trust. The Bureau of Indian Affairs was able to persuade Congress to renew trusteeship annually after the twenty-five-year period specified by the Dawes Act had expired. The decline of tribal autonomy throughout the state came long before the allotment process began. Allotment, however, did mean the demise of some villages; yet abandonment of the land and dispersal of many tribelets occurred mostly before the major allotment procedures got underway. Indians who remained on reservations came to rely heavily upon the government ration system. As a result these Indians increasingly got into the habit of refusing to support themselves by work.

In allocating them land, the poorest plots went to them and the best were sold to white settlers. Even when Indians were lucky enough to be awarded good land, they were so inexperienced with legal ownership that they were tricked into selling their best holdings. But, worst of all, the Indians, with little experience in managing land, made a poor adjustment to a white environment. The Dawes Act came almost too late to benefit a people who needed charity as much as government definition of their status. Some who claimed that the Indian functioned best in his own environment—as a member of a tribal group rather than as an individual—lived to see the Dawes Act repealed by the Indian Reorganization Act of 1934. From that date onward to 1953, the government restored tribal life, a handicraft culture, and a reservation society to the Indian. By the time of this change in official policy, of course, great numbers of Indians had left the reservations for good. Only about a dozen bands out of four dozen in the state registered with Indian Reorganization Act authorities. Through the years private, state, and national organizations, among them the Northern Indian Association, the Indian Rights Association, the Sequoia League, the Indian Board of Cooperation, and the California League for American Indians, have made a contribution to the betterment of Indian conditions in California. One testimonial to their efforts is the Sherman Institute, near Riverside; this school was privately founded in 1901 with government encouragement to afford the Indian children of southern California practical industrial and handicraft training.

With a few such exceptions, however, Caucasian efforts to help the California Indian have failed. The Indian himself has at times seemed to resist progress, at least in the sense that whites define the term. Some tribal groups did win favorable land-tenure court decisions, federal and state. Beginning in the 1930s, two California attorney generals, Earl Warren and later Robert Kenny, sought payment of $1.25 per acre from Washington for lands allotted the Indians as their property. As a result, the rights of "treaty Indians" came to be appraised at $17,500,000. But, in 1944, after fifteen years of litigation, the Indians were finally awarded only $5,165,863.46. This sum, furthermore, was placed in the United States Treasury—to be made available by congressional appropriation under confining terms.

Governmental niggardliness had once again characterized United States–Indian relations.

After World War II legal claims against the federal government were lodged by Indians throughout the nation, in which professional historians became involved as consultants. Pursuant to the Ute case, won outside California, the United States Supreme Court from 1948 to 1950 awarded 3,337 acres of Palm Springs land to seventy-one surviving members of the Agua Caliente band of the Cahuilla Indians. Because these Indians remained unsatisfied with that allotment, Congress in 1959 passed an additional law of equalization on their behalf. They thereby achieved a commanding position in real estate ownership at the popular resort town, receiving in excess of thirty thousand acres. The Palm Springs Indians held about two thousand acres of this land in "tribal tenure," including the land on which their spa is located.

In addition, hearings before a federal Indian Claims Commission during the 1950s and 1960s led to a federal decision that California's Indians held an aboriginal title to at least 64 million acres of land for which they were to be paid approximately 45½ cents per acre, totaling $29 million. Each Indian was to receive about $150 as a result of legal action.

Despite the government's past failures in dealing with native Americans, there are today more Indians in California (about two hundred thousand) than in any other state. Less than 25 percent live on reservations. They are of mixed descent and are mostly urbanites who have migrated into the state from elsewhere, as did their ancestors.

Selected Readings

A basic work is R. F. Heizer and M. A. Whipple, eds., *The California Indians: A Source Book* (Berkeley, 1951). Cook, *The Conflict Between the California Indian and White Civilization* and Helen Hunt Jackson, *A Century of Dishonor* (New York, 1881), recount the devasting pressures exerted on the Indians by the whites. Consult the Harper Torchbook reprint edited by Andrew F. Rolle (New York, 1965). See also George W. Manypenny, *Our Indian Wards* (Cincinnati, 1880), and a more specific article, William H. Ellison, "The Federal Indian Policy in California," *Mississippi Valley Historical Review* 9 (June 1922), 37–67.

Two books by Imre Sutton focus upon dispossession and legal treatment of Indian land claims: *Indian Land Tenure* (New York, 1975) and *Irredeemable America* (Albuquerque, 1986). On earlier Indian administration see Edward Everett Dale's *The Indians of the Southwest* (Norman, Okla., 1949). See also C. E. Kelsey, "The Rights and Wrongs of California Indians," Commonwealth Club of California *Transac-*

tions for 1909–10 (San Francisco, 1910), and C. C. Painter, *Condition of Affairs in Indian Territory and California* (Philadelphia, 1888).

On Beale's reservation system see Stephen Bonsal, *Edward Fitzgerald Beale: A Pioneer in the Path of Empire, 1822–1893* (New York, 1912), and Helen S. Giffen and Arthur Woodward, *The Story of El Tejón* (Los Angeles, 1942), as well as Richard E. Crouter and Andrew F. Rolle, "Edward Fitzgerald Beale and the Indian Peace Commissioners in California, 1851–1854," Historical Society of Southern California *Quarterly* 42 (June 1960), 107–32. J. Ross Browne, *The Indians of California* (San Francisco, repr. 1944), and John W. Caughey, ed., *The Indians of Southern California* (San Marino, 1952), treat the condition of the California Indian in the nineteenth century.

On Indians and the discovery of the Yosemite see Lafayette H. Bunnell, *Discovery of the Yosemite and the Indian War of 1851* (Los Angeles, 1911), and Annie R. Mitchell, *Jim Savage and the Tulareno Indians* (Los Angeles, 1957), as well as C. Gregory Crampton, ed., *The Mariposa Indian War, 1850–1851: Diaries of Edward Eccleston* (Salt Lake City, 1958). A little-known revolt is described in William Edward Evans, "The Garrá Uprising: Conflict Between San Diego Indians and Settlers in 1851," California Historical Society *Quarterly* 45 (December 1966), 339–49.

Regarding the Modoc War, Jeff. C. Riddle—son of Wi-ne-ma, the Modoc heroine—and Frank Riddle, an American miner, together wrote *The Indian History of the Modoc War and the Causes That Led to It* (San Francisco, 1914). Keith A. Murray has produced *The Modocs and Their War* (Norman, Okla., 1959). See also Max Heyman, *Prudent Soldier* (Glendale, 1960), a biography of General E. R. S. Canby, and Erwin N. Thompson, *Modoc War: Its Military History and Topography* (Sacramento, 1971). A contemporary account of that conflict by an officer who participated in it is C. T. Brady, *Northwestern Fights and Fighters* (New York, 1907). Another firsthand account is A. B. Meacham, *Wigwam and War-path, or The Royal Chief in Chains* (Boston, 1875).

Regarding the struggle for defense of Indian civil and land rights see: Kenneth Johnson, ed., *K-344, or the Indians of California vs. the United States* (Los Angeles, 1966); David G. Shanahan, "Compensation for the Loss of the Aboriginal Lands of the California Indians," *Southern California Quarterly* 57 (Fall 1975), 297–320; and George H. Phillips, *Chiefs and Challengers: Indian Resistance and Cooperation in Southern California* (Berkeley, 1975).

CHAPTER 26

The Workingmen
and the
New Constitution

RECOVERY FROM the devastating national panic of 1873 was slow; and the dry winter of 1876–1877 ruined California's grain harvest and added to the travails, already described, of ranchers. As a result, numerous farm hands were unemployed and discontented. Such workers slept in barns, were not permitted to eat with their employers, and lacked basic sanitation facilities. Bands of tramps infested California's dusty roads. Unemployed workers flocked to the cities, seeking public relief. Hordes of the unemployed were anxious to work for wages of $2 per day. Labor riots in large Eastern cities also encouraged discord out West. Workingmen renewed demands for unionization, and demonstrated vigorously for the eight-hour day as one means of sharing jobs more widely.

Kearney and the Workingmen

A forceful labor leader arose to give direction to this dissatisfaction. Denis Kearney, a native of County Cork, Ireland, had arrived in California during 1868, having followed the sea from boyhood. In personal habits he was industrious and frugal. In appearance he was short and stout, with coarse features and dark eyes. Clothed in a low-cut waistcoat, he was a forceful speaker who displayed a crude epigrammatic skill and possessed the power to sway audiences with intemperate language. A San Francisco freight-draying business, which he purchased in 1872, prospered until Kearney's incendiary utterances caused merchants to withdraw their patronage.

Kearney constantly injected the race issue into labor agitation. He harangued crowds of workers, reiterating the popular slogan, "The Chinese Must Go!" As unemployment increased, Kearney charged heatedly that the Chinese were competing unfairly. The fact that 22,000 Chinese immigrants arrived in California's ports in 1876 added fuel to the flames Kearney helped light. San Francisco papers of the period, usually antilabor as well as anti-Chinese, reported that Kearney's "shoulder-striking hoodlums," recruited among disgruntled workers, tormented edgy Chinese. The city's anti-Chinese labor riots of July 1877 posed an emergency that the police proved inadequate to meet. Kearney's men threatened even to seize control of the state. Consequently, a new Committee of Safety was formed by aroused citizens, under the presidency of William T. Coleman, "The Lion of the Vigilantes." This group equipped itself with 6,000 hickory pick handles with which to quell rioters along the waterfront. Below the palaces of Nob Hill millionaires, irate workers continued to prowl the streets looking for hapless Chinese, newly landed from Canton. At the Pacific Mail Steamship Company docks, one July night, the situation grew acute. A two-hour fight occurred before Coleman's vigilantes could subdue workers who sought to prevent the landing of more Chinese from ships in the bay. Coleman's committee restored peace and prevented rioters from damaging municipal and private property.

On September 21, 1877, several months after these violent labor conflicts, Kearney and various other militant organizers officially founded the Workingmen's Party of California. Previously, labor had been organized into ineffective subgroups, among them an amorphous San Francisco Trade and Labor Union. With 15,000 men unemployed within that city, Kearney determined to dramatize their plight by making his protests felt at the municipal and state levels of government. His strategy was to charge corruption and to demand more representation for labor. On the day he announced the founding of the party, Kearney declared that every Workingman should add a musket to his household effects, and predicted that within a year at least 21,000 laborers would be "well armed, well organized, and well able to demand and take what they will, despite the military, the police, and the 'safety committee.'"

Kearney delighted workers with his threats of violence. The open-air meeting held on Sunday afternoon, September 23, 1877, in a vacant lot in front of San Francisco's new City Hall, was the first of a series of sessions in which Kearney pleaded for the support and active cooperation of laborers in the Workingmen's movement. On one occasion the fiery Irishman suggested that "a little judicious hanging" would be the best course to pursue toward "robber-capitalists."

Kearney's organizing of a new labor party proceeded swiftly, but his speeches grew ever more inflammatory. One of his largest meetings took place during October of 1877, at the sandlot location, with three thousand persons attending. A few days later, Kearney and six associates were arrested in San Francisco and put in prison. His incarceration served only to increase his following. After two weeks in prison, Kearney resumed his unrestrained attacks upon public officials.

In January 1878, a group of unemployed Workingmen set out for San Francisco's City Hall to demand "work, bread, or a place in the county jail." Before they reached their destination their numbers had swelled to 1,500 marchers. The mayor pleaded that he was powerless to help them. At another mass meeting the workers threatened to "blow up the Pacific Mail Steamship Company's dock and steamers," to bomb the Chinese quarter, and to use firearms and "infernal machines" to destroy "marked men." In this charged atmosphere Coleman's militia reassembled once more, a United States Navy man-of-war arrived to protect the government mail docks, and more of Kearney's firebrand followers were thrown into prison. An alarmed legislature passed an act making it a felony to incite a riot or to commit acts of violence against persons or property.

On January 21, 1878, the Workingmen's party held its first state convention, inveighing against a government that "has fallen into the hands of capitalists and their willing instruments." Exercising influence in municipal elections, the Workingmen's party became a force in state politics. In 1878–1879 it elected various state Supreme Court judges, eleven state senators, and sixteen assemblymen. Despite Kearney's vigor, disintegration began to appear in the party ranks after a rumor spread that he had accepted railroad money and was corruptible. Kearney's integrity and loyalty to his workers continued to be impugned within the labor movement in a whispering campaign that led to his removal from office at the end of 1878. Kearney's opponents hoped, by his ouster, to combat mounting charges of labor recklessness with which his leadership had been tarred by the press and by conservative bankers and merchants.

Kearney's political influence remained considerable. He was the spokesman of a movement that, though naïve, was significant as the first organized attempt to rally the forces of labor in California. Many of the reform measures he advocated, which were advanced for their time, ultimately were adopted. These included the now-familiar eight-hour day, a statewide public school system (particularly for vocational education), reform of the banking system, and restrictions upon business profiteering and land monopoly. Kearney's Workingmen were more antimonopolistic than anticapitalistic. Yet, in an age when business still felt little urge to apologize for its abuses, they were considered dangerous radicals and their leader reprehensible.

California's Second Constitutional Convention

While the Workingmen's movement was gaining in size and strength, California moved toward revision of its constitution. The constitution of 1849 had endured long beyond the expectation of its framers. It had been formed to meet the needs of a frontier area anxious for admittance to the Union, and its inadequacy in the face of new problems was apparent. Indeed, the legislature had several times recommended drawing up a new constitution, but had been sidetracked. Among the defects of the old constitution were outmoded provisions for public finance, the lack of a system for safeguarding public lands, an unrealistic tax-apportionment system, and the absence of machinery for improving labor conditions. Also, it provided no effective control over railroads and public utilities at a time when discontent with the railroads was rising.

By the fall of 1877 California's politicos decided that the state needed a new constitutional convention. When the convention assembled, on September 28, 1878, seventy-eight delegates registered as nonpartisan, fifty-one as representatives of the Workingmen's party, eleven as Republicans, ten as Democrats, and two as independents. Of the 152 delegates only two—both Workingmen from San Francisco—were natives of California. Indian residents and those of Spanish background were not represented. The largest occupational group was made up of lawyers; fifty-nine delegates were members of the bar. Farmers had the next largest representation, thirty-six in all. Thirty-five delegates were of foreign birth.

In general, the delegates spoke for three main power groups. In descending order of influence these were: (1) capitalists and corporations, including large landholders, represented by expert legal counsel and incumbent state legislators; (2) aggrieved farmers eager to reform existing railroad, water, and monopoly practices as well as unfair taxation; (3) city laborers, who owned even less property than heavily mortgaged farmers, and whose anticonservative interests were similar to those of that group. As the convention got under way, much time was tal n up with trivial points of order, appeals from the chair's decisions, and questions of personal privilege. There was even prolonged discussion of whether to admit "phonographic reporters." Propositions for constitutional provisions were put forth in an almost endless procession. The discontent of the farmers and laborers found frequent expression; nearly every Workingman had a separate motion to present.

Taxation and the Railroad Issue

A topic of major importance at the convention was taxation, including assessment, collection, and the exemption of property from taxes. Various proposals were advanced in favor of a poll tax, an ad valorem tax on all property, an income tax, a graduated tax on large estates, and suspension of taxes for citizens already in debt. Most of these measures were proposed by advocates of heavier taxation of the rich; and it became obvious that conservative interests would seek to block tax reforms.

Two delegates representing an Independent Taxpayer's party assumed a prominent position in the debates over taxation, alleging that the bulk of future taxes would be shouldered by the poor unless constitutional reform were devised to equalize the tax burden. This party had, indeed, previously come into being with the object of backing legislators "who would command the confidence of the whole people, and who would be free from the control of rings and corrupt combinations." Those who opposed this reformist group dubbed it the Dolly Varden party, after the softhearted, yet wily, coquette in Charles Dickens's novel *Barnaby Rudge*. The Independent Taxpayer delegates were able to marshal such support from the Workingmen and other reform groups that they achieved passage of their principal proposal: California's State Board of Equalization was empowered by the convention to assess *all* property taxable by the state government. The board was to consist of one member from each congressional district, and its duty would be "to equalize the valuation of taxable property in the several counties, and also to assess the franchise, roadway, roadbed, rails and rolling stock of all railroads operated in more than one county in the state."

Californians had heard their legislative sessions called the "legislature of a thousand steals," because of collusion between politicians and railroad officials. Further, the railroads were responsible, in the opinion of many, for fulminating racial and labor conflict by their importation of thousands of Chinese. The farmers at the convention were anxious that control of the Southern Pacific should be a prominent part of the agenda. They charged that the railroad fraudulently influenced local elections, rigged high freight rates, and favored large shippers through secret rebates. In particular, the Southern Pacific's quarrels with farmers who had settled on railroad lands in the state's Central Valley blackened the reputation of the railroad.

The constitutional convention was bound to reflect the pressures of farm groups. By the 1870s, local "farmer clubs" had been absorbed by the national Patrons of Husbandry, or the Grangers, who stood solidly for the reduction of freight rates and for the lessening of public expenditures. The Grangers, in fact, aided by such reformers as Henry George (to be discussed at length in Chapter 27), succeeded in making the railroad magnates the whipping boys of late-nineteenth-century life. George claimed that such monopolies were damaging the poor and rewarding the rich. Dissatisfied farmers were joined by equally discontented laborers, who also felt that California's economy, dominated by railroad interests, was at the service of the rich and powerful. The Democrats, reflecting this sentiment sooner than the Republicans, officially came to favor the reduction of railroad rates, the prohibition of railroad discriminations, and revocation of special privileges enjoyed by corporations and large landowners.

Although a State Railroad Commission was created, its powers were not extensive and were only partially enforced. Individual commissioners bowed to the blandishments of the railroads. Railroad attorneys, working with sympathetic judges, could keep tax liens tied up in legal proceedings for years. The state was forced to accept whatever the railroad chose to pay. Government reforms, particularly at the state level, did not cut deeply, and the hardships that the farmers suffered on account of railroad abuses continued for many years after the constitutional convention.

In 1880, at Mussel Slough, near the town of Hanford in Kings County, a bitter dispute between farmers and the railroad resulted in the loss of several lives. Various settlers, after improving land along the slough—"sold" to them by the railroad—were confronted with a delay in the conveyance of their land titles by the Southern Pacific Company. The enraged homesteaders claimed they had been tendered the land under irrevocable conditions, only to have railroad officials change these terms. The law was, nevertheless, technically on the side of the railroad, and Southern Pacific representatives tried to evict the settlers. A battle ensued between the two groups in which seven persons were shot to death and an eighth badly wounded. A number of settlers were then tried because they had resisted the law, and were sent to prison for protecting what they believed to be their property.

The railroad's land-management policies, as dramatized by this incident, and its further struggles with farmers, caused tension against it to mount steadily. One has only to read Frank Norris's book, *The Octopus*, to realize how central the railroad was to late-nineteenth-century California and why public opinion turned against it as the symbol of malevolent wealth. Another novel, Josiah Royce's *The Feud of Oakfield Creek*, trenchantly criticized the railroad's practices.

Other Major Issues at the Convention

Although reform-minded delegates at the constitutional convention were united in opposition to the railroad, they split over proposals to control banks. Opposition to banks had been voiced publicly for years. Local bankers, however, were essential to the farmer; bank stockholders and directors represented interests identified with agriculture. Consequently, the Grangers sided with country bankers against measures for reform of banking practices, while nonpartisans joined the Workingmen's party in attacks against city banks. Prolonged debate developed over a constitutional revision that bank directors or trustees should be liable to creditors and stockholders for moneys embezzled or misappropriated by bank officers. Banks circularized depositors against controls on credit firms. They charged that discrimination against financial institutions was implied. When a convention vote was forced, however, the measure was carried.

One labor delegate clamored for the insertion in California's new constitution of clauses embodying Kearney's slogan, "The Chinese Must Go!" A number of anti-Chinese clauses were adopted (later held to be in conflict with the United States Constitution) that prohibited employment of Chinese by corporations. Section III forbade Chinese employment "on any state, county, municipal, or other public work, except in punishment for crime." Condemnation of Asiatic "coolieism," or contract labor, as "a form of human slavery" also became part of the constitution.

California's public school system was given what remains its basic shape, though it has been modified by subsequent amendments. The University of California, which had been created by a legislative act of March 23, 1868, was accorded the legal status of a constitutional corporation. Other matters determined by the convention of 1879 concerned granting divorces, state rights of eminent domain, and definition of state water rights. The section of the new constitution formulated to safeguard California's public waters and shoreline would long thereafter be cited in support of her claims to oil tidelands. The convention also had brought before it the issue of woman suffrage by delegates who pleaded for political equality of the sexes. Champions of the measure, however, met with little success; although Wyoming had enacted woman suffrage as early as 1869, California was not to achieve it until 1911.

Public Reception of the Constitution

The convention continued its deliberations for 157 days. Numerous pressure groups, including the Workingmen, banks, the Grange, and the railroads, had confused and slowed down the work of the convention. Indeed, by their incessant lobbying they hindered reform.

In the balloting over ratification, both the Republican and Democratic parties supported the constitution, although individual Republicans opposed its adoption on the grounds of its antirailroad features, which were actually mild. Many conservatives, of course, felt differently. Former Governor Fredrick F. Low, a lifelong Republican, deplored, in his reminiscences, the fact that both the San Francisco *Bulletin* and *Call* accepted money from the railroads to fight the constitutional convention's railroad reforms. Republican Governor Booth, too, believed railroad reform necessary.

Although the constitution was ratified by a majority of California's voters, little public enthusiasm was shown for the new fundamental law of the state. The constitutional convention had failed to achieve its most pressing objectives. Its restraints upon corporations proved disappointing, and relations between capital and labor continued as unhappy as before. Henry George considered the power of California's largest land monopolists unbroken.

California's current unwieldy constitution consists of the document produced by the convention of 1879 plus more than 300 amendments. It is seven times as long as the Constitution of the United States. Many amendments are statutory, having a debatable place in the organic law, and they present serious difficulties in interpretation of the constitution. Actually this constitution is a code of laws assembled in catalogue fashion, rather than a frame of government.

Dissolution of the Workingmen

Closely connected with the constitutional convention were the fortunes of Kearney's Workingmen's movement. Although Kearney was not a delegate, his representatives pushed for the reforms he suggested. Conscious of their inexperience, Kearney's men put forth their views with such vehemence that they scared off potential supporters, including the farmers who guarded their freedom with equal conviction. On the other hand, sometimes the Workingmen's blunt tactics were effective. Their proposal for an eight-hour day on public works projects was the signal for especially warm debate. Here was the essence of radicalism; yet, the majority voted in the eight-hour day.

The Workingmen reached the peak of their political power at the time of the constitutional convention. The men elected by the party as public officials were as a rule unsuccessful office holders. The failure of labor legislators to secure reform measures made workers dissatisfied both with the movement and its leaders. By February 1880, when Kearney was again arrested for his vociferous sandlot speeches, the split between him and other party stalwarts had widened. Two years later, Kearney stated: "There is no Workingmen's party now, and it would take a telescope larger than Lick's to find a vestige of the giant that shook not only the state but the nation." The wily Irish labor leader retired from politics, inherited a large fortune, and "went soft" in the years until his death in 1907.

The Workingmen, although unsuccessful in achieving their reform program, did make labor's wishes publicly known. The new constitution's restrictions against land monopoly, against the railroads, and against the power of corporations had been gained in large part because of the Workingmen's agitation. The Workingmen were also racists who transformed the Chinese issue into a national one; they were partly responsible for passage of the Federal Exclusion Act of 1882. The Workingmen's demands—an eight-hour day, fixed salaries for government jobs, a bureau of labor affairs—rubbed off onto the two major parties. Labor, although temporarily sidelined, would later request more specific reforms from the Democratic party in particular.

Selected Readings

Regarding the labor movement in California a seminal article is Ralph Kauer's "The Workingmen's Party of California," *Pacific Historical Review* 13 (September 1944), 278–91. Henry George wrote an article entitled "The Kearney Agitation in California" for *Popular Science Monthly* 17 (August 1880), 433–53. James Bryce's noted *American Commonwealth* (New York, 1891) also discussed "Kearneyism," though Kearney objected to Bryce's description. Regarding early labor organization see, in addition, Lucile Eaves, *A History of California Labor Legislation* (Berkeley, 1910); J. C. Stedman and R. A. Leonard, *The Workingmen's Party of California* (San Francisco, 1878); and two books by Ira B. Cross, *Frank B. Roney: Irish Rebel and California Labor Leader* (Berkeley, 1931), and *History of the Labor Movement in California* (Berkeley, 1935). There is material on Denis Kearney in George H. Tinkham, *California Men and Events: 1769–1890* (Stockton, 1915). An admirable biographical study that includes an account of social unrest in the late nineteenth century is Charles Albro Barker's *Henry George* (New York, 1955). See also Arthur N. Young, *The Single Tax Movement in the United States* (New York, 1916), and Henry George, Jr., *Life of Henry George* (New York, 1900).

The following books about the constitutional convention of 1879 are helpful: *Debates and Proceedings of the Constitutional Convention of the State of California* (3 vols., Sacramento, 1880); Winfield J. Davis, *History of Political Conventions in California* (Sacramento, 1893); and Carl B. Swisher, *Motivation and Political Technique in the California Constitutional Convention, 1878–1879* (Claremont, 1930).

The San Francisco *Chronicle* was the only journal to support the

Workingmen and the Sacramento *Record-Union* was a railroad organ. The *Chronicle* referred to the *Record-Union* as the "Stanford organ, circulation about 1750." The San Francisco *Examiner* represented the farmers' viewpoint, while the *Alta California* tried to remain neutral.

Regarding California tax problems before the turn of the century, see C. C. Plehn, "The Taxation of Mortgages in California," *Yale Review* 8 (May 1899), pp. 35ff. Criticism of the railroads, which led to constitutional attempts to control them, is highlighted in Gordon W. Clarke, "A Significant Memorial to Mussel Slough," *Pacific Historical Review* 18 (November 1949), 501–4. In the same journal, consult Irving McKee, "Notable Memorials to Mussel Slough," 17 (February 1948), 19–27, and John A. Larimore, "Legal Questions Arising From the Mussel Slough Land Dispute," *Southern California Quarterly* 58 (Spring 1976), 75–94.

CHAPTER 27

California Culture, 1870–1918

CALIFORNIA'S CULTURE REPRESENTS a fusion of two traditions—the Spanish and the Anglo-American. Writers and artists have drawn heavily on the picturesque Spanish heritage. They have also sought to recapture the vanished world of frontiersman and miner. This rediscovery, though often of a past no more than legendary, has infused California's cultural atmosphere. At the same time, a self-conscious pride in the new state's material achievements characterized the work of its first American chroniclers. There also developed in California literature a trend toward realistic description and a critical sense of protest.

By 1870, the pioneer phase of California's history had generally ended. No longer an outpost of civilization, California was ready for a more refined culture. Popular enjoyment of artistic performances was continually increasing, especially at San Francisco, where an enthusiastic theater movement flourished. A number of wealthy patrons were now in a position to encourage prose, poetry, art, and learning. They founded museums and galleries and financed opera houses and symphony orchestras. Furthermore, creative impulses, though transplanted from the East, were becoming sufficiently strong to give Californians a measure of cultural independence.

By far the most numerous of the creative groups active in California during the late nineteenth and early twentieth century were the writers. It is not easy to determine precisely what literature is native to a locale. Many of California's outstanding authors have been born elsewhere, though their writing is set in the state of their adoption and their style influenced by experiences in California. Thus they are in a real sense "California writers." Helen Hunt Jackson was originally a New England writer of children's stories. Mark Twain, the author of narratives set in the Far West, came from Hannibal,

Missouri, and wrote much of his best work not in California but in Hartford, Connecticut. Bret Harte, whose writings became cherished Californiana, was a native of New York who spent the latter part of his life in England. Joaquin Miller, hailed as "Poet of the Sierra," came from Indiana by way of Oregon. Three of California's most trenchant critics, Frank Norris, Henry George, and Ambrose Bierce, were also born outside the state.

Women Writers, Critics, and Developers

Since the time of the mythical Queen Calafía, the role of women in California history has been ignored by most historians. Notable among the women who contributed to California's new culture was Helen Hunt Jackson. After her first visit to the state in 1872, she combined an interest in the mistreatment of Indians with a concern for the decay of the old Spanish tradition. Exploiting these themes nationally, Jackson published a number of articles in *Century Magazine*. These and her book *A Century of Dishonor* (1881) stirred up considerable interest in the Indian. However, her *Ramona* (1884) did not achieve the desired effect of arousing the public's indignation for the Indian cause; readers instead took *Ramona* to be a true picture of California's idyllic and peaceful Arcadian past and her writings to be a truthful account of its missions.

In addition to Jackson, other women influenced California's society. In 1876 Helena Modjeska, a Polish actress, established a short-lived Utopian colony at Anaheim. The controversial Isadora Duncan spent her youth in the Bay area before going on to world fame as a dancer.

A vivid character of a different type was "Mammy" (Mary Ellen) Pleasant, a black operator of a San Francisco boardinghouse in the 1850s. Had she, however, not been described as a procuress, a blackmailer, and a backer of John Brown's raid upon Harper's Ferry, we would know little about her. A former slave, she became involved in causes beyond running houses of assignation. By lending other blacks money at reasonable rates of interest, she built a fortune, which she used to aid their fight to secure rights of testimony in the courts. This was gained by a legislative act of 1863. She also successfully sued two San Francisco streetcar companies who barred her people from riding the city's streetcars. Less well known is Charlotta Bass, editor of the *California Eagle*, southern California's first black newspaper.

California proved receptive to literary pursuits by women. In 1893 the state legislature named Ina Coolbrith California's first poet laureate. Gertrude Stein settled in Oakland from 1879 to 1892 before going on to Paris where, in 1903, she met the young San Franciscan Alice B. Toklas, with whom she was to share the rest of her life. Both women blossomed outside of California.

In 1899 the arch-feminist Mary Austin traveled west from Illinois with her family to homestead land near Bakersfield. Until 1905 she taught school in various Owens Valley towns. During those lonely but fruitful years she grew deeply attached to the land and its people. Her writings reveal a fascination with the effects of physical environment upon human beings and, in particular, an intuitive feeling for Indians and the wilderness in which they were forced to live. Austin wrote incisive stories and articles for Lummis's magazine and produced a penetrating early volume, *The Land of Little Rain* (1903). Her best-known book, it consists of fourteen sketches of the people, animals, and land south of Yosemite and north of Death Valley. It is this southern Sierra country to which Mary Austin devoted years of personal observation. She also published such historical romances as *Isidro* (1905), almost venerative in its description of this region. In *The Basket Woman* (1904), *The Flock* (1906), and *California, Land of the Sun* (1914), she transmitted to readers a sense of the West's sagebrush and sand and a feeling for desert symbols. After 1911 she lived at Carmel, Paris, London, New York, and finally, at Santa Fe, but her interest in the West and California remained constant.

Other women celebrated the glories of California's past. Among these was Gertrude Atherton, who spent most of her life in San Francisco, where she was born in 1857. A wealthy woman, she traveled widely; her novels ranged in background from ancient Greece, France, and Germany to the West Indies and California. Among her California best sellers were *The Splendid Idle Forties* (1902) and *The Californians* (1898); the latter is a thin re-creation of Spanish California's society as it met the tests of Yankee invasion. She wrote thirty-seven books in forty years. Her last was *My San Francisco* (1946), an intensely felt retrospective work. In a similar vein was Kathleen Norris (sister-in-law of Frank Norris), also a native San Franciscan, who, after 1910, wrote dozens of sentimental books for young women.

Kate Douglas Wiggin combined a career of public service with her writing. After training the majority of California's first kindergarten teachers, she went on to a writing career in New York; but she remained famous for the free kindergartens she established for poor children. Wiggin wrote moralizing books for girls, among them *A Summer in a Cañon* (1889). A colleague of Mrs. Wiggin's, Joaquin Miller, once wrote, "See Yosemite Valley first and then the Silverstreet kindergarten." Sarah Brown Cooper, a devotee of Wiggin's, helped to establish 287 kindergartens throughout the United States and abroad by 1895; these were based on the San Francisco model, established in 1863. Mrs. Cooper's good work was followed by that of Emma Marwedel, a German who in 1876 opened the California Model Kindergarten. She used the methods of Frederick Froebel, "father of kindergartens," and was sponsored by Caroline Severance, the reformer and pioneer club woman who in 1875 had moved from Boston to California.

Severance came to Los Angeles with a head full of ideas for changing its sleepy pueblo environment. She established its first book club and, indeed, the city's public library. Severance also founded the Friday Morning Club. Its members advocated reform of the juvenile detention system and led a campaign to keep politics out of school board elections. They also sought to save the giant sequoias, established "El Camino Real" signposts to mark the route between missions, helped develop the Los Angeles Philharmonic Orchestra, and worked to bring a branch of the University of California to Los Angeles (later UCLA). Severance also sought to gain the vote for women, which was achieved in 1911; she established important charities and was a champion of the rights of children as well as of women. At age ninety-one she wrote, "We have come to the dawn of a glorious tomorrow; a landmark in the most sacred crusade of the ages, when woman is heroically released from the bondage and superstitions of the past, and liberated from the political black list in our free country."

Among the women's clubs that sprang up at Los Angeles were the influential Wilshire Ebell Club and nearby Pasadena's Shakespeare Club. They spread female attention beyond church and home and became centers of social warmth, reaching a national peak of 2 million members by the 1920s. Some of the largest clubs were in California where there were 600 such organizations. After women won the right to vote, however, they were lured away to other activities, including sports, theatrical groups, politics, and education. For their time these clubs were an important means of personal transcendence and mutual reinforcement for women.

Better known than Severance, especially in northern California, was the beneficent Phoebe Apperson Hearst, mother of the publisher William Randolph. Like the banker Amadeo Pietro Giannini, she established her own foundation at the Berkeley campus of the University of California, which became an important additional means of support for research and future building.

Yet another account of generous female philanthropy arose from the humblest of origins, black slavery. A Georgia slave, Biddy Mason, crossed the plains in 1851 with her three slave daughters, driving a herd of sheep behind her master's wagon train. After reaching California, he planned to take Biddy's family to Texas, a slave state. But their master was stopped at the California border by a sheriff with a writ preventing him from taking blacks out of a "free" state. Biddy found work as a nurse in Los Angeles at $2.50 per day. With her savings she purchased several parcels of land. Refusing to sell property, even at a handsome profit, she continued to buy lots. During the real estate boom of 1887 she lived to see land that she had bought for $250 soar in value to $200,000. She used her wealth to found a nursery school, frequently visited the city jail, paid the expenses and taxes for her church, and supplied groceries to indigent families. Her home became a refuge for stranded and needy settlers. She died in 1891 as one of the most affluent property owners in California.

California's womenfolk demonstrated continuing versatility, despite the limitations placed upon them. Harriet Williams Russell Strong, for example, was an agriculturist, civic leader, and water developer whose family moved to California in 1854, when she was ten years old. Her husband, Charles Strong, had purchased 220 acres of semi-arid land in southern California from Pío Pico, the last Mexican governor. Located near the present city of Whittier, the property, Rancho del Fuerte, became known as the Strong Ranch. After his death she planted walnuts and other crops. To increase production, she studied marketing as well as irrigation and flood control. From 1887 to 1894 she took out patents on a sequence of storage dams and various household inventions. Strong became known as the "walnut queen" and "pampas lady" (for she also grew pampas grass), won election as the first woman member of the Los Angeles Chamber of Commerce, and gained national fame by her agricultural product exhibits at the 1893 World's Columbian Exposition at Chicago. Strong founded the Wilshire Ebell Club of Los Angeles in 1894. She was active in the Friday Morning Club, the Ruskin Art Club, and in the Los Angeles Symphony Association. She was also a strong advocate of flood control and water supply measures and supported the federal aid program to dam the waters of the Colorado River.

Another woman of real distinction was Alice Constance Austin who in 1918 designed an entire utopian socialist city known as Llano del Rio. Tied to the California "arts and crafts" approach (a back-to-the-basics movement inspired by England's William Thorris), she sought the collectivization of domestic work; in her architectural scheme a central kitchen and laundry facility was to be connected to outlying kitchenless houses by an underground railway. Her work provided a complex synthesis of reformist ideals.

Most historians remain unaware that in the late nineteenth century women entered male-dominated fields in California in respectable numbers. The Los Angeles city directory for 1890 listed 27 female physicians and 260 male doctors. The ratio of women to men steadily increased throughout most of the nineteenth century. The 1850 federal census showed only 7,017 females in California to 85,850 males. By 1890 the figures jumped to 508,071 females among 700,059 males.

Finally, one woman, who arrived from Indiana in her twenties, had an ongoing effect upon the legal profession. This was Clara Short-ridge Foltz. She studied law on her own and eventually procured passage of a legislative act that permitted women to practice law. In fact, she was the first female admitted to the state bar and also the first woman attorney to plead before the California Supreme Court. Foltz also became an important force in California politics in the 1880s.

Early Reformers

The earliest "California School" of writers had either concentrated on the wonders of the state or caricatured its raw society in a spirit of horseplay, evoking humor by the crude use of dialect and bad grammar. By the 1870s their writing had become less flamboyant. Writers had begun to deal with social reform; the vulgarity of the post–Civil War period was soon to bring forth Henry George, Frank Norris, and Jack London, who subjected the capitalistic order to strong attack, while Josiah Royce, Ambrose Bierce, and Helen Hunt Jackson published influential works on social, political, and economic problems. One of the most provocative thinkers, creator of a "theory of the leisure class," was Thorstein Veblen, who taught at Stanford University from 1906 to 1909. After a period of residence in the East, he returned to California in 1926 and lived there until his death.

Henry George, restless and unorthodox, had held half a dozen jobs along the San Francisco waterfront before he turned to the economic analysis that made him world famous. He had been a seaman and a printer and had tried to support himself by prospecting for gold. George once reminisced: "I was, in fact, what would now be called a tramp. I had a little money, but I slept in barns to save it and had a rough time generally." Then, in an atmosphere of labor turbulence and high unemployment, George became a newspaper reporter and editor with an ambition to voice the complaints of the working peo-ple. While developing his ideas in San Francisco, he wrote for the *Californian* and four other journals. Despite the fact that he had almost no formal schooling, his writings, among them tracts sup-porting the movement for an eight-hour working day in the 1870s, attracted wide attention. George personally set the type for some of these activist tracts.

He evolved an appealing "single-tax" theory in his book *Progress and Poverty* (1880). In this volume George protested against the pres-ence of poverty and wealth side by side in so rich a land, and charged that large absentee land monopolists and speculators were collecting an "unearned increment"—which he regarded as a malicious form of rent—from their vast properties. Thus, George felt, at the height of the labor unrest of the late nineteenth century, that the wealthy were further enriching themselves at the expense of the downtrodden. George was obsessed with the significance of land use in human history. In California, idle land was everywhere before his eyes, and he may have exaggerated the importance of the issue. His book nevertheless sold three million copies, making George a champion of the landless "laboring masses" and winning him the respect even of persons who opposed his socialistic ideas. Having attained national prominence, he moved to New York and became a professional pamphleteer, lecturer, and propagandist for liberal causes; in 1886 he ran against Theodore Roosevelt for mayor of New York City.

Another California thinker who wrote in a reformist vein was Josiah Royce. Born in 1855 at Grass Valley, Royce had little in his pioneer background to suggest that he would one day sail out of San Francisco to teach and to write books about philosophy at Harvard. After graduating from the University of California in 1875, Royce studied in Germany. He then returned to the United States for further instruction at Johns Hopkins University. Like Henry George, he published his initial writing in California. He too was incensed at abuses of the land monopolists and of the railroad. By 1882 he was on the Harvard faculty. Royce became, along with William James, one of the most influential American philosophers, basing his theories on the principle of individuality and human will rather than upon the role of the intellect. An idealist and nonconformist, Royce expressed his distaste for railroad domination in his novel *The Feud of Oakfield Creek* (1887). Royce's most important book about his native state was *California . . . A Study of American Character* (1886). Royce, unlike Henry George, concerned himself more with politics than with economics, and his criticisms of society were philosophical.

A spiritual ally of Royce and George was Charles Howard Shinn, who became a forceful anti-monopolist and conservationist. His *Mining Camps: A Study in American Frontier Government* (1885) is a minor classic. Shinn wrote in the tradition of "the great amateurs," among them Francis Parkman, Hubert Howe Bancroft, Hiram M. Chittenden, and, later, Bernard De Voto. Shinn's *The Story of the Mine* (1897) and his *Graphic Description of Pacific Coast Outlaws* (reprinted 1958) combine industry and a sense of the dramatic in history.

Frank Norris also became a bitter critic of monopolies in general and the railroads in particular. Born in 1870, Norris grew up in California. He turned to the realistic techniques of the French novelist Emile Zola in his quest for the most powerful literary style with which to present his views, and became a leader in the movement toward realism in American writing. Shortly before his death at the age of thirty-two Norris wrote about his work: "I never truckled. I never took off the hat to fashion and held it out for pennies. I told them the truth. They liked it or they didn't like it." Norris's most famous work was, of course, *The Octopus* (1901). It etched in pitiless detail the clash between the railroads and the farmers, describing the rails over which the latter had to transport their wheat as oppressive steel tentacles. *The Octopus*, together with Norris's other novels, *McTeague* (1899), *The Pit* (1903), and the posthumous *Vandover and the Brute* (1914), won him wide critical acclaim as a "romantic realist" and as an important figure in the history of American social protest.

The writing of Frank Norris exerted a deep influence upon Jack London. London's realism combined a strong romantic strain with a sense of social conscience. In such popular works as *The Call of the Wild* (1903) and *The Sea Wolf* (1904), London celebrated the untamed savage brutality and primitiveness of nature, displaying both his skill as a storyteller and his sensitive feelings for his fellow men. He lacked restraint and finish, but showed a genuine talent for characterization, particularly of the passionate egos of his almost superhuman heroes. London was strongly influenced by his early environment. From boyhood onward, his life became intimately associated with San Francisco Bay: "It is worthless to give the long sordid list of occupations, none of them trades, all heavy manual labor. . . . At 15 left home and went upon a Bay life. . . . I was a salmon fisher, an oyster pirate, a schooner sailor, a fish patrolman, a longshoreman, a boy in years but a man among men." London described this type of life in *The Cruise of the Dazzler* (1902) and in *Tales of the Fish Patrol* (1905). His early struggle to make a living as a writer is the subject of the autobiographical novel, *Martin Eden* (1909), which emphasizes his dissatisfaction with society. His later works, reflecting tension over the shortcomings of the American industrial order, led him to champion socialism as a means of righting the wrongs of mankind. Both *The Iron Heel* (1908) and *The Revolution* (1910) reveal how London was attracted to Marxism as an economic and political alternative to democracy. Although he donated money to socialist groups (including one that projected an IWW (Industrial Workers of the World) "invasion" of Lower California as late as 1911), London became discouraged with revolutionary causes. By the year of his death, 1916, at age forty, he was no longer a Socialist party member. London's total literary production was astounding: in seventeen years, he turned out some fifty books filled with adventure, primitive violence, and class struggle. Long after his death, California dedicated a Jack London State Park to his memory. It is located in the Valley of the Moon in Sonoma County, where he did much of his last writing while battling melancholia and alcoholism. There one can still see the ruins of Wolf

House, built on his earnings, which burned before he could occupy it.

A writer of a different sort, the brilliant, acid-tongued, and vindictive Ambrose Bierce, had the distinction of dominating the California literary world for decades with his witty and opinionated diatribes. His journalistic targets were many, from disreputable politicians to untalented young authors. Bierce delivered contemptuous judgments with gusto, and his satire was gruesome and amusing at the same time.

He saw himself as a sensitive man in a corrupt age, against which he jeered. Bierce became the censorious figure of California letters. By the use of derision and cynicism, this complex and deeply pessimistic man pummeled readers unceasingly. From the late 1880s onward, his criticisms of society appeared in the columns of young William Randolph Hearst's San Francisco *Examiner*; like Hearst, Bierce gained as many enemies as adherents. Hearst was then a militant progressive who, by hiring this "Devil's Lexicographer," launched devastating attacks against the Southern Pacific railway interests. Readers were also attracted by Bierce's tales of sardonic humor, horror, and mystery, which resemble those of Poe. Bierce included, in popular collections of his own, such especially admired stories as *A Horseman in the Sky* and *The Damned Thing*. *The Dance of Death* (1877), a literary hoax in the writing of which Bierce was a collaborator, and *The Monk and the Hangman's Daughter* (1892), a short novel, went through many printings. Perhaps his most famous book was *The Devil's Dictionary* (1911), composed of a series of ironic definitions. Bierce's disappearance in 1913, when he was seventy, is as mysterious as his most controversial writings. It is assumed that, dissillusioned and tired, he went to revolution-torn Mexico and died there.

Writers of Reminiscence and Nostalgia

Participants in the dramatic events of California's past frequently recorded their reminiscences. Among these was William Heath Davis, whose *Sixty Years in California* (1889) and posthumous *Seventy-Five Years in California* (1929) give one a view of the society that grew to maturity while Davis was at San Francisco. Such chroniclers highlighted the drama and heroism of pioneer hardships and drew heavily on their own experiences in the American conquest or the gold rush. Their accounts are a repository of historical data, entwined with sentimentality, legend, and folklore. Major Horace Bell's *Reminiscences of a Ranger* (1881), the first exclusively English-language book printed in Los Angeles, deals with the period following the 1850s. Harris Newmark's *Sixty Years in Southern California* (1916) presents a view of the social and commercial life of southern California through the eyes of a successful Jewish merchant. These accounts can be supplemented by Sarah Bixby Smith's memories of life on a sheep ranch in the 1870s and 1880s, entitled *Adobe Days* (1925), and Jackson A. Graves, *My Seventy Years in California* (1927).

There were also writers who glorified the Hispanic heritage. Representative of this nostalgic tradition was the New Englander Charles Fletcher Lummis, eccentric literateur and Harvard acquaintance of Theodore Roosevelt. Lummis's *The Land of Poco Tiempo* (1893) and *The Spanish Pioneers* (1893) set the trend for books of adulation about the *dolce far niente* (leisurely) existence that supposedly prevailed in early California. Bizarre in his mannerisms, Lummis wore a green corduroy suit, with a Spanish sombrero on his head and a red sash wrapped around his middle. He lived out his own distinctively bohemian interpretation of Spanish colonial life in El Alisal, the house he constructed from boulders on the edge of Los Angeles's Arroyo Seco. Infatuated with the cult of Spain, Lummis dedicated himself to the restoration of the missions and the saving of Indian-Spanish folk traditions. From 1895 to 1902 he edited *The Land of Sunshine*, which later became *Out West* a journal extolling the beauties of life "at the right hand of the continent." On its pages appeared the first English translations of Father Serra's diary, Costanso's journal, and Benavides's memorial. Contributors included David Starr Jordan, Joaquin Miller, Edwin Markham, Mary Austin, Jack London, Eugene Manlove Rhodes, Frank Norris, Mrs. John Charles Fremont, Mrs. George Custer, Gutzon Borglum, Maynard Dixon, Edward Borein, Ina Coolbrith, and William Keith.

Lummis presided over construction of the Southwest Museum, located between Pasadena and downtown Los Angeles. He built it, in 1913, in that revived "mission style" of architecture which, alas, featured concrete rather than adobe construction.

Also writing prior to World War I were two authors whose works were rooted in the ethnology, folklore, and natural history of the state: George Wharton James and Charles Francis Saunders. James was for years employed by the Southern Pacific Railroad, and the books he wrote for publicity purposes kept romantic memories alive, praised the wonders of nature, disseminated Indian lore, and promoted California as a place to live. Among James's most widely read books were *In and Out of the Old Missions* (1905), *Through Ramona's Country* (1907), and *The Heroes of California* (1910). After 1912, as editor of Lummis's magazine *Out West*, James exerted considerable influence in attracting tourists to southern California. Saunders, a Quaker naturalist from Pennsylvania who sought the fascination of the southern California backcountry, wrote such charming books about the state as *Under the Sky in California* (1913), *With the Flowers and Trees in California* (1914), and *Finding the Worthwhile in California* (1916). Saunders's simplicity of expression won him an audience among readers of all ages.

Stewart Edward White, a more prolific author, had spent his boyhood in California but had later moved away. After publishing his first book, *Westerners* (1901), he resettled in California. Among White's books, which were frequently serialized in the *Saturday Evening Post* and other Eastern journals, were *The Blazed Trail* (1902), *The Cabin* (1910), *Gold* (1913), and *The Forty Niners* (1918). His *The Saga of Andy Burnett* (1947), along with his *The Long Rifle, Ranchero, Folded Hills,* and *Stampede*, tells the story of a young man's trek across the mountains to Carmel and of the friction between the Hispanic and Anglo-Saxon ways of life. In general, one would have to classify the work of White, along with that of Atherton, Wiggin, and Norris, as insubstantial but entertaining, reflecting the national taste for Western deserts, mountains, and moral heroes and heroines.

The production of literature designed to gratify this taste continued until World War I and even after. Walter Nordhoff's *The Journey of the Flame*, which appeared in 1933, written under the pseudonym Antonio de Fierro Blanco, was a fictional reminiscence of life in Spanish Baja California by the son of a prominent resident, German-born Charles Nordhoff. The elder Nordhoff had written publicity pieces for the railroads, including *California for Health, Pleasure and Residence* (1874) and *Peninsular California* (1888). Other treatments of California's past and current glories, half fiction and half truth, maintained the sentimental tradition of Lummis's *Out West*. Few of California's descriptive writers after the middle of the nineteenth century were major artists. Incurably romantic and obsessed with the picturesque, they achieved popularity only because these qualities suited the reading public of their times.

Poets

Among the best-known poets of California in this period was Joaquin Miller (Cincinnatus Hines Miller), dubbed by himself and admirers "Poet of the Sierra." Miller first went to San Francisco in 1870, where he came to be included in the circle of Bret Harte. That year he published at his own expense *Pacific Poems*, a romantic celebration of California and the West which made him famous. Acclaimed in England as a "frontier poet," he capitalized upon his popularity by touring both that country and the European continent. The English poet William Michael Rossetti introduced Miller at Pre-Raphaelite literary soirées, where Miller read his long-winded poetry dressed in chaps and sombrero, a red shirt, baggy trousers complete with suspenders, cowhide mining boots, and a sealskin coat. Miller loved to play the part of a bearded, uncouth Western rustic—in short, to act out Harte's stereotype of the miner. After he returned from his European excursion he built "The Hights" (as he spelled it), a quaint cliffside home in the Oakland hills. For years, until his death in 1913, he was one of California's most prominent figures. Although Miller achieved respect and adulation in his own day, despite his exaggerations and eccentricities, today he is ranked as a literary mediocrity.

The theme of California as a pastoral paradise also dominated the thin writings of Ella Sterling (Cummins) Mighels, whose *Story of the Files* (1893) and *Literary California* (1918) caused the state legislature to award her the title "Literary Historian of California." The writings of John Steven McGroarty, particularly his *Mission Play*, staged annually at San Gabriel after 1912, were in this same glamorized tradition. Two other California poets were Edward Rowland Sill and Edwin Markham. The Connecticut-born Sill graduated from Yale in 1861, then came to California by sea via Cape Horn. He held a variety of jobs, including the position of post office clerk at Sacramento, and from 1874 to 1882, that of English professor at the University of California. Then he forsook teaching for full-time writing. A man of wide intellectual attainments, Sill stressed the California locale in much of his poetry and prose, including *Venus of Milo* (1883) and *Christmas in California* (1890).

Although born in Oregon, Edwin Markham grew to manhood on a ranch in California. He also gave up teaching, in 1899, to write poetry. Markham remained in California over forty years, from 1857 to 1901, and bespoke its praises in his book, *California the Wonderful* (1914). His best-known work is *The Man with the Hoe and Other Poems* (1899). Markham's inspiration for the title poem of the volume came from the French painter Jean François Millet; but this protest against the brutalization of downtrodden farmers, composed in striking blank verse, may well have been suggested to him also by years spent in a ranching environment at a time when economic conditions were acute. The poem catapulted him to international fame. Markham saw his poem translated into forty languages, and it reputedly earned him more than $250,000.

Little humor accompanied the many late-nineteenth-century paeans to California's past glories and natural wonders. An exception was the doggerel of Bret Harte and, later, of Gelett Burgess. Burgess was a surveyor for the Southern Pacific Railroad before he became an illustrator and minor poet. By the turn of the century his verse "The Purple Cow" was being recited all over the country:

> I never saw a purple cow
> I never hope to see one

> But I can tell you anyhow
> I'd rather see than be one.

Just as Harte deplored the popularity of his poem "The Heathen Chinee," the work for which he was perhaps most widely known, so Burgess came to regret the renown this verse attained:

> Oh, yes, I wrote the Purple Cow
> I'm sorry now I wrote it
> But I can tell you anyhow
> I'll kill you if you quote it.

This zany piece had originated in *The Lark*, a whimsical publication that Burgess published from 1895 to 1897.

Historians and Commentators

By the end of the nineteenth century two amateur compilers of history, Zoeth Skinner Eldredge and Theodore H. Hittell, had made use of the autobiographical accounts of the first generation of pioneers to produce multi-volume histories of the state. These men, in spite of their lack of professional training, wrote fully and sometimes quite capably concerning the major events of the past. Clearly the best of California's amateur chroniclers, however, was Hubert Howe Bancroft, San Francisco bookseller and publisher, who between 1875 and 1890 painstakingly compiled a series of books about the Pacific Coast from Alaska to Latin America. His books numbered thirty-nine stout volumes, whose 30,000 pages were only partly written by himself. In fact, he set up a virtual "history factory" production system, with an able staff of paid assistants to interview numerous early residents.

At the heart of the Bancroft series were seven heavily footnoted volumes on California. Although Bancroft was an untrained historian, his books on the whole were comprehensive if not well integrated. Less well known is the fact that a woman collaborator, Frances Fuller Victor, wrote substantial sections of his multi-volume *History of California*. Bancroft's invaluable manuscript and book collection, assembled in the West, in Europe, and in Mexico, was ultimately sold to the University of California at Berkeley for $250,000, less $100,000 donated by Bancroft. His collection, which also includes newspapers, maps, diaries, and memorabilia, forms the core of the university's Bancroft Library.

After World War I, a band of scholars took on the task of structuring the history of California in a more objective and authoritative

The naturalist, John Muir. (Photography by Bradley and Rulofson, San Francisco [no date]. By courtesy of The Bancroft Library, University of California, Berkeley.)

manner. At the state university in Berkeley, anthropologist Alfred L. Kroeber turned his attention to the Indian past. Historians Herbert E. Bolton, Charles E. Chapman, and Herbert I. Priestley dealt with the Spanish period.

A number of writers of nonfiction were attracted by California's natural wonders and by its plant and animal life. John Muir was the most popular of these naturalists. No writer has shown such feeling for the majesty of the Sierra peaks and for the great valley of the Yosemite. Scottish-born, but educated in the United States, Muir spent much of his life tramping the California backcountry; he became a defender of its forests, mountains, and wildlife. President Theodore Roosevelt listened with special care to Muir's advice about the preservation of America's native flora and fauna. One result of this was government action on behalf of wilderness areas. Muir died

in 1914, leaving behind books that are still widely read, among them
The Mountains of California (1894, revised 1911), *Our National Parks*
(1901), *Stickeen* (1909), *The Yosemite* (1912), and *Steep Trails* (1918).
Other naturalists included the brothers Joseph and John Le Conte,
who produced their best-known geographical writings and mountain
sketches in California. The Le Contes were joined by David Starr
Jordan, later president of Stanford University, whose *Alps of the King
and Kern Divide* (1907) testified to his skill as a writer-naturalist. This
work ranks with Clarence King's *Mountaineering in the Sierra Nevada*
(1872). King, a Yale-educated geologist, included John Muir in a
circle of friends that numbered John Hay and Henry Adams.

Visiting foreign celebrities turned their attention to California. In
1882 the English aesthete Oscar Wilde included the state in his na-
tionwide lecturing tour. Perhaps the most renowned visiting Englishman was Robert Louis Stevenson, who in 1880 published an essay
entitled "The Old Pacific Capital" in *Fraser's Magazine* in London.
This dealt with Monterey and, along with Stevenson's *The Silverado
Squatters* (1884), it recalled his idyllic stay in California during 1880.
Despite his poor health he had a pleasant visit, and that year he was
married there to an American woman whom he had followed from
Europe. Stevenson's account of a sojourn at Monterey was included
in *Across the Plains, With Other Memoires and Essays* (1892). This piece
is a portrayal of the sleepy pueblo, which Stevenson saw as about to
be overcome by an avalanche of tourists whom he called "millionaire
vulgarians of the Big Bonanza." Stevenson's unpublished manuscript
Arizona Breckonridge, or A Vendetta of the West was also probably written
in California. He made one final nostalgic trip through San Francisco
in 1888 on his way to the South Seas, where he died.

Before and after the turn of the century a host of well-known native
American writers were also drawn to the California locale. Typical
of such authors was Charles Warren Stoddard, whose *Poems* was edited in 1867 by Bret Harte, with whom he had been associated in
contributing to San Francisco's *Goldern Era* and in working on the
Overland Monthly. He was for a time secretary to Mark Twain.

Journalism

Mention has been made of San Francisco's pioneer literary journals
and of California's earliest newspapers, the *Californian*, the *California
Star*, and the *Alta California*. By 1854, San Francisco had twenty-two
newspapers and journals. In southern California the San Diego *Herald* and the Los Angeles *Star* were the two main papers of the 1850s.
In 1853 the humorist George Derby for a time took over editing the
Herald, converting it into a satirical sheet that lampooned the imi-

tativeness of other California newspapers. The San Diego *Herald* eventually gave way to the *Union*, as at Los Angeles the *Star* made way for the *Times*. The *Times* and the *Union* then became the major papers of southern California's two largest cities.

California newspapers of the late nineteenth century were in the main four-page affairs, with five to seven columns of small type. On the front page they ran several columns of advertisements, including patent-medicine claims, notices by quack doctors who promised to alleviate the severest bodily aches and pains, and ads for such merchandise as high-buttoned shoes, canvas sails, pink velvet vests, tenpenny nails, and "long-nine" cigars. The rest of the front page was generally devoted to news from the outside world. Before the completion of the transcontinental telegraph in 1861, this news was weeks, even months, behind the times.

In 1865, at San Francisco, Michael and Charles De Young established the *Chronicle* as a theatrical journal. In the next year it dropped the word "Dramatic" from its masthead and, by printing "telegraphic news," was soon on its way to becoming a general paper. Another journal that emerged at San Francisco was also rooted in the arts. The *Argonaut*, founded in 1877, maintained a high standard of workmanship that contrasted markedly with existing newspapers by pirating Eastern news dispatches and features. A refreshing journalistic alternative, the *Argonaut* featured original literary pieces.

At Sacramento, after 1883, Charles K. McClatchy gave new life to the Sacramento *Bee*, founded in 1857. For several generations it was to remain, along with the Fresno and Modesto *Bees*, other members of the same hive, an authoritative voice in the Sacramento Valley. At Los Angeles, General Harrison Gray Otis acquired the *Times* in 1881. This paper, whose ownership passed into the hands of Harry Chandler and his descendants, played a vital role in the growth of Los Angeles; it became embroiled in a number of civic issues, among them the Free Harbor struggle, the Owens River water controversy, and union fracases. At Santa Barbara Thomas Storke's *News Press* also grew to be the oracle of that community. After 1900, centralization of control characterized journalism, with the established "newspaper families" extending their domain over most California dailies. The De Youngs, the Hearsts, the McClatchys, the Storkes, and the Chandlers all built influential newspaper chains.

Music and Drama

California has long provided receptive audiences for musical performances. San Francisco's opera season came to be among America's most celebrated. From 1879 onward, the Tivoli Theater and Opera

House in that city offered a year-round schedule of performances. Within the walls of this theater many distinctive events were staged, including the reputed first performance of Pietro Mascagni's one-act opera *Cavalleria Rusticana* in 1890. At the last musical performance to be held in the Tivoli, on November 23, 1913, another Italian composer, Ruggiero Leoncavallo, conducted his *I Pagliacci*.

In 1911 the symphony orchestra of San Francisco became the first in the nation to be assisted regularly by public funds. Prior to World War I many performers, including some of international fame, were attracted to the state. Among them was Adelina Patti, the most celebrated soprano from the end of the Civil War to the turn of the century. Others, such as Ernestine Schumann-Heink and Lotte Lehman, liked California so much that they settled there. Mesdames Nellie Melba, Luisa Tetrazzini, and Amelita Galli-Curci were other divas feted in California. Tetrazzini, who made her North American debut at the Tivoli in 1905, became the darling of San Francisco's opera fans and, incidentally, had a gourmet recipe for chicken named after her—probably at San Francisco. Still other popular stars, operatic and symphonic, were Beniamino Gigli, Geraldine Farrar, Theodore Chaliapin, Giovanni Martinelli, Ignace Jan Paderewski, Artur Schnabel, and Arturo Toscanini. On the very night of the San Francisco earthquake and fire of 1906 the great Italian tenor Enrico Caruso sang the role of Don José in Bizet's *Carmen*, while elsewhere in the city the young Shakespearean actor John Barrymore was giving one of his earliest San Francisco performances.

Drama, like music, was in the late 1800s warmly supported by Californians. Long before Hollywood, actors and actresses were drawn to California. San Francisco was the first Western city to support a professional theater on a large scale. Only New York, in fact, surpassed its record of hundreds of performances each year. Shakespearean plays produced in San Francisco after 1870 included *The Merchant of Venice, Richard III, Hamlet, Othello*, and *Macbeth*. Sheridan's *School for Scandal, The Rivals*, and *Pizarro* were also frequently performed, as were the plays of Bulwer-Lytton. In addition to these were such dramas dealing with local scenes as Augustin Daly's *Horizon*, Bret Harte's *Two Men of Sandy Bar*, and Joaquin Miller's *Danites in the Sierras*. Minstrel, variety, and vaudeville shows charmed other patrons of theatrical productions.

The most outstanding actor to appear in California during this period was Edwin Booth, whose name was synonymous with that of Hamlet in the minds of theatergoers throughout the country. In 1876 Booth, this time without his father Junius, came back to San Francisco for an eight-week engagement. He smashed all attendance records for the dramatic stage in the United States, with hundreds turned away each night from the theater in which he played. That season

Market Street from Third Street, San Francisco, looking east, before the earth-quake and fire of 1906. (H. G. Hills Collection; by courtesy of The Bancroft Library, University of California, Berkeley.)

a young San Francisco boy managed to get a walk-on part alongside Booth. His name was David Belasco. With San Francisco as his base, he played more than 170 parts in 100 plays. In 1882 Belasco headed east to new prominence on the New York stage, where he produced, incidentally, some of the plays in which Lotta Crabtree, who had charmed lonesome miners during the gold rush era and who remained popular, appeared.

At the suggestion of Edwin Booth, the Polish actress Helena Modjeska went to San Francisco in 1876; she achieved prominence in the roles of Lady Macbeth, Ophelia, and Cleopatra. An entirely different type of performer, Lillian Russell, also came to California in 1881, the year after she began her career. By that time the city supported twelve different theaters. In one of these, blond Miss Russell appeared in the revue *Babes in the Woods* attired only in a blouse, purple tights, and high-buttoned shoes. Although female tongues wagged, hundreds of males applauded her performances vigorously. After the turn of the century the Western-born actress Maude Adams packed large audiences into San Francisco's theaters to see her incomparable performances of J. M. Barrie's *Peter Pan* and *The Little Minister*, while the native San Franciscan David Warfield pursued a career under the guidance of Belasco. Warfield joined forces with Oliver Morosco, author, impresario, and theater owner, to present a number of productions in San Francisco and elsewhere along the Pacific Coast.

Since 1872 San Francisco's Bohemian Club, founded by newspapermen looking for a quiet refuge after hours, began to admit actors and artists. Shortly thereafter, Henry Edwards, English actor and member of the stock company at the California Theatre on Bush Street, became the second president of the club. In 1878, when Edwards departed for New York City, an overnight farewell picnic was held for him at Paper Mill Creek in Marin County. Because it was so successful, the next year the Bohemians traveled to Duncan's Mills on the Russian River. That outing was notable as the occasion for the first al fresco performance of Shakespeare's *As You Like It*. The exclusive Bohemian Club owns yet today 2,700 acres along the Russian River, in a redwood forest known as the Bohemian Grove, still the scene of club productions.

Higher Education

Aside from literary, musical, and dramatic activity, the cultural growth of California during the late nineteenth century can be measured by its educational advances. Compulsory attendance of grammar school students was first instituted in 1874, and later came to be applied to all persons between the ages of eight and eighteen.

The first institutions of collegiate rank were founded by church endowment, and they almost all suffered shortages of money and difficulties in obtaining faculty. The Catholics established various institutions before the turn of the century, the first of which was Santa Clara University, founded in 1851 as a preparatory school. Later Loyola University, the University of San Francisco, Saint Mary's, and Immaculate Heart College were begun by Catholic religious orders.

Among institutions established by Protestants was the College of the Pacific; today located in Stockton, it was begun at San Jose by the Methodists in 1851 as the University of the Pacific, the name it readopted. In 1879 the same denomination founded the University of Southern California, later to become an independent institution. Mills College, situated in the Oakland suburbs, traces its history to 1852; it is now the oldest women's college in the Far West. At Palo Alto, Stanford University was founded in 1890 by Leland Stanford as a memorial to his only son, and became the most richly endowed of all the private universities and colleges of the West. Stanford gained early prominence through its first president, David Starr Jordan, a nationally known naturalist.

In southern California, Occidental College was founded in 1887, and Pomona College only a few months later. The Associated Colleges of Claremont (including Pomona, Scripps, Claremont University College, Harvey Mudd, and Claremont McKenna College) grew out of the founding of Pomona. In 1901 the Quakers established Whittier College, and in 1909 the Baptists founded a college at Redlands, later called Redlands University. By the early twentieth century, most of these colleges achieved intellectual independence and gave up their sectarian connections, but they retained the traditions under which they had been founded.

The privately endowed institutions in California, meanwhile, had come to be supplemented by a state university and college system. In 1868 the University of California was formally created by a bill of the state legislature. Henry Durant was its first president, followed two years later by Daniel C. Gilman. When Gilman resigned in 1875 to accept the presidency of Johns Hopkins University, he was succeeded by the scientist John Le Conte.

Symbolic Faith in Progress

Californians, like other Americans, have commemorated their pride in human progress, cultural and material, through state exhibitions, county fairs, and other celebrations. The Panama–Pacific Exposition of 1915 was a symbolic highlight of California's pre–World War I era. Although half the world was plunged into war as its exhibits neared completion, this exposition (and another held the same year at San Diego's Balboa Park) proclaimed the state's progress since the turn of the century. Public enthusiasm for the exposition was tremendous. Beginning in the summer of 1915, crowds exceeded all expectations. Much attention was given to the new communication with the East Coast made possible by the opening of the Panama Canal, and the establishment of the first telephone connection between San Francisco and Chicago. Displays of art, agriculture, machinery, food, and other hallmarks of progress were paraded before 19 million visitors. Mirror pools, potted palm trees, amusement facilities, and a central promenade completed the effect of eleven large plaster-of-paris palaces in which the exhibits were housed.

San Francisco could take satisfaction in its theaters, libraries, churches, and university across the Bay, as well as in more newspapers than the city of London. Presidents Grant, McKinley, and Roosevelt enjoyed gold-service banquets in the Palace Hotel's Palm Court on Market Street. In that same hostelry Diamond Jim Brady once downed six dozen oysters before astonished onlookers. After 1900, in a golden age of *gourmandiserie*, it was possible to obtain a meal, with the best Napa claret, at Papa Coppa's for less than fifty cents. In an atmosphere reminiscent of *la bella Italia* his restaurant offered *tortellini al brodo, lasagne,* and a dessert of *zabaglione.* Visitors could find still another brand of hospitality at Leveroni's Cellar, the Bella Union, or the Bank Exchange Saloon, the latter located in the historic Montgomery Block. The Cliff House, near the city's Seal Rocks, offered an incomparable view of the Pacific.

Before the great fire of 1906 absorbed its energies in reconstruction, and before prohibition and civic reform chastened San Francisco, it was one of the most amazing cities in North America. Much of its cosmopolitan charm has lingered on. The city's faults are America's faults, but San Francisco's virtues are its own.

The generation that came to maturity between the Civil War and World War I possessed an unshakable faith in progress. Though condemnation of the railroads, labor strife, and political corruption caused alarm, California's basic optimism remained predominant. The reformist criticisms of George, Norris, and London were not allowed to trouble the state's self-possessed tranquillity. California's romantic chroniclers and prophets of success proved more attractive than its peddlers of gloom.

Selected Readings

An anthology of California writing is Joseph Henry Jackson's *Continent's End: A Collection of California Writing* (New York, 1944), and a bibliographical essay is Lawrence Clark Powell, *Land of Fiction* (Los Angeles, 1952). For the southern part of the state see Franklin D. Walker's *A Literary History of Southern California* (Berkeley, 1950). His *San Francisco's Literary Frontier* deals with the first generation after the gold rush.

On Henry George see Jacob Oser, *Henry George* (New York, 1974), and Kenneth M. Johnson, "Progress and Poverty—A Paradox," California Historical Society *Quarterly* 42 (March 1963), 27–32. In addition to Charles Shinn's *Mining Camps* (repr. New York, 1948), he wrote *The Story of the Mine* (New York, 1896) and *Graphic Description of Pacific Coast Outlaws* (repr. New York, 1958).

John Muir left behind *The Story of My Boyhood and Youth* (Madison, Wis., 1965). Also see Stephen Fox, *John Muir and His Legacy* (Boston, 1981). Ambrose Bierce is the subject of Walter Neale, *Life of Ambrose Bierce* (New York, 1929) and Paul Fatout, *Ambrose Bierce: The Devil's Lexicographer* (New York, 1967). Edmund Wilson, *Patriotic Gore* (New York, 1962) includes a section on Bierce. Frank Norris is treated in Franklin D. Walker, *Frank Norris* (Garden City, N.Y., 1932), and Ernest Marchand, *Frank Norris: A Study* (London, 1942). On Jack London, consult Joan London, *Jack London and His Times* (New York, 1939); William McDevitt, *Jack London's First* (San Francisco, 1946); the fictionalized biography by Irving Stone, *Sailor on Horseback* (Boston, 1938); and Richard O'Connor, *Jack London* (New York, 1964).

Women's travails are depicted in: Mary Jane Megquier, *Apron Full of Gold* (San Marino, 1949), letters edited by Robert Glass Cleland; also see Elinor Richey, *Eminent Women of the West* (Berkeley, 1975), and Dorothy Gray, *Women of the West* (Millbrae, Calif., 1976). See also the bibliography by Joan Hoff Wilson and Lynn Bonfield Donovan, "Women's History: A Listing of West Coast Archival and Manuscript Sources," *California Historical Quarterly* 55 (Spring 1976), 74–83; Christiane Fischer, "Women in California in the Early 1850s," *Southern California Quarterly* 60 (Fall 1978), 231–54; David J. Langum, "California Women and the Image of Virtue," *Southern California Quarterly* 61 (Fall 1977), 245–50; Thelma Lee Hubbell and Gloria R. Lothrop, "The Friday Morning Club: A Los Angeles Legacy," *Southern California Quarterly* 50 (March 1968), 59–90; and brief biographies of Caroline Severance, Harriet Strong and Biddy Mason in Lothrop's "Three Southern California Heroines," *Brand Book XV*, The Westerners Los Angeles Corral (Los Angeles, 1978). See also Lothrop's "Westering Women and the Ladies of Los Angeles. . . ," *South Dakota Review* (Summer 1981), 41–67. Helen Holdridge, *Mammy Pleasant* (New York, 1959) is a questionable account of her dramatic life and times. Two other women leaders are studied by Valerie Mathes, "Helen Hunt Jackson: Official Agent to the California Mission Indians," *Southern California Quarterly* 63 (Spring 1981), 63–77; Ruth Odell, *Helen Hunt Jackson* (New York, 1939); and Elizabeth McPhail, *Kate Sessions, Pioneer Horticulturist* (San Diego, 1976). Finally, consult Doyce B. Nunis Jr., "Kate Douglas Wiggin: Pioneer in California Kindergarten Education," *California Historical Society Quarterly* 61 (1962), 291–307.

Regarding Mary Austin, consult Thomas M. Pearce, *The Beloved House* (Caldwell, Idaho, 1940), and her own autobiography, *Earth Horizon* (Boston, 1932), as well as Helen M. Doyle, *Mary Austin: Woman of Genius* (New York, 1939). Treatments of Charles F. Lummis are: Edwin Bingham, *Charles F. Lummis, Editor of the Southwest* (San Marino, 1955); Dudley Gordon, *Charles F. Lummis: Crusader in Corduroy* (Los Angeles, 1972); and Turbese Lummis Fiske, *Charles F. Lummis: The Man and His West* (Norman, Okla., 1975). See Martin S. Peterson, *Joaquin Miller: Literary Frontiersman* (Stanford, 1937). Informative as to Stevenson's stay in California is Anne Roller Issler, *Our Mountain Heritage, Silverado and Robert Louis Stevenson* (Stanford, 1950), and Katharine D. Osbourne, *Robert Louis Stevenson in California* (Chicago, 1911).

Historiography is treated in Harry Clark, *A Venture in History: The Production, Publication, and Sale of the Works of Hubert Howe Bancroft* (Berkeley, 1973), and John W. Caughey, *Hubert Howe Bancroft: Historian of the West* (Berkeley, 1946). Also suggestive of historical scholarship is *Greater America: Essays in Honor of Herbert Eugene Bolton*

(Berkeley, 1945). Newspapers are examined in Edward C. Kemble, *A History of California Newspapers* (New York, 1927), reprinted from the Sacramento *Union* of 1857. John P. Young's *Journalism in California* (San Francisco, 1915), and John Bruce's *Gaudy Century: The Story of San Francisco's Hundred Years of Robust Journalism* (New York, 1948), and by Ella Sterling (Cummins) Mighels in *The Story of the Files* (San Francisco, 1893). There is a *History of the Los Angeles Star* by William B. Rice (Berkeley, 1947). A newspaperman's autobiographical memoir of Fremont Older's San Francisco *Bulletin* days is R. L. Duffus, *The Tower of Jewels: Memories of San Francisco* (New York, 1960). See also Mrs. Fremont Older, *San Francisco, Magic City* (New York, 1961), by the widow of one of its brilliant newspaper editors.

Early-twentieth-century drama forms a part of *Memories and Impressions of Helen Modjeska: An Autobiography* (New York, 1910). This can be supplemented by *Portrait of America: Letters of Henry Sinciewicz*, translated and edited by Charles Morley (New York, 1959). Consult also William Winter, *The Life of David Belasco* (2 vols., New York, 1918); Constance Rourke, *Troupers of the Gold Coast: or The Rise of Lotta Crabtree* (New York, 1928); Parker Morell, *Lillian Russell: The Era of Plush* (New York, 1940); and Eleanor Ruggles, *Prince of Players: Edwin Booth* (New York, 1953).

Developments in higher education are in William W. Ferrier, *Origin and Development of the University of California* (Berkeley, 1930). See also his *Ninety Years of Education in California* (Berkeley, 1937), and Verne A. Stadtman, *The University of California, 1868–1968* (New York, 1970), as well as Albert G. Pickerell and May Dornin, *The University of California, a Pictorial History* (Berkeley, 1969). Consult also Andrew Rolle, *Occidental College: The First Seventy-Five Years, 1887–1962* (Los Angeles, 1962). See too Charles W. Cooper, *Whittier: Independent College in California* (Los Angeles, 1967), and Helen Raitt and Bernice Moulton, *Scripps Institution of Oceanography: First Fifty Years* (Los Angeles, 1967). Edith R. Mirrielees, *Stanford: The Story of a University* (New York, 1959); Charles Burt Sumner, *The Story of Pomona College* (New York, 1914); Manuel P. Servin and Iris A. Wilson, *Southern California and its University, A History of U.S.C., 1880–1964* (Los Angeles, 1969); John R. Thelin, "California and the Colleges," *California Historical Quarterly* 56 (Summer 1977), 140–63 and (Fall 1977), 230–49 are informative. W. W. Ferrier's *Henry Durant* (Berkeley, 1942) deals with the first president of the University of California, while a biography of Stanford's first president is Edward M. Burns, *David Starr Jordan: Prophet of Freedom* (Stanford, 1953). Consult also *The Memoirs of Ray Lyman Wilbur*, edited by Edgar Eugene Robinson and Paul Carroll Edwards (Stanford, 1960), and Benjamin Ide Wheeler's *The Abundant Life* (Berkeley, 1926). Irving G. Hendrick, *California Education* (San Francisco, 1980) is a brief history of that subject.

A biography of a leading cleric is John B. McGloin's *California's First Archbishop: The Life of Joseph Sadoc Alemany, 1814–1888* (New York, 1966). John W. Robinson, "Charles Francis Saunders: A Quaker Botanist in Southern California," *Southern California Quarterly* 60 (Summer 1978), 143–53, concerns a gentle and affectionate Pasadenan.

An overview of the period is Kevin Starr's *Americans and the California Dream, 1850–1915* (New York, 1973). He focuses upon southern California in *Inventing the Dream: California Through The Progressive Era* (New York, 1985).

Mental health is the subject of Richard W. Fox's *So Far Disordered in Mind: Insanity in California, 1870–1930* (Berkeley, 1978), while domestic life is treated in Robert Griswold, *Family and Divorce in California, 1850–1890* (Albany, N.Y., 1982).

CHAPTER 28

Twentieth-Century Progressive Politics

In California, as throughout the nation, the period between 1900 and the outbreak of World War I stands out as one during which the discontent of farmers was directed at the railroad and meat-packing monopolies and banking, finance, and manufacturing trusts. City workers opposed the influence of big business over government, and focused anger upon corrupt machine politics at the municipal level. A group of reform-minded journalists, who came to be known as "muckrakers," joined these agrarians and city workers in exposing corrupt big-business practices and in championing close control of large trusts, or industrial combinations.

The beginning of the new century had seemed to augur no spectacular political or economic changes. No state or national leader had yet arisen to head the crusade for reform. In the presidential campaign of 1900, California voted for the conservative William McKinley over William Jennings Bryan, as did the nation as a whole. By 1904 the national mood had shifted toward liberalism, however, and the state again followed the prevailing political pattern. It supported Theodore Roosevelt, who had become the standard-bearer of reform. But in the ensuing gubernatorial campaign, it elected Republican James N. Gillett, a machine candidate. The popular belief was that the control of the state lay behind the scenes, rather than with either of the major parties. The real power was the Southern Pacific Railroad.

Combating the Railroad

For half a century, indeed, beginning with the construction of the railroad, its political activities were closely involved with the course of California history. At first the purpose of the railroad's founders in entering practical politics was to maintain their monopoly as to rates and services. Railroad lobbyists and emissaries—principally William F. Herrin of San Francisco and Walter Parker of Los Angeles— were adroit dispensers of money on behalf of their cause. At Sacramento, when the legislature was in session, Herrin, as chief counsel of the Southern Pacific, saw to it each week that a round-trip ticket to San Francisco was left on the desk of every member. Annually the railroad did bribe a sizable number of the forty members of the state senate and even more members of the assembly. The railroad also regularly subsidized newspaper editors with monthly payments. It hoped thus to obtain favorable publicity in a state where a kind word for the railroad was a rarity, and where, in fact, the railroad could be denounced with little fear of offending anyone, except the local ticket agent.

The Mussel Slough tragedy had added ugliness to the railroad's reputation. George, Norris, and Royce had complained in their books that the power of the railroad was free from regulation and control. Even before development of the Southern Pacific, the Central Pacific had been charged with being the "third party" in state politics, with having "its leaders, its managers, its editors, its orators, its adherents" everywhere, and with bearing no allegiance to the people of the state. Especially resented was the notion that the railroad was outside the law. The constitution of 1879 had made provision for a Board of Railroad Commissioners; but this measure had been ineffective in regulating freight and passenger rates. The railroad had gained so powerful a grip on the press that opposition seemed futile. Such independent newspapers as the Sacramento *Union* were subjected to relentless opposition, because of their criticisms of the railroads.

Farmers had long been hostile to the railroad because of its discrimination against small customers and its under-the-table rebates for favored shippers. Ranchers resented the failure of the state to control the railroad's power. A series of exposés included public airing in 1883 of the incriminating Colton letters. David D. Colton, a retired brigadier general of volunteers, had been a close associate of Huntington, Stanford, and Crocker during the period after 1874 when they were lobbying for government bills and subsidies to establish the Southern Pacific network from Yuma into Arizona and New Mexico. Although General Colton possessed only a minor interest in the company, Huntington wrote him frankly and frequently. His letters provided a cumulative picture of Huntington's manipulation of men and events as chief political agent for the company in Washington. After Colton died suddenly in 1878, his widow was dissatisfied with the financial settlement that she received from her husband's former colleagues. Her protests to them were poorly received because General Colton had had a falling out with Huntington before his death. Five years later the unhappy Mrs. Colton released several hundred of the personal and business letters Huntington had written to her husband.

Long lists of corruptible officeholders came out of the correspondence, in the course of which Huntington had indiscreetly discussed the costs of obtaining passage of legislation that would favor the railroad. The Colton letters, by providing an inside view of Huntington's use of power to influence legislation, supported the popular conviction that the railroad had established a government within a government. In 1887, when Huntington was called to appear before the United States Railway Commission, he admitted that he would have considered it perfectly proper to pay the salaries, fees, and expenses of the entire Arizona territorial legislature in order to get legislation passed. As Huntington put it: "My record as a business man is pretty well known among business men and there is nothing in it I am ashamed of."

After revelation of the Colton letters, Huntington came in for further notoriety in connection with repayment of government advances that had made possible construction of the Central Pacific. Although the Big Four had voted themselves huge dividends, they had made no attempt during their greatest prosperity to pay off these government loans. Congress had begun in 1878, with passage of the Thurman Act, to consider legislation to compel the railroad company to retire the thirty-year bonds on schedule, but Huntington had used every means to prevent such measures. Within a few years he was left alone to carry on this fight and that against the building of rival transcontinental systems; Hopkins died in 1878, Crocker in 1888, and Stanford in 1893.

Each of the four men had amassed a fortune in excess of $50 million. Toward the end of the century a financial writer estimated Huntington's fortune to be $70 million. He owned enough railroad trackage to connect the North and the South Poles, and he could travel from Newport News, Virginia, to San Francisco without ever riding on anyone else's rails. He also owned timber stands, sawmills (in which he employed his nephew, Henry E. Huntington), steamship lines, and coal mines. During the 1880s and 1890s, Huntington continued to maintain that the railroad had performed a public service. He thought that the thirty-year debt bonds (at 6 percent interest) that the railroad was obligated to repay should be replaced by ninety-nine-year obligations at 1.5 percent interest. He restated his conviction that he had operated within the business ethics allowable in an age later labeled as dominated by "robber barons."

The national press, however, charged that Huntington wanted what amounted to cancellation of the railroad's debts to the government.

And the San Francisco *Examiner*, under young William Randolph Hearst, kept up a barrage of criticism against Huntington. In 1896 Hearst sent Ambrose Bierce to Washington to cover Huntington's activities. Bierce wired his paper daily descriptions of Huntington's testimony before congressional committees. Bierce's reports exposed to wider public view Huntington's questionable respect for honesty, his vindictiveness, and, above all, his lack of concern for interests other than those of the railroad. These articles, accompanied by cartoons that showed Huntington leading the governor of California around on a leash, proved instrumental in defeating his refunding proposals.

Another public controversy that dogged the last days of Huntington's career was the "free-harbor" fight. By 1890 Los Angeles had achieved a population of over 50,000 persons. The city was on its way toward becoming the largest in California. Only one deficiency threatened to halt this expansion—lack of a harbor. Ships still docked at the roadstead of San Pedro–Wilmington, surrounded by mud flats, sand hills, and dank sloughs. It was clear that federal funds alone could build the docks, sea walls, slips, and passages necessary for a modern harbor, although some persons maintained that private interests should manage construction of the harbor. Since two sites, San Pedro–Wilmington and Santa Monica, were available, a bitter fight developed over the future location of an expanded harbor. The Huntington interests favored construction of a deep harbor at Santa Monica, principally because the Southern Pacific controlled all the approaches to that location. Angeleños, however, knew that if Congress should select Santa Monica, their future harbor would be a port constructed for the benefit of Huntington and his company.

Determined to forestall awarding federal funds to Santa Monica, an aroused Los Angeles citizenry organized a Free Harbor League whose object was to secure the appropriation for San Pedro. The term "free harbor" sprang from the feeling that the new port should not be dominated by the railroad. The Terminal Railroad, a minor competitor of the powerful Southern Pacific, had access to San Pedro, a fact that gave Los Angeles some assurance that access to its future harbor would not be the exclusive province of the Huntington monopoly. Otherwise, critics of the Southern Pacific felt, it would set whatever freight rates it wanted, and govern the loading and unloading of harbor cargo. Senator Stephen M. White allied himself with the Free Harbor Leaguers, as did the Los Angeles *Times* and the city's Chamber of Commerce. Senator White, a persuasive orator, battled for three years, from 1893 to 1896, to prevent Huntington from having federal funds allocated to Santa Monica. The free-harbor fight ended with San Pedro designated as the site of Los Angeles's

port, epitomizing the distrust of the Southern Pacific that had been
built up in the public mind.

In 1900, the flinty Collis P. Huntington reached the end of his
life. Shortly after his death, his nephew, Henry, sold control of the
Southern Pacific to E. H. Harriman. Henry formed out of seventy-
three existing local lines a new interurban railway system to serve
the Los Angeles area, known as the Pacific Electric Railway Company.
But the nephew was never quite able to rid himself of the stigma of
his uncle's primitive capitalism. Only when the magnificent Henry
E. Huntington Library and Art Gallery was founded in San Marino,
after the turn of the century, did the memory of the Huntington
name begin to mellow in public esteem.

One should not, however, conclude that the power of the railroad
was weakened by the death of the last of the Big Four. William F.
Herrin, chief counsel of the Southern Pacific under the Big Four,
remained a strong power in state politics, a power that even the
progressive movement found hard to challenge. Yet the tide of reform was gaining impetus from the presence of a reform-minded
president, Theodore Roosevelt, in the White House.

To charge what the traffic would bear was natural in the nineteenth
century. Long unheard was the notion that a regulatory commission
should decide passenger and freight rates according to a "fair" profit.
In 1910 the railroads capitulated to precisely such regulation after
years of public pressure.

The Attack on Municipal Corruption

The American people now seemed ready to clean up the country,
including all levels of government. In an era when Charles Evans
Hughes was exposing insurance scandals in New York, the regime
of Governor Robert M. La Follette of Wisconsin was meticulously
investigating the corruptive power of lumber and rail interests in
that state. Meanwhile, the best-known of the muckrakers, Lincoln
Steffens, strongly interested in "good government," exposed the corrupt alliance of business and politics in city after city, in articles later
collected as *The Shame of the Cities*. Steffens, who had spent his boyhood in Sacramento, devoted new concern to California.

San Francisco was ripe for an investigation. From 1897 to 1901,
the city had enjoyed a moderate administration under Mayor James
D. Phelan, a financier of inherited wealth. Then, on January 8, 1902,
a labor-backed political machine, the Union Labor Party, captured
the city administration and installed a theater musician, Eugene E.
Schmitz, as mayor, with Abraham Ruef, a clever attorney with a
handlebar mustache, as the power behind the throne. Ruef had once

been idealistic about politics. With Schmitz, however, Ruef collected bribes, blackmailed legitimate businesses, and extorted graft through protection rackets—with all these payments under the guise of attorney's fees to Ruef. They forced the purchase of liquor, cigars, and special licenses on gambling establishments and bilked French restaurants known to have prostitution cribs upstairs. The Ruef–Schmitz team levied tribute, too, upon municipal employees, the Pacific Gas and Electric Company, the Home Telephone Company, and the city's streetcar system. Ruef saw himself as a future senator, and Schmitz planned to run for governor.

In 1905 the San Francisco *Bulletin* began publishing articles by Fremont Older, its reformist editor, excoriating the city regime. Older, former mayor Phelan, and sugar magnate Rudolph Spreckels were about to begin a campaign to overthrow Ruef and Schmitz when disaster struck San Francisco. This catastrophe was to throw new light on the city's administration.

The San Francisco Earthquake and Fire

At 5:16 A.M. on April 18, 1906, a massive earthquake shook the ground along the San Andreas Fault from Salinas in the south to Cape Mendocino in northern California. A rumbling noise awakened thousands at San Francisco. Then came a terrifying grinding sound as flimsy buildings were twisted off their foundations. More substantial multi-storied brick structures cascaded into the streets. Yawning fissures opened up in the earth. Almost every chimney in the city was so cracked that passersby were in danger. Short-circuited electric wires, which fell into the city's streets, set off fires that swept through block after block of residences. When volunteer firemen attached their hoses to hydrants, no water came out of the mains. Not only were pipes broken, but in some instances, the city's fire hydrants had never even been hooked up to its water system.

Firemen fought fanatically, without water, to stamp out the advancing flames. But the fire moved relentlessly from downtown toward Powell, Polk, and Van Ness Streets. Panic-stricken property owners stood on the roofs of buildings with strips of carpet, beating out the flames. Many persons who refused to heed the warnings of police and firemen not to stand too close to the fireline lost their lives when debris fell on them. General Frederick Funston, commandant of the Presidio of San Francisco, charged into the city and proceeded to dynamite more than a quarter mile of mansions along Van Ness, one of its most beautiful streets. Explosion as well as burning took an awesome toll in the fire, which raged for three days and two nights before it burned itself out. Both Nob Hill and Chinatown were left

*Earthquake damage, San Francisco. City hall from Larkin Street, April 23,
1906.* (H. G. Hills Collection, photography by T. E. Hecht; by courtesy of The
Bancroft Library, University of California, Berkeley.)

*Earthquake damage, San Francisco. Valencia Street, between 17th and 18th
streets, April 23, 1906.* (H. G. Hills Collection, photography by T. E. Hecht; by
courtesy of The Bancroft Library, University of California, Berkeley.)

in ruins; almost the entire northeastern part of the city, an area of four square miles extending from the Southern Pacific Depot on the south to Telegraph Hill on the north side, lay in debris. Over five hundred city blocks had been destroyed, and along with them most of the city's business houses, banks, churches, and newspaper offices. The total property loss in San Francisco was placed at $200 million, and 452 people had lost their lives. At nearby Palo Alto, Stanford University's newly constructed buildings were also largely demolished.

Despite relief shipments sent from all over the world, 300,000 homeless people were forced to live for weeks in army tents pitched on vacant lots and in Golden Gate Park. Campers, some clad in their best Sunday clothes, munched on rations of shredded-wheat biscuits and drank beef tea. Hundreds of tins of corned beef were distributed by the Red Cross. By standing in lines several blocks long, children could get free oranges and milk.

Reform

Even as the work of rebuilding the devastated city began, and a new and wider Market Street rose from the ashes, plans for the destruction of the Ruef–Schmitz machine were formed. Older, Phelan, and Spreckels were joined in their cleanup efforts by a young attorney, Francis J. Heney, who, as a United States prosecutor, had indicted fraudulent timber operators in Oregon. Older persuaded President Roosevelt to lend to the California reform group, along with Heney, the ace detective William J. Burns, whose cooperation in the timber-fraud trials had resulted in the conviction of prominent politicians.

After months of detective work, the great "San Francisco graft prosecution" began in November 1906 with the indictments of Ruef and Schmitz for extortion. Masses of incriminating evidence were piled up, in addition, against executives of the city's public utility corporations. Patrick Calhoun, president of the United Railroads of San Francisco, and his company's chief counsel, Tirey L. Ford, were indicted on charges that they had paid a quarter of a million dollars to bribe the San Francisco Board of Supervisors in order to substitute elevated trolleys for cable cars. Whereas the bribe takers, Ruef and Schmitz, were condemned for crookedness, the bribe givers, Calhoun, Ford, and other indicted officials of such firms as the Parkside Realty Company and Pacific States Telephone and Telegraph Company, were regarded differently by the public and newspapers. It was argued that the business community had been blackjacked into making deals with Union Labor politicians who ran the city. Although this logic could hardly acquit the bribe givers of dishonesty, a number

The defense in the great San Francisco graft prosecution of 1906–1907. Henry Ach, one of Abraham Ruef's attorneys, in whispered conversation with Ruef. San Francisco police chief Biggy at left. (Carl Hoffman Papers; by courtesy of The Bancroft Library, University of California, Berkeley.)

of legal technicalities were produced at the trial of Calhoun and Ford, and they finally escaped conviction for bribery. The intermediary to whom they had paid a fee was Ruef. Although the political boss of San Francisco, he was not technically an officeholder. The underground government of the city was indeed evasive.

During the graft trials Fremont Older and his fellow reformers not only were subjected to numerous indignities, including social ostracism by their peers, but on several occasions experienced near-violence. Older was kidnaped and taken by train to Santa Barbara. He believed that there was a plot to kill him, and that this failed only because a hired gunman lost his nerve. After being "found," Older was returned to the trial by police officials. Next, the house of the principal witness, a San Francisco supervisor, was blown up. Documents intended for use in the graft prosecutions were stolen out of private homes and offices. On November 13, 1907, a prospective juror who had been challenged by the prosecution because of a criminal record arose in the courtroom during Ruef's trial, drew a gun, and shot Chief Prosecutor Heney in the head, wounding him almost fatally. Though the motive for the shooting was probably resentment at the exposure of the man's prison record, when he committed suicide it was charged that he had done so to avoid testifying about whether he had been hired to murder Heney.

The San Francisco graft trials lasted more than two years. Of all the defendants, only Abe Ruef finally went to the penitentiary. He was sentenced to fourteen years for bribery, but after four years and seven months at San Quentin, he was freed. Ruef benefited from public concern over anti-Jewish activities. He owed his freedom mostly, however, to the man who had fought hardest to see him condemned— Fremont Older. In 1911 that crusader, troubled by qualms of conscience over the use of Ruef as a scapegoat by others as guilty as he, launched a campaign in the pages of the *Bulletin* to free Ruef. Older now considered the broken Ruef fully repentant. The editor's compassion may have been partly traceable to a speech of Theodore Roosevelt's in which the president had warned the public to be careful about attacks on public servants. "Especially should we beware," Roosevelt had cautioned, "of attacking the men who are merely the occasions and not the causes of disaster." As for Ruef's political associate, Mayor Schmitz, the state Supreme Court had reversed his conviction. Members of the Schmitz family, who regarded Ruef as an unmitigated liar, resented the fact that their reputation was tarnished by questionable evidence against Schmitz. Although guilty of negligence, evidence suggests that Schmitz may not have taken the bribes he was charged with having received. Indeed, he denied ever receiving a dishonest dollar, and his trial in 1912 exonerated him because of evidence insufficient to obtain a conviction.

The spirit of municipal reform, meanwhile, was resulting in action at Los Angeles. In that city a "good government" movement took shape under Dr. John R. Haynes, a wealthy physician and severe critic of the influence of the Southern Pacific. Haynes was concerned about the favorable stand that United States Justice Stephen J. Field, a Californian, took toward large corporations. He also criticized business influence over state courts. But Haynes was primarily interested in local government. As early as 1895 he had fathered a Direct Legislation League to move power out of the hands of the city bosses into those of the electorate. His ideas gave shape to the moralistic, middle-class crusade already under way against corruption. Haynes, and men like him, led the fight in denouncing municipal and state "boodlers," seeking to replace them in public office with honestly elected citizens. Their ideal was to make government responsive to public sentiment, to limit the power of corporations, especially the Southern Pacific, as well as that of wheedling legislators. One of Haynes's acts was the establishment of a foundation bearing his name, with the goal of raising the moral standards of public life.

Through the influence of Dr. Haynes and civic-minded fellow citizens, Los Angeles became one of the first cities in the nation to
adopt the measures of initiative, referendum, and recall as part of
its charter. During 1909 the electorate forced Mayor Arthur C. Harper to resign after he became involved in a sugar company stock
speculation. Harper had received the support of the Southern Pacific
machine while running for office, a fact that did not help the mayor's
popularity.

Success in using these new techniques for strengthening the power
of voters provided an example for other California cities, as did the
San Francisco graft trials—even though culprits remained unpunished. Soon reform elements sought the resignation of graft-tainted
officials at Sacramento, Oakland, Fresno, and Santa Barbara.

The Lincoln–Roosevelt League

On August 1, 1907 a new political alignment within the Republican
party, the California progressives, formed the Lincoln–Roosevelt
League. The founders of the league were liberal Republicans, who
used the names of both of their greatest party leaders to symbolize
freeing the Republican party in California from domination by corrupt interests. The president himself gave his blessing to the group,
which was made up of well-educated business and professional men.
The platform of the Lincoln–Roosevelt League pledged to free the
state from domination by the Southern Pacific, reflecting the changing national mood regarding regulation of business.

In 1910 the league ran Hiram W. Johnson—a stocky little man in
a tight vest with the gleam of reform in his eye—as its candidate for
governor. Johnson had achieved fame in the last days of the San
Francisco graft prosecutions, which he had taken over after Heney
was shot. Now forty-four, a stubborn and steel-nerved politician,
Johnson knew how to put the diffuse talents of his supporters to use.
During his 20,000-mile automobile campaign, over rocky, unpaved
roads, two powerful newspapermen, Edward A. Dickson of the Los
Angeles *Express* and Chester A. Rowell of the Fresno *Republican*,
proved of great service to Johnson. With their help he won the governorship against four candidates and led progressive Republican
legislators to Sacramento.

The Lincoln–Roosevelt League succeeded in an objective that neither the Republicans nor the Democrats had been able to accomplish
in a generation—the overthrow of one of the nation's most entrenched political systems. The legislature of 1911 racked up a record
that was the envy of progressives in every state of the Union, receiving praise from Theodore Roosevelt. Measures providing for in-

itiative, referendum, and recall were among the first to be adopted. Then came bills designed to cut down on the prerogatives of political machines and bosses. Previously the parties had nominated senatorial candidates within politically safe conventions. The Direct Primary Law, originally passed in 1909, and amended in 1911 and again in 1913, secured nomination of candidates by the voters themselves.

The state legislature of 1911 also added a total of twenty-three amendments to the constitution, all subsequently adopted by the voters. These amendments concerned such vital issues as control of public utilities, workmen's compensation, regulation of weights and measures, conservation of natural resources, income-tax provisions, and women's suffrage. Other progressive measures included a "blue-sky" law for protection of the securities investor, a civil-service law, laws providing for mothers' pensions, and the establishment of a minimum wage for women and minor children. There were also bills that provided for nonpartisan elections and permitted cities to adopt the commission form of government.

The reforms seem routine today, but in their time the measures enacted by the California progressives were major innovations. A black spot in the record of these reformers, however, was their insistence upon Asiatic exclusion. One writer has called Johnson and his retinue racists whose liberalism did not extend to minority groups. Yet one should remember that both liberals and conservatives before World War I were opposed to unrestricted immigration.

The major achievement of the progressive victory in California was the retreat of the Southern Pacific from state and local politics. Belatedly recognizing the disadvantage of its unpopular operations, the corporation professed to welcome the opportunity "to divorce itself from its former relations to politics." As governor, Johnson, along with the state legislature, made sure that the railroads would be the servants and not the masters of the people. By the use of cross-filing, progressive candidates after 1912 could become the nominees of more than one party. Indeed, henceforth a candidate's affiliation need not even be identified on primary ballots. This allowed progressives to retain Republican registration and to influence that party's structure. California's historically generous educational system also stems from the progressives.

Our generation, having forgotten their pioneering efforts to civilize corporations, is less grateful for the progressive legacy. The progressives became victims of change in intellectual fashion.

Progressive Decline

By 1912 progressives had become deeply involved in the movement to found a third national political group, the Progressive party, under

*Hiram Johnson (Republican), governor 1910–1917;
United States senator, 1917–1945.* (California State
Library.)

the leadership of Theodore Roosevelt. This "Bull Moose" party was
to split the Republicans into a reformist wing that provided an alternative to old guard conservatives represented by Roosevelt's successor, President Taft, and to city political machines of the Democratic party. Roosevelt was nominated for the presidency on this
ticket, with California's Governor Johnson as his running mate. The
pair carried the state by a narrow margin that year, but lost the
national election. Johnson's excursion into national politics retarded
his reform program in the next session of the legislature. Disorga-
nized by defeat, the California progressives lost much of their drive.
These former fire-eaters later became tired reformers. Johnson was,
nevertheless, returned to the governorship under the Progressive
party banner. His second administration was primarily concerned
with reorganizing inefficient departments, enforcing dormant regulations, and invigorating the state's creaky political machinery.

The confusion engendered in the election of 1912 made itself felt again in the presidential campaign of 1916, when Charles Evans Hughes ran on the regular Republican party ticket against President Woodrow Wilson. As part of a national reform effort, Johnson ran for the United States Senate. Wilson's victory in 1916, by only 3,700 votes, was due partly to Johnson's antipathy to Hughes. Both men stood aloof from each other. In August 1916, Hughes visited California with campaign advisers but kept in poor contact with Governor Johnson. Moreover, a feud had broken out between the Republican party's central committee and Johnson. Hughes did nothing to heal the breach while in California. Not only did Hughes offend labor-union members by eating in a San Francisco club that displayed an open-shop sign; he also scarcely realized the extent of Johnson's egotism and power in his home state. Both men were momentarily in the same hotel, the Virginia of Long Beach, without meeting. Johnson felt snubbed by Hughes. With Republican victory the goal of both, their advisers were at fault in allowing such a tense situation to develop.

Johnson, resentful toward Hughes, had failed to campaign vigorously for his fellow Republican. Had he done so any more than half-heartedly, he might have swung the state for Hughes, but its electoral votes went to Wilson, leaving Hughes only twelve votes short of the presidency. Some asserted that it was the California vote that lost Hughes the election. But he also lost Ohio, Montana, Nebraska, Kansas, Maryland, Missouri, and Oklahoma; California was reflecting a national pattern. Furthermore, California could then cast only thirteen electoral votes—in contrast, for example, to Ohio's twenty-four. California's contribution to Wilson's "gallon of victory" was not necessarily the vital fourth quart.

Johnson's race for the Senate in the election of 1916 had been worrisome, in view of recent Progressive defeats. He was anxious not to alienate potential Democratic voters, and this may be one reason why he had not worked hard for Hughes or criticized Wilson strongly. Johnson won the seat (with both the Progressive and Republican nominations) by almost 300,000 votes. He kept the senatorship for nearly thirty years, until his death in 1945.

National issues eclipsed the now-defunct Progressive movement. Like other states, California ratified the Eighteenth Amendment to the federal Constitution by vote of its legislature in January 1919, thus becoming the twenty-fifth of the states to approve Prohibition. Numerous towns in southern California had already adopted local prohibition; but, chiefly because of its large vineyards and wine interests, California was erroneously supposed to be a stronghold of "wet" forces.

After the election of Warren Harding to the presidency in 1920, California reverted to orthodox mainline Republicanism. In the decades between the two world wars the state gave its vote to Coolidge and Hoover. Not until the New Deal era of Franklin D. Roosevelt was there any significant change in this voting trend. Meanwhile, the old Progressives had to campaign under other labels.

Despite their eclipse in the period after World War I, the progressives had made an ineradicable mark on the history of California. They not only had cleaned up state and local government but had also improved its efficiency. Without seeking to destroy the capitalistic economic structure, they had called attention to its weaknesses. Although self-righteous, their criticisms of society occurred in an atmosphere of reasonableness. Their goal, "to kick the Southern Pacific out of state politics forever," was attained. Had the Republican party in 1912 not split into conservative and reform wings, the Progressive campaigns might have gone even further.

Selected Readings

Violence in the San Joaquin Valley during the 1880s is described in J. L. Brown's *The Mussel Slough Tragedy* (Fresno, 1958), and in Irving McKee, "Notable Memorials to Mussel Slough," *Pacific Historical Review* 17 (February 1948), 19–27. Financial involvements of the railroad are the subject of an article by H. J. Carman and C. H. Mueller, "The Contract and Finance Company and the Central Pacific Railroad," *Mississippi Valley Historical Review* 14 (December 1927), 326–41. A pro-company apologia is Cerinda W. Evans, *Collis Potter Huntington* (2 vols., Newport News, Va., 1954). Consult also David Lavender, *The Great Persuader* (New York, 1970), and Ralph N. Traxler, "Collis P. Huntington and the Texas and Pacific Railroad Land Grants," *New Mexico Historical Review* 34 (April 1959), 117–33. Railroad involvement in the free-harbor controversy is the subject of Charles D. Willard, *The Free Harbor Contest at Los Angeles* (Los Angeles, 1899), and Edith Dobie's *The Political Career of Stephen Mallory White* (Stanford, 1927).

The alliance between politicians and the railroads is discussed in Norman E. Tutorow, *Leland Stanford, Man of Careers* (Menlo Park, Calif., 1971), and Ward McAfee, *California's Railroad Era, 1850–1911* (San Marino, Calif., 1973); also see Morley Segal, "James Rolph, Jr., and the Early Days of the San Francisco Municipal Railway," California Historical Society *Quarterly* 43 (March 1964), 3–18, as well as Judd Kahn, *Imperial San Francisco: Politics and Planning, 1897–1906* (Lincoln, Nebr., 1980).

One of the great books of its time is J. Lincoln Steffens, *The Autobiography of Lincoln Steffens* (2 vols., New York, 1931). The leading work on the reform movement in California prior to World War I is George E. Mowry, *The California Progressives* (Berkeley, 1951). See also Spencer C. Olin, *California's Prodigal Sons: Hiram Johnson and the Progressives, 1911–1917* (Berkeley, 1968) as well as his survey, *California Politics, 1846–1920* (San Francisco, 1981). Concerning corruption in San Francisco, see Walton Bean, *Boss Ruef's San Francisco* (Berkeley, 1952); an older source on the same subject is Franklin Hichborn, *The System* (San Francisco, 1915). Elements of the graft prosecutions in that city emerge from Fremont Older, *My Own Story* (San Francisco, 1919), and Evelyn Wells, *Fremont Older* (New York, 1916), as well as from Steffens's account. A charming popularization is Bruce Bliven, "The Boodling Boss and the Musical Mayor," *American Heritage* 11 (December 1959), 8–11, 100–104. More flamboyant and recent is Lately Thomas, *A Debonair Scoundrel: An Episode in the Moral History of San Francisco* (New York, 1962). Corrective accounts are Robert Del Pippo, "Eugene E. Schmitz, 1864–1928: 23rd Mayor of San Francisco, An Historical Reassessment," M. A. Thesis, University of San Francisco, 1965, and James P. Walsh, "Abe Ruef Was No Boss," *California Historical Quarterly* 51 (Spring 1972), 3–16.

Regarding the San Francisco earthquake and fire of 1906 see William Bronson, *The Earth Shook, the Sky Burned* (New York, 1959); Monica Sutherland, *The Damndest Finest Ruins* (New York, 1959); John C. Kennedy, *The Great Earthquake and Fire, San Francisco 1906* (New York, 1963); and Gordon Thomas and M. M. Witts, *The San Francisco Earthquake* (New York, 1971).

An inside view of the Hughes-Johnson misunderstanding of 1916 is Edward A. Dickson, "How Hughes Lost California in 1916," *Congressional Record* (Washington, D.C., August 19, 1954). One should also read F. M. Davenport, "Did Hughes Snub Johnson?" *American Political Science Review* 40 (April 1949), 321–32. Informative as to Progressive techniques is J. Gregg Layne, "The Lincoln–Roosevelt League," Historical Society of Southern California *Quarterly* 25 (September 1943), 79–101. Analysis of Governor Johnson's role is in A. Lincoln, "Theodore Roosevelt, Hiram Johnson, and the Vice Presidential Nomination of 1912," *Pacific Historical Review* 28 (August 1959), 267–83. Another election is described in H. Brett Melendy, "California's Cross-Filing Nightmare: The 1918 Gubernatorial Election," *Pacific Historical Review* 33 (August 1964), 317–30. More on cross-filing is in Franklin Hichborn, "The Party, the Machine, and the Vote: The Story of Cross-filing in California Politics," California Historical Society *Quarterly* 38 (December 1959), 349–57, and 39 (March 1960), 19–34; and James C. Findley, "Cross-filing and the Progressive Movement in California Politics," *Western Political Quarterly* 12 (September 1959), 699–711.

A description of what happened to the reform frenzy is Jackson K. Putnam, "The Persistence of Progressivism in the 1920's: The

Case of California," *Pacific Historical Review* 35 (November 1966), 395–411. Other works include: Thomas G. Patterson, "California Progressives and Foreign Policy," California Historical Society *Quarterly* 47 (December 1968), 329–42; Eric Falk Petersen, "The Adoption of the Direct Primary in California," *Southern California Quarterly* 54 (Winter 1972), 363–78; and John L. Shover, "The California Progressives and the 1924 Campaign," *California Historical Quarterly* 51 (Spring 1971), 17–34.

CHAPTER 29

Material Growth

THE SAN FRANCISCO EARTHQUAKE and fire, the most cataclysmic event in the history of California, sharply set back the growth of the city's population. On the other hand, the heavy damage gave years of booming employment to the building trades. Suppliers of plumbing, hardware, roofing, and similar products prospered. Civic leaders demanded a rebuilding of the city on a grander scale than ever before.

Further south, once the struggle over the location of Los Angeles's new harbor ended, Angeleños went on to develop a great new port. In 1909, legal consolidation of the coastal towns of San Pedro and Wilmington with Los Angeles occurred as the result of an intricate piece of political gerrymandering. A connecting "shoestring" of land only five hundred feet wide, stretching more than fifteen miles to Wilmington, had been annexed to Los Angeles to provide an extended harbor district that represents a significant engineering achievement for its time. Because the harbor was protected only haphazardly from the sea by Point Fermin, War Department engineers had to construct an elongated breakwater to protect both shipping and wharves.

These new port facilities, whose construction was followed by opening of the Panama Canal in 1914, made Los Angeles one of the world's most important harbor cities. By 1924, Los Angeles had eclipsed San Francisco in total annual tonnage and had become the biggest port on the Pacific Coast. Situated on the great circle route to the Orient, Los Angeles harbor continued to enjoy an enormous growth in the 1920s. Meanwhile, the city was becoming a labyrinth of steel and concrete, expanding rapidly as a population shift occurred from northern California southward. Los Angeles pushed its boundaries over the Hollywood Hills toward San Fernando. On the west it came to bound Culver City and northward to adjoin Burbank, Glendale, Pasadena, Alhambra, Vernon, Huntington Park, South Pasadena, Torrance, Inglewood, Gardena, Hawthorne, El Segundo, and Long Beach. From the foothills of the Santa Monica Mountains the city encompassed the Verdugo Hills and eventually included more than 450 square miles of land. "L.A." has been referred to as "a group of suburbs in search of a city."

Urban transportation was vital in the growth of both San Francisco and Los Angeles. After 1915, as the northern city increased in size, Francis Marion Smith, "the borax king," developed the Key Route Electric Railway to supplement the city's Peninsular Electric Railway, which found a counterpart at Los Angeles in Henry E. Huntington's expansion of his network of "big red electric cars," the Pacific Electric. At its height the latter transportation web operated nine hundred cars over eleven hundred miles of track. By the mid-1920s Los Angeles County contained more than forty incorporated cities within its limits, and its transport facilities were already strained.

Further south, John D. and Adolph Spreckels poured millions of dollars into the development of San Diego, including the renowned Hotel del Coronado (1887). After the turn of the century, Katherine Tingley and her Theosophists began their colony at Point Loma. As the Horton House of the 1870s gave way to the U.S. Grant Hotel, few even remembered William Heath Davis's shaky attempts to build San Diego in the 1850s. The city's 1908 welcome of President Theodore Roosevelt's "Great White Fleet" ushered in the era of San Diego as a naval center. Its development reached eastward to the Imperial Valley and southward to Tijuana—described in 1905 as "a wide place on a poor road." By 1915 San Diego saw the appearance of a Hispanic architecture boom, begun at San Diego's Panama–California Exposition. There followed the development by the Ryan Aeronautical Corporation of Charles E. Lindbergh's world-famous airplane, the "Spirit of Saint Louis." Among the other personalities who helped to make San Diego better known were E. S. Babcock, Ellen Browning Scripps, and U. S. Grant, Jr., as well as the controversial Charles B. Hatfield, "The Rainmaker."

California and World War I

The prosperity of California was stimulated by World War I. Though the state was remote from zones of combat, it became involved in the national war effort. A few Eastern factories were beginning to establish branches in the San Francisco Bay area. Eastern capital attracted new immigration westward and pulled California closer toward the nation's total economic life.

Before World War I heavy employment had centered around food processing, including packing and canning, as well as lumber, mineral, and oil production. These activities flourished with renewed vigor, while the war encouraged diversification and industrial maturation. Demand for San Joaquin Valley cotton grew because of its use in the millions of new uniforms that had to be supplied to soldiers. Taking up the slogan, "Food Will Win the War!" the state also sent huge quantities of grains, fruits, meats, and vegetables into storehouses. California contributed more than 150,000 soldiers to the Allied forces, especially to the Ninety-first Division, which saw service in the Battle of the Argonne in France. As it had in the Civil War, California also gave generously to Liberty and Victory Loan drives, in each case exceeding the state quota.

When peace came, the economy of California had been lifted onto a new plateau of production of goods and services. A housing boom gave birth to dozens of new towns. In southern California these included San Clemente, a community of red-tile-roof houses on the ocean, the resort center of Palm Springs on the desert, and Lake Arrowhead Village in the mountains. Avid realtors developed large tracts of countryside into sites for furnace-less plaster palaces and multi-storied buildings. The suburbs of cities became dotted with small frame bungalows, which retired Iowa farmers might buy for as little as $1,000, as well as more expensive homes for those who preferred white "Spanish-style" stucco with palm trees in their yards. Aggressive tourist promotion by local chambers of commerce had been instrumental in creating this housing boom, which ended in 1929.

Developments in Mining

During World War I, demands had never been greater for gold and silver, as well as for soda, potash, and quicksilver. Miners developed new methods of extraction that increased production markedly. Hydraulic mining, which necessitated the digging of ditches and the construction of earthen dams, devastated hundreds of square miles of rich agricultural lands. Millions of tons of earth washed into the Yuba, Bear, and American rivers, filling their beds with boulders and yellow mud, known as "slickens." Before the 1920s, dredger mining had replaced the hydraulic method. The dredge was floated on a scow in an artificial pond fed by a ditch. A chain of heavy buckets brought up sand, rocks, and gravel, from which gold was washed out. Dredge engineers, like hydraulic engineers, created desolate wastes by sluicing out great piles of sand and rock.

The state mined increasing amounts of silver, copper, lead, quicksilver, manganese, tungsten, platinum, asbestos, diatomite, and marble. With the development of the automobile, prodigious quantities of asphalt and cement were required for highways, creating a new industry. Borax, or sodium borate, had been mined commercially since 1885, when the famed twenty-mule teams began to haul this mineral, used as a cleanser, out of Death Valley. By the 1920s California ranked second among the states in total mineral production, despite a lack of coal and iron deposits.

The Rise of the Oil Industry

From the time of the mission padres, petroleum was known to exist in the subsoil. Roaming cattle would fall into the tar and pitch sumps of southern California, as animals of prehistoric times had done. From the Mexican period onward, Angeleños had used asphalt, a sticky form of petroleum, for roofing. The first usable oil may have been found at Pico Canyon near San Fernando, but the earliest verifiable oil well in California was drilled in 1861 in Humboldt County. The next year a further venture was undertaken in Contra Costa County, near Martinez. Wildcatters also dug shallow wells all over the Santa Susana Mountains near Ventura, as well as at Santa Barbara and further north in the Humboldt Bay region.

Meanwhile, the first actual oil production west of Pennsylvania occurred in California's Ventura County without the drilling of wells. This operation had begun in 1859, after a whale-oil merchant investigated oil seepages near Los Angeles. On property belonging to Major Henry Hancock, he erected a small pot-still with which he produced semiliquid asphaltum. When Hancock drove him off the ranch, the entrepreneur set up a second still along the Ventura River.

By 1864 a touring professor of chemistry from Yale College, Benjamin Silliman, Jr., after seeing the oil seepages in Ventura County, wrote glowing reports on their commercial possibilities. The result of his account was the formation of two companies to exploit California oil resources, both firms controlled by the Pennsylvania Railroad. A combine, the Philadelphia & California Petroleum Company, drilled a well near the Camulos Ranch and seven other wells in the Ojai region between 1865 and 1867. One of the latter was California's first gusher.

Not until after the turn of the century were techniques developed for making a satisfactory illuminant from California crude oil, which is heavy and asphaltic-based. In the mid-1860s, crude oil was sold as fuel, without refining, as it came from the wellheads. After this initial frenzy of the 1860s died away, the oil industry entered a dormant period that was not interrupted until the mid-1870s, when the California Star Oil Company began drilling in southern California's Newhall Basin.

Scores of other small firms followed the California Star Oil Company. In no industry was competition fiercer than in oil refining. Because so many wells were dug and refineries set up, the market was glutted, and prices fell. The frenzied rush to new sites was reminiscent of the gold mania of 1848–1849. Few operators survived this experimental, if exciting, period of speculative enterprise. Despite the production of kerosene for illumination, tar for roofing, and oil for lubrication, the petroleum industry in those years before the invention of the internal-combustion engine suffered from limited markets and primitive operational techniques. In 1879 California Star became the Pacific Coast Oil Company, corporate ancestor of the Standard Oil Company of California. Pacific was then the dominant oil company of the state. By 1884 many companies had failed or been absorbed by larger operations.

California's oil industry of the early 1890s was revitalized by two men who were to profit greatly from vast underground reserves. These were Lyman Stewart and Edward L. Doheny. Stewart had made his first fortune, as a young man, in the oil rush at Titusville, Pennsylvania. In 1883, after overproduction occurred in the eastern United States—where monopolization quickly set in—Stewart headed west to begin a new career. Provided with land leases by T. R. Bard and the Pacific Coast Oil Company, Stewart spent several lean years prospecting for oil, forming, in 1890, the Union Oil Company. Two years later he struck a prodigious well in Adams Canyon, Ventura County, which flowed down the canyon into the Santa Clara River until it could be capped. This gusher alone produced 1,500 barrels of oil per day for Stewart.

The career of Edward L. Doheny is one of the most colorful in the history of American capitalism. Born in Wisconsin in 1856, Doheny started work as a government surveyor. In 1876, as a youth of twenty, he drifted into the Black Hills just as Dakota Territory was experiencing a silver and gold rush. Doheny next headed for Arizona and then Kingston, New Mexico, where another rush was under way. He worked as a mucker and hard-rock miner along the Mexican border, then as a miner in the Mojave Desert of California. With this experience and some money behind him, Doheny came to Los Angeles in 1892. On the streets of the city he noticed that brea, or tarry pitch, clung to the wheels of passing carriages and carts; he traced this substance to an oil seepage near Westlake Park. With a prospector friend, Charles A. Canfield, Doheny leased a city lot and began to dig. When they had, by the use of pick and shovel, reached a depth of fifty feet, the pair struck a pocket of gas that almost asphyxiated them. They then employed a driller who at 600 feet brought in a well with a capacity of forty-five barrels per day. This started a frantic oil boom that caused 2,300 wells to be dug in Los Angeles within the next five years.

A strange new skyline sprang up in the old pueblo, still no more than a formless community of muddy and crooked streets. Greasy little refineries were noisily hammered together, most of them shanty-like structures consisting of a few boards, with an iron drum for a still, and a "worm" in which oil vapors could be condensed. Derricks were erected in both front and back yards. Some Angeleños became wealthy, but others got nothing for their trouble except expensive drilling bills, uprooted gardens, and clouds of dry dust that coated their houses. A rich oil field surrounded La Brea pits where, in 1875, amateur paleontologists found the first remains of prehistoric animals—the skeleton of a saber-tooth cat that had been trapped in the tar seeps. By 1897 oil production in the Los Angeles area, including nearby Puente and Fullerton, had risen to 1,400,000 barrels per year. Five years later the figure reached 9,000,000 barrels.

Meanwhile, Doheny and other operators were having trouble marketing surplus oil. They sold some of it for spraying dusty streets and also persuaded manufacturers of pipe to use an oil coating to prevent rust. In October 1894, Doheny's competitors, the Union Oil Company, succeeded in converting a railroad locomotive, fitted with a tender and tank, into an oil burner for demonstration purposes. After successful runs near Santa Paula, the engine was used on the Cajon Pass grade to pull a string of loaded cars in an attempt to create a market for excess oil. The saving in adapting locomotive engines from coal to oil amounted to as much as 25 percent in daily operations. The Santa Fe Railroad agreed to pay $1 a barrel for oil, a price that seems low today but was appealingly high then. Prior to 1899 oil fluctuated in price from $1.50 downward to a few cents a barrel. By 1901, the Southern Pacific Railroad bought five hundred tank cars and built fifty storage tanks, marking its conversion, like the Santa Fe, from coal to fuel oil.

Encouraged by this new market, the oil industry embarked upon expanded operations at Coalinga in Fresno County, at Bakersfield, and along the Kern River. Doheny branched out to Peru and Mexico, where he not only drilled for oil but also developed techniques of paving automobile roads with asphalt. Such development of the industry was accompanied by extensive construction of equipment, especially tank cars and pipe lines, in order to handle the outpouring of California's oil fields. Once the needs of the automobile were felt, state oil production shot up to 77,697,568 barrels in 1910.

The Oil Boom of the 1920s

In the 1920s new discoveries took place in the San Joaquin Valley and in the Midway-Sunset, Lost Hills–Belridge, Elk Hills, Wheeler Ridge, and Kettleman Hills areas. In these zones oil was found in synclinal geological formations marked by domes. But expenses were high and risks great, with most wildcat wells turning out to be dry holes. In southern California new wells were brought in at Whittier, Fullerton, Coyote Hills, Montebello, Richfield, Compton, Torrance, and Inglewood. Along the coast, or near it, wells were drilled at Watsonville, Santa Maria, Ventura, and Newhall. But the greatest strikes were made in 1920 at Huntington Beach, near Los Angeles, and in 1921 at Santa Fe Springs and Signal Hill. These three fields contained such vast pools of oil that their discovery upset national prices and glutted existing storage facilities. Greater capital and experience were needed to exploit such vast underground reserves.

The Stewart interests, having converted themselves into the modern Union Oil Company, continued to look for new markets. Moving away from such simple products as kerosene, axle grease, and candle wax, Stewart encouraged development of a safe oil burner for marine engines. His firm also commissioned tanker vessels to transport oil to overseas markets, making California's industry a global one. A new company, the Tidewater Associated Corporation, was formed when fifty small companies in Kern County banded together to take better advantage of the opportunity to supply the new oil-burning railroad locomotives. The Pacific Coast Oil Company had become the Standard Oil Company of California, part of a national producing, refining, and marketing trust. In 1911, however, by Supreme Court decree, the Standard trust group was ordered dissolved. Having resumed its independent status, the Standard Oil Company of California proceeded to develop the Huntington Beach area. Meanwhile, Union Oil concentrated on Santa Fe Springs, while the third major field, Signal Hill, saw increasing activity on the part of the Shell Oil Company.

At Signal Hill, Indians had used this hillock, some 300 feet high, as a place from which to signal aborigines on Catalina Island, across the channel from Long Beach. Later, during Spanish times, it had served as a beacon for passing ships. In 1920, Shell of California spent $110,000 to lease part of the hill. Two years later Signal Hill reached a production of 244,000 barrels daily from 265 wells. By 1924, California ranked first in the production of petroleum products, with an output worth $333,292,000. This figure represented about 70 percent of the dollar value of the state's mineral production that year. Throughout the 1920s California led in Western oil pro-

"Spudding in" ceremonies in Compton, September 21, 1926. (Historical Collections, Security Pacific National Bank.)

duction, though new oil centers evolved in Texas, Louisiana, Oklahoma, and Wyoming during the succeeding decade.

Doheny attracted notoriety through his eagerness to obtain the Elk Hills reserves. This episode produced charges of corruption that led into the cabinet of President Warren G. Harding. It was revealed that on November 30, 1921, Doheny had secretly dispatched a satchel with $100,000 in it to Secretary of the Interior Albert B. Fall, "an old prospector friend" who officially held control of the Elk Hills reserves and of others at Teapot Dome, Wyoming. Secretary Fall claimed that the money was only a loan, but a scandal followed the revelation that he planned to lease these oil reserves to Doheny. In 1923, both Fall and Doheny were indicted for conspiracy to corner national resources. In 1928, Fall was convicted and sentenced to prison, although Doheny escaped punishment; in effect, he was acquitted of giving the bribe that Fall was convicted of taking.

The pioneer oil speculators of Doheny's generation lived in an age when California's oil reserves bubbled out of the earth, spilling uncontrolled down city streets, over gardens, and across vacant lots. It was common for promoters to convey prospective buyers of oil stock by the busload to auction sites, where retired preachers made fortunes hawking lots in tents pitched in a revival atmosphere. Great opportunities for corruption existed. In 1921 Courtney C. Julian, a Canadian-born oil driller, boomer, and supersalesman, advertised for funds in Los Angeles newspapers and raised $175,000 in one fortnight. He organized the Julian Petroleum Company, known as "Julian Pete," on the basis of a few wells leased on the edge of Signal Hill. After Julian had satisfied a few original stockholders with lucrative dividends, he was able to lure new investors with the testimonials of the first group. Then, by selling bogus stock in his dummy corporation, he made several million dollars. In 1925, after a public audit of his operations was demanded by outraged holders of worthless stock, he fled the state. Next Julian entered the mining stock business, bought a radio station to broadcast smears against his enemies, was accused of mail fraud, sailed for Shanghai one step ahead of the law, and committed suicide there in 1934.

In spite of an occasional checkered career such as that of Julian, oil development was to play an important role in California's economy. The industry, however, continued to suffer from overproduction, a boom-and-bust psychology, and from poor conservation methods. In the 1920s a veritable fever of speculation in real estate and in the stock market afflicted the nation and the state. The need arose to curtail output by agreements among major producers, but such arrangements led to charges of monopoly and price fixing. In later years production was cut back by other factors, including dwindling reserves and demands for conservation. Drilling techniques that

Oil field in the Central Valley. (By courtesy of Chevron Corporation.)

left millions of barrels of unrecoverable crude petroleum below the surface of the earth aroused public opinion to the need for government action. As time passed, regulation and taxation were imposed, yet the oil industry was able to obtain tax deductions based on high exploration costs and need for depletion allowances.

After 1929, a peak year of oil production, new discoveries, a mile below the surface, made Santa Fe Springs the state's largest producer. The Wilmington field caused a serious problem in the Long Beach area when land began to subside. Both Texas and Louisiana were forging ahead of California in oil production, although growing demands encouraged a search for new reserves. The average life of the best-producing wells was only twenty-five to thirty years; as production zones reached a mature phase, most wells had to be drilled deeper than 1,000 feet. These circumstances led drillers to look toward the ocean for new sources of oil, years before ocean wells were sunk elsewhere. In the 1930s they tapped offshore reserves from rigs anchored into the ocean floor. Development of the port of Long Beach, which was begun in 1938, financed in large measure by proceeds from drilling a rich field along its waterfront, created a new legal question—whether the state or federal government owned tideland oil resources. Final determination would have to await future legal decisions.

California's oil production, in the years following the first decades of the twentieth century, continued to climb until it reached a million barrels per day. Still later, however, it was to slip downward, making it necessary for the state to import foreign crude from Indonesia and Saudi Arabia.

From 1900 to 1930, California's oil industry had been dramatically spurred by the discovery of large new pools, by the development of better refining techniques, including the catalytic cracking process, and by new demands for fuel for factories, automobiles, trucks, and airplanes.

The Coming of the Automobile

There were not many cars on Western highways in the first years of the twentieth century. By 1919 there were fewer than 7 million passenger cars registered in the entire United States. Then, in the 1920s, the auto underwent a transformation from a sputtering plaything of the rich, which frightened ladies and horses, to a necessity of the working masses. Quantity production of the inexpensive Model T Ford, whose price dropped to $280, increased the number of cars nationally to over 23 million by 1929. Just under 2 million of these were the property of Californians. Numerically, this far exceeded that of other Western states (Nevada, 31,915; Arizona, 109,013; Utah, 112,661; Oregon, 269,007); and on a per capita basis, the California registration was the largest in the United States. Meanwhile, as tractors replaced horses on farms, and buses took the place of trolleys in the larger cities, mechanized transportation of all forms became common.

The auto markedly stimulated roadside enterprise. Service stations sprang up everywhere, providing—in addition to gasoline and minor adjustments—free air, road maps, and restrooms for the convenience of dusty motorists. Repair shops and garages to fix stubborn self-starters, inert spark plugs, and faulty brakes were indispensable to car owners, who were thereby relieved of such anxieties as the need to know such terms as *magneto, differential,* and *generator.* Supply houses were established to install seat covers, batteries, and side curtains. The growth of tourism led to the development of motels, which were locally owned until the national hotel chains arrived in California.

The manufacturers of new windshields, rubber tires and tubes, and automobiles remained centered in the large cities of the East. Only as demands increased did they move facilities to California. Its motorists sometimes felt that the state was functioning as a colonial appendage of large Eastern corporations.

Along with the phonograph, radio, and movies, the auto broke down the isolation of those who lived on farms and ranches. It also emancipated city workers, who came to use "the machine" for pleasure trips on weekends and during holiday periods. Gradually, too, automobiles stimulated the decentralization of cities, making it possible for people to live at some distance from their work. In the years from 1910 to 1930 California began to pull itself out of the mud, as rutted country lanes were converted into two-laned ribbons of concrete. These, in turn, gave way after the 1930s to four-lane macadamized highways, which remained in use until the advent of still larger freeways in the 1940s. The $18 million voted for road construction in 1910 seemed like a pittance a few years later. Highway routes 66, 70–99, and 101, major arteries, were built in part with federal funds. These highways changed the face of the California countryside, aiding the development of raw settlements in wild and empty deserts.

The automobile made for a new type of landscape. Railroad towns were displaced by crossroads with garages, filling stations, hot-dog stands, and tourist bungalows. Gypsy fortune tellers joined concessionaires desirous of doing business with unwary Easterners who drove past neon-lighted stucco booths shaped like a half orange. From these glared such highway signs as "All the Orange Juice You Can Drink for 10 Cents" and "Palmistry Will Tell Your Future in California."

Favorable climatic conditions, low gasoline prices, and ready access to desert, beach, and mountain helped to make Californians automobile-minded. Thousands of tourists were brought to the state each year by advertising which emphasized California's constant sunshine. The most popular resorts were the beaches from Santa Barbara to San Diego, Catalina Island, Lake Tahoe, Sequoia and Lassen National Parks, the Yosemite Valley in the High Sierra, the Russian River above San Francisco, Palm Springs on the desert, and Big Bear and Lake Arrowhead in the San Bernardino Mountains. Death Valley too became a winter tourist attraction. The control of traffic was a matter of great complexity, especially at Los Angeles and San Francisco, where congestion was heaviest. Meanwhile public transportation suffered a decline. At Los Angeles the interurban system established by the Pacific Electric Company perished in the interwar years. Railroads were forced to close down branch lines as buses and trucks took advantage of shorter routes between cities. Though accidents continued to mount, so did the demand for new cars. Whole boulevards, notably Figueroa and Alvarado Streets in Los Angeles, and

Broadway, looking south from Second Street, Los Angeles, June 8, 1889, at the opening of the cable car route. (C. C. Pierce Collection; by courtesy of The Huntington Library, San Marino, California.)

Pasadena Freeway, one of the first in the nation, mid-1950s. (Historical Collections, Security Pacific National Bank.)

Van Ness Avenue in San Francisco, came to be monopolized by auto dealers.

An Age of Prosperity

In the 1920s and 1930s, despite a national economic depression, California's domestic and foreign trade expanded. Increases in tourism and the growth of the mining, hydroelectric power, and cinema industries all helped to gain prominence for the state. The automobile and its subsidiary industries were largely responsible for this expansion. The assembly plants of Ford, Chrysler, and General Motors, the tire-production establishments of Firestone and Royal, and such firms as Libby-Owens-Ford Glass and Exide Batteries gave employment to thousands. Throughout the depression years, 1930 through 1937, automobile production remained surprisingly stable.

Accompanying a shift of population to such suburbs as Oakland and Long Beach, there arose a need to finance new residential and manufacturing construction. Banks were now consolidated into large-scale institutions capable of loaning millions of dollars annually. In 1929, a merger created the Security First National Bank of Los Angeles. This gave southern California one of the country's largest banks. The largest of all was the Bank of Italy, later the Bank of America. Founded in 1904 at San Francisco by Amadeo Pietro Giannini, son of an Italian immigrant, it developed a system of branch banking that came to dwarf other banks. Geared to the needs of the small depositor, Giannini's system spread beyond the boundaries of the state, and even of the nation. For a time the Bank of America became the largest bank in the world, helping to gain financial status for San Francisco, where its headquarters remained.

The growth of California during the interwar period is mirrored in the record established by its largest city. In 1921 Harry Chandler, who had become the publisher of the Los Angeles *Times*, called a conference to examine ways by which the tourist trade might be increased. The businessmen and real estate boosters who attended helped him form the "All-Year Club of Southern California," designed to advertise the wonders of Los Angeles in Eastern newspapers. In the heady spirit of the 1920s, this organization did much to attract new residents as well as visitors.

By 1930, 2,300,000 people lived within a thirty-mile radius of the city. Yet, only in the early thirties did "L.A." develop a genuine civic center, with its new Spanish-style Union passenger railroad terminal and nearby complex of government buildings. Between 1930 and 1940 the city also celebrated its 150th anniversary, was host to the Tenth Olympiad in a new coliseum, saw the arrival of the first streamlined transcontinental trains, built an observatory at Griffith Park, constructed a metropolitan water system, and laid the groundwork for what was to become a wartime aircraft industry.

Meanwhile, San Francisco strengthened its opera, symphony orchestra, and museums, improved Golden Gate Park, and built the remarkable Bay bridges to supplant ferry boats previously in operation. On May 27, 1939, the day the Golden Gate Bridge opened, 200,000 people walked across the span. That same year San Francisco was host to the Golden Gate International Exposition, the "World's Fair of the West." Exactly 17,041,999 persons paid the entrance fee for this largest exposition ever held west of Chicago. The island in the middle of San Francisco Bay, site of the fairgrounds, was to have become an airport after the fair, but because of World War II it became a naval base instead.

San Francisco has always been a tourist mecca, with its exotic Chinatown, cable cars, restaurants, Coit Tower, and Golden Gate, through which ships stream in a constant procession. During the 1930s the city's shipyards, drydocks, and canneries continued expansion; but this was also a period of experimentation. Captain Robert Dollar made San Francisco the home port of steamship companies, while the city was becoming an air center. On November 22, 1935, Pan American Airways' "China Clipper" soared off to establish the first air link between North America and the mainland of China.

The spectacular growth of California's population during the twenties and thirties was part of a larger pattern. This increase has gone on unabated since the gold rush. By 1940, on the eve of World War II, the state's population numbered 6,907,387. Los Angeles was a metropolis of 1,504,277 persons, and San Francisco one of 634,536. Outside San Francisco, commuters found new "bedrooms" in the suburbs of Alameda, Oakland, Berkeley, and Burlingame. With the promise of further expansion ahead, the contrast between the nineteenth and twentieth centuries was to become even more marked. Like other urban centers, California would become overdeveloped as to population but underdeveloped in the means for dealing with its most pressing problems.

Selected Readings

A study of the transition of a town to a city is Oscar Osborn Winther, "The Rise of Metropolitan Los Angeles, 1870–1900," *Huntington Library Quarterly* 10 (August 1947), 391–405. The role of climate in this growth is discussed by Winther in "The Use of Climate as a Means of Promoting Migration to Southern California" (San Marino, 1959). Health as a migration factor is the topic of John E. Baur's

200,000 people walk north across Golden Gate Bridge at its opening on May 27, 1939. (By courtesy of the San Francisco Chronicle.)

Health Seekers of Southern California (San Marino, 1959). The transportation system that supported the growth of Los Angeles is the subject of Spencer Crump's *Ride the Big Red Cars: How Trolleys Helped Build Southern California* (Los Angeles, 1962). The phenomenal growth of Los Angeles is examined too in W. W. Robinson, *Los Angeles from the Days of the Pueblo* (Los Angeles, 1959), and in Andrew Rolle, *Los Angeles: From Pueblo to City of the Future* (San Francisco, 1981). Construction of Los Angeles harbor is discussed in Charles A. Matson's *Building a World Gateway* (Los Angeles, 1945).

San Francisco is the subject of A. R. Neville, *The Fantastic City* (Boston, 1932), and Charles C. Dobie, *San Francisco's Chinatown* (New York, 1936). Frank Parker has paid tribute to a civic symbol in *Anatomy of the San Francisco Cable Car* (Stanford, 1946). The harbor is described in William Martin Camp, *San Francisco, Port of Gold* (New York, 1947), while Robert W. Cherny and William Issel, *San Francisco* (San Francisco, 1981) is a general history.

The role of banks in urban growth is developed in *The Biography of a Bank: The Story of Bank of America* (New York, 1954), by Marquis James. Descriptions of the oil industry are in Frank F. Latta, *Black Gold in the San Joaquin* (Caldwell, Idaho, 1949). See, regarding the Union Oil Company, Frank J. Taylor and Earl M. Welty, *Black Bonanza* (New York, 1950). A brochure, produced by the American Petroleum Institute, is *California's Oil* (New York, 1948). Consult also R. G. Percy, "The First Oil Development in California," *California Historian* 6 (December 1959), 29–30. Regarding Doheny, see I. F. Marcosson, *The Black Golconda* (New York, 1924). Doheny and Stewart are both treated in Ruth S. Knowles, *The Greatest Gamblers* (New York, 1959). Other oil history sources include: Gerald T. White, *Formative Years in the Far West, A History of Standard Oil Company of California and Predecessors Through 1919* (New York, 1962); W. H. Hutchinson, *Oil, Land, and Politics: The California Career of Thomas Robert Bard* (Norman, Okla., 1965); and Walker A. Tompkins, *Little Giant of Signal Hill: An Adventure in American Enterprise* (Englewood Cliffs, N.J., 1967). Spectacular photos are in Kenny Franks and Paul Lambert's *Early California Oil: A Photographic History, 1865–1940* (College Station, Tex., 1985).

Regarding "the automobile era," see Phil T. Hanna, "The Wheel and the Bell," *Westways* 42 (December 1960), 41–56, and Mark S. Foster, "The Model-T, the Hard Sell, and Los Angeles's Urban Growth: the Decentralization of Los Angeles During the 1920's," *Pacific Historical Review* 44 (November 1975), 459–84. Mostly pictorial are Bruce Henstell, *Los Angeles, An Illustrated History* (New York, 1980), and his *Sunshine and Wealth: Los Angeles in the Twenties* (San

Francisco, 1985), as well as David Gebhard and Hariette Von Breton, *Los Angeles in the Thirties* (Santa Barbara, 1975). More detailed is Willis Miller, "The Port of Los Angeles–Long Beach, 1929–1979, A Comparative Study," *Southern California Quarterly* 65 (Winter 1983), 341–78.

CHAPTER 30

Water, Conservation, and Agricultural Growth

THE MIGRATION INTO the state that accompanied the automobile could not have been supported without water. Larger cities and small farming communities alike were obliged to find new sources when local wells and streams began to fail them. Only in 1884 did a state-wide irrigation convention meet in Riverside to discuss water usage. Not until 1887 did state legislators pass the Wright Act, providing for water-conservation districts. From 1900 onward, however, hundreds of millions of dollars were spent on dams, wells, canals, reservoirs, and aqueducts. Especially in semiarid southern California, irrigated agriculture—once ridiculed by farmers—became wide-spread. At the same time new communities of the southland were wisely building upon the conservation experiments of George Chaffey, who had led the way toward replenishing dwindling water supplies of older communities.

Los Angeles and the Owens Valley

Los Angeles displayed particular interest in Chaffey's diversion of streams, creation of lakes, and storage of subsurface water. Located at the center of a dry belt of settlements, Los Angeles faced a genuine water crisis by 1904, when it became apparent that the city reservoirs were barely able to take in enough water to equal their outflow. The city *had* to find new sources of water. Its solution to the dilemma was to tap the Owens River in the far-off southern Sierra—a scheme that became one of the most controversial projects in the history of the state. In 1904, Chief City Engineer William Mulholland, with the support of his predecessor in the office, Fred Eaton, recommended that a bond issue be put on the ballot to provide for construction of a $25 million aqueduct that would traverse the 238 miles from the Owens Valley to Los Angeles. Mulholland and Eaton argued that building such an aqueduct was the only way to relieve shortages created by continued reliance upon the Los Angeles River, an uncertain underground stream that was then the city's major water source.

Construction of a pipe and flume system across the Mojave Desert, to catch the melted snow of the southern Sierra, began in 1908. Utilizing an army of several thousand workers, Mulholland completed his complex network of tunnels and trenches in less than five years. In November 1913, to commemorate a feat considered second only to the building of the Panama Canal, a celebration was held at the San Fernando Valley spillway where the aqueduct terminated. About these festivities the faraway New York *Times* reported on November 5:

> Thousands of citizens went, this morning, to the head of San Fernando Valley, 23 miles north of the city, and saw General Adna R. Chaffey lift the gates which turned into the San Fernando reservoir a flow, assuring to the city 260,000,000 gallons of water every 24 hours. . . . Field pieces of the National Guard fired a salute, a band played and the crowds waved flags and shouted as the gates were opened. Fifteen thousand automobiles were parked in a neighboring field.

In spite of glowing newspaper accounts, controversy developed over the project. Violent criticism of Mulholland and the Los Angeles city fathers came from ranchers and farmers forced to evacuate their Owens Valley homes under threat of eviction. Sportsmen who loved to fish in the valley, as well as outdoorsmen and naturalists, joined in the chorus of protest. In *The Story of Inyo* (1922), W. A. Chalfant aired charges of corruption and intrigue, while a newspaperman, Morrow Mayo, wrote a book entitled *Los Angeles* (1933) that included a section on "The Rape of Owens Valley." Although both Chalfant and Mayo exaggerated the facts, their emotional accounts came to be accepted by historians. The reputation of Los Angeles as a looter of water resources from a pastoral paradise has persisted to the present day, with many critics convinced that private interests benefited most from the Owens Valley Project.

Mayo charged that a syndicate of bankers and real-estate operators, organized to develop the Van Nuys area of the San Fernando Valley, formed the pressure group that bought up fallow land with the purpose of making a financial killing when the valley was irrigated by Owens River water. Mayo's allegation is subject to dispute, in view of the involvement of the United States Reclamation Service, in whose judgment the Owens Valley Project was a necessity for Los Angeles. Residents of the four Owens River towns of Big Pine, Lone Pine, Bishop, and Independence were, however, led to believe that the land syndicate profited unfairly at their expense, because the properties of the syndicate were able to draw upon huge reservoirs outside Los Angeles to store Owens water.

These citizens of the Owens Valley appealed in vain to the chief forester of the United States, Gifford Pinchot, and to President Theodore Roosevelt. Roosevelt sided with Los Angeles. He even ordered the Bureau of Reclamation to extend existing government "forest" lands into the valley. These lands were then made available to the Los Angeles aqueduct. Meanwhile, dispossessed Owensites continued to regard that project as a swindle rather than as a piece of aggressive vision. Pathetic stories in the national press dwelt upon the privations inflicted upon them because of the beastly aqueduct.

Next certain Owens Valley residents engaged in three events against that menace to them. The first took place on August 17, 1923, when ranchers near Big Pine armed themselves with rifles and stood guard over the headgate of Big Pine Ditch to prevent diversion of water from the Owens River into the aqueduct. Next May, a spillway near Lone Pine was dislodged by dynamite and large pieces of the aqueduct were torn away. The last in the series of attempts to damage Los Angeles's new water facilities was the opening of the Alabama wastegates, five miles north of Lone Pine, on November 16, 1924. The protesters turned the flow of the aqueduct into the bed of the Owens River. When this show of force too was unavailing, concerted opposition by valley residents collapsed.

Throughout the 1920s the charge was repeated that Los Angeles had coerced landowners into selling property for unfair prices. City officials countered these accusations by pointing out that the average price paid was $145 per acre, as opposed to a normal price of around $100 per acre. Nevertheless, the seizure of the Owens River had given the city an unsavory reputation in the mountain areas of the state. The slogan "Remember the Owens Valley" reminded northern legislators for years to come of the seizure of land for water-development purposes.

In 1928 renewed criticism of William Mulholland arose when a dam he had constructed in San Francisquito Canyon near the town of Saugus, part of the Owens Aqueduct, collapsed. Close to midnight on March 12 of that year, an avalanche of water cascaded down the narrow Santa Clara Valley to Santa Paula, fifty miles away. Houses, trees, telephone poles, bridges, and railroad tracks were swept away, with 385 people losing their lives. Courageously, Mulholland accepted the blame for having built his dam on a weak and friable bedrock and clay substratum, and thus ended his career of public service on an unhappy note.

From the beginning of the Owens Valley Project it had many defenders who emphasized its contributions to Los Angeles and to the valley itself. Supporters pointed to new roads in the Owens Valley, constructed and improved in connection with building the aqueduct. Valley residents who once sold alfalfa were able to turn to more profitable enterprises serving the Sierra tourist trade, opening new highway businesses. The city of Los Angeles reimbursed those whose homes and farms had been confiscated, in addition to paying for the lands of owners willing to sell out. The aqueduct was recognized as an engineering achievement that would benefit hundreds of thousands of people and insure growth of an important city. The new water supply also made feasible establishment of power generation, capable of producing cheap electricity for thousands of homes and factories. With the subsequent addition of Crowley Lake, a large storage reservoir on the eastern slope of the Sierra, Los Angeles was able to garner yet another source of water from the upper Mono basin.

San Francisco too had to cope with a water shortage in the early years of the twentieth century. Although located in an area of heavier rainfall, the city's demands for water would soon exceed the supply. Civic leaders had long been eyeing the Hetch Hetchy Valley near Yosemite National Park as a source of water. John Muir and other naturalists, however, objected strongly to the San Francisco plan, which would inundate the scenic valley, diverting water from the Tuolomne River. Their protests to the United States Department of Interior retarded construction of the proposed dam for years. Federal authorization, however, came in 1913 when Franklin K. Lane, former city and county attorney of San Francisco, became secretary of the interior. San Francisco finally completed its Hetch Hetchy aqueduct and power network in 1931. Although the project cost the then-phenomenal price of $100 million, it proved less than essential to the city's growth.

The Boulder Canyon Project

By 1923, while controversy over the Owens Valley Project was still a public issue, Los Angeles faced much the same conditions that had led it to embark on that water-development measure almost twenty years before. The city was adding 100,000 new residents per year to its population, which was approaching a total of 2 million. To solve the disparity between daily intake and outflow of city reservoirs, desperate means were considered. Consultations with occult rain makers, Indian medicine men, water dowsers, and other "weather experts" confirmed the belief that construction of new dams was the best solution to the water shortage.

As early as 1922 representatives of Colorado, Wyoming, Utah, New Mexico, Arizona, Nevada, and California met in Santa Fe to sign a Colorado River Water Compact. This document provided for development of the basin of that river for use of the participating states. Although Secretary of Commerce Herbert Hoover cooperated in the allotment of water rights to these states, it was not until 1928 that a law (the Swing–Johnson Bill) was passed by the United States Congress to permit construction of the dam in Boulder Canyon that was basic to the proposal. The project was to be undertaken jointly by the federal government, the states, and municipalities. The aims were to protect the Imperial Valley against recurrent threats of flooding, to provide a multi-state water reserve, and to generate hydroelectric energy for an expanding Southwest.

A federal bill of 1930 allocated almost $11 million to begin construction. Most of the major cities of Los Angeles County formed a Metropolitan Water District to coordinate water and power distribution for southern California. In 1931 the district floated a bond issue of over $200 million for construction. The Depression blunted sale of the bonds, but the federal government's new Reconstruction Finance Corporation assumed a share of the financing of the Boulder Canyon Project. In fact, this project became one of the nation's most important public works, supported by the government in an effort to ameliorate the Depression. The enterprise, with Hoover Dam in Boulder Canyon as its dominant structure, was, for its time, one of the largest construction jobs in the world. The dam, 1,282 feet high, required the combined efforts of six large construction companies employing 10,000 workers; the latter had to be housed in a new town, Boulder City, built expressly for the purpose. An artificial lake 242 miles long, Lake Mead, was constructed in connection with the dam, as well as a complicated system of conduits, flumes, reservoirs, and pumping plants to transport water from the lake. Despite opposition from private utility companies, Army engineers, and the state of Arizona, Hoover Dam, with its storage facility, Parker Dam, was completed on March 1, 1936. Huge generators pumped electrical energy into homes, farms, and industrial plants throughout the Southwest.

Piercing its way through six mountain ranges, the aqueduct provided a lifeline to the communities drawing upon it. The Metropolitan Water District erected a costly diversion dam to deflect water westward for 242 miles to Los Angeles. The Imperial Irrigation District, similarly diverted Colorado River water at Imperial Dam, above Yuma, Arizona, and transported it 80 miles along the 200-foot-wide All-American Canal, to the Imperial Valley. A 125-mile extension of this canal, to serve the Coachella Valley, was not completed until 1948. Without the Boulder Canyon Project, southern California could not have expanded commercially and industrially as it has. Hoover Dam, furthermore, safeguards the Imperial Valley and communities surrounding the Gulf of California from spring floods, storing water to be released during periods of shortage.

Water for the Central Valley

Farther north, in the interior of the state, the 1930s saw California's farmers becoming concerned over water supplies needed for agricultural growth. The solution seemed to lie in channeling flood waters into the furrows of dusty farms located far from the rivers. One of the most obvious sources of water was the 400-mile-long Sacramento River, with its average annual runoff of 22,230,000 acre-feet. (An acre-foot of water is the amount that will cover one acre to a depth of one foot—or 43,560 cubic feet.) The Sacramento's drainage area covers almost thirty thousand square miles. Its source is a small lake on one of the peaks of the Klamath Mountains near the Oregon border. It flows eastward from this point, then turns south to Suisun Bay, northeast of San Francisco Bay. Many tributaries help swell it along the way; among the largest are the McCloud, Pit, Feather, Yuba, Bear, and American rivers, which rise on the sides of the Sierra and Cascade ranges. Between Redding and its mouth, the Sacramento River drains the valley that, like California's capital city, was named for it.

By the time the courts banned hydraulic mining in 1884, the channel of the Sacramento was so silted that navigation was closed to all but vessels of the shallowest draft. The same situation caused extensive flooding, so that in the 1930s flood control and water conservation along the river basin were overdue. Millions of dollars of damage occurred in the state's Central Valley every time its rivers went on the rampage, with the cities of Stockton, Visalia, Oroville, Yuba City, and Marysville being particularly vulnerable. In addition to the Sacramento, the San Joaquin River, a twisting stream that joins the Sacramento from the south, then flows into San Pablo Bay (an arm of San Francisco Bay), played an essential part in the history of conservation in the Central Valley. To redistribute the flow of both rivers, a new plan for harnessing their water passed the state legislature in 1933. This scheme, the Central Valley Project, also proposed to generate large quantities of electric power by impounding part of the waters of the Sacramento, the San Joaquin, and lesser streams. Massive opposition to the measure was posed by private utility companies, particularly the Pacific Gas and Electric Company, but when these companies sponsored a public referendum in 1933, California voters upheld the Central Valley Project.

With this issue settled, there still remained the problem of raising money to build such extensive facilities. When a state bond issue of $170 million could not be sold on account of the Depression, the state appealed to the federal government for assistance under the National Industrial Recovery Act. As a result, California's water program in the Central Valley was declared a national reclamation project. Congress, in a Rivers and Harbors Bill of 1935, authorized the expenditure of $12 million for construction of Shasta Dam, north of Redding, as a first step of the Central Valley Project. Begun in the late 1930s, along with the Friant Dam near Fresno, the dams of this project were designed to store almost as much water as all the other reservoirs in California (totaling 600 or more). Shasta Lake, the construction of which was completed in 1945, is capable of storing 4,500,000 acre-feet of water. In addition, two major water arteries, the Friant-Kern Canal and the Delta-Mendota Canal, were to channel water through the San Joaquin Valley.

Completion of the Central Valley Project was delayed by controversy that continued to rage throughout the 1930s and 1940s as to who should build and control water and power facilities. The struggle came to involve the Bureau of Reclamation, Corps of Engineers, state Department of Public Works, municipal water systems, and private utilities. These companies maintained their policy of obstructionism to public-works programs branded as unfair socialistic experiments. Further opposition to government participation came from large landowners, who fought the 160-acre limit on land for which any one owner could receive water from any Bureau of Reclamation project.

Conservation: Water, Forests, and Power

"No state has gained more than California from the artificial application of water, or has more at stake in the extension of its use," once wrote Elwood Mead, the pioneer conservationist after whom Lake Mead was named. Irrigation is essentially a form of conservation, Mead believed, as did Theodore Roosevelt and other early conservationists. The reclamation of water resources early in the twentieth century came to be accompanied by a belated concern over depletion of the timber and mineral wealth of the Far West. Although the idea of conservation had grown through the years of the pro-

Giant redwood trees overwhelming visitors on one of many inviting pathways. These trees are in Stout Memorial Grove, Del Norte County. (By courtesy of Redwood Empire Association.)

gressive movement, effective regulatory steps had yet to be taken.

Within only a few generations whole forests had been ruthlessly denuded by fire and ax. A fortunate exception had occurred in the case of the Muir Woods, one of the world's greatest redwood stands, which was spared through the efforts of the nature lover William Kent. Located on the side of Mount Tamalpais, this timber was about to be logged in 1903, when Kent borrowed $45,000 to buy the land and turn it over to the federal government as a national preserve. In general, however, lumber companies were permitted to exploit forest resources, with no provision for replacement or selective cutting. By the early twentieth century the close connection between overcutting and periodic floods had become clear. Some of the choicest lands in the state had already been ruined by man-made erosion. Animals, like the bighorn mountain sheep, had been reduced to a few scraggly specimens in zoos. John Muir and John Burroughs demanded the creation of parks to protect the magnificent sequoias and coast redwoods, as well as the wild life of the countryside.

As early as 1889, Major John Wesley Powell had promoted a study of water sites and had made recommendations for their preservation. In 1911, California created a State Conservation Commission and, two years later, a State Water Commission. These agencies began to put into operation the latest advances in scientific forestry. Lumbering companies, which first resisted controlled management of government forest preserves, came eventually to see the merits of reforestation. During 1924–1925 alone, the California Forest Protective Association planted a million and a half young redwoods and Douglas firs, as well as spruce and cedar trees, on the cutover lands of Mendocino, Del Norte, and Humboldt counties. The original belt of forest in those three counties had once been twice the size of Rhode Island. To prevent further depletion, private and government projects of this sort became common. During the Depression years of the 1930s, the Civilian Conservation Corps (CCC) carried on extensive replanting along the wilderness trails.

During this period the National Park Service and the California State Division of Beaches and Parks labored to preserve the natural beauties of the state and to prepare more recreation sites. California came to include within its boundaries twenty-two national forests, four national parks, and eight national monuments, in addition to 150 state recreational areas. Among national parks and monuments are Yosemite, Sequoia, Lassen, the Devil's Postpile, and Channel Islands. The state park system includes Big Basin Redwoods, Point Lobos, Humboldt Redwoods, and Morro Bay. Several private organizations, notably the Sierra Club, have also made great efforts on behalf of the preservation of natural wilderness areas.

As the population grew, demands for electrical energy became insatiable. From 1900 to 1923 the Southern California Edison Company alone increased generating capacity from 12,000 horsepower to 500,000 horsepower. By 1928 this huge utility was serving more than 300 cities and towns over an area of 55,000 square miles, with a customer population of 2 million. Meanwhile, the Pacific Gas and Electric Company transmitted power throughout central and north-

Rio Nido Beach in the Russian River district in Sonoma County. (By courtesy of Redwood Empire Association.)

ern California, servicing thirty-eight California counties from hydroelectric plants constructed in some of the highest valleys of the Sierra.

Continued Agricultural Advance

California's agricultural development reaped inestimable benefits from new water and power supplies, as well as from land-conservation measures. As in other farm areas of the country, agricultural yield in California spiraled upward while the acreage of the average farm decreased and the value of farm land boomed. In 1850 California's 872 major ranches had averaged 4,500 acres, valued at only $2 per acre. By 1900 7 percent of the state's farm owners controlled 63 percent of its agricultural lands. Twenty years later the number of farms had increased to 117,670, and by 1935, a peak of 150,360 was reached. (The figures indicate a reverse trend twenty years later, when the number of farms declined to 123,074, while the average size increased to more than 300 acres.)

The major problem of the interwar years was not agricultural production but, rather, finding the means to increase sales and consumption of the variety of products that California grew. As elsewhere in the country, crops were plowed under during the Depression of the 1930s, at the very time when refugees from the Dust Bowl regions of the Middle West were going hungry. To sustain a profitable price level, vineyardists, orange-grove owners, and ranchers redoubled their search for markets to absorb the greater yields that resulted from better spraying, fertilizing, and irrigating crops. Prohibition worked a particular hardship upon grape growers and wineries, which tried to market their products in nonalcoholic forms such as "wine bricks" and grape bars.

The fruit and vegetable farms of the Central Valley came more and more to resemble big-business operations, in their impersonality and efficiency. A cheap, exploitable migrant labor market, widespread unemployment, mechanization, and specialized production combined to boost output.

Fresno, in the San Joaquin Valley, a city served by two railroads and various truck lines, reflected the new pattern of growth. It became a clearing center for the distribution of fruit and vegetables, cotton, livestock, wine, dairy products, raisins, dried apricots, and prunes. In addition, it became a supply center for nearby mountain recreation sites and tourist traffic, and a local headquarters for petroleum, hardware, grocery, and appliance firms. Other valley towns—Stockton, Visalia, Madera, Merced, Modesto, and Bakersfield—also grew into important market centers.

Selected Readings

A view of the Owens Valley country, before it was despoiled, forms part of Mary Austin's *The Land of Little Rain* (New York, 1903). Her book *The Ford* (New York, 1917) includes a graphic presentation of the intrigues of irrigation and oil in California. The 1928 holocaust in the Santa Clara Valley is the subject of Charles Outland's *Man-Made Disaster: The Story of the Saint Francis Dam* (Glendale, 1962).

Regarding the Boulder Canyon Project one can read Ray Lyman Wilbur and Elwood Mead, *Construction of Hoover Dam* (Wahington, D.C., 1935), and George A. Pettit, *So Boulder Dam Was Built* (Berkeley, 1935). David O. Woodbury, *The Colorado Conquest* (Indianapolis, 1941), and P. L. Kleinsorge, *Boulder Canyon Project* (Stanford, 1941), deal with the same subject.

More on the struggle over water appears in Norris Hundley, *Water and the West: the Colorado River Compact and the Politics of Water in the American West* (Berkeley, 1975), and William L. Kahrl, *Water and Power: The Conflict Over Los Angeles' Water Supply in the Owens Valley* (Berkeley, 1982). On the same subject is Abraham Hoffman, *Vision or Villainy: Origins of the Owens Valley–Los Angeles Water Controversy* (College Station, Tex., 1981); see also Hoffman's "Did He or Didn't He? Fred Eaton's Role in the Owens Valley–Los Angeles Water Controversy," *Journal of the West* 22 (April 1983), 30–38, and Robert Matson, *William Mulholland, A Forgotten Forefather* (Stockton, 1978).

Also useful is Philip Ross May, *Origins of Hydraulic Mining in California* (Oakland, 1970). John Upton Terrell, *War for the Colorado River*, volume 1 of which is entitled *The California–Arizona Controversy*, and volume 2, *Above Lee's Ferry—The Upper Basin* (Glendale, 1965).

The Central Valley Project is the subject of Robert de Roos, *The Thirsty Land: The Story of the Central Valley Project* (Stanford, 1948), and Viola P. May, *Shasta Dam and Its Builders* (n.p., 1945). Merle Armitage, *Success Is No Accident: The Biography of William Paul Whitsett* (Yucca Valley, Calif., 1959) deals with one of the developers of the state's water resources. A survey is S. T. Harding, *Water in California* (Palo Alto, 1961). See also C. Raymond Clar, *California Government and Forestry From Spanish Days* ... (Sacramento, 1959). Problems of flood control and their relation to mining are discussed in California Department of Public Works *Bulletin No. 26*, "Sacramento River Basin," (Sacramento, 1931); Kenneth Thompson, "Historic Flooding in the Sacramento Valley," *Pacific Historical Review* 39 (November 1960), 349–60; and Robert Kelley, "Taming the Sacramento: Hamiltonianism in Action," *Pacific Historical Review* 34 (February 1965), 21–49. The growth of a major utility in the development of water and power is charted by Charles M. Coleman, *P. G. & E. of California: The Centennial Story of the Pacific Gas and Electric Company, 1852–1952* (New York, 1952).

An early opponent of the exploitation of the natural resources of California was John Muir. From the 1870s onward, in dozens of articles for the San Francisco *Bulletin*, the *Overland Monthly*, and *Harper's*, Muir stressed this theme. See C. R. Bradley, *Reference List to the Published Writings of John Muir* (Berkeley, 1897). *The Life and Letters of John Muir* (2 vols., Boston, 1924), edited by William Frederic Bade, reveals Muir's deep interest in conservation. So do his previously unpublished journals, edited by Linnie M. Wolfe as *John of the Mountains* (Boston 1938). Also significant are Muir's *The Mountains of California* (New York, 1894), and *Our National Parks* (Boston, 1901). Holway R. Jones, *John Muir and the Sierra Club: The Battle for Yosemite* (San Francisco, 1966), is a tribute published by the organization he founded in 1892. Francis P. Farquhar, *History of the Sierra Nevada* (Berkeley, 1965), is the best history of those mountains. A mimeographed biography entitled *William Kent, Independent*, by Elizabeth T. Kent (Kentfield, 1950), honors the conservationist who saved the Muir Woods.

The relationship of farming to water development is in Clarke H.

Chambers, *California Farm Organizations* (Berkeley, 1952). The topic is treated in Carey McWilliams, *Factories in the Fields* (Boston, 1939). Another work regarding California's agricultural growth is Marion Clawson, *Longterm Outlook for Western Agriculture* (Berkeley, 1946).

The interest in nature shown by Clarence King's *Mountaineering in the Sierra Nevada* (New York, 1905) has continued in the Sierra Club *Bulletin* (1897–). A useful volume is Francis P. Farquhar, *Place Names of the High Sierra* (San Francisco, 1926). Regarding the California backcountry, see also Joseph H. Le Conte, *Rambling Through the High Sierra* (San Francisco, 1899); Roderick Peattie, *The Sierra Nevada* (New York, 1947); Oscar Lewis, *High Sierra Country* (New York, 1955); and W. Storrs Lee, *The Sierra* (New York, 1962). Concerning the sequoias, see Norman Taylor, *The Ageless Relics* (New York, 1962), and Susan Schrepfer, *The Fight to Save the Redwoods* (Madison, Wis., 1983). More general is Roderick Nash, *Wilderness and the American Mind* (New Haven, 1967).

CHAPTER 31

Labor in
an Industrial Age

CALIFORNIA'S MASSIVE GROWTH of population did not occur without continuing political and economic dislocations. The blue-and-gold tourist folders that urged visitors to spend winters in "the golden state" scarcely hinted that serious social problems brewed beneath the surface of its outwardly easy-going way of life. Infectious real estate advertisements of the state's attractions stood in contrast to underlying social discontent.

From the 1870s, when Denis Kearney had harangued the masses on the windy sandlots of San Francisco, California's working men had vigorously asserted their rights. After the turn of the century, tensions between laborers and employers grew more pronounced. Through their own Union Labor Party, workers continued to speak out against the concentration of economic power in the hands of financiers and shipping tycoons. Labor also raised a strong voice of protest during the Ruef–Schmitz scandals in San Francisco. That city became one of the most effectively organized labor strongholds in the country, a center from which labor agitators operated vigorously in the interior and in the coastal valleys of the state. Even after labor had proved its power in a number of cases, however, the relation between capital and labor was characterized by strain, disorder, and frequent clashes.

The IWW

After 1905 the Industrial Workers of the World, a socialist-oriented group of dissident unionists organized at Chicago that year, turned its attention to the Far West. The IWW was developing in order to organize California's seasonal and part-time workers into "One Big Union." Among these migratory laborers were field hands, lumberjacks, and cannery workers not welcome to join the American Federation of Labor, which was organized along craft lines. Hours of labor on most farms and ranches were long and the pay extremely low, while conditions in farm labor camps were deplorable. Furthermore, use of farm machinery annually lessened the need for harvest workers.

These conditions drew the attention of revolutionary IWW leaders. Agitators set to work throughout the state, their greatest activity occurring in the years 1908 to 1912. By 1910, union organizers had recruited about one thousand migratory farm laborers as members of a dozen locals in California. National IWW membership, incidentally, reached no more than 60,000 at its zenith; revolutionary unionism in America has never had a widespread following. However, the IWW, urging radical reform of the economy, stirred the souls of migrant workers. Those who became members of the IWW were referred to contemptuously in rural newspapers and farm journals as "Wobblies," belonging to an "I Won't Work" movement, while local police officials regarded the volatile organization as an outlaw labor group. Soapbox orators were arrested at rallies sponsored by the IWW, fire hoses were turned on its members, and field workers were warned not to join IWW locals. Municipal officials took no action when organization headquarters in various cities mysteriously burned.

In spite of such harassment, the IWW persisted. After inflammatory incidents with local police, the most serious of which took place at Fresno and San Diego, various municipalities adopted stiff regulations aimed explicitly against the IWW. The terror in which municipal officials held the IWW was based on its ideology. Subscribing as it did to the Marxian concept of class struggle and to syndicalist and anarchist ideas, the organization was undeniably a threat to California's status quo. Both organized and unorganized workers also distrusted the "Wobblies" because of their attempts to obtain equal status for Chinese and Mexican workers. Employers naturally hated the IWW techniques of on-the-job recruiting and quick strikes—usually unannounced. Though its leaders were jailed, clubbed, and even killed, the "Wobblies" continued their radicalism.

The longstanding IWW campaign to organize migratory workers reached a peak of violence on August 3, 1913, on a large hop farm near Wheatland in the Sacramento Valley. At stake were the conditions under which itinerant laborers—men, women, and children— were forced to live and work on the farm, known as the Durst Ranch.

Virtually no provision had been made to house them decently or to provide sanitation. Eight toilets existed for 2,800 persons. The owners of the ranch had advertised for many more workers than they could actually use and then paid the ones they hired wages as low as seventy-five cents per day. A ranch-owned store held back 10 percent of meager wages, forcing field hands to purchase food and supplies at inflated prices. The workers, under the leadership of Blackie Ford, head of the IWW local, called a strike. Then, when a sheriff's posse sought to arrest Ford and other ringleaders, a pistol was fired, and a full-scale riot followed. The sheriff and the local district attorney, as well as several workers, were killed. Governor Hiram Johnson called out the National Guard and brought in private detectives to investigate; as a result of the incident the IWW organization was virtually dismantled in the Sacramento Valley. Ford and a colleague were convicted of murder and sentenced to life imprisonment.

The Wheatland Riot nevertheless led to attempts to improve the welfare of migratory workers. The California legislature, its attention drawn to the problem of seasonal labor, passed several bills toward this end, though such measures were not effective. A new Commission on Immigration and Housing did what it could to achieve decent working conditions but was hampered by lack of power. Those ranchers who imported thousands of extra workers each season to pick peaches, grapes, cotton, and hops still claimed they could not afford to furnish individual dwellings to part-time laborers. They argued that because the harvest season lasts only a few weeks, such housing, vacant much of the year, is impractical to maintain. Labor leaders contended that this reasoning was a poor excuse for the continued inhumanity with which workers were treated.

The prewar era seemed to breed discontent. Late in 1913, a disgruntled agitator who called himself "General" Kelley marched an "army" of several thousand unemployed workers to Sacramento to demand relief. They resembled Jacob Coxey's army of ragamuffins, which, in 1895, had marched to Washington from Ohio with similar demands. Kelley's men were driven off by armed guards after attempting to camp on capitol grounds.

Bombing of the Los Angeles *Times*

In 1910, several years before the Wheatland Riot and before Kelley's fruitless march to Sacramento, the labor movement became involved in an ill-conceived event. The bombing of the Los Angeles *Times*, set back the labor movement in California for many years. The blast occurred at 1:07 A.M. on October 1, just as the newspaper's mechanical force was getting the *Times* to press. Twenty persons were

Destruction by fire of the Los Angeles Times *Building, 1910.* (C. C. Pierce Collection, photograph by C. C. Tarter; by courtesy of The Huntington Library, San Marino, California.)

killed and many more injured and the *Times* building was reduced to a mass of rubble. The disaster influenced deeply the future editorial philosophy of the *Times*. Tension between the paper and labor organizers had been of long duration, and after the bombing mutual suspicion increased even more. The owner of the *Times*, General Harrison Gray Otis, blamed irresponsible labor leaders for the bombing, particularly members of the International Association of Bridge and Structural Iron Workers, then involved in a local strike. Conversely, the voices of labor, denying that a bomb had caused the blast, accused the *Times* of criminal negligence in operating a plant which union spokesmen called a gas-leaking firetrap. It was only after a lengthy trial that the incident was established as an act of union violence.

In 1911 three labor agitators—Ortie McManigal and James B. and John J. McNamara—were brought to trial, accused of organizing the bombing. Labor retained the renowned attorney Clarence Darrow, known for his vigorous opposition to both violence and capital punishment. The testimony against the McNamara brothers was far too incriminating for Darrow to win their acquittal. Acting on his advice, they changed their pleas from not guilty to guilty and, after a compromise with both prosecution and judge, they were sent to the state penitentiary. The good offices of the crusading journalist Lincoln Steffens were used to arrange this compromise, by which the McNamara brothers changed their pleas in exchange for the prosecution's dropping the pursuit of other suspects. James drew a sentence of life imprisonment and John one of fifteen years. McManigal was freed because he had "turned state's evidence," thereby making it possible for government officials to indict his accomplices.

Not only was public opinion vociferous in denouncing the bombing, but criticism was also voiced over Darrow's compact on behalf of the McNamara brothers. This may have been Darrow's only way of saving the lives of the McNamaras, who confessed to the *Times* dynamiting. Darrow himself was indicted for jury bribery in this case, although he was later acquitted. Unfortunately for union leaders, the bombing so blackened their reputation that labor disturbances were equated, particularly after the outbreak of World War I, with lack of national patriotism. The *Times* bombing helped to kill off the militancy that had characterized the American labor movement.

Continued Labor Strife

The advent of war was to create a heavy demand for both skilled and unskilled workers, which raised wages, particularly in urban areas. Apprehensive about the spread of union activity, management urged upon labor the open shop as a temporary war measure. As public agitation on behalf of the open shop became pronounced, union leaders grew discontented. The issue was the source of new irritation between capital and labor. In 1916 violence again erupted.

President Wilson had proclaimed July 22 of that year "Preparedness Day," when the nation was to demonstrate its unity and fitness for service in case war were ever declared. At San Francisco advocates of the open shop helped organize a patriotic parade as a Preparedness Day demonstration. Meanwhile, a serious longshoremen's strike was under way. The combination was enough to make employers and union organizers edgy about their differences. In the midst of this uneasy situation a suitcase containing a bomb, left by someone on a city sidewalk, exploded at 2:06 P.M., killing nine persons and injuring forty others.

Two union leaders, Thomas J. Mooney and Warren K. Billings, were arrested and accused of the crime. In 1913, Billings had been convicted of carrying explosives. Although he had claimed to be the victim of a "frame-up," he had been sentenced to two years in Folsom Penitentiary. Newspapers joined in the strong public feeling over the Preparedness Day incident and the Mooney–Billings trial, dealing in rumor and innuendo. The press circulated a story on January 3, 1917, the day the trial began, that Mooney and Billings had been part of a conspiracy of anarchists who had plotted to assassinate Governor Hiram Johnson. There was also talk connecting the two men with "Reds" from abroad supposedly converging on California to spread the new doctrine of bolshevism. Both Billings and Mooney presented alibis to clear themselves of the Preparedness Day bombing. Mooney produced three photos of himself and his wife on the roof of a Market Street building viewing the parade. A streetside clock conveniently located in the background showed the time to be 1:58, 2:01 and 2:04 P.M., just prior to the bombing. Despite this and other evidence for the defense, Mooney was sentenced to be hanged, and Billings received a life term in the state penitentiary.

A rally in Petrograd, Russia, helped to focus international attention on the case. The White House was deluged by protests from labor leaders. President Wilson appointed an investigative committee, whose overall conclusion was that there was insufficient evidence to find anyone guilty. As a result of Wilson's intervention, in the interest of wartime unity, Mooney's punishment was commuted to life imprisonment. Nevertheless, the public remembered that during the trial the prosecution had proved Mooney's association with the McNamara brothers—convicted earlier of the explosion of the Los Angeles *Times*.

Californians held to the feeling that Mooney and Billings were dangerous: "They may not be guilty of the bomb explosion, but they belong where they are." From the moment Mooney and Billings went behind the bars of San Quentin Penitentiary, however, labor embarked upon a twenty-year campaign to free the two men, calling them martyrs of an "American Dreyfus case." Labor sympathizers maintained that Mooney and Billings had been adjudged guilty only because of association with anarchistic antiwar exiles. Their case continued to attract attention all over the world. In contrast to previous hostility on the part of the press, thousands of lines of newspaper and magazine copy were written on behalf of Mooney and Billings. Grave charges of perjured testimony during the trial were made in their favor by Fremont Older, the reformist San Francisco newspaperman who had attacked the Ruef–Schmitz machine and who himself came to be called an anarchist by antiunion critics. In 1939, after repeated petitions and appeals, Governor Culbert L. Olson pardoned Mooney as the first act of his administration. Mooney died soon thereafter. Billings was pardoned much later by Governor Edmund G. Brown.

Following the Preparedness Day bombing, the open shop reigned in California for a number of years. In 1919, during the repressive atmosphere of the postwar years, California adopted a Criminal Syndicalism Law to control labor leaders. The act, resulting from public fear of the spread of communism after the Russian Revolution of 1917, forbade any form of violence in labor disputes. Anyone convicted of "labor violence" could be sentenced to as much as fourteen years' imprisonment. Radical ideas of foreign origin were not to be welcomed in postwar California, which gave its full support during this period to Prohibition and "100 percent Americanism."

The Criminal Syndicalism Law ultimately caused the arrest and imprisonment of persons accused of encouraging the overthrow of law and order. It was invoked to discourage union agitators in such tense situations as the 1923 San Pedro strike, various cannery strikes during the 1930s, and work stoppages from 1933 to 1934 among vegetable, fruit, and cotton pickers of the Imperial and San Joaquin valleys. Ordinarily these repressive measures were administered by local and state police. But at Salinas, in 1936, growers recruited a "citizen's army" to put down a strike by migrant lettuce pickers. Equipped with shotguns and pick handles, the army "got the lettuce picked," broke the strike, and disbanded offending unions.

The fierceness of California's Criminal Syndicalism Law was illustrated by the arrest of the writer Upton Sinclair for reading the United States Constitution aloud in public. The San Pedro strike of 1923, led by the IWW, had elicited the sympathy of Sinclair, then a young reform-minded writer. Confrontation with the Los Angeles commercial establishment helped Sinclair to launch the American Civil Liberties Union in southern California. The major punitive effect of the law, however, fell squarely where its advocates had intended—upon labor leaders. This legislation, as well as municipal ordinances and public pressure, combined in a few years to kill off what remained of the IWW and other radical groups in California.

Selected Readings

Early labor struggles are described in Martin Zanger, "Politics of Confrontation: Upton Sinclair and the Launching of the ACLU in Southern California," *Pacific Historical Review* 38 (November 1969), 383–406, and in Carleton Parker, *The Casual Laborer and Other Essays* (New York, 1920). A primary source is William D. Haywood, *Bill Haywood's Book* (New York, 1929). Consult also Wallace Stegner's novel *The Preacher and the Slave* (Boston, 1950), a literary picture of the "Wobblies." Another analysis is that of Robert L. Tyler, "The I.W.W. and the West," *American Quarterly* 12 (Summer 1960), 175–87. John Dos Passos utilizes the "Wobblies" as part of his criticism of American capitalism in *U.S.A.* (New York, 1939). Yet another novelist, Stewart Holbrook, is somewhat more objective in "The Last of the Wobblies," *American Mercury* 62 (April 1946), 467–68. Paul

F. Brissenden, *The I.W.W.: A Study of American Syndicalism* (New York, 1920), is an older technical analysis. See also Louis Adamic, *Dynamite: The Story of Class Violence in America* (New York, 1935), and William J. Burns, *The Masked War. . . .* (New York, 1913). Burns was a prominent detective in the *Times* bombing case. The most recent and comprehensive study of the "Big Red Scare" is Robert K. Murray, *Red Scare: A Study in National Hysteria, 1919–1920* (Minneapolis, 1955). Specifically dealing with the Preparedness Day incident are Ernest J. Hopkins, *What Happened in the Mooney Case* (New York, 1932), and by Thomas J. Hunt, *The Case of Thomas J. Mooney and Warren K. Billings* (New York, 1929), and the interesting but not fully reliable *Frame-Up: The Incredible Case of Tom Mooney and Warren Billings* (New York, 1967) by Curt Gentry. Adela Rogers St. Johns's *Final Verdict* (New York, 1962) tells the story of her attorney father, Earl Rogers, who was involved in saving Clarence Darrow from the charge of bribing the jury in the Los Angeles *Times* bombing. *The Autobiography of Upton Sinclair* (New York, 1962) is full of details about his involvement in California labor struggles.

Books that touch upon the tensions described in this chapter include Bernard C. Cronin, *Father Yorke and the Labor Movement in San Francisco, 1900–1910* (Washington, D.C., 1943); Frederick L. Ryan, *Industrial Relations in the San Francisco Building Trades* (Norman, Okla., 1936); Grace H. Stimson, *Rise of the Labor Movement in Los Angeles* (Berkeley, 1935); and Paul S. Taylor, *The Sailors' Union of the Pacific* (New York, 1923). Articles include Thomas W. Page, "The San Francisco Labor Movement in 1901," *Political Science Quarterly* 17 (December 1902), 664–88; Ed Rosenberg, "The San Francisco Strikes of 1901," *American Federationist* 9 (January 1902), 15–18; Lillian Symes, "Our American Dreyfus Case," *Harper's* 161 (May 1931), 641–52; E. Guy Talbott, "The Armies of the Unemployed in California," *Survey* 32 (August 22, 1914), 523–24; Walter V. Woehlke, "Bolshevikis of the West," *Sunset* 40 (January 1918), 11–13, 73, 82; and Gerald D. Nash, "The Influence of Labor on State Policy: The Experience of California," California Historical Society *Quarterly* 62 (September 1963), 241–57. See also Norris C. Hundley, Jr., "Katherine Philips Edson and the Fight for the California Minimum Wage, 1912–1913," *Pacific Historical Review* 29 (August 1960), 271–86. Consult also: David F. Selvin, *A Place in the Sun: A History of California Labor* (San Francisco, 1981); Alexander Saxton, *The Indispensable Enemy: Labor and the Anti-Chinese Movement in California* (Berkeley, 1971); Louis B. and Richard S. Perry, *A History of the Los Angeles Labor Movement* (Berkeley, 1963); and Richard H. Frost, *The Mooney Case* (Stanford, 1968).

CHAPTER 32

The Depression Years

AFTER THE COLLAPSE of the stock market in October 1929, President Herbert Hoover's administration seemed powerless to stop the downward economic spiral. Late in 1932, through the Reconstruction Finance Corporation, the federal government allocated emergency funds to individual states. These were supposed to "trickle down" to individual citizens through their municipalities. Such aid, however well-intentioned, did not prove effective.

In California swarms of quasi-residents, in search of jobs and spiritual roots, moved about in the frontier tradition, hardly knowing what level of government authority to obey or to appeal to for help. Unemployment spread, and the strength of California unionism decreased. Not only did transient farm labor remain unorganized; unemployed city workers too found themselves in intense competition for jobs. The bargaining power of local union leaders was further weakened; labor spokesmen were in no position to demand the closed shop, or to insist upon better working conditions of any sort.

In the presidential elections of 1932, the Democratic candidate was Franklin Delano Roosevelt, governor of New York. Roosevelt's campaign took him to the major cities of the Far West, which responded to his magnetic appeal. Roosevelt offered genuine hope to those who were downhearted and discouraged. Californians had tired of hearing that speculation in the stock market was the primary cause of the Depression. They were more interested in the solution of local problems than in national issues.

At the Commonwealth Club in San Francisco on September 23, 1932, Roosevelt described in somber terms the concentration of private enterprise in the United States into large business concerns. "Put plainly, we are steering a steady course toward oligarchy, if we are not there already," he said. Roosevelt went on to speak of every man's right to life and to a comfortable living, and declared, "Our government, formal and informal, political and economic, owes to everyone an avenue to possess himself of a portion of that plenty sufficient for his needs, through his own work." When election day came, California voted overwhelmingly for Roosevelt.

But while he campaigned, the situation was growing worse. Overproduction of both agricultural and commercial commodities caused unemployment to spread. Once-prosperous industries, farms, and real-estate developments were mired down by the Depression. Within a few months banks, as the result of runs on their holdings by worried depositors, were threatened with collapse. To allow time for the state legislature to devise protective legislation, California Governor James Rolph, Jr., ordered a three-day bank holiday on March 2, 1933. By March 4, the day of President Roosevelt's inauguration, almost every state governor had imposed severe restrictions on withdrawals. On the same day Rolph extended the California bank holiday for three more days.

The country faced economic paralysis, with the scarcity of money in some cases reducing business to a barter system. Hope ran high that Roosevelt's "New Deal" would quickly be put into effect. Because Roosevelt demonstrated that he viewed the crisis as far from insoluble, Californians as well as other Americans looked to him for crucial leadership.

The "Okies" and "Arkies"

Although California's relief activities—carried on through a State Relief Administration—were far from adequate to meet emergency conditions, thousands of migrants descended upon the state in the Depression years. California, fearful of the burden on its economy, warned migrants not to come there to seek jobs. Rumors of high wages out West, however, caused many to make a trip they were later to regret.

Among the newcomers were 350,000 farmers from the parched Dust Bowl areas of the Middle West; these were known as "Okies" or "Arkies," from their origins in Oklahoma or Arkansas. Their trek overland in rickety flivvers and jalopies, with brooms and pails tied onto vehicles heaped with mattresses, children, and blankets, has been described in John Steinbeck's novel *The Grapes of Wrath*. Most of these migrants arrived in California during 1935 and in the four years thereafter. Because the labor situation was so gravely depressed, even responsible citizens supported legislation to close the border to indigents. Later, in 1941, the United States Supreme Court declared such laws unconstitutional.

Farm owners became accustomed to paying starvation wages that the newcomers were forced to accept. Faced with bankruptcy, the owners claimed they could not possibly spend money they did not have to improve the working conditions of refugees. Both the AFL and the CIO battled almost in vain in the pear orchards of Marysville, in the packing sheds of Bakersfield, and in the canneries of Fresno to organize migrant workers. In 1933–1934, after a wave of field strikes, a group of farm owners, the Associated Farmers of California, organized themselves as "an educational agency to inform the public about the type of personnel leading the agricultural strikes." This anti-labor group came to number forty thousand members, and proved more than a match for the ineffective United Cannery, Agricultural, Packing and Allied Workers of America, CIO, to which few migrant workers belonged.

After 1930 Californians turned for gubernatorial leadership to James ("Sunny Jim") Rolph, Jr., longtime mayor of San Francisco. Rolph was a familiar figure on horseback at parades and pageants. Although folksy, and convivial, "Sunny Jim" was a curious choice to make in a time of great emergency. He had no idea how to cope with massive unemployment and poverty. Furthermore, he opposed almost any reform of California's tax structure and signed legislation that caused taxes to fall unfairly upon persons of the lowest income. A sales tax on food came to be blamed upon Rolph, who also made the mistake of endorsing a brutal jailbreak lynching. When he died in 1934, "Sunny Jim" was succeeded by the lieutenant governor, Frank Merriam, who resembled President Hoover in his conservatism over what must be done to fight the Depression.

Folksinger Woody Guthrie mocked the ineptitude of the stuffy Merriam in one of his ballads. He also captured the spirit of intolerance over what to do about the Okies and Arkies. This prejudice was born of a combination of insecurity and shame concerning fellow Americans caught in a tragic social and economic web. California laborers, already hard pressed, saw these impoverished invaders as willing to live in ghastly "Hoovervilles" and to endure sluggings and beatings by alleged "deputy sheriffs." Steinbeck portrays the Okie as he faced slow starvation or prosecution for vagrancy. Guthrie, like Steinbeck, embodied the Depression years. Born in an Oklahoma oil boom town, he went on the road at thirteen, spent several years at Los Angeles, where he sang on a radio station for "the little man" and "the drifting families," voicing both strength and bitterness in his "talking blues":

> We got to old Los Angeles broke,
> So dad-gum hungry we thought we'd choke,
> And I bummed up a spud or two

And my wife cooked up potater stew . . .
Fed the kids a big batch of it,
But that was mighty thin stew . . .
So dad-gum thin you could pretty nearly
Read a magazine through it . . .
If it had been just a little thinner,
I've always believed,
If that stew had been just a little bit thinner,
Some of our senators could have seen through it.*

Like Steinbeck, Guthrie felt that California was being misused by
selfish, scared people:

California's a Garden of Eden
A paradise to live in or see . . .
But believe it or not,
You won't find it so hot
If you ain't got the Do-Re-Mi.†

Guthrie, who composed over a thousand songs, is best remembered
by his "folk national anthem" entitled *This Land Is Your Land*.

This land is your land and this land is my land,
    From California to the New York Island,
    From the redwood forest to the Gulf Stream waters,
    This land was made for you and me.
As I went a walking that ribbon of highway
    I saw above me that endless skyway,
    I saw before me that golden valley,
    This land was made for you and me.
I roamed and rambled, and I followed my footsteps
    To the sparkling sands of her diamond deserts,
    All around me, a voice was sounding,
    This land was made for you and me.
When the sun come shining and I was strolling,
    The wheat fields waving, the dust clouds rolling,
    A voice was chanting and the fog was lifting,
    This land was made for you and me.‡

---

*Talking Dust Bowl, words and music by Woody Guthrie. TRO © copyright 1961
Ludlow Music, Inc., New York, N.Y. Used by permission.
† Do-Re-Mi, words and music by Woody Guthrie. TRO © copyright 1961 and 1963
Ludlow Music, Inc., New York, N.Y. Used by permission.
‡This Land Is Your Land, words and music by Woody Guthrie. TRO © copyright 1956
and 1958 Ludlow Music, Inc., New York, N.Y. Used by permission.

Mexicans and Filipinos

The problem of providing housing and food was aggravated, for relief agencies, by the need to care for increased numbers of Mexicans. These refugees slipped over the border, where they came into sharp competition with other laborers. California was becoming more industrial, but it scarcely needed such an influx of workers during the Depression. Most Mexican newcomers remained in the vicinity of Los Angeles, where they formed the largest expatriate community in the world outside of Mexico.

Serious problems of education, housing, and assimilation developed around California's Mexican minority. Forced to accept unpleasant jobs at low wages or to remain unemployed, they clung to their language, clustered in their own organizations, and retained separate tastes and outlook. Later, youthful Mexican gangs—known during and after World War II as *Pachucos*—got into trouble with police on the streets of east Los Angeles and other communities. Carrying switchblade knives in their trouser pockets and razor blades in their long hair, they were a source of chagrin to older and more sober Mexicans, as well as to *Anglos*. In 1943, discharged Navy and Marine veterans, in addition to what the press called "white hoodlums," rioted against the "Zoot suit Pachuchos." Unfortunately public opinion associated the latter with Mexican residents in general.

Members of another minority group, the Filipinos, were also willing to work long hours for little money. They, thus, competed strongly for scarce jobs as houseboys, laundry workers, restaurant dish washers, and fry cooks. During the Depression years unemployed whites resented them thoroughly. Sentiment against Filipino farm laborers led to the Watsonville riot of 1930, and also to a disturbance at Salinas in 1934, in which they were brutally manhandled. By the mid-1930s, proposals for the exclusion of Filipinos were heard in the California legislature. The state offered them free transportation home if they promised not to return to the United States. When World War II broke out, those Filipinos who had remained in California enlisted in the Navy, where some became mess boys on the staffs of admirals. California's Filipinos, like the Chinese and Japanese, met demands for their exclusion from the state. Economically such workers from other countries may have been comparable to the Okies and Arkies; but there remained a basic difference—the Dust Bowl refugees were not foreigners. Filipinos and Mexicans were.

Utopian Schemes

California's climate also attracted thousands of older people, many of them unable to work. The oldsters seemed to believe that sunny

California would, in one way or another, sustain them. Some were
dependent on a modest income, which was seriously reduced by the
nation's economic difficulties. Others had suffered from the collapse
of banks. These elderly people tended to be attracted by schemes
that promised to alleviate their hardships by redistributing the uneven national and state wealth.

Among such plans was the movement known as technocracy.
Technocracy's chief advocate was Howard Scott, an engineer who
wanted to create a utopian society by eliminating poverty. Scott proposed to place technical experts in control of industry and government. Equipped with blueprints, he explained the intricacies of his
proposed engineering–civilization in abandoned drug stores, garages, and unrentable buildings.

Like technocracy, the other utopian plans that the Depression years
encouraged were identified with a particular personality. One of these
was the controversial Upton Sinclair, who had been, since the Progressive era, a crusading author and journalist. In 1920 he unsuccessfully sought a congressional seat for the first time. Two years
later he ran for the Senate, and in 1926 and 1930 became the Socialist
candidate for governor (even before World War I, a significant socialist movement had existed in California). Sinclair's last attempt at
public office was in 1934, when he sought the Democratic nomination
for governor. The experimental program he proposed appealed to
party leaders as the best possibility of ridding the state of long years
of Republican rule. Sinclair's EPIC ("End Poverty in California")
plan was tailormade for the discontented and downhearted. He advocated a monthly pension of $50 for widows, the aged, and the
handicapped, and, like Henry George earlier, championed inheritance and income taxes, a tax on idle land, and stimulation of employment. Sinclair believed that homeowners should be exempt from
taxation and that state ownership of farms and factories would cure
unemployment. He also urged a scrip currency to replace hard-to-
get dollars.

Although Sinclair's plan held much the same appeal for the unemployed as Roosevelt's New Deal, then moving into high gear, Sinclair did not gain the president's endorsement. Roosevelt considered
Sinclair's program impractical. Others also regarded Sinclair as an
extremist visionary whose socialist notions were unworkable. During
the most bitterly contested of California's gubernatorial elections,
the conservative press, radio, and movie industry united in a campaign against Sinclair. But the reactionary nature of this opposition
gained supporters he might not otherwise have had, though not
enough to secure his election. Sinclair's opponent was the bland tra-
ditionalist Frank F. Merriam, who had in 1934 succeeded to the

governorship upon the death of Governor Rolph. In November, Merriam received 1,138,620 votes as against Sinclair's 879,537.

The discontented groups who had fought for Sinclair's victory did not give up his ideals. Instead, they turned to even more radical messiahs. It was an age when reactionary radio orators and pundits of every description gained huge followings by advocating measures to cure the ills of mankind. Among these was Dr. Francis E. Townsend, a retired physician who sold real estate at Long Beach. With the slogan "Youth for work and age for leisure," he proposed in 1934 his Townsend Old Age Pension Plan, a supposedly foolproof scheme that would provide a monthly pension of $200 for every person over the age of sixty—provided each payment was spent within one month. A 2 percent federal tax upon business transactions was to support the plan. Townsend's plan was not so much a pension scheme as a means of eliminating aged workers from jobs that "belonged to younger persons." Principal opposition to the plan came from those who feared it would pyramid taxes.

Townsend led a national "crusade" through his homey newspaper, *The Townsend Weekly*, and through the five thousand clubs organized in his name. Up to 1937, even after a congressional investigation resulted in his conviction for contempt of Congress, his movement flourished among the elderly. Although national Townsend Club membership was estimated at from 3 to 10 million, Dr. Townsend's plan aroused still wider opposition among those who considered its provisions unsound. Even Sinclair opposed it as economic madness. Subscribers to Townsend's newspaper continued to read it long after his plan had any chance of adoption.

In 1938 yet another visionary plan—the "Thirty Dollars Every Thursday," or "Ham and Eggs," proposal—suggested a pension to every unemployed person over the age of fifty. The scheme was to be financed by the sale of state bonds and by a gross income tax on individuals and businesses within California. The purchase of a two-cent stamp (in order to make each $1.00 warrant negotiable per week) had the appeal of "producing" $1.04 at the end of fifty-two weeks. The additional four cents "gained" was to be used to administer the program. Payment of state taxes would be by scrip or warrants. Pushed by professional politicians in the state elections of 1938, the measure came close to adoption, despite the fact that well-informed critics labeled it economic irresponsibility. This movement, as well as the cure-all EPIC plan and Dr. Townsend's pension scheme, can best be understood in terms of the despair and confused thinking of the Depression years. The failure of Roosevelt's New Deal to endorse locally improvised plans doubtless contributed to their end. Nevertheless, California's welfare agitation of the early 1930s helped speed passage of the Social Security Act of 1935, a more realistic national approach to security.

Federal Relief and Work Programs

A series of congressional measures, most of which survived Supreme Court tests of their constitutionality, enabled Roosevelt to deliver on his campaign promises of a New Deal featuring relief, recovery, and reform. Dozens of new federal agencies, known by alphabetic abbreviations of their titles, were established to perform functions designed to bring back prosperity. Often these organizations worked in partnership with state agencies.

Mention has been made of the use of federal funds to construct Hoover Dam and of the national government's participation in the Central Valley Project. Other federally financed power, reclamation, flood-control, and navigation projects were to affect markedly the future of California. By the middle 1930s the short-term relief benefits of massive government aid had become everywhere evident. In California, as elsewhere throughout the nation, destitute people depended upon weekly government checks to sustain them until they could get jobs. In addition to this direct relief, unemployed young men were given jobs in the Civilian Conservation Corps (CCC). This project pushed through construction of mountain trails and firebreaks on federal forest lands or in the six new state parks established in California during 1933. Other young people in college were aided by National Youth Administration (NYA) money. Their fathers, meanwhile, worked on Works Progress Administration (WPA) or Public Work Administration (PWA) construction projects.

Though bitterly resisted by conservatives, these activities were effective in alleviating economic hardship. Their cost, moreover, came to seem modest in the light of expenditures during World War II and after. Certainly no state benefited more from the federal relief program than California, where hundreds of new schools, parks, roads, and beach facilities built during the Depression—in addition to the larger-scale projects previously mentioned—contributed materially to its development then and in the years that followed.

The Olson Administration and California's Governors

Despite the popularity of the New Deal—which helped Franklin Roosevelt to sweep the state in four successive national elections—there was only one Democratic state administration during the first half of the twentieth century. Until Governor Culbert L. Olson came to power in 1938, Californians had not seated a Democratic chief executive since Governor James H. Budd, who left office in 1899. Only an occasional Democrat had been elected to the legislature.

Most of the latter governors came from modest origins; like Olson, few were highly educated. Fewer of them, like Hiram Johnson or Earl Warren, became national figures. Only one governor of California has gone on to become president of the United States, although two became vice-presidential candidates and one became chief justice of the United States Supreme Court. Because of their disparity in background, it is difficult to compare them, or even to rate their administrations.

The reform movement that had come into prominence in the early years of the century had been largely led by the progressives, who were of Republican origin. The Republican party in California, in fact, was then generally more liberal than in the nation as a whole. Conversely, the Democratic party in the state had never built up a tradition of progressivism and reform. Even regarding Prohibition, which wreaked havoc upon a basic California industry, winemaking, the Democrats were politically timid.

Nevertheless, the reaction against Republican President Hoover that accompanied the Depression made it possible for William Gibbs McAdoo, former secretary of the treasury under President Wilson and director general of the railroads during World War I, to build up a Democratic machine in California during the early 1930s. McAdoo, Wilson's son-in-law, was elected to the Senate from California in 1932. That year the rangy McAdoo had stridden to the platform at the Democratic party convention in Chicago to cast California's forty-four votes for FDR. With this switch of the Golden State, Roosevelt, within minutes, received the Democratic nomination. By 1938, however, Sheridan Downey defeated McAdoo, then seventy-five years old, for the Democratic nomination to his Senate seat, despite a trip to California by President Roosevelt to endorse McAdoo. Downey went on to win a striking victory in the election also. On the same ticket, Olson, who had served a term in the state senate, was elected governor; in this office he followed the placid Republican administration of Governor Merriam, who had defeated Sinclair in 1934.

Olson was a frank advocate of FDR's ideas and, as a former backer also of Sinclair's EPIC plan, he stood for reformist policies. But he suffered the misfortune of becoming governor during the last stages of the Depression, when public pressure for liberal measures had abated. Although Olson tried to solve California's migrant-labor situation, an economy-minded Republican legislature enticed even Democrats into withdrawing support of Olson's reform program. In attacking agricultural problems, Olson also came up against the Associated Farmers, which opposed government meddling with the seasonal labor situation. Not only was Olson unable to secure passage through the legislature of his principal social measures, but his administration was wracked by the bungling of numerous appointees. His first official act—the freeing of Tom Mooney in 1939—remained his most dramatic one. In more conventional times such a governor might have been more successful. Soon liberal-minded Republicans, led by Attorney General Earl Warren, would have little trouble reclaiming the governorship from a besieged Olson.

Renewed Labor Agitation

As more industries moved to the West Coast the growth in the numbers of urban workers offered new opportunities for labor leaders to strengthen their power. Following the upswing of business after the recession of 1937, the CIO attracted previously unorganized laborers who were encouraged by the industry-wide bargaining techniques of John L. Lewis, the vigorous and effective CIO president. Lewis personally turned his attention to unskilled laborers in California's fields and factories who had once been the target of IWW organizers. Not until decades later would it be possible to unionize farm laborers.

Ripe, however, for immediate labor organization was the San Francisco waterfront. There, since the 1890s, the Coast Seamen's Union had agitated for better working conditions. Its leader was Andrew Furuseth. Born in Norway in 1846, he had sailed before the mast for years, and then had come to San Francisco; there he became a waterfront organizer and pioneer crusader for seamen's rights. He had dedicated himself to the extermination of such evils as "buckoism," "the crimp," and boardinghouses run by, or for the benefit of, maritime companies. Sailors were forced to pay a fee to the "crimp," a labor broker, in order to obtain employment. Similarly, the operators of boardinghouses, attracting seamen by providing them with beds, meals, and clothing on credit, charged exorbitant prices. Then these operators, with scores of unemployed seamen deeply in their debt, turned men over to the masters of ships with whom they were in league. The sailors were in no position to bargain over wages. Enraged by these practices, Furuseth fought for seamen's rights over many years. When, at his death in 1938, his ashes were thrown into the sea, the old man was honored by all maritime workers for his devoted service to the Sailors' Union of the Pacific which carried on his work.

Waterfront workers at San Francisco, still dissatisfied, considered their Longshoremen's Association a company union through which shippers controlled hiring and labor conditions. This was actually an open-shop situation. The prevailing discontent paved the way for the entrance of radicalism into the maritime labor movement, which now acquired new leaders. Among these was Harry Bridges, a spellbinding Australian-born longshoreman who operated a hydraulic winch on the Embarcadero, San Francisco's wharfs. He began to attract attention in the early 1930s by complaining that a speedup of waterfront operations, to reduce the costs of handling vessels in port, caused many accidents among the longshoremen. The maritime firms countered by stating that tonnage had declined yearly because of the unrealistic demands of waterfront workers.

His enemies called Bridges a dangerous alien radical, if not a Communist. But thousands of longshoremen up and down the Pacific Coast stood behind his authoritarian ILA leadership. By 1934 he staged a strike that affected shipping from San Diego to Seattle. The militant Bridges wanted a minimum thirty-hour week at wages of a dollar an hour. He also objected to the "shape-up" system of hiring longshoremen, by which shipping-company foremen selected workers the company wanted. Bridges charged that favoritism and pandering to company demands determined whether a worker was employed, instead of union seniority. Bridges ultimately obtained a system of hiring halls under union control.

The center of the great maritime strike of 1934 was San Francisco. The ILA tied up traffic in and out of the port for ninety days. In sympathy with longshoremen, other workers went out on strike too. Sailors marched off their ships; warehousemen quit their jobs; teamsters abandoned trucks and lift vans. Hundreds of ships lay idle in San Francisco Bay, while cargoes rotted and rusted on piers and in warehouses.

The attempt by employers to use strikebreakers only aggravated matters. On July 5, "Bloody Thursday," an especially violent episode erupted, in which the San Francisco police moved against picket lines with tear gas. Before it was over, two union pickets had been shot to death, and over 100 men, including police, had been wounded. On July 14, ILA leaders appealed to all unions not already involved in the sympathy strikes to join in protesting the action of the police. Almost 150,000 workers of all descriptions stopped work for three days. The entire San Francisco area was paralyzed, in the most severe disturbance the city had undergone since the earthquake and fire of 1906. The governor called out the National Guard to protect state property. This move intensified the resentment of riotous strikers, as did the action of "vigilantes" who wrecked "radical" meeting places.

Internal disputes among union leaders helped end the strike. The more conservative ones felt that the general strike damaged the interests of unionism; this was too high a price to pay for a short-term victory against management. As allied union members returned to work, only the longshoremen remained out on strike. Eventually these were prevailed upon to "work" specified ships and to submit their demands to the arbitration of a Presidential Longshoremen's Board. The longshoremen won concessions from management, including higher wages and joint control of their own hiring halls. However, fourteen agitators seized or arrested in the strike were later deported as aliens residing unlawfully in the United States. Though the strike had resulted in a quasi-victory for labor, the public was not to forget that the price had been violence.

Settlement of this strike by no means brought peace to the San Francisco waterfront. Shorter labor stoppages occurred throughout the later 1930s. A jurisdictional altercation between Bridges and other labor leaders continued until Bridges took his longshoremen into the CIO. Bridges remined controversial. Because of his power, demands were made for his deportation from 1936 onward. The congressional Committee on Un-American activities charged that the ILWU and other CIO unions were under Communist leadership and control. One of the chief witnesses accused Bridges of being a Communist who used unions for Communist purposes. The courts upheld Bridges's radical unionization techniques. Personally explosive, he retained power along the Pacific Coast and Hawaii.

During the mid-1930s demands for unionization spread to Los Angeles, the center of the "American Plan," as the open shop was known. By 1935, the port of San Pedro had been unionized. Pressures filtered back from the city's waterfront into Los Angeles proper. Next, the plasterers, hod carriers, plumbers, typographers, tire workers, steam fitters, and auto workers became more adamant in their demands upon management.

By the end of the 1930s a new era of negotiation had begun in the relations of California labor and management. Harry Bridges called strikes an "obsolete weapon," while Roger Lapham, chairman of the board of the American-Hawaiian Steamship Company (and later mayor of San Francisco) stated, "I do not believe that employers should organize to break unions." Though still distrustful of one another, both sides had learned to cooperate for their mutual benefit. Meanwhile, the New Deal encouraged collective bargaining through the National Labor Relations Board. Labor came to look upon the federal government as a friend who would respond to its demands. A handful of disgruntled workers felt that government could do more to relieve Depression conditions. Conversely, some businessmen were convinced that the coddling of labor, accompanied by pump-priming measures, could not restore prosperity. For the most part, California capital and labor joined in the national struggle to find some way out of the economic darkness.

William Randolph Hearst

Against the background of the grave social dislocations of the Depression years the figure of William Randolph Hearst stands out in particular relief. Born into a wealthy family at San Francisco in 1863— his father, Senator George Hearst, had created a mining fortune— young Will attended Harvard and, in 1887, at the age of twenty-four, was handed the San Francisco *Examiner* to manage. Through his willingness to invest vast amounts of his father's money, Hearst made the *Examiner* the most powerful paper on the West Coast. His reputation as a young and energetic publisher was first made by attacks on the Southern Pacific Railroad. At first the young Hearst appeared in the role of a reformist crusader; but by the 1930s he bore little resemblance to the liberal of earlier decades. Hearst came to believe that reform had gone far enough and that conservatism must reverse the power of labor unions, of government, and, in particular, of New Dealers.

Throughout his eighty-eight years Hearst was an enigma even to close associates. Though outwardly shy, he made his power felt even at the international level through his chain of some thirty newspapers, thirteen magazines, and several radio stations. Hearst came to be associated with a remarkable number of issues and events. Prominent among these were the Spanish-American War (which he almost surely helped cause); hatred of the two Roosevelts (although by one of the choicest ironies of history he had in large measure obtained the presidential nomination of the second one); antivivisection; opposition to United States entry into both World Wars; suppression of radical minorities; and distrust of internationalism. In promoting his prejudices, Hearst achieved mixed results. Thinking persons were offended by his convictions, and nearly always repelled by his taste. But mass public tastes made the Hearst press popular.

At the heart of Hearst's empire were his newspapers. He bought papers all over the country and applied to them the techniques of reckless spending and reporting that had made the *Examiner* successful. There was a sameness about their sensational reportage, as well as about their slanted editorials that appealed to a less-than-educated readership. These newspapers were the archetypes of yellow journalism—the despair of Hearst's critics. In California's Depression decades, as the "Chief" grew more conservatively eccentric, the Hearst press was one of the bulwarks in the way of economic or political reform. Even conservatives shunned Hearst as he moved toward the extreme right. The Hearst machine spewed hate at both President Roosevelt and Governor Olson, and fulminated against all attempts to "tinker" with the currency, to "coddle" the unemployed, and to "socialize" the country.

The headquarters of Hearst's domain was his San Simeon estate, on the rocky coast between San Luis Obispo and Monterey. In the interwar years "the Lord of San Simeon" poured $35 million into the construction of an immense castle there. Stocking it with art treasures from all over the world, Hearst made San Simeon a rendezvous for guests drawn from the fields of the movie industry, art, music, literature, and public affairs.

Hearst, like his mother, Phoebe Apperson Hearst, was given to subsidizing philanthropic and educational institutions. Nevertheless, there were many who felt that he could easily have used more of his annual income (at times $15 million) for other purposes than to gratify his acquisitive impulse. In 1935 his far-flung personal empire was valued at $200 million. His holdings included seven castles; warehouses full of antique furniture, hundreds of paintings, and tapestries; ranches on which he raised 10,000 beef cattle; several zoos, hunting lodges, and beach homes.

Orson Welles's 1940 film *Citizen Kane* drew a picture of the personal imperialism of the aging genius. As times changed, the anachronism of "Citizen Hearst," as one of his biographers calls him, became more apparent. After World War II the Hearst dynasty crumbled. By the mid-1960s his two major papers, the San Francisco *Examiner* and the Los Angeles *Examiner*, gave way to the *Chronicle* and the *Times*. The *Examiners*, both morning papers, had to be merged with the Hearst evening newspapers to meet the competition of suburban dailies and radio and television newscasts, and to deal with rising production costs, lowered advertising, and falling circulation.

Selected Readings

On the Dust Bowl migration see Walter J. Stein, *California and the Dust Bowl Migration* (Westport, Conn., 1973), in addition to the novels of John Steinbeck, and the treatment by Dorothea Lange and Paul S. Taylor, *An American Exodus: A Record of Human Erosion* (New York, 1939). The story of the California social crusaders, including Dr. Townsend, is told in Luther Whiteman and Samuel L. Lewis, *Glory Roads: The Psychological State of California* (New York, 1936). A book that is more statistical than descriptive is Abraham Holtzman, *The Townsend Movement: A Political Study* (New York, 1963). Regarding the Prohibitionists see Gilman Ostrander, *The Prohibition Movement in California* (Berkeley, 1957). See also Abe Hoffman, "A Look at

Llano: Experiment in Economic Socialism," *California Historical Society Quarterly* 40 (September 1961), 215–36.

On Sinclair, the basic book is his own *I, Candidate for Governor—and How I Got Licked* (Pasadena, 1935). See also Fay Blake and H. M. Newman, "Upton Sinclair's Epic Campaign," *California Historical Quarterly* 63 (Fall 1984), 305–19; Judson Grenier, "Upton Sinclair: A Remembrance;" *California Historical Society Quarterly* 47 (June 1969), 165–69; and Grenier's "Upton Sinclair: The Road to California," *Southern California Quarterly* 56 (Winter 1974), 325–36, which appeared in an entire issue of that journal devoted to Sinclair.

Related to the reform movement are Woodrow C. Whitten, *Criminal Syndicalism and Law in California* (Philadelphia, 1969), and Philip Taft, *Labor Politics American Style: The California State Federation of Labor* (Cambridge, Mass., 1968), which traces activities, organization, and personalities from 1901 until its merger with the AFL-CIO in 1958.

The references on labor in California given in the Selected Readings for Chapter 31 are pertinent to this chapter. See also Mitchell Slobodek, *A Selective Bibliography of California Labor History* (Berkeley and Los Angeles, 1964). The best biography of a California maritime labor leader is Hyman Weintraub's *Andrew Furuseth: Emancipator of the Seamen* (Berkeley, 1959). This can be supplemented with Robert Knight, *Industrial Relations in the San Francisco Bay Area, 1900–1918* (Berkeley, 1960), and Paul S. Taylor, *The Sailors' Union of the Pacific* (New York, 1923). Alexander Saxton, "San Francisco Labor and the Populist and Progressive Insurgencies," *Pacific Historical Review* 34 (November 1965), 421–38, discusses labor from 1890 to 1914. Charles Norris, *Flint* (New York, 1940), is a novel that depicts agitation in the San Francisco shipyards during the middle 1930s. San Francisco's crippling strike of 1934 and other labor disturbances are discussed in Ira B. Cross, *History of the Labor Movement in California* (Berkeley, 1935). More specific are Mike Quin, *The Big Strike* (Olema, 1949), and Paul Eliel, *The Waterfront and General Strike . . .* (San Francisco, 1934).

H. Brett Melendy and Benjamin F. Gilbert's *The Governors of California* (Georgetown, Calif., 1965), is the only overall study of the state's governors.

California's New Deal years are treated by Robert E. Burke, *Olson's New Deal for California* (Berkeley, 1952). John Phillips, *Inside California* (Los Angeles, 1939), is an anti-Olson view. Oliver Carlson, *A Mirror for Californians* (Indianapolis, 1941), takes a look at the same period. Olson's successor is the subject of Irving Stone's *Earl Warren: A Great American Story* (New York, 1948).

Concerning Hearst, see Oliver Carlson and Ernest S. Bates, *Hearst: Lord of San Simeon* (New York, 1937); John Tebbel, *The Life and Good*

Times of William Randolph Hearst (New York, 1952); John K. Winkler, *William Randolph Hearst: A New Appraisal* (New York, 1955); and W. A. Swanberg, *Citizen Hearst: A Biography of William Randolph Hearst* (New York, 1961).

Two studies of the zoot suit riots at Los Angeles are: Ralph S. Banay, "A Psychiatrist Looks at the Zoot Suit," *Probation* XII (February 1944), 81–5, and Mauricio Mazón, *The Zoot Suit Riots* (Austin, Tex., 1984). Another minority is the subject of Harold A. De Witt, "The Watsonville Anti-Filipino Riot of 1930," *Southern California Quarterly* LXI (Fall 1979), 291–302.

CHAPTER 33

Twentieth-Century Cultural Developments

AFTER 1900, the turbulence of an expanding society resulted in many forms of intellectual ferment. Some of this experimentation was misdirected and confused, embracing the derivative and the mediocre. In the first part of the present century artistic improvisation sometimes took strange forms.

Faddists and Cultists

During the first quarter of the century, southern California was descended upon by migrants armed with numerous solutions to mankind's dilemmas, from economics to health. The mild climate and cheap housing helped attract members of bizarre social and religious cults who had been discontented elsewhere. With them they brought ideas—sincere for the most part—that even tolerant natives found difficult to accept. A few diet faddists went so far as to preach that they could conquer illness by mixing "spiritual power," "mushroom-burgers," and date milk shakes. Among the new arrivals were such religious fundamentalists as the Rev. Robert P. Shuler of Kentucky and Dr. Billy Sunday, the radio evangelist. They were joined by Yogi mystics, Swami palm readers, rainmakers, Hindu fakirs, and occultists of every description. Earnest devotees—including sentimental elderly persons and aging movie queens—joined to venerate their chosen spiritual leaders.

Theosophy, a sect following Buddhist and Brahman theories, gained loyal adherents in California. The theosophists sought knowledge of

417

God by mystical insight and philosophical speculation. "The Purple Mother," Katherine Tingley, established a Point Loma Theosophical Community near San Diego about 1900. It lasted until shortly after her death in 1929. In the 1920s the theosophist Annie Besant also came west and settled in the Ojai Valley below Santa Barbara. There she brought "The New Messiah," one Krishnamurti, to preside over her small flock of converts. Until her death in 1933 this rival of Katherine Tingley looked upon her Ojai community as the cradle of a "new civilization."

Another woman who played a part in religious pentecostal faith-healing was Aimee Semple McPherson, a dynamic evangelist who founded the Four Square Gospel Church in Los Angeles. Full of verve and loud of voice, Mrs. McPherson, or Sister Aimee as she was called, practiced conversion and therapeutic redemption through vigorous evangelism. On occasion she scattered religious tracts from an airplane; at other times she held prayer meetings in a boxing arena. A talented showwoman who sometimes wore the white uniform and gold braid of an admiral, Sister Aimee had a potent appeal for the downhearted and lonely. From the platform of Angelus Temple, she exhorted the multitudes to follow her into mortal combat with the devil. For twenty years she broadcast religious services over radio station KFSG. In 1925 the station wandered off its assigned wavelength. Herbert Hoover, then secretary of commerce, ordered the station's license suspended, whereupon Sister Aimee cabled him: "PLEASE ORDER YOUR MINIONS OF SATAN TO LEAVE MY STATION ALONE. . . . YOU CANNOT EXPECT THE ALMIGHTY TO ABIDE BY YOUR WAVELENGTH NONSENSE. . . ." In 1926 Sister Aimee walked into the ocean and was presumed to have drowned. Eight days later she reappeared with a tall tale that she had been kidnapped, and was given a grand reception at Los Angeles. The story, however, was exposed as questionable, if not false. Mrs. McPherson died in 1944. By that time she had accumulated a great deal of property and had added more than two hundred branch churches to her denomination. She had offered her followers not only the entertainment of bell ringers and xylophone bands; she also gave material aid to the sick and needy who gravitated toward southern California, craving her unorthodox form of prayer and guidance.

In recent years the cinema has treated the Los Angeles of Sister Aimee's era in such films as *Chinatown* (1975). The exploitation of local themes by merchandisers of history has also spread to television, where her story was presented as a TV special during 1976. Sister Aimee was a notable expression of that occultism for which "L.A." was becoming known. One sees the same phenomenon in the "funeral park." These stereotyped establishments, found throughout southern California, are advertised as vales for the departed. Their stock in trade is the glossing over of death as associated with the mundane cemetery or graveyard of the past. Swaddled in euphemisms, mourners are presented with a glowing vision of the hereafter as a desirable place to go, in happiness. The crudities of this approach have lent themselves to the lampooning of satiric authors, especially Aldous Huxley and Evelyn Waugh.

Asked why he had settled in southern California, Huxley once quipped, "I stopped there on my way to India, and because of inertia and apathy remained." Los Angeles had an influence on the way Huxley wrote. A critic of man's outdated Victorian pomposities, Huxley grew cynical; yet he sought solutions that might satisfy man's animal and spiritual needs. In *After Many a Summer Dies the Swan*, Huxley mocked ostentation and personal hollowness. He became impressed with eastern mystical thought and began to attend meetings of the Vedanta cult, accompanied by yet another "southern California Englishman," Christopher Isherwood. He hated the grotesquely palatial residences of the Hearsts and of the movie magnates and lampooned advertisements for funeral parks ("the Beverly Pantheon, a Personality Cemetery"). Huxley also experimented with mescaline, seeking to improve his visions of Buddhism, wrote about Utopias, and peopled his novellas with mystics searching for God in a semiarid paradise of orange groves and eternal sunlight.

California came to be seen as peculiarly hospitable to occultism, as a final resting place where odd practitioners were tolerated long after stable social patterns had become the rule elsewhere. Ideas and movements that embarrassed the rest of the nation gave southern California a reputation for the bizarre. Delusional behavior impaired its sense of reality. In the individual such behavior is associated with mental regression to infantile stages. In their delusions, some persons saw, heard, and even met angels as well as demons.

Literary Trends

During the early twentieth century, writers from all over the nation continued to visit California, as Mark Twain, Bret Harte, Helen Hunt Jackson, and Mary Austin had done. Some were more distinguished by their industry than by their literary finesse. A notable example of a writer who came to California before World War I and made a fortune there was Zane Grey. Prior to settling in Altadena, where he built a Zuni-style terraced house, Grey had been an Ohio dentist with experience also as a professional baseball player. Grey soon was writing at least one and sometimes two Western novels per year. The most popular of these was his *Riders of the Purple Sage* (1912). His work was stereotyped and pedestrian, but its exploitation of the color and, loosely speaking, of the history of the West achieved popularity. He influenced subsequent pulp writers of Western fiction by setting a style that was undeviating as to plot but was highly marketable. More than sixty of Grey's books were printed in large editions. His production was far in excess of immediate—as opposed to long-term—demand; and although he died in 1939, Grey's manuscripts continued to be published long after his death.

In the same tradition of literary mass production was Harold Bell Wright. First an artist and later a minister, Wright was the author of several dozen novels set in the West. At about the time he moved to California he published his first successful work, *The Shepherd of the Hills* (1907). Wright's *The Winning of Barbara Worth* (1911), focusing upon the reclamation of the Imperial Valley from the desert, sold more than a million and a half copies. His other best-selling novel, *The Eyes of the World* (1914), also used southern California as a literary backdrop. Wright's major characters were conceived as absorbing strength from an environment on the edge of the wilderness. This theme of nobility springing from the soil never seemed spontaneous, however, and his books are not highly regarded today. Another subliterary arrival in southern California was Gene Stratton Porter, author of the popular *A Girl of the Limberlost* (1909).

More significant American writers also came to California. One of these was Hamlin Garland, who had achieved fame as celebrator of the "middle border," in works based on his native Middle West. Toward the end of his life Garland moved to Hollywood and spent his last years there. Little of major importance marked this period, although Garland did produce in California his *Roadside Meetings* (1930), *Companions on the Trail* (1932), and *My Friendly Contemporaries* (1932). He also absorbed the local environment, writing about spiritualism and psychic phenomena. Another prominent author, Theodore Dreiser, spent several years in Hollywood during the 1920s and settled there in 1938, staying on until his death in 1945. Like Garland, he turned to other interests in these later years, producing *The Bulwark* (1946), a minor work published after his death, which stresses spiritual values in the life of the individual. A laborer with a different purpose was Will Durant, a popularizer of history.

Between the two world wars European intellectual refugees, attracted by a wonderful climate and an atmosphere of freedom, found both variety and surprise in southern California. Los Angeles's universities and colleges gave them what their old cultures had once provided. Among the foreign-born writers were Aldous Huxley, Thomas Mann, and Christopher Isherwood. In addition to the previously mentioned attacks by Huxley and Evelyn Waugh on what they considered to be the macabre "cemetery culture" of the region, the lampooning of quackery and faddism in religion and economics has been a favorite sport among visiting writers. Satirists, more often than not Englishmen, have depicted the exotic unreality of California, its commercialism, the vapidity of Hollywood, or the harsh realities behind the new fortunes being coined there. Conversely, California has been called a boneyard for aging British intellectuals. Huxley grew philosophical about the confusion he saw, while Isherwood continued to focus on the Berlin he had known between the wars. Mann and his daughter Erika came to California as refugees from Nazism, and the themes he dealt with were far from the land in which they had sought refuge. Between the wars Sadakichi Hartmann, a Japanese-born historian of art and an aesthete, wrote plays, took bit parts in the movies, and, at San Francisco, produced strange and exotic poetry.

Among other poetic craftsmen was George Sterling, known for his romantic sonnets, which were musical in style. He produced most of his work at Carmel on the Monterey peninsula, where he settled after writing his first poetry in a studio of San Francisco's Montgomery Block. Sterling, in Jack London's words, "looked like a Greek coin run over by a Roman chariot." His *Testimony of the Suns* (1903) was imaginative and honest. In 1926, Sterling killed himself in San Francisco's Bohemian Club.

Robinson Jeffers is today considered the greatest poet California has produced. Jeffers, after graduation from Occidental College, went to live at Carmel and there built with his own hands an imposing stone residence named Tor House. With his wife and sons he spent the rest of his life in that solid house. Jeffers set forth powerfully his feelings about man's depravity, which he contrasted with the nobility of the Carmel coastline. Symbolic in his themes, Jeffers made man out to be an insignificant and unworthy child of nature. He once wrote, "Cut humanity out of my being, that is the wound that festers." His respect for the primeval and for the wonders of the universe itself were what first drew admirers to his stark poetry and what kept them reading his works. Jeffers was at his best in such long narrative poems as *Roan Stallion* (1925) and *Be Angry at the Sun* (1925). In his later years, *Medea* (1947), a tragedy adapted for poetic drama from Euripides, also brought him acclaim. Early in 1962 he died in his beloved Tor House.

The reformist writers of twentieth-century California were in the tradition of Henry George, Frank Norris, and Jack London. Among them was Upton Sinclair, another in the long line of literary imports. Like London and Norris, he had a profound desire to correct social ills. Sinclair came to California after World War I, having already written his novels *The Jungle* (1906) and *The Money-Changers* (1908). He had an extraordinary career, at the same time exerting leadership in countless causes. Almost everything he stood for was detestable to business interests, and his platform, as divulged in his book *The EPIC Plan for California* (1934), was inflammatory in its utopianism. But Sinclair's writings commanded worldwide attention. There is no question that such books as *The Jungle* achieved specific reforms. In later years Sinclair wrote the Lanny Budd series which began with *World's End* (1940), and continues through nine more novels to *O Shepherd Speak!* (1949).

Recent California Novelists

The best known of the "California novelists" is John Steinbeck, born at Salinas in 1902. In his early books *The Pastures of Heaven* (1932) and *Tortilla Flat* (1935), Steinbeck discovered himself as a writer through using the people and setting of the Salinas Valley, much as William Faulkner relied on a mythical county in Mississippi. Steinbeck's work portrays both character and terrain, and frequently reflects the author's anger with injustice; the latter quality gives it a kinship with works of such other reformists as Frank Norris and his contemporary, Sinclair. Steinbeck's most important novel, *The Grapes of Wrath* (1939), probably won him the Pulitzer Prize. It displays a sociological, almost a polemical bent. The book chronicles the plight of Oklahoma farmers forced by Dust Bowl conditions of the early 1930s to move westward and become "fruit tramps" in California. In its description of these rootless, deprived hangers-on, Steinbeck achieved a trenchantly dramatic impact. He later found raw material for his writing in society's harsh treatment of other minority groups. For a time, however, Steinbeck's writing lost its earlier vitality. His long novel *East of Eden* (1952), again set in the Salinas locale, was only moderately effective as a symbolic analysis of evil. *The Wayward Bus* (1947) and *Sweet Thursday* (1954) were even less significant. Although no one could be sure that his next book would not be a minor classic, *The Winter of Our Discontent* (1961) was not such a book. His *Travels With Charley in Search of America* (1962) was merely attractive.

As Steinbeck had done, William Saroyan discovered rich literary lore in the agricultural area where he was born. Saroyan's work is largely set in the countryside around Fresno and reflects his Armenian origins in the San Joaquin Valley. His novels and plays, including *My Heart's in the Highlands* (1939), *My Name is Aram* (1940), and *The Beautiful People* (1942), present a group of rural characters who are rhapsodically individualistic, if not eccentric. Saroyan is better known for his short stories. In these, an assemblage of warm and attractive people, reflecting the author's kindly assessment of human nature, are depicted as inhabiting a carefree dream world.

Following World War II Steinbeck and Saroyan did not recapture

Jagged stretch along the coast of Sonoma County in Northern California. (By courtesy of Redwood Empire Association.)

the youthful audiences that had once been their admirers. Replacing them in popular favor, much good writing began to come out of the colleges and universities of the state. At Stanford Wallace Stegner was earning acclaim for books set in the American West, among them *Mormon Country* (1942) and *The Big Rock Candy Mountain* (1943). Like Stegner, Mark Schorer (*The State of Mind*, 1947) and Henry Nash Smith (*Virgin Land*, 1950) were professors who combined writing with teaching. Richard Armour, on the faculty of Scripps College, made a name for himself as the "playful poet," with light verse reminiscent of Gelett Burgess.

Academic writers also developed historical themes, in both fiction and nonfiction. At Occidental College, historian Robert Glass Cleland produced entertaining narratives on the fur trade, the California ranches, and the American West. At the University of California George R. Stewart, in such books as *Fire* (1948) and *Sheep Rock* (1950), spanned history and literature in a workmanlike way. Stewart's earlier *Bret Harte* (1931) and *Ordeal by Hunger* (1936) fall more definitely within the category of nonfiction, while his *East of the Giants* (1938) and *Storm* (1941) are fictional works. Also writing fiction in a Western setting was Walter Van Tilburg Clark, on the faculty of San Francisco State College. There he taught students techniques developed in his

The Ox-Bow Incident (1940) and *The Track of the Cat* (1949). Another professor who wrote popularly in the postwar years was Eugene Burdick, of the University of California. His *The Ninth Wave* (1956) is a fictional view of California politics as seen by a trained observer. With William J. Lederer, Burdick went on to write *The Ugly American* (1958), a book that created a national stir by its critique of Americans abroad, especially the most bumptious of those government officials administering foreign-aid programs in other lands. Burdick collaborated with another college teacher, Harvey Wheeler, on *Fail-Safe* (1962), a novel that predicted an accidental nuclear holocaust.

The best-known novel of Niven Busch, *California Street* (1959), concerns a San Francisco newspaper dynasty. He has also written *Duel in the Sun, The Hate Merchant,* and *The Actor.* James Edmiston's *Home Again* (1955) is a poignant criticism of the government's removal of Japanese-born Americans from the Pacific Coast during World War II. A related theme runs through Abraham Polansky's *A Season of Fear* (1956), an indictment of the public attitude toward minority groups. San Francisco Chinese form the backdrop of C. Y. Lee's tasteful *The Flower-Drum Song* (1956), which became a musical play and film.

The list of prominent postwar writers includes Jessamyn West, a Quaker educated at Whittier, whose *The Friendly Persuasion* (1945) was transformed into a prize-winning movie script. Her *South of the Angels* (1960), like James M. Cain's *The Postman Always Rings Twice* (1934) and *Mildred Pierce* (1941), is set in southern California. Similarly, Judy van der Veer skillfully described the San Diego backcountry in *Brown Hills* (1938) and *November Grass* (1940). John Fante, in *Ask the Dust* (1940), *Wait for the Spring, Bandini* (1938), and *Dago Red* (1940), and Joe Pagano (*Golden Wedding*, 1943) have portrayed an Italian-American background of life in the Far West.

Another successful literary Californian was Erle Stanley Gardner. Admitted to the California bar in 1911, he began writing about criminal topics as an avocation. Gardner is best known as the creator of Perry Mason, a detective-lawyer who as the supersleuth hero of innumerable books and television shows has received something of the adulation won earlier by A. Conan Doyle's Sherlock Holmes. Gardner, like other writers, found California congenial as an atmosphere in which to work but drew many of his themes from elsewhere. So did Edgar Rice Burroughs, originator of the banal Tarzan stories, Rupert Hughes, and James Hilton, all popularizers who kept up a voluminous production. On a level of descending importance were Stuart Lake (*Wyatt Earp*, 1931), Paul Wellman (*The Iron Mistress*, 1951), and Ernest Haycox (*The Earthbreakers*, 1952). Outpacing each of these writers in sales is Louis L'Amour, all-time best-selling author of Westerns. Beginning with *Hondo* (1952), his several dozen novels have sold millions of copies.

A totally different type of writer was Henry Miller, born in Manhattan in 1891. Most of his work was autobiographical; his best-known books are *Tropic of Cancer* (1934) and *Tropic of Capricorn* (1938), written during his expatriate period abroad. For many years Miller lived on a mountaintop overlooking the Pacific Ocean at Big Sur. His book *Big Sur and the Oranges of Hieronymus Bosch* (1956) describes his life in California. He takes his reader on a firsthand tour of human depravity, and his central statement is that man has lost the art of living and that "until this collosal, senseless machine which we have made in America is smashed and scrapped there can be no hope."

A group reflecting Miller's influence grew up in the 1950s. Prominent among these spokesmen of the "Beat Generation" were Jack Kerouac and Allen Ginsberg, who made San Francisco their headquarters. Both expressed the frustrations of impatient young people who abhorred postwar society. Kerouac coined the phrase "Beat Generation" to describe disillusioned associates whom he portrayed in his writings. Ginsberg joined Kerouac in publishing his writing in *Neurotica*, a journal built on "beat" compositions that reflected a rebellion against "squares"—those mediocre conformists who lived a safe but dull existence. Defying society's conventions, the "beatniks" clustered about the *café espresso* houses of San Francisco and the west side of Los Angeles.

These bearded bohemians aroused critics, who felt they deserved the unpopularity they sought. As if to anticipate the Hippie rebellion of the 1960s, their poetry readings, jazz festivals, and "kookie" artistic displays at Sausalito generated only mild interest, even among the young of the 1950s. The "beatniks" thought they were modern and avant-garde, which perhaps they were for a while. Probably the most representative of their works is Kerouac's *On the Road*. Ginsberg's *Howl* (1956) was called on the one hand a tedious collection of raucous, wordy, and complex poems; on the other, friendly critics found some astonishing effects in this book. Ginsberg and Kerouac's writings were considered intense and challenging by some, but adolescent and unrewarding by others. On occasion, the "beats" could become humorous; they encouraged the social commentary of the comedian Mort Sahl, a former University of California student who made a fortune in such nightclubs as San Francisco's Hungry i and Hollywood's Crescendo, as well as through records and television.

Periodical and Book Publishing

In the mid-twentieth century, the penetrating regionalism that had characterized the early California press gave way to national editorial standardization. Hearst's fulminations about the Southern Pacific and General Otis's tirades against local labor bosses in the Los Angeles *Times* were replaced by syndicated news and editorial opinion provided by Eastern wire-service media. The California press remains characterized by lack of variety and a high degree of monopolization. Even in large cities one or two papers control the news media.

California has not yet produced a major book publishing firm, but it has numerous fine printers. Both typographers and book dealers have established a tradition for distinctive printing, supported by the Book Club of California and the Zamorano and Roxburghe Clubs. They produce books mostly in limited editions, with regional appeal. The University of California Press, Stanford University Press, the Arthur H. Clark Company, and Fearon have, however, instituted commercial operations resembling those of publishing firms of the eastern seaboard. Meanwhile, other commercial presses have sprung up at or near San Francisco in the postwar period, notably Wadsworth, W. H. Freeman, North Point Press, Hesperian, and Angel Island. In the 1980s Harcourt Brace Jovanovich moved its headquarters from New York to San Diego.

Music and Drama

In the early twentieth century, the most important musical institutions in California were the Tivoli Opera House and the San Francisco Symphony. The Tivoli closed in 1913, but the San Francisco Opera Company filled the gap ten years later. After 1932 it was given a home, the War Memorial Opera House, the first such municipal structure in the United States. The San Francisco Symphony, since its founding in 1911, has benefited from the leadership of outstanding conductors who improved its quality. In southern California, the Los Angeles Philharmonic Orchestra, founded in 1919, has attracted such conductors as Carlo Maria Giulini and André Previn. Since 1921, open-air concerts at the Hollywood Bowl have given both musicians and conductors an outlet for their talents.

In the interwar period early resident songwriters Charles Wakefield Cadman and Carrie Jacobs Bond were replaced by others. Ferdinand Rudolph (Ferde) Grofe, an arranger, and composer of the *Grand Canyon Suite*, began his career as an "extra" piano player at the Old Hippodrome Theater on San Francisco's Barbary Coast. On the eve of World War II foreign composers sought refuge in California, among them Arnold Schönberg and Igor Stravinsky.

Los Angeles has been a point of origin for many musicals that have gone on to long Broadway runs. Among these have been *Show Boat*, with Paul Robeson, *Roberta*, with comedian Bob Hope, *Peter Pan*, starring Mary Martin, as well as *Kismet* and *Song of Norway*. Among the celebrated creators of musicals who came from elsewhere to work in California were Jerome Kern, Oscar Hammerstein, Sigmund Romberg, and George Gershwin. The Civic Light Opera Company staged a majority of these performances over a period of more than fifty years. Today the Mark Taper and Ahmanson theaters feature regular productions. Most of the plays of Neil Simon have been produced locally before their national runs.

The Films and Television

Hollywood, which became the world's film capital, has drawn to California its greatest publicity in modern times, both good and bad. The development of the first motion-picture techniques in the United States was not, however, confined to Hollywood. In 1872 Eadweard Muybridge, a photographer, was commissioned by former Governor Leland Stanford to take action shots of Stanford's race horse, named Occident. Stanford had bet a friend $25,000 that horses, while trotting, took all four hooves off the ground at one time during their stride. In order to prove this, Muybridge, with the aid of the engineering staff at Stanford's Southern Pacific Railway, lined up twenty-four cameras along a race track at Palo Alto. Fine wires were then stretched across the track. As the horse broke these, a camera shutter was released, with the result that a series of photographic prints were taken at stated intervals. The illusion was created that the horse was in motion when projection of the individual exposures onto a screen in rapid succession produced what was in essence a moving picture. Muybridge's achievement attracted attention to the possibility of designing a motion-picture camera. Credit for its invention, however, is usually but erroneously given to Thomas Alva Edison and his assistants.

For some years after the development of movie cameras, the production of films was largely confined to New York and New Jersey. About 1907, however, producers, actors, and scenario writers began to swarm toward Hollywood, for two main reasons. First, California's year-round good climate and variety of scenery made it an ideal location for motion-picture production. Second, the state was far from Eastern debt collectors eager to hound movie producers, and from the interference of New York State's motion-picture patent law, with its injunctions against producers who infringed upon the patents held by Edison and other developers of cinema equipment. The fugitive producers with their bootleg cameras had little capital with which to build a new industry. In southern California, however, since labor costs were lower than elsewhere, they could operate on a shoestring budget if they pooled resources. They rented second-hand equipment, painted their own sets, improvised lighting techniques—did everything possible to save money. In 1913 when Samuel Goldwyn, Jesse Lasky, and Cecil B. De Mille came west to produce *The Squaw Man* in a barn at the corner of Selma and Vine Streets, they had only a few thousand dollars and an unknown actress, Clara Kimball Young. This picture, and those that followed, enriched the producers as orders poured in from hundreds of former vaudeville houses and nickelodeons now transformed into movie parlors.

In addition to these independent producers from New York, film organizations began to grow up in California. One of the first of these was the Selig Polyscope Company, which in 1907–1908 filmed *The Count of Monte Cristo* near Los Angeles. Selig built a studio the next year at Edendale, a Los Angeles suburb. In 1909 the Bison Studios of New York arrived in Hollywood, followed by the Pathé organization and Biograph. The Vitagraph, Kalem, and Edison film companies appeared shortly thereafter. By 1914, when most of the Eastern companies had sent work forces to California, seventy-three firms were producing pictures in California. In those early years of the industry, a film company could grind out a "Western" every other day.

A sleepy little village founded by Kansas prohibitionists before the turn of the century, Hollywood had a town ordinance as late as 1903 that forbade driving more than two thousand sheep down Hollywood Boulevard at any one time. Hollywood, almost overnight, was transformed into the center of the film world.

During the early years of the film industry, it passed through a megaphone-and-custard-pie-comedy phase that drew to it both hacks and persons of talent. That era gave rise to the stereotype of the autocratic director, clad in riding breeches and wearing his cap backward, who shouted orders at droves of extras employed to fill the background of his pictures. Among the most imaginative men who came west to "shoot pictures" was David Wark Griffith, producer of *The Birth of a Nation*. Due to its high cost of production ($100,000), this was the first American picture to command a two-dollar admission fee. It opened at Clune's Auditorium in Los Angeles on February 8, 1915, and ultimately grossed $20,000,000. This was also the first film to be honored with a showing at the White House, where President Wilson is said to have remarked, "It is like writing history with lightning."

With the development of a "star system," the production of films became fantastically expensive. Outside the marquees of klieg-lighted premières, traffic stopped while fans ogled their favorite stars. Charlie Chaplin, who became famous all over the world, was an English comedian whose background was pantomime. With Mary Pickford, soon known as "America's Sweetheart," Chaplin worked for Mack Sennett's Keystone Company. In two years Chaplin's salary skyrocketed from $150 to $10,000 a week. Both of these stars were to command salaries in excess of $1 million a year. Theda Bara, Dustin Farnum, Harold Lloyd, Lillian Gish, Rudolph Valentino, and Greta Garbo were other performers whom fans idolized. The cowboy stars William S. Hart, Tom Mix, and Ed ("Hoot") Gibson became the heroes of countless small boys. A few of this group of actors had punched cattle on the range and were fine horsemen, as was the rustic comedian Will Rogers. In a category of her own, each week Pearl White left silent-film audiences breathlessly awaiting the next installment of *The Perils of Pauline*, a serial first produced in 1914.

World War I led to the collapse of movie making in Italy, Germany, and England. As a result, Hollywood producers gained control of the world movie market. Mergers and consolidations, brought on by postwar competition and price cutting, reduced the number of studios to a handful. By 1923 more than 20,000 actors and actresses were working before cameras, their weekly payroll amounting to over a million dollars.

The Hollywood of the 1920s is almost beyond recall today. In those lush years the flow of cash through the box offices staggered even the most avaricious of filmdom's pioneers. A baronial self-confidence led the movie moguls to festoon their studios with boastful pennants that read: "More Stars than There Are in Heaven" and "Hollywood, the Greatest Show on Earth." This was the era of matinee idols duly equipped with white silk shirts, bevies of aspiring starlets, sixteen-cylinder racing cars, and thirty-room white stucco palaces. Movie queens such as Pola Negri and Gloria Swanson spent thousands for perfume alone, helping to make Hollywood one of the most talked-of towns in the world. Gossip concerning the industry and its stars was unquenchable. As early as 1923 the New York *World* wrote: "Hollywood has no art galleries, no institutions of learning aside from primary schools and kindergartens—nothing that makes the slightest pretense to culture, civic or otherwise. . . . But Beauty, ye gods, the place is choked, blocked, heaped to the gunwales with female beauty. One has to elbow beauties out of the way to make a passage down Hollywood Boulevard."

The stars' private lives drew criticism. In 1921, the career of comic Roscoe ("Fatty") Arbuckle was shattered by a scandal concerning the death of a young would-be actress in the course of a wild party in a hotel in San Francisco. Not only were Arbuckle's comedies thereafter banned from the screen in many communities, but a civic outcry for new moral standards was voiced. Sentiment for censorship grew so strong that in 1922 the major producers banded together to form the Motion Picture Producers and Distributors Association. Will H.

Hays, former postmaster general of the United States, was brought to Hollywood at a salary of $100,000 to impose discipline upon the industry. The Hays Office, which he headed for many years, was intended to restrain the industry from filming objectionable material. The Hays office encouraged the "moral ending," a phenomenon that did much to transform honestly controversial pictures into vehicles for pious platitudes.

Among the technological innovations that contributed to Hollywood's success, one of the most dramatic was the addition of a sound track to the movie film strip. *The Jazz Singer* was the first motion picture with sound. This "talkie," starring song-and-dance man Al Jolson, revolutionized the industry when it appeared in 1927. "Stars" with squeaky, high-pitched voices vanished and were replaced by the Clark Gables, Spencer Tracys, Claudette Colberts, and Joan Crawfords. Sound pictures, attracting larger crowds than ever, led to the building of bigger theaters.

Brassy promoters encouraged a national craving for cheap entertainment combining the attractions of melodrama, vaudeville, and the circus. For twenty-five cents, in a carpeted atmosphere of popcorn and Coca Cola, America's moviegoers—who numbered at least 50 million each week by the late 1920s—supported an industry built on opportunistic agents, stunt men, writers, scene painters, and thousands of hangers-on. Original and creative ideas often were squelched in the interest of money making. Only half-smiling could Hollywood's most famous lion roar *"Ars gratia artis"*—"Art for art's sake"—the caption that accompanied his every appearance. Actually, commercial considerations almost always triumphed over artistic ones. In those profitable years director-producer Cecil B. De Mille indulged his audiences with pretentious "historical" productions such as *The King of Kings* (1927) and *Cleopatra* (1934), whose purpose was spectacle, not significance. Such pictures were eminently vulnerable to the charge of tasteless vulgarity. De Mille himself once said, "Your poor person wants to see wealth, colorful, interesting, exotic." His films, with hundreds of paint-bedaubed extras, chariot races, and papier-mâché replicas of the monuments of antiquity, set an unfortunate pattern. Hollywood came to worship the "colossal" and "stupendous" as elephantine epics became the norm and showmanship triumphed over art.

The commercialism of the movie producers can be partially attributed to their early insecurity. William Fox was originally a cloth sponger on New York's Lower East Side. Marcus Loew moved from dealing in furs to operating a penny arcade. Samuel Goldwyn was a glove salesman. Carl Laemmle, a German immigrant, managed a Wisconsin clothing store. Louis B. Mayer, who became one of the richest and most powerful of these pioneer "cellulords," began as a rag collector. Unprepared for making artistic judgments, such men simply tailored films to the public taste.

Boy-meets-girl plots, big-laugh comedies, mawkish family dramas, and song-and-dance extravaganzas furnished an escape to viewers, especially during the Depression years. Hollywood set the fashion for impressionable adolescents in dress, home furnishings, and married life; it clearly promoted the standardization of "culture." Many films were subject to the charge of glorifying violence, corruption, and sex. In the 1920s civic groups claimed that film titles had become too sensational, promising unwholesome attractions for the young and innocent. Representative of such titles were *Ladies Must Dress, Parlor, Bedroom, and Bath, The Love Flower, Old Wives for New, Paid to Love, The Price She Paid,* and *Theodora Goes Wild.* Parents resented the suggestive environment of darkened theaters and came to feel that the movies undermined morals, while churches accused the movie makers of marketing films that were spiritually debasing. One newspaper ad of the 1930s spoke of a movie featuring "beautiful jazz babies, champagne baths, midnight revels, petting parties in the purple dawn, all ending in one terrific smashing climax that makes you gasp."

The studios paid large sums of money for movie scripts. Writers drawn to Hollywood included F. Scott Fitzgerald, Nathanael West, William Faulkner, and Clifford Odets, while George and Ira Gershwin, David Rose, Vincent Newman, Dmitri Tiomkin, and Miklós Rózsa joined the fold of studio songwriters. This kind of talent was allowed, on rare occasions between the wars, to produce excellent films like *All Quiet on the Western Front* (1930), *The Informer* (1935), and *Citizen Kane* (1940). In the late 1930s the industry turned to foreign stars and themes to counter competition from such producers as England's Sir Alexander Korda. Among the new names were British actors Ronald Colman, Leslie Howard, and Robert Donat, as well as the Irish actress Greer Garson. The movies they made, such as *Mrs. Miniver* and *Goodbye, Mr. Chips,* earned for Hollywood a new measure of respect. Movies of substance, however, were more the exception than the rule.

One of the last big moneymakers of the pre-television age was *The Best Years of Our Lives* (1946), starring Fredric March and directed by William Wyler. This production won most of the Academy Awards that year. At the same time Hollywood continued to flood the country with B-grade pictures, which it turned out in larger numbers than ever after 1945. A few postwar titles are illustrative: *Vice Raid, Drag Strip Girl,* and *High School Confidential.* Films of this type could hardly save the industry from sagging theater attendance while the costs of making movies rose steadily as stars demanded larger shares of the profits. Increasingly high taxes absorbed another large part of Hollywood's revenues. After 1948 government antitrust suits forced the major "Big Five" studios to divest themselves of lucrative theater chains.

Gloom settled over Hollywood as it was beset by competition from paperback books, phonograph records, and such recreations as bowling, waterskiing, and boating. By the late 1940s producers and directors found it financially and artistically advantageous to film pictures out of the country, particularly at studios in Rome, Paris, and London.

The old studio system has itself been replaced by other modes of production. The film empires of Mayer and Goldwyn are no longer economically affordable. Contract artists in Hollywood's early years did not face the pressures of administration and finance that afflict the industry today. The details of administration were once shouldered by an Adolph Zukor, who ruled Paramount Studios for more than forty years and who, in 1975, was still on its board of trustees at the age of 103.

A new generation of producer-directors replaced such pioneers. This different breed was known for achievements in both acting and writing. A few had directed plays on the New York stage. In the 1950s director Elia Kazan and actor Marlon Brando were among those who contributed a directness of approach to films, qualities that the Hollywood moguls had shunned as unprofitable. Films like *On the Waterfront*, however, attracted new audiences.

The role of the cinema has been pervasive. During World War II especially, this universal art form greatly increased contacts between nations. The movies have given many foreigners their first impression of the United States. The film reached into the lives of millions, not only as entertainment but also as a means of instruction, for movies have been used to train workers. In addition, film versions of *Anna Karenina, Wuthering Heights,* and *War and Peace* made these works familiar to many who would never have read them.

The cinema has also been characterized by such unique developments as Walt Disney's fantasies and cartoons, newsreels, and documentaries. Among other new forms that Hollywood developed were the independent production of films, home movies, educational films, color films, drive-in theaters, wide-angle screens, and three-dimensional productions.

The 1970s saw a long-awaited revival of interest in big-budget films. Francis Ford Coppola, Dino de Laurentis, and Carlo Ponti (all of whom happened to be of Italian origin), produced films that resembled the earlier epics. The new titles included *The Godfather, Jaws,* and *King Kong.* Some big-budget films, however, "bombed"; among these were such titles as *Heaven's Gate, One From the Heart,* and a new genre of "brat-pack" productions. By the 1980s home video cassettes severely cut into film revenues. But a virtually new industry resulted from this adaptation.

Hollywood was hardest hit by television, which offered free home entertainment. It too was a film medium, although its formats differed from those of Hollywood. In time, television had great influence upon the movies. In imitation of television techniques, a wave of more realistic pictures was produced by "independents." Few old-time directors, writers, or producers successfully shifted to TV production. Its marketing demands were totally different. Survival of the film industry came to depend upon the production of short films for television, as Los Angeles became a West Coast center of television transmission by the national networks. Cable TV production also amounted to a virtually new industry, far beyond the silent films of early Hollywood days.

Fine Arts and Architecture

In the 1930s, artists reflected a consciousness of the disturbed economic and social conditions of the day that was parallel to the concern of writers such as John Steinbeck. Among the new painters of the 1930s were Phil Dike, Barse Miller, and Rex Brandt. First among California's sculptors was Gutzon Borglum, who began his career by studying art at San Francisco in the late 1880s. Ultimately he was commissioned to carve the features of four American presidents in the granite cliffs of Mt. Rushmore, South Dakota; his work achieved national fame. Another California sculptor and book illustrator, Joe Mora, also became well known outside the state, as did printmaker and painter Edward Borein. Mora settled at Pebble Beach and Borein opened a studio at Santa Barbara.

Outstanding among California's pioneer photographers were Carleton E. Watkins, Eadweard Muybridge, and Arnold Genthe. Watkins, a chum of railroad magnate Collis P. Huntington during boyhood days in New York, worked during the 1850s at San Francisco and, in 1861, was one of the first to photograph the Yosemite Valley. His pictures helped to influence public opinion in favor of legislation to establish Yosemite as a national park. Due to the benefactions of Huntington, Watkins traveled all over the West. Regrettably, almost all of his photographic plates and his fine collection of daguerrotypes were destroyed in the San Francisco fire of 1906. Unable to recover from the shock of losing his life's work, Watkins was committed to the state insane asylum at Napa in 1910 and died there. Mount Watkins, a massive granite peak atop the Yosemite chasm, is named after him.

Muybridge was English-born; his original name was Edward Muggeridge. Before he undertook the experiments for Leland Stanford that contributed to the development of the motion-picture camera, his views of the Yosemite Valley and of Alaska were exhibited across America and Europe. In 1873, Muybridge also took unique photographs of the Modoc Indian War. His work marked a great advance in the art of photography.

A third distinguished California photographer was the German-born Genthe. At San Francisco, after 1898, Genthe set up a remarkable studio. Holder of a Ph.D. degree, he was among the earliest photographers to develop his work as a distinctive art form. Genthe altered photographic techniques by the use of backlighting, and was experimental in his application of focus. Women enjoyed sitting for portraits by the handsome young Genthe. After the 1906 San Francisco fire and earthquake, he wandered along the city's streets, recording the devastation. Genthe's photos caught the shock on the faces of men, women, and children of the stricken city. He lived in San Francisco until 1911. His years in California had made a permanent mark upon Genthe, one of the great American photographers.

The California photographers best known today are Edward Weston and Ansel Adams. Adams's black-and-white photos are sharp, vivid, and penetrating. Much of his work is devoted to the landscape of the Yosemite Valley. His is a latter-day complement to the superb oil paintings done in the Sierra before World War I by Chris Jorgensen. The majestic spirit of California's land, water, and air governs the artistic impulse of Adams and Weston. Other painters, watercolorists, and etchers follow in this tradition. Weston achieved an international reputation with his black-and-white photography, published in various books. Carmel was his home and his lens explored without rest the landscape of the Monterey peninsula. Weston died in 1957, having spent fifty years capturing subtleties of light and shadow. "Without ceremony," according to his Carmel neighbor, the poet Robinson Jeffers, Weston "taught photography to be itself, not a facile substitute for painting, or an anxious imitator."

As early as the 1920s art colonies at Carmel, Santa Barbara, and Laguna Beach reflected deepening interest in sculpture, painting, mosaic-work, and architectural design. Art institutes, among them Otis, Chouinard, the Art-Center school, and museums grew in their stature. The Huntington Art Gallery in San Marino obtained many more paintings of the English Renaissance, while the Crocker Art Gallery at Sacramento and the De Young Museum in San Francisco enlarged their collections. The Southwest Museum at Los Angeles likewise improved its holdings of Indian materials.

In the post–World War II era California artists, like the novelists, moved away from art that reflected the social compassion and consciousness of the 1930s. This had been representational in approach. Now nonobjective or abstract forms predominated. The earthy, personal, and highly individualistic work of the Italian-born painter Rico Lebrun is representative of this movement. Lebrun is best known for "The Crucifixion" (1950), an immense tryptich. Some artists, of course, continued to paint in the representational style, and at times intolerant critics wielded enough influence to secure the removal of "offending" works of painting and sculpture from museum exhibitions. Statues commissioned for public buildings were especially subject to criticism. Yet the public came increasingly to tolerate innovations in artistic technique and execution.

One of the most bizarre artistic phenomena in modern California is the work of an Italian immigrant, Simon Rodia, builder of the Watts Towers. Located near Los Angeles, these novel creations were fashioned out of bits of glass, tile, and artifacts garnered from junk heaps. Rodia built the first tower in 1921. Five years later, when Los Angeles annexed the town of Watts, Rodia became involved in a long conflict with the city because he had no building permit and because the towers were considered unsafe. While demolition and condemnation hearings dragged on for years, Rodia, who said he wanted to build something big, went on with thirty-three years of erecting a gigantic fantasy of concrete, steel, and rubble. His towers were called by art appreciators a paramount achievement of twentieth-century folk art in the United States. When tested for safety, these filigree and mosaic-covered structures proved so strong that they could not easily be pulled down, even by steel cables attached to tractors. In 1954, at the age of eighty-one, Rodia tired of his project and left Los Angeles. Public bickering over whether the towers were structurally sound left him embittered. He felt rejected by the society for which he had, as a monument of love, built the towers. Rodia never returned to Los Angeles. Why had he built the towers so strong? he was once asked. He replied, "If a man no have feet, he no stand."

Architecture was marked by improved housing standards and an increase in public affluence. In the 1890s the adobe or Mexican ranch-style house inspired a "mission revival" architecture that featured plaster walls, phony arches, and imitation tile construction of a pretentious "Spanish style." From 1910 to 1930 this style shared popularity with the wooden California bungalow of architects Charles Sumner Greene and Henry Mather Greene. The principal product of the arts and crafts movement of the early twentieth century, the structures were usually surrounded by a garden set between cacti and palm trees. These happy dwellings combined the eclecticism of European chalets with Asian ornamentation. The word bungalow is itself derived from Bengal.

"Modern" architects, among them Frank Lloyd Wright, Rudolph

M. Schindler, and Richard Neutra, built some of their first experimental structures in California, where architecture had already become a fascinating hodgepodge of affronts to one's sensibility. It is not unusual to find adjacent examples of Queen Anne style, Hawaiian or Oriental vestiges, Tudor or Jacobean mansions, French château affectations, Georgian or Mount Vernon colonial, Cape Cod fishermen's cottages, Egyptian and Mayan inspired houses, or Hopi Indian dwellings replete with ladders.

After 1900, at San Francisco, it was the age of the architects Willis Polk, Bernard Maybeck, and John Galen Howard. Polk was the designer of the Ferry building and one of the planners of the city's Civic Center. He also constructed the Hallidie Building, called the world's first glass skyscraper. Maybeck and Howard became, successively, the planners of the University of California at Berkeley, aided by the benefactions of Phoebe Apperson Hearst. Maybeck collaborated with Polk in designing architecture for the Panama Pacific International Exposition of 1915.

At San Diego, after 1893, Irving Gill built exceedingly original residences. Utilizing concrete, which he coated with plaster, Gill reduced the use of ornamentation. Although the best-known San Diego architect, he was not chosen as a designer for that city's Panama Pacific Exposition of 1915. Rather, the honor went to a devotee of Spanish colonial architecture, Bertram Goodhue, whose buildings ushered in a Hispanic revival that affected the California white-stucco-and-red-tile faddism of the period after 1910. Except for his leaner, more angular Los Angeles Public Library, Goodhue's designs utilized the Churriguresque motif that had pervaded Spanish and Mexican architecture in the eighteenth century.

At Los Angeles after 1926, Neutra achieved renown because of his radical building designs and city plans. By the mid-1930s the Spanish-style house, once so popular in California, had begun to give way to more functional experiments. Neutra's and Wright's most modernistic houses were designed for Californians who desired to replace Italian mannerist homes or Victorian residences. Both architects stressed the practical in residential construction for "outdoor living." Their modernistic split-level houses offered greatly increased living space, wide windows, and enclosed recreation areas. Well suited to the California environment, this architecture contributed to evolution of the popular ranch-style residence.

Educational Advances

Just as the nineteenth century saw the founding of private collegiate institutions, the twentieth witnessed the growth of state-financed pub-

University of California, Berkeley, central campus dominated by its "campanile." (University of California photograph by Dennis Galloway.)

lic campuses. In 1919 the State Normal School at Los Angeles became, by legislative act, the University of California, Southern Branch. Ten years later this rapidly growing public institution—now called the University of California at Los Angeles, or UCLA—moved onto a new campus at Westwood, near Beverly Hills. With its original campus at Berkeley, the state university improved its faculty, broadened the curriculum, and expanded its multi-campus system.

California's state college system, a newer development, grew out of a group of loosely related normal schools and teachers' colleges. Renamed the state college and university system, their scope widened beyond teacher preparation to include full training in the liberal arts and sciences. Also participating in public education are some ninety junior colleges.

California's educational offerings include a large-scale "extension" system of training beyond high school. Emphasis upon the applied arts is an important aspect of California's adult education program. After World War II the Ford Foundation founded at Palo Alto a Center for Advanced Study in the Behavioral Sciences, which aims to serve behavioral studies as the Institute for Advanced Studies at Princeton, New Jersey, serves the physical sciences.

In the sciences California has demonstrated special prominence during the past three-quarters of a century. The California Institute of Technology at Pasadena, founded in 1890 as the Polytechnic or Throop College of Technology, was in the 1920s transformed into a virtually new institution by astronomer George Ellery Hale and pioneer atomic physicist Robert A. Millikan. After Millikan was awarded the Nobel Prize in 1923, he drew around him philanthropists and teachers who lent distinction to "Caltech." Caltech specialized in physics, biology, and genetics. In the late 1950s its Jet Propulsion Laboratory designed and supervised the manufacture of the United States's first artificial earth satellites. The institution also became deeply engaged in missile development and, on June 2, 1966, achieved the first soft landing on the moon. The Jet Propulsion Laboratory remains a center of research for America's space program in conjunction with the National Aeronautic and Space Administration.

Another research center is the Lawrence Radiation Laboratory of the University of California at Livermore. Cyclotrons exist at both the Berkeley and Los Angeles campuses of the university. Its scientific facilities, medical schools, observatories, and institutes expanded rapidly. Another university campus specializing in science, the Scripps Institute of Oceanography at La Jolla, operates research vessels throughout the Pacific area. Also at La Jolla is the Salk Institute for Biological Studies, founded in the name of Jonas Salk, the research physician who has been given major credit for development of the first poliomyelitis vaccine.

In the field of astronomy the Lick Observatory at Mount Hamilton—technically also a campus of the University of California—was one of the first major observatories established in the United States. It has been in operation since 1874. Better known is the Mount Wilson Observatory, whose 100-inch telescope operated from 1917 to 1985. Located at Mount Palomar in San Diego County is a 200-inch telescope, in operation since 1948.

A Modern Culture

Associated with California's educational and scientific institutions are many centers of twentieth century cultural activity. California possesses two major historical societies, at San Francisco and Los Angeles, both of which produce quarterlies for their members. Several research libraries publish books and professional journals. In the humanities and social sciences the Henry E. Huntington Library and Art Gallery at San Marino, the Bancroft Library of the University of California, Berkeley, and the Hoover Library of War, Revolution, and Peace at Stanford are internationally known. The Bancroft Library is a research center of Western American history. The Huntington Library has become a center for studies in English and American literature and history. Its treasures include the *Gutenberg Bible*

(1455), and the art collection has a sizable group of paintings by English artists, among them Thomas Gainsborough's "Blue Boy." Two amusement parks, Marineland and Disneyland, are educational and recreational reservations.

In 1932 Los Angeles was the site of the Olympic games, building a coliseum in which Mildred (Babe) Zaharias, the greatest woman athlete in the world, performed. California was host to the Olympics again in 1984. Pasadena's Rose Bowl is known as the granddaddy of all the annual bowl games. In addition to the Los Angeles Dodgers and the San Francisco Giants, baseball teams include the San Diego Padres, the Angels at Anaheim, and the Oakland Athletics. The Rams and the Clippers of the National Football League are based at Los Angeles. In the field of golf Billy Casper and Gene Littler came from San Diego, while Johnny Miller and Ken Venturi are from San Francisco. All became internationally known champions. In tennis California has produced Richard "Pancho" Gonzalez, Jack Kramer, and Dennis Ralston. Women tennis players include Billie Jean King and Tracy Austin. In horse racing Eddie Arcaro is well known at Santa Anita, Hollywood Park, and Bay Meadows, the state's major tracks. Long before the Ontario speedway was built, Rex Mays and Pete De Paolo were accomplished drivers.

Although Eastern critics continued to poke fun at Los Angeles, the city grew steadily in cultural awareness and cosmopolitanism. For whatever reasons, from the mid-1960s onward it demonstrated a new vitality and energy, shrugging off its detractors with a refreshing self-esteem. By 1964 the city completed a music pavilion, the first structure of a $35 million cultural center. Creation of resident repertory, ballet, and opera companies, as well as the emergence of nineteen symphony orchestras in Los Angeles County by 1967, underscored the rising interest in "culture." The Los Angeles County Art Museum was also completed in 1965 at a cost of almost $12 million. During the 1970s the benefactions of Norton Simon at Pasadena and J. Paul Getty at Santa Monica led to the creation of two world-class museums that they named after themselves.

These activities were evidence to some that cultural leadership within the state had shifted from north to south: a new Los Angeles arts council began to coordinate music center activities; funds were raised for a California Institute of Arts; a museum of the communications industry opened in Hollywood; and Los Angeles became a major book-buying and art-collecting market, the latter led by a new generation of "business collectors," such as Norton Simon.

The awakening of southern California seemed antithetical to the pattern established by the flood of midwestern migrants in the early 1900s. W. C. Fields once labeled Los Angeles "Double-Dubuque," while Sinclair Lewis called it "the retreat of all failures." The earlier farm-born conservative materialism had, indeed, contributed to cultural stagnation. Various forces seemed to change the pragmatic shallowness of the immediate past, the first of which was a shift in the incoming population toward persons with professional skills. Second was the continued prosperity of southern California's new industries and, third, the emergence of community leadership. After World War II, despite the fact that magazines, newspapers, and books continued to satirize southern California as a superficial "land of pop and honey," "L. A.," the city that had played host to Stravinsky and Brecht, was in the midst of cultural excitement.

A special aspect of California's emerging society included the influx of thousands of scientists and engineers, drawn by its burgeoning aircraft, electronics, and missile establishments. The Rand (Research and Development) Corporation at Santa Monica, a semipublic agency created by the United States Air Force to carry on strategic studies by "brainstorming" techniques, brought together philosophers, political scientists, physicists, and mathematicians. They created a "think tank," or "R & D" intellectual "industry." Similar to Rand, but more technical are the Space Technology Laboratories of Thompson, Ramo, Wooldridge at Canoga Park, overseers of the United States Air Force's Ballistic Missile Division. Hughes Aircraft and International Telephone and Telegraph are among the companies with specialized research facilities in California. The Standard Oil Company of California has established at Richmond and La Habra a California Research Corporation whose exclusive activity is research. At San Diego the Hopkins Laboratory, sponsored by the General Dynamics Corporation, and the United States Navy Electronics Laboratory, stress "pure research."

Selected Readings

Analyses of California's best-known modern novelist are Brian St. Pierre, *John Steinbeck: The California Years* (San Francisco, 1984); Harry T. Moore, *The Novels of John Steinbeck* (Chicago, 1939); Nelson Valjean, *John Steinbeck, The Errant Knight* (San Francisco, 1975); and Martin Stoddard, *California Writers* (New York, 1984), which also stresses the relationship between Steinbeck and Jack London's work.

William Saroyan's *My Name is Aram* (New York, 1940), and *The Human Comedy* (New York, 1943) are partly autobiographical. Edmund Wilson, *The Boys in the Back Room: Notes on California Novelists* (San Francisco, 1941), deals with James M. Cain, William Saroyan, and John Steinbeck. On Jeffers see Lawrence Clark Powell, *Robinson Jeffers: The Man and His Work* (Pasadena, 1940); Frederick J. Carpenter, *Robinson Jeffers* (New York, 1952); Radcliffe Squires, *The Loyalties of Robinson Jeffers* (Ann Arbor, Mich., 1956); and Melba Berry Bennett, *The Stone Mason of Tor House* (Los Angeles, 1966).

A blending of art and literature is Carl Oscar Borg and Millard Sheets, *Cross, Sword, and Gold Pan . . .* (Los Angeles, 1936). See also Helen Laird, *Carl Oscar Borg and the Magic Region* (Layton, Utah, 1984), and Edith Hamlin, "Maynard Dixon, Artist of the West," *California Historical Quarterly* 53 (Fall 1974), 361–71. Regarding architecture see Frank J. Taylor, *Land of Homes* (Los Angeles, 1929), and Richard Neutra's *Mystery and Realities of the Site* (Scarsdale, N.Y., 1951). Colonial architecture is studied in Kurt Baer's *Architecture of the California Missions* (Berkeley, 1958). An examination of the nineteenth century is Harold Kirker, *California's Architectural Frontier* (San Marino, 1960). This can be supplemented by Geoffrey E. Bangs, *Portals West: A Folio of Late Nineteenth Century Architecture in California* (San Francisco, 1960). Consult also Randell L. Makinson, *Greene & Greene: Architecture as a Fine Art* (Santa Barbara, 1977).

Recent architecture is described in Esther McCoy's *Five California Architects* (New York, 1960) and *Richard Neutra* (New York, 1960). See also Frank Harris, ed., *A Guide to Contemporary Architecture in Southern California* (Los Angeles, 1951): Joseph A. Baird, Jr., *Time's Wondrous Changes, San Francisco's Architecture, 1776–1915* (San Francisco, 1962); and David Gebhard and Robert Winter, *A Guide to Architecture in Southern California* (Los Angeles, 1965). Consult also Gebhard's "The Spanish Colonial Revival in Southern California, 1895–1930," *Journal of the Society of Architectural History* (May 1967). Regarding printing, see James D. Hart's *Fine Printing in California* (Berkeley, 1960). Ward Ritchie, "Fine Printing in Southern California," in *A Bookman's View of Los Angeles* (Los Angeles, 1961) is also useful.

Examples of photography, and commentary upon it, are in Joyce R. Muench, ed., *West Coast Portrait* (New York, 1946), and Edward Weston, *My Camera on Point Lobos* (Boston, 1950), as well as Charis Wilson Weston and Edward Weston, *California and the West* (New York, 1940). Ansel Adams has reproduced his photographs (with Nancy Newhall) in *This Is the American Earth*, published by the Sierra Club (San Francisco, 1959), and *Yosemite Valley* (San Francisco, 1959). Early photography is discussed in Mary V. Jessup Hood and Robert Bartlett Haas, "Eadweard Muybridge's Yosemite Valley Photographs, 1867–1872," California Historical Society *Quarterly* 42 (March 1963), 5–26. Haas has also written *Muybridge, Man in Motion* (Berkeley, 1976).

Jeanne Van Nostrand has produced two histories of California art: *The First Hundred Years of Painting in California* (San Francisco, 1980), and *San Francisco 1806–1906 in Contemporary Painting, Drawings, and Watercolors* (San Francisco 1975). See also D. C. McCall, *California*

Artists, 1935 to 1956 (Bellflower, Calif., 1981). Rico Lebrun, *Drawings* (Berkeley, 1961), describes what has shaped a contemporary painter's viewpoint. Also consult Harvey Jones, *"Masterpieces of the California Decorative Style* (Santa Barbara, 1980).

A portrait of one of Hollywood's producer-directors is Richard Batman, "D. W. Griffith: The Lean Years," California Historical Society *Quarterly* 44 (September 1965), 195–204. A study of the movies is Leo C. Rosten, *Hollywood: The Movie Colony, the Movie Makers* (New York, 1941). Histories of the movie industry include Benjamin B. Hampton, *A History of the Movies* (New York, 1931), and Maurice Bardeche and Robert Brasillach, *A History of Motion Pictures* (New York, 1938). See also Terry Ramsaye, *A Million and One Nights* (New York, 1926). The problem of censorship is analyzed in Raymond Moley, *The Hays Office* (New York, 1945). Another analysis is Lewis Jacobs, *The Rise of the American Film* (New York, 1939). Skillful in its satire of movie making is Harry Leon Wilson's novel, *Merton of the Movies* (Garden City, N.Y., 1922). Hollywood during the Depression years is the subject of Nathanael West's novel *The Day of the Locust* (New York, 1939). Better-known fiction works are Budd Schulberg, *What Makes Sammy Run* (New York, 1941), a novel about the drive for power in Hollywood, and F. Scott Fitzgerald, *The Last Tycoon* (New York, 1941). A semiallegorical treatment is Libbie Block, *The Hills of Beverly* (New York, 1957).

A look at one of the movie moguls is Bosley Crowther, *Hollywood Rajah: The Life and Times of Louis B. Mayer* (New York, 1960). See also A. R. Fulton, *Motion Pictures: The Development of an Art from Silent Films to the Age of Television* (Norman, Okla., 1960), and Edward Wagenknecht, *The Movies in the Age of Innocence* (Norman, Okla., 1962). Fred J. Balshofer and Arthur C. Miller, *One Reel a Week* (Berkeley, 1967), discusses the pre–World War I era of film making, while George N. Fenin and William K. Everson, *The Western, From Silents to Cinerama* (New York, 1962), gives a composite view of the cinema. Kenneth MacGowan, *Behind the Screen: The History and Techniques of the Motion Picture* (New York, 1965), is a detailed account minus the "beautiful people" approach. A "requiem for a dream town," written with sensitivity, is Beth Day's *This Was Hollywood* (New York, 1960). Two books that look at Hollywood folklore and peculiarities are Hortense Powdermaker, *Hollywood: The Dream Factory* (London, 1951), and Mervyn Le Roy, *It Takes More Than Talent* (New York, 1953). A description of Los Angeles and Hollywood during the interwar period is Edmund Wilson, "The City of Our Lady, the Queen of the Angels," in *The American Earthquake* (New York, 1958).

Joseph Henry Jackson edited such anthologies as *The Western Gate* (New York, 1952) and *Continent's End* (New York, 1944). A life of Aimee Semple McPherson is Nancy Barr Mavity, *Sister Aimee* (Garden

City, 1931); a later treatment of the same subject is Lately Thomas, *The Vanishing Evangelist* (New York, 1959). Robert Bahr, *Least of All Saints: The Story of Aimee Semple McPherson* (Englewood Cliffs, N.J., 1979) unfortunately manufactures conversation.

A whitewash of southern California's commercialized "cemetery culture" is Adela Rogers St. Johns, *First Step Up Toward Heaven* (Englewood Cliffs, N.J., 1959), whereas Evelyn Waugh's satire *The Loved One* (Boston, 1948), and Aldous Huxley's *After Many a Summer Dies the Swan* (New York, 1939) debunk it all. There are also studies of utopian colonies, including Robert V. Hine, *California's Utopian Colonies* (San Marino, 1953) and his *California Utopianism: Contemplations of Eden* (San Francisco 1981), as well as Emmett A. Greenwalt, *The Point Loma Community in California, 1897–1942* (Berkeley, 1955).

A collection of literary pieces is edited by Robert Pearsall and Ursula Spier Erickson, *The Californians: Writings of Their Past and Present* (San Francisco, 1960). Other anthologies are Richard Lehan, *Los Angeles in Fiction* (Albuquerque, 1981), and Robert Kirsch and William Murphy, *West of the West* (New York, 1967). A bibliographical essay is Lawrence Clark Powell's *Land of Fiction* (Los Angeles, 1952). A lampooning of southern California is Cynthia Lindsay, *The Natives Are Restless* (New York, 1960). Another examination is Jessamyn West's *South of the Angels* (New York, 1960).

On the "beatniks," consult Gene Feldman and Max Gartenberg, eds., *The Beat Generation and the Angry Young Men* (New York, 1958); Thomas Parkinson, ed., *A Casebook on the Beat* (New York, 1961); and Lawrence Lipton, *The Holy Barbarians* (New York, 1959).

CHAPTER 34

Wartime Problems

DURING THE YEARS PRECEDING World War II, Californians had become disturbed over the threat posed by the European dictators and the Japanese military clique. The unexpected attack upon Pearl Harbor in Hawaii by Japanese dive bombers on December 7, 1941, created a new mood. Californians soon heard of the surrender of Sumatra, Borneo, and the Philippines. A strange anxiety ran through California.

The war years brought economic dislocations and social tensions. Manpower problems, rationing, transportation difficulties, and the need of housing defense workers were the order of the day. Military training camps, shipyards, and aircraft factories had to be constructed quickly. Nothing must impede the job of getting planes, tanks, and guns to the fighting front. California's war industries drew workers from all parts of the United States. The state dismantled its border "bum blockade" against "Okies" and "Arkies," encouraging workers to flock westward for employment in its new war plants. Local chambers of commerce focused attention upon getting industries to move to California, or to establish branch plants in the West.

Japanese Relocation

Long before Pearl Harbor, security had become a paramount consideration. During 1940, the state legislature passed the Dilworth Anti-Spy Bill, the Slater Anti-Sabotage Act, and the Tenney Anti-Subversive legislation. Before the war, feeling against the Japanese had been mounting. The wartime atmosphere of suspicion was harmful to race relations. By 1940 there were 120,000 Japanese in California. As they became more affluent, these immigrants experienced

444

the jealousy of white competitors and became more vulnerable to the old bugaboo that Asians were unassimilable. As fishermen, cannery workers, and agriculturalists they still awakened the hostility of Caucasian competitors. Japanese truck farmers, in particular, more firmly entrenched than ever in the state's agricultural system, aroused envy.

After the Pearl Harbor attack, apprehension spread to the mainland, especially during 1942 after a lone Japanese submarine surfaced at Goleta, near Santa Barbara, and fired a shell that splintered the end of a wooden jetty. Frightened residents put their houses up for sale and made plans to flee. On February 25, 1942, the Los Angeles *Times* erroneously reported that Japanese planes had bombed that city, damaging defense installations. Antiaircraft fire had indeed been shot into the sky against imaginary aircraft, and the jittery populace was ready to assume the worst.

Many of the Japanese were second-generation Nisei (Japanese-Americans born and educated in the United States). There was no evidence that any were disloyal. But this did not alter public demands that the Japanese be interned. They were forced to sell homes, businesses, and land at a fraction of its value. Radios, cameras, and all "suspicious" personal effects were confiscated by federal agents.

By order of General John L. DeWitt, head of the Western Defense Command from 1941 to 1943, some 112,000 West Coast Japanese, two-thirds of them American citizens, were subject to relocation. Thousands were, thus, taken from their homes and businesses and herded into the interior. Among them were Issei (persons born in Japan), Nisei, and Kibei (American-born but partly educated in Japan). This move was at the insistence of Earl Warren, state attorney general before he became governor. Warren was influenced by such nativist groups as the State Grange, the American Legion, the Native Sons and Daughters of the Golden West, and the State Federation of Labor. Together these sponsored the California Joint Immigration Committee, through which they voiced their views. Some Japanese were given the choice of "relocation" along the eastern seaboard. Others were sent to security camps in California and to Heart Mountain, Wyoming, Topaz, Utah, and other internment centers outside California.

Few had the courage to speak out against internment of "enemy" aliens. In 1942, however, the German-born novelist Thomas Mann protested before the Tolan Committee. Other artists, including Lion Feuchtwanger, Bruno Frank, and Arturo Toscanini, sent telegrams to Washington, as did atomic physicist Albert Einstein, writer Cesare Borgese, and the Italian exile Count Carlo Sforza. Their efforts were fruitless.

At Tule Lake, Manzanar, and other California internment centers

Japanese evacuees lived behind barbed wire under military guard. They were charged with no crime but were considered potential enemies by the Department of the Army. No defender, in the government or outside it, arose to invoke the protection of the Constitution on their behalf.

Although no identifiable cases of sabotage occurred, only in 1944 were the first internees allowed to leave the relocation centers for coastal areas. By 1946 their incarceration had ended.

Only about 65,000 of the Japanese who had been forced to leave the West Coast ever returned. Some settled in the Middle West and in the East. Historians who have studied this forced evacuation in the calmer postwar years have concluded that it was a grievous violation of constitutional rights. But the United States Supreme Court has never fully conceded that the government was culpable and has refused to indemnify Japanese who appealed to the court.

Only long after World War II did California's Japanese gain sympathy for their grievances, and then on moral rather than legal grounds. Yet a remarkable change occurred in the public attitude toward the Japanese. Whereas Californians had once believed that wartime Japan was little more than a nation of savages, a new respect flowered after Japan's defeat. Occupation troops acquired a taste for Asian life, some marrying Japanese brides. Americans, mesmerized by German technology, showed the same appreciation toward the makers of Japanese transistor radios and autos. The Nisei had acquitted themselves magnificently during the war as members of the highly decorated 442nd Regimental Combat Team, as professional men, or, in the case of Pat Suzuki, a graduate of San Jose State College, as star of the 1956 Broadway musical, *Flower Drum Song*.

The Japanese-Americans constituted only a tiny fraction of United States population, but their success story is unmatched by any other minority. In a Horatio Alger sense they have "outwhited the whites." Education, a low crime rate, and professional attainment have given them the reputation of model citizens. Only in recent years have young Japanese-Americans begun to challenge the materialism and acceptance of "the system" with which their parents identified.

A Wartime Footing

Earl Warren, California's most renowned modern governor, and attorney general from 1939 to 1943, had a warm and attractive personality. He was, furthermore, a skilled political leader. A progressive-minded Republican, Warren stayed clear of feuds within his own party. His vigorous campaign against Olson showed Warren to be the most talented Republican strategist in many decades. Warren's views were relatively nonpartisan, and he seldom mentioned either of the two leading political parties if he could avoid it. Like old Hiram Johnson, whose picture was the only one that hung in Warren's office, he called himself a Progressive. Also like Johnson, he attracted moderate voters of all parties. Always informal in manner, Warren projected a reassuring image in difficult times. Because of the war, a moratorium on politics and labor difficulties characterized the Warren era. The waterfront strikes that had rocked the coast were a thing of the past. Most industrial disputes were handled now by voluntary arbitration; on occasion the governor himself was the arbitrator, for his judgment and good faith were trusted by all sides. Warren spent three terms at Sacramento, being easily reelected in 1946 and 1950.

The population influx during World War II was far in excess of that during World War I. Not only did thousands of defense workers pour into the state; soldiers, sailors, and airmen came by the hundreds of thousands for military training or to be shipped overseas. Military posts became virtual cities, with their own supply, transportation, and postal facilities. In south-central California, Camp Roberts housed upwards of 50,000 men. Another big army depot was Fort Ord, located between Monterey and Salinas. Camp Pendleton, near Oceanside, became a massive West Coast base for the marines, who played a large role in the Pacific campaigns during World War II. San Diego, Long Beach, and Mare Island, already major naval bases, increased their facilities manyfold. And there were newly expanded air training centers at March Field, the El Toro Marine Air Depot, and the Alameda Naval Air Station. San Francisco and Los Angeles became huge troop embarkation centers.

Even before the attack on Pearl Harbor, California had begun to shift from peacetime to "defense" production. On the Richmond, Oakland, and San Pedro waterfronts the Todd and Bethlehem shipyards in 1941 hammered out ships for the allied powers. Huge appropriations from the United States Maritime Commission also reopened shipbuilding installations at Sausalito and Vallejo that had been idle since World War I. The shipyards of the Henry J. Kaiser enterprises began to build hundreds of cruisers, destroyers, cargo carriers, and auxiliary vessels. The labor force at Kaiser's Richmond Yard alone came to number more than 100,000. Kaiser controlled Calship at Los Angeles and also constructed, with the help of a Reconstruction Finance Corporation loan, the largest steel mill in the West in a vineyard at Fontana.

Numerous firms that produced steel products, chemicals, textiles, and machine tools had been on a wartime footing before 1941. Others quickly converted, after Pearl Harbor, to the production of tanks, jeeps, and munitions. Heavy industry was introduced to California on a massive scale. As civilian workers poured into the state, its towns expanded overnight. Vallejo jumped from a population of 20,000 in 1941 to 100,000 in 1943. New housing projects built with government money mushroomed. Thousands of workers dwelt in trailer parks or in substandard housing and commuted to work, traveling as much as three or four hours per day. Crowding and strain were the order of the day.

The Aircraft Industry

No segment of the California economy grew more rapidly than the aircraft industry. Airplanes had been produced in the state since before World War I. When World War II came, an aircraft center was already in being there.

In 1910 when publisher William Randolph Hearst had put up $50,000 for the first pilot who could fly from California to the East Coast in thirty days or less, no one claimed the prize. But that same year the first public aviation meet in America was held on the Dominguez Ranch near Los Angeles. This event drew almost 200,000 spectators, who saw Glen Curtis make the first successful West Coast flight, which lasted for all of two whole minutes. Barnstorming "air circus" stunt flyers and wealthy enthusiasts created a market for airplanes. At first these craft were held together with baling wire. Eventually standardization led to improved construction.

Southern California's airplane designers and builders began shortly after World War I to construct a variety of aircraft. Among these was Donald Douglas who learned his trade with Glenn L. Martin, an airplane engineer. At Los Angeles, Martin had established his own company in 1912 but, in 1929, moved to Baltimore. Southern California's aircraft designers broke into the national news in 1927 when Charles A. Lindbergh, "The Lone Eagle," commissioned San Diego's Ryan Aeronautical Corporation to build his *Spirit of Saint Louis*, in which "Lindy" flew the Atlantic.

One of the giants of the American aircraft industry, the Lockheed Aircraft Company, was founded by Malcolm and Allan Loughead, who sold the company in 1932 to other owners, among them banker Robert E. Gross. Gross, the dominant figure in the development of the company, represented a reversal of the standard formula for success in the aircraft industry. Unlike aviation's earlier barnstorming heroes, Gross entered the field as a cautious businessman, heading a corporation that was all but moribund. Then Lindbergh, Wiley Post, and Amelia Earhart began to set flying records in the company's planes. In 1933, Gross helped develop the twin-engined Electra, which earned Lockheed an international reputation.

Mines Field Airport, Inglewood, 1933. (Photograph by Fairchild Aerial Surveys, Inc.; Historical Collections, Security Pacific National Bank.)

In 1935 the output of California's aircraft industry had reached $20 million annually. By 1941, placement of orders for warplanes by foreign governments and by our own government made California vital to the rearmament program of the "free nations" of the world. The Douglas and Lockheed plants were the cornerstones of American airpower. Douglas-trained workers who had never previously operated an acetylene welding torch or a rivet gun put together Havoc Nightfighters for the British, Liberators, Flying Fortresses (B-17s), transports, and dive bombers. At Burbank, Lockheed produced Hudson bombers for Britain, the P-38 fighter, the Ventura, and the 128-passenger Constitution. Lockheed employed a work force of 90,000 persons during the height of the war and was responsible for 6 percent of all United States plane production. During the war years this company built 20,000 planes.

Other plants, notably Consolidated Vultee (founded by Gerard Vultee), which later became part of the General Dynamics Corporation, Douglas, North American, Northrop, and the Hughes aircraft companies, expanded spectacularly during World War II.

World War II was one of the major turning points of California history. It speeded up industrialization, aided by an outpouring of government funds. The war also accelerated economic development and urban growth. Except for Japanese-Americans, minorities were henceforth accepted more readily, including blacks, Hispanics, and women—all sorely needed in the war effort. War's end also saw the emergence of California as a new portal to the outside world.

Founding the United Nations

In April 1945, as the war in Europe was drawing to a close, representatives of forty-six nations met at San Francisco to transform a wartime alliance against the Axis powers into a permanent structure for world peace. Despite almost constant disagreement between American and Russian delegates, all but disrupting the conference, the UN Charter was signed at San Francisco on June 26 by the delegates of all nations participating. On October 24, 1945, the new organization came into being. Thus San Francisco is forever associated with the UN Charter, whose purpose, as stated in its opening words, is "to save succeeding generations from the scourge of war." Among the reporters covering this event was a young, recently demobilized veteran named John F. Kennedy.

Selected Readings

Discrimination against Mexicans and Japanese has become a subject of popular interest. In her novel *Tumbleweeds* (New York, 1934), Marta Roberts portrays the demoralization of a Mexican couple dependent upon relief in California during the Depression decades. Cornelia Jessey uses her *Teach the Angry Spirit* (New York, 1949) to lament the hardships of life in the Mexican district of Los Angeles during World War II. Carey McWilliams presents a sympathetic view of another foreign group in *Prejudice: Japanese-Americans, Symbol of Racial Intolerance* (Boston, 1944). The Army version of Japanese relocation, published by the United States War Department, is *Japanese Evacuation from the West Coast* (Washington, D.C., 1943). See also Stetson Conn, "The Decision to Evacuate the Japanese from the Pacific Coast, 1942," in Kent Roberts Greenfield, *Command Decisions* (New York, 1959), and Conn's *Guarding the United States and Its Outposts* (Washington, D.C., 1964), which details army plans to evacuate aliens from the West Coast. An evacuee, Miné Okubo, has given her impressions of internment in *Citizen 13660* (New York, 1946). More critical is Morton Grodzins, *Americans Betrayed: Politics and the Japanese Evacuation* (Chicago, 1949), and the previously cited book by ten Broek, Barnhart, and Matson, *Prejudice, War, and the Constitution*. The evacuation of the Japanese has given rise to studies that are condemnatory, sociologically and politically. Among these are: Roger Daniels and Harry Kitano, *American Racism* (Englewood Cliffs, N.J., 1969), and Daniels' *Concentration Camps USA: Japanese Americans and World War II* (New York, 1971), as well as Kitano's *Japanese Americans, The Evolution of a Subculture* (Englewood Cliffs, N.J., 1969). See also Bill Hosokawa, *Nisei, the Quiet Americans* (New York, 1969), as well as Jeanne Wakatsuki and James Houston, *Farewell to Manzanar* (Boston, 1973). Already mentioned are Thomas and Nishimoto's *The Spoilage* and Thomas's *The Salvage*. Also suggested is Leonard Bloom and Ruth Riemar, *Removal and Return . . .* (Berkeley, 1949). See also Edward N. Barnhart, "The Individual Exclusion of Japanese Americans in World War II," *Pacific Historical Review* 29 (May 1960), 111–30; Audrie Girdner and Anne Loftis, *The Evacuation of the Japanese-Americans During World War II* (New York, 1969); Michi Weglyn, *Years of Infamy* (New York, 1976); and John Modell, *The Economics and Politics of Racial Accommodation: The Japanese of Los Angeles, 1900–1942* (Urbana, Ill., 1977). Consult also Earl Warren's *Memoirs* (New York, 1977).

The literature concerning aviation is scattered and diverse. A history of sorts is Kenneth M. Johnson, *Aerial California: An Account of Early Flight in Northern and Southern California, 1849 to World War I* (Los Angeles, 1961). The story of Charles A. Lindbergh's epochal flight, with details about the building of the "Spirit of Saint Louis" in California, is told in his book *We* (New York, 1927). With attention to California is Hugh Knowlton, *Air Transportation in the United States: Its Growth as a Business* (Chicago, 1941); another is Elsbeth Freudenthal, *The Aviation Business* (New York, 1940). The worldwide wartime implications of the aircraft industry are set forth in H. H. Arnold, *Global Mission* (New York, 1949). Postwar prospects are the subject of Bernard A. McDonald, *Air Transportation in the Immediate Post-War Period* (Buffalo, 1944). A company history is Western Air Lines, *Wings Over the West: The Story of America's Oldest Airline* (n.p., 1951). See also Arlene Elliott, "The Rise of Aeronautics in California, 1849–1940," *Southern California Quarterly* 52 (March 1970), 1–32.

Government in wartime is the subject of Martin J. Schiesl, "City Planning and the Federal Government in World War II: The Los Angeles Experience," *California Historical Quarterly* LIX (Summer 1980), 127–143.

CHAPTER 35

California after World War II

As RECONVERSION TO a peacetime economy began, the possibility of business mortality among war-born plants worried civic leaders. Domination of postwar manufacturing by companies that had grown big during the war was another threat. A third source of anxiety concerned future employment of the great numbers of people the war had drawn to the state. These new residents were mostly wage and salary workers, rather than professionals. A high number of California veterans returned to the state. More than 300,000 service personnel from other parts of the country persuaded their families to join them among the orange groves.

A gratifying number of the G.I.s who poured back into California found satisfactory work. Furthermore, most of the persons who labored in the state's shipyards in 1943, as well as the majority of its aircraft workers, succeeded in obtaining postwar employment. The migration into the state generated new employment to take the place of war industry. Emergency relief to veterans under the G.I. Bill of Rights helped take up the slack in unemployment. Governor Warren and the legislature had set aside revenues collected during the war as a "rainy day fund." A California State Reconstruction and Reemployment Commission supervised economic reconversion.

Diversification and New Industry

The war not only gave new life to manufacturing; it also helped diversify industrial development. This adjustment was long overdue in California, where economic organization was clustered around too few major industries, among them orange growing, the movies, and oil. The war, furthermore, made the state increasingly prominent in

452

the economy of the nation. It allowed California to draw a larger share of per capita income and population than ever before. Rising freight costs made it economical for national firms to establish permanent branches in California. A specialized labor pool on the West Coast also encouraged Eastern manufacturers to move their plants. In addition to the well-established aircraft industry, significant expansion occurred in the manufacture of refrigeration equipment, technical instruments, heating and cooking apparatus, chemicals, hardware, and cosmetics for national markets.

California products gained prominence in the postwar era. Among these were wearing apparel (especially sportswear), jewelry, and footwear for women. Los Angeles continued as an automobile assembly depot second only to Detroit. As a tube and tire center the city came to service much of the West. Before the war, smelting and refining of ferrous metals within the state had occurred on an insignificant scale. After 1943, however, Kaiser's Fontana mill in southern California began to process iron ore from Eagle Mountain and tungsten from the Rand Mountains. After the war secondary cities, among them Oakland, Stockton, Fresno, San Jose, and San Diego, received a share of the industries attracted to California.

Boom

Wartime facilities had been temporary. Now apartments, homes, schools, and public facilities had to be built. Business construction boomed. In 1947 alone Los Angeles built 215 new factories; 392 others were constructed that year in the San Francisco Bay area.

There seemed to be no end to the migration into the state as the once tranquil paradise became crowded with people and automobiles. In 1940 California had a population of 6,907,387; it ranked fifth among the states. Eight years later, by 1948, with a population of 10,031,000, the state passed Illinois and was contesting with Pennsylvania the right to call itself the nation's second largest state. By 1950, when the population reached 10,586,223 (up 53 percent from 1940), Californians could speak of their state as the second largest. It had a birth rate that was two and a half times its death rate. Despite the noxious fumes of smog, which made city throats rasp and eyes smart, its rate of growth was uncomfortably spectacular. The state's highways became so jammed that it recorded the highest accident rate in the nation, and its schoolrooms grew so crowded that some schools were forced to offer classes in several shifts daily.

Until quite recently it was not publicly acceptable to question the heedless overbreeding that occurred nationally as well as in California during the postwar era. In those years of spreading housing tracts, veterans of the war achieved a form of status by founding new family units.

The Korean War further aggravated housing shortages. Although families doubled up and tripled up, public housing projects were resisted. Meanwhile, California of the 1950s experienced one of the great construction booms of all time. In small towns and big cities alike, acres of raw, green lumber framework, stacks of bricks, and sacks of cement went into thousands of new dwellings. Large-scale tract development occurred at the new postwar cities of Westchester, Lakewood, and West Covina in southern California and at Burlingame and Lafayette in the North. Unincorporated communities, such as Saratoga, Campbell, Monte Sereno, Los Altos, and Milpitas in Santa Clara County, as well as Pacifica and Woodside in San Mateo County, incorporated as new cities.

Transportation

Closely tied to these projects was the development of new highways, including San Francisco's East Shore and Bayshore freeways. In 1947, a ten-year highway construction program was voted by the state legislature. By 1955, excluding city streets and federal highways, California had 136,570 miles of roads, of which about half were surfaced. Some four hundred highway common carriers and bus lines were engaged in the transportation of passengers and freight. The state spent more than $1 million per working day on new freeways and highways.

Highway engineers planned a 12,500-mile statewide freeway system to link all cities in the state with a population of 5,000 or more persons, and to tie these into the federal highway system. Automotive industries and services became a key element in the state. Organizations like the Automobile Club of Southern California grew politically powerful. By 1967, California had more drivers and cars (nearly a one-to-one ratio of registered drivers to registered vehicles)—almost 10 million of each—and consumed more gasoline than any other state in the union. The Los Angeles area was the largest and fastest-growing gas and petroleum fuel market in the world.

Meanwhile, traffic congestion grew critical. Los Angeles County alone had 4.5 million vehicles in 1967. Although the legislature in 1964 had approved a Southern California Rapid Transit District (RTD) to plan intracity transportation, obstacles were numerous. Irate citizens blamed politicians, the lobbying of used and new auto dealers, and the threat of high taxes for delays in developing an alternative to transportation by the internal combustion engine.

Supporters of an expanded highway network pointed out that Cal-

California freeway intricacies. (By courtesy of Chevron Corporation.)

ifornia's metropolitan areas would remain automobile-oriented. By 1966 the state was receiving $350 million per year in federal highway grants. Mass rapid transit other than by automobiles remained in the planning stage, except at San Francisco, where construction of the Bay Area Rapid Transit District proceeded after public opposition halted freeway construction in 1964.

Californians had made virtually no provisions for surface movement of their mass society other than by automobile. The British minister of transport during the 1960s called Los Angeles a "concrete desert" whose environment had been brutalized by the automobile. To him, reliance upon the auto as a single approach to mass rapid transit had made that city the world's most horrible example of non-experimentation. By 1970 the Sierra Club's president reiterated this low opinion of Los Angeles, calling the city "a mistake, an utter disaster, one of the most irrational things man has ever done."

San Francisco's freeway revolt resulted in failure to complete the Embarcadero Freeway as the city also struggled to keep the state's

Panhandle Freeway out of Golden Gate Park. Freeway revolts occurred in communities conscious of their uniqueness. At Laguna Beach and Pasadena too citizens stood up to the state highway commission. But highway planners balanced the cost of a freeway against savings to drivers in travel time and money. The formula did not measure the social losses to a community when a freeway was rammed through it, bisecting residential areas, slashing through parks, destroying historic sites, cutting through redwood stands, and blighting the landscape. A similar short-sighted philosophy governed proposed dam construction, flood control projects, and other public works. By stressing efficiency, public agencies seemed to rationalize landscape destruction. Occasionally freeways were kept out of beauty spots, as at Laguna Beach, at Prairie Creek in Jedediah Smith Redwoods Park, and at Upper Crystal Springs Lake along the Junípero Serra Freeway—but only after prolonged public clamor.

At San Francisco a haughty spirit of self-celebration did not always help civic reform. In other communities as well there was reluctance to change. Symbolically, Carmel's residents resisted installation of sidewalks and house numbering, even though this meant no home mail delivery. Thus not every Californian, especially the conservationists, agreed that change meant progress.

The Automobile Club of Southern California continued to oppose rapid transit beyond buses and autos. Major oil companies and auto dealers, too, discouraged rapid transit. These critics charged that public transportation systems could not survive upon densities of four to six families per acre without some form of subsidy. Each year's delay led construction costs to grow astronomically, because of inflation. Local rapid transit advocates continued to seek state offshore oil revenues and a percentage of motor vehicle taxes with which to begin construction. No longer could railroad lines be relied upon to furnish public transportation.

At San Francisco progress on mass transit was better. In 1962, supposedly tradition-bound San Franciscans adopted the BART System to connect the cities of the east bay. Tunnels under the bay would link them with subway stations on the peninsula. One by one the bay cities had implored the state public utilities commission to suspend their antiquated, unprofitable passenger operation.

Los Angeles and San Francisco both undertook reconstruction of their central civic areas during the 1950s and 1960s. At Los Angeles, around a central mall that covered 228 acres, new, twenty- to forty-story buildings were constructed to house federal, state, county, and city government offices. Another massive face-lifting project was redevelopment, with federal aid, of a blighted area, Bunker Hill, into a high-rise residential and commercial site.

As the shift from single-family homes to apartments continued, the

Los Angeles skyline changed markedly. Construction became vertical rather than horizontal. Rising land costs made it uneconomical to build single-family dwellings in downtown areas. A new style of architecture was converting downtown Los Angeles and its Wilshire district into multi-storied apartments and office buildings, built of "high-rise" lightweight metal and much window glass. In 1956, repeal of the 140-foot height limit on buildings was followed by construction of the first modern skyscrapers.

At San Francisco in the 1950s the process of building skyward was accelerated. The city built Candlestick Park, new home of the former New York Giants baseball club. The James Lick Freeway, bisecting the city with a system of viaducts and overpasses, also opened to traffic. San Francisco's population grew almost imperceptibly in the postwar years. As compared to Los Angeles, which possessed room for expansion, San Francisco, confined to a peninsula, was forced to utilize its land space carefully.

Defense Spending: The Korean and Vietnam Wars

Continuing heavy defense expenditures by the federal government underwrote a large share of California's postwar construction. After 1950, the manufacture of military aircraft became a more permanent business. A new round of government orders opened up branch plants of the major aircraft companies that had been closed since World War II. California increasingly possessed what amounted to a "nongovernmental civil service," that is, aircraft, missile component, and instrument workers who had come to rely upon government contracts for jobs. This made for employment vulnerability whenever defense expenditures were cut. The "cold war" with the Soviet Union, however, indicated a steady need for military production.

The establishment in 1954 of the Air Force's Space Technology Laboratory at Inglewood and Canoga Park, and the founding of the IBM Research Laboratory at San Jose and of Astronautics Inc. in San Diego further immersed California in missile, rocket, and outer-space research and technology. A significant event of the late 1950s was the activation of the nation's first privately financed nuclear power plant at Vallecitos. The new Pacific Missile Range became a major launching site. Vandenberg Air Force Base changed nearby Lompoc from a rural town, concerned with mining diatomaceous soil and flower raising, to a city of thirty thousand persons.

The term "Federal City" came to be applied to Los Angeles, where a close relationship between its economy and the central government flourished in the 1960s. Critics averred that industry in that munic-

ipality was more responsive to Washington than to Sacramento as
business and municipal leaders became involved in classified negotiations with the national capital.

So much reliance on the federal government for housing, transportation, and flood control grants diminished the role of government. The mayors of Los Angeles wanted local control but continued
to rely upon outside government funds. Meanwhile they governed
timidly. Fletcher Bowron emerged as the best of the postwar Los
Angeles mayors, pushing for reform in the late 1940s of the police
department and championing public housing for the poor. Norris
Poulson, his successor as mayor after 1953, integrated the police and
fire departments, interesting himself also in attempts to control air
pollution by putting pressure on Detroit's auto makers. But the postwar mayors, at San Francisco also, eroded their local power base,
eliciting more and more government contracts and testifying increasingly before Washington congressional committees in search of
federal funding. All of this helps us to understand why California's
cities never produced mayors of the stature of Fiorello La Guardia
in New York or Willy Brandt in Berlin.

As a center of science and technology the state's position was second to none. Here was the largest complex of military production
in the nation. The Los Angeles region became better known for its
missiles than for its movie premières. Several hundred companies,
which employed more than 100,000 persons, settled within a mile
of its international airport.

In the 1950s came the jet age. The first jet experimental flight
was by Chuck Yeager at Edwards Air Force Base, a desolate moonscape on the Mojave Desert. In 1954 this was followed by the super-
sonic flight of X-15, a combination of rocket and airplane.

Since California had taken the lead over other states as a defense
contractor of complex weapons systems, it became a target for critics
of concentration of defense and space spending. In 1962, 40 percent
of the $6.1 billion in prime contracts for military developmental,
test, and research work went to California. The presence of a "university–industrial" complex was a catalyst in building a sophisticated
engineering and manufacturing force. By 1968 more than one-third
of California's industrial production was in the defense and space
fields.

California's former "defense" industry was changing and inventive. In the early 1960s North American's El Segundo plant developed the prototypes of the B-70 bomber, the most powerful yet designed, and produced the X-15 as well as the guidance and control
systems of the Boeing Company's Minuteman missile. North American's Rocketdyne Division powered the ascent of thirty-six out of
forty of the first American space probes. Rocketdyne also developed

the H-1 Saturn engine. North American coordinated its efforts with those of the National Aeronautic and Space Administration, Caltech's Jet Propulsion Laboratory, and the Space Technology Laboratories, operated for the Air Force by Thompson, Ramo, Wooldridge, Inc. North American was the prime contractor of the Apollo moonship, while Rockwell International became the prime contractor for NASA's Space Shuttle Program.

The Lockheed corporation of Burbank and Sunnyvale, like North American, remained active both in missile and aircraft production. Its F-104 Starfighters were used throughout the world. Lockheed, in addition to producing the Polaris submarine missile for the United States Navy, was the prime contractor for the Midas system of detecting ICBM (intercontinental ballistic missile) firings. Lockheed played a part as well in the development of the Agena and Polaris missiles and in the Samos "spy-in-the-sky" satellite. By the 1970s Lockheed's L-1011 widebodied jet transport became a major air carrier.

Competing with that airplane was the McDonnell-Douglas DC-10. That firm has also manufactured the Thor-Able booster rocket, with the aid of the Aerojet General Corporation of Azusa and North American's Rocketdyne Division. Douglas also worked on the Nike-Zeus and Skybolt ballistic missiles.

At San Diego, Convair (later General Dynamics), builder of the F-106 Delta Dart and the 880 jet airliner, also grew into a missile-designing organization. Its prize product was the Atlas ICBM, a missile with a range of almost 10,000 miles.

Through the 1960s the transformation of the aircraft industry into the present day aircraft-missile-electronics complex continued under conditions of rapid population growth and industrialization. Aerospace is a capital goods industry. It is extremely sensitive to economic conditions and to the business community's expectations of what capital needs may be. The industry's largest single customer is the government of the United States. The government's needs are not necessarily influenced by the rise and fall of the business cycle, yet spending cutbacks in military and space hardware, coupled with the occasional slowdown of the economy, have had dramatic effects on the aerospace industry.

Each government cutback in defense-space contracts leaves the state's economy vulnerable. A kind of secondary civil service force of thousands of employees has been created. The Vietnam War helped to make the aerospace industry a permanent feature of California's economic life. It has evolved from equipment manufacturing into a research format that provided long-range military planning plus hardware for both the defense industry and outer space explorations. A large percentage of the "contract dollars" awarded by the National

Aeronautics and Space Administration goes to California research and development projects.

More than 200 electronics firms operate plants in the peninsular suburbs south of San Francisco alone. Among these "black box" makers are: IBM, ITT, Ampex, Hewlett-Packard, Western Electric, Raytheon, Remington Rand, Sylvania, Sperry-Rand, Zenith, Motorola, Philco, and General Electric. Today the phrase Silicon Valley connotes electronic specialization worldwide.

Economic Growth

More and more invested wealth, corporate and real estate, has come to be centered in the state, which has moved beyond economic regional domination into national leadership. Few states top California in per capita income. By 1976 the personal income of Californians advanced to $155 billion. That year median family income was $16,865, regrettably eroded by continuing inflation.

Modern California has been described as "America only more so." Internationally too the state has become powerful. Some nations have economies that are puny by comparison. If California were a separate nation, it would be one of the largest economic forces in the world. If Los Angeles, Orange, San Bernardino, Riverside, and Ventura counties alone were a separate nation, the region would rank eleventh in production capacity among the countries of the world. In recent years the state's "gross product" has been exceeded only by the United States itself, the Soviet Union, West Germany, France, and Japan. California's "GNP" is triple that of Communist China.

Postwar Politics

When President Eisenhower called Governor Earl Warren to Washington in 1953 to become chief justice of the United States, California's "Warren era" of politics came to a close. Warren, although head of the Republican party in the state, based his administration upon both Republicans and Democrats. In nonpartisan ways he pressed for reform of workmen's compensation, prison conditions, and old-age pensions. He liked to refer to welfare measures as progressive and middle-of-the-road, rather than as liberal.

When Warren moved to Washington, he left behind a weak Republican state central committee. Sectional rivalries grew so serious that statewide political cooperation became almost impossible as three ambitious Republicans assumed prominence. Lieutenant Governor Goodwin J. Knight, a party regular, succeeded to the governorship.

Knight remained in office for five years, until 1958. The second leader to step into the limelight was Senator William F. Knowland. In 1945 Warren had appointed the thirty-seven-year-old Knowland to the United States Senate to fill the post left by the death of Hiram Johnson. Knowland was reelected in 1952. The third politician to inherit part of Warren's power was Richard Milhous Nixon, who rose to greater power. In 1945 party leaders who opposed Warren selected Nixon, then a young Navy veteran, to run for the seat of liberal congressman Jerry Voorhis, incumbent Democrat in Nixon's home district. Nixon won and in 1950 ran for the Senate against Helen Gahagan Douglas, wife of film star Melvyn Douglas. Nixon suggested that those opposing him were lacking in patriotism and in anticommunist conviction. This sentiment was to mar Nixon's reputation for years to come. Nevertheless, Nixon developed staunch adherents, and became a national figure, known especially for his stand on internal security.

No issue of the postwar years aroused greater tension within California than did the fear of communist infiltration. This was the McCarthy period of unproven accusations of treason against persons in public office. Nixon's career was furthered by the passage of the restrictive Mundt-Nixon Immigration Act and by his role in the trial and conviction of former State Department aide Alger Hiss for perjury, in connection with accusations of espionage. State Senator Jack B. Tenney headed a committee that claimed to have detected communists in California's government and educational circles. A remedy for uprooting subversives in public life was to require teachers and government employees to sign a "loyalty oath." The resulting atmosphere encouraged public timorousness and conformity.

Beginning in 1949, a "test-oath" controversy raged on the campuses of the University of California. Professors who refused to sign a noncommunist oath imposed upon them by the regents of the university were dismissed. Ultimately the state supreme court ruled this oath invalid, on the ground that the power to require it belonged to the legislature, not to the university regents. In 1950, the legislature's Levering Act required an even more elaborate oath of all state employees. In the meantime the University of California had lost some of its most talented and independent-minded faculty members to other colleges and universities. In 1958, another California loyalty oath was struck down by the United States Supreme Court.

From 1952 until 1960, Vice-president Nixon, second-ranking member of the Eisenhower administration, occupied the most prestigious position of any California Republican. Yet, Nixon, Knowland, and Knight benefited from an almost solidly Republican press. Joseph Knowland, father of Senator Knowland, owned the Oakland *Tribune*, which threw its support to Knowland's son in every political campaign. The Los Angeles *Times* gave strong support to at least one and sometimes all of the three Republican leaders. The Hearst chain of newspapers had usually been conservative Republican in outlook since the early New Deal period. The San Francisco *Chronicle*, although the most liberal major newspaper in California, supported Republicans at election times. The Sacramento, Modesto, and Fresno *Bees* were generally independent newspapers. Thus, Los Angeles, San Francisco, San Diego, Oakland, and Fresno—the largest cities in the state—remained without actively Democratic papers.

The three Republican leaders also benefited from the fortuitous political device of cross-filing. From 1913 until 1959, when the privilege was abolished, any candidate could file for the nomination of more than one party. In California, where Democratic registration has traditionally been heavier than Republican, cross-filing worked in favor of the Republican candidate. The majority of the successful candidates for public office captured both nominations. Campaigning as a nonpartisan, any candidate who won the nomination of both parties could capitalize upon the large proportion of voters who were independent. This tended to produce dull elections in which candidates avoided controversial issues. Too often each side sought to show conservative voters that its candidate was not too liberal while demonstrating to liberals that he was not too conservative.

Candidates also relied upon professional public relations firms to publicize their campaigns. California is known for the activity of such organizations, whose purpose is to use mass media to develop public sentiment in favor of a particular candidate or ballot proposal. Such firms have devised many of the campaign posters, slogans, and clichés of California's recent political history.

In addition to public relations firms, there existed in California a less excusable variety of political lobbying. During the 1940s and early 1950s Artie Samish, the "Mr. Big" of California politics, ran the "Third House" of the California legislature. He became the spokesman for truck and bus lines, liquor and beer interests, race tracks, and for confidential clients who paid fat fees. Samish treated the legislature with contempt, romping arrogantly through its halls as though he had prerogatives superior to those of its members. Samish was exposed in *Collier's* magazine, however, and in 1953, he was convicted of evading federal income taxes.

Nearly 400 organizations are represented at the state capitol. These pressure groups include organized business, labor, agriculture, the professions, and ecology advocates.

Recapture of California by the Democrats

In 1958 the Republican hegemony in California came to an end. A political squabble within the party helped cause its ouster. Senator

Knowland, who wanted the governorship, forced Governor Knight out of the race for reelection. Democratic state Attorney General Edmund (Pat) Brown was given an unexpected advantage in his battle for the governorship with Knowland.

Like Warren before him, Brown had conducted nonpartisan political campaigns, avoiding close association with his own party. He was a vigorous candidate, a native son, and a Catholic. Brown touted liberal reform, and attracted thousands of new voters. He garnered not only the support of his own party but that of independents and was swept into the governorship.

Although there had been a Democratic majority of registered voters since 1934, California had elected Republican governors for more than fifty years, except for the Olson regime, in 1938. Many new Democratic voters had moved into the state. An infectious enthusiasm among young Democrats also generated interest within that party and reinvigorated it by a grass-roots door-to-door campaign.

Pat Brown faced controversial statewide problems, including traffic and smog control, water development, and a debate over capital punishment, because of the case of Caryl Chessman, the "red light bandit." Chessman's execution had been delayed for twelve years during which he argued his own defense, claimed mistrials, and wrote best-selling books about the injustice of capital punishment. He presented Brown with a legal dilemma. His impending execution caused worldwide criticism to be focused on the state's death penalty. On May 2, 1960, Chessman finally died in San Quentin's gas chamber, after Brown refused him a last stay of execution. Brown personally opposed capital punishment but, in the absence of a state law terminating the practice, the governor saw no alternative but to send Chessman to his death.

In 1960, when Vice-president Nixon became the nominee of the Republican party for the presidency, Brown figured prominently in that election. At the Democratic National Convention held in Los Angeles's new Sports Arena, he helped to win the presidential nomination for Massachusetts Senator John F. Kennedy. Nixon, the native son, won his state by a narrow margin, but his victory proved insufficient to prevent Kennedy's election.

Two years later Nixon challenged Brown for the governorship. Nixon's political future then seemed at stake. Failure to win his native state might impair the forty-nine-year-old Republican's chances of remaining a national figure. The campaign was bitter. Nixon accused Brown of being soft on communists and of bungling administration of the state, and pledged the death penalty for "big-time dope peddlers." He promised to drop "chiselers" from the welfare rolls and held out the hope of lower taxes and greater efficiency at Sacramento. Brown defended his record on education, water development, and welfare. Both sides brought lawsuits to stop circulation of pamphlets described as "smears." All indications were that the election would be close. Nixon lost heavily and assailed press coverage of his campaign, although he had received support of many more of California's large newspapers than had Brown.

At the time, most political pundits thought that Nixon's political career was over. Little did they know that only one year later, in 1963, President Kennedy would be murdered. No one could imagine that the Vietnam years would also give Nixon a chance to rebuild his political image and that he would go on to a great presidential victory that would, in turn, be stained by deceitfulness during the Watergate investigations.

In the early 1960s, the California Democratic Council, which had built up a statewide organization, began to disintegrate. The CDC was especially critical of Governor Brown's timid leadership of the party and his allowing factionalism to develop. This infighting resembled the bloodletting that had wrecked California's Republican party in 1958. The state's independent maverick Democrats included Samuel William Yorty, elected mayor of Los Angeles in 1961, who had bolted the party in 1960 to back Nixon against Kennedy. Assembly Speaker Jesse Unruh, a Democrat who, like Yorty, had ambitions for higher office, became a lone wolf who guarded his powerful role in Sacramento. Democratic malcontents found themselves with a fractured party on their hands.

Assembly speaker Unruh was for a time a national figure. Had the Kennedy brothers survived, he would have played a major role in their administrations. After losing the speakership he became a critic of the overlapping of state, county, and city governments. Resembling the Populists and Progressives of an earlier age, he voiced complaints against oil companies, housing-tract speculators, and moneyed interests interfering with the political process by the use of lobbyists with the support of a "political ripoff" system. But Unruh had to fight against his image as a "Big Daddy" politico in an unsuccessful Los Angeles mayoralty race against Tom Bradley, a black leader who won in 1973. Earlier, in 1970, the New York *Times* had urged the election of Unruh against film star Ronald Reagan in the gubernatorial race that year: "The Reagan–Unruh contest has significance far beyond California," the *Times* said in an editorial. "Ronald Reagan personifies nonissue politics. His approach is based on a contempt for serious discussion of real problems; it relies on glamorized images projected in carefully controlled public appearances and in intensive television advertising."

The special-interest groups that backed Reagan, as Unruh suggested, did have an enormous influence on the state legislature. Reagan won, subsequently opposing attempts to stop water pollution and to obtain mass transportation, thereby encouraging inefficient automobiles that befouled the air with smog.

Although the Democrats controlled California politics from 1958 to 1966, the state has been in Republican hands during most of its history. By the 1960s a new voting pattern emerged in California. Two political extremes—the far right and the far left—became widely developed in the state. Hyperconservative rural Southerners and retired elderly folk, yearning for the simplicity of earlier days, disliked "big government" and looked distrustfully at the young and restless "human tumbleweeds" who, without money and responsibility, flooded into the state. The ultra-conservative John Birch Society maintained its headquarters in California. Despite California's progressive past, nonpartisanship gave way to right-of-center sentiment. All the while Reagan, and Nixon before him, projected the image of being moderates, accusing their opponents of extremism. By 1968 such a new party, the Peace and Freedom advocates, opposed the Vietnam War but stood little chance of success. Their championing of civil rights also was about to be drowned by an ultra-rightist tidal wave.

Selected Readings

Sources for the political and economic development of California in the postwar years include John D. Weaver, *Warren: The Man, the Court, the Era* (Boston, 1967), and Leo Katcher, *Earl Warren: A Political Biography* (New York, 1967). Richard M. Nixon's *Six Crises* (New York, 1962) sums up his own career; see also Earl Mazo, *Richard Nixon: A Political and Personal Portrait* (New York, 1959), and William Costello, *The Facts About Nixon . . .* (New York, 1960). These should be supplemented by Horace Jeremiah (Jerry) Voorhis, *Confessions of a Congressman* (New York, 1947).

The articles by Lester Velie that exposed Samish's operations were entitled "The Secret Boss of California," *Collier's*, August 13, 1949, pp. 11–3, 71–3, and August 20, 1949, pp.12–3, 60, 62–3. These have been updated by Arthur H. Samish and Bob Thomas, *The Secret Boss of California* (New York, 1971). An article that throws light on election procedures is Frances M. Carney, "Auxiliary Party Organizations in California," *Western Political Quarterly* 11 (June 1958), 391–92. Similarly analytical is Currin V. Shields, "A Note on Party Organization: The Democrats in California," *Western Political Quarterly* 7 (December 1954), 683 ff.

The use of professional public relations advisers in elections is treated in Robert J. Pitchell, "The Influence of Professional Campaign Management Firms in Partisan Elections in California," *Western*

Political Science Quarterly 11 (June 1958), 286 ff. See also Eugene C. Lee and William Buchanan, "The 1960 Election in California," *Western Political Quarterly*, 16 (March 1961), 309–26.

Analyses of perplexing state problems include William L. Thomas, Jr., *Man, Time, and Space in Southern California* (Washington, D.C., 1961), and Winston W. Crouch and Beatrice Dinerman, *Southern California Metropolis: A Study in Development of Government for a Metropolitan Area* (Berkeley, 1964). The process by which city and county units have merged or sought to maintain their identity from "metropolitanization" is examined in Richard Bigger et al., *Metropolitan Coast: San Diego and Orange Counties* (Berkeley, 1958). Two studies of urbanization in the San Fernando Valley are Richard E. Preston, *The Changing Landscape of San Fernando Valley Between 1930 and 1964* (Northridge, 1966), and Robert Durrenberger, Leonard Pitt, and Richard E. Preston, *The San Fernando Valley: A Bibliography* (Northridge, 1967).

Regarding urbanization in northern California, there is Mel Scott's *The San Francisco Bay Area: A Metropolis in Perspective* (Berkeley, 1965). Edward Eichler and Marshall Kaplan, *The Community Builders* (Berkeley, 1967), focuses upon the development of new towns.

Useful are Kathleen C. Doyle, *Californians: Who, Whence, Whither* (Los Angeles, 1956) and "Economic Survey of California," *California Blue Book* (Sacramento, 1958), published by the State Chamber of Commerce. See also A. E. Karinen and D. W. Lantis, "Population of California: 1950–1961," *Annals* of the Association of American Geographers 51 (December 1961), and *California Statistical Abstract* (Sacramento, 1958). The State Department of Finance publishes an annual publication entitled *California's Population.*

Books that deal with California government and politics include Leo J. Ryan, *Understanding California Government and Politics* (Palo Alto, 1966); Winston W. Crouch, Dean E. McHenry, John C. Bollens, and Stanley Scott, *California Government and Politics* (3d ed., Englewood Cliffs, N.J., 1964); Robert A. Walker and Floyd A. Cave, *How California Is Governed* (New York, 1953); Dean R. Cresap, *Party Politics in the Golden State* (Los Angeles, 1954); Bernard L. Hyink, Seyom Brown, and Ernest W. Thacker, *Politics and Government in California* (6th ed., New York, 1969); and Henry A. Turner and John A. Vieg, *The Government and Politics of California* (2d ed., New York, 1964). A helpful anthology is David Farrelly and Ivan Hinderaker, eds., *The Politics of California: A Book of Readings* (New York, 1951). See also Winston W. Crouch, *The Initiative and Referendum in California* (Los Angeles, 1950), and Joseph A. Beek, *The California Legislature* (Sacramento, 1957).

Somewhat more historical is Joseph P. Harris, *California Politics* (3d ed., Stanford, 1961). A book for young people is Anne B. Fisher's *The Story of California's Constitution and Laws* (Palo Alto, 1953).

California's loyalty-oath controversy is the subject of David P. Gardner, *The California Oath Controversy* (Berkeley, 1967). Postwar economic activity is the subject of Frank L. Kidner, *California Business Cycles* (Berkeley, 1946). See also James L. Clayton, "Defense Spending: Key to California's Growth," *Western Political Quarterly* 15 (June 1962), 280–93; Ewald T. Grether, *The Steel and Steel-using Industries of California* (Berkeley, 1946); and George H. Hildebrand, *The Pacific Coast Maritime Shipping Industry, 1930–1948* (2 vols., Berkeley, 1952).

CHAPTER 36

Confrontation:
The Beleaguered
Sixties

THE 1960s STAND OUT as an era of great unrest, violent behavior, and intemperate language, in which the dominant voices and figures were those of youth. Dissatisfaction with existing institutions run by "the Establishment" formed the keynote of militants who called themselves the New Left or the Radical Left. The tone of the period was shrill as government and institutions came under attack, sometimes physically as well as ideologically.

Beleaguered politicians and estranged voters seemed to offer few solutions. In California's history the threat of violence (let alone overt acts) has repeatedly turned voters away from liberal candidates for office. From the cotton strikes in the central valley during the early 1930s through the era of Upton Sinclair, left-wing extremism has ruined the fortunes of liberal reformers. The student and university revolts of the 1960s continued the trend. Well into the 1970s historians could note with dismay the failure of bond issue after bond issue having to do with rapid transit, pollution, schools, and governmental reorganization of city charters. As an economic recession settled on the nation after 1969, the voter's faith in government diminished. A depersonalized complexity settled upon California.

How to cope with one of the world's first mass societies became a fundamental problem of our time. In a way, California's experiences with congestion served as an early warning system for the rest of America. A brutalized society and environment became a possibility in the age of the computer.

Superficial prosperity and material wealth masked uneasiness beneath the surface. "Street people," sometimes extolling homosexu-

468

ality ("Gay Liberation"), or strumming guitars and shaking rattles in a drugged trance, would soon disconcert middle-class conformists. A new type of conformity, based on long hair, defiant dress, and back-to-nature health foods characterized the hippie code.

The Hippies

In the 1960s California felt the alienation from society of a wide variety of young persons. The disgust of a new type of rebel grew so great that an "underground culture" emerged. Instead of expressing open aggression against parents, hippies took a cool look at modern life, decided it was beyond hope, and "dropped out." Cloistered in the ghettoes of San Francisco, Oakland, or Venice West, they grew resentful of the war in Vietnam, which took millions of dollars for armaments, while bigotry, poverty, and ignorance seemed to be troweled over. Disgust over automation, the suppression of individuality, and with what they considered shallow materialism and phony morals led to further estrangement.

In California especially the hippie generation sought salvation in a life-style that involved the use of "psychedelic" colors discovered under the influence of drugs. While preoccupied with the search for "inward values," in pockets of communal living the hippies emphasized love and the sharing of food and property. Hippiedom—the Haight–Ashbury district of San Francisco—became a national focal point, and on weekends Haight Street was jammed with "straight" sightseers, sometimes bringing traffic to a halt.

Magazines and newspapers, as well as radio and television stations, featured descriptions of these young rebels. Parents did not understand how their children, who had enjoyed superior advantages, could leave middle-class homes and, in the language of disillusioned youth, "turn on, tune in, and drop out." But in the 1960s youth was not impressed by materialism; the fact that California had half the swimming pools in the United States during the 1960s was a statistic not celebrated by the young. They were more apt to regret the failures of conservationists in a struggle to create even a small national redwoods park on the California coast. California's Galanos-designed dresses, the cotillion balls of the society page, and the coming out of debutantes were far from the interests of experimenters with marijuana and Zen who paid no taxes.

Hippies let their hair grow, dressed as they pleased, and often wore no shoes. Parents frequently saw only outward appearances and seldom listened to their ideas, or so their children believed. Young rebels expressed these in what came to be known as the "underground press." The Los Angeles *Free Press* was sold at curbside along the Sunset Strip. In the Bay Area the Berkeley *Barb* and San Francisco *Oracle* also assumed a semisubversive anti-Establishment stance.

Following the lurid publicity and the ogling tourists who frequented the Haight-Ashbury district came commercialization. Furthermore, the hippie movement itself did not diminish avarice, aggressiveness, and other shortcomings in its adherents. Their ghetto resembled everyone else's; it too was ridden by illegitimacy, murder, suicide, and drug addiction. Distrust gradually arose among those who came to feel that their way of life had proved no better than society's. Drugs such as LSD may have given new depth and meaning to a few users; to others, "bad trips" did not sustain personal growth but sometimes represented a temporary fling or permanent tragedy. For the drug user, however, reentry into the dull routine of one's society proved difficult, for drugs deadened the drive to work and produce. Sociologists and psychologists felt that the hippies raised valid questions about society's ethics; yet malcontents did not provide solutions. Critics of the hippies believed that they refused to face real issues and that this constituted a form of hypocrisy.

When their vague ideals were not accepted by the public at large, scores of hippies left San Francisco to start communes in rural areas. Others took up meditation, taught by eastern religions. Looking inward to find peace without drugs was another approach, but the use of drugs remained widespread. Some advocated loosening state and federal penalties concerning the use of marijuana. Others hoped that the hippies would, in time, go back into the mainstream of California society and try to improve it.

Student Unrest and the Vietnam War

Reflective of the impatience of students, the mid-1960s stood in contrast to the placidity of "the silent generation" during the 1950s. After 1963, student demonstrations occurred on California's campuses, particularly at the University of California at Berkeley. There were also protest rallies at San Francisco State College and other collegiate centers. A "Free Speech Movement" at Berkeley kept the university in the headlines. This movement erupted as a displacement of anxiety from society to the colleges and universities, although they were hardly repressive institutions. Agitators insisted upon a greater voice in university administration and in curriculum design. The right of political assembly was particularly dear to activists. Student drama, journalism, and music came to reflect their discontent. Wide-eyed young fans of the folksingers Bob Dylan and Joan Baez wanted action as well as words. Idealistic students of the 1960s also lived in an age of political assassination, during which President John Kennedy, Dr.

Martin Luther King, Jr., and Senator Robert Kennedy were gunned down. It was easy to blame these senseless murders on "the Establishment."

Following massive sit-ins during the fall of 1964, the Free Speech Movement became unpopular. Its vagueness was not long supportable, and the blatant use of obscenity by its leaders led to demands that police move onto the Berkeley campus when order could not be maintained. Ronald Reagan, before he became governor, repeatedly spoke of the need to clean up Berkeley's left-wing extremism. By late 1964 conditions grew so serious at Berkeley that the normally benign Governor Brown ordered state police to break up a student sit-in. More than 700 youths, not all of them students, were dragged out of Sproul Hall, the administrative center, and jailed. Almost 600 of these were pronounced guilty of illegal trespassing and resisting arrest. At San Francisco State College its president, semanticist S. I. Hayakawa, who went on to become a senator, personally confronted rebellious students, earning some public acclaim thereby.

One writer has called the 1960s a period which saw "the ungluing of America." The San Francisco Bay area became a center of agitation for black rights and against the Vietnam War. Students threatened to burn draft cards, defied law and order, and remonstrated against "the Establishment." They resented the presence on campus of representatives from napalm-producing firms as well as armed-service recruiters. As an unwinnable war dragged on, rioters blocked the Oakland Induction Center, turning in draft cards and repudiating educational draft deferments. The war never generated widespread support.

California undergraduates in the 1960s wished to expand their role on the campuses of the state university, questioning the wisdom of conservative, business-oriented regents, who had been appointed for sixteen-year terms by past governors. Students were impatient also with the depersonalization of academic life and argued for decentralization of the university, which eventually did take steps to reorganize its campuses. Small undergraduate colleges similar to those at Oxford represented a student ideal, partly realized by the founding of new campuses at Santa Cruz and San Diego. At Berkeley, faculty study groups sought to find added ways to reduce mechanization and to disarm hostility by sharing authority. A 1967 faculty committee recommended means by which teaching could be reinvigorated and the university decentralized so that students did not feel warehoused. But later, under the Reagan administration, public distrust of the state university would reach new heights.

In 1967 the regents of the University of California dismissed its president, Clark Kerr. Conservative members of that board felt that he had been wishy-washy toward student militants. His firing high-lighted tension between academia and the public at large. California's academic community was clearly in disfavor with a large segment of the electorate. Repeated confrontations between demonstrators and university officials had convinced the public that left-wing professors and administrators were spineless allies of student activists. Universities and colleges alike became targets for critics from both the left and the right.

At a time when the tax base staggered under expanding educational budgets (which competed with accelerating welfare and health care costs), disgusted voters began to favor bond issues for police protection rather than for students and teachers. Taxpayers, confused by the mystique of revolt, believed that the state's colleges and universities should teach students only those skills with which they could make a living, and nothing else. Such critics did not feel that state-operated campuses should become seats of public criticism, or distasteful dramatic and artistic productions. At Berkeley, a city in which the university dominates the community, power only temporarily remained in the hands of older residents who showed scant understanding of the radically different younger generation. The "generation gap" was a reality.

The Oldsters

In the sixties the hippies dramatized divisions between the generations. Although these rebels had mostly faded off the landscape by the 1970s, not so its oldsters. These "senior citizens," (a euphemism to mask society's guilt over their treatment) continued to crowd the welfare rolls. Not all of them had the means to enter "retirement communities," such as Leisure World. A visitor from England quipped, "Either the aged stay home or just don't age. Everyone in California looks young."

Thus far, the economy had proved expansive enough to allow integration of aged persons into the labor market. But, as long as per capita income remained the highest in the nation, oldsters would be strongly attracted to California and were a potential charge on the welfare rolls. Elderly people were confused by the complexity of California's sheer mass.

They looked in vain for political leadership that would better understand their problems. Certain communities favored the elderly as long as they had the means to support themselves. Santa Barbara, once called the home of America's rich unburied dead, gave way to San Clemente, "the cemetery of the living." This retirement center included, for a time, a disgraced former president of the United States.

Wetbacks and Migrants

One of the unsolved problems that continued to face California in the 1960s concerned migratory labor. Agriculture requires large numbers of hand laborers. They hoe and thin sugar beets, cut spinach, feed livestock, and prune vineyards. During winter and summer, fruit, vegetable, and cotton pickers range throughout the state looking for work. In the 1960s uncertain market conditions and an oversupply of workers kept wages depressed. For migrant laborers, traditionally nonunionized, a bad freeze or drought drastically reduced their income. Even today they live in substandard housing, are not fed adequately, and their children seldom complete a grade-school education. In California and throughout the United States their way of life has been described as a "harvest of shame."

In California migrants after World War II came into severe economic competition with Mexican farm workers. The debased condition of cherry pickers and almond harvesters has not improved markedly, in part due to the competition of laborers from Mexico. By the thousands these *braceros* were imported into California precisely because they formed a cheap and willing labor pool. Among them were *alambristas*, wetbacks who came into California "under the wire." The low wages they received as supplementary farm laborers north of the border seemed opulent by Mexican standards. In 1942, Public Law 78 had made their in-migration legally possible, but in 1964 the law expired and clandestine immigration increased. Throughout the postwar era illegal wetbacks were shepherded across the Rio Grande into Texas and other parts of the rural Southwest. Man-snatching *coyotes*, or middlemen, made a business of secreting laborers, marketing whole labor crews to employers.

Unprotected by interstate agreements to control or improve their conditions, migrants wandered from farm to farm, following the harvests as birds follow the sun. Women and children slept nightly in abandoned barns, frame shacks, adobe huts, empty corrals, on straw in warehouses—any place where rent was not demanded. Some hovels in which they lived had dirt floors, or tin roofs with no ceilings. Cheesecloth or flour sacks hung over window openings to keep insects out, but flies, attracted by primitive toilet facilities, found their way into sleeping areas. Poorer "houses" were patched together from scraps of lumber, flattened oil cans, old signboards, or tar paper. They had no indoor pipes or cooking facilities. Migrants cooked outside over open fires in warm weather and out of inside washtubs when it rained.

The IWW had tried unsuccessfully to unionize the Central Valley, and later, in the 1930s, the AFL and CIO also failed. During 1960, however, the Agricultural Workers Organizing Committee obtained wage increases of 12 to 17 cents for each box of peaches picked and from 15 to 17 cents per box for tomatoes. In 1961 the Teamster's Union signed a union-shop contract at Salinas with various large ranches. But these were sporadic gains, without general significance. The Council of California Growers insisted that their unstable and unpredictable "industry" did not lend itself to traditional unionization. They claimed that once a crop was ready for harvest, strikes were an impossibility, as they could not shut down picking operations to negotiate.

Seasonal farm laborers, since before Steinbeck wrote *The Grapes of Wrath*, wanted union recognition, better housing and working conditions, unemployment insurance, and the right to bargain collectively. Farm owners often refused to discuss these demands; some even dusted strikers with insecticides. In 1965 at Delano (a Central Valley town) scab laborers imported by the growers, however, met aggressive picketers who shouted "Viva la Huelga!" while firing marbles with slingshots. Labor organizers of the farm workers imposed a statewide boycott upon Delano grapes and beverages. A few chain stores agreed not to stock these items. Leaflets explaining the boycott flooded into stores that had not agreed to ban such merchandise. The strike was also backed by the Congress of Racial Equality (CORE) and student groups, with support from local clergymen.

Personally leading the farm workers was Cesar Chavez, a magnetic idealist who had spent his youth in the labor camps of Imperial Valley. Chavez and his grape strikers marched 300 miles to Sacramento (in the manner of Coxey's Army in 1893) to protest working conditions. In August 1966, Chavez began to reap the fruits of his organizing efforts when grape pickers employed by the powerful Di Giorgio Fruit Corporation voted in favor of Chavez's U.F.W. union against the Teamsters, who had tried to organize them. By the fall of 1967 Chavez had also struck against the Giumarra Vineyards—the largest table-grape growers in the world.

In February 1968, Chavez completed a twenty-five-day hunger fast, which was brought to an end primarily because he feared violence. Senator Robert Kennedy joined him at the close of the fast, expressing sympathy (after the senator's assassination Ethel Kennedy, his widow, continued the family's support for Chavez). The year 1968 saw nine smaller strikes among California's farm workers and intensification of the boycott against purchasing grapes.

By the summer of 1970 the big grape strike approached its fifth year. Many believed that the growers would never give in. But Chavez intensified picketing, inviting student groups to help the farm labor cause. In June 1970, a group of Central Valley grape growers agreed to sign contracts. They were followed by a majority of Coachella growers.

Chavez's persistence produced a minimum wage for his pickers of $1.70 per hour, an unheard-of rate of pay. Crates containing union-picked grapes displayed the United Farm Workers Union label. The walls of resistance erected by the grape growers came tumbling down as the majority of growers signed labor contracts.

By late 1970 the UFWU was admitted into the AFL-CIO. "Brown power" had never before attained such results. Chavez, speaking out against depersonalized agribusiness, labor contractors, and "body merchants," sought to enhance the dignity of his union's members. He turned to challenging the lettuce-growing "industry," moving the battle from the San Joaquin and Coachella valleys to the Salinas Valley. There he faced the same management attempts to break a strike that he had encountered with the grape growers. On December 4, 1970, he was jailed without bail for refusing to obey an injunction. This court action drew further national attention to his lettuce boycott and he was released. But trouble in the fields was not over.

The Chicano Struggle

In the 1960s "Viva la Huelga," "Viva la Causa," and "Viva Cesar Chavez" became rallying phrases for students, labor reformers, and churchmen throughout the southwestern states. Civil rights marchers participating in the "black revolution" also lent their experience, time and heart to help the struggle to unionize farm workers. Shy and sad in appearance, Chavez became the charismatic mobilizer of a once despised heritage. His checkered shirt and blue jeans characterized a wish to remain close to his people. He came from their ranks and knew what it was to do "stoop work," picking grapes or harvesting lettuce all day long. He made up for lack of a formal education by extensive reading; the autobiography of India's Mohandas Gandhi had a profound effect upon him. Like Gandhi, he refused to allow violence to enter into his fight for Chicanos and other farm workers. Chavez, a reformer with an olive branch, drew the attention of both major political parties to the inarticulate Mexican-American segment of the state's population.

In 1963 California's Mexican-Americans were shocked by the assassination of President Kennedy. A fellow Catholic, he had been nominated for the presidency at Los Angeles, hub of the Mexican-American population, and had campaigned with special vigor among the "Viva Kennedy" clubs organized during the 1960 presidential campaign. Early in 1964 Kennedy's successor, President Lyndon Johnson, scheduled a series of unprecedented conferences in Los Angeles with Mexico's President Lopez Mateos. These covered the whole range of United States relations with Mexico. In addition to discussing the sharing of Colorado River water and the *bracero* problem, the two chiefs of state dealt with the social reforms championed by Kennedy's Alliance for Progress program throughout the Americas. Astute observers of local politics did not, however, miss the importance of the setting in which the Democratic party had chosen to hold these talks, or the emerging political role of the Mexican-Americans. Los Angeles contains the largest Mexican population of any city in the United States.

Widespread dissatisfaction continued in California's Mexican-American community. Less than five years after President Kennedy's death their grief was to be repeated. In June 1968, his brother, Senator Robert Kennedy of New York, was assassinated at Los Angeles following a stunning presidential primary victory in which the Mexican-Americans had strongly participated.

While the discrimination directed against them may not seem so overt as that which blacks encountered, a large percentage of California's adult population of Mexican background was employed in unskilled occupations. Statistically they were several years behind the blacks in scholastic achievement, and four years behind nonminority citizens of the state. In the five states of Texas, New Mexico, Colorado, Arizona, and California there were millions of schoolchildren with Spanish surnames whose language and culture exposed them to bigotry. The problems of Mexican-Americans include the interrelated complexities of low income, unemployment, migration, school retardation, low occupational aspirations, and problems that attend the intrusion of one culture upon another.

The Californian of Mexican descent continued to live on a smaller per capita income than any other group in its population, including blacks. Some California *Latino* leaders referred to their people as *desgraciados*, or "born without grace." For a populace so proud of its heritage, such a status was humiliating.

Stereotyped attitudes toward Mexican-Americans have grown in California since the Treaty of Guadalupe Hidalgo deceptively guaranteed a defeated people equal rights with other residents. But years of employment as stoop laborers in the fields cast Mexican-Americans in an inferior role. Their children endured segregated seating in schools and special handling at the hands of white Anglo-Saxon Protestant (or WASP) authorities. Some Mexican-American children dropped out of school by the time they reached the eighth grade, the legal limit within which a child must attend classes. Such a child, who joined his or her parents in the fields, also joined the ranks of thousands sidetracked from further education. A few converts to the "Anglo" social order were content to move into grass-green, middle-class neighborhoods.

Slowly the Chicano community began to shake off its inexperience in politics. New leaders were voted onto city councils and into the state legislature and federal congress. After 1962 the Mexican Political Association was only one of several new Chicano political organizations. Restiveness among California's Mexican-Americans, however, remained far from allayed.

In March 1968, demonstrations and boycotts by Mexican-American students and teachers occurred in seven Los Angeles high schools. The city's school board was forced to promise implementation of various reforms (after maintaining that it would not do so "on a shotgun basis"). Among these was the appointment of at least one black school principal to replace a white principal as well as alleviation of restrictions on hairstyles and clothing, more bilingual instruction, and a modernized industrial training program for minority-group students who would not go on to college. Accused of sparking the school walkouts were members of a group called the "Brown Berets," whose goal stood in contrast to the "Green Berets" of the United States Army in Vietnam. Their leaders sought to unite *"La Raza"* (the race) in the barrios of California. Wearing clothing that resembled the revolutionary garb of Fidel Castro and his Cuban followers, these critics carried signs that read *"Viva la Revolucion!"*

California's Chicano leaders went from generalized protest toward nonglittering but more practical organization. But hopes to build a new politial party, *La Raza Unida*, dissolved into fracticidal disputes as weary activists turned toward the nonviolent ideals of Chavez, the only nationally known figure of Mexican-American heritage. Only slowly was a new leadership forged in the barrios of east Los Angeles and south San Francisco. More and more young Chicanos were coming out of the colleges and universities who were anxious to replace members of the older generation, labeled Tio Tacos—"Uncle Tacos," a parallel for Uncle Tom.

California's Blacks and Watts

The inequities that faced California's black population also cried out for reform. Even after statehood was achieved in 1850, blacks could not give testimony against Whites in a court of law. Although California joined the union as a free state, the Fugitive Slave Act (1852) got applied in such a way as to discriminate against blacks. The oldest black newspaper in the state, *The California Eagle*, has been published at Los Angeles since 1879. Black communities grew slowly until the 1880s, after which larger numbers of nonwhites piled into nascent ghettoes, including custodians, waiters, cooks, railroad porters, domestics in the homes of the rich, handymen, and gardeners. The economic stimulus of World War I attracted still more blacks westward.

By 1944 the Japanese district of Los Angeles ("Little Tokyo") felt the inroads of 80,000 new black residents. Blacks also moved into Pasadena, San Francisco, and Oakland, but they were not welcomed in "lily-white" communities at Glendale and San Marino. Blacks, however, founded an all-black community at Val Verde Park in the Tehachapi foothills, as well as a Los Angeles-based insurance corporation, and a few resorts. From the 1950s through the 1960s California's black populace grew by 91 percent, while its overall population increased by only 48 percent. During the same decade over 350,000 blacks moved to California.

Blacks not only entered white neighborhoods; in the professions, in sports, and in the political world they slowly challenged white supremacy. Dr. Ralph Bunche, a graduate of UCLA, went from a State Department career to become under secretary at the United Nations; Jackie Robinson began his baseball prominence at Pasadena Junior College; Tom Bradley, a city councilman, became mayor of Los Angeles in 1968.

Crowded into dilapidated lower-class neighborhoods, blacks chafed at prejudice, segregation, and social deprivation. In southeast Los Angeles the sprawling ghetto of Watts became an especially unwholesome sore spot. Although its streets were lined with palm trees, it was a crowded slum nonetheless, and bound to produce violence. California's blacks detested the rank legal and extralegal discrimination they suffered. True, the Rumford Fair Housing Act, passed by the legislature in 1963, broadened prohibitions against discrimination to include the sale or rental of certain categories of private dwellings. Yet large segments of the population pressed for its repeal. Along with the 1959 Unruh Civil Rights Act (which had outlawed housing discrimination by business establishments), the Rumford Act formed the heart of the state's laws against discrimination in housing. In 1964 the voters adopted Proposition 14, which nullified the state's open-housing provisions. This setback for blacks occurred on the eve of the Watts riots. Not until 1966 did the state supreme court strike down Proposition 14.

The August 1965 Watts uprisings epitomized the malaise of disenchanted blacks. Hundreds of rioters, shouting the antiwhite epithets "Burn, Baby, Burn" and "Get Whitey," looted stores, set buildings afire, and shot at firemen and police. Governor Brown ordered National Guard troops into Los Angeles to help local police restore order and to establish a curfew. The riots, which lasted for six days, caused the deaths of thirty-five persons, injury to six hundred others, and $40 million in damage. Some 4,000 persons were arrested, mostly in a square-mile burned-over area.

One rioter told a reporter: "Everywhere they say 'Go to California! California's the great pot o'gold at the end of the rainbow.' Well, now we're here in California, and there ain't no place else to go, and the only pot I seen's the kind they peddle at Sixtieth and Avalon." The Watts outbursts underscored a sense of hopelessness that grew out of economic misery, a diffuse black family structure, envy of the white man's luxuries, and resentment against "Establishment" forces of law and order. Antiwhite rowdyism, however, made these upheavals only party racial. The search for material goods led black marauders to sack furniture stores filled with television sets, freezers, and high fidelity phonographs—as if to defy the white monopoly on success. Key terms or phrases repeated after the Watts riots depicted the problems of inner-city streets: discrimination, anarchy, mob violence, looting, illegitimacy, drug addicts, venereal disease, employment inequality, police brutality, attacks on policemen and school teachers.

The Watts disturbances, among the first serious racial conflicts in the postwar United States, did little to alter hatred of disenchanted poor blacks toward whites. There resulted, nevertheless, some moves toward reform, one of which involved building a cultural center at Watts as well as a hospital. Educated blacks from ghetto areas were listened to with greater attention than before. Yet there was a continuing failure to delve deeply into the roots of interracial misunderstanding, although local police attempted to open up a dialogue with blacks in order to reduce community tensions. The McCone Commission, appointed by Governor Brown immediately after the Watts outbreak to study the reasons for the riots, indicated that Watts needed much better transportation and recreational facilities. White businessmen also tried to widen employment opportunities, in order to assuage rootless young blacks, but the killing (sometimes between competing youth gangs) continued. In the midst of a 1968 summer Watts festival, several persons were killed in encounters with the law.

California's racial history once seemed like a model one when compared with that of some other states. Revamping run-down neighborhoods and pouring money into welfare programs, the state had never sponsored a poll tax. Although its cities long had separate Mexican-American and Chinese sectors, impacted black sections did not emerge until after World War II. Schools were officially integrated long ago.

Yet disguised bigotry remained among California's voters. Even after the Watts riots, attempts were made in the legislature to repeal the Rumford Act, although California stood to lose millions of dollars in federal redevelopment funds for nonsegregated neighborhoods. In summary, while conditions for blacks improved after the Watts riots, a rising level of expectation accompanied dissatisfaction over slowness in achieving parity with whites. "Black power" advocates and impatient, sometimes idle, young blacks expected quicker action on the promises of legislators, and sponsors of such national anti-poverty programs as "Head Start" and "Upward Bound."

Selected Readings

Works that reach back to the beginnings of the black experience in California include the following: James de Abajian, compiler, *Blacks and Their Contributions to the American West: A Bibliography* (Boston, 1974); Kenneth Goode, *California's Black Pioneers* (Santa Barbara, 1973); James A. Fisher, "Political Development of the Black Community in California," *California Historical Quarterly* 50 (September 1971); 256–66; Francis N. Lortie Jr., "San Francisco's Black Community, 1870–1890," a thesis (1970) available as a reprint (San Francisco, 1973); Thurman A. Odell, "The Negro in California Before 1890," *Pacific Historian* 19 (Winter 1975), 321–45; Lawrence B. De Graaf, "The City of Black Angels: The Emergence of the Los Angeles Ghetto, 1890–1930," *Pacific Historical Review* 39 (August 1970), 323–52; De Graaf's "Recognition, Racism, and Reflections on the Writing of Black History," *Pacific Historical Review* 44 (February 1975), 22–51; and E. Berkeley Tompkins, "Black Ahab: William T. Shorey, Whaling Master," *California Historical Quarterly* 51 (Spring 1972), 75–84. See also F. Ray Marshall, *The Negro and Organized Labor* (New York, 1965).

Literature on the Watts riots is substantial. Basic is the McCone Commission report, *Violence in the City: An End or a Beginning* (Los Angeles, 1965), supplemented by Jerry Cohen and William Murphy, *Burn Baby Burn: The Los Angeles Race Riot, August, 1965* (New York; 1966), which reproduces photos taken during the riots. Other accounts are Spencer Crump, *Black Riot in Los Angeles: The Story of the Watts Tragedy* (Los Angeles, 1966), and Robert Conot, *Rivers of Blood, Years of Darkness* (New York, 1967), which includes case histories, interviews, and sociological material concerning the Watts riots.

Regarding Watts also see Nathan Cohen, *The Los Angeles Riots: A Socio-Psychological Study* (New York, 1970); Robert M. Fogelson (compiler) *The Los Angeles Riots* (New York, 1969), which includes the McCone Commission Report and objections to it; as well as Paul Bullock, ed., *Watts: The Aftermath* (New York, 1970), as viewed by the residents of Watts; and Joseph Boskin and Victor Pilson. "The Los

Angeles Riot of 1965: A Medical Profile of an Urban Crisis," *Pacific Historical Review* 29 (August 1970), 353–65. More literature on blacks is at the end of Chapter 21.

General statements regarding immigrants are in George E. Frakes and Curtis Solberg, eds., *Minorities in California History* (New York, 1971). See also Moses Rischin, "Immigration, Migration, and Minorities in California: A Reassessment," *Pacific Historical Review* 41 (February 1972), 71–90, which contains good statistics but is repetitious.

An updated bibliography regarding Chicanos follows Chapter 38. Here are earlier studies: Paul S. Taylor has written an imposing series of research monographs on the role of Mexicans in the United States. His *Mexican Labor in the United States* (Berkeley, 1928–34), a multivolume study, is basic. Volume 1 is entitled *Imperial Valley*. With Dorothy Lange Taylor, he also published *An American Exodus: A Record of Human Erosion* (New York, 1939). Carey McWilliams treats this same subject in his previously mentioned *Factories in the Fields*, as well as in *North from Mexico* (Philadelphia, 1949). In a similar vein is Ruth D. Tuck, *Not with the Fist* (New York, 1946). Useful also is Harry Schwartz, *Seasonal Farm Labor in the United States* (New York, 1945). Leonard Pitt's *The Decline of the Californios: A Social History of the Spanish-Speaking Californians* (Berkeley, 1966), treats the Mexican-American story from 1846 to 1890. A modern discussion in relation to a vital California crop is N. Fogelberg and A. W. McKay, *The Citrus Industry and the California Fruit Growers Exchange System* (Washington, 1940). See also California State Chamber of Commerce, *Migrants: A National Problem and Its Impact upon California* (San Francisco, 1940), and N. Ray Gilmore and Gladys W. Gilmore, "The Bracero in California," *Pacific Historical Review* 32 (August 1963), 265–82. See also Mark Reisler, "Always the Laborer: Anglo Perceptions of the Mexican Immigrant," *Pacific Historical Review* 45 (May 1976), 231–54.

Studies of Mexican-Americans that concern their role in agriculture include John Gregory Dunne, *Delano: The Anatomy of the Great California Grapeworkers Strike* (New York, 1967); John C. Elac, "The Employment of Mexican Workers in U.S. Agriculture, 1900–1960," Ph.D. dissertation, UCLA (1961); James F. Rooney, "The Effects of Imported Mexican Farm Labor in a California County," *American Journal of Economics and Sociology* 20 (October 1961), 513–21; W. Willard Wirtz (U.S. Secretary of Labor), *The Year of Transition: Seasonal Farm Labor* (Washington, 1966); Ernesto Galarza, *Merchants of Labor: The Mexican Bracero Story* (San Jose, 1964); Otey M. Scruggs, "The Evolution of the Mexican Farm Labor Agreement of 1942," *Agricultural History* 34 (July 1960), 140–49; and Truman E. Moore, *The Slaves We Rent* (New York, 1965). More general are Manuel P.

Servín, "The Pre-World War II Mexican-American: An Interpretation," California Historical Society *Quarterly* 45 (December 1966), 325–28; Fernando Penalosa, "The Changing Mexican-American in Southern California," *Sociology and Social Research* 51 (July 1967), 405–17; and Michael Mathes, "The Two Californias During World War II," California Historical Society *Quarterly* 44 (December 1965), 323–32.

The Division of Fair Employment Practices, California Department of Industrial Relations, has published a series of pamphlets, including *Californians of Spanish Surname* (1964); *Negroes and Mexican Americans in Southeast Los Angeles* (1966); *Negro Californians* (1963); and *Californians of Japanese, Chinese and Filipino Ancestry* (1965).

Clark Kerr, *The Uses of a University* (New York, 1963), relates higher education to the needs of a technological society. More immediately focused upon California is Arthur G. Coons, *Crises in California Education* (Los Angeles, 1968). Seymour M. Lipset and Sheldon S. Wolin, eds., *The Berkeley Student Revolt: Facts and Interpretations* (New York, 1965), will inevitably be followed by similar books, as will the first "life" of Ronald Reagan (with Richard Hubler), *Where's the Rest of Me?* (New York, 1965). A survey of recent California politics is Eugene C. Lee, ed., *The California Governmental Process: Problems and Issues* (Boston, 1966). Publicist Thomas M. Storke's battle against the John Birch Society is described in his *I Write for Freedom* (Fresno, 1963), with a preface by Adlai Stevenson. Charles M. Price ed., *Consensus and Cleavage: Issues in California Politics* (San Francisco, 1968), is a compilation. Reaching further back, are the readings edited by Leonard Pitt, entitled *California Controversies: Major Issues in the History of the State* (New York, 1967).

CHAPTER 37

A Menaced Life-style?

IN THE 1960s pressing physical as well as human problems had begun to afflict California in painful ways. As hundreds of thousands of new residents pushed into the state each year, environmental concerns grew urgent. These included overcrowded schools, hospitals, mental health facilities and sanitariums, a freeway system that was clearly outmoded, the need for reapportionment, taxation, water shortages, juvenile delinquency, and air pollution. Unending debate as to how best to handle these difficulties raged both in the press and in legislative halls. A glance at some of the physical problems that beset California should be helpful to an understanding of the human challenges discussed in the last chapter.

Smog

Los Angeles and San Francisco have been plagued by one of the most baffling problems that can afflict any city—air pollution in the form of smog. This term is a combination of the words smoke and fog. The persistent, choking, bluish haze grew more uncomfortable each year. It dirtied buildings, reduced visibility, irritated eyes, angered tourists, and created a public furor. Almost every politician promised to do something about the emission of fumes. As early as 1947, Los Angeles organized a County Air Pollution Control District, which spent millions of dollars trying to banish the fumes. Yet the city banned backyard incinerators only in 1957. Until a state law allowed the APCD to override local jurisdiction, its air pollution ordinances could not be applied to the sixty-three municipalities that surrounded Los Angeles. The control of industries that produced sulphurous petrochemicals became part of the APCD program, as did laboratory investigation to determine factors responsible for smog.

Los Angeles is located in a saucerlike basin that suffers from the lowest wind velocity of any major city of the United States. If the air could escape the surrounding rim of mountains, where the atmosphere grows cooler with altitude, the condition would not be so troublesome. But bright sunshine on hot, sunny days causes photochemical regrouping of exhaust gas molecules. Then smog ozones form and the sulphurous plumes billowing out of industrial smokestacks refuse to go away. Hydrocarbons from auto exhausts and vapor leaks from gas tanks also contribute to the smog.

Like the San Francisco Bay area, southern California remains a distinct province of the state. Its contrasts are immense as the visitor flies into the Los Angeles Basin on a clear night over an endless network of sparkling lights. Columns of automobiles crowd the freeways. The beauty of this scene is in contrast to the pall of smog that may envelop the region on the next day. Crowding has produced a profligate waste of energy that contributes to mortality rates from emphysema, bronchitis, lung cancer, and coronary insufficiency. Air pollution has also been related to asthma, respiratory infections, and allergies.

Although smog once seemed less of a problem in the north, San Francisco in 1955 organized an Air Pollution Control District. This consisted of nine counties in the bay area that banned open rubbish fires. Municipal dumps, which deposited layers of filthy air over the bay on windless days, were forced to cover-and-fill city refuse. But full smog control was never achieved. At Los Angeles after 1956, when the concentration of pollution reached a prescribed level, local industries were notified to reduce the burning of fuel. Business firms were forced to burn only natural gas from May through October.

Legislative action to control auto exhausts was painfully slow, although this was clearly the main cause of smog. Meanwhile Californians experienced year-round smog conditions, even during the winter months. In addition to human suffering, growers of leafy field crops, including lettuce and spinach, complained that their smog losses ran into the millions. The reduction of fruit and vegetable yields is also demonstrable. The leaves of avocado and orange trees affected by smog dry up and turn gray and splotchy.

Reapportionment, Taxes, and the Constitution

Another continuing problem was the political imbalance between the northern and southern parts of California. In the earliest years of statehood, when the southland was distinctly rural, spokesmen at the state capital for the ranchos and pueblos of the south found themselves pitted against powerful representation from "the City," or San Francisco. Virtually all important state appropriations were spent in northern California, where the bulk of the population resided. The state's earliest schools, hospitals, colleges, and other institutions were in the north.

Southern California's growth, however, reversed the population pattern. Today, southern Californians refer to the mountainous, thinly populated northern regions of the state as "cow counties," a term once used to describe Los Angeles. That city, although now the population center of the state, as late as the 1960s felt hampered by a northern rural minority in the legislature that drained it of tax money. San Francisco frequently sided in the legislature with the rural, central-northern counties, also voting with farm lobbyists to block reapportionment of the legislature.

In northern mountain counties of California, one voter had more representation in the state senate than did four-hundred Los Angeles voters. The north had possessed the bulk of California's population when county lines were drawn. Nonurban northern areas frequently vetoed measures dealing with increased freeway construction, water development, flood control, taxation, smog prevention, and education. By 1964 the struggle between northern and southern California took a turn in favor of the south when the United States Supreme Court ordered both houses of all state legislatures apportioned on a "one man, one vote" basis.

At the national level, in the redistribution of congressional seats and electoral votes, resulting from the 1960 census, California added eight seats to its thirty in the House of Representatives, giving it a total of forty electoral votes (the formula is one vote for each state's seat in the House of Representatives plus two for its senators).

Revision of the state constitution is another matter of concern to reform-minded citizens. The last major revision of California's constitution was in 1879. Since then it has been amended over 300 times and has grown to 75,000 words, ten times the length of the United States Constitution. It is exceeded in bulk only by the constitution of India and that of Louisiana. The state constitution, which resembles a telephone book in bulk, contains provisions that should be in the statutory law of the state, and not in the constitution. For example, the constitution provides that the legislature "shall have no power to prohibit wrestling and twelve-round boxing contests in the State of California." The constitution requires that the trustees of the Huntington Library shall make an annual report to the secretary of state. Any person who fights a duel with deadly weapons or who accepts a challenge to fight a duel, or acts as second, shall be prohibited from holding public office or voting in California.

Los Angeles sprawl, 1954. (By courtesy of William A. Garnett. © 1954 by William A. Garnett.)

The Forty-Four Counties of
Northern California

```
0        50        100       150
|_____|_____|_____|
              miles
```

Water and Society

By the late 1940s even Hoover Dam and the Boulder Canyon Project could not permanently provide water for southern California. In Kern County alone, underground wells were being overdrafted by 260 billion gallons per year. Overdraft of underground resources in coastal locations caused the intrusion of seawater into freshwater deposits. In the Los Angeles basin and to the north, in Suisun Bay and along the Sacramento–San Joaquin Delta, such intrusions caused serious pollution.

As we have noted, federal measures to control the Sacramento and San Joaquin rivers and to generate hydroelectric power were authorized in the 1930s under the Central Valley Project. Its chief units included Shasta Dam (completed in 1945), near the northern end of the Sacramento Valley, and the smaller Friant Dam (completed in 1942), near the headwaters of the San Joaquin, drained by the Friant–

The Fourteen Counties of
Southern California

Kern Canal. Another canal, the Delta–Mendota, was placed in operation in 1951. Folsom Dam, twenty miles above Sacramento, on the American River, went into operation in 1955. That year construction of the federally financed Trinity River Project, yet another unit of the Central Valley Project, was begun. By 1960, after more than a quarter-century of effort and the expenditure of $1 billion on its water development, the Central Valley Project had placed Fresno, Kern, and Tulare among the nation's ten most productive farm counties.

None of these developments provided a permanent solution to water needs outside the San Joaquin Valley. The major sources of water remained badly distributed geographically. Along California's northwest coast the Sacramento, the San Joaquin, and the Eel, Mad, and Klamath rivers continued to empty most of their water into the ocean. A new approach to water resources had to be found. As early as 1948, advocates began to speak up for the Feather River Project.

Flood control activity combined with conservation. (Department of Water Resources.)

The Feather, the most important tributary of the Sacramento River, has a seasonal runoff about one-fifth that of the entire Sacramento drainage basin. To harness the waters of the Feather a large reservoir capacity was needed, consisting of costly dams and more than eight hundred miles of canals, tunnels, lakes, siphons, and penstocks. This project was only part of an $11 billion statewide plan that would be under construction until the year 2020. During 1957, site clearance began on "the world's largest dam," the 730-foot-high Oroville Dam, located on the Feather River above Sacramento—the first step toward the largest construction project in California, a great "natural stairway" of untapped hydroelectric power and water.

Debate over whether state or federal funds should be used—added to political sectionalism between northern and southern California—slowed down the Feather River Project. Even after construction had begun on Oroville Dam, the legislature remained locked in discord over whether to complete it and whether to build the dam projected to accompany it—San Luis Dam, 310 feet high, in Merced County. An adamant stand by southern legislators against appropriating money for water that could be recaptured by northern "counties of origin" contributed to a ten-year stalemate. The north required flood control as urgently as the industrializing, parched south needed water. Protection of the towns of Yuba City, Butte, and Marysville from floods also had to be weighed against the need for life-giving water to southern California.

Critics feared the enrichment of "corporation farmers" whose thousands of productive acres would be nourished by water paid for by others. Another stumbling block to adoption of the Feather River Project was its great cost. Largely, however, the issue was the north's interests as opposed to the south's.

Not until after the election of Governor Brown in 1958 was the legislative deadlock broken. He deserves credit for persuading representatives of competing counties that it was in their best interest to stop squabbling over the future of California's water. In 1960 California voters endorsed Brown's water bond program and the long-delayed Feather River Project began to be built in earnest. It called for no less than the transfer of water from northern California to points as far south as San Diego County. Protection of northern rights in the "counties of origin" is implicit in the plan, the world's biggest water-transport system.

The Feather River Project was begun in a region of steep-walled canyons and forested mountains, comprising some of the most breathtaking scenery in the West. The project provides for fish and game protection as well as flood control and conservation. There are one thousand miles of trout streams in the Feather River Country, with bass, steelhead, and shad available in the river itself.

This massive project transfers runoff water to areas of shortage for municipal and industrial use and for irrigation. This last purpose is crucial, since 95 percent of California's crops are grown on irrigated land. The new water network was to consist of sixteen dams, eighteen pumping stations, nine power plants, and miles of aqueducts, canals, and pipelines. "The California Aqueduct's" north-south artery includes the Detal Project, with its network of canals and pumping stations in the Sacramento–San Joaquin Valley. Transporting this water into southern California posed a big construction problem, as the Tehachapi Mountains form a barrier between that area and the San Joaquin Valley. Water must be lifted over the Tehachapis and then sent via tunnels bored through the mountain ridges. To receive Feather River water, after it arrives at the state's terminal reservoir at Castaic, the Metropolitan Water District constructed a 300-mile system of feeder lines.

A disappointing alternative to California's costly water transport problem has been desalination of water. The popular conception of the economic feasibility of converting ocean water into freshwater has little foundation in fact. However, in 1967 President Johnson announced that the federal government would help to build the largest desalination plant in the country near San Diego.

Tunnel through Tehachapi Range bringing northern water into arid Southern California. (Department of Water Resources.)

By the mid-1970s Californians had begun to experience second thoughts about the water conservation programs they had authorized a decade earlier. One aspect of those programs came under particular attack. This was a forty-three-mile peripheral canal around the Sacramento–San Joaquin Delta. That flume had been planned to divert water to pumping plants. Ecologists, however, maintained that the canal would destroy nature's balance of water fowl and fish life along the sloughs of the delta. Following the Arab oil boycott of 1974, the electricity costs needed to pump Feather River water southward to southern California greatly increased monthly utility bills. As a result, environmental home insulation projects suddenly became popular.

Conservationists have also awakened to the damaging relationship between water management and soil pollution. Salt and chemicals stay in the soil and are sometimes drained into wildlife refuges or into the ocean. This has resulted in deformities among some species of life. Toxics like selenium are particularly dangerous, causing high abortion rates among cattle and sheep. Humans too are so affected by contaminated wells that fears have arisen that one day California will choke on its own sludge.

Agriculture: "Factories in the Fields"

Aggressive water development has made possible steady economic expansion of California, for most of its farms depend upon artificially supplied water. California has become an industrial state without ceasing to be an agricultural one. It has consistently led the nation in gross income from agricultural products. California is first nationally in the production of almost forty crops, and no state even comes near its production of fruits and vegetables. Forty percent of all the fruit consumed in the United States is grown in the state.

Year after year, California has topped other states in agricultural production. It continues to produce virtually every crop, indeed more than 275, from cut flowers to kelp. Even fish are harvested artificially. Though faced with heavy competition from Florida, the state still dominates the nation's citrus production. Today's cattlemen breed, feed, ship, and sell their own livestock; a few even grow the alfalfa and sorghum used in cattle fattening. Rancher-farmers rely upon two-way radios to keep contact with employees; they operate motor pools and buy costly harvesters, tractors, and automatic potato pickers. This mechanization is a far cry from the nineteenth century's horse-drawn plows, haystacks, and milk wagons.

Agriculture has yielded large areas of farmland to real estate subdivisions, industrial plants, and space-consuming highways. Real estate promoters "process the desert" to prepare new housing tracts.

Despite California's rich land potential, successful production was achieved only after bitter conflict between small and large landowners. Modern agribusiness, far from being inevitable, resulted from a complex of forces operating over the last century or more. These included the virtually unchecked ability of large farm interests to shape public policy. As a result, government's expanding agricultural subsidies—public irrigation development, tax-funded research, marketing assistance, price supports, and subsidized labor projects—have primarily benefited large-scale enterprises. Corporate farming has come to reign in California, not because of impersonal environmental or economic forces, but rather because of conscious social choice manifested through a political process in which the power of the large-scale enterprises has been decisive.

As a result, the small farm is frequently incapable of grossing an income sufficient to allow it to compete successfully. Consequently, it is tending to be replaced by large, mechanized agribusinesses. These corporations include the Kern County Land Company, whose hold ings in the Central Valley are gargantuan. The Irvine Ranch Company once operated a vast acreage in Orange County and has become the major landowner in Imperial County as well. In the San Joaquin Valley, the DiGiorgio and Sawyer fruit and vegetable farms produce millions of dollars of income annually. The Maggio Company in the Imperial Valley is the largest single grower of carrots in the United States. The Brock Ranches near El Centro, and the Antle Ranches, growers of Salinas lettuce and carrots in the Imperial Valley and Arizona, are among the leading producers of vegetables in the nation.

These corporations have not only increased the size of the average farm but have consolidated agriculture operations within the state. Large growers extended their operations into shipping and processing, cementing in cattle-feeding pens, lettuce and truck garden sites, orange groves, and orchards. Heavy in-migration has made the sight of orange orchards, once the symbol of southern California, a memory of the past. There was a time when the very name Orange County held a special enchantment. As late as 1930, orange growing was the first agricultural crop in the state, with dairies second and livestock third. But orange groves occupied land that soared to $20,000 per acre during the 1950s. As ten newcomers stepped across the state line in search of sunshine and a better life, California lost one more acre of farm land.

Five million acres of California's primeland continue to disappear as each year passes. Yet, in 1985 the state led in the production of forty-seven agricultural commodities, accounting for over 90 percent of the national output of almonds, apricots, artichokes, broccoli, dates, figs, grapes, clover seed, nectarines, olives, persimmons, pomegranates, and walnuts. In addition, the state produced at least three-quarters of the nation's asparagus, cauliflower, garlic, lemons, honeydew melons, safflower, and tomatoes. California remains the leading producer of eggs in the United States. Grapes, more than half of which are crushed for wine and brandy, rank as the most valuable fruit harvest. Most of the wine consumed in the United States originates in California. In addition to wine production and bottling, a large food-processing industry comprises fruit and vegetable canning and freezing operations. Some of these involve poultry, dairying, and fish

Mt. Shasta, a towering volcanic peak of the Cascade Range, reflected in a mill pond. (Union Pacific Railroad.)

canning. Fish and shellfish landed at California ports exceed the largest catch of any state in the Union.

In recent years California has been losing agricultural markets to competitors in Texas, Arizona, and Latin America, where wages are lower. The virtual monopoly which the state once enjoyed in growing and processing many foods has disappeared. Mexico, Guatemala, and

Ecuador have all entered the fruit and vegetable processing field. Some growers and packers of such crops as beans, broccoli, celery, and lettuce have gone out of business after being forced to pay wages of over $7 per hour.

Who Owns the Oil?

California, once second only to Texas as an oil-producing state, has in recent years found its production curve leveling off. The state consumes all the oil it produces, yet uses so much fuel that it is on an import basis. During World War II, when the need for oil vastly increased, exploration was stepped up and prospecting techniques improved. When California became an oil-importing state after the war, attention was given to its valuable offshore oil resources. This in turn gave rise to the tidelands controversy, a battle for jurisdiction over the vast deposits that extend outward many miles from the shoreline. Various southern states claimed that state limits of jurisdiction extended for ten miles out to sea. Under international law, three miles was the accepted jurisdiction of a nation. California leased tideland drilling rights to private companies and reaped large royalties from these leases. In 1947, furthermore, Supreme Court decisions established the "paramount rights" of the federal government to offshore oil reserves.

The seaboard states, however, continued to maintain rights beyond the federally recognized three-mile limit. Because the offshore jurisdiction of neither state nor federal government was firmly established, California extended its claims as far as thirty miles out to sea. The status of California's tidelands remained nebulous until 1965, when the Supreme Court denied almost all of California's claims to submerged tidelands oil, valued at more than $1 billion. Only Monterey Bay, less than 100,000 acres of the 6 million acres claimed by the state, was awarded to California. The high court's decision appeared to end a twenty-year dispute, unless the national Congress passes a law granting California underwater rights to San Pedro, Santa Monica, and San Luis Obispo bays. The chance for enactment of such legislation is faint.

Long Beach after World War II leased offshore reserves to independent oil operators in defiance of both state and federal claims. Only after a lengthy dispute was a three-way agreement reached between the federal government, the state, and California costal municipalities. The state had to agree to spend a sizable part of its oil and gas revenues for beautification of polluted beach sites and of cramped picnic and camping areas. Residents and tourists today flock

The Richmond refinery of Chevron U.S.A. Inc. (by courtesy of Chevron Corporation.)

to recreational facilities made possible from these offshore oil funds. Tidelands oil revenues were also earmarked for water development.

Care, however, must be exercised that coastal waters do not become forested with offshore drilling rigs on platforms that rival thirty-story buildings in height. The State Lands Commission limits drilling to operators who have leased thousands of acres of beach land, from north of the Ventura County line beyond Carpinteria to Gaviota. Federal-state tension over offshore oil drilling has grown particularly angry along the Santa Barbara channel. In the 1960s, oil spills led to the formation of a group called GOO (Get Oil Out).

Paradoxically, although Californians seek to curtail the oil industry, new discoveries occurred off Point Arguello in the 1980s. Large reserves exist beneath the Santa Maria Basin. Billions of barrels of oil are locked beneath the sea as far north as Morro Bay. The federal government continues to pressure the state for full exploitation of this treasure.

A Brutalized California

Past migration was relatively insignificant compared to California's modern growth. During the ten years following 1950, state population swelled by about half a million persons each year. The 1950s saw an increase of 48.5 percent, or 5,130,981. Of these persons, 70 percent settled in southern California. A flight to the suburbs altered the drawing power of California's largest cities. By 1960, about 90 percent of the population clustered around nine metropolitan areas, less than 5 percent of California's land area.

As long as the boom in California's defense industry lasted, millions of new workers could be absorbed. With mechanization and the leveling off of defense contracts, however, no new mammoth growth industry was available to stimulate California economically. Only space technology (which eventually put American astronauts on the moon) promised future expansion. The cost of space ventures, furthermore, was frightful.

A widening stain of confusion marred the shift in the postwar years from an agricultural to an industrial way of life. This period of turmoil featured explosive growth, the results of which were not entirely healthy. Vulgarization of the social environment accompanied physical deterioration. California had arrived at a postindustrial stage of economic development with few roadmarks to guide its future.

As frontier rurality developed into an industrial milieu, the missions and ranchos of the Spanish period made way for Hollywood, oil derricks, aircraft factories, steel mills, residential subdivisions, and television studios. The grape vineyards and orange groves of the early twentieth century surrendered to tourist attractions, housing projects, and jet-propulsion laboratories. The noxious fumes of smog and serious state and municipal problems damaged the charm that California once held for health seekers, tourists, and outdoor lovers. Traffic congestion grew so acute that new freeways were obsolete, indeed dangerous. Without helicopter surveillance and air-to-ground radio reports, traffic jams became impossible to control.

Dynamite and bulldozers damaged unique scenic wonders and gouged the landscape with deep scars. Buzzing chain saws logged the noble redwoods. Instant cities slobbered over the countryside. Sleazy suburbias, cluttered with unsightly billboards, marred the landscape. In a single generation California was on the way toward ruining the unique Mediterranean climate of southern California.

The National Park Service has estimated that there were once more than 2 million acres of redwoods between Monterey Bay and southern Oregon. Now only a fraction of that virgin forest remains. During the 1960s these tallest of trees continued to be logged at the rate of a billion board feet per year. Were it not for the "Save the Redwoods League" most of the virgin forests would have vanished.

Only some 10 percent of the state is still farmland. The Bay region's population is spilling over into the once tranquil wine-growing Napa and Livermore Valleys. Conservationists have suggested establishment of national agricultural reserves, just as seashore and historical areas have been created.

Not all urbanization has led to spoliation. An unusual land development has been the opening up of the Irvine Ranch in Orange County. In 1864 James Irvine with three partners purchased Rancho San Joaquin. By 1889 he had expanded the Irvine Ranch to 105,000 acres. His holdings, six times the size of Manhattan, extended twenty-two miles inland from the coast. Later his son incorporated the holdings to form the Irvine Company. The company leased nearby land on which to run sheep and cattle and to raise barley, potatoes, wheat, and, later, citrus. In 1960 a master plan was drawn up for development of Irvine's agricultural lands. A new campus of the University of California was built on land donated by the company to the state. New planned communities replaced the rancho past.

Other instances of protecting the environment include restoration by San Francisco of its Palace of Fine Arts, the last remnant of its 1915 Panama Pacific International Exhibition. Along the Marina Shoreline visitors see a 160-foot-high domed rotunda on the east and a semicircular 48-foot-high gallery on the west, the tour de force of the architect Bernard Maybeck. Nearby, the Victorian Ghirardelli chocolate factory has also been restored as a place to wine, dine, and shop. Conversion of an adjacent antique cannery near Fisherman's Wharf and of the city's cable-car barn (whose machinery has been repainted in gay colors) combines preservation of historic sites with today's functional needs.

Repeated demands have been made that San Francisco Bay be filled in to accommodate more population. In 1965 the state legislature created a Bay Conservation and Development Commission, to stop the Berkeley city council from doubling that city's area by expanding into the bay. Steadily criticized also were the Atomic Energy Commission tapline at Woodside, despoliation of scenic coastlands and redwoods, and the unsystematic use of arable lands. Neon signs, haphazard garbage disposal, and the lack of parks in urban areas offended thinking persons. Threats to such green belts as San Francisco's Golden Gate Park and Los Angeles's Elysian Park were unceasing.

Avaricious developers continue to locate cheaply constructed tract homes in areas isolated from centers of employment. These houses quickly fall into disrepair. Deserted by working folk, neighborhoods lapse into the hands of the unemployed or of migrants. Ulcerated nests of poverty, ugly slum conditions, and a shrinking countryside press in upon local government while junkyards and ramshackle houses undermine community pride.

Inattention during the 1940s and 1950s to the long-term consequences of a spiraling birthrate caused massive construction in sub-

San Francisco. (Courtesy of William A. Garnett. © 1954 by William A. Garnett.)

sequent decades of new schools, libraries, airfields, fire stations, and recreation centers. Critics of the failure to provide enough public parks and playgrounds have been somewhat appeased in Los Angeles by the development of Disneyland, Marineland, and other recreation centers. But the amusement parks so popular in today's California are a synthetic alternative to its lost greenery. Instead, an "artificial landscape" consumes much of the countryside.

Lewis Mumford first made us aware of the senseless cannibalism of the modern "gridiron cities." As more freeways are developed to transport workers in a hivelike environment, traffic congestion mounts. Not only do California's freeways erase the countryside; they also take valuable land off the public tax rolls. Freeways consume up to twenty-eight acres of land per mile of construction. An interchange uses up to eighty acres. By the late 1960s, the San Francisco Bay area alone lost an estimated twenty-one square miles of countryside every year, while southern California surrendered seventy square miles annually to concrete ribbons and "urban sprawl." When taxes go up, due primarily to shortsighted zoning, farmers are forced to sell valuable agricultural land.

At Los Angeles, this squandering is at its worst. Two-thirds of its center is occupied by streets, freeways, parking facilities, and garages. Regulations require building contractors to furnish one parking space per habitable room. In 1985 a bid for construction of one downtown garage alone came in at $34 million; this was almost sure to involve a further "cost overrun." That structure's cost per single auto space was estimated at $17,000, which reminds one of the steep price which Angeleños pay for not having devised proper public transportation. Repeated failure to provide mass transport has also speeded dispersal of Los Angeles toward its suburbs.

As the shift from single-family homes to apartments continued, the urban skyline of California changed markedly. There was radically increased vertical construction. Rising land costs made it uneconomical to build single-family dwellings in numerous areas. Repeal in 1956 of the 140-foot height limit on buildings was followed by construction of the first modern skyscrapers. A central-city boom began with construction of a new Music Center, the forty-two-story Union Bank Building, and the fifty-five-story Atlantic Richfield–Bank of America complex (a West Coast version of New York's Rockefeller Center). Urban residents, however, continued to orient their lives around suburban shopping centers. Berry patches, raw dirt and even oil refineries were quickly transformed into slick high-rises, industrial "parks," and high-tech research centers.

As the tide of life rushed up through California's valleys, overwhelming the countryside, thousands of new ranch-style houses were hammered together. Peacefulness departed, replaced by the whine of rubber tires on concrete and the clatter of overhead aircraft. Repeatedly, engineering-minded planners placed maintenance of California's scenic beauty low on their order of priorities. Keeping the traffic moving and providing high-tension power lines seemed more important than saving the cities.

It took Los Angeles until 1972 to announce plans for voluntary recycling of waste products. While a city like Laguna Beach was able to fight off freeway and high-rise building threats, it met continuing pressures from developers and the state Department of Highways. Daly City and Pacifica seemed to be architectural and planning mistakes. In southern California the City of Commerce became an industrialized moonscape, spreading its urban rot as did Fontana's steel plants.

A few communities successfully resisted growth. Corona, in 1976, passed a no-growth city ordinance. Petaluma restricted construction of new housing to 500 units per year. The construction industry blamed environmentalists for frustrating home buyers, violating citizen's rights, and obstructing unfettered movement. Antigrowth statutes remained unpopular. Ingrained attitudes continued to equate growth with progress. Environmentalists remained on the defensive, having to face the charge that they were irrational freaks standing in the way of California's future.

In 1971 coastline preservation bills began to be sponsored in the state legislature. Attempts were made to sever coastal protection from cities and towns, which had transformed the coast into a playground for private greed. All through the 1970s legislators struggled with how to implement an overall coastal plan. The siting of atomic and electric generation plants along the seashore proved to be a particularly thorny issue. Nuclear safety remained a major worry of conservationists. Diablo Canyon and San Onofre, where two controversial reactors are located, have become slur terms.

Meanwhile a democratic society continued its endless debates about a future which was fast arriving. California faces the emergence of "super-cities" that have begun to stretch northward from San Diego and beyond Los Angeles, moving toward Santa Barbara and San Luis Obispo. This urban stain runs east and west from Riverside, Sierra Madre, and Pasadena to the seaside. In northern California too a second sprawling complex threatens to become a continuous metropolis around the fingers of San Francisco Bay—with offshoots into the valleys northward, southward, and inland from the bay.

While the megalopolis inundates the land, urban sprawl is erasing impractical artificial boundaries. Smaller cities have become economically, socially, and politically obsolete. As new entities evolve out of redistricting, some communities fight to maintain local autonomy. Society requires cooperation between the older city and county units of government and such new agencies as metropolitan water districts, transit authorities, and air pollution control districts. But urban blight continues.

Selected Readings

Data on water development are in publications of the State Water Resources Board, notably *Water Resources of California* (Bulletin No. 1, Sacramento, 1951), and *The California Water Plan* (Bulletin No. 3, Sacramento, 1957). See also Mary Montgomery and Marion Clawson, *History of Legislation and Policy Formation of the Central Valley Project* (Berkeley, 1946). A study of the relationship of politics to water development is Vincent Ostrom, *Water and Politics: A Study of Water Policies and Administration in the Development of Los Angeles* (Los Angeles, 1953). Also see Erwin Cooper, *Aqueduct Empire: A Guide to Water in California, Its Turbulent History, and its Management Today* (Glendale, 1968). Invaluable is *The California Water Atlas* (Sacramento, 1979).

Criticisms of Los Angeles include Christopher Rand, *Los Angeles, the Ultimate City* (New York, 1967), and Alison Lurie, *The Nowhere City* (New York, 1966). More objective but less imaginative is Robert M. Fogelson, *The Fragmented Metropolis, Los Angeles, 1850–1930* (Cambridge, Mass., 1967). Consult also John L. Chapman, *Incredible Los Angeles* (New York, 1967). Raymond F. Dasmann. *The Destruction of California* (New York, 1965), reflects the shock of a biologist and zoologist concerning what has been happening to California, as does his *California's Changing Environment* (San Francisco, 1981). Even more critical is William Bronson's *How to Kill a Golden State* (New York, 1968). Another look at the sullied landscape that man is creating appears in Richard Lillard, *Eden in Jeopardy, Man's Prodigal Meddling With His Environment: The Southern California Experience* (New York, 1966).

Surprisingly, no fully satisfactory book has yet been written regarding the smog problem. Government reports do exist, however, beginning with *Air Pollution and the Public Health* (Sacramento, 1957). The Air Pollution Foundation has also published *The Air Pollution Problem: An Appraisal* (San Marino, 1960).

A discussion of the offshore oil controversy is Ernest R. Bartley, *The Tidelands Oil Controversy* (Austin, 1953). This is an expansion of the same author's "The Tidelands Oil Controversy," *Western Political Quarterly* 2 (March 1949), 135–53. Another useful article is Robert B. Krueger, "State Tidelands Leasing in California," *U.C.L.A. Law Review* 5 (May 1958), 427–89. The United States Supreme Court ruled that California should temporarily refrain from leasing its offshore oil lands in *United States* v. *California*, 332 U.S. 19 (1947). The effects of spillage are detailed in Robert Easton, *Black Tide: The Santa Barbara Oil Spill and its Consequences* (New York, 1972).

Reforestation and other challenges to the environment are presented in Ronald F. Lockman, *Guarding the Forests of Southern California* (Glendale, 1981).

CHAPTER 38

The Seventies

CALIFORNIA REACTED TO the changes which overwhelmed it by accommodating rather than by analyzing. The weakness of its political party structure impeded coherent social action programs. Furthermore, rising expectations made it difficult to curtail material growth. No one really had foolproof answers to solving the central problem of our time: how to handle and restrain the turbulent, often contradictory, drives of a mass society. Furthermore, California's growth reflected national trends as did a new wave of conservatism that began to surface after the death of President Kennedy in 1963.

The New Conservatives

California's gubernatorial election of 1966–1967 was held in an atmosphere of concern over an increased crime rate, high property taxes, and civil disturbances—including riots in the black sections of its largest city and student rebellions at the state university in Berkeley. Racial tension and charges of fiscal irresponsibility also lurked in the background as Governor Edmund (Pat) Brown sought a third term against screen actor Ronald Reagan. Brown projected the untrue image of a tired campaigner heading a bungling administration.

Reagan had been president of the Screen Actors Guild and proudly stressed his political inexperience. He made excellent use of money provided by conservative businessmen to finance effective television appearances. A veteran of more than fifty motion pictures, in which he had frequently played the role of the "nice guy who doesn't get the girl," Reagan projected relaxed self-possession before television cameras. He convinced the electorate that he was a moderate, morally indignant over massive government social welfare programs. Reagan also quieted old disputes inside California's Republican party.

Despite a continuing Democratic party advantage in voter registration, Reagan swept into office, defeating Governor Brown by nearly a million votes. In 1967 the Republicans not only controlled the state but also both of its national senatorial posts. With the Warren tradition in limbo, the Republican party was dominated by new faces proposing budget slashes of 10 percent in all departments, causing a storm of demonstrations by students and teachers, as well as mental health and welfare advocates. Reagan's campaign promises had included tax reform, especially for the elderly and for business. Now voters waited patiently for the tax relief their new governor promised. In order not to raise taxes, the new administration hoped to make government more frugal. When the governor proposed a sales tax on food, Democrats reacted furiously.

Although Reagan's critics charged him with backward negativism, he signed a liberal law on abortion. His desire to curtail government services by restricting property taxes was beaten through the initiative program. Despite a 1968 movement to recall the governor, he remained popular.

Reagan's "anti-intellectualism," as academics saw it, was applauded by the public at large. The new governor's budget cuts were resented by welfare and education advocates. As a start, Reagan proposed to slice $40 million from the $491 million requested by the state college and university systems for 1967–1968. Educators remonstrated that the overall effect of such cuts was to injure "quality education." Next, Reagan hoped to do away with student freedom from tuition fees in California's university and state college system. Opponents argued that the governor's retrenchment maneuvers would deprive the poor of a college education. He contended that most college students came from middle-income families, and the public should not be taxed to subsidize them. Reagan settled, temporarily, for no increase in existing charges, but subsequently both the state university regents and state college trustees moved toward higher charges. His efforts to crimp the universities were checked by the regents. Reagan, however, did play a role (as a member of the Board of Regents) in the 1967 ouster of university President Clark Kerr.

Late that year Reagan proposed to trim state public assistance agencies and to close eight mental health clinics in urban areas. Another uproar greeted these curtailments. Whenever protests mounted, Reagan held back temporarily from announced courses of action. Critics called Reagan's administration one that governed by crisis. Ultimately, he did effect significant fiscal cuts; but, in the case of the state's mental health program, he relented.

One of the biggest Reagan economy targets was in funds for medical care of the elderly, the indigent, and other welfare recipients. He proposed slashes of up to $210 million in such programs and also called for changes in eligibility requirements. Reagan hoped "to squeeze fraud and abuse out of California's welfare system." He feared the possibility of perpetuating poverty "by substituting a permanent dole for a paycheck."

In order to save money, toll collectors on bridges were forced to surrender revolvers, which were then sold. Travel by state employees was curtailed, as was the use of teletype and telephone services and the purchase of equipment and supplies. The governor's office suspended the publication of road maps, brochures, pamphlets, and a park and recreation magazine. Reagan announced that some $50,000 was saved in typewriter ribbons and $2 million in the state's phone bill during the first few months of his governorship. The governor also sold a state-owned airplane. Mostly, his economies were effected by item vetoes in legislative appropriation bills.

Reagan ran up against the momentum of state growth as well as ingrained and costly governmental programs. Early in 1968 he first announced a deficit of $210 million in the "Medi-Cal" program alone. The governor's conservative backers in the legislature placed great emphasis on public order. In 1967 Reagan proposed six bills to deal with crime control, only one of which was enacted—a law that tripled the minimum penalty for rape, robbery, or burglary in cases where victims were injured. A stronger gun-control law passed the legislature in part because of a national mood toward such controls; also because a Black Panther group, armed with unloaded weapons, scared the legislature witless by bursting into that body while the law was being debated. True to his promises, the governor tried but failed to gain repeal of the controversial open-housing law. Reagan also had trouble gaining passage of tighter obscenity laws, or the establishment of county welfare fraud units, or the institution of a merit system for judges.

As early as 1968 Reagan was a contender for the Republican presidential nomination. But, at that time, he met the opposition of more moderate Eastern party leaders, who preferred fellow Californian Richard Nixon. Back in California critics charged that Reagan achieved unity among California's Republicans by coddling all wings of the party. Other critics, instead, saw an administration filled with businessmen who served on task forces and commissions without pay while urging the loosening of state controls over business. Labor hated Reagan. When farm labor grew short during the 1967 harvest, the governor sent convicts to help harvest crops. He also ordered use of employable welfare recipients where labor shortages existed. Labor called such moves a subsidy to growers.

The eight Reagan years seemed quixotic at best, a period of missed opportunity for reform and the achievement of little order over un-controlled state growth. Late in 1974 a newspaper appraisal of "Reagan's Reign" was subtitled "Footprints, But No Permanent Monuments or Scars." Reagan's eight years in office were seen as a checkpoint rather than as a turning point in California's political development. In stemming the growth of government, he was defeated by a variety of factors. Rampant national inflation lay beyond the control of any state governor. A hostile Democratic legislature was determined to thwart surface solutions to deep-seated government problems. He hardly displayed much understanding of the intricacies of the state's infrastructure, boasting a philosophy of government that hearkened back nostalgically to the days of Calvin Coolidge. Legislative inertia too made it difficult to overhaul a lumbering bureaucracy in Sacramento.

Reagan's vetoes against government spending did act as a brake against an even more rapid rate of growth of state services. But welfare rolls actually increased under Reagan. His attempts to coax state employees into voluntarily working on holidays showed how distant he was from entrenched civil servants. The number of such employees was about the same when he left office as when he became governor. Although he was no "idea man," his staff did computerize time-consuming state operations. But it was difficult to attack a relatively efficient and honest civil service system. The Reagan administration, however, stopped construction of a number of new state buildings and facilities sanctioned by the legislature. Dissident state college and university personnel were also "kept in their place" by a governor who reaped public acclaim by cracking down on unruly students as well.

By 1974, California's voters had tired of Governor Reagan. The youth and race revolutions seemed to be over, as young and old alike searched for a new face in government. Little did they then guess that Reagan would one day become president of the United States. While he bided his time, waiting for the Republican nomination, California turned toward more moderate leadership without seemingly giving up its conservative mood.

Jerry, Son of Pat Brown

In the spirit of the 1970s California's new governor, Edmund (Jerry) Brown, Jr., repeatedly reminded his audiences that there was a limit to what government could undertake. He criticized the "spending philosophy" of old New Dealers like his father. Although an advocate of civil rights, racial integration, and ecology, Brown proved to be more of a fiscal conservative than his father.

Young Brown (only 37 years old when he became governor) was first elected California's Secretary of State. He used that office as a ladder to the governorship. Upon assuming that position Brown said that he had absolutely no national political aspirations. In 1975 he even refused to attend the National Governors Conference, claiming to be more concerned with state problems of unemployment, illegal immigration, crime, medical insurance, and the plight of farm workers. Local issues (such as fighting the highway and auto lobbies, which wanted more freeways) seemed to overwhelm larger national interests at the beginning of his term. Truly complex social dilemmas did indeed face Jerry Brown.

By 1976 young Brown entered the national primaries as a "favorite son" candidate. He offered an appealing style, blending fiscal austerity and idealism. In a year during which Jimmy Carter swept the country to gain the Democratic party nomination, Brown for a time also became a refreshing politician in post-Watergate America. An English journal called Brown the "Little Prince" of United States politics, pointing out how he had been heavily influenced by a book entitled *Small is Beautiful* by the Keynesian economist, E. F. Schumacher. But Brown was loath to acknowledge his debt to this source or to discuss publicly such touchy issues as "gay" liberation and socialism.

With the Reagan years over, and the wave of fear about mass riots having subsided, Brown spoke to the aspirations of younger educated persons. For a while he seemed to provide the counterculture's response to post-Vietnam disillusionment with big government, big business, and big unions. Half of California's population was under the age of twenty-nine. These products of the 1950s "baby boom" felt comfortable about Brown. In California, increasingly called a "media state," Brown, like Reagan, came off as a good TV performer. His flair for manipulating symbols—his refusal to live in a new governor's mansion or to use an executive jet plane and official limousines—struck voters favorably. Like Reagan, he skillfully used press and television to overcome California's weak party structure.

Although Jerry Brown was absorbed with serious state problems, some of these had national implications. Young Californians who believed that what they think today America does tomorrow saw Brown's brand of politics as the wave of the future. Even in Orange County, Protestant home of Richard Nixon and the world's first drive-in church, Brown, an unmarried ex-Jesuit ascetic who dabbled in Zen, was popular. Reminiscent of Reagan, Brown repeated the idea that his program was "to confront the confusion and hypocrisy of big government, that's what's important."

As young Brown began to think about reelection, cries of "fake" were heard among discontented followers. Willie Brown, a black San

Francisco Democrat, said he was tired of being misled by a man who was like "a bowl of Jello." Jerry Brown remained vulnerable to public disenchantment over this refusal to make firmer ideological commitments. But his "creative inaction" caused reformers to fume. For them, the admonition to lower their expectations, "for we are entering an era of limits," was not enough of a program to entice fickle voters. Brown's "think small" convictions were no substitute for a solid record of achievement. When Brown finally decided to campaign for the presidency, even close adherents charged that he had abandoned the ship of state at Sacramento.

As with Reagan, the public expected magical solutions to difficult problems because both governors had promised so much. During 1975 a malpractice crisis inundated the medical community. This concerned the soaring rates which physicians had to pay for insurance in case they lost malpractice suits. Hundreds of physicians throughout the state temporarily ceased practicing medicine until the governor promised relief. His response, couched in verbiage, was no more than a reassurance that his administration would continue to "monitor" the rise of insurance premiums. No clear plan emerged to solve the problem that Brown characterized as "beset by rising costs and few easy solutions."

The governor's boyish charm and rhetoric made him sound like an old-fashioned Populist as well as a monk committed to personal sacrifice in order to achieve social change: "We're going to have to work harder," he stated in a 1976 speech to the California Democratic Council. "It's going to take a lot more pain and suffering before we can get to where we have to go. . . . The price of democracy is discipline." The response to Brown's intonations continued to be not all favorable. One assemblyman chided the young governor's inaction: "I've heard that goddamned sanctimonious speech too many times. He lectures everyone—people who know a lot more about public policy than he does. . . ."

Although the second Governor Brown's style featured decision making through indecision, protests against his reform record were not entirely fair. While he did not seem particularly gifted with consistent or orderly thinking, Brown did act upon some convictions. A new state Office of Appropriate Technology was the first such agency in America to advocate climatically and environmentally designed buildings; it sponsored wind power, solar heating, home organic farming, and bioconversion (use of human waste to produce energy). Brown also appointed unprecedented numbers of women, minority members, and consumer advocates to state regulatory commissions. He sought to unmask privilege in the legal, educational, and medical fields that prospered in the name of professionalism. Although he infuriated members of these groups, he modestly stated, "I throw out a lot of thoughts and ideas, and some of them don't go anywhere, but some of them gather their own momentum."

The young governor took advantage of public criticism against big government and massive technology, attacking the number of units in government that continued to multiply like spores in a cake of yeast. By 1977 more than 2,500 agencies of government existed in Los Angeles county alone. That county then supported 102 commissions headed by 1,178 commissioners. Inactive commissions had been on the books for decades. Four separate commissions, in addition to the police, reviewed drug problems alone. Despite duplication and waste, inaction prevented sorely needed reform.

"Brown Power" and the Migrant Poor

Although Cesar Chavez had struggled in the 1960s to organize the farm workers, large segments of California's agricultural labor force remained unorganized. In the next decade he ran into opposition not only from California's growers but also from the Teamsters Union of America. In addition to charging discrimination and low wages, in 1973 Chavez claimed that large corporate growers were spraying their crops with poisonous pesticides. In the Imperial Valley, at the state capitol at Sacramento, and in Washington the antipesticide attack on growers and chemical companies was launched by his United Farm Workers Union at a critical point in Chavez's efforts to organize lettuce pickers. In 1973 his greatest enemy, the American Farm Bureau Federation, claimed that some fruit pickers received $6.44 per hour, or in excess of $200 per week, and that a picker could make more than $10,000 per year. A 1973 government study, however, reported that the average per-hour pay for farm labor nationally was $1.97 and that the average per-hour rate on California farms was $2.44.

Critics of Chavez not only accused him of misrepresenting the plight of his farm workers; they also leveled charges of irresponsible authoritarianism against him. Corporate interests hammered away at what they called his revolutionary and leftist leadership, called him "the hero of the limousine liberals" and a labor boss who "corralled thousands of farm workers to join his union, denying them free elections."

Chavez's greatest enemy turned out to be the rival Teamsters Union. In addition to organizing leaders and truckers, most of California's lettuce pickers worked under Teamster contracts. In April 1973 Chavez told a Coachella union meeting, "We're fighting for our lives." Only three years had passed since his victory over the grape industry. The contracts he had signed were expiring. Meanwhile the

Teamsters were ready to negotiate what Chavez termed "sweetheart contracts" with the growers.

Chavez was, however, backed by AFL-CIO leaders who labeled the Teamsters a corrupt union. Meanwhile, the Teamsters claimed to represent thirty thousand farm workers, mostly in "row crops," such as tomatoes and lettuce. Chavez's UFWU estimated its own membership as between thirty and forty thousand, depending on seasonal fluctuations. Their leader was convinced that the Teamsters were working with major growers to break his power over these workers. On April 17, 1973, Chavez decided to order both a strike and boycott against growers who produced grapes under contracts with the Teamsters. He charged that the Teamsters had reinstituted labor recruiting that "could lead to the same lousy conditions the workers had for years before our contract." One field hand told a newsman: "This is the ranch where I work. If the Teamsters are here, I'll sign with them. If it's Chavez, I'll go with him." Another worker said: "I'm not for or against anybody. If I get work I'll work. The UFWU is good, but it has drawbacks. It sometimes is run inefficiently." Farmhands, caught in the middle of a jurisdictional dispute, did not fully understand the conflict; but they remained grateful to Chavez for having improved their lives, not only in terms of wages but also in bringing such amenities as ice water into stifling labor camps.

Mexican-American pickers resented the intrusion of the Teamsters into Chavez's controversy with the grape growers. In 1975 George Meany, head of the AFL-CIO, called the back-door Teamster contracts totally immoral. But growers complained that Chavez ran his union in a chaotic fashion, that crucial messages were undelivered, that agreements were broken, and that his hiring halls were a farce. One grower complained, "It isn't easy dealing with a man who thinks he is a saint, but who doesn't mind going back on his word." Such growers seemed determined to stop Chavez at almost any price. He threatened a system that had served them well for years. The compliant work force on which they could rely was no longer intact.

Chavez charged that collusion between the Teamsters and the growers led to illegal payoffs to Teamster officials in a conspiracy to destroy his union. At both Washington and Sacramento he called for investigations of "union busting." A Senate Labor and Welfare Committee did come to California to investigate Chavez's charges of a conspiracy against him.

By 1977, Chavez succeeded in patching together his second working agreement with the Teamsters. Chavez, who favored the nonviolent methods of Martin Luther King and Gandhi, remained far from inactive. His was a crusade that spread beyond the arena of agricultural labor. Chavez and the UFWU flag became symbols to California's Chicanos, who comprise over 80 percent of the Chicanos in the United States. They looked to Chavez for leadership in organizing the urban *barrios*, bursting with impatience.

Population Decline

After the mid-1950s California experienced one of the great population shifts in the history of the United States, reaching a peak of 338,000 new residents in 1962. Los Angeles had become the most populous county in the United States. Thereafter the migration began to slow and then fell considerably. After heavy layoffs in the aerospace industry in the late 1960s, the downtrend accelerated.

The core cities were the first to lose population. People of affluence and education sought to escape racial conflict as well as urban congestion by a flight to the suburbs. In 1974 Los Angeles County experienced its first population drop in 123 years. Most of that out-migration represented a spill-over into Orange and Ventura counties. Los Angeles County, by 1976, stabilized its population at about 7 million persons. But by far the fastest growth occurred in Orange County, once dotted with orange groves.

Notable changes in the populations of California's major cities occurred during the 1970s. San Diego by 1975 had solidified its rank as the second largest city, with a population of 773,400. Third-place San Francisco had dropped to a total of 666,100. San Jose had become number four, while Oakland had been relegated to sixth place, preceded by Long Beach. Sacramento, the capital, was eighth in population that year, followed by Anaheim, Santa Ana, and Fresno.

Despite the drop-off in population, California managed to grow by 19.5 percent from 1970 to 1980. An American love affair with the Sun Belt cities of the Southwest accounted for some of this growth. But, it was also partly due to a tremendous increase of foreign-born migrants. By 1981, more people moved into the state from abroad than from other states. Foreigners from Latin America and Asia seemed undeterred by the fact that the median price for a home was more than 50 percent higher than the national average. A great deal of Hong Kong and Taiwanese wealth entered the state.

California had been the first-ranked state in population since 1964. After the 1980 census, its seats in the United States House of Representatives rose to forty-five, the largest delegation of any state. By 1986, its population was approaching 26 million persons. This figure does not include illegal immigrants, principally from Mexico and Central America. More than 50,000 Vietnamese refugees became legal residents after the fall of Saigon.

Another new feature of California's population growth has also emerged. A diversity of sexual behavior patterns has greatly increased the visibility of homosexuals or "gays." At San Francisco especially the homosexual community grew exponentially from 1965 to 1985. Perhaps a sixth of its population (more than 100,000 persons) today are acknowledged homosexuals. Their affluence and political power has led them to be courted by aspiring politicos. A tragedy involving Mayor George Moscone and a member of the Board of Supervisors, Harvey Milk, an avowed homosexual, occurred in 1979. Both men were shot to death in San Francisco's city hall by a disgruntled former official, but in the shadows lurked the still-unexplained homosexual issue.

Meanwhile another change in the population pattern accompanied the rise nationally of a new brand of young urbanite. The upwardly mobile aspirants to success, power, and material wealth, called "Yuppies" for Young Urban Professionals, took the place of the hippies of past decades. At Los Angeles, San Francisco, and San Diego they sought careers in such better-paid professions as law, medicine, and banking.

Transit Snags and the Energy Crisis

Into the 1980s Californians, enamored of the automobile, made little progress toward developing mass rapid transit. The public attitude remained provincial; most persons were woefully uninformed about the benefits of fixed light-rail systems operating elsewhere throughout the world. Repeated government-sponsored feasibility studies only served to confuse the transportation issue. An imaginative high-speed "bullet train" plan that would have linked San Diego to Los Angeles was finally scrapped in 1984. Time, money, and the patience of its developers simply ran out.

Despite the gasoline crunch of the 1970s, California's ambitious freeway program also had to be curtailed. Inflation and lessened tax receipts cut down the amount of roadway that could be built. Yet dependence upon cars remained unabated. San Francisco did manage to build its Bay Area Rapid Transit (BART) system, but Los Angeles continued to flounder in liberating itself from autos. Indifference, poor press and political leadership, and public ignorance about the benefits of rapid transit condemned that city to inaction. Bond issue after bond issue was voted down by the electorate. Even urban transit enthusiasts were depressed by the skyrocketing construction and operating estimates. The BART system was to have cost $920 million when approved by the voters in 1962. As its first segment opened in 1972, the price was up to $1.6 billion. The system would have cost more than $5 billion if built in the late 1970s. A valiant county supervisor, Baxter Ward, labored in vain for the construction of a

232-mile "Sunset Coast Line" to be built along freeway medians and shoulders, flood-control embankments, and on existing railroad rights-of-way. The project could have serviced forty-four cities at a cost of $5.8 billion, but voters themselves helped to scuttle each such project. Repeated failure of rapid transit proposals had become a predictable pattern.

In 1973 the Arab oil embargo showed how the state was vulnerable to political and economic negatives that afflict cities as well as nations. At Los Angeles, initial fear of gas shortages quickly gave way to inertia. In 1976 a comprehensive rapid transit proposal again appeared on the ballot and was voted down for the third time in nine years. Los Angeles went back to its fume-spewing bus system. The opening of bus lanes along the freeways was a poor substitute for a fixed-rail system.

Related to past failures of mass rapid transit has been the growing scarcity of gasoline in a state that was once a major exporter. A diminished supply of low-sulfur fuel oil reminded Californians of their energy vulnerability and past prodigality. California's oil fields had helped to float World Wars I and II on a sea of surplus oil, now vanished. As a result, emergency measures had to be taken, allowing cities in the smog-plagued Los Angeles Basin to burn conventional fuel oil.

In California the internal combustion engine has won a total victory over every other means of surface locomotion. There is evidence that in the 1940s bus and auto manufacturers, as well as the oil, tire, and car dealers, had helped destroy the world's largest interurban transport system, which had served southern California well. As late as 1945 the Pacific Electric Railway still carried 110 million passengers between fifty-six communities.

Enslaved by autos, today's "gridiron cities" devour and "pave over" their landscape. In a hivelike environment, not only do freeways erase the countryside; they also take valuable land off the public tax rolls. California's freeways resemble the state's water transfer system; they represent legislative and engineering triumphs, but both scar the landscape. Downtown areas of California's largest metropoli are squandered by the streets and freeways of a myopic automania.

Recession Fears and Educational Burdens

California was once thought to be recession proof. But the energy crisis and intermittent cuts in government contracts reminded the state of its dependence upon outside forces. Between 1967 and 1971, following reduction of military spending after the withdrawal of troops from Vietnam, the number of aerospace jobs declined from a high of 616,000 to fewer than 440,000. California's treasury went from a surplus of $2.9 billion in 1979 to a deficit of $541 million in 1983. Yet the state, with only 9.6 percent of the nation's population, still received 11.2 percent of the federal budget in 1980. The fate of California remained so intertwined with that of Washington that they seemed inseparable.

Massive voter dissatisfaction with the tax system touched off a tax-payer revolt. In 1978, Howard Jarvis's property tax reduction initiative (Proposition 13) passed by a landslide. The measure was so successful that he encouraged similar tax rebellions in states throughout the nation. The expanded educational program was at the heart of the heavy burden shouldered by California's taxpayers. Inflation had increased the expenses of operating the public schools, although some teachers' salaries lagged behind those of garbage collectors. The "war baby" boom was over and it became more difficult to pass school bond issues that competed with other pressing needs. Meanwhile, education had become the largest single item in the state budget. An obsolete tax structure placed much of the burden for education on local property taxation. The passage of bond overrides declined precipitously as taxes skyrocketed.

Expansion of the state college and university system had placed new fiscal burdens on the taxpayers at a time when the job market for college graduates had shrunk. Despite the existence of more than 10,000 state PTA's, the standards and quality of teaching, from kindergarten through the graduate-school years, was widely questioned. The turmoil of the 1960s had encouraged a serious leveling effect upon the grading system which threatened to become permanent. Colleges and universities found it necessary to introduce courses in basic English and Mathematics due to the poor test performances of entering high school graduates who came to college without thorough instruction in basic academic skills possessed by previous matriculants.

Reagan and the second Governor Brown had little success in curbing California's bloated educational system, from grade schools through college. The proliferation of campuses for higher education had greatly increased budgetary demands on the state treasury. Each governor preferred to believe the inflated projections of future enrollment prepared by their staffs. Furthermore, Brown failed to apply toward the educational field those skills that he demonstrated in dealing with labor relations, civil service pay, and environmental concerns.

Selected Readings

The history of recent California politics has been handled in a spotty way. Written from the political analyst's viewpoint is Michael P. Rogin and John L. Shover, *Political Change in California* (Westport, Conn., 1970). Carey McWilliams, ed., *The California Revolution* (New York, 1968) is an uneven collection of essays. Another book of readings is Royce D. Delmatier, Clarence F. McIntosh, and Earl G. Waters, eds., *The Rumble of California Politics, 1848–1970* (New York, 1970).

When the younger Brown sought the presidency, a spate of books appeared about him and his father: John C. Bollens and G. Robert Williams, *Jerry Brown in a Plain Brown Wrapper* (Pacific Palisades, 1978); J. D. Lorenz, *Jerry Brown: The Man on the White Horse* (New York, 1978); Robert Peck, *Jerry Brown: The Philosopher Prince* (New York, 1978); Roger Rapoport, *California Dreaming: The Political Odyssey of Pat and Jerry Brown* (Berkeley, 1982) and Orville Schell, *Brown* (New York, 1978).

Also in a popular vein are Gladwin Hill, *Dancing Bear: The Inside Look at California Politics* (New York, 1968); Bill Boyarsky, *The Rise of Ronald Reagan* (New York, 1968); and Joseph Lewis, *What Makes Reagan Run? A Political Profile* (New York, 1968). Edmund G. Brown, Sr., has written two books about recent politics: *Reagan and Reality: The Two Californias* (New York, 1970), and (with Bill Brown) *Ronald Reagan, the Political Chameleon* (New York, 1976). Lou Cannon's *Ronnie and Jesse: A Political Odyssey* (New York, 1972) concerns Reagan and Unruh. Another comparison is Gary Hamilton and Nicole Biggart, *Governor Reagan, Governor Brown* (New York, 1984).

Overblown is Kenneth Lamott's *Anti-California: Report From Our First Parafascist State* (New York, 1971). More substantial are Jackson K. Putnam, *Modern California Politics* (San Francisco, 1980), and Putnam's *Old Age Politics in California, From Richardson to Reagan* (Stanford, 1970).

Chicano labor and racial strife has elicited a number of books. In addition to the sources listed at the end of Chapter 36, see Francisco Balderrama, *In Defense of La Raza* (Tucson, 1982); Roger Daniels and Spencer C. Olin, eds., *Racism in California: A Reader in the History of Oppression* (New York, 1972); George D. Horowitz, *La Causa: The California Grape Strike* (New York, 1970); Ralph de Toledano, *Little Cesar* (New York, 1962); Ernesto Galarza, *Barrio Boy* (Notre Dame, Ind., 1971), as well as his *Spiders in the House and Workers in the Field* (Notre Dame, Ind., 1970); Leo Gobler, Joan W. Moore, and Ralph Guzman, *The Mexican-American People* (New York, 1970); and Joan London and Henry Anderson, *So Shall Ye Reap* (New York, 1970).

Books about Cesar Chavez include: Ronald B. Taylor, *Chavez and the Farm Workers* (Boston, 1975); Jacques Levy, *Cesar Chavez: Autobiography of La Causa* (New York, 1976); Peter Matthiessen, *Sal Si Puedes* (New York, 1969); James Terzian and Kathryn Cramer, *Mighty Hard Road: The Story of Cesar Chavez* (Garden City, N.Y., 1970); and Mark Day, *Forty Acres* (New York, 1970). Also see Linda and Theo

Majka, *Farm Workers, Agribusiness, and the State* (Philadelphia, 1982), as well as Daniel E. Cletus, *Bitter Harvest: A History of California Farmworkers* (Ithaca, N.Y., 1981), and Lawrence J. Jelinek, *Harvest Empire: A History of California Agriculture* (San Francisco, 1979). Excellent on irrigation reform is Donald J. Pisani, *From the Family Farm to Agribusiness* (Berkeley, 1984). Ellen Liebman, *California Farmland* (Totowa, N.J., 1983) is unfortunately turgid.

Readable but dated are Carey McWilliams, *Brothers under the Skin* (Boston, 1951) and, his *North from Mexico* (Philadelphia, 1949); see also Matt S. Meier and Feliciano Rivers, *The Chicanos* (New York, 1972); Raul Morin, *Among the Valiant* (Los Angeles, 1963); Leonard Pitt, *The Decline of the Californios: A Social History of the Spanish-Speaking Californians* (Berkeley, 1966); and Julian Samora, ed., *La Raza: Forgotten Americans* (Notre Dame, Ind., 1969). Manuel Servin, ed., *The Mexican-Americans: An Awakening Minority* (Beverly Hills, Calif., 1970) is a series of readings of varying quality.

On Chicanos consult Charles Wollenberg, ed., *Ethnic Conflict in California History* (Los Angeles, 1970); also the August 1973 *Pacific Historical Review*, a special issue entitled "The Chicano," as well as Gilbert Cruz and Jane Talbot, *Chicano Bibliography, 1960–1972* (Austin, Tex., 1974). *The Chicanos* by Gilberto Lopez y Rivas (New York, 1974) is another general volume. More recent scholarship includes: Albert Camarillo, *Chicanos in California* (San Francisco, 1985), and his *Chicanos in a Changing Society* (Cambridge, Mass., 1980), as well as Ricardo Romo, *East Los Angeles: History of a Barrio* (Austin, Tex., 1984). See also Rodolfo Gonzalez, *I Am Joaquin* (New York, 1973) and Edmund Villaseñor, *Macho* (New York, 1973), as well as Mauricio Mazón, *The Zoot-Suit Riots* (Austin, Tex., 1984). Regarding educational problems of Mexican-American children see Herschel T. Manuel, *Spanish-Speaking Children of the Southwest* (Austin, Tex., 1958). See also Wayne Moquin, ed., *A Documentary History of the Mexican Americans* (New York, 1971).

Indians and Asians are in Robert F. Heizer and Alan F. Almquist, *The Other Californians: Prejudice and Discrimination under Spain, Mexico, and the United States to 1920* (Berkeley, 1971). The history of blacks in California has aroused less attention than other minorities. See, however, Rudolph Lapp, *Afro-Americans in California* (San Francisco, 1979); W. Sherman Savage, *Blacks in the West* (Westport, Conn., 1976); and Douglas Daniels, *Pioneer Urbanites: A Social and Cultural History of Black San Francisco* (Philadelphia, 1980).

CHAPTER 39

An Era of Limits?
Into the 1980s

To OUTSIDERS, California's fascination remains magnetic. Visitors today, like those 150 years ago, still come under its persuasive spell. The richness of the land, diversity of natural wealth, beauty of the landscape, and mildness of its climate were all advertised long before chambers of commerce were organized. But, beyond the boosterism in the letters of hide and tallow traders, seamen, and gold hunters lay other, almost indefinable, qualities. These gave California that special glamour which few other locations have known.

Most Californians still optimistically think of their state as golden. Nicknamed "the Golden State," its state colors are gold and blue, the official flower is the golden poppy, and the state fish is the golden trout of the High Sierra. The world's love affair with California, however, remains both delight and curse. Consumerism reigns over a materialistic and technologically oriented society that frequently exalts means over ends. Tensions between urban and rural communities, divisions among wealthy and poor, as well as those that separate the old and young, unbalance state loyalties. Yet variety and experiment remain part of the current scene. Just as the Sierra Club guards the back-country, San Franciscans take parochial pride in such historic symbols of the past as their cable cars, restaurants, and palatial hotels. Los Angeles, instead, focuses upon the modern.

In 1985 that city faced continuing controversies over building a Metro Rail system. Questions arose as to the safety of boring through the seeping underground methane gas pools that lay along its route. Were it not for the tenacity of a small coalition of business and labor interests, as well as members of the Los Angeles congressional delegation, the project would again have been derailed. In December, following a long legislative battle, President Reagan signed a spending bill that promised $429 million for construction of the subway's first 4.4 miles. There remained complex negotiations between the local Rapid Transit District and a reluctant Republican administration as to the degree of federal funding. Critics still contended that the $3.3 billion projected to build an 18.6-mile line was too costly. Furthermore, a major westside rerouting, to avoid the potentially dangerous methane gas areas, escalated its budget. Tunneling was to start in 1986, despite opposition of Reagan's administration, which repeatedly withheld construction funds voted by the United States Congress.

Meanwhile the population pressures and confusions of the computer age have disoriented formerly confident Californians. Some have left the state in quest of more stable surroundings and better job opportunities. Meanwhile, a tendency to let matters drift has often sidelined long-range planning. Some of California's most pressing problems—the scummy air, garbage-strewn shorelines, shoddy neighborhoods, racial tensions, traffic congestion, crime, and violation of the natural landscape—have become limiting factors upon the state's future.

A Growth of Maturity?

California, however, affords unusual opportunities for self-indulgence. The splendor of its mountains and beaches provide unique recreational escapes. Some live out their fantasies with few restrictions indeed. Tolerance of bizarre life-styles and personal narcissism has been widespread in an era of drug use alongside the selective influence of the movie, TV, and record industries.

Some clichés about urban life are, however, changing. San Francisco, which once possessed an image of stateliness, has seen its southern rival, Los Angeles, challenge its supremacy. "L.A.," no longer the plastic heartland of craziness, has acquired a new urbanity. While a fantasy land of citrus groves has lost some of its past charms, the city has narrowed the gap between Bible Belt values and contact with a much wider world. Still suburban in outlook, southern California defies governmental coordination, partly because, in earlier years, land speculators were virtually guaranteed a birthright to create further blight.

The Frustrations of Planning

Democracy's greatest sin has been described as the tendency to drift aimlessly, without sense of direction. This was characteristic of California's frontier development. City planners were virtually unknown

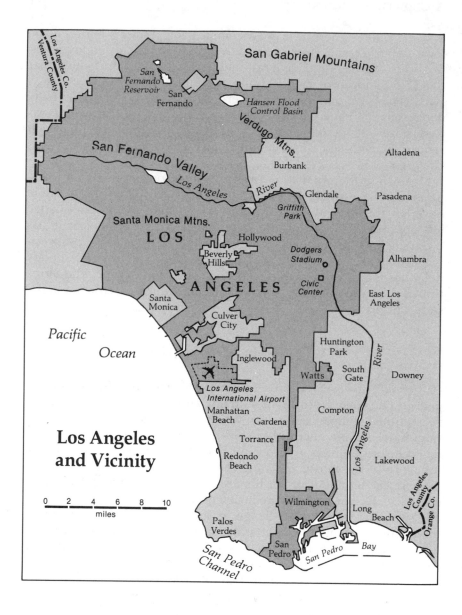

Los Angeles Co.
Ventura County

San Gabriel Mountains

San Fernando Reservoir

San Fernando

Hansen Flood Control Basin

Verdugo Mtns.

Altadena

Burbank

San Fernando Valley

Los Angeles River

River

Glendale

Pasadena

Santa Monica Mtns.

Griffith Park

Hollywood

LOS

Beverly Hills

Dodgers Stadium

Alhambra

ANGELES

Civic Center

East Los Angeles

Santa Monica

Culver City

Huntington Park

River

Pacific

Ocean

Inglewood

Watts

South Gate

Downey

Los Angeles International Airport

Manhattan Beach

Gardena

Compton

Los Angeles

Los Angeles and Vicinity

Torrance

Redondo Beach

Lakewood

Los Angeles County
Orange Co.

0   2   4   6   8   10
miles

Wilmington

Long Beach

Palos Verdes

San Pedro

San Pedro Bay

San Pedro Channel

High rise in Los Angeles, Spring 1976. (Photograph by V. R. Plukas.)

before 1910. Emergency "planning" during the later New Deal era made the word itself a suspect term. Today, in an age of mass complexity, purposeless waste and unplanned building sometimes lead to environmental chaos.

The state's problems are not peculiar to California alone. Any society which is constantly reassured that its virtue derives from the consumption of more and more goods is bound to see humane virtues sorely tested. Yet, in this age of roaring traffic and clogged megalopoli, some Californians do seek to salvage their expansive style of shuttle living as well as to revitalize ugly city cores and polluted suburbs. Along with the look-alike supermarket chains, pool-flanked houses, sports cars, and outdoor barbeques, a sense of unity is required to knit the state together. Freedom from formality is not enough to solve pressing social problems. Unless the diverse backgrounds of California's bewildered newcomers can be harnessed, its industrial parks, pedestrian malls, and endless housing projects can produce further environmental distortions. It is a long path from the leafy environment of rich suburbias to the solution of gnawing slum problems. Finally, if slowly, a powerful environmental movement has recently emerged to challenge unchecked material growth. Relatively few Californians would admit that the ugliness they see around them is born of arrogance toward the land and its resources. Outsiders continue to deplore California's ostentation—one of the themes in Neil Simon's 1976 play, *California Suite*.

During 1976, in his first message to the state legislature, Governor Jerry Brown highlighted the importance of preserving the quality of California's life. But he soon encountered the frustrating limits of planning. Despite the fact that an increasingly complex society requires more planning, its management had become an uphill fight. Public distrust of government planners was widespread. California's second Governor Brown came to see his role as presiding over a scaled-down set of expectations.

The young and outwardly ascetic governor did attain such long overdue legislative achievements as a strengthened coastline protection bill, a land mark agricultural labor relations law, laws governing construction of nuclear power plants, legislation closing business tax loopholes, and reform of the state's sixty-year-old system of sentencing prisoners. There was less progress in combating unemployment, and no reform of public school financing, with its heavy reliance on local property taxes.

As never before, unprecedented criminal violence that no governor could stop gave California a tarnished reputation. After the longest trial in its history, cult leader Charles Manson was convicted in 1971 of the murder two years before of an actress and six other persons. Three women accomplices had gladly joined his "family" in these crimes. In February of 1975 the Federal Bureau of Investigation and local police were baffled by the sensational kidnapping of Patricia Hearst, an heiress of the newspaper dynasty. That May a group which called itself the Symbionese Liberation Army was cornered by the Los Angeles Police Department in a bloody shootout that ultimately did lead to finding her.

Other bizarre criminal adventures also marred the state's image, among them the weird Reverend Jim Jones's flight from San Francisco to Guyana and the 1978 mass murder-suicide there of his People's Temple followers. The assassinations of San Francisco's Mayor George Moscone and Councilman Harvey Milk, only a few weeks later, further stained San Francisco's and California's allure as well. Songsters no longer belted out the words "California, Here I Come" in quite the same way as had Al Jolson back in 1921.

Perhaps Brown's strongest achievements as governor were in enforcing clean-air laws and controlling pesticides and toxic wastes. He worked for several years to complete the state water project begun by his father, only to see the controversial peripheral canal project defeated by the voters in 1982. He also battled the federal government over the issuance of licences for offshore oil drilling. His environmental zeal fitted the "era of limits" and of "lowered expectations" which he championed. His equally strong record on affirmative action for minority employment actually unbalanced the all-white, male power structure.

As time passed, Jerry Brown came to be labeled "Governor Moonbeam" by critics because of his indecisiveness. In 1978 he originally opposed lobbyist Howard Jarvis's Proposition 13, which proposed slashing state property taxes. Then, when the measure passed, he embraced it. Seriously unbalanced state budgets allowed Brown's enemies to call him a fiscal incompetent. Growing attacks also developed against his appointee as Chief Justice, Rose Bird, the first woman named to such a high office. Charging that she presided over a lax supreme court, conservative members of the state bar repeatedly sought her recall and that of some of the other six hundred judges Brown had appointed. A fourth of these were women, blacks, or Latinos who were alleged ultraliberals whose decisions weakened criminal prosecution throughout the state. Brown appointed more than 1,600 women to state office and many minority members of both sexes.

Another issue that contributed to a reputation for indecisiveness was his handling of the invasion by the Mediterranean fruit fly during 1980–1982. A confirmed environmentalist, he was opposed to authorizing use of a powerful chemical spray against the "Medfly." As infestation spread, Brown, who had become a scapegoat, reversed his original order forbidding spraying. Also, Brown's appointments to a new Agricultural Labor Relations Board that he had created were so heavily weighted toward Cesar Chavez's United Farm Workers Union that the governor alienated nearly all the state's growers.

Brown, once a generational hero, had trouble finding his ultimate niche in history. He not only outraged the agricultural and financial communities, but lost his youthful constituents as they grew up and slipped away. Former hippies of the 1960s became upwardly mobile Yuppies who preferred dwelling sedately in white-collar, high-tech surburbias to "roughing it" in ascetic, monastic simplicity. Controversy had become too big a part of Brown's single-minded political style. Finally, former adherents were angered by the governor's presidential aspirations, which took him away from the state for months on end.

In comparing the leadership styles of Governors Ronald Reagan and Jerry Brown, one finds that the former delegated important powers to his staff, whereas Brown, although a good idea man, was limited as an executive. Both Reagan and Brown were unable to scale down the size of government. Both leaders were less effective than Governor "Pat" Brown in getting their ideas passed by the state legislature. Both featured ideological symbolism over tangible achievement. Reagan as governor resembled Reagan as President— charismatic but seldom a hands-on leader. Brown, who never actually had a chance to be president, deluded himself entering futile primary campaigns in other states. By 1982, after losing the governorship, he was easily defeated in a race for the United States Senate by San Diego Mayor Pete Wilson. Another Republican, George Deukmejian, had already become the Republican governor that year. The eight stormy years of the second Brown's political era were over.

With a Californian again in the presidency, Reagan's home state became one of the biggest gainers. Despite past cutbacks in government contracts, 22 percent of the nation's defense spending remained rooted in California although only 7 percent of its work force was in military production. As a result, by 1985 the state retained a surplus of federal spending of over $10 billion, or $395 million above the taxes which Californians sent to Washington. That year their state obtained 50 percent of all prime contracts for new nuclear plant systems. In 1984 the Hughes Aircraft, Lockheed, and North American corporations each received orders ranging from $1 billion to almost $3 billion for work on such projects as the Trident, Tomahawk, and Minuteman missile systems.

In the fiscal year 1985 the Pentagon awarded $153.5 billion in military and civilian contracts. California companies won $29.1 billion of these, or more than 20 percent of the total while New York was runner-up with some $10 billion of defense orders, or 7 percent of these awards.

Ethnic Growth and Economic Expansion

In unexpected ways California has become increasingly cosmopolitan. Los Angeles, one of the largest Mexican cities in the world, is also America's second-largest Jewish community—larger than those in Paris, London, or Buenos Aires. California's black, Japanese, Korean, Chinese, and Filipino populations have all expanded. So has the number of American Indians, many arriving from other states. Presidents Kennedy, Johnson, and Carter issued directives and signed laws increasing the number of Asians eligible to enter the country from Hong Kong, Taiwan, and Korea. Many refugees have come to San Francisco's Chinatown, traditional center of America's West Coast Orientals, after a 1968 Immigration and Nationality Act provided for abolition of the national origins quota system. Following the fall of Vietnam in 1975, California was called upon by the federal government to accept a substantial number of Vietnamese refugees.

Today Monterey Park, an eight-square-mile enclave on the edge of the San Gabriel valley, has come to be called "Little Taipei." It is a haven for flight capital from Taiwan and Hong Kong; even modestly well-off immigrants bring in savings of $50,000. Some Asians arrive with hundreds of thousands of dollars in their suitcases. Their first stop may be at the local Mercedes dealership, and the second at the office of a real estate broker of Asian background. The Chinese who today arrive in California are no longer coolies imported to lay down railroad tracks. Some 22 percent of Monterey Park's Asian adults have a college degree.

Displaced California residents complain of feeling like foreigners in their own country. Prime commercial space in Monterey Park is as expensive as in downtown Los Angeles. Chinese restaurants, bars, and movie theatres spill over into Alhambra, San Gabriel, and Montebello. With schools overcrowded and traffic approaching grid-lock, criminal activity has also broken out, spawned by youth gangs as well as by old-country criminal tongs specializing in protection rackets.

Southern California has sustained such a strong in-migration of new residents that Los Angeles is being called a new Ellis Island. By 1980 only 27 percent of the students in the city's schools were Caucasians. So-called Anglos fell in number to less than 50 percent of the city's population by the middle 1980s. Neither the media nor other civic institutions had prepared California for such an ethnic explosion.

By 1983, with a population of well over 25 million, the state remained the nation's most populous. More than 14 million persons—approximately 60 percent of its inhabitants—then lived in Los Angeles County or in adjacent Orange, Riverside, and Ventura counties, which were no longer exclusively agricultural. By then milk and cream topped California's list of farm products, followed by cattle and calves. Grapes ranked third in its output while cotton was fourth. California still grows more carrots, cauliflower, and celery than any other state, while it produces 91 percent of the nation's wine.

A recent national farm depression has, however, affected California agriculture. Some farmers, seeking to profit from the land boom of the 1970s, added to the size of their farms, buying land on credit. Overproduction in the 1980s, as well as depressed prices and shrinking markets, has made it impossible for others to keep up mortgage payments. Also there have been few buyers for land bought at inflated prices. Some farmers, therefore, face bankruptcy and have moved out of farming. Corporate farms have also suffered.

Meanwhile, by 1984, California received $28 billion worth of defence contracts, twice the total receipts from farming. The state remains the leading American source of tungsten, and its mines contribute major quantities of gold, silver, iron ore, mercury and other minerals. California has dropped to fourth among the states in oil production and is the seventh national supplier of natural gas.

"The Duke"

Long identified with "law and order" issues, veteran Republican legislator George Deukmejian was elected attorney general of California in 1978. Author of the state's death penalty initiative and the "Use a Gun, Go to Prison" laws, he decided to run for governor in 1982

California Population Growth Projections by County

County	1980	2000	2020
Alameda	1,109,100	1,276,000	1,373,900
Alpine	1,100	2,200	3,400
Amador	19,500	34,900	48,800
Butte	144,900	225,800	300,600
Calaveras	21,000	48,000	73,300
Colusa	12,900	16,800	19,300
Contra Costa	658,200	836,000	970,800
Del Norte	18,300	21,600	24,100
El Dorado	86,700	169,900	245,900
Fresno	516,900	698,700	841,200
Glenn	21,500	29,700	35,900
Humboldt	109,000	125,400	137,000
Imperial	92,700	142,000	180,700
Inyo	17,900	22,400	25,400
Kern	406,400	612,700	778,100
Kings	74,200	100,400	113,100
Lake	36,900	83,600	120,700
Lassen	21,900	37,700	52,500
Los Angeles	7,490,400	8,474,200	9,002,500
Madera	64,000	116,800	154,000
Marin	222,800	238,500	239,900
Mariposa	11,200	20,000	28,400
Mendocino	67,100	93,100	113,000
Merced	135,600	198,400	244,100
Modoc	8,700	12,600	14,500
Mono	8,700	17,400	28,300
Monterey	292,000	385,300	432,800
Napa	99,200	118,100	132,700
Nevada	52,700	122,900	177,800
Orange	1,942,200	2,605,400	3,017,800
Placer	118,400	226,300	337,700
Plumas	17,400	23,600	28,700
Riverside	668,900	1,200,100	1,607,900
Sacramento	787,700	1,186,600	1,508,500
San Benito	25,200	40,200	54,700
San Bernardino	903,100	1,597,800	2,177,900
San Diego	1,874,800	2,849,000	3,494,400
San Francisco	680,800	674,800	626,700
San Joaquin	350,200	513,600	667,300
San Luis Obispo	156,900	256,700	349,600
San Mateo	587,700	630,300	613,400
Santa Barbara	299,700	373,800	412,500
Santa Clara	1,299,100	1,592,500	1,763,600
Santa Cruz	189,400	271,500	335,400
Shasta	116,800	164,100	202,600
Sierra	3,100	5,500	8,100
Siskiyou	40,000	50,500	54,400
Solano	237,300	397,200	520,600
Sonoma	301,500	443,500	559,000
Stanislaus	267,900	403,900	521,300

California Population Growth Projections by County (*Continued*)

County	1980	2000	2020
Sutter	52,600	70,900	80,800
Tehama	39,100	57,900	72,700
Trinity	12,000	18,500	23,200
Tulare	247,500	362,200	455,800
Tuolumne	34,300	57,500	80,400
Ventura	532,000	838,500	1,117,200
Yolo	114,000	158,800	191,900
Yuba	49,800	61,500	64,900
Total	23,771,000	31,414,000	36,862,000

Courtesy of the Los Angeles *Times* (1985).

because "attorney generals don't appoint judges but governors do." This son of Armenian refugees represented the city of Long Beach at the capitol for sixteen years, serving four years in the Assembly and twelve in the Senate. In seeking the governorship, he followed two well-known predecessors in the attorney general post, Earl Warren and Edmund G. "Pat" Brown.

When he took office in January of 1983, Deukmejian inherited severe financial problems. The proposed state budget, after five successive deficits, seemed headed for a sixth. Wielding the "item veto," more than any previous governor, he made deep cuts. The belt tightening was painful and subsidized groups complained bitterly, especially entrenched advocates of educational expansion. With new budgetary restraints in place and with the onset of a national economic recovery, the financial picture turned around dramatically in Deukmejian's first year. As both "the Duke's" popularity and the state's fiscal position improved, major new funds were reallocated to education and other previously curtailed programs. Deukmejian's low-key, business-like approach earned him high marks from the press and the public and grudging respect from his adversaries.

Voters perceived this governor as a good manager without the presidential ambitions of a Jerry Brown or Ronald Reagan. Also, during his first term at least, he had luck on his side. Revenues came back into balance; there were no prison riots, no breakdown of the state's medical or mental health system, no power black-outs, no Medfly crisis. Without being smug or boastful he turned decision-making to his advantage. By 1986, the public perception was of a reliable, solid, public steward. His performance was rated higher in the polls than that of either Reagan or Brown. During the 1982 campaign, and in preparation for the 1986 election, Deukmejian projected the image of a highly capable public servant content to do a good job in Sacramento. With no severe economic recession in sight, and barring a major administration scandal, his chances for reelection in 1986 were good indeed.

The Twenty-third Olympiad

After fifty years and amid controversy, doubts, and pessimism concerning prospects for a successful venture, the Olympic Games returned to Los Angeles in 1984. Opponents cited the financial debacle suffered in Montreal in 1976, the terrorist attack in Munich in 1972, and other probable difficulties in staging another Olympiad. As finally worked out, the organizers avoided the outlay of public funds by obtaining corporate sponsorships, selling television rights at a high figure, using existing housing at universities, and training 50,000 volunteers. An alleged lack of security became the official excuse for the last-minute withdrawal by Soviet bloc nations. Few believed the boycott was anything but retaliation for the American pullout from the 1980 Moscow Games to protest the Soviet invasion of Afghanistan. There were also dire prophecies of dangerously toxic levels of air pollution and gigantic traffic snarls, or "terminal gridlock" as one critic put it.

From the spectacular Hollywood staging of the ceremonies, to performances by the athletes, to the carefree exuberance of throngs of spectators, the 1984 Summer Games exceeded all expectations and disappointed the doomsayers. Highlights were frequent and television coverage exhausting. Memorable scenes included former Olympic decathlon winner Rafer Johnson running up the steps to light the Olympic flame, Mary Lou Retton nailing a perfect ten in the gymnastic competition, Mary Decker's agony after stumbling in the 3,000-meter run, British decathlon champion Daley Thompson's joyful victory run around the track waving the Union Jack, and the superb diving performance of Greg Louganis. Great human interest stories developed around victories by cancer victim Jeff Blatnick in wrestling and recently injured Joan Benoit in the first Olympic marathon for women. While the absence of the Russians lessened the level of competition—notably in wrestling, gymnastics, weight lifting, and track and field—and the boycott by East German athletes produced almost a clean sweep by American swimmers, the first time Olympic participation by the People's Republic of China made ideology seem of slight importance.

As orchestrated by Peter Ueberroth, whose feat won him a "Man of the Year" cover on *TIME* magazine, the games even earned a profit. Grim predictions concerning unmanageable traffic and smog failed to come true. Shuttle busses, rescheduled vacations, and an unanticipated decline in tourists, along with an exodus of forewarned

Surfer, photographed from a jetty at Newport Beach, executes a turn. Photo by Ker; courtesy of *Surfer Magazine.)*

locals, combined to produce smoothly flowing freeways. This second Olympiad had an exhilarating effect upon the morale of Californians. Pride surged as a world-class accomplishment was carried out with great success.

Without "pay as you go financing," the Olympic Games would never have materialized. By the mid-1980s Californians had become adamant in their demands for fiscal responsibility. As a result, the voters finally authorized a public lottery system after years of resistance to that idea. It went into effect during 1985, giving promise of an important increase in revenues for education and other state services.

Future Directions

Because of the verbal barbs hurled against them, Californians have grown used to rolling with the punches. Since the days when Sinclair Lewis called the state "the retreat of all failures," such criticism has been recurrent. Another novelist, Joan Didion, a native Californian, in an essay entitled "How Can I Tell Them There's Nothing Left?" has described today's frantic pursuit of fun amidst tacky bungalows and motels: "Here is where the divorce rate is double the national average and where one person in thirty-eight lives in a trailer. Here is the last stop for all those who came from somewhere else, for all

The Los Angeles Music Center. (Photography by Duane C. Alan.)

those who have drifted away from the cold and the past and the old ways." Historian Henry Steele Commager, yet another critic, maintains that California has become "a society that worships open air and play rather than work." Television producer Norman Lear says that the weather attracts "emotionally unwrapped people." Others believe that there is too much sun in California and that the summer heat turns people into crazed, fun-loving nerds.

Despite such fulminations, Californians have retained a brand of confidence not to be found elsewhere. They continue to boast that what happens to them will soon be copied elsewhere. Consumer trends within the state are closely studied by national manufacturers. A great many new ideas are first launched in California, as a 1985 poll by *Science Digest* has affirmed. This publication canvassed 1,200 corporations, universities and colleges, scientific and engineering associations, nonprofit institutions with research and development programs, and government agencies involved in research. The magazine selected "the year's top 100 innovations, and the men and women behind them." Out of twenty-seven states, plus the District of Columbia, reflected in the final findings, twenty of the one hundred innovations claimed California as their place of origin (New York was second with thirteen followed by Pennsylvania with ten).

About the state's powerful mesmerizing effect, one English wag recently remarked: "I have seen the future and it plays." The conversion of the ocean liner *Queen Mary* into a Long Beach hotel, or the moving of London Bridge out onto a barren desert, have baffled foreigners. Such flexibility is, however, unique. Few areas can claim to be the world's entertainment center. Detroit or Tokyo could never become another Los Angeles—the mystique is not the same.

From the 1960s onward, California became a center of openness to change in life-styles. Sexual freedom and experimentalism have been warmly embraced by trusting adherents. To this day some converts remain happy "doing their own thing." But freedom from traditionalism and conformity has its perils. Personal transcendence has also made for drug and pornography centers which exist side by side with synthetic religious communes and strange therapies. Rooted in both present and future, Californians tend to pay little attention to their past. Traditional systems of social ranking and historic hierarchies of leadership have become blurred. Even distinctions between reality and fantasy become twisted.

But all is not chaos in today's California. Significant technological growth continues as humans step boldly into a non-terrestrial future. This process began when the astronomer Edwin Hubble developed a new theory of the expanding universe ("The Big Bang") at the Mount Wilson Observatory near Pasadena. Later, Californians helped to place the first astronauts on the moon. Today's scientists, who labor in California's space-age "think factories," form a talent pool that may permanently alter life on earth. But there are dangers in technology too. Will Californians go on venerating freeways and surrender more land to the automobile? Or will they choose to move toward greater orderly growth and less blighting of the environment?

Despite its many faults and past mistakes, California's freer style of life and work continues to attract international attention. Critics may call some Californians sports-mad loungers in a lotus land, but they also see them as anything but staid and brittle. The big, the new, and the innovative, however, do not assure that unique will to excel that characterized fifth-century Greece, Republican Rome, or Europe's Renaissance cities. California has not been favored by any such direct cultural inheritance. Instead, it has fused a frontier rurality with today's urbanism—a wrenching challenge indeed. Perhaps Californians will one day leave materialism behind, searching for a new sense of beauty that can provide them a window into a less clouded more serene future.

Selected Readings

The most recent culture of California has not been treated in a systematic fashion. The following, however, are useful references: George H.

Knoles, ed., *Essays and Assays: California History Reconsidered* (San Francisco, 1973), Lawrence Clark Powell, *The Creative Literature of the Golden State* (Los Angeles, 1971), William Storrs Lee, ed., *California, A Literary Chronicle* (New York, 1968), Leslie Freudenheim, *Building With Nature: Roots of the San Francisco Bay Tradition* (Santa Barbara, 1974), Mellier Scott, *Partnership in the Arts: Public and Private Support of Cultural Activities in the San Francisco Bay Area* (Berkeley, 1963). Arthur Bloomfield, *The San Francisco Opera, 1923–1961* (San Francisco, 1961), concerns the growth of culture in the Bay area.

Consult also Harold Kirker, "California Architecture and its Relation to Contemporary Trends in Europe and America," *California Historical Quarterly* 51 (Winter 1972), 289–305, George A. Pettit, *Berkeley: The Town and Gown of It* (Berkeley, 1973), John and LaRee Caughey, eds., *Los Angeles: Biography of a City* (Berkeley, 1976), Reyner Banham, *Los Angeles, The Architecture of Four Ecologies* (London, 1971), John D. Weaver, *El Pueblo Grande: Los Angeles* (Los Angeles, 1973), and Doyce B. Nunis, Jr., ed., *Los Angeles and its Environs in the Twentieth Century* (Los Angeles, 1973), a bibliography. A glance at the tensions exerted upon a middle-class southern California suburb is Richard M. Elman, *Ill-at-Ease in Compton* (New York, 1968).

Contemporary California is treated as a social laboratory by an English reporter in a book entitled *In the Future Now* by Michael Davie (London, 1972). Similar glib generalization is Joel Kotkin and Paul Grabowicz, *California Inc.* (New York, 1982), which postulates the notion that business elites somehow control California. Scott Bottles, *Los Angeles and the Automobile: The Making of the Modern City* (Berkeley, 1987) does not concern the auto as much as suburbanization. The author reaches some pessimistic conclusions about mass transportation.

The leading newspaper at Los Angeles has given rise to three books: Marshall Berges, *The Life and Times of the Los Angeles Times* (New York, 1984) is virtually an in-house product and uncritical. Robert Gottlieb and Irene Wolt, *Thinking Big: The Story of the Los Angeles Times* (New York, 1977) is entertainingly wider in scope. William Wilson, *The Los Angeles Times Book of California Museums* (New York, 1984) is written by the newspaper's art critic.

A recent anthology is Jonathan Eisen and David Fine, *Unknown California* (New York, 1985). Useful also is Judson Grenier, ed., *A Guide to Historic Places in Los Angeles County* (Dubuque, 1978). Helpful for biography is Carol Dunlap, *California People* (San Francisco, 1982). Finally, an impressionistic interpretation is David Brodsley, *L.A. Freeway: An Appreciative Essay* (Berkeley, 1981).

Joan M. Jensen and Gloria Lothrop, *California Women: A History* (San Francisco, 1987) updates a hitherto neglected subject.

Appendix

The Governors of California

SPANISH REGIME, 1767–1821

(Dates of service in the case of each governor are from assumption to surrender of office.)

Gaspar de Portolá
November 30, 1767, to July 9, 1770

> From May 21, 1769, Portolá was *commandante-militar* for Alta California. From July 9, 1770, to May 25, 1774, the position of comandante was filled by Pedro Fages; and from May 25, 1774, to February 1777, by Fernando Rivera y Moncada.

Matías de Armona
June 12, 1769, to November 9, 1770

Felipe de Barri
March ?, 1770, to March 4, 1775

> Governor of *Las Californias*, residing at Loreto.

Felipe de Neve
March 4, 1775, to July 12, 1782

> In February 1777, Neve took up residence at Monterey. Rivera y Moncada went south to assume the lieutenant governorship at Loreto. The acting lieutenant-governor, pending Rivera's arrival, was Joaquín Cañete.

Pedro Fages
July 12, 1782, to April 16, 1791

> On July 18, 1781, Rivera y Moncada was killed on the Colorado River, and Joaquín Cañete served as lieutenant-governor until November 1783, when he was succeeded by José Joaquín de Arrillaga.

José Antonio Roméu
April 16, 1791, to April 9, 1792

José Joaquín de Arrillaga
April 9, 1792, to May 14, 1794

> During this period, Arrillaga was lieutenant-governor and comandante of Lower California, and governor of *Las Californias ad interim.*

Diego de Borica
May 14, 1794, to March 8, 1800

José Joaquín de Arrillaga
March 8, 1800, to July 24, 1814

> Until March 11, 1802, when he died, Pedro de Alberni was *comandante-militar* for Alta California. The decree making Alta California a separate province bore the date August 29, 1804, and it reached Arrillaga November 16.

José Darío Argüello
July 24, 1814, to August 30, 1815

> Governor *ad interim.*

Pablo Vicente de Solá
August 30, 1815, to November 10, 1822

> Held over from Spanish regime to November 1822.

MEXICAN REGIME, 1821–1847

Luís Antonio Argüello
November 10, 1822, to November ?, 1825

> Until April 2, 1823, Argüello's authority derived from the Spanish Regency. After that date it derived from Iturbide as Agustin I. After November 17 it derived from the *Congreso Constituyente* (National Congress). In March 1823, Iturbide named Naval Captain Bonifacio de Tosta governor of Alta California. In 1824 José Miñón was appointed governor of Alta California but declined the office.

José María de Echeandía
November ?, 1825, to January 31, 1831

> Antonia García was appointed as Echeandía's successor, but the appointment was revoked.

Manuel Victoria
January 31, 1831, to December 6, 1831

José María de Echeandía
December 6, 1831, to January 14, 1833

> De facto *jefe político* and *jefe militar* in the district south of, but not including, Santa Barbara.

Pío Pico
January 27 to February 16, 1832

> *Jefe político* by appointment of the *Diputación* for only twenty days.

Agustín Vicente Zamorano
February 1, 1832, to January 14, 1833
De facto *jefe militar* only in the district north of and including Santa Barbara.

José Figueroa
January 14, 1833, to September 29, 1835
Early in 1833 Figueroa asked to be relieved of office. On July 16, 1833, José María Hijar was appointed *jefe político*, but the appointment was revoked by Mexico's President Santa Anna on July 25. On July 18, 1834, Figueroa withdrew his request to be relieved.

José Castro
September 29, 1835, to January 2, 1836
From October 8, 1835, to January 1, 1836, the position of *jefe militar* was held by Nicolás Gutiérrez.

Nicolás Gutiérrez
January 2 to May 3, 1836

Mariano Chico
May 3 to August 1, 1836

Nicolás Gutiérrez
August 1 to November 5, 1836

José Castro
November 5 to December 7, 1836
Castro was *jefe militar* until November 29, when he was succeeded by Mariano Guadalupe Vallejo. He then became acting governor.

Juan Bautista Alvarado
December 7, 1836, to December 31, 1842
Until August 7, 1839, Alvarado was governor *ad interim*. On June 6, 1837, Carlos Carillo was appointed governor, and on December 6 he assumed office at Los Angeles, but was arrested and deposed by Alvarado on May 20, 1838.

Manuel Micheltorena
December 31, 1842, to February 22, 1845

Pío Pico
February 22, 1845, to August 10, 1846
By the departmental junta Pío Pico was declared governor *ad interim* on February 15, 1845. José Castro served as *jefe militar* for the same period.

José María Flores
October 31, 1846, to January 11, 1847

Andrés Pico
January 11 to January 13, 1847

AMERICAN GOVERNORS UNDER MILITARY RULE
(Dates given are beginning of term.)

Commodore John D. Sloat
July 7, 1846

Colonel Richard B. Mason
May 31, 1847

Commodore Robert F. Stockton
July 29, 1846

General Persifor F. Smith
February 28, 1849

Captain John C. Frémont
January 19, 1847

General Bennett Riley
April 12, 1849

General Stephen W. Kearny
March 1, 1847

GOVERNORS OF THE STATE OF CALIFORNIA
Dates given are date of inauguration

Peter H. Burnett
Ind. Dem. Dec. 20, 1849

William Irwin
Dem. Dec. 9, 1875

John McDougal
Ind. Dem. Jan. 9, 1851

George C. Perkins
Rep. Jan. 8, 1880

John Bigler
Dem. Jan. 8, 1852

George Stoneman
Dem. Jan. 10, 1883

John Neely Johnson
Amer. Jan. 9, 1856

Washington Bartlett
Dem. Jan. 8, 1887

John B. Weller
Dem. Jan. 8, 1858

Robert W. Waterman
Rep. Sept. 13, 1887

Milton S. Latham
Lecomp. Dem. Jan. 9, 1860

Henry H. Markham
Rep. Jan. 8, 1891

John G. Downey
Lecomp. Dem. Jan. 14, 1860

James H. Budd
Dem. Jan. 11, 1895

Leland Stanford
Rep. Jan. 10, 1862

Henry T. Gage
Rep. Jan. 4, 1899

Frederick F. Low
Union Dec. 10, 1863

George C. Pardee
Rep. Jan. 7, 1903

Henry H. Haight
Dem. Dec. 5, 1867

James N. Gillett
Rep. Jan. 9, 1907

Newton Booth
Rep. Dec. 8, 1871

Hiram W. Johnson
Prog. Rep. Jan. 3, 1911

Romualdo Pacheco
Rep. Feb. 27, 1875

William D. Stephens
Rep. Mar. 15, 1917

Friend W. Richardson
Rep. Jan. 8, 1923

Clement C. Young
Rep. Jan. 4, 1927

James Rolph, Jr.
Rep. Jan. 6, 1931

Frank F. Merriam
Rep. Jan. 7, 1935

Culbert L. Olson
Dem. Jan. 2, 1939

Earl F. Warren
Rep. Jan. 4, 1943

Goodwin F. Knight
Rep. Oct. 5, 1953

Edmund G. Brown
Dem. Jan. 5, 1959

Ronald Reagan
Rep. Jan. 5, 1967

Edmund G. Brown, Jr.
Dem. Jan. 5, 1975

George Deukmejian
Rep. Jan. 5, 1983

Index of
Authors Cited

Index

551

California: A History, Fourth Edition, was copyedited by Anita Samen. Production editor was Brad Barrett. James A. Bier drew the maps; Carolee Lipsey and Martha Kreger proofread the copy; Frances Rolle compiled the index. The text was typeset by Impressions, Inc., printed by Malloy Lithographing, Inc., and bound by John H. Dekker & Sons.

The cover and text were designed by Roger Eggers. Cover photo: Art Brewer © 1985.

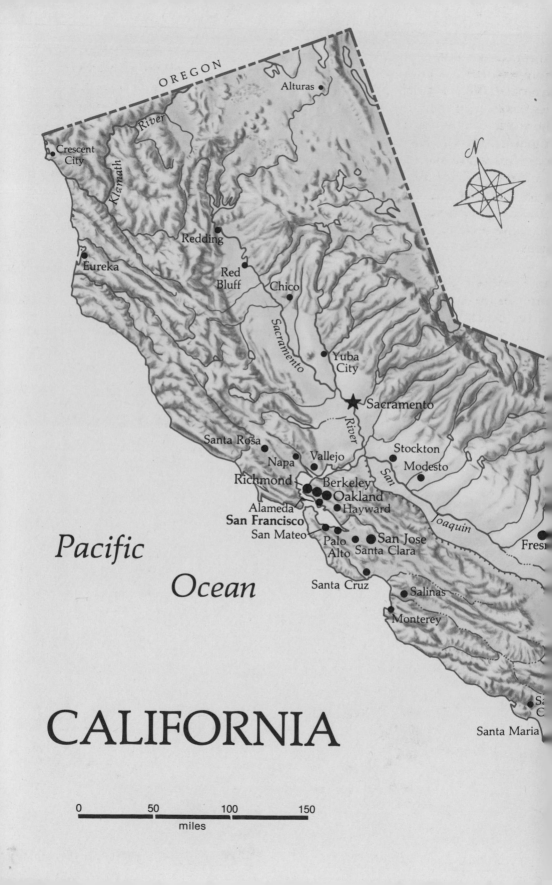

OREGON

Alturas

Crescent
City

Klamath River

Redding

Eureka

Red
Bluff

Chico

Sacramento

Yuba
City

★ Sacramento

Santa Rosa

Napa

Vallejo

Stockton

Modesto

Richmond

Berkeley

Oakland

Alameda

Hayward

San Francisco

San Mateo

Palo
Alto

Santa Clara

San Jose

River

San

Joaquin

Fres

Pacific

Ocean

Santa Cruz

Salinas

Monterey

Sa
C

Santa Maria

CALIFORNIA

N

0   50   100   150
miles